Julius Margolin. Courtesy of Beit Aba, the archive of Aba Ahimeir, Ramat Gan, Israel.

Journey into the Land of the Zeks and Back

A *Memoir of the Gulag*

JULIUS MARGOLIN

Translated by
STEFANI HOFFMAN

Foreword by
TIMOTHY SNYDER

Introduction by
KATHERINE R. JOLLUCK

OXFORD
UNIVERSITY PRESS

OXFORD
UNIVERSITY PRESS

Oxford University Press is a department of the University of Oxford. It furthers
the University's objective of excellence in research, scholarship, and education
by publishing worldwide. Oxford is a registered trade mark of Oxford University
Press in the UK and certain other countries.

Published in the United States of America by Oxford University Press
198 Madison Avenue, New York, NY 10016, United States of America.

Library of Congress Cataloging-in-Publication Data
Names: Margolin, Julius, 1900–1971, author. | Hoffman, Stefani, translator. |
Snyder, Timothy, writer of foreword. | Jolluck, Katherine R., writer of introduction. |
Margolin, Julius, 1900–1971. Doroga na Zapad. English.
Title: Journey into the land of the Zeks and back : a memoir of the Gulag /
Julius Margolin ; translated by Stefani Hoffman ; foreword by Timothy
Snyder ; introduction by Katherine R. Jolluck.
Other titles: Puteshestvie v stranu Zëka. English | Road to the West.
Description: New York : Oxford University Press, 2020. |
Identifiers: LCCN 2020020756 (print) | LCCN 2020020757 (ebook) |
ISBN 9780197502143 (hardcover) | ISBN 9780197502167 (epub) | ISBN 9780197502150
Subjects: LCSH: Convict labor—Soviet Union. | Political prisoners—Soviet
Union—Biography. | Penal colonies—Soviet Union. | Political persecution—Soviet Union.
Classification: LCC HV8931.R8 M2813 2020 (print) | LCC HV8931.R8 (ebook)
| DDC 365/.45092 [B]—dc23
LC record available at https://lccn.loc.gov/2020020756
LC ebook record available at https://lccn.loc.gov/2020020757

1 3 5 7 9 8 6 4 2

Printed by Sheridan Books, Inc., United States of America

Contents

Foreword

by Timothy Snyder

WE SPEAK OF memory, but memory is empty without witness. It is too much to expect that all who suffer speak. Yet without witness, memory devolves into propaganda that serves the moment. Julius Margolin asks whether the real Russia is the one that celebrates victory over Nazi Germany on Red Square, or the one that exists in the uncharted universe of concentration camps that he calls "the land of the zek." He wrote in 1946 and 1947, right after five years of Soviet penal servitude; the question is still pertinent in the Russia of the twenty-first century. Margolin was himself a "zek," a convict, who survived incarceration in the largest concentration camp system during its most murderous period.

We call the Soviet camps the Gulag, after the title of Alexander Solzhenitsyn's much later book, published in 1973. Had Margolin's book been published when he wrote it, "zek" and "land of the zek" would be the terms we use now. This first complete collection of Margolin's texts about the camps, published as a whole in English translation, arrives at a time when we know a great deal about them. When documents became available after the end of the USSR in 1991, historians sought to balance the experiences of the prisoners with those of the guards, the camp directors, the politburo, Stalin himself. We know certain things that Margolin did not: the locations of most of the camps, the numbers of registered prisoners and deaths, the names of those who persecuted them. Yet without the voices of the witnesses, even such knowledge is not enough. If memory is challenged by witness, history is enriched by it.

Only a very few memoirs of concentration camps, and only a scarce handful of memoirs of the Gulag, give a sense of what it was like on the inside. Margolin gives a reason: to become a zek was to lose the points of reference that would make the experience intelligible to others: "No one retains his original form. Observation is difficult because the observer himself is deformed. He, too, is abnormal." In this sense the title of this book is perfectly chosen. Margolin recounts the five years between his deportation from Soviet-occupied Poland in 1940 and his return to postwar Poland in 1946 and then his subsequent departure for Palestine via France. It is a mark of his honesty that he records his own decline; it is a mark of his recovery that he was able to write this book. This literary and philosophical memoir is not simply an unmatched historical record; it is also a deep moral judgement. Tens of millions of people passed through the Gulag; only a few were able to write searching and reliable books about it. This one is perhaps the best.

Margolin was a philosopher, which made him a special witness. Born the son of a doctor in the predominantly Jewish town of Pinsk in what was then the western Russian Empire, he studied for a while in revolutionary Russia and then completed a doctorate in philosophy in Berlin. He called himself a Polish Jew and spent most of the 1930s in Poland, mainly in Łódź. In 1936 he and his family moved from Poland to Palestine. He was in Poland settling some necessary business when Germany invaded on 1 September 1939. Like about a quarter million Jews in western Poland, he fled eastward before the Germans. The Soviet Union invaded Poland from the east on 17 September. Like many of those Jews, Margolin tried to find a way out. When he failed, he returned to his parents in Pinsk, where he lived through the annexation of eastern Poland and the imposition of the Soviet system.

Margolin defines himself as a European and as a "man of the West." He was forty years old when he entered his first concentration camp, old enough to have seen something of the world and to start a family, but young enough to react with flexibility. He had a strong sense of decency and normality: human rights and truth were basic concepts. He had the vocabulary and concepts of a philosopher with a strong interest in literature: he never lacked for words or concepts in an environment that beggared description. He was a native speaker of Russian, the language of the camps, but also a native speaker of Polish and Yiddish, the languages of the prisoners with whom he was sentenced.

As Margolin saw matters from Łódź or Pinsk in late 1939 and early 1940, the Nazis and the Soviets had together destroyed Europe. The Molotov-Ribbentrop pact of August 1939, and the joint German-Soviet invasion of Poland that followed, was the end of the life he thought he was leading. Poland, from which he had emigrated but for which he had sympathy, was destroyed by its powerful neighbors. In Pinsk Margolin watched as local resources, grain and meat, were directed by Soviet power to the Nazi ally, even as Germany invaded western Europe. Both Nazi Germany and the Soviet Union declared that the Polish state did not exist; this created a basic problem of access to law and protection for tens of millions of people who were subject not to a conventional occupation but to annexation and colonization. In Margolin's case, he was sentenced to five years of hard labor in a camp for having the wrong papers.

His choices were constrained by the joint action of Nazi and Soviet power. Jews could flee Germans, but would find themselves in territory that would become Soviet. Margolin is a keen observer of what happened in eastern Poland under Soviet rule: the deportation of elites, the subjugation of the economy, the closing of all independent organizations. Many Jews wanted to go back: "as late as spring 1940, Jews preferred the ghetto to the Soviet equality of rights." Many Jews did in fact return. Those like Margolin who stayed were expected to take Soviet citizenship. Jews who did not were deported to special settlements in Soviet Kazakhstan and Siberia in June 1940. A few weeks after that, Margolin was sent to a camp in the Russian far north to fell trees.

During Margolin's first year as a zek, the Soviet Union and Nazi Germany were allies. His forced labor served an economy that supplied the Wehrmacht. We might be tempted to think of this as ironic; for Margolin it was simply the end of his world: "Both sides were inhuman reflections of everything we held dear and sacred." There was nothing surprising, for him, in "Russia's alliance with Nazi Germany." A Jew in Soviet confinement, he had to endure pro-Nazi propaganda: "The rare Soviet newspapers that landed in the camp were full of pro-German publicity." The Soviet press was reprinting the speeches of Nazi dignitaries. "In line with Hitler's successes," Margolin recalls, "antisemitism increased in the camp." Although he was a Polish Jew, and well aware of Polish antisemitism, no one called him a kike until he was in a Soviet camp.

Margolin knew Germany well but never saw a Nazi camp; he left the country in 1929, four years before Hitler came to power. The comparisons were, however, unavoidable. A young German Jew who feared Nazi terror found his nightmares realized in a Soviet camp. Jews who had been in Dachau said that Soviet servitude was worse. Margolin also noticed that young fascists with whom he was imprisoned admired the camp structure. They agreed with its basic organizing principle: the strong should survive, the weak perish.

Margolin and his fellow inmates were evacuated eastwards from the camp on Lake Onega when Nazi Germany invaded the Soviet Union on 22 June 1941. Some four million people were in Soviet camps when Hitler betrayed Stalin and Nazi Germany invaded its ally. In the next two years some

2.5 million more Soviet citizens were sentenced to the camps. Between 1941 and 1943, chaotic transports and drastic shortages made a camp sentence even more dangerous than before. About half a million deaths were officially registered in the camps in those years; the true figure is likely far higher.

Margolin survived these conditions, observed them, chronicled them, and analyzed them with unparalleled clarity and insight. In extraordinary descriptions, we learn about what he called "the fatal year 1942" when around him "zeks were falling like grass." He and his fellow prisoners talked about which kinds of grass and which kinds of bark could be eaten. With great precision and without pathos he describes, for example, digging in a canal downstream from an outhouse looking for edible material left over from swill for pigs.

Margolin's great subject was dehumanization: the reduction of zeks in their own minds to hungry beasts, and in the minds of their bosses to laboring machines. Everyone was hungry all the time. Food was rationed so that the more productive got more than the less: "The means of coercion was hunger." A prisoner can be brought "to a bestial condition where the moment of satiety becomes the culminating point of every day, the sole stimulus of his actions."

To be treated only as an instrument of labor destroyed a sense of self-worth. "Only a free person," Margolin wrote, "knows the joy of free labor, and for him this labor is meaningful because it serves a goal that he chooses and in which he believes." It is physically difficult to fell trees all day in a north Russian forest, as Margolin did in his first labor assignment. Yet he notices the spiritual costs as well: "The surest way to make a person ludicrous and contemptible is to force him systematically to do work that he is incapable of doing, in the company of people who are superior to him in strength and skill." People are reduced to the quantity of labor they perform: "I myself was not worth anything. My right to life was measured by the percentage of the work norms that I fulfilled."

The sheer pointlessness was an element of the suffering. Margolin labored poorly, punished for actions that he could not regard as a crime, sentenced by a state of which he was not a citizen, serving a regime he abhorred. After the war, Margolin read Jean-Paul Sartre and laughed at Sartre's idea that alienation was something experienced by bourgeois French people. He saw Sartre's complaint about the absence of absolute meaning in existence as a temptation to seek it in politics, in a system such as communism. As a prediction of Sartre's politics, this was correct. Margolin actually experienced something very much like a pure alienation and wrote about it with a skill that should have been humbling to those who wrote about what they did not know.

Margolin is a chronicler not only of the cruelty and suffering of others but also of the disappearance of the self. In his prose the physical and institutional structure of the camp figures as a threat not just to life but to any sense of what living might mean. Throughout the book, for example, he returns to his constant difficulty in keeping clothed. These passages concern the extreme cold—and basic dignity: "The moment arrives when we no longer have anything of our own. The state dresses and undresses us as it pleases." Poland is destroyed and Palestine is far away; he has no contact with the people who mattered to him before his sentence; "family ties are liquidated." It pains him that his wife and son and Palestine do not know what has happened to him. The continuity of life itself is broken, the accumulation of moments, days, and memories that is the oxygen of our consciousness. Prisoners "gradually forgot about our past," as the present became a matter of mechanical repetition and animal survival.

Margolin survived physically, thanks to his languages, his friendships with camp doctors, his canniness, and a good deal of luck. He almost died several times, and his gifts as a writer are perhaps most apparent in his recollections of those moments. Yet perhaps the central experience was not malady but dehumanization. He is saddest about the day when he first robbed from a fellow prisoner, the day when he first struck another man in the face. Even as Margolin gave way physically and spiritually to the system, he never lost his sense of human value. In circumstances where such behavior was understandable and even necessary for survival, he still remembers it as wrong, and as damaging to himself. The Polish philosopher Leszek Kołakowski said that when we choose the lesser evil we must remember that it is evil. This is a challenge in daily life; that Margolin could retain this level of ethical reflection in the camp is miraculous.

Margolin never lost his capacity to see his fellow zeks as human. He takes care to describe the particular conditions of his fellow Jews, who were the majority of his campmates at the beginning. He explains that Poles, with whom he shared a language and a country, were the group closest to Jews in the camp. Margolin befriends Ukrainians, with whom, as he recalls, Jews had an uneasy history. Ukrainians were sent to the Gulag in disproportionate numbers before, during, and after the war; in Margolin's book they have a voice.

Margolin knew that he was an unusual witness. Concluding his book in 1947, at a time when the world did not know about the Gulag and did not want to learn, he writes, rather formally, that on "the basis of my five-year experience, I affirm that the Soviet government, utilizing specific territories and political conditions in its country, has created a subterranean hell, a kingdom of slaves behind barbed wire, inaccessible to world public opinion." Margolin correctly anticipated that the very moral emptiness that he experienced would become an argument of the defenders of the Soviet regime. What he opposed was the total abandonment of ethics, the open nihilism and its attendant sadism: "Might is right; everyone lies; everyone is a scoundrel; fools must be taught a lesson."

The defense of the Soviet system, before the war, during the war, after the war, and even today, was that the abandonment of humanity served some goal. What Margolin experienced as an emptiness could be seen from a distance as a stage in history. Hunger, dehumanization, and mass death in wastelands were necessary to reach a greater good. This is what Sartre, for example, believed, and similar defenses of the Gulag are mounted even now, in Russia and beyond. Margolin's experience directly contradicts this wishful thinking: "What I saw in five years of my stay in the Soviet subterranean kingdom was an apparatus of murder and oppression acting blindly." He turns the argument from determinism around: "The Soviet regime's crime is not justified but, on the contrary, aggravated and accentuated if it turns out that there is no other way of reinforcing the power of those in the Kremlin than the monstrous camp system of contemporary slavery and millions of anonymous deaths."

Margolin had no patience with relativism, or what we today call whataboutism. It is no defense of Soviet mass killing to point out that the Nazis committed worse crimes. The Soviet camp system, he noted, was older, larger, and more durable than the Nazi one. It was wrong to "justify the Soviet camps by asserting that Auschwitz, Majdanek, and Treblinka were much worse." As Margolin saw matters, the Nazis and the Soviets had together destroyed Europe in 1939. Neither side was right in the war that began in 1941, and so defending one by referring to the crimes of the other was a logical mistake. Margolin was himself physically trapped between the two systems. But human freedom, for him, was the ability to judge both on higher criteria, rather than on the terms their alliance or their clash seemed to force.

Margolin has a final word for those who would shrug their shoulders at the history of Soviet concentration camps in the belief that in so doing they are somehow serving progress. "The people who justify Soviet camps, who say 'Let them sit in camps' or 'Perhaps this is not true' or simply 'What do we care?' may consider themselves anti-fascists and wear a mask of rectitude. It is clear to me that these people are preparing a second edition of Hitler in the world." If you lose your concern for the facts of history, you have lost your concern for humanity. If you choose evasion and propaganda, then the anti-fascists lose out to the fascists, the better evaders and the better propagandists. The act of truthfully recording human suffering, by contrast, is also the act of affirming human value. The dignity of recalling detail is also the dignity of passing judgement. As a matter of individual ethics and also as a matter of democratic pragmatism, no "trampling on human rights should remain anonymous."

Witness undoes anonymity, and judgment girds an ideal. Margolin thought that democracy transcended a shallow quarrel between Right and Left. The Right was not bound to defend fascism, and the Left was not bound to defend the Soviet Union. And no one was bound to identify with Right or Left. The trap of us-and-them was dehumanizing. What humanized was an active moral concern for truth, access to the historical record, and the freedom to express what was learned. Although every democracy is flawed, as he recognized, the flaws can be seen as such. When the witness and judgment of individuals informs the discussion and choices of citizens, a democracy can be corrected and renewed.

Acknowledgments

by Stefani Hoffman

I FIRST READ this powerful narrative in the abridged Russian version in 1975. Ever since, I have wanted to share with English readers Margolin's timeless, exquisitely expressed wisdom and humanity and his passionate denunciation of injustice and evil. I want to express my unbounded gratitude to those who made this possible. I am deeply grateful to Susan Ferber, executive editor at Oxford University Press. Her vision, energy, and dedicated attention accompanied all stages in the preparation of this volume. My heartfelt thanks go to Leona Toker and Misha Shauli for their invaluable help and support. They were instrumental in initiating an English translation, and both of them not only carefully read the entire translation but also provided significant help in elucidating the text.

My thanks go to Luba Jorgenson, whose archival work established the full Russian text. Her work was supported by Antoine Jaccottet, whose press Le Bruit de Temps published her revised and completed French translation of the entire work. I would like to acknowledge the contribution of the late Inna Dobruskina, who researched and digitized Margolin's work, and thank Yossi Ahimeir, chairman of the Jabotinsky Institute in Israel, for offering his expertise about background information on Margolin's life. Additional thanks to Melissa Yanuzzi, Oxford senior production editor, who is overseeing final production stages.

Special thanks to my husband, Allen Hoffman, for his kind help in refining the text.

I am pleased that this publication fulfills a cherished aspiration of Julius Margolin's son, Ephraim, for whose continuing support I am grateful.

I also want to thank The Hebrew University of Jerusalem for affording me a hospitable place to work.

Introduction

by Katherine R. Jolluck

THE TITLE OF this book, *Journey into the Land of the Zeks and Back*, suggests that it is a kind of travelogue to a mysterious place. Indeed, Julius Margolin, writing just after the Second World War, notes that the "country" he describes "does not appear on a Soviet map nor is it in any atlas" (5). By "Land of the Zeks" he is referring to the Gulag, Stalin's system of forced labor camps throughout the USSR, though that term became widely known in the West only much later, after the publication of Aleksandr Solzhenitsyn's *Gulag Archipelago* in 1973. For his own designation Margolin uses *zek*, the Russian slang term from the abbreviation of the word *zakliuchennyi* or *z/k*, meaning convict, a prison or forced labor camp inmate. He describes himself as a tourist of a "special sort" to this land, one who did not choose his own route; rather, "the Soviet regime decreed it" (6). This is a travelogue to a monstrous place, along the lines of Jonathon Swift's *Gulliver's Travels*: fantastical, ironic, and bitter.

Margolin describes this realm with the eyes of a journalist and pen of a literary stylist, vividly portraying its terrain, conditions, regimen, and inhabitants. An outsider to the system, he is keenly attuned to its peculiarities and contrasts them to the world that he and his readers call home. He writes not from preconceived notions, but from personal experience, explaining his time in the land of the zeks as a Westerner and, uniquely for the era of his writing, as a Jew. Margolin was also a philosopher and describes the Gulag in the most basic human terms, probing the logic behind the development of the camp system: the mechanisms of control; its effects on the human body, psyche, and personal relations; the reasons the system continued unchallenged; and the dangers it posed to humanity.

A citizen of independent Poland, with a residency permit for Palestine, Margolin initially held what he considered the typical position toward the USSR of the progressive and the radical European intelligentsia: that of "benevolent neutrality."[1] He had read many of the popular accounts of trips to the Soviet Union in the 1920s and '30s. At the time, left-leaning individuals visited the land of the Revolution and came back full of praise, either not seeing or discounting evidence of anything adverse. This tendency was amplified in the aftermath of World War II, when the Red Army pushed Nazi forces across eastern Europe all the way to Berlin, liberating country after country from the fascists. Criticism of the USSR was anathema to liberals and progressives, to almost any antifascists in the early post-war years. It was precisely at this time, June 1945, when Margolin was released from a Soviet labor camp after serving a five-year sentence, which was then followed by nearly a year in internal exile. Returning first to Poland and then to Palestine in 1946, he furiously wrote his account of his time in the Soviet Union. He insists, however, that the book is not a memoir: "It is too goal-oriented for that, and it relates not to the past, which people who have grown wise with experience recall in their declining years, but to the present" (502).

Fueled by the desire to broadcast "the absurd and tragic disparity between the 'tourist' literature and Soviet reality," he penned the book to shatter the illusions and awaken the consciences of those who hailed the victors of Stalingrad and Berlin and who looked to the USSR as a shining example for the future. One cannot support democracy, Margolin insists, and tolerate the outrage of slavery. "As long as the democratic world is reconciled to the existence of reservations of slavery in the Soviet Union," he writes, "there is no hope of averting the threat of slavery in our own midst" (507). Although written about a country that no longer exists, the book speaks to our present, as well, for it deals with timeless issues of power, dehumanization, resilience, and complacency.

JULIUS MARGOLIN HAS been described in a variety of ways: as a Russian Jew, Polish Jew, Belarus-born Israeli writer, Litvak writer, Russian-speaking Polish philosopher, Israeli intellectual of Russian origin, and even a Lithuanian writer. The confusion is not so surprising. Though he ultimately settled in Israel, Margolin was born to Jewish parents and raised in the diaspora. Moreover, his hometown of Pinsk experienced ten different stewardships in the twentieth century, as Russians, Germans, Poles, Soviets, and Belarusians fought to control the territory containing his birthplace. Named Iulii Borisovich

Margolin, he was born on October 14, 1900, in Pinsk, then located in Russia's Pale of Settlement. After changing hands several times between the Russians and the Germans in the course of the First World War, and between the Poles and the Russians in the subsequent Polish-Soviet War, Pinsk was incorporated into the reborn Polish state in 1920. During the Second World War, the Soviets annexed eastern Poland in 1939, including Pinsk, lost it to the Nazis in 1941, and finally reincorporated it into the USSR in 1945. Today it is in the Republic of Belarus.

Pinsk was predominantly a Jewish town in the early twentieth century, when Margolin was born, with Jews making up approximately three-quarters of the population. Russians constituted thirteen percent of the inhabitants and Poles seven percent while the town still lay within the Russian Empire, but that ratio changed drastically after Pinsk's 1920 incorporation into Poland.[2] Though Margolin heard Yiddish, Polish, and Lithuanian spoken around him, his family spoke Russian, and his early education took place in Russian institutions, first at a local elementary school, later at both a high school (1915–1919) and then the Higher Institute of Public Education (1920–1922) in Ekaterinoslav (from 1925 Dnepropetrovsk, now Dnipro).[3] By his own description, Margolin "took root in Russian culture."[4] In the words of Inna Dobruskina, who organized and publicized Margolin's manuscripts, "By language, upbringing, and culture, he was Russian, one of the best representatives of the Russian Jewish intelligentsia."[5] Above all, he considered himself a Jew, reportedly stating that when that did not suffice to describe his origins, he did not care whether he was called a Pole or a Russian.[6] Still, Margolin reports that when the outbreak of the Second World War caught him in Poland, he felt "sincerely upset" at "the Polish tragedy," to which "the sentiments of a Polish Jew" tied him (9).

After completing his studies in Ekaterinoslav in 1922, Margolin moved to Germany, enrolling in 1923 in the department of philosophy of the University of Berlin. Active in the Russian émigré community, he published on Russian literature and in the Russian-language newspaper *Nakanune* (*On the Eve*). In 1926 Margolin married Eva Spektor, a fellow philosophy student who also hailed from the Russian Pale of Settlement; their son Ephraim was born that same year. Margolin completed his dissertation, entitled "The Fundamental Phenomena of the Intentional Conscience," and received his doctoral degree in 1929.[7] The young family subsequently moved to Poland, settling in the central city of Łódź, where Margolin worked as a writer and journalist. In Łódź, which had the second largest Jewish population in interwar Poland, he became engaged in Zionist thought, publishing the book *The Idea of Zionism*, in Polish, in 1937.[8] He also became a follower of Vladimir (Ze'ev) Jabotinsky and his Betar movement, a Revisionist Zionist youth movement popular in Eastern Europe, especially Poland, in the interwar period.[9] While in Łódź, Margolin also published a book in Yiddish on the philosophy of poetry, entitled *The Construction of an Artistic Work*.[10]

Margolin and his family traveled to the British Mandate of Palestine in 1936. So that his wife and son could settle in Tel Aviv, Margolin borrowed one thousand British pounds (current value of $70,000), a payment necessary to qualify for an immigration visa. To repay that loan, Margolin had to manage a textile plant in Łódź for the next three years.[11] He, too, obtained a residency certificate for Palestine but also retained his Polish citizenship, and journeyed to Łódź in May 1939, intending to return to Tel Aviv on September 3. However, on September 1 the Nazis invaded Poland. The Wehrmacht captured the city of Łódź a week later and, valuing its industrial capacity, soon annexed it to the Third Reich. Before that happened, Margolin fled the city for Warsaw, but quickly left the capital with a wave of refugees headed eastward, away from the Germans.

Unbeknownst to any of Poland's inhabitants, the east would soon be fraught with different dangers, for Germany and the USSR had recently concluded a secret agreement to carve up the Polish state. The Nazi-Soviet Pact, also known as the Molotov-Ribbentrop Pact, signed on August 23, 1939, was a nonaggression treaty that also included secret protocols providing for the division of the Polish state between the two powers.[12] The Soviet Union's partition amounted to fifty-two percent of Polish territory, along with 13.5 million of its inhabitants. The majority of these inhabitants (roughly two-thirds) were members of the national minorities, most numerously Ukrainians, Belarusians, Jews, and Lithuanians, some of whom were unfavorably disposed toward the interwar Polish state, which maintained an increasingly difficult relationship with them. Throughout the interwar period the Polish government sought to extend its control over the eastern portions of the country, settling ethnic Polish military veterans and civilian colonists, called *osadnicy*, there to serve as a Polonizing element. The government established the Frontier Defense Corps (KOP) to protect the eastern border, but also to quell internal unrest and spread Polish propaganda. In 1930 military and police forces carried out operations to "pacify" increasingly violent Ukrainian nationalists in the southeast.[13] As in most of Europe in the 1930s, Jews in Poland faced growing antisemitism. Antisemites characterized the Jews as ungrateful to their hosts, accused them of weakening the nation, and linked them to communism. Resentment of the Jews resulted in economic boycotts, beatings, and anti-Jewish riots. After 1935 the government gave in to popular antisemitism, instituting administrative measures to weaken Jews' role in the economy and to reduce their presence in academic institutions.[14]

The Soviets used the tensions present among the inhabitants of eastern Poland to their advantage. First, they exploited the turmoil experienced by the population in the wake of the Nazi onslaught, which was compounded by uncertainty at the appearance of Red Army tanks and troop columns crossing the border. The Soviet Union invaded from the east on September 17 without a declaration of war. Local inhabitants initially assumed that the Red Army had come to help fight the German Wehrmacht. The Polish-Soviet Non-Aggression Treaty of 1932 had been renewed in 1934 for ten years, which lent credence to this interpretation.[15] In many places Soviet soldiers themselves announced their purpose as fighting the Germans; some even waved white flags upon arrival. Masking their true intention of turning eastern Poland into a part of the USSR, other Soviet soldiers proclaimed that they had come to liberate their brethren, the Belarusians and Ukrainians, fellow Slavs, from the "yoke" of the Poles. As a result, in towns throughout the region locals came out to greet the Red Army, offering flowers, waving red banners, and erecting triumphal arches. Individuals of all ethnicities were reported to have welcomed the Soviet army in some areas. Margolin himself writes: "Not only the Jews but also Poles, Ukrainians, and Belarusians opened their hearts to the Soviet Union. They all regarded the arrival of Soviet troops not as a conspiratorial and cynical partition of Poland but as a fortuitous obstacle impeding Hitler" (19). Ethnic Poles in the east, who had the most to lose, were the most reticent and suspicious of the Soviets.[16]

The day Red Army troops crossed the border, September 17, found Julius Margolin in the town of Czortków (now Chortkiv, in Ukraine). Upon learning of the Soviet invasion, Margolin and his traveling companions—each with a foreign passport or residency permit—fled to the Polish-Romanian border, hoping ultimately to make it to their distant homes. Romanian soldiers refused to let Jews enter the country, and Margolin's group went to the city of Lwów (now Lviv), soon to be incorporated into the Ukrainian Soviet Socialist Republic. Here Margolin came face to face with the reality of the Soviet invasion. "There was no longer a war but there was an upheaval in political, social, and daily life, whose source was not internal but external, dictated by Moscow," he writes. "Liberation from the Germans turned into conquest" (21). Historian Jan Gross similarly describes the essence of the Soviet invasion in his book title *Revolution from Abroad*. Seeking to Sovietize the territory, to transform it according to its own model, the occupier quickly shut down local and national institutions and overturned existing hierarchies of authority.

Ethnic Poles were replaced by Ukrainian, Belarusian, and Russian speakers in schools, governmental agencies, and cultural bodies. The ruble replaced the *złoty* as legal tender, wiping out pre-war savings and devastating businesses. Land and personal property were confiscated and redistributed; as families found their domiciles requisitioned by Soviet officers and officials, they joined the refugees from the German occupation in seeking limited shelter in the new circumstances.[17] Shortages of goods, including bread, quickly arose, making queues ubiquitous. According to Gross, the chaos was not simply a byproduct of the invasion, but deliberate, a "perfectly sensible strategy." It was, he explains, "a stage in the subjugation of the local people to a new, distant, and absolute authority . . . that very shortly results in a weakening of the community bonds around which resistance would be likely to crystallize against impending measures."[18]

In late October, after several weeks of propagandizing, cajoling, and threatening, Soviet authorities held compulsory elections with a predetermined outcome throughout the territories of eastern Poland. These elections sanctioned delegates to national assemblies in what were now called Western Belorussia and Western Ukraine. Several days later these assemblies voted unanimously to request incorporation into the USSR, which the Supreme Soviet in Moscow quickly granted.[19] Unable to secure permission to cross the border into Romania in order to return to Palestine, Margolin found Lwów unbearable and decided to return to his hometown, Pinsk, where his parents still resided.

There Margolin continued his quest for a visa to leave, which proved impossible. Since the new regime no longer recognized the Polish state or its documents, it could not, he was told, stamp a Soviet exit visa in his Polish passport. Margolin once again traveled to the Romanian border, but learned that it was sealed; he decided to try his luck elsewhere and headed up north in late December to the new border with Lithuania, hoping to reach the city of Wilno (now Vilnius). Margolin viewed the city as the "gates of freedom" since it now belonged to an ostensibly independent state.[20] However, he was turned back on the road to the border and interrogated by the NKVD, the Soviet secret police. The officer believed his excuse for being near the state boundary and released him. "Three months later," Margolin observes, "I would not have gotten off so easy" (32). Indeed, the new authorities intensified their efforts to arrest anyone caught attempting to cross the former Polish frontiers, either to Lithuania, Romania, Hungary, or the General Government—the other side of the new German-Soviet border, which cut through the middle of the recently-defeated Polish state.[21] Tens of thousands of people were arrested for trying to cross a state boundary in the first month of the occupation alone.[22] Convicted of border transgressions under Article 120 of the Belorussian and Ukrainian Criminal Codes, such individuals typically received a sentence of five years of hard labor.[23]

Attempting to leave Soviet-occupied Poland constituted just one of many crimes for which inhabitants of eastern Poland were incarcerated by Soviet authorities. Mass arrests began soon after the invasion, singling out national and local leaders in the military, political, economic, religious, and cultural spheres. Initially the regime targeted Polish army officers, government officials, policemen, landowners, business and administrative elites, and the clergy.[24] The victim pool expanded to include anyone the regime considered to be "socially dangerous" or "unreliable"—in other words, people who did not conform to the demands of the new system. While no precise data has yet been established, estimates of the total number of individuals in eastern Poland arrested by Soviet authorities from September 1939 to June 1941 reach 250,000.[25] They were charged and sentenced ostensibly according to Soviet law, which stipulated punishments that tended to be far out of proportion to the infractions. Charges were routinely fabricated. Additionally, the accusations frequently referred to behavior not criminalized in Western law, for the Soviet regime considered many individuals guilty simply because of their class origins, occupation, political allegiance, or national identity, and convicted them for alleged counterrevolutionary activities or as "enemies of the people."

The dragnet spread ever wider. In December 1939 the Politburo began making plans for a vast assault on Polish society—the deportation of civilians to the interior of the USSR. The first deportation was executed on the night of February 10–11, 1940. It primarily affected military settlers (*osadnicy*), but also included civil servants, local government officials, police officers, forest workers, and small farmers. Critically, entire families were taken, regardless of the age of their members. The number of individuals deported totaled at least 140,000. Sent to work in the forests of Siberia and the Arctic North of Russia, the deportees lived under the supervision of the NKVD.

The deportation of the military settlers and their families was just the first of four major operations that occurred during the wartime Soviet occupation of eastern Poland. The second took place on the night of April 12–13, 1940, removing the families of persons who had previously been arrested or taken as prisoners of war, or who fled abroad or went into hiding. This group, sent primarily to Kazakhstan, numbered between 61,000 and 66,000. Two months later, on June 29, 1940, another deportation began, involving 76,000 to 78,000 individuals. At this time the regime targeted the so-called refugees (*bezhentsy*) who had fled from German-occupied Poland; they were distributed in many different areas in European Russia, the Far North, and Siberia. The fourth deportation occurred one year later, from late May to mid-June 1941. An estimated 88,000 persons were taken away at this time, with ethnic Poles representing just over forty percent. The others came from Lithuania, Latvia, Estonia, and Moldova, all of which the Soviet Union annexed in June 1940, fulfilling the secret protocols of the Molotov-Ribbentrop Pact of 1939. This deportation operation was still in progress when the German army invaded the USSR on June 22, disrupting all Soviet administrative activity in its western territories and prompting the hasty evacuation of Soviet authorities.

Recent estimates of the total number of women, men, and children forcibly exiled to the USSR from eastern Poland from 1939 to 1941 range from 315,000 to 400,000.[26] Some scholars assert that the total number of deportees reached nearly one million, as Polish authorities had estimated during the war.[27] Regardless of the exact number, it is clear that hundreds of thousands of civilians never charged with any crimes were torn from their homes and exiled by administrative decree. The deportations, writes historian N. S. Lebedeva, constituted an "inseparable part of the Stalinist policy of destroying the state structure of Poland and Sovietizing western Ukraine and western Belorussia."[28]

Hence it was into an atmosphere of increasing terror that Margolin returned to Pinsk at the beginning of 1940, after failing to reach the Lithuanian border. He witnessed the arrest of Polish governmental officials there and the first deportation, in February, of the military settlers: "[I]n a characteristic Soviet measure, they were not simply removed from their posts but also liquidated as a population group. They no longer were among us. The *osadnicy* followed them" (35). Another upheaval began in March 1940 with the passportization campaign. Though all of the inhabitants of the annexed Polish territories became, in the eyes of the new rulers, de facto Soviet citizens, each was required to accept a Soviet passport and, importantly, register with the new authorities. Accurate lists of names and addresses constituted an important tool for control and assisted in the planned deportations. Pressure was applied on the locals to accept the new passports through propaganda and threats, as well as access to living quarters and jobs.[29] Refusal to renounce Polish citizenship in favor of a Soviet passport rendered one "disloyal," punishable by arrest or deportation as a "dangerous element."

The refugees from German-occupied Poland, which included Margolin, had a different choice to make in the spring of 1940: they could accept a

Soviet passport or register to return to the German zone. The choice was especially stark for Jewish refugees, including those, like Margolin, whose home was in Palestine or elsewhere. "[V]oluntary acceptance of Soviet citizenship could in the future cut off the path of return," he writes, "Refusing it meant handing oneself over to the Gestapo" (59). Late in 1939 the German and Soviet governments agreed to repatriate refugees from their respective partitions. As part of the process, German evacuation committees were set up in the Soviet zone, registering those who wished to return to the western side of Poland. Prepared to accept up to 70,000 individuals, they had 164,000 petitioners. Westward evacuations began in April. A total of 66,000 individuals, including approximately 1,600 Jews, thus returned to the German partition.[30] In facing this dilemma, Margolin made the decision to register to return to German-occupied Poland, explaining his reasoning as follows:

> Both prospects were absurd for me. I wanted to go to Palestine, to my home and family, where, on the basis of a certificate and visa, I ought to be able to go at any time. In no way did I want to accept Soviet citizenship, but in March 1940, the only way I could legally avoid receiving a Soviet passport was to register to return to the German-occupied sector of Poland" (59).

Since his Palestinian visa had recently expired, he telegraphed his wife there, requesting that she obtain an extension. He then waited in Pinsk with other refugees for his expected departure to the German zone and for his visa extension, which came too late.[31] Margolin uses a striking metaphor to describe his situation: "I was like a fly who has landed on a sticky leaf with the inscription 'Death to the flies,' and although it is illiterate, does not know what glue is, and understands nothing, none of this is necessary—in a split second, it is mortally afraid and bewildered: it is impossible to break away! Something irremediable and terrible has happened" (58).

The third wave of deportations (June 1940) targeted the refugees from Nazi-occupied Poland. The ones who had applied to the German commission to return to that side but were not accepted, predominantly Jews, seemed especially dangerous in Soviet eyes. If they wanted to leave, they clearly had to be enemies of the Soviet Union. Ironically, the Soviet response of deportation or arrest saved many of their lives. While the Jews who returned to German-occupied Poland were eventually killed by the Nazis, many of those sent to the Soviet interior made it through the war alive. Only ten percent of Poland's pre-1939 Jewish population survived the Second World War (380,000), two-thirds of them in the Soviet Union.[32]

Margolin did not receive permission from the Germans to return to Łódź or Litzmannstadt, as the Nazis renamed it. In June 1940 a Soviet policeman took him for a "talk" at the station. He later reflected, "When I crossed the threshold at the police station . . . I immediately ceased to be a human being" (72). Margolin was cursed at, subjected to a body cavity search, had his possessions confiscated, and then taken to a crude NKVD prison. The charge leveled against him: violation of the passport regime; he was residing in the USSR without documents. Possession of a Polish passport meant nothing. As the interrogator explained, "The passport of a nonexistent state is not a passport" (76). This crime was exacerbated by Margolin's desire, declared by registering with the German repatriation commission, to leave the Soviet Union. Margolin tried to defend himself and explain his situation, realizing only later that, as a naïve European intellectual, he made a grave error. "I paid with an extra two years of my sentence for the cheap pleasure of pressing my interlocutor to the wall, for verbal stubbornness," he reflects (75).

Thus began Margolin's five-year ordeal as a Soviet zek, a prisoner (followed by nearly a year as an exile), the story of which takes up the bulk of his book. After six weeks in the Pinsk prison, Margolin was loaded onto a prisoner transport train, which he calls "the wandering coffin." He echoes the descriptions of the civilian deportees, who recounted the terrible conditions they endured on the transports over several weeks. "They were trains," wrote one, "that we Poles never even dreamed existed."[33] Like them, Margolin felt bereft at moving eastward across the border: "With each day, we were farther and farther from our past. It was not an ordinary journey. It was a journey to the other world. And we knew that when it ended, we would leave the coffin; everything around us would be different." (94).

He was let out of the coffin in the Karelo-Finnish Republic, also known as Karelia, in the far northwestern part of Russia. There, on the northern tip of Lake Onega, Stalin had established the Belomorsko-Baltiiskii camp (Belbaltlag) in 1931 to provide the labor to construct the Baltic–White Sea Canal. When the canal opened in 1933, it was proclaimed "an important victory for the USSR on the frontline of industrialization and the strengthening of the defense capability of the nation."[34] The building of the canal represented the first instance of massive-scale construction by forced labor in the USSR. Since it was completed quickly and supposedly on budget, "corrective labor," as it was called, became a model to emulate in Stalin's industrialization drive. As a result, "By the mid-1930s, the Gulag was the Soviet Union's largest construction organization," writes historian Oleg Khlevniuk. "The Soviet dictatorship felt justified in its conclusion that prison labor offered a mobile and cheap

solution to the nation's infrastructure problems."[35] After the canal's comple-
tion the camp was renamed the Baltiisko-Belomorskii Kombinat (BBK) or
Baltic–White Sea Industrial Complex. Its inmates labored to maintain the
canal and also worked in timber felling, agriculture, and construction.[36]

At the transit camp where he first disembarked from the train, Margolin,
an intellectual, was astonished to hear the news that they would be sent to
labor in the forest. "Never before had there been such people assigned to
felling trees," he notes when this came to pass. "Westerners, Polish Jews, a
scrawny people dressed in elegant suits, speaking foreign languages, and not
understanding anything around them" (114). That camp, Square 48, was just
one sector of hundreds more that comprised the BBK. Margolin estimated
that it held over 1,000 prisoners, mostly from Poland, both Jews and non-
Jews. At this point they were in an unusual position: none of them had actually been sentenced so were technically not prisoners. Since they were in a
corrective labor camp, its head informed them, they had to work and follow
camp rules.

A month after arrival, authorities in Moscow issued their sentences.
Margolin received five years in a labor camp as a "socially dangerous element" for violation of the Soviet passport regime.[37] Life became increasingly
more difficult as he and the other "Westerners," as he refers throughout the
book to those brought from Poland, began to weaken from excruciating
labor, malnutrition, and worsening weather conditions. Margolin himself
could barely manage to complete thirty percent of the required work quota
or norm, for which he received starvation-level food rations. Convinced of
the "Westerners'" inability and unwillingness to work, the authorities began
mixing them with Soviet prisoners, whom they believed would show the
newcomers how to work.

With the influx of Soviet zeks, Margolin thus became acquainted with
the infamous Soviet *urki*, the notoriously vicious professional criminals,
who lacked all scruples and terrorized other inmates. Camp authorities favored common criminals in general over those convicted on political charges
and did little to stop the predatory behavior of the hardened criminals. In
memoirs of the Gulag, which have been written almost exclusively by former
political prisoners, tales of the *urki* abound.[38] The politicals lived in fear of
the *urki*, who robbed, assaulted, raped, and murdered other prisoners. These
powerful criminals habitually played cards for other people's clothing and
even lives. "When it came to women," writes a Polish woman also sent to the
Gulag, "they played for the right to rape."[39] Margolin notes that the Soviet
urki "entered our milieu like wolves into a flock of sheep" (141). At various

points throughout his time in the Gulag he had his food taken away, all his possessions stolen, and was nearly strangled to death by *urki*.

During the first ten months of his sentence, Margolin had one source of solace: letters from his mother in Pinsk. While he was forbidden to send or receive letters from abroad, and therefore could not communicate with his wife and son in Palestine, mail continued to flow between the Gulag and the annexed territories until war broke out between Germany and the USSR. Indeed, many Polish citizens incarcerated and deported deep into the Soviet Union credited the packages they received from home with saving their lives.[40] At one point Margolin's mother even sent him his new visa for entry into Palestine, which had arrived in Pinsk; authorities confiscated it and used it as further evidence of his guilt. For camp inmates, a package from loved ones not only provided needed nutrition and objects to barter, but "was a greeting from home, a sign of love and evidence of fidelity. . . . We again felt like human beings and found new reserves of resistance" (217).

This communication and assistance ended abruptly in June 1941, when the Nazis invaded the Soviet Union. The last letter Margolin received from his mother informed him of his elderly father's death. He learned much later that his mother had been shot by the SS in 1942 during the liquidation of the Pinsk ghetto.

The German attack on the Soviet Union was an unmitigated disaster for the people who fell under Nazi occupation. As a border region, the Karelo-Finnish ASSR was vulnerable to invasion, so Margolin's camp, along with twenty-seven other labor camps in the western USSR, was soon evacuated.[41] The inmates traveled primarily on foot; in Margolin's case, they walked twelve hours per day, for over three hundred miles, eastward to the Arkhangel'sk region. Their destination: the Kargopol camp (*lag*). Opened in 1937, it housed over 25,000 prisoners before the evacuees arrived.[42] A Polish writer also arrested by the Soviets in 1940 and sentenced to hard labor, Gustaw Herling-Grudziński, spent time in Kargopolag as well and described it in another of the early published Gulag memoirs, *A World Apart*.[43] In Kargopolag Margolin was held at Kruglitsa, the medical camp, and Osinovka, the penal sector.[44]

July 1941 brought astounding news to the Poles: an agreement between the London-based Polish government-in-exile and the Soviet Union. Needing an ally after the calamitous invasion by the Wehrmacht, the Soviets restored diplomatic relations between the two governments. The Sikorski-Maiskii Pact of July 30, 1941, had two major provisions. First, it called for the formation of a Polish army in the USSR to fight the Nazis, set up under the command of a Pole, General Władysław Anders, who had been imprisoned in Moscow.

Second, it promised "amnesty to all Polish citizens who are at present deprived of their freedom on the territory of the USSR either as prisoners of war or on other adequate grounds."[45] Though the rapprochement between the two governments proved short-lived, beginning in the late summer of 1941 waves of Poles started flowing from all over the Soviet Union to its southern regions, in search of outposts of the newly-formed Anders Army.[46]

Not all of the detained Poles were released, as Margolin himself learned. "From the beginning," Jan Gross writes, "the Soviet authorities were reluctant to implement the agreement signed with the Polish government; many Poles were never informed of the amnesty, others were not released from confinement."[47] One problem centered around whom Soviet officials considered Polish citizens: often they equated citizenship with Polish ethnicity, thereby excluding the Jews, Ukrainians, and Belarusians from eastern Poland likewise deported and incarcerated. In October 1941 some of Margolin's fellow "Westerners" began to be released from the camp; he was not. His complaint to the authorities elicited the explanation that as a person of non-Polish nationality, the amnesty did not apply to him. As many Polish Jews had been released, Margolin rejected this reasoning, but his further appeals brought no replies, only an allusion to the fact that he had had contact with foreign consulates.

Bereft of hope, Margolin remained in the camp, exhorted constantly to work. His health and spirits progressively deteriorated. The spring of 1942, a difficult time for the Soviet population at war, was excruciating for inmates of the Gulag. The death rate in the camps in 1942 reached five hundred times that of 1940, at 176 per one thousand prisoners.[48] Margolin writes of eating grass, nettles, saltbush, old frozen potato scraps, and boiled leather in order to stave off death by starvation. When sent to the lumber camp of Onufrievka, Margolin had little hope of survival, but, in his words, "A miracle happened" (349). An inmate-doctor declared him medically unfit for hard labor and granted his request to be sent back to Kruglitsa, the medical settlement. For a time Margolin was assigned to light labor, but when food rations decreased yet again near the end of 1942, he no longer had the strength for that job. Severely malnourished, his weight had dropped from 80 kilos (176 lbs.) to 45 (99 lbs.). After falling unconscious, he was examined by a physician, a free worker, who declared him an invalid, unfit for physical labor.[49] Margolin's status as an invalid elated him, as he believed it provided the grounds for his release.

In 1939 Stalin had banned all early releases from the camps, including those for medical reasons. However, soon after the outbreak of war with Germany, as the number of sick and disabled inmates grew to more than one-third of the total camp population, the Soviet government decreed amnesties for several categories of invalids and others who were not work-capable. Approximately 650,000 prisoners were thus discharged in 1941. The releases, writes historian Golfo Alexopoulos, "were primarily motivated by the desire to unload the Gulag's 'ballast.' "[50] Over the next few years, as the rate of prisoners who had "completely lost their labor capability" continued to rise, more exemptions were granted to Stalin's earlier ban, and Gulag officials again were allowed to use local courts to release incapacitated inmates.[51]

In this regard, however, Margolin experienced his second disappointment in camp. "The first time they arbitrarily excluded me from the amnesty for Polish citizens in the winter of 1941," he writes. "In 1943, they kept me in camp despite my decommissioning" (398). He was no longer required to work, so he "declared a grand vacation" (409) and turned to philosophical writing, which had helped him survive when he first landed in a camp hospital. Before too long, however, Margolin needed to work, as the food ration for invalids consisted of a watery soup and 400 grams (less than one pound) of bread per day. He also sought to avoid being dispatched to a special camp section for invalids, which camp authorities used to reduce the costly burden infirm prisoners posed. Indeed, a medical-sanitation department director reported that in her camp's invalid section "living conditions were nonexistent."[52] Margolin took up various jobs in the gardens, the vegetable warehouse, and the clothes-drying room; he even became the brigade leader of the invalids. The latter position gave him access to additional rations of bread, which resulted from mistakes in the ledgers or in the cutting of rations. "I was thus fed on account of the disorder and imperfection of the camp mechanism," Margolin explains: "All of us in camp were caught in a net and incessantly were seeking some loophole in it. We lived like people shut in a basket who survive on the air that the sides of the basket let in" (441).

The rapprochement between Moscow and the London Polish government of the summer of 1941 quickly fell apart. As tensions mounted, the Anders Army was evacuated across the Caspian Sea to Iran.[53] Relations between the two governments collapsed completely in April 1943 after the German army discovered mass graves in the Katyń forest of approximately 4,400 Polish army officers and reservists, a fraction of the—we now know—roughly 22,000 prisoners who were murdered on western Soviet territory.[54] The officers and civilians had been deported from Poland in 1939 and secretly executed on the orders of Stalin and Lavrentii Beria, head of the secret police, in the spring of 1940. Until 1990 the Soviet government insisted that these Polish citizens had been murdered by the Nazis.[55] Stalin used the refusal of the Poles to accept the Soviet denial of responsibility as an excuse to break relations with the Polish London government; he then began creating organizations of Polish communists that would be ready to take power once Polish territory was liberated by the Red Army from the Nazis. This included a military force, commanded by Lieutenant Colonel Zygmunt Berling, who had likewise been interned as a POW in 1939. Soviet authorities had isolated Berling from his fellow Polish officers as someone sympathetic to the communist cause.[56] In May 1943 the Soviets sanctioned the formation of the Tadeusz Kościuszko Infantry Division. As it grew, Stalin allowed it to be expanded, in August, to the Polish Corps, under the now promoted General Berling. In the spring of 1944 this corps was in turn enlarged and reorganized into the Polish First Army. Though still under Berling's command, more than half of its officers were Russian—most of the Polish officers had been executed, and thousands of surviving members of the Polish military left with the Anders Army. The Berling Army, as it was called, operated under Soviet subordination.[57]

At this point, May 1944, some of the Polish citizens still in the camps were examined for fitness to join the Berling Army, Margolin included. Not surprisingly, given his weakened state, he was declared unfit for service. Soon afterward, though, Margolin arbitrarily lost his status as an invalid, and in July 1944 he and the other Poles too infirm for military service were sent to Vorkuta, a camp located above the Arctic circle. Established in 1932 to exploit the reserves of coal there, "by the late 1930s and early 1940s it had become one of the fastest growing and deadliest prison camp complexes in the Soviet Union," notes one historian.[58] "I understood that I would not return alive from Vorkuta," Margolin thought, upon learning their destination (453). It was, in fact, miraculous that he survived. Luck intervened, again in the form of a sympathetic doctor. At the Kotlas transit center, en route to Vorkuta, Margolin encountered a physician who had helped him several years earlier in Kruglitsa. This man enlisted the aid of the resident doctors, who kept him from the departing transports, allowing him to have an "underground" existence.

Still, at Kotlas Margolin's health continued to deteriorate, and eventually he was moved to the hospital block for patients with medical complications. Diagnosed with "alimentary dystrophy"—the Soviet euphemism for the wasting away of the intestinal muscle due to starvation—his invalid status was restored. He notes with irony that, just as the war was ending beyond the camp, the carnage continued inside it: "Month after month, lying on the cot, forgotten by the entire world, even by my enemies, I watched as people were dying" (490). Margolin avoided that fate under the care of Dr. Veniamin Berger, a Lithuanian Jew similarly arrested and sent to the Gulag. Later Margolin credited Berger with having "saved my life, pulled it from the clutches of the most vile and humiliating death—from starvation. In the Kotlas camp where we met, he slowly and patiently put me back on my feet—in the literal sense of the word."[59]

In June 1945 Margolin's term of imprisonment ended, and he was released. Typically discharged inmates were barred from the major cities and border regions, and certainly from leaving the country. Having to choose a place to go on the spot, Margolin decided upon the Altai *kraj* (region), where he knew Dr. Berger had a friend. Located in Western Siberia, the Altai *kraj* borders Kazakhstan; many of the families of arrested Poles were exiled there in 1940 and 1941, as were peoples from the Baltic states in 1941. Margolin set off on the long journey southward, to the town of Slavgorod, to find Berger's friend. That man, Leonty Soloveichik, himself an exile from Lithuania, took Margolin under his wing for the next nine months.[60]

As the political situation began to crystallize in Poland at the war's conclusion, Kremlin leaders concluded a treaty with Poland's provisional government, which they themselves had established. This government, dominated by pro-Soviet communists, agreed to a population exchange with the Soviet Union. The relevant part of the treaty of July 6, 1945 restored Polish citizenship to Poles and Jews who had been exiled to the USSR and called for their evacuation to Poland. More than 230,000 individuals boarded trains between February and April 1946, this time traveling westward.[61] Margolin was included in this repatriation, and he left Slavgorod in late March 1946, departing from the Soviet Union for good.

Upon reaching Poland, Margolin went immediately to Łódź, "the city where I had spent ten years of my life and from which I had fled in 1939" (528). He stayed there for four months, wandering the streets, looking for a familiar face. Before the war, between 230,000 and 250,000 Jews lived in Łódź; when the city was liberated by the Soviets early in 1945, approximately 1,000 remained. Polish Jews who survived the war quickly moved to major cities, including Łódź, so that when Margolin arrived there the Jewish population had reached 30,000.[62] But his people had "disappeared in broad daylight" and he "moved among shadows." "It was inconceivable that in this city," he bemoans, "where I had known hundreds of people and could not walk a hundred meters without encountering a reciprocal glance, gesture, or word in greeting, now no one recognized me" (531).

While in Łódź Margolin obtained both a passport and a visa for Palestine. He left Poland on August 29, 1946. Only when the plane flew over the western Polish border did he feel that his Soviet adventure was over and he was free. When he landed in Paris he had his first contact with family in nearly eight years—his wife's brother, Alexander. Alexander and his wife helped Margolin travel to Marseilles, where ships departed for Haifa. After a three-week wait, he boarded the Greek steamship *Heliopolis*, in September 1946, and journeyed once again to Mandatory Palestine.

Margolin returned to Tel Aviv, to his wife and son, who had not known of his whereabouts for years. "When he returned, after nearly a seven-year absence," his son Ephraim later recalled, "he had broken front teeth and strange, round eyeglasses. He had white hair, but his moustache was still red."[63] At this point Margolin was only forty-six years old. He immediately took up the cause of Jewish Zionists remaining in the Soviet camps, appealing to Jewish leaders in Palestine and abroad to come to their aid.[64] At the end of 1946 Margolin publicized the plight of Dr. Berger, who cared for him in Kotlas, and had been a prominent Zionist in Lithuania before the war. Margolin stressed Berger's unjust incarceration and continued suffering in the Gulag to rally Western Jews to intervene on behalf of all the Jews still languishing in the camps. He wrote about Berger in his first article "after seven years of silence," while still onboard the *Heliopolis* (570). It was published as an open letter in the Yiddish-language paper *Forverts* (*The Forward*) in New York, the Hebrew-language *ha-Hevrah* (*Society*) in Tel Aviv, and the Russian-language *Sotsialisticheskii Vestnik* (*Socialist Herald*) in Paris. In the piece Margolin declared: "The 'Berger Case' is the affair of all our people, Jews, who gave their lives to Zionism and, living in Poland, Lithuania, the Baltic states, had nothing to do with the Soviet Union before the war. Now they are considered 'Soviet citizens'—and the Soviet country can find no other use for them than slavery." Failing to react to such injustice, he continued, signals moral decay and inevitable political decline.[65] Margolin's letter met with silence. Margolin's son recalls that his father, immediately after arriving in Palestine, went to Haifa to meet the family of Dr. Berger; they were communists and told him that he was lying about the existence of labor camps in the USSR.[66]

Margolin's principal endeavor upon his return to Palestine was writing this book, which he did in Tel Aviv from late 1946 through 1947. Just as his appeals to Jewish leaders in Palestine met with little response, so too did his book manuscript. Margolin had advance warning of this reaction while on the steamship to Haifa. As he explains in the concluding chapter of this book, he shared the article he was writing about Veniamin Berger with a passenger from Tel Aviv, who cautioned him: "No one in our country is ready to accept such things. It will be very difficult to make people listen to you." Pointing to several public figures on the ship, the man continued, prophetically: "You attacked communism and therefore your truth has no meaning for them. By this single article, you drew a sharp line between them and yourself" (577).

Indeed, Margolin met with continued opposition in socialist-oriented Palestine/Israel, as opinion of the Soviets was high among Jews due to the Red Army's success in defeating the Nazis. And since Soviet support was necessary for the creation of the state of Israel, no one wanted to alienate this critical power. Unable to get his book published in Israel, Margolin looked to France. He sent the manuscript to Roman Gul, a Russian émigré, who published several chapters in his monthly Russian-language journal, *Narodnaia pravda* (*People's Truth*), early in 1949. Gul praised Margolin's text, writing, "I do not know a single work on the concentration camps equal in strength to this manuscript."[67] Gul passed it on to Boris Souvarine, one of the founders of the French Communist Party and a former executive member of the Communist International (Comintern); he had broken with the Party in the 1920s and became a fierce critic of Stalin. Souvarine helped to get excerpts published in the French conservative daily *Le Figaro* later in 1949 and to find a publisher for the larger work.[68] It was translated and published in 1949 in abridged form as *La condition inhumaine. Cinq ans dans les camps de concentration soviétiques* (*The Inhuman Condition: Five Years in Soviet Concentration Camps*).[69]

Left-leaning French intellectuals did not welcome talk of concentration camps in the USSR. Historian Michael Christofferson explains that as the Cold War began, "intellectual politics became increasingly binary and Manichean in its logic"; the American and Soviet sides seemed to represent the only existing options.[70] When Victor Kravchenko, a Soviet defector, published his book *I Chose Freedom* in France in 1947 (*J'ai choisi la liberté*), the communist-leaning journal *Les lettres françaises* denounced him as a fraud and accused him of fabricating his claims about Soviet labor camps. Kravchenko sued the journal for libel and, in a much publicized and debated trial, won.[71] According to scholar Tony Judt, however, "in fact the impression left was of a communist moral victory,"[72] due to Kravchenko's shady character, "pompous mannerisms," and apparent connections with American officials, which sharply contrasted with the prominent and respected witnesses who opposed him.[73]

After the publication of his own book, Margolin was caught up in a similar trial, as a witness for a French political activist named David Rousset. A leftist but not a communist, Rousset had fought in the resistance during the war and was imprisoned by the Nazis in Buchenwald and several other camps.[74] In November 1949 he published an appeal in the conservative paper *Le Figaro littéraire* to survivors of the Nazi concentration camps to help him investigate whether parallel camps existed in the USSR. Rousset insisted that the initiative to create a commission to inspect Soviet camps was not about judging the Soviet Union. Rather, it was a purely humanitarian concern, above politics.[75] As historian Emma Kuby reports, Rousset claimed that "he could not stand by while fellow men endured the same abjection he had once experienced."[76] The communist attack appeared immediately in *Les lettres françaises*, written by Pierre Daix, who stressed his moral authority as a fellow Nazi concentration camp survivor to denounce Rousset. Attributing Rousset's appeal to anticommunist sentiments, Daix accused him of making up evidence of Soviet camps.[77] Rousset sued for libel, and the trial began in late 1950.

With one exception, Rousset invited only Gulag survivors with leftist political leanings to testify on his behalf as they could not easily be discredited by the communists. Margolin was the exception. In July 1950 Rousset had written to Margolin that Jewish survivors had a particular duty to participate in the trial.[78] Margolin himself, in a document penned after the trial's conclusion ("The Paris Report"), explained that though he was not a socialist, Rousset reasoned that as a Jew he could not be dismissed by the defense as a fascist.[79] Margolin flew to Paris and testified at the trial. "Despite my five years of hard labor, I was in court for the first time in my life," he reflected. "At that moment I did not feel like a witness, but a prosecutor."[80] During the trial the defense lawyer, voicing a common sentiment among the Left, told Margolin, "Hitler killed six million Jews, and I consider it inappropriate for a Jew to oppose the state that saved the Jews." Margolin retorted, "Hitler shed enough Jewish blood, and there is no need to attribute Stalin's victims to him as well."[81]

Rousset won his suit, and the trial has been credited with forcing more French intellectuals to address the issue of the forced labor camps in the Soviet Union.[82] He did create his desired organization, the International Commission of Inquiry against the Concentration Camp Regime (CICRC). Headquartered in Brussels, it was active until 1960. Margolin tried to establish a commission in Israel to take part in this international body, but found no interest. "In 1950, there were more open defenders of the Soviet camps there," he declared, "than people with the courage to openly stand against them."[83] When he and a few others seeking to create an Israeli union of former prisoners of Soviet concentration camps hung flyers up in Tel Aviv in 1954, "The proclamations, which dared to remind the citizens of Medinat

Israel of the fate of Russian Jewry, were torn, torn, torn to pieces, destroyed systematically and thoroughly."[84]

Twenty years after the Rousset trial, Margolin wrote bitterly about the response his participation and subsequent calls for action received at home:

> The trial was, in general, ignored by the Israeli press, despite the fact that an Israeli journalist and Russian Jew, a resident of Tel Aviv, the author of a famous book about Soviet camps, took such a prominent part in it. Maybe not "in spite of," but precisely because of this. It is unpleasant for a Jew—I am also an Israeli citizen—to speak at a trial that annoys the Soviet government, and alongside non-Jews as well.[85]

He was also angered by the fact that only a dozen people showed up to listen to his public presentation of his report on the trial. "I was counting on a larger audience, but it was not found for me in Israel," he wrote.

Margolin spent the 1950s and '60s, until his death in 1971, working as a freelance journalist and writer in Tel Aviv, publishing mostly in the Russian-language press. He wrote several books on Israel and Jewish history.[86] Above all, he felt an urgent need to fight against the labor camps in the Soviet Union and to keep such camps from appearing elsewhere in the world. Millions could be reached, Margolin thought, through film, and he hoped to write a screenplay called *The Country of the Zek.*" In a 1953 letter he wrote that he wanted "to convince someone like Darryl Zanuck that that country is no less interesting than Java or Bali, and that it is worth building a copy of a Soviet camp, without mystification, on 2 hectares in Hollywood . . . and make a film."[87] Nothing seems to have come of this idea.

Margolin wrote tirelessly about the Gulag and the plight of Jews in it. In the early 1950s he also traveled to Europe and the United States, and even Bombay, to speak on these topics.[88] He never found a political home in Israel. A follower of Jabotinsky and Revisionist Zionism, Margolin rejected the leftist Labor or Socialist Zionists who dominated Israeli politics. Initially he was drawn to Herut, a right-wing nationalist party founded in 1948 by Menachem Begin. Also a member of Jabotinsky's Betar before the war, Begin had similarly been exiled to the USSR from eastern Poland in 1940.[89] Margolin broke completely from Herut in 1954, angry that Begin had voiced no concern for the plight of Soviet Jews. He was convinced that Begin had "virtually destroyed" the revisionist party founded by Jabotinsky.[90]

As time went on, Margolin took up the cause of Soviet Jews in general and their inability to emigrate. He collaborated with the Society for Assistance to Soviet Jewry (MAOZ), which was created in 1958 to pressure the Israeli government to enable Soviet Jews to make *aliyah*, to move to the Land of Israel. Until the end of his life he was outraged that the taboo on the issue of the Soviet camps seemed to apply to the general situation of Soviet Jewry. In 1970, one year before his death, Margolin explained this silence as follows: "At the core is extreme caution (to say the least) regarding the Soviet government and Soviet ideology—both among those who understand that the persecution of Jewish culture and the national movement is inseparable from the whole Soviet system, and those who, without understanding, feel it, and therefore avoid open resistance to communism as such." "There are always Jews who delay or moderate the protest against communism," he lamented, "even when it comes to the central problem of Jewish existence."[91] Margolin died of leukemia in Tel Aviv on January 21, 1971, at the age of seventy.

MARGOLIN'S MAGNUM opus consists of two books, presented here for the first time in English.[92] The longest, *Journey to the Land of the Zek*, chronicles his life from September 1939 through his release from the Gulag in June 1945. He completed this manuscript in October 1947. The second, *The Road to the West*, was written several years later. Both were written in Russian.

Margolin could not find a publisher for *Journey to the Land of the Zek* in Israel. Nor could he interest any of the large presses in Britain or the United States, even with the help of the writer Arthur Koestler. In a letter of January 1949 Koestler reported to Margolin his lack of success in finding an English-language publisher for the book, but affirmed his conviction "that England and America, from all points of view, are more important for the publication of your book than France."[93] But it was France that proved the most propitious for Margolin's work. Early in 1949 *Narodnaia pravda* (*People's Truth*), a Russian-language journal based in Paris, printed four chapters from the manuscript.[94] The French newspaper *Le Figaro* ran a series of ten translated excerpts under the title "Five Years in Soviet Concentration Camps" in October of the same year. The French publishing house that accepted Margolin's manuscript, Calmann-Levi, insisted on shortening it and changing the title. Its editors cut several entire chapters and pages throughout the work. The abridged book, translated by Russian émigré writer Nina Berberova and Mina Journot, appeared in Paris in November 1949 under the title *La condition inhumaine. Cinq ans dans les camps de concentration soviétiques* (*The Inhuman Condition: Five Years in Soviet Concentration Camps*). Margolin explained to

Boris Souvarine, who had helped him find the publisher, that the new title was a response to André Malraux's 1933 novel *La conditione humaine* (*The Human Condition*), which was sympathetic to communism.[95]

In the United States only Russian émigrés were interested in Margolin's account, and in 1952 a Russian edition was published by the Chekhov Publishing House in New York. This version was more severely abridged, omitting the first seven chapters of the manuscript—all those dealing with Margolin's time on Polish territory under the Nazi and Soviet occupations—as well as other scattered chapters and pages throughout the original. The New York editors cut more than one-third of Margolin's text, leaving him aggrieved. The author shared his frustrations with Mark Vishniak, a Russian émigré who taught at Cornell University and served as *Time* magazine's specialist on Russian affairs, in a November 1952 letter:

> I felt like an artist from whose painting they scraped off forty percent of the paint or cut off part of the canvas, under the pretext that "it doesn't fit in the frame." With someone like Koestler, I suppose, they would not dare to cut 250 pages from the book, but they treated me like a provider of "information": choose what is more interesting, the rest in the basket. Many pages that are strong and necessary for its integrity are gone.[96]

These severely abridged versions were all that readers could access for the next sixty years.

Margolin also voiced dismay that the New York publisher had no plan to distribute the book in Israel, whose left-leaning Russian-speakers he considered a critical audience. Copies of the Russian edition were smuggled into the USSR and passed around illegally as *tamizdat*—literature published abroad and circulated underground, like the self-published writing similarly distributed, which is known as *samizdat*. Russian writer and literary critic Benedikt Sarnov noted that when Aleksandr Solzhenitsyn's "One Day in the Life of Ivan Denisovich" appeared like a bombshell in the Soviet press in 1962, he had already read quite a few camp manuscripts in *samizdat*. He continued: "I also read the wonderful book by Iulii Margolin, *Journey to the Land of Zek*, which was published already in 1952 in New York."[97] Misha Shauli, who disseminated underground literature in Kiev in the early 1970s and recently edited the first complete Russian version of Margolin's book, recalled hearing from several former dissidents that Margolin's book was smuggled into the USSR in the mid-1950s and circulated in the dissident underground of Moscow, Leningrad, and the Baltic states.[98] A German translation of the abridged version was published in Munich in 1965.[99] The 1952 Russian language edition was reprinted in Israel in 1976 by the Society for the Preservation of the Memory of Dr. Julius Borisovich Margolin; it was again printed in Israel in 1997 and in Moscow in 2008.[100]

In 2010 the first complete edition of Margolin's *Journey to the Land of Zek* was published in French by Le Bruit du Temps, as *Voyage au pays des Ze-Ka*. Working with the full manuscript, a copy of which has been preserved in the Central Zionist Archive in Jerusalem, Luba Jurgenson, a professor at the Sorbonne, revised the original French edition. She restored the omitted parts, as well as Margolin's original title.[101] Since Jurgenson's publication renewed interest in Margolin and made the entire text available, it has been translated into other languages. In 2013 both Polish and German translations of the complete version were published.[102]

None of these editions of Margolin's account of his tribulations under Soviet rule include the denouement, however. Margolin's smaller second book continues the story from his post-release stay in the Altai *kraj*, repatriation to Poland, short stay in France, up to his return to Palestine in 1946. This book, *The Road to the West*, was completed in the early 1950s. Its first chapter was published in the Hebrew newspaper *Herut* at the end of 1951.[103] Margolin noted that he was working on the book in his letter to Vishniak, dated November 30, 1952. The following year two chapters were published in a Russian-language journal with footnotes stating that they came from his forthcoming book, and a letter to Margolin from an assistant in Paris late in 1954 indicates that the book had just come out there.[104] However, researchers have not been able to locate such a publication in France, Russia, or the United States.[105]

In October 2012 this second part of Margolin's chronicle was published as a separate book in Paris as *Le livre du retour* (*The Book of Return*).[106] The volume contains eight additional autobiographical chapters on Margolin's childhood. At the end of 2013 Carmel Publishing House in Jerusalem issued a Hebrew translation of the complete *Journey to the Land of the Zek* that includes a slightly abridged version of *The Road to the West*.[107] In 2016 the first complete Russian version of *Journey to the Land of the Zek* was published together with *The Road to the West* in two volumes in Israel by the Jabotinsky Institute, with the permission of Ephraim Margolin (Julius's son).[108]

IT IS IRONIC that the English-speaking public can access Margolin's masterful account of the Gulag only in 2020, for it was among the early survivor accounts to be published and one of the first to offer a comprehensive and detailed description of how the system of forced labor camps functioned and the effects it had on inmates. The American reading public tends to credit Aleksandr Solzhenitsyn with bringing knowledge of the Soviet labor camps to the world with his monumental work, *Gulag Archipelago*. But that was published only in 1973—almost a quarter-century after the abridged version of Margolin's book appeared in print in French translation.

According to literary scholar Leona Toker, the first few Gulag memoirs were published in Europe in the late 1920s, by survivors who had managed to escape to the West. In the early 1930s several more accounts appeared, written by individuals who were "bought out" of the Soviet Union for hard currency, which Stalin needed for his industrialization campaign. Toker explains that these early memoirs had little effect on Western public opinion. The accounts lacked mutual confirmation and contained inaccuracies, information gathered from hearsay, and sensationalism. More importantly, these former inmates deplored the Soviet regime from the start, so were easily dismissed by intellectuals predisposed to support the progressive social experiment launched by the Bolshevik revolution. To left-leaning individuals, both these memoirists and the camps they described appeared to be marginal phenomena.[109]

The next wave of camp memoirs began appearing in the West on the heels of the Second World War. Polish citizens who had been deported and incarcerated in the Soviet Union from 1939 to 1941 produced the first of these works; most of these authors got out of the USSR with the Anders Army in 1942.[110] They constituted the first large group of people—more than 100,000—to have left that country after having spent time in Soviet prisons, camps, and deportation settlements. The Anders Army itself had collected tens of thousands of testimonies from evacuated Polish citizens in 1942 and 1943, both in hopes of tracing the whereabouts of its missing officers (whose graves were only discovered in 1943) and for use in pleading the case for the restoration of Poland's eastern border in an expected postwar peace conference.[111] These materials provided the basis for several books on the Soviet Gulag in the late 1940s.[112] The best-known Gulag memoir from the group of exiled Poles was *A World Apart* by Gustaw Herling-Grudziński, who was imprisoned in Kargopolag. Published in England in 1951, with an introduction by British intellectual Bertrand Russell, the book received acclaim for its stark and detailed portrayal of camp life, its focus on the enduring humanity of fellow inmates, and its high literary quality.[113]

Although Margolin was neither amnestied in 1941 nor evacuated with the Anders Army in 1942, his work belongs to this second set of Gulag memoirs. Like his fellow Polish citizens described above, he was an outsider to the Soviet world, dragged into its penal system unjustly, but ultimately able to leave the country and return to Europe, which he called home. And like these other Polish citizens, he felt an urgent need to tell the world about what he had endured and the system that wrought the heinous realm of the forced labor camps. This he shares with other foreign survivors of the Gulag who wrote about their camp experiences soon after World War II, some of whom testified along with Margolin in 1950–1951 on behalf of David Rousset, who fought the claim that he had fabricated evidence of Soviet forced labor camps. Unlike the survivors who wrote in the late 1920s, these memoirists "went public as witnesses not only in the literary but also in the juridical sense of the word," writes Toker, "and put the issue of Soviet concentration camps on the public agenda."[114]

In contrast to leftists such as Rousset, who insisted that he singled out the Soviet labor camps for attack rather than the Soviet system itself, Margolin sought to break all illusions about the supposed accomplishments of the communist regime and the order it had created. He made his position clear in the first article he wrote after his release:

> The seven past years have made me a convinced and passionate enemy of the Soviet system. I hate this system with all the strength of my heart and with all the energy of my thoughts. Everything that I saw there filled me with horror and disgust for the rest of my life. Everyone who was there and saw what I saw will understand me.[115]

Margolin aims to explain this foreign world, the Land of the Zek, to people in the West who can have no inkling of its alien processes, values, and destructiveness.

Margolin's documentary intent is evident from the start of his book, as he details the process of Sovietization in eastern Poland after the 1939 invasion. While he shares his personal travails, he provides only minimal details and puts them aside to record what he sees around him: the devastation of local economies, communities, and cultural institutions; the disillusionment of the population with the reality of Soviet rule; the tragic fates of acquaintances, particularly Jews who returned to the German-occupied zone.

Some parts of Margolin's account read like a sociological study of an obscure country. He describes the physical terrain of the camps, the material conditions, daily procedures, rules, and disciplinary practices. In the voice of a neutral observer, Margolin records labor norms and food rations, the procedures for logging, working in the bathhouse and clothes drying room, and the cheating and mendacity involved in getting through a day's labor. We learn about the regulations for sending letters, receiving packages, and appealing one's sentence; hygienic conditions, prevalent illnesses, and the available medical care; sex and love among the inmates. The book contains a primer on camp lingo and a long discussion of the work of the Cultural-Educational Sector, which sought to "re-educate" prisoners. More than a decade before Solzhenitsyn's "One Day in the Life of Ivan Denisovitch" appeared in the Soviet press, chronicling a typical day of a zek, Margolin penned chapters devoted to the routines, activities, and adaptations of the inmates as well as their camp bosses. Various types of prisoners receive focused attention in Margolin's opus, including fellow Polish Jews, other "Westerners" taken from Soviet-occupied territories, former communist officials, peasants, women, Catholic and Orthodox priests, Old Believers, intellectuals, members of the Soviet national minorities, and the vicious professional criminals (*urki*). Margolin recounts conversations with all such people, at times recording their stories as an ethnographer, at others conveying his emotional reactions to their tragedies, as well as to the friendships and betrayals he experienced with them.

Throughout it all, Margolin has a keen sense of the absurd and manages to convey aspects of his Gulag existence with irony. He reports, for example, being "liberated" from his possessions by the *urki* (157–158). He describes himself as "the guest from Europe, raised on Kant and Husserl, with eyeglasses and the look of an astonished sheep" (145). A difficult conversation with an NKVD agent is recounted in Margolin's characteristically sardonic style:

> Here I realized that the operative was not strong in geography: he thought Palestine was in Germany. But it was too late to teach him geography. In general, it can be dangerous to get into disputes with representatives of the political police. With NKVD operatives in the forests of the Russian north, it is simply senseless. You can never know what will come of it (138).

In this case, it cost Margolin his coveted office job in the camp.

A philosopher and thinker, Margolin includes in his book disquisitions on a variety of topics, including the nature of Europeans and of Asians, the essence of the Soviet system, and the process of dehumanization in the camps. According to Toker, he was probably the first to discuss the latter topic.[116] For Margolin, logical thought served as a means of self-preservation. In fact, as a form of resistance to the degradation caused by camp life, he completed three philosophical treatises over the course of his imprisonment: "The Theory of Falsehood," "The Doctrine of Hate," and "The Doctrine of Freedom." At a transit prison en route to Vorkuta a guard confiscated all of Margolin's papers, including these manuscripts, and dumped them in the trash. Reflecting on the loss of this unique work, which could never again be created, Margolin lamented: "One should also erect a monument to the unknown destroyed book—the one that was destroyed at the hands of the annihilators of the spirit, the one that was crushed in embryo, and the one that was not allowed to reach readers" (460).

Among Margolin's most detailed and moving discussions—at times documentary, at others very personal—are those about the stages of dehumanization and the effects of starvation on the body and spirit. He recalls eventually beating up a man who constantly stole from him; though it made him a hero in the eyes of others, he felt regret and disgust. Early on, Margolin records the condition and behavior of the *dokhodiagi*, the "goners," he encountered in the camp. These were the prisoners who had become so starved and both physically and morally depleted that they lost their human image (174). The Nazi concentration camps had an analogous figure, the *muselmann*. Later on Margolin himself "skidded to the lowest point of physical decline." "There was no mirror in camp, I did not know how I looked, and I did not care," he relates with intense pain and shame. "I saw myself reflected in my pitiful neighbors, hideous goners. I did not shave for weeks, slept in my clothes, and I was disgustingly filthy" (538). Long before the psychological consequences of long-term deprivation and abuse became familiar topics, Margolin also provided astute observations on the phenomenon of camp neurosis, "the painful deformation of the human psyche caused by a long stay in camp conditions" (353). This was all part of the Soviet process of "reforging" individuals, like some pieces of steel. Human beings carried no greater value to Soviet leaders than physical resources and objects for exploitation. "Soviet corrective labor camps are a gigantic and unique factory," he concludes, "producing spiritual cripples and psychopaths" (363).

One of the issues absent from the other early published Gulag memoirs is the fate of Jews. Margolin's Jewishness is central to his identity and central to his story. He reports facing antisemitism throughout his experience, from Poles in Warsaw after the invasion, and Romanian border guards, to Soviet citizens of all types. Given their common enemy, Poles and Jews got along well in the camp, he writes, despite their increasingly troubled relationship back at home before the war. He adds that Polish antisemitism paled in comparison to the Russian variety, which he calls "massive and elemental" (232). Margolin encountered antisemitism daily from officials as well as fellow inmates, and he comments that the Soviet zeks, whom he considered representative of ninety percent of the Russian population, approached Jews with "much concentrated malice, poison, and seething hatred" (236). Besides relating this hostile atmosphere, Margolin shares the

stories of many Jews similarly seized by the occupying Soviets and deposited
in the Gulag. He was fortunate to encounter a series of exiled doctors, many
of them fellow Jews, who intervened in his camp trajectory, keeping him
from especially destructive labor or destinations, providing extra care, and
essentially saving his life. The plight of these Jewish doctors became the initial focal point of Margolin's efforts to alert the world about the camps
after his own release. Additionally, Margolin pays tribute to the Jews who,
duped by the German commission offering them the chance to return to
their homes in Nazi-occupied Poland, ended up going to their slaughter. So
too the Polish Jews who accepted Soviet passports and remained in eastern
Poland, only to be killed when the Nazis overran that territory. Already
in 1940 Margolin is convinced that the only hope for the Jews is Zionism
(68–69).

Besides identifying as a Jew, Margolin sees himself fundamentally as a
Westerner, a European. He is aware of the disjuncture between his own
thinking and expectations and those of the new Soviet rulers from the very beginning of the invasion. He refers to himself and others struggling to adjust to
the new system instituted in 1939 as "naïve European intellectuals." Margolin
feels this dissonance keenly on the transport from Pinsk to the labor camp in
Russia's Far North. He shares the tremendous shock and anxiety expressed
by countless Polish deportees at crossing the border into Russia, which they
experienced not simply as leaving their own country, but the world as they
knew it. "With a great cry we crossed the Polish border and went to a completely foreign and hostile land," recalled one of the deported Poles. "Europe
remained a long way off," wrote another, "behind us."[117] Margolin, too,
recounts the stark differences he saw once he crossed the Polish border, where
"our European concepts were, evidently, inapplicable to these people" (92). To
most of the Polish exiles Russia was unambiguously Asia. Margolin concurs
that Russians are not Europeans: "But they are not Asians," he counters. "It
is Eurasia—and they are an intermediary people." He continues: "They took
the negative aspects, the worst from each culture. They combined European
anxiety, dualism, and torturous intellectual inquiries with Asiatic despotism
and suppression of the personality" (96).

Margolin describes the journey into the Soviet Union as an even more profound rupture than did many other Polish exiles—he was separated not just
from Europe, but from the earth's surface, from human memory, from history.
"It was an unbridled descent; a demonic, invisible force led us into the heart
of night, to a subterranean kingdom from which there was no return. With
each day, we were farther and farther from our past. It was not an ordinary

journey. It was a journey to the other world" (94). It was the "World Apart," the "Inhuman Land," the "Dark Side of the Moon" that his compatriots described in their books published around the same time, an analogue to the "House of the Dead" that Feodor Dostoevsky depicted after his incarceration in a tsarist labor camp in Siberia nearly sixty years earlier.[118] Reflecting on Dostoevsky's book, Margolin notes that his own account describes not simply a "Dead House" but "an entire Dead Kingdom" (354).

Neither Margolin nor his fellow exiles from Poland and the Baltic states, whom he delineates from Soviet zeks as "Westerners," could adapt to this Dead Kingdom. He notes acidly, "The Westerners do not know how to do anything—neither to open a lock with a nail, scrape off plywood with glass, light a lamp without matches, nor to work on a hungry stomach" (124). At various times he tried to describe "our ways" to noncomprehending Soviets, officials and fellow inmates. Margolin felt it was even harder for the Jews deported from Poland to adjust to this world; in his case, "sixty generations of scholars and individualists, who had not been serfs, hindered me from resigning myself and submitting my neck to the camp yoke" (227).

Margolin understood his identity as a Zionist Jew and as a Westerner to be inextricably linked. While aboard the steamer headed from France to Palestine in 1946 he felt that, though the ship was traveling eastward, he was really going West (569). In an unpublished manuscript from 1950 entitled "The Key to My Biography," he wrote that his whole life experience taught him that his home is the Land of Israel, Israel's place is in the West, and "the way to the West and way of the West—are ways to freedom."[119] For Margolin, humanism, and the freedom of human beings to think, develop, and act, constituted the essence of the West and the antithesis of the Soviet Union. The Soviet system meant human degradation—unbounded humiliation and demoralization. The greatest tragedy was to be found in the Gulag, for, in Margolin's words, millions of people "were reprocessed here into wood for export, minerals, gold, material goods, and simply human chaff doomed to annihilation" (244). The monstrous system of forced labor camps, in Margolin's estimation, represented not simply an incidental aspect of the Soviet system, but a fundamental component. He believed that the regime was based on false theoretical premises and constituted a system of violence. "The forced labor camp," he writes, "derives from the essence of the Soviet regime and is inseparable from it. They are two sides of the same coin" (505).

Ultimately, Margolin considered the Soviet camps to be worse than the Nazi ones. He recognized the horrendous and unjust suffering that occurred in Hitler's camps; however, they represented a temporary aberration in Europe that was inevitably defeated. In contrast, the Soviet camps constituted a massive, long-term, and well-developed system. In a discussion with a Soviet zek in the midst of the war, Margolin thus explained his conclusion: "You can't compare Nazi camps with yours. Neither in scale nor in essence. There is a thorn there that Europe will soon tear out of its body. Your camps are a durable system, the logically, well organized culmination of the regime. Europe can exist without Hitler and his camps. But the Soviet regime cannot exist without camps" (245). The fact that Soviet leaders cloaked their practices and institutions behind a smokescreen of propaganda particularly enraged Margolin. Claiming to create a New World, based on lofty and humanitarian principles, the Soviet regime was instead enslaving millions of innocent people, committing an "unparalleled pogrom of the spirit and execution of human hearts," that could have no justification whatsoever (363). Only the Nazi concentration camps, however, faced condemnation. No one was challenging the Soviet version, either within or without the USSR.

This stark reality led Margolin to heap scorn on Western intellectuals, who, at the time of his writing in the late 1940s, uniformly failed to denounce the Soviet Gulag. At best, some of them believed there was nothing they could do or feared that open protest might endanger relatives still incarcerated. Margolin condemned such individuals as weak. He criticized as indecent the many more who simply refused to see or hear anything that countered their notions of Soviet communism as a revolutionary and well-meaning system. The worst of these, Western communist fellow-travelers, accepted the camps as a necessary aspect of progress. Margolin felt particular repulsion for the latter, as they often were writers and thinkers exercising moral authority and commanding high respect in their societies. After the defeat of Hitler, the problem of the Soviet camps had to be a central concern for Western humanists and freedom fighters. Again underlining the connection between his Jewish and Western identities, Margolin concluded: "In my opinion, the attitude toward the problem of Soviet camps is the touchstone in evaluating a person's decency, just as is one's attitude toward antisemitism" (506). He devoted the rest of his life to raising awareness of and trying to combat the overlapping atrocity of the Soviet labor camps and the "monster that has lurked in the depths of our historical scene," the persecution of the Jews in the USSR.[120]

Notes

1. Central Zionist Archive (hereafter CZA), Jerusalem, A536/49, Iulii Margolin, "Vesti iz Rossii. Delo Bergera (otkrytoe pis'mo)," 1946. Available at http://www.rjews.net/raisa-epshtein/articles/margolin/6.htm.

2. Steven L. Guthier, "The Belorussians: National Identification and Assimilation, 1897–1970. Part I: 1897–1939," *Soviet Studies* 29, no. 1 (1977): 45. According to the Polish government's 1921 census, Poles constituted nearly 17 percent of the population of Pinsk. The diminished Russian population was presumably included in "Others," who made up 2.2 percent; White Russians, as Belarusians were then called, reached nearly 10 percent. Azriel Shohet, *The Jews of Pinsk, 1881 to 1941* (Stanford, CA: Stanford University Press, 2012), 2; 459.

3. S. N. Chizhik [I. A. Dobruskina], Fakty iz biografii Iu. B. Margolina, Avtorskii sait Raisy Epshtein: Iulii Margolin i Golda Elin, at http://www.rjews.net/raisa-epshtein/j_margolin.html.

4. CZA, A536/51, Iulii Margolin, "Kliuch k moei biografii (sekretno)," Oct. 30, 1950. Available at http://www.rjews.net/raisa-epshtein/articles/margolin/10.htm.

5. I. A. Dobruskina, Vstuplenie k nastoiashchei publikatsii, Iu. B. Margolin, Puteshestvie v stranu ze-ka, at http://margolin-ze-ka.tripod.com/introduction.html.

6. D. Rousset, G. Rosenthal, T. Bernard, *Pour la vérité sur les camps concentrationnaires: Un procès antistalinien à Paris* (Paris: Ramsay, 1990), 115, cited in Anna Maria Jackowska, "Julius Margolin—świadek zagłady żydowskiej w obozach sowieckich. Przyczynek do dziejów zimnej wojnej," *Dzieje Najnowsze* 43, no. 3 (2011): 101.

7. Iulii Margolin, *Grundphänomene des intentionalen Bewusstseins* (Berlin: Ebering, 1929).

8. J. Margolin, *Idea syonizmu* (Warsaw-Łódź: Wydawnictwo Atid, [1937]).

9. The name comes from the Hebrew acronym for the Joseph Trumpeldor League, which was named for a Zionist activist and army veteran who was killed in 1920. Menachem Begin, prime minister of Israel from 1977 to 1983, was a leading member of Betar in Poland before World War II. Daniel Kupfert Heller, *Jabotinsky's Children: Polish Jews and the Rise of Right-Wing Zionism* (Princeton, NJ: Princeton University Press, 2017), 1–4.

10. J. Margolin, *Der oyfboy fun a ḵinsṭlerish ṿerḵ* (Warsaw: Farlag Oyś, 1939).

11. Misha Shauli, editor of the 2016 Russian edition of Margolin's book, telephone conversation with translator, Stefani Hoffman, January 23, 2020. Ephraim Margolin conveyed this information to Shauli in a conversation in Israel in February 2014.

12. While this aspect of the treaty became known in the West in 1945, the Soviet government denied its existence until 1989. In that year Mikhail Gorbachev signed a resolution admitting the "probable" existence of the protocols. See *Izvestiia*, December 27, 1989. Only in 1992 did the Communist Party of the Soviet Union make the original protocols public. See *Izvestiia*, October 30, 1992.

13. On national relations in Poland between the wars see Aleksandra Bergman, *Sprawy Białoruskie w II Rzeczypospolitej* (Warsaw: PAN, 1984); Andrzej Chojnowski, *Koncepcje polityki narodowościowej rządów polskich w latach 1921–1939* (Wrocław: Nakład Narodowy im. Ossolińskich, 1979); Jerzy Tomaszewski, *Rzeczpospolita wielu narodów* (Warsaw: Czytelnik, 1985); Wojciech Wrzesiński, ed., *Między Polską etniczną a historyczną* (Wrocław: PAN, 1988).

14. The literature on interwar Polish-Jewish relations is large. See for example: Joseph Marcus, *Social and Political History of the Jews in Poland, 1919–1939* (Berlin: Mouton Publishers, 1983); Władysław Bartoszewski, *Ethnocentrism: Beliefs and Stereotypes. A Study of Polish-Jewish Relations in the Early Twentieth Century* (Cambridge, UK: University of Cambridge, 1984); Chimen Abramsky, Maciej Jachimczyk, and Antony Polonsky, eds., *The Jews in Poland* (London: Basil Blackwell, 1986); Jerzy Tomaszewski, *Najnowsze dzieje Żydów w Polsce* (Warsaw: PWN, 1993); Celia Heller, *On the Edge of Destruction: Jews of Poland between the Two World Wars* (Detroit: Wayne State University Press, 1994); William Hagen, "Before the 'Final Solution': Toward a Comparative Analysis of Political Anti-Semitism in Interwar Germany and Poland," *Journal of Modern History* 68, no. 2 (1996): 351–81; Robert E. Blobaum, ed., *Antisemitism and Its Opponents in Modern Poland* (Ithaca, NY: Cornell University Press, 2005); Antony Polonsky, Hanna Węgrzynek and Andrzej Żbikowski, eds., *New Directions in the History of the Jews in the Polish Lands* (Boston: Academic Studies Press; Warsaw: POLIN Museum of the History of Polish Jews, 2018).

15. According to the Soviet government, the Polish state had ceased to exist due to the German invasion and the flight of the Polish government. The deputy people's commissar for foreign affairs of the USSR delivered a note to this effect to the Polish ambassador in Moscow on the morning of September 17. The note also announced the nullification of the 1934 pact between the Soviet and Polish governments.

16. Poles deported to the interior of the Soviet Union widely and angrily reported that Jews, Ukrainians, and Belarusians welcomed the Red Army in September 1939. Many members of the national minorities had good reason to do so. However, both at the time and long afterward, ethnic Poles tended to single out members of the national minorities for participating in such actions, accusing them of betraying the Polish state and collaborating with the Soviets to the detriment of the Poles. It must be noted, as Margolin does in his text, that some Poles also participated in welcoming the Soviets, seeing them as fellow fighters against the Nazis. And some Poles also worked with the Soviets during the occupation. Finally, it is important to remember that many Jews, Ukrainians, and Belarusians remained loyal Polish citizens and bemoaned the fall of Poland. See Katherine R. Jolluck, *Exile and Identity: Polish Women in the Soviet Union during World War II* (Pittsburgh, PA: University of Pittsburgh Press, 2004), 196–99; Jan T. Gross, *Revolution from Abroad: The Soviet Conquest of Poland's Western Ukraine and Western Belorussia* (Princeton, NJ: Princeton University Press, 1988), 28–35; Jan

T. Gross, *Neighbors: The Destruction of the Jewish Community in Jedwabne, Poland* (Princeton, NJ: Princeton University Press, 2001), 152–67.

17. Hoover Institution Archives (hereafter HIA), Stanford, CA, Władysław Anders Collection, 1939–1946 (hereafter WAC), Box 48, Vol. 21, No. R2153; Box 41, Vol. 8, No. 10685; Box 54, Vol. 36, No. R7835.

18. Gross, *Revolution from Abroad*, 69.

19. See Gross, *Revolution from Abroad*, 71–113.

20. After the First World War the city became part of Poland, known as Wilno, but the Soviets granted it to the state of Lithuania after their invasion of Poland in September 1939. In October the Lithuanian government signed an agreement putting it firmly in the Soviet security zone, effectively losing its foreign policy independence, and allowing Red Army troops to be stationed there. See Sarūna Liekis, *1939: The Year That Changed Everything in Lithuania's History* (Amsterdam; New York: Rodopi, 2010), 123-53. In August 1940 Stalin annexed Lithuania, along with Latvia and Estonia, to the Soviet Union as constituent republics.

21. In a study of women in eastern Poland arrested and incarcerated in the USSR, Katherine Jolluck found that border transgressions accounted for the highest number of arrests, 44 percent of the total. See Jolluck, *Exile and Identity*, 25.

22. N. S. Lebedeva, "The Deportation of the Polish Population to the USSR, 1939–41," *Journal of Communist Studies and Transition Politics* 16, nos. 1–2 (2000): 36.

23. Krzysztof Jasiewicz, "Obywatele Polscy aresztowani na terytorium tzw. Zachodniej Białorusi w latach 1939-1941 w świetle dokumentacji NKWD/KGB," *Kwartalnik Historyczny* 101, no. 1 (1994): 118.

24. In addition to arresting Polish civilians, the Soviets interned Polish army officers and reservists; by late September they had taken 240,000 POWs. Approximately 42,000 of them, men of lower rank, were sent home; 25,000 were assigned to work on construction and metallurgy projects. Another 14,500 of them were sent to special internment camps in the western USSR. On December 3, 1940, the Soviet Politburo decided to arrest all registered officers of the Polish Army. Lebedeva, "The Deportation of the Polish Population," 30–32. The officers sent to the special camps were subsequently shot, along with 7,000 other prisoners from Poland, in the spring of 1940. See ns 54–55 below.

25. Jolluck, *Exile and Identity*, 7, 10–12.

26. Aleksander Gurjanow, "Cztery deportacje 1940–41," *Karta*, no. 12 (1994): 114–36; "Sprawozdanie z dyskusji dotyczącej liczby obywateli polskich wywiezionych do Związki Sowieckiego w latach 1939–1941," *Studia z dziejów Rosji i Europy Środkowo-Wschodniej* 31 (1996): 117–48; *Zbrodnicza ewakuacja więzień i aresztów NKWD na kresach wschodnich II Rzeczypospolitej w czerwcu - lipcu 1941 roku. Materiały z sesji naukowej w 55-rocznicę więzniów NKWD w głąb ZSRR. Łódź, 10 czerwcu 1996 r.* (Warsaw: Główna Komisja Badania Zbrodni Przeciwko Narodowi Polskiemu, 1997), 8–9; Lebedeva, "The Deportation of the Polish Population," 28–45.

27. V. S. Parsadonova, "Deportatsiia naseleniia iz Zapadnoi Ukrainy i Zapadnoi Belorussii v 1939–1941 gg.," *Novaia i noveishaia istoriia* 2 (1989); Korzon, in "Sprawozdanie z dyskusji," 127; Marek Tuszynski, "Soviet War Crimes against Poland during the Second World War and Its Aftermath: A Review of the Factual Record and Outstanding Questions," *Polish Review* 44, no. 2 (1999): 200; Andrzej Paczkowski, "Poland," in *The Black Book of Communism: Crimes, Terror, Repression*, edited by Stéphane Courtois et al. (Cambridge, MA: Harvard University Press, 1999), 370–71.

28. Lebedeva, "The Deportation of the Polish Population," 28.

29. Gross, *Revolution from Abroad*, 188–89.

30. Grzegorz Hryciuk, "Deportacje ludności Polskiej," in *Masowe deportacje radzieckie w okresie II wojny światowej*, edited by S. Ciesielski, G. Hryciuk and A. Srebrakowski (Wrocław: Instytut Historyczny Uniwersytetu Wrocławskiego, 1994), 53.

31. Margolin's visa extension came through in September 1940, when he was already in a Soviet forced labor camp.

32. Shimon Redlich, *Life in Transit: Jews in Postwar Lodz, 1945–1950* (Boston: Academic Studies Press, 2011), 53.

33. HIA, WAC, Box 36, Vol. 2, No. 1907. See also: Jolluck, *Exile and Identity*, 17–19.

34. Doc. no. 56, July 27, 1933, in *Gulag v Karelii, 1930–41*, edited by V. G. Makurov (Petrozavodsk: Karel'skii nauchnyi tsentr, 1992), cited by Christopher Joyce, "The Gulag in Karelia 1929–1941," in *The Economics of Forced Labor: The Soviet Gulag*, edited by V. V. Lazarev and Paul R. Gregory (Stanford, CA: Hoover Press, 2003), 167. Writer Maxim Gorky toured the canal site and in 1934 edited an official, celebratory book on its construction: *Belomorsko - Baltiiskii kanal imeni Stalina: Istoriia stroitel'stva, 1931–1934 gg.* (Moscow: OGIZ, 1934). It presented a humane view of the use of convict labor. The book was published in English a year later: *Belomor: An Account of the Construction of the New Canal between the White Sea and the Baltic Sea* (New York: H. Smith and R. Haas, 1935).

35. Mikhail Morukov, "The White Sea–Baltic Canal," in *The Economics of Forced Labor*, 162.

36. Oleg V. Khlevniuk, *The History of the Gulag: From Collectivization to the Great Terror* (New Haven, CT: Yale University Press, 2004), 363; Joyce, "The Gulag in Karelia," 168. Although the first forced labor camp was set up by Lenin in 1920, on the Solovetsky Islands, Stalin created the vast system that would spread across the entire Soviet Union and engulf millions of individuals. The Politburo decided to establish the complex network of camps in 1929. On the early history of the Stalinist camps, see Khlevniuk, *History of the Gulag*, 9–53.

37. On the common use of this label to categorize and criminalize people, see David Shearer, "Elements Near and Alien: Passportization, Policing, and Identity in the Stalinist State, 1932–1952, *Journal of Modern History* 76, no. 4 (2004): 835–81.

38. See, for example: Margarete Buber-Neumann, *Under Two Dictators* (New York: Dodd, Mead & Co., 1949), 72; Elinor Lipper, *Eleven Years in Soviet Prisons* (Chicago: Henry Regnery Co., 1951), 93, 95, 148, 150, 157;

Aleksandr Solzhenitsyn, *The Gulag Archipelago*, translated by Thomas P. Whitney (New York: Harper & Row, 1973), Vol. I, 499–508; Vol. II, 126, 177, 233–35, 425–26; Varlam Shalamov, *Kolyma Tales*, translated by John Glad (New York: W. W. Norton, 1980), 107–27; Hilda Vitzthum, *Torn Out by the Roots: The Recollections of a Former Communist* (Lincoln: University of Nebraska Press, 1993), 172.

39. HIA, WAC, Box 44, Vol. 13, No. 13971. See also: Jolluck, *Exile and Identity*, 165–66, 254–59, 271–76; Valery Chalidze, *Criminal Russia: Essays on Crime in the Soviet Union*, translated by P. S. Falla (New York: Random House, 1977), 64, 70; Robert Conquest, *The Great Terror: A Reassessment* (New York: Oxford University Press, 1990), 314–15, 326.

40. Jolluck, *Exile and Identity*, 60, 131.

41. Approximately 750,000 prisoners were evacuated from the border regions. Edwin Bacon, "'Glasnost' and the Gulag: New Information on Soviet Forced Labour around World War II," *Soviet Studies* 44, no. 6 (1992): 1079.

42. Khlevniuk, *History of the Gulag*, 359.

43. Gustav Herling, *A World Apart* (London: Heinemann, 1951).

44. For another account by a Polish Jew imprisoned at Osinovka, see Alexander Harris, *Breaking Borders: One Man's Journey to Erase the Lines that Divide* (Bloomington, IN: iUniverse, 2008). Harris was arrested for trying to cross the Lithuanian border in 1940.

45. Polish-Soviet Agreement, July 30, 1941, Appendix E, in George V. Kacewicz, *Great Britain, the Soviet Union, and the Polish Government in Exile (1939-1945)* (The Hague: M. Nijhoff, 1979), 231.

46. Relations between Stalin and the Polish London government quickly deteriorated and in 1942 General Sikorski, prime minister of the Polish government-in-exile, sought the removal of the Anders Army from Soviet territory. Two evacuations of Polish citizens took place, in March–April and then August 1942. Nearly 115,000 Polish citizens thus left the USSR, traveling to Iran and then points beyond. See Julian Siedlecki, *Losy Polaków w ZSRR w latach 1939–1986* (London: Gryf Publications, 1987), 126, 134; Irena Grudzińska-Gross and Jan T. Gross, eds., *War through Children's Eyes* (Stanford, CA: Hoover Institution Press, 1981), xii–xvi.

47. Grudzińska-Gross and Gross, *War Through Children's Eyes*, xxv.

48. Bacon, "'Glasnost' and the Gulag," 1080.

49. "Free workers" refers to individuals who lived outside the boundaries of Gulag camps and worked within the camps themselves or with the prisoners at labor sites, particularly on industrial and construction projects. See Oleg Khlevniuk and Simon Belokowsky, "The Gulag and the Non-Gulag as One Interrelated Whole," *Kritika* 16, no. 3 (2015): 487–88.

50. Golfo Alexopoulos, *Illness and Inhumanity in Stalin's Gulag* (New Haven, CT: Yale University Press, 2017), 140. See also 136–40.

51. Alexopoulos, *Illness and Inhumanity*, 143–47. Some scholars believe that releasing prisoners close to death was a means of reducing the camps' dismal mortality rates. Alexopoulos, *Illness and Inhumanity*, 157–58.

52. Alexopoulos, *Illness and Inhumanity*, 115; for more, see 110–16.

53. The Anders Army, formally the Polish Armed Forces in the East, was renamed the Polish Army in the East in September 1942. In 1943 it became part of the newly created Second Polish Corps, also led by Gen. Władysław Anders, and subordinated to British command. At the end of 1943 the Second Polish Corps was transferred to fight on the Italian peninsula. See Józef Garliński, *Poland in the Second World War* (New York: Hippocrene Books, 1985), 178–79, 214, 231–34, 251–56, 270–72. Anders' memoir of this period was published in Polish and English in 1949: *Bez ostatniego rozdziału: Wspomnienia z lat 1939–1946* (Newtown, Wales: Montgomeryshire Printing Co., 1949); *An Army in Exile: The Story of the Second Polish Corps* (London: Macmillan, 1949).

54. For writing on the Katyń massacre before the Soviet admission of guilt, see: Joseph Czapski, *The Inhuman Land* (New York: Sheed & Ward, 1952); Janusz Zawodny, *Death in the Forest: The Story of the Katyn Forest Massacre* (Notre Dame, IN: Notre Dame University Press, 1962); Stanisław Iwianiewicz, *W cieniu Katynia* (Paris: Instytut Literacki, 1976); Louis Fitzgibbon, *Katyn* (New York: Charles Scribner's Sons, 1977).

55. See *Izvestiia*, no. 105 (April 14, 1990): 1, 4. The documents released by Mikhail Gorbachev included information on the killing and location of the mass graves of the additional 17,400 prisoners, bringing the total number of murdered Polish army officers, reservists, and civilians to approximately 22,000. The inmates of the three special camps established in 1939, plus another 7,300 Polish men and women held in Soviet prisons, were executed in April and May of 1940. Besides the Katyń forest, near Smolensk, mass graves were also located near Kalinin (now Tver) and Kharkov (now Kharkiv). The relevant documents were turned over to the Polish government in 1992 and published: *Katyń. Dokumenty ludobójstwa. Dokumenty i materiały archiwalne przekazane Polsce 14 października 1992 r.* (Warsaw: Instytut Studiów Politycznych Polskiej Akademii Nauk, 1992); *Katyń. Dokumenty zbrodni*, 2 vols. (Warsaw: Trio, 1995). The most critical documents can be found in English translation in Anna M. Cienciala, Natalia S. Lebedeva, and Wojciech Materski, eds., *Katyn: A Crime Without Punishment* (New Haven, CT: Yale University Press, 2007).

56. Berling initially joined the Anders Army in 1941 and was supposed to evacuate with it to Iran in 1942. He decided instead to remain on Soviet territory and work with Soviet authorities.

57. Garliński, *Poland in the Second World War*, 155–59, 192–98, 250–51.

58. Alan Barenberg, *Gulag Town, Company Town: Forced Labor and Its Legacy in Vorkuta* (New Haven, CT: Yale University Press, 2014), 3.

59. CZA, A536/49, Margolin, "Delo Bergera."

60. By carrying an uncensored letter from the couple to their daughter in France, Margolin commenced the long process of bringing Soloveichik and his wife, Lina Grigorevna, to Paris in 1948. See 513, n 5. He wrote about the Soloveichiks and their departure from the USSR in Iu. B. Margolin, "Chudo v Slavgorode." Available at http://margolin-ze-ka.tripod.com/article03.html.

61. This population was to be "exchanged" for Russians, Ukrainians, Belarusians, Rusyns, and Lithuanians on Polish territory, who would be taken to the USSR. The treaty excluded displaced Ukrainians and Belarusians—though they were pre-war Polish citizens—from returning to Poland. Albert Kaganovitch, "Stalin's Great Power Politics, the Return of Jewish Refugees to Poland, and Continued Migration to Palestine, 1944–1946," *Holocaust and Genocide Studies* 26, no. 1 (2012): 67–68. See also: Jan Czerniakiewicz, *Repatriacja ludności polskiej z ZSRR, 1944–1948* (Warsaw: Państwowe Wydawnictwo Naukowe, 1987).

62. Redlich, *Life in Transit*, 62, 54.

63. Patricia Corrigan, "Philosopher's Long-Buried Story of Gulag Finally Sees Light," *J.: The Jewish News of Northern California* (February 11, 2011), at https://www.jweekly.com/2011/02/11/philosophers-long-buried-story-of-gulag-finally-sees-light/. For more comments regarding Margolin's exile and return made by his son, see Ephraim Margolin, American Friends of the Hebrew University, "Spotlights," September 4, 2017, at https://www.afhu.org/2017/09/04/ephraim-margolin/.

64. CZA, A536/52, Iu. Margolin, "Obrashchenie k rukovoditeliam evreiskoi obshchestvennosti," Tel Aviv, November 20, 1946. Available at http://www.rjews.net/raisa-epshtein/articles/margolin/8.htm.

65. CZA, A536/49, Margolin, "Delo Bergera." See also *Sotsialisticheskii vestnik,* no. 12 (December 27, 1946): 275–78.

66. Ephraim Margolin, Personal correspondence with author, February 2, 2020.

67. S. N. Chizhik, Sud'ba odnoi proklamatsii, at http://www.rjews.net/raisa-epshtein/articles/margolin/5.htm.

68. See Jackowska, "Julius Margolin," 106.

69. Jules Margoline, *La condition inhumaine. Cinq ans dans les camps de concentration soviétiques*, trans. Nina Berberova and Mina Journot (Paris: Calmann-Lévy, 1949).

70. Michael Scott Christofferson, *French Intellectuals Against the Left: The Antitotalitarian Moment of the 1970s* (New York: Berghahn Books, 2004), 32.

71. The book first came out in the United States in 1946: Victor Kravchenko, *I Chose Freedom: The Personal Political Life of a Soviet Official* (New York: C. Scribner's Sons, 1946). The French version was published by Editions S.E.L.F. in 1947. On Kravchenko's reception and trial, see Carolyn J. Dean, *The Moral Witness: Trials and Testimony after Genocide* (Ithaca, NY: Cornell University Press, 2019), 63–71; Tony Judt, *Past Imperfect: French Intellectuals, 1944–1956* (New York: New York University Press. 2011), 105, 112–13; Christofferson, *French Intellectuals*, 31–34. For Kravchenko's own account of the trial, see Victor Kravchenko, *I Chose Justice* (New York: C. Scribner's Sons, 1950).

72. Judt, *Past Imperfect*, 113.

73. Emma Kuby, "In the Shadow of the Concentration Camp: David Rousset and the Limits of Apoliticism in Postwar French Thought," *Modern Intellectual History* 11, no. 1 (2014): 156.

74. Rousset had gained acclaim for the two books he wrote about the Nazi camps: *L'univers concentrationnaire* (Paris: Éditions du Pavois, 1946); *Les jours de notre mort, roman* (Paris: Éditions du Pavois, 1947). For more on Rousset's life, see: Kuby, "In the Shadow," 151–56.

75. Dean, *The Moral Witness*, 73.

76. Kuby, "In the Shadow," 148. Elsewhere Kuby concluded, however, that "the commission was conceived as a vehicle for highlighting embarrassing similarities between Hitler's atrocities and Stalin's vast network of Gulag labor camps." Emma Kuby, "Survivors against Concentration Camps," *Dissent* (July 2, 2019).

77. Kuby, "In the Shadow," 165.

78. Kuby, "In the Shadow," 157 n 36.

79. Iu. B. Margolin, "Parizhskii otchet," 1951. Available at http://margolin-ze-ka.tripod.com/1951-1.html.

80. Margolin, "Parizhskii otchet." While in Paris, he also published four articles in the French press, gave a lecture, and spoke on the radio.

81. Margolin, "Parizhskii otchet." Rousset and others published excerpts from the courtroom proceedings soon after the trial: David Rousset, Théo Bernard, and Gérard Rosenthal, *Le procès concentrationnaire pour la vérité sur les camps: extraits des débats* (Paris: Éditions du Pavois, 1951).

82. Judt, *Past Imperfect*, 114; Dean, *The Moral Witness*, 80.

83. Margolin, "Parizhskii otchet."

84. Iu. B. Margolin, "Sud'ba odnoi proklamatsii," 1954. Available at http://margolin-ze-ka.tripod.com/1954-1.html. "Medinat Israel" comes from the Hebrew and means "State of Israel."

85. Iu. B. Margolin, "Predislovie k 'Parizhskomu otchetu,' ot avtora - 20 let spustia," 1970. Available at http://margolin-ze-ka.tripod.com/1951-2.html.

86. Margolin published the following books in Israel: *Izrail'—evreiskoe gosudarstvo* [pub. under pseud. Aleksandr Galin] (Tel Aviv: Omanut, 1958); *Evreiskaia povest'* (Tel Aviv: Izd-vo MAAIAN, 1960); and *Diamat: kritika sovetskoi ideologii* (Tel Aviv: MAOZ, Obshchestvo bor'by za osvobozhdenie evreev iz SSSR, 1971). Several more books of his writings have been published posthumously: Iulii Margolin, *Povest' tysiacheletii; szhatyi ocherk istorii evreiskogo naroda* (Tel Aviv: Obshchestvo po uvekovecheniiu pamiati Iu. B. Margolina, 1973); Iulii Margolin, *Nesobrannoe* (n.p.: Obshchestvo po uvekovecheniiu pamiati d-ra Iuliia Borisovicha Margolina, 1975); Iulii Margolin, *Nad mertvym morem* (Tel Aviv: n.p., 1978); Julius Margolin, *Le livre du retour* (Paris: Le Bruit du Temps, 2012); Julius Margolin, *Le procès Eichmann et autres essais* (Paris: Le Bruit du Temps, 2016). Some of his articles were translated into English and published in the journals *Commentary* and *The New*

Leader. Excerpts of his book *Evreiskaia povest'* (*A Jewish Tale*) were published in English in Maxim D. Shrayer, ed., *An Anthology of Jewish-Russian Literature: Two-Centuries of Dual Identity in Prose and Poetry*, Vol. 2 (New York: M. E. Sharpe, 2007), 484–97.

87. HIA, Mark V. Vishniak, Papers (hereafter MVVP), Box 7, Correspondence, folder "Margolin, Iulii, 1951–1962," Letter from J. Margolin, Tel Aviv, April 8, 1953. Darryl Zanuck was a prominent Hollywood film producer and studio executive at the time.

88. In 1950 he spoke at the UN Economic and Social Council; in 1951 at the Congress of Cultural Workers in Bombay; in 1953 at the Nadezhda Society in New York and the Union of Russian Jews in Paris; and in 1956 at the editorial meeting of the magazine *Posev* (*The Sowing*) in Frankfurt am Main. Chizhik, Sud'ba odnoi proklamatsii. The text of the first talk was published in German: Iulii Margolin, *Sklavenarbeit hinter dem Eisernen Vorgang. Auszug aus einer Erklärung des in Polen geborenen zionistischen Gelehrten Dr. Julius Margolin* (Düsseldorf: n.p., 1950).

89. He also wrote a memoir of the experience: Menachem Begin, *White Nights: The Story of a Prisoner in Russia* (London: Macdonald, 1957).

90. Iu. B. Margolin, "Problemy evreiskogo natsionalizma," *Novyi zhurnal* 341 (1955): 210–23; quoted in Chizhik, Sud'ba odnoi proklamatsii.

91. Margolin, "Predislovie."

92. Since there was no "official" version of *The Road to the West* the translator, Stefani Hoffman, decided to omit two chapters. One ("Galya") was a fictional piece; the second ("Letter from the Road") was publicistic. Neither piece added to Margolin's story. Hoffman included the short section Margolin entitled "Paris" in Chapter 5. Finally, she added the chapter on Slavgorod from other pieces Margolin wrote to fill in the gap in his story.

93. Arthur Koestler, Letter to Julius Margolin, January 18, 1949. Reproduced by Dobruskina, Vstuplenie k nastoiashchei publikatsii, at http://margolin-ze-ka.tripod.com/commentary01.html.

94. *Narodnaia pravda* (February 1949): 22–27. Cited by Dobruskina, Vstuplenie k nastoiashchei publikatsii.

95. Jackowska, "Julius Margolin," 106. Malraux's novel was translated into English as *Man's Fate*.

96. HIA, MVVP, Box 7, Correspondence, folder "Margolin, Iulii, 1951–1962," Letter from J. Margolin, Tel Aviv, November 30, 1952. I am indebted to Misha Shauli for bringing this document to my attention.

97. Benedikt Sarnov, "Iavleniie Solzhenitsyna," *Grani*, October 30, 2012. Available at https://graniru.org/Culture/Literature/m.208097.html.

98. Misha Shauli, Personal correspondence with author, December 21, 2019.

99. Julius Margolin, *Überleben ist Alles. Aufzeichnungen aus sowjetischen Lagern* (München: J. Pfeiffer Verlag, 1965).

100. Iulii Margolin, *Puteshestvie v stranu Ze-ka* (Tel Aviv: Obshchestvo po uvekovecheniiu pamiati d-ra Iuliia Borisovicha Margolina, 1976); Iulii Margolin, *Puteshestvie v stranu Ze-ka* (Tel Aviv: MAOZ Sionistskoe natsional'noe dvizhenie, 1997); Iulii Margolin, *Puteshestvie v stranu Ze-ka* (Moscow: AST; Zebra E, 2008).

101. Julius Margolin, *Voyage au pays des Ze-Ka*, trans. Nina Berberova and Mina Journot, rev. and completed by Luba Jurgenson (Paris: Le Bruit du Temps, 2010).

102. Julius Margolin, *Podróż do krainy zeków* (Sękowa, PL: Czarne, 2013); Julius Margolin, *Reise in das Land der Lager* (Berlin: Suhrkamp Verlag AG, 2013).

103. J. Margolin, "'A Train Traveled West.' It's the first chapter of the book *Road to the West* by Julius Margolin," *Herut*, December 21, 1951.

104. Iu. Margolin, "Galya," *Novyi zhurnal*, no. 33 (1953): 105–23; Iu. Margolin, "Non Omnis Moriar," *Novyi zhurnal*, no. 35 (1953): 59–71. CZA, A536/53, Sarana Gurion, Letter to Iu. and E. Margolin, Paris, November 30, 1954. Available at http://margolin-ze-ka.tripod.com/commentary04.html.

105. Inna Dobruskina explains her failed attempts to locate this publication at I. A. Dobruskina, Kommentarii k nastoiashchei publikatsii, Iu. B. Margolin, Puteshestvie v stranu ze-ka, at http://margolin-ze-ka.tripod.com/commentary04.html. Excerpts from *Road to the West* were published in *Novoe russkoe slovo* (July 12 and 13, 1956) and *Russkaia mysl'* (November 27, December 4, and December 11, 1969).

106. Julius Margolin, *Le livre du retour* (Paris: Le Bruit du Temps, 2012).

107. Iulii Margolin, *Masa l'Eretz Haasirim*, translated by Idit Shaked (Jerusalem: Carmel, 2013). This volume omits two chapters from *The Road to the West*, "Galya" and "The End of Maria," which the publisher considered irrelevant to the work as a travelogue genre.

108. Iulii Margolin, *Puteshestvie v stranu Ze-ka i Doroga na zapad*, 2 vols., edited by Misha Shauli (Jerusalem: Studio Click Ltd., 2016).

109. Leona Toker, *Return from the Archipelago: Narratives of Gulag Survivors* (Bloomington, IN: Indiana University Press, 2000), 30–33.

110. The first of these books were published in Polish: Józef Czapski, *Wspomnienia starobielskie* (Rome: Oddział Kultury i Prasy, 2 Korpusu, 1944); Melchior Wałkowicz, *Dzieje rodziny Korzeniewskich* (National Committee of Americans of Polish Descent, 1944); Józef Czapski, *Na nieludzkiej ziemi* (Paryż, Instytut literacki, 1949). The English translation of the latter came out in 1951 as *The Inhuman Land* (London: Chatto & Windus, 1951); it was republished in 2018 by the New York Review of Books as *Inhuman Land: Searching for the Truth in Soviet Russia, 1941–1942*. The first memoir I have found from the exiled Poles published in English is Ada Halpern, *Liberation, Russian Style* (London: Maxlove Publishing Co., 1945).

111. Jolluck, *Exile and Identity*, xiv–xviii.

112. Sylvestre Mora and Pierre Zwierniak, *La justice soviétique* (Rome: Magi-Spinetti, 1945); Anonymous, *Dark Side of the Moon* (London: Faber & Faber, 1946); David Dallin and Boris Nicolaevsky, *Forced Labor in Soviet Russia* (New Haven, CT: Yale University Press, 1947). (In a 1989 edition of *Dark Side of the Moon* the author was revealed as Zoë Zajdlerowa.) Some of the documents were used in a wider condemnation of the USSR written at the same time: Bronisław Kuśnierz, *Stalin and the Poles: An Indictment of the Soviet Leaders* (London: Hollis & Carter, 1949). The U.S. Department of State analyzed the Polish testimonies for a 1952 report on the Soviet Gulag. HIA, U.S. Department of State, Office of International Information, No. 61022, Inside Soviet Slave Labor Camps, 1939–1942: An Analysis of Written Statements by 9,200 Former Prisoners.

113. See n 43. The book was praised as "a masterpiece which should be read for its humanity," one that surpassed Dostoevsky in its intensity. Quoted in Katarzyna Zechenter, "Obituary: Gustaw Herling," *Guardian* (July 7, 2000).

114. Toker, *Return from the Archipelago*, 37. This list includes Margarite Buber-Neumann, Elinor Lipper, Jerzy Glickman, and Valentin Gonzalez (El Campesino). See Toker, *Return from the Archipelago*, 37–45.

115. CZA, A536/49, Margolin, "Delo Bergera." This part of Margolin's article was quoted by U.S. Senator Thomas Dodd in the introduction to a report he commissioned for a Senate subcommittee. Robert Conquest, "The Human Cost of Soviet Communism," Subcommittee to Investigate the Administration of the Internal Security Act and Other Internal Security Laws of the Committee on the Judiciary, United States Senate (Washington, DC: U.S. GPO, 1970), 3. Dodd (and Conquest) incorrectly identify Margolin as a "prominent Lithuanian Jewish leader."

116. Toker, *Return from the Archipelago*, 39.

117. HIA, WAC, Box 45, Vol. 13, No. 14220; Box 42, Vol. 9, No. 10754.

118. See ns 43, 110, 112. Dostoevsky's masterpiece, *Zapiski iz mertvogo doma* (*Notes from the House of the Dead*) was first published in serial form in 1860–62.

119. CZA, A536/51, Margolin, "Kliuch k moei biografii."

120. Margolin, "Parizhskii otchet."

Glossary

The items in capital letters are acronyms formed from Russian words.

ATP—Administrative-Technical Personnel. Refers to the barrack housing those people. Conditions there were better than in an ordinary barrack.

Article 58—article in the Soviet criminal code most frequently used to arrest political opposition under charges of counterrevolutionary activity or treason.

balanda—watery camp soup.

BBK—Baltic–White Sea Canal, one of the large systems of penal forced labor camps in the Soviet Union.

BUR—barrack of reinforced regime; a disciplinary barrack.

bushlat—long-sleeved quilted jacket lined with cotton wadding worn in labor camp.

cheteze: ChTsZ—Chelyabinsk tractor factory; term for camp footwear made without size or form from the rubber of old tractor tires.

ChOS—special supply unit in labor camp.

etap—the Russian word *etap* refers to a transfer from one camp or prison to another, often by rail and/or ship, sometimes with sections on foot.

Gulag [technically GULAG]—acronym for Main Administration of Camps—the government agency in charge of the Soviet forced labor system. Owing mainly to Solzhenitsyn's *The Gulag Archipelago*, the term has come to refer in general to the punitive camp system in the Soviet Union.

Intelligentsia, *intelligent* [individual]—in the Soviet period, the term referred to anyone who engaged professionally in mental labor. The term derives from the group (not from one particular class of society) of intellectuals in nineteenth century Russia, many of whom were committed to a variety of moral, spiritual, legal, or political reforms in tsarist Russia.

kolkhoz—collective farm in the Soviet era.

oblast—an administrative and territorial division in some republics of the former Soviet Union. Usually, the *oblast* carried the name of its administrative center. It is translated variously as "province," "area," "zone" or "region." The use of the last term may be problematic as "region" is also used as the translation of a smaller administrative subdivision, "raion."

OBLLIT—Regional department of the People's Commissariat for Public Education in charge of publications, i.e., censorship.

OBLONO—Regional Department of Public Education [employer of Margolin in the city of Pinsk].

pridurki, *pridurok*—prisoner who landed an easy job by camp standards, either an office job or one that merely was not physically demanding.

selkhoz—agricultural farm.

SHIZO—penalty isolator.

Stakhanovite—term borrowed from usage outside the camp to indicate person who overfulfills the work quota. The term derives from the legendary work of a Soviet miner, Aleksey Stakhanov (1906–1977), whose (partly staged) record achievements were cited as a model in the Soviet period.

Third Sector—office representing the security/intelligence forces that policed prisoners and free employees.

TsTRM—central technical repair warehouse.

URB—Registration-Distribution Office, also referred to as the Second Sector; it dealt with distribution and registration of forced labor in camp.

urka, [pl.] *urki*—hardened camp bandit or thief who unscrupulously exploited the others' weakness or stupidity; member of the criminal underworld.

zek—Russian slang term from the abbreviation of the word *zakliuchennyi* or *z/k*, meaning convict, a prison or forced labor camp inmate.

Journey into the Land of the Zeks and Back

Trapped in the USSR
Sept. 1939–June 1940

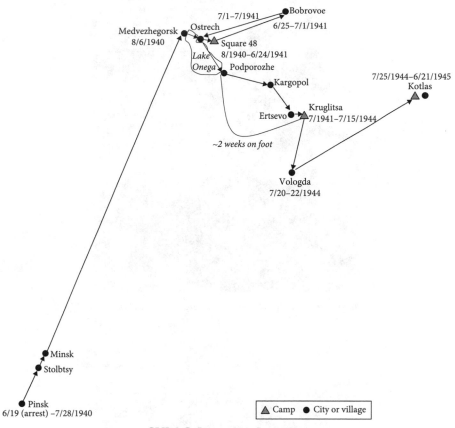

Bobrovoe
7/1–7/1941
6/25–7/1/1941

Medvezhegorsk
8/6/1940

Ostrech

Square 48
8/1940–6/24/1941

*Lake
Onega*

Podporozhe

Kargopol

7/25/1944–6/21/1945
Kotlas

Kruglitsa
Ertsevo 7/1941–7/15/1944

~2 weeks on foot

Vologda
7/20–22/1944

Minsk

Stolbtsy

Pinsk
6/19 (arrest) –7/28/1940

△ Camp ● City or village

GULAG: June 1940–June 1945

Julius, Eva, and Ephraim Margolin in Łódź, Poland, 1930.

Julius Margolin at the beach, Tel Aviv, 1950s.

Journey to the Land of the Zek

Prologue

I HAD PLANNED to travel to the Soviet Union long before the start of World War II.[1]

At the time, I was living in Łódź, Poland. Interest in the Soviet Union was considerable in that country. Indeed, interest in the communist country was different in Paris and New York from that in Poland, where people remembered 150 years of tsarist occupation and the war of 1920; moreover, the two countries had a common border and Russia had always been both a real threat and a nearby temptation. The Communist Party was illegal in Poland. There were no grounds for it in an agrarian, Catholic country with weakly developed industry and a negligible proletariat. About ten to fifteen percent of Jewish youth were under the sway of communism. God knows what communism meant to the miserable dreamers of the Polish ghetto. In the 1930s, the *Pamphlets* of Karl Radek and *Historical Materialism* of Bukharin were sold from carts on the streets of Łódź. On the day of Lenin's death in January, the anniversary of the three "Ls,"[2] a red flag appeared on the telegraph wires, and Jewish youth broke the glass windows in Jewish-owned shops on Piotrkowska Street. The radical intelligentsia read aloud Broniewski's[3] poems about "the furnaces of Magnitogorsk." In Warsaw theaters, Kirsanov's *Granada*[4] was recited to loud applause.

---

1. The heading in Russian reads literally: "Instead of an Introduction."

2. The three communist leaders, Lenin, Liebknecht, and Luxemburg died in January.

3. Władysław Broniewski (1897–1962), Polish poet, was a communist sympathizer in the 1930s. Magnitogorsk is an industrial city in the Ural Mountains, whose iron and steel industries developed in the Soviet period. Composed in 1933 when the poet was in a Polish prison, the lines read: "two furnaces were fired today in Magnitogorsk."

4. Margolin's mistake; M. Svetlov wrote the poem.

Tourists traveled the routes of the Soviet travel bureau Intourist to become familiar with the great country of the Revolution. Many returned after a week's stay in Moscow with a box of Soviet chocolate and pleasant memories. A two-week tour enabled one to visit Ukraine. The resorts of the Caucasus and Central Asia were open to those who could afford a three- to four-week tour. Thus, André Gide visited Gori, Stalin's birthplace, and Sieburg[5] visited the Red Arctic. Everyone who could write conveyed his own impressions about the Soviet Union.

In the years of my Soviet imprisonment, I recalled that literature. It included some well-crafted reportage, full of subtle observations, wit, and brilliance. As a whole, however, all this literature was childish prattle. Neither the skeptics nor the enthusiasts had any understanding of the Soviet Union; they did not have the right to write on a subject about which they knew so little. Now the absurd and tragic disparity between this "tourist" literature and Soviet reality is evident to hundreds of thousands of people like me who wound up deep in the Soviet hinterland during the war years.

In addition to institutionalized tourist visits, during the years of Polish independence, there was another sort of travel about which the newspapers were silent. At all times, illegal renegades were crossing the border, people who did not want to remain in capitalist Poland and sought the promised land, "the homeland of all workers," in search of justice and freedom. We do not know the fate of these people. Why didn't we hear from any of them? They were not famous writers or delegates from America. When they disappeared like a stone in water, no one took an interest in them. They were insignificant people, anonymous, sawdust, attracted to the lodestone of a dream about a better world. It would have been, however, most worthwhile to question them. Their truthful and nonliterary report would have said much more than volumes of official propaganda. Many of them are living in the Soviet Union, and it is a shame that they are unable to tell us about themselves.

In the city of Biała-Podlaska, a Jew had a stall where he sold soda water. His children became rebels: they did not pray to God and did not want to hear about Polish kindness or distant Palestine. When the younger son grew up and became convinced that there was little hope of a revolution in Biała-Podlaska, he arranged with the peasants on the border to take him to the Soviet side. That was in 1931. I met him eleven years later in a Soviet camp, in the great and populous country of the zek [Russian abbreviation z/k for the

---

5. Friedrich Sieburg (1893–1964) was a German journalist who traveled frequently to the Soviet Union and published his impressions from there.

word "convict," *zakliuchennyi*], and I heard his story, which was similar to thousands of others.

The country of the zek does not appear on a Soviet map nor is it in any atlas. It is the sole country in the world where there are no disputes about the Soviet Union, no delusions, and no illusions.

Melman, the owner of his own engineering firm, lived in the city of Lublin. If his relatives are still alive, here is a report on one who disappeared without a trace. Engineer Melman was an independent and stubborn person. He could not stand the Polish regime, and he crossed the border with a group of "dissatisfied" people. They were sent directly from the border post to prison and from there to a labor camp, where I met him. At that time, after several years of incarceration, he was an unusually taciturn person, broad-shouldered, with a darkened face and gloomy mien. I think by that time he no longer had any convictions. His goal was not to die in a camp, but he did not succeed. He died of an intestinal obstruction in the spring of 1944 in the Kruglitsa corrective labor camp in the Arkhangelsk region. Someone gave him two extra meal tickets and his body, which was unaccustomed to normal food, did not hold up.

The year 1937 was fatal for "illegal" tourists. That was the year of the great purge in the Soviet Union. Among the millions dispatched to camps were those who had arrived from abroad to reside in the Soviet Union. It made no difference whether they had arrived legally or illegally.

I remember a young nurse in a camp infirmary.

"Why were you arrested, nurse?" "My papa came from Latvia." "How old were you when you arrived?" "Eight." This is not a conversation of two crazy people. In the Soviet Union, everyone understood this exchange without explanations.

I did not arrive in Russia via Intourist and did not cross the Polish border in the dark of night; I was a tourist of a third, special sort. I did not need to travel to Russia—it came to me. The route was a special one that we did not hear about from Intourist. I did not observe Russia from the window of the Metropol Hotel or from the window of a restaurant car on a train. I saw it through the barred window of a prison car, from inside the barbed wire of camps, and I covered hundreds of kilometers on foot when the cursing guards goaded the crowd of prisoners in stages through the forests and the impoverished *kolkhozes*[6] of the north; I crossed the Urals twice—in a cattle

---

6. Soviet collective farms.

car and on the third bunk of a rough train car, where the presence of foreign correspondents is not permitted; I lived in the Siberian backwoods, like everyone else went to work, and carried in my pocket the document of which Mayakovsky was so proud: a Soviet passport good for five years.[7] I do not have this document any longer, which is why I am able to write things about the Soviet Union that our wise men did not dream of and about which people with Soviet passports do not write.

People who sympathize with the Soviet system assume that my itinerary was infelicitously chosen and diverted me from famous Soviet routes. I was not in the battle for Stalingrad; I did not take Berlin. Had I been there, perhaps I would have written differently? Perhaps. I did not choose my route; the Soviet regime decreed it.

The world knows everything about Stalingrad but nothing about the camps. Where is the truth of Russia, at the Victory Parade on Red Square or in the country of the zek, which does not exist in the atlas? Evidently, we must take these things together in their entirety and interconnection. I have no illusions; I saw underground Russia. I *saw* it. Let those who pin their hopes on the country of the Soviets take this "material," too, into consideration and harmonize it with their conscience as best they can.

---

7. Margolin was in error: The poet Vladimir Mayakovsky wrote about a Soviet passport for travel abroad, to which ordinary Soviet citizens were not entitled. Margolin, who was not a citizen of the USSR, had only a residence permit.

I

September 1939

IN THE SUMMER of 1939, we did not believe there would be a war. Each of us knew that war was inevitable but no one was prepared for it to start tomorrow. Reality showed that the Polish army was not prepared, nor were the democracies in Western Europe or over the Atlantic. Jews of the city of Łódź—a quarter of a million people doomed to death—were the least prepared of all. For several days before catastrophe struck, demonstrators marched through the streets of Łódź with placards "Deprive the Germans of Polish citizenship!" Passing through the Jewish streets, the demonstrators yelled: "Jews, your turn will come, too!" Two weeks later, Łódź was in German hands.

On the eve of the war, the Poles explained to French news correspondents that Poland was sufficiently strong to oppose Germany without the help of the Soviets. Two weeks later, they would have welcomed this help on their knees, with flowers and triumphal arches. It was, however, too late. On September 17, 1939, the Red Army invaded Poland as Hitler's ally.

In the summer of 1939, we did not believe in war. Thousands of people who did not need to be in Poland and could have left heedlessly remained there. The Jewish population en masse stayed put. On one side was Hitler; on the other was the entire world. It seemed unbelievable that Germany would dare to fight on two fronts.

Only on the evening of August 23, 1939, did it become clear that war was coming. That evening the world learned of Stalin's pact with Hitler. You can compare our feeling of horror upon hearing this news with that of visitors to the zoo who, in front of their eyes, see the tigers' cell open. The hungry beasts rise, and the door of their cell is wide open. That is just what the "leader of the peoples" did on August 23: he let loose a crazed beast on Europe—and gave his blessing to the German army to plunge into Poland. Tens of millions paid with their lives for this "wise move" that corrupt pens have elegantly defended. For the crime of August 23, Russia paid with an ocean of blood and terrible suffering. It was not the shortest way to destroy Hitler; rather it was the shortest way to destroy Europe. The rout of Europe began in September 1939 with Stalin's blessing. The "leader of the peoples" could be satisfied with the outcome of his game although his original calculation was not justified. The "clash of the predators," as the events of 1939–1940 were called in the Soviet version, speedily had to be renamed "the great defensive war of world democracy." The malicious smile of Soviet rulers while observing the world-wide conflagration very rapidly turned into an expression of horror. For us, little people whose blood is traded on the political market, August 23, 1939, is a gloomy, ill-fated date.

Between September 1 and 17, we experienced the pathetic spectacle of the collapse of Poland. A state with a population of thirty-six million, an entire world, full of good and evil, of historical traditions and millennia-old culture, collapsed like a house of cards. The war was lost in the very first half hour, when the Polish forces near Poznan did not withstand the attack of the German tank divisions.

The morning began normally on that first day of September in Łódź. The telephone rang on the desk in one of the offices of the firm where I was working. The person at the table picked up the receiver, and suddenly his face turned crimson, his eyes widened, and he began to yell wildly into the receiver: "What, what's that?"

I rushed to him: "Did something happen at your home?" He dropped the receiver: "The Germans bombed Warsaw, Cracow, Lvov.[1] It's war!"
Łódź was not attacked from the air on that day. The following morning, however, we were awoken by explosions. . . . German squadrons drifted above the city in a triangular formation. The sparse anti-aircraft fire did not disturb or hinder them. . . . We could see that the sky above our heads already belonged to Hitler: the moment that the planes flew above, I understood that nothing hindered them from dropping bombs on any square or street in the city; if they did not do so, it was because of the German command's good will. We had imagined war differently.

On the third day, the air sirens went off incessantly. Normal work halted; there was no normal communication, nor any news about the course of military operations except for the German ones. Disaster advanced. On the night of the third day, in blind, eyeless, darkened Łódź, I encountered the

---

1. Now Lviv, in independent Ukraine.

first crazed woman. The crazy woman lurched along the sidewalk in the dark, wringing her hands, and muttering disjointed words. Perhaps her family had just been killed by a German bomb and she no longer knew where her home or her place was. An avalanche of human grief descended after her. I did not recognize the familiar streets of the peacetime city; they had turned into a jungle, with death hiding in its dark ravines.

The Germans crawled forward like a monstrous, cold reptile, and every evening we would hear the voice of Fritzsche,[2] nasal, slow, poisonously malicious, full of mocking exultation and threats. The German radio broadcast to Poland would begin with the Polonaise of Moniuszko.[3] To this day, I cannot hear that triumphant, sweeping melody without shuddering, as if a swastika were engraved across it. I left Łódź at dawn on the fifth day. I received a phone call early in the morning: "We have a place in the car. We shall wait for fifteen minutes." That morning the Germans were 50 kilometers from the city. I took my briefcase and went out to the street. It was a clear September morning. "It might take a month until I return home," I thought. "I need to take an overcoat." I returned. I took down a summer coat from the hook but put it back. And I took—just in case—a sturdy fall coat with the label of the Łódź store Einigkeit. I left the city with this "Einigkeit" and a briefcase, into which for some reason the distressed maid stuffed house slippers. Unlike other Jews, I knew exactly where my home was. My home was in Palestine. My family had been there since 1936, and that summer I was in Poland as a guest. The only things linking me to Poland were my Polish passport and . . . the sentiments of a Polish Jew.

One can now talk about the patriotism of Polish Jews in the past tense. There are no longer any Polish Jews. Poles who can do without us and our allegiance now live on Berek Joselewicz[4] Street. That morning, however, when I began my epic refugee wanderings, I was sincerely upset, and the Polish tragedy distanced from my mind the single thing that I should have been thinking about—the tragedy of my own people. In the twenty years of its

---

2. Hans Georg Fritzsche (1900–1953), head of the Radio Division in the Third Reich.

3. Stanisław Moniuszko (1872–1819), composer who was considered the father of Polish national opera.

4. Berek Joselewicz (1764–1809) was a Jew who fought for Polish independence. He was a colonel in the Jewish regiment in the Kosciusko uprising in 1794. During the Napoleonic wars, he fell in the battle of Kock in 1809.

independence, Poland of the Legions[5] had committed three crimes for which it now had to pay: three mistakes, each of which represents a crime before the court of history and the human conscience. The first crime by a people who had just thrown off the yoke of national enslavement was its policy toward national minorities. Belarusians, Ukrainians, Lithuanians, and Jews were persecuted and deprived of equal rights in the Polish state. The second crime was the inhuman, rapacious ideology of the Polish rightists—political cynicism in domestic relations, which, especially after Piłsudski's[6] death, led to the popularization of Hitlerite methods in Polish society and distorted the moral features of the Polish nation with a grimace of antisemitism—until the present day. The third crime was foreign policy, unwillingness to defend European democracy, which in 1938 took the form of an act of shameful betrayal, when Poland aided Germany in the division of Czechoslovakia and thus wound the rope around its own neck. Hitler used Poland's help to crush Czechoslovakia, and a year later, Russia's help to crush Poland. It was the same method and the same reliance on the blind greed and venal cynicism of his partners.

The car took us away from Łódź. On both sides of the road we passed groves, fields, and meadows bathed in the summer sunlight; the Polish land, a live target for murder, stretched in front of us. German airplanes accompanied us as we drove the 130 kilometers to Warsaw. The bombing crews regarded the stroll over Poland as harmless, amusing sport. The towns through which we traveled, slowing our speed, were filled to overflowing with people and overloaded wagons. Panic burgeoned in front of our eyes. Late at night, a mass exodus from Łódź began, when tens of thousands streamed out of the doomed city. We preceded this wave by fifteen hours.

Parting forever with the peaceful Polish countryside on that day, I thought about the country which, in Piłsudski's words, was "doomed to greatness" but was unable to become great. Chopin[7] and Piłsudski represent two extremes of the Polish spirit: Chopin's music, lacking any firmness or masculine strength,

---

5. Term used to describe Poland between 1926 and 1939, during which time its leaders belonged to the Polish Legions, which were founded during World War I, with the goal of independence.

6. Józef Klemens Piłsudski (1867–1935) was a Polish national hero who served as chief of state (1918–1922) and first marshal. From 1926 until his death in 1935, he was considered the de facto leader of the Second Polish Republic. Unlike his political opponent, Roman Dmowski, leader of the rightist National Democrat party, Piłsudski favored a multi-ethnic Poland.

7. Frédéric François Chopin (1810–1845) was Poland's most famous composer. A child prodigy and virtuoso pianist of the Romantic era, he achieved international renown for his works, composed primarily for solo piano.

and Piłsudski's exploits, heroic but lacking ultimate depth and a universal perspective. There was no real middle ground between the two, no political tact or ability to create something new that was not clouded by pride. Chopin and Piłsudski remained without followers. It is not true that Poland is "second-rate Europe," in the words of some unintelligent person. Poland is the real Europe. Adam Mickiewicz and Juliusz Słowacki, Bolesław Prus and Stefan Żeromski[8] were first-rate Europeans. Poland, however, was never in the avant-garde; it was always the rear guard of Europe, a border zone with all its disadvantages and dangers. . . . On that day of departure, its courtyards and village wicker fences and church spires were dear to me, and I wished that Poland could emerge from this terrible trial renewed and free, a genuine participant in the great democratic revival of Europe, in which I believed. It did not even occur to me that Hitler or Stalin could emerge victorious in this war.

Warsaw was boiling like a cauldron in the pause between two air raids. Saxon Square was crowded with cars that had arrived from afar. There were no rooms in the Hotel Europa. There was no gas for the car, and we lost two days in search of fuel. On the fifth day of the war, daily railroad service had halted, and it was a matter of luck to get on a train. I spent the night in the outskirts of the city. At night, the radio woke up the city's residents, broadcasting an alarm: "The Germans have broken through; dig trenches!" Everyone left the apartment where I was sleeping. I also got up so as not to remain alone in a stranger's home. At two in the morning, I arrived at the empty Saxon Square. A yawning guard met me at the entry to the Europa Hotel. "No one is here; all the Jews ran away!" he said, looking at me intently, as if amazed that I had remained. I asked about my companions. "They left!" he said indifferently. There was nothing to do; I took a room and went to sleep, planning in the morning to purchase a backpack and cross the Vistula River on foot.

Early in the morning, however, the first people whom I saw in the hotel lobby were my companions from Łódź. The information that I had received at night was incorrect. On September 7 at 11:00 a.m., we left Warsaw. Over the first few kilometers until Minsk,[9] we moved slowly in a dense throng. An unimaginable jumble swirled on the highway: pedestrians, equestrians, and baby carriages became entangled with heavy trucks; buses with carts and horse-drawn carriages; vans with passenger cars and handcarts loaded with shabby belongings. Women were walking, holding children by the hand;

---

8. Famous Polish literary figures and thinkers.

9. The reference is to a town in Poland, not the capital of Belarus.

young people went as if on a hike, with packs and sacks. Having moved into
the middle, we were unable to get out and proceeded with the general stream.
Suddenly, German planes appeared, flying low (we did not see any Polish
planes until the Romanian border). The crowd hurriedly dispersed in all
directions. We also left our Buick and lay down in a potato field near a fence.
On that day, however, they did not bomb the refugees. Only on the following
morning, terrible scenes played out on the road to Lublin, and for meters, the
highway was drenched with blood.

We gradually managed to extract ourselves from the traffic jam, and after
Minsk (30 kilometers beyond Warsaw), the road was free. We had not yet
escaped from the range of air fire. All the cities on our way were showered
with bombs. The Germans were everywhere at once. We passed through
burning Siedlce; people were hollering; a policeman was savagely beating a
woman with a rubber club as she tried to escape from him. We rushed through
villages where huts were ablaze. The buzzing from on high never ceased. We
stopped before Międzyrzec, waiting for the end of the shelling. We thought
that with one more thrust ahead, we would escape from the war and all that
would remain would be the summer heat and the undisturbed silence of the
rural road, where a wagon with a bearded, sleepy Jew plodded along.

Finally, we entered Brest and stopped on Jagiellonski Street. I got out,
stretching my legs, and immediately a person approached, smiling and offering his hand. "Don't you recognize me?" It was a lawyer whom I had met
in another city seven years ago. "I am a local resident; you can spend the night
at my place."

Upon hearing what was going on in Warsaw and about the wave of refugees
that followed us, our host ran to buy a wagon and horse in order to be prepared to flee. We brought to Brest the panic from which we had fled. . . . The
next morning, we left for Volhynia.

The front flowed on behind us but at 200 kilometers after Warsaw, nothing
was known about the real situation. The Poles placed their hopes on some
phantasmagoric aid from the West, on the English air force, a French breach
of the Siegfried Line, or the intervention of the Red Army. The officers lied
to the solders; local leaflets reported in enormous headlines about the Polish
cavalry's breakthrough into Eastern Prussia, the bombardment of Berlin, and
a French invasion into the Saar region.

In Kovel, we found a homey Jewish province, neglected gardens and
wooden porches, spacious yards, and an inn overcrowded with distinguished
guests from Warsaw. Barefoot children, with fingers in their mouths, looked
at the unusual guests sitting on the protective mound of earth next to the

inn—women in elegant travel suits, plump Łódź factory owners, and the very deputy mayor of Warsaw. At the end of the street, there was a kibbutz, where Jewish youth were undergoing training for future life in Palestine. Portraits hung on the walls; no longer useful literature lay on the tables. Everything was too late. "Run away from here," I wanted to tell them. "Don't rely on your elders anymore. You cannot expect anything from them; they don't know anything; they are not responsible for anything. . . ." It was, however, too late to convince or converse with them.

At night we passed through Lutsk in a convoy of cars with dimmed lights.

Our next stop was Rivne. The city was full of refugees from Cracow and Lvov and evacuated institutions. Ministers of the disbanded government, detained in Rivne, told yarns about a force mustered for a counterattack against the Germans and discreetly disappeared in the direction of the Romanian border. Abandoned cars, useless because of the lack of fuel, stood along the roads. Their owners willingly exchanged a car for a horse and wagon. We still had gas but we had to hide the car to keep the military authorities from requisitioning it. The stores and stalls were either closed or empty; after the political collapse, the fabric of everyday life began to unravel: a deficit of food products and goods and the absence of any notion of what would happen tomorrow. In Tarnopol, Galician Jews with long side-locks, wearing black frocks, astonished us with their complete calm. It was as if everything had no direct relation to them. Relying on God, they decided once and for all not to anticipate events and to wait until one could again carry on trade.

In a narrow Tarnopol alley, I heard words of poisonous hate, pogromist remarks about Jews from the mouths of young Polish nurses in khaki equipped with gas masks. They could not wait. . . . These were sisters or mothers of the six-year-old children who later attacked old people and women and tore out their hair—with their little hands. The Tarnopol crowd already showed the first symptoms of demoralization and expectation of a new regime. Special refugees were there: Polish families from the region that were fleeing to the city in fear of Ukrainian reprisals.

On September 15, we arrived in Chortkiv.[10] Circumventing the military barrier, we burst into this picturesque town whose beautiful mountainous locale recalled Italian landscapes. It was forbidden to enter Chortkiv. Therefore, half a kilometer before the town, we got out of the car and made our way into the city on foot. Shimkevich, our driver and friend, drove the car off the road

10. Now part of Ukraine, under Polish control it was called Czortków.

and passed through back courtyards and side alleys. One of our group had a brother in the city. We were received with warm hospitality. It was quiet and calm here; after ten days on the road, this was a real oasis. We reproached ourselves for having ignored the beauty of Chortkiv during peace time and were prepared to stay there for some time . . . until the situation clarified itself.

The situation became clear sooner than we thought. September 17 was a quiet summer morning in Chortkiv. I woke up and went to the municipality to request a pass to Zalishchyky. To my surprise, the municipal office building was utterly empty. The office doors were wide open; desk drawers were open, and not a soul was in the corridors. A picture of hasty flight. In a back room, two administrative aides were standing and looking at the sky, where a flock of airplanes were circling.

"That's their planes, no doubt!" said an aide with a trembling voice.

I presented my request, but he hardly listened to me.

"Yes, go where you want, for god's sake. . . . What kind of permits are you looking for now?"

I went out onto the street, not understanding a thing. I dropped in on a neighbor and turned on the radio.

At that moment, the radio broadcast Vyacheslav Mikhailovich Molotov's[11] speech: a solemn communiqué to the world that at dawn today, in view of the collapse of the Polish state, the Red Army crossed the border in order defend the kindred peoples of Western Ukraine and Belorussia.[12]

An hour later, we hurriedly fled Chortkiv. Our gas might just suffice to reach the Romanian border. We circumvented columns of Polish troops; the soldiers were looking toward the horizon to see whether Soviet tanks were coming, and the officers explained to them that the Red Army was coming to their aid.

They blocked our way at Zalishchyky. We feared that the Soviet advance units would overtake us, and we decided to continue on to Sniatyn, 150 kilometers further. At 1:00 p.m., we arrived at Sniatyn, five kilometers from the Romanian border. There we learned that the border was hermetically sealed. Just two days ago, it had been possible to cross it for money. But now, not even money helped. The Romanians placed a triple cordon of troops at the border. It was impossible to break through.

---

11. V. M. Molotov was the Soviet foreign minister at the time.

12. Now independent Belarus.

We had nothing to lose. Each of us had family abroad: I in Palestine, the others in Paris and London. Each had a foreign passport in his pocket. With the approach of darkness, we drove to the border.

In Sniatyn, we saw Polish airplanes for the first time: eight planes formed a circle over the city, bidding farewell to Poland, and headed over the River Prut. Sniatyn was the sole point where the Polish army was fully motorized; there was no infantry. At the border stood a 4-kilometer-long line of army vehicles, trucks, and passenger cars requisitioned by the army. At night, the Romanians stood in three rows, moving slowly in the gloom. The road teemed with people; it was full of resonating voices, signals, and agitated bustle. We missed our only chance: we should have abandoned our wonderful Buick, melted into the crowd, and crossed the border with a group of soldiers under the cover of darkness. But we were still novices: how could we suddenly decide to risk adventures and hardships? Our powerful black car seemed like a reliable bulwark, like a ship in the night on the open sea in the midst of a storm. We saw that it was not the sole civilian car in line. We passed the night in nervous anticipation, in measured advance toward the treasured border where a Romanian officer stood under an arch with his flashlight and counted the number of soldiers in each car: "Next! Next. . . ."

Our turn came at dawn. They allowed us to go five meters beyond the border. Alongside the Romanian officer stood a Polish one, who helped to identify and catch Jews. "Documents!" and on our driver's passport he read, "Shimkevich, Moishe." The rest were no better. They ordered us to get out of the car and return. The car went to the Romanians. "We won't give cars to the Bolsheviks!" the Romanian explained in German. Nearby a Frenchman who was also stopped was cursing. They explained the matter to him in an aside: by chance, a passenger in the car was a Jew. The matter was immediately settled: they removed the Jew, the happy Frenchman tootled off. It's good to be a Frenchman.

We fought for the right to retrieve our suitcases. A fierce downpour ensued. Under the pouring rain, we dragged back to Sniatyn on foot with our suitcases. It was not a triumphal procession. At the outskirts of the shtetl, I must have looked rather pitiful, as a Jewish woman came out of her house and invited me to rest and drink some tea. That was my debut in the role of a homeless vagabond.

On the same day, a group of Palestinian Jews made a final attempt to make their way home: they suggested that the Romanian authorities allow them to ride a bus under police convoy to Constanta, where they could directly board a steamship. We stood half a day on the border bridge, awaiting a telephone reply from nearby Chernivtsi. In the end, they drove us away with curses. It turned dark. We decided that we would know better what to do in the morning.

The next day was cloudless and sunny, music was playing, and the whole town was on its feet: Soviet troops had entered during the night. A red banner waved from the high tower of the city hall; armored cars stood in the square, and the city bustled with people. The Red Army men stood surrounded by a dense crowd. Each one was in the center of a circle where people showered him with questions and crowded in to look, as if at a miracle. Dozens of improvised meetings took place. The good-natured soldiers, not showing a bit of surprise or embarrassment, answered all the questions. My journey into Russia was beginning, although at that moment, I did not even suspect it.

Ukrainian farmers in traditional white outfits wanted to know the price of bread, and a shoemaker asked about the price of shoes. Everyone was interested in the wages in the Soviet Union and all were overwhelmed by the extraordinary well-being of the Soviet citizens. "I myself am a shoemaker," said a freckled fellow, grinning and waving a sharp edged bayonet. "I was earning up to one thousand rubles."

"And how much do shoes cost?"

He winked and asked: "How much do they cost by you?"

They named a price.

"Well, by us, for example, it's the same," the fellow said without hesitating. A group of Red Army men formed a circle:

> *Apples and pears blossomed,*
> *Clouds floated above the river,*
> *Katiusha came to the river bank . . .*

The melody of "Katiusha" pleased everyone. . . . Just three days ago, no one in Sniatyn expected these songs. Polish aviators in handsome black jackets, officers in horned caps, and the civilian Polish population were bewildered, trying to understand what had happened, not believing their eyes.

Only years later, when I was already in the Soviet Union, did I understand what a farce those cheerful Red Army men had carried off on that clear morning, how they had lied totally with such inspiration, those Yaroslavl and Ural lads, how they had made fools of us, telling us about boots for 16 rubles and the *kolkhoz* paradise. Apparently, they had been instructed to that effect, or their unique Russian patriotism inspired them to get the better of the Poles. I must say, the Jews immediately had some suspicions: hearing that "There is everything," "We have everything," they began to pose trick questions, "And do you have Copenhagen?" It turned out, "Of course, there is Copenhagen, too, as much as you want! . . ." The picture became clearer when the military police ordered all stores to open, declaring that the zloty was equal to the ruble, and an avalanche of Soviet buyers pounced upon the stores. "A ruble for a zloty!" They received for nothing the vestiges of bourgeois abundance as a reward to the victors. Later, I saw commanders enter empty stores in Lvov and, unable to read Polish, they would ask what was being sold there. It did not matter to them what they could buy—nails, suitcases, bathing suits. As they didn't inquire about the price, the Jews would first modestly add ten or twenty percent, but later they realized that these people needed everything at any price.

Three years later in a Soviet forced labor camp, I met a prisoner who was one of those who in September 1939 "liberated" Western Ukraine. I asked him about his impression of the first "abroad" that he had seen. From him I learned the thoughts of the Red Army soldiers who had told their audience on the streets of Sniatyn about Soviet well-being. "Rokitno, where I wound up, is a small village, but the fellows were simply blown away when they saw how many good things there were in the apartments. Mirrors and a record player, and they still complained about how bad it was. Well, we thought, just wait, darlings, with us you'll forget how to complain. In particular, the stores with textiles were astonishing—goods were not only on the shelves behind the counter but also on the customers' side. Enough! They don't live like we do. Immediately they started to hide goods, but nevertheless, I found a way, and you won't believe how much cocoa I bought! At fifteen rubles a kilo, and before us, they say, they sold it for kopecks. It's too bad that they sent us back, and we didn't get to enjoy things. . . ."

We lived in Soviet Sniatyn until the end of September. It was a marvelous early autumn. I lived on the outskirts in a little house with a glass-enclosed veranda and front yard where aster and hollyhocks blossomed under the window. My landlady, an old Pole, lived alone with a similarly old servant, and both were deathly afraid. In the morning, I would descend a bluff to the river to bathe. Blue hills stood on the other side of the Prut River; that was Romania. After a few days, groups of Poles began to return from there: the Romanians treated them roughly, forced them into a camp in an open field, ordered them to dig up potatoes for their meals, and seized their valuables.

In Sniatyn it was idyllic: the market was full; Soviet commanders were busy with purchases and impeccably polite. The population organized a welcome for the Red Army. They decorated the city, and about seven hundred people marched past the military governor's building with red flags and shouts of "Welcome," and "Hurray!" The majority were Jews. Several Ukrainians marched behind. There were no Poles. If one considers that the approximately five thousand Jews of Sniatyn had every reason to be grateful to the Soviet regime, then the percentage of Jewish enthusiasm was relatively low. The Poles, however, did not see those thousands who remained home. For them it was a "Jewish demonstration." That evening, a patriotic Polish woman, a teacher, bitterly complained to me about Sniatyn Jews.

It was difficult for us to leave the Romanian border. We did not give in; we sought guides, and waited for an opportunity. How long could we remain without attracting the attention of the Soviet authorities? In the evening, in a private home, we would gather to listen to the radio—our only link to the outside world. Warsaw was still holding out; the Red Army was advancing; we still awaited miracles on the Western front. The sleepy border town was an island of quiet.

The roofs of the Ukrainian huts were decked out with golden corn and gourds. The Soviet administration was located in the white building of the Zionist Organization with a Star of David on the front facade. And we, the Europeans who had lost our way, to whom all this seemed like a dream, instead of reading "Ecclesiastes," subscribed to the still open private library and read nonstop Montherlant,[13] an antisocial and anarchistic writer, author of brilliant paradoxes, our enemy Montherlant, future flunky of Vichy.

No one was willing to take us across the border. Finally, we presented our foreign passports decorated with many visas to the commandant's office and humbly requested an exit visa. The dashing, mustachioed commanding officer disdainfully twirled in his hands the blue booklets with the Polish eagle on the cover. The telephone rang. The commander grimaced and barked into the phone: "What kind of master of pharmacology? Please drop these titles! The time of the gentlemen and the academics is over! From the pharmacy? Then say from the pharmacy!"

Then turning to us: "Who are you?"

We explained to him in pure Russian, dropping all titles, who we were, and the officer offered us free refugee passage to the capital of Western Ukraine, Lvov.

---

13. Henri de Montherlant (1896–1972), French writer who collaborated with the Nazis.

2

Encircled

IN SEPTEMBER 1939, the Red Army occupied half of the Polish state.

Unable and unwilling to fight, Polish forces did not resist. In random clashes, several hundred were killed and two thousand wounded. This was that "jointly spilled blood" that, according to Stalin's telegram to Hitler, was supposed to lay the foundation for Soviet-Nazi friendship. The population welcomed the Red Army as a guardian angel. Not only the Jews but also Poles, Ukrainians, and Belarusians opened their hearts to the Soviet Union. They all regarded the arrival of Soviet troops not as a conspiratorial and cynical partition of Poland but as a fortuitous obstacle impeding Hitler—"Up to here and not one step further."

Communiqués enthusiastically reported that German divisions were retreating before the Red Army. The government-appointed administrator of Rivne ordered the construction of a triumphal arch and ordered local delegations to welcome the arriving troops. Polish police wearing white gloves welcomed the Red Army with bouquets of flowers. The news that Soviet forces were approaching the Vistula evoked a burst of enthusiasm in besieged Warsaw: relief was approaching. Never in the history of the two peoples, in the history of these two lands, had there been a more favorable moment to close old accounts, to liquidate age-old quarrels, with joyous recognition and gratitude to bring together Poles and non-Poles and begin a new era. All of us could have been bought cheaply then.

At that time, millions of despairing people fled the German invasion. The German assault and Polish national defeat left only one exit—toward the East. The Poles turned to their fraternal Slavic neighbor. The Jews sought the protection of the great Republic of Freedom. Socialists and democrats appealed to the country of the Revolution.

By chance, a friend of mine, a homeowner and member of the Pinsk city council, a peaceful bourgeois, was delayed at that time in a boarding house in Otwock near Warsaw. A German lieutenant entered the salon of the boarding house, saw Jewish faces, shuddered and said, "How horrible, so many Jews!" and left. In the evening, they began to register them. When the Pinsk homeowner's turn came, an idea crossed his mind. He proudly puffed out his chest and said, "I am a Russian communist." The German lieutenant silently glanced at him without saying a word. The next day, they permitted him to leave. He was unlucky, however: he wound up in an internment camp, and sat for several days in an open field with a crowd of refugees until the Germans expelled them to the Russian border. German cavalrymen drove the crowd with whips for 15 kilometers. The appearance of a Russian guard was a turning point in my friend's life. He ran up to him in tears, embraced him, and began to kiss his face, his bayonet, and coat. The Red Army man smirked and said, "Take it easy, brother; take it easy; now it will be better!"

Everyone believed that it would be better. A month later in my native Pinsk, I realized that my homeowner was no exception. Jewish youth were demonstrating on the streets of Pinsk with portraits of Stalin and . . . Pushkin.[1] Very few of these unfortunate youths understood that on the other side of the River Bug, half of Polish Jewry would pay with their lives for their celebration.

Our eyes were not opened immediately. We found enormous pandemonium in Lvov.[2] The destruction was still fresh. Death announcements covered the walls of houses. It was impossible to force one's way to the center of town. Trucks with Russian soldiers drove by, squadrons were marching, the megaphones of mobile radio stations were blaring, and the cafes and restaurants were overflowing. A million refugees and soldiers. Golden autumn leaves covered the main Boulevard of Legions, where platforms had hastily been erected, with columns decorated with slogans, wooden and plywood monuments designed to appear like marble. This imitation marble was symbolic: from a distance, it seemed like an impressive obelisk but up close—hastily slapped together boards with garish inscriptions. The wooden decorations looked rather pitiful among the bronze and Baroque of the old Polish city, but nearby were tanks and armored cars made of genuine steel.

---

1. They thus demonstrated their enthusiasm for both the current Soviet state and traditional Russian culture.

2. Now Lviv, in independent Ukraine.

Lvov still remembered the first Russian occupation of 1914. Then, the tsarist army brought trucks with flour; this time they did not bring any flour. They placed fresh flowers, however, at the monument to Mickiewicz on Mariacki Square. Moreover, there were Yiddish radio broadcasts. No one was touched yet. They registered refugees and Polish army officers. As soon it became clear, however, that the Soviet regime came to seize power, hordes of Poles began to leave for the German side. In October, Lvov looked like a temporary camp, a spectacle of confusion and unrest. Crowds storm foreign consulates on the eve of their closing. Agitated foreigners attempt to leave. Groups of refugees arrive daily from the West; many have walked on foot for 600 kilometers. Notices about missing children and broken families are hanging everywhere. Jews from Vienna and Silesia tell horror stories about how they were evicted and expelled over the Soviet border.

At the Lvov intersections, loudspeakers bellow military communiqués about German victories. Chopin's unworldly melody, grotesquely amplified like a crazed bull, cuts into the street crush. Chopin on the street is louder than the car horns. They are selling *Chervonyi Shtandard*, *Pravda*, *Izvestiya*, and Russian language textbooks. Everywhere portraits of the leaders and advertisements for Soviet films are hanging.

There was no longer a war but there was an upheaval in political, social, and daily life, whose source was not internal but external, dictated by Moscow. Liberation from the Germans turned into conquest. Although there was no front, the city looked like it was near a war zone. Gigantic queues formed, where hundreds of people stood in line in the autumn mud for bread, vodka, and a handful of candies. Innumerable little restaurants and snack bars also sprang up, where refugees served refugees, shady little dens full of speculators or "former people," where everyone spoke in whispers about the possibility of escaping to Hungary or getting to Romania. We were, however, already encircled. The nationalization of factories and banks, the division of land, exhibits that mounted photographs of enormous Soviet cities and of the marvels of technology, but nearby—terrible destruction in the cities and the impossibility of finding work. The Soviet regime announced the enlistment of those willing to work deep inside Russia: free transport and one hundred rubles for the trip.

Trainloads began to leave from Lvov to the Donetsk basin. Simultaneously, we were isolated, the borders were closed—except for the inner one, across which an unauthorized, semi-illegal stream of refugees flowed from German-occupied Poland into Soviet Poland and in the opposite direction. In particular, the border with the Soviet Union was closed. One could not travel in either direction without special permits, which were not issued to private individuals.

Immediately upon arriving in Lvov, I went to the military police head-quarters on Wałowa Street to request a laissez-passer to cross the border to Romania. Seemingly, a simple matter. I was living permanently in Tel Aviv, where I had an apartment and family; I had come from there in May. The war caught me on my way home. My visas and foreign passport were all in order. They ordered me to return in a week. A week later, they ordered me to appear in another two weeks. Each time I found new people in the headquarters who had no idea what I needed. Palestine, a certificate, a visa were all incompre-hensible words; and documents in Polish were inaccessible. Finally, they told me that the civil authority would decide matters of a laissez-passer after the plebiscite.

This plebiscite—about annexing Western Ukraine and Belorussia[3] to the Soviet Union—will remain in my memory as a model of an election farce. The results were determined in advance as are the results of any elections or-ganized by a military regime with the complete support of the administrative apparatus (or the administrative apparatus with the complete support of the military force), with the exclusion of opposition and absence of independent public supervision. On the day of the plebiscite, I left home and returned only at eleven o'clock in the evening. I had firmly decided not to participate in the plebiscite. Upon my return, I learned that a policeman had come for me twice—"Why doesn't he vote?"—and he promised to come a third time. I had no choice and went to the polling booth. There I demanded that my name be removed from the voting list. I explained that I was in Lvov in transit, I was living abroad and did not think that I had the right to decide the issue of the political future of Western Ukraine. This did not help. "You can vote," they told me; "We have nothing against it." I categorically refused. They told me that no one was forcing me, but they would mark me as someone who evaded voting. I went to the Soviet officer in charge of the polling place and showed him my identity card issued by the Tel Aviv municipal police in April of that year. This card was not a substitute for a passport, but the English text made an impression on the officer. He phoned the Central Election Commission and reported that the list of voters included an Englishman who did not want to vote. "Cross out the Englishman!" they told him, and I left victorious. Those whose names had not been crossed out voted as they were

---

3. Now the independent state of Belarus.

supposed to, and the Soviet regime took possession of Western Ukraine and Belorussia in a completely "legal, democratic way."

Our meetings with the Soviet commanding officers took place in the rooms of the Bristol restaurant, where even in daylight people dined under electric lighting, in the noisy, polyglot crowd, amidst drapery and velvet, accompanied by the clamor of dinnerware, and odors of frying, as the old waiters looked sadly at the decline of the former first-class Polish restaurant, and the young ones snapped at the guests and made critical remarks to them. The officers were not haughty and were sociable (to a certain degree). When we asked, "How is it possible that the Soviet Union signed a pact with fascists?" they invariably answered that it was "politics," but war with the fascists was inevitable. There were Jews among them, who would ask us what it was like to live with the Poles and what was going on in Palestine. They would ask with the complete sympathy of people who "could understand" although the issues did not concern them directly.

The formidable colonel who occupied a room in my friends' apartment behaved differently. In the evening, he would appear in the study and listen together with everyone else to the radio broadcast from Moscow. When foreign radio broadcasts began, however, he would get up and disappear. In principle, he was not interested in what the foreign broadcasts were saying, evidently considering such curiosity unworthy of a Soviet individual. Shortly, the authorities requisitioned the apartment and the entire house, and my friends were moved to a smaller, more modest apartment.

It was a damp, inclement fall, and nothing advanced with regard to my departure. Why had the contact with our families abroad been cut off? I imagined the fear of my dear ones, who had not received any news from me since the start of the war. Why was it impossible to go home? Why did I have to sit in this odious, alien city? And how long could one sit on one's suitcases without money or a salary? The thought of getting a job with the Soviets did not occur to me. I had to leave, not "get settled." I felt like a chauffeur who has been detained in high gear at a guard post: the motor is humming but no one lifts the barrier. . . . The time comes when one has to turn off the motor, get out and sit on the road. . . . How much longer?

I could not stop moving, driven by thoughts of home and impatient waiting. I could not imagine that they simply would not let me go home. Had someone told me that, I would have thought he was joking. While standing on the threshold of the jungle, I was thinking in categories of European justice. The friends with whom I had left Łodz did not have a Palestinian certificate or visa as I did. At the end of October, they therefore decided to travel to Vilna,[4] which the Red Army had just then transferred to Lithuania. They succeeded, and ultimately were able to leave Lithuania for Europe. One of them made it to New York, another to Brazil, and a third to Australia. I, too, made it to Palestine but my journey lasted . . . seven years.

At that time, still well fed and living in relatively normal conditions, I acutely felt my solitude, isolation, and the absurdity of my situation. Eventually, my stay in Lvov became unbearable. On the second day after the plebiscite, I took the train to Pinsk, the city of my childhood, which more than once in my wanderings served me as a rest station and refuge from misfortunes.

The city of my mother! But first, a switch in Rivne and one in Łuniniec. Rivne marked the end of the Ukraine with its white bread and sugar. The landscape became more barren as I traveled northward—Belarusian mists, lakes, dreary plains, damp groves, and deserted stations with piles of firewood. At the railroad station in Rivne, I was shocked at the sight of an incredible group of ragamuffins. I had never before seen such people in Poland: a crowd of youths in astonishing rags and tatters, worn-out shoes, some barefoot, in women's blouses, with fantastic rags wound around the neck. I was not the only one who looked in amazement at this crowd: from what slum had they appeared? It turned out that they were freshly mobilized recruits from Leningrad, who were going to do their military service. There was not one whole pair of trousers among them. It was as if we were peeking into another world, and everyone became somewhat uneasy. . . .

Soviet Belorussia began at the train station in Łuniniec, whose walls were covered with slogans and red cloth. The railroad stations here look solemnly monumental, like genuine "state institutions," with all the magnificence of the constructions from the time of Tsar Nicholas II: buffets with palms in planters, heavy doors, high windows and doorways—an imposing contrast to the pitiful little wooden houses and cobblestone roads behind them. The peasants were wearing *bast* shoes and leg wrappings, with canvas sacks on their backs; the Jews were not like those in Galicia or "Kongresówka"[5]; they were special, LITVAKS, Pinsk Jews, shortish and red-faced, with healthy, coarse features, round heads, small, lively eyes—a breed that is dear to my heart and which, it seems, is recognizable at the end of the world.

4. Now Vilnius, capital of Lithuania.

5. Congress Poland, the territories that were annexed to the Russian Empire after the Congress of Vienna in 1815.

The capital of the Pinsk marshes had turned into a Soviet city! The transition was easier than in Lvov because there were no language problems. People in the Polesia region had always spoken Russian; it was the language of the village, and every Jew could speak it. On the other hand, no one knew Belarusian, the new state language—neither villagers nor city dwellers. Jewish schoolchildren, who until now confused only Polish with Russian, now mixed up three Slavic languages and were thoroughly confused.

Pinsk buzzed and hummed like an orchestra tuning its instruments before the conductor's appearance. The conductor had arrived but no one knew what kind of music he would play. . . . The city was full of enthusiastic people who only yesterday had been illegal, frightened-to-death people, refugees, Soviet arrivals, concealed enemies, and dull ordinary citizens, who were neither enemies nor friends, and waited to see what would happen.

I could not permit myself such an indulgence. Upon arriving in Pinsk, I immediately went to OVIR, the department for visas and registration of foreigners. It was not hard for me to convince the illiterate and good-natured fellow with whom I spoke that I was not a local and had to travel to Palestine. Clearly, he had no objections to that. But he did not have the authority to issue visas. He had to send a request to the Belarusian capital, Minsk. Seeing how difficult it was for the head of the regional OVIR to form the letters on paper, I took his pen from his hand and wrote the request for him. . . . I do not know whether it was ever sent to Minsk. I think that the fellow simply sent it over to the next street, to the regional NKVD, or Soviet Gestapo, where there were people more intelligent than he was. An invisible noose, which every inhabitant of the Soviet country wears, had already been slipped over my neck, and I soon began to feel it.

With the arrival of the Soviet regime, old Doctor Margolin,[6] a long-time resident of Pinsk, was deprived of his pension, which the Lublin Medical Fund had been paying him regularly for eight years. I arrived just in time to deal with his financial affairs. The director of the Social Welfare Office was another Margolin—a thin Jewish member of the Komsomol, who had not yet adjusted to the sudden transition from underground work to the "summit of power." Intimidated, he clumsily tried to stave off the masses of human sorrow that were beating down the doors of his office. Old pensioners, invalids, widows, all those maintained by the Polish state besieged him, and there were no funds or formal basis for helping them. The payments of the

6. Julius Margolin is writing about his father, Boris.

Soviet regime were insufficient for lodging and food or for milk for toothless
mouths. Something clearly was not right: dream and reality did not match.
The old people were weeping, and this lad in an open Russian shirt with a
prominent Adam's apple and bulging eyes looked at them in embarrassment
and pity. Two Margolins spoke about a third. It turned out that according to
Soviet law, a doctor who had served the state for twenty-five years had the
right, if he became an invalid, to a pension equal to half of his last salary. The
difficulty was that old Doctor Margolin, whose service had begun at the end
of the previous century, was, understandably, unable to present documenta-
tion from his work places. Who could certify his work during the cholera
epidemic along the Volga in 1897? Even his work in the Pinsk hospital, which
the director of the welfare service himself knew about as he used to come
to Doctor Margolin's office as a child, could not be certified because the
archives were missing, and the hospital itself had burned down several years
ago. Without the documents, the Welfare Office could not pay. "Nothing?"
asked one Margolin in distress. "Nothing," sighed another Margolin. There
remained only the allowance for the poor, which the municipality paid at the
rate of 20 rubles a month (the price of 10 liters of milk). I glanced at the line
of sick, disabled, bandaged old men with canes and blind old women who had
clearly overstayed their time in this world, and I blessed the fate that brought
me in timely fashion to Pinsk in order to help my aged father. The communist
revolution was a rather unprofitable matter for him. And again—as at the
Rivne railroad station—an icy wind blew in from the half open door.

Time was passing and there was still no answer from Minsk. We spoke
very pleasantly with the head of OVIR, and finally he told me that there was
no formal possibility of stamping a Soviet exit visa on my Polish passport.
"We don't recognize the Polish state, which means that we can't put a visa on
Polish documents. It's a different matter if you accept Soviet citizenship. As a
Soviet citizen, you will then have the right to request an exit visa."

I asked, "If I return to you in a week with a Soviet passport [identity
document], will you be able to exchange it for a foreign travel document?"
"Well, no," said the OVIR head, "I don't deal with that matter. Perhaps, then,
however, it will be possible to write to Minsk about your request." I immediately realized that things were not going well. I left Pinsk and hurried to the
Romanian border, to the already familiar Sniatyn.

It was the start of December. In passing through Lvov, my caution
prompted me to take from an acquaintance a promissory note from a Sniatyn
merchant and an official letter stating that I was entrusted with settling
this debt.

The Lvov train arrived in Sniatyn at ten o'clock in the evening, and the two dozen arriving passengers were taken under guard to the railroad police. Things had changed in three months, and it was forbidden to approach the border without serious reasons. The arriving passengers were all locked up until the morning, when they were sent back on the Lvov train. I was the only one who satisfactorily explained the reason for my arrival and received permission to enter the city.

It was the dark of night when the horse-driven carriage left the station (it was 3 kilometers to the city). We were stopped half way at a guard post, and again I had to present my documents. "Do you have matches, comrade?" asked the Red Army soldier. Neither he nor I had matches. In the total darkness, the soldier made do with touching my identity document and ordering the driver, "Get moving!"

In dormant Sniatyn, I managed with difficulty to reach the inn and knock on the window. The innkeeper remembered me from September and greeted me like an old friend. In a few minutes, I was sleeping under an enormous down quilt in the sole guest room. For three days, I remained in empty, depopulated Sniatyn. The refugees had left, the Poles were disappearing, and my Polish landlady from September had disappeared somewhere. An iron comb had swept through the population of the border town. The owner of the house where we had listened to the radio three months ago, a former merchant, now engaged in making sausages. I was categorically advised not to cross the border. They had just caught the son of the local shoemaker, a former Komsomol member, in an attempt to cross the border, and it was not known what became of him. He had disappeared mysteriously. Even a cat could not cross the border. The mysterious disappearances of people noticeably unnerved Sniatyn Jews, who were accustomed to knowing the exact addresses of their own, even in prison. The people who disappeared left no traces, they did not even write letters—how very strange! When Russians were asked about it, they merely laughed and replied with a proverb: "If you know a lot, you'll age quickly."

The Romanian border turned out to be impenetrable, but there remained the Lithuanian one to the north. I reproached myself for not having gone there immediately. How much time had been lost!

Again Lvov! I seemed to have landed at a noisy intersection, into a motley crowd of people who felt that the ground had been swept from under their feet, and they were desperately floundering about—they included moneychangers, wheeler-dealers, ordinary people selling watches and their last remaining possessions, and also new bureaucrats, turncoat careerists, and Soviet civil servants. Many of my acquaintances had fully integrated as engineers or leaders of enterprises; some had taken work trips to Moscow or Kiev[7] and were full of impressions. In many homes, the disorder and devastation were masked, concealed by a simulation of everyday comfort: as in the past, people set the table and conducted "normal" conversations, but a bed had already been set up in the dining room; the landlady prepared "reserves"; suddenly, inexplicably, they would begin to speak in a whisper. Hundreds of thousands of people in Lvov led a strange, unreal, temporary existence: it was as if they were dreaming everything that was happening to them. These people were not leading a natural, free way of life that had developed organically and corresponded to their desires. It was a huge masquerade for the benefit of an alien regime that itself wore a mask, did not say what it thought, and went its own conspiratorial way.

A threat hung in the air, a pile of suppressed thoughts, hidden feelings, a heap of distrust, lies, fear, suspicions, the impotence of private life, which had already been mined and was ready to explode at any minute: the cursed atmosphere of Stalinism or of any dictatorship, the atmosphere of violence, multiplied by the pain of the military defeat, disruption, disintegration, and separation. There were thousands of people like myself, who, on the eve of the war, had arrived from abroad. There were grandmothers who had come from afar for a month to spend time with their grandchildren and had landed in the Soviet Union; Palestinian youth who suddenly felt as if they were illegal; foreigners, who wanted nothing more than permission to leave as soon as possible because being "alien" in Soviet conditions is a crime.

New people constantly became part of this jumble—from the West, from the Nazi zone, refugees who did not look back. One evening I heard a familiar knock on the door. I opened: on the threshold stood my best friend and companion, Mieczysław Braun—straight from Łódź.

In his youth, Mieczysław Braun belonged to a group of poets called "Skamander," and his poems were included in all Polish school anthologies. In 1920, he was wounded near Radzymin defending Warsaw from the Bolsheviks. The time came, however, when Polish society began to boycott him as a Jew. A Polish patriot and a European, Braun had traversed a difficult path from socialism and assimilation to Zionism. He returned to his people, and in the summer of 1939, he wrote an excellent poem, "Assimi," devoted to the epic of illegal immigration. On the deck of a ship traveling to the

7. Now Kyiv, capital of Ukraine.

shores of Palestine, Mieczysław Braun envisioned among the youth a figure in an old-fashioned loose cloak and wide-brimmed hat: Heinrich Heine,[8] returning home. The stanzas of "Assimi" still ring in my ears but no one will hear them any more: people and the treasures of their hearts, their words, and their thoughts lie buried in the enormous grave of Polish Jewry.

That evening Mieczysław told me about his misfortunes. He left Łódź together with his wife on the eve of the city's fall. They walked for several hundred kilometers, spent the nights in peasant huts, and in the daytime moved with the human stream. German tanks overtook them near the border at the River Bug. A month after the start of their journey, they had to return to "Litzmanstadt," as the Germans had renamed Łódź. Their apartment had been plundered and occupied by the Germans. Braun settled on the edge of the city and for six weeks did not go out. He kept busy reading the complete works of Tolstoy. After six weeks, it was announced that Jews had to wear a yellow patch. For 700 zlotys, a Łódź priest whom he had once done a big favor agreed to drive him to the border in a car decorated with a swastika. "In exchange," the priest told him, "when the Red Army comes to Łódź, you will take me to the German border." Evidently, at that time, the Łódź Germans were not too optimistic about Germany's military fortunes.

A kilometer from Ostrów-Mazowiecka, the German dropped him off and hurried away. It was already dark when Braun entered the village, and he was astonished by the empty streets. The village seemed to have died, and there was no trace of Jews. Braun entered the Polish hotel at the market. There he passed himself off as a Pole. He was a tall, blue-eyed blond, and no one would have taken him for a Jew. The innkeeper was astonished to see a guest in the evening: street traffic was prohibited in the evening; he was lucky that he had not run into a police patrol. It turned out that the night before there had been a massacre of Jews in Ostrów-Mazowiecka.

This village was overflowing with refugees. A fire broke out the morning before, and the Germans accused the Jews of arson. This was the signal for a pogrom. Horrible scenes played out at the market where they assembled the entire Jewish population. The Jews started fleeing from the village; the Germans shot at them. Finally, they rounded up 350 people and drove them to the cemetery. In addition, they took thirty Poles, including a servant from the hotel where Braun was staying. Upon his return, he told the innkeeper that at the cemetery the Germans separated the women and children from

---

8. An allusion to the famous German poet (1797–1856), who was born into a Jewish family but converted to Christianity.

the men. They ordered the men to dig a grave. They dug silently; only the women and children shrieked. Two refugees approached the German lieutenant. They had an eight-year-old daughter and they offered the lieutenant all the money that they had if he would let the daughter return to the village. They did not ask anything for themselves. The German took the money, took out his revolver, and shot the girl in front of her parents. All 350 people were gunned down. The sight of little children's hands, feet, and heads flying in all directions from the bullets made a strong impression on the Poles. Then the Poles were ordered to bury the corpses. They dawdled. The Germans gave them a choice: 20 zlotys each for the work or a bullet. The Poles buried the corpses.

Braun listened, nodding, and tried not to show his agitation. He was the only guest in the hotel, which was occupied by the German police. The innkeeper, who lived in the neighboring house, was about to leave, but Braun decided to detain him because he was afraid to remain alone with the Germans. He started to tell jokes and tales non-stop and drank with him until late at night, and when the innkeeper recollected the time, dawn broke, and the night had passed.

In the morning, the servant took him to the neighboring village, and Braun spent the second night in a hut at the border. That night the Germans searched all the huts for Jews and found them in each hut. Braun's Aryan appearance saved him. The German poked him and shone a flashlight in his eyes: "Who is this?" "A relative," said the landlady. The German looked at the document. "Czech?" he asked. Braun did not argue, and they left him in peace.

As soon as the Germans went away, the landlady demanded that he leave the hut. Alluding to the Mother of God and the heart of a Pole, Braun managed to convince the peasant to accompany him. The peasant agreed only when Braun turned his pockets inside out, showing him that he was giving him all his money—down to the last penny. They crossed a grove, passing so close to a German guard that they heard voices. Braun carried a backpack and the peasant his suitcase. They reached a clearing, and the peasant indicated with his hand: "Over there are the Russians." And he turned to leave. "What about my suitcase?" called Braun. The peasant merely started to walk faster. Braun could not chase after him and went in the opposite direction. At midday, he reached a train station on the Russian side where a Soviet train was standing. A nurse who took pity on him let him into the officers' car, and he arrived in Lvov without any trouble. It would not be worth telling this story were it not for the astonishing fact that Mieczysław Braun, who was received with honors in Lvov and welcomed into the Polish section of the Soviet Writers' Union with all the consequent material benefits, three months later willingly crossed the border in the opposite direction, to the very same Germans about whom he had no illusions. Later on, I shall discuss what impelled him to return.

In the second half of December 1939, via the Baranowicze-Vilna rail line, I arrived in Lida, on the Lithuanian border. Vilna was then the desired goal, the gates of freedom. I had a backpack on my back and very little money in my pocket. Lida had neither the Ukrainian-Moldavian repleteness of Sniatyn nor the bustle and restaurants of Lvov. Severe cold, poverty, destruction, and boarded up stores prevailed. The foreheads of the crowds of people filling the boardwalks spelled out why they had arrived. The city was overcrowded; it was impossible to squeeze in anywhere. For several days, I slept on the floor in a tiny room at the home of casual acquaintances. They were a young couple, both refugees; the husband was unemployed, the wife a skilled worker at the Rigavar boot factory. I witnessed their bitter poverty, as the salary at the factory was not enough even for bread, and they had sold their last belongings. After a few days, I left for an apartment that was an assembly point for those trying to cross the border illegally. It was a den, with a certain romance. At night the apartment turned into a crash pad—they set up folding beds, families hung up sheets as partitions, but it was so cold that, even fully dressed, I was unable to fall asleep. I would get up in the darkness and walk among the sleepers, taking coats down from the hooks to wrap myself in them. At dinnertime, rabbis would gather, bearded Jews in fur hats who were trying to escape the Soviet impiety and reach the Lithuanian Jerusalem. They would carry on discussions around the table, in which I could not participate, on topics such as: "If one of the four fringes of the 'tsitsis'[9] is missing, can one consider that the law is fully complied with or is it only three quarters fulfilled?"

We soon formed a group of seven and reached an arrangement with a guide. I did not have enough money but my companions agreed to give me credit until Vilna, where I hoped to pay them back. The icy wilderness of Lida, my illegal existence, the sneaking around, the dirt, cold, anguish, senseless confusion of those days wore me down. Finally, on the morning of December 28, we received the signal to leave.

---

9. Specially knotted ritual fringes, or tassels, worn at the corners of a garment by observant Jewish men.

We each gave the Belarusian guide an advance of 150 rubles. Our belongings were loaded onto sleds; we went on foot, and we soon stretched out in a line along the road. It was a clear, frosty morning. We were supposed to traverse several kilometers from Lida, wait until evening at a peasant's farm, and cross the border at night. Thousands of people had crossed the border before us in this spot.

We did not get far, however. Armed men suddenly came out of a little house near the road; it was our bad luck that a police guard post had been set up that very morning. They sent us back. They halted the sled, on which women were sitting with a heap of our things. There was nothing I could do but go to the sled. In a few minutes, they led us under escort together with the sled back to Lida.

We waited several hours for our turn at the NKVD. They interrogated each of us separately in a large room with several tables. I said that I was going to Radun, a village 18 kilometers from Lida.

"Why, then, with sleds, when there is a daily bus to Radun?"

I explained that it did not make sense for me to stand in line in the cold half a day for a bus ticket when in the same time I could get there with a horse and even by foot.

"Why Radun?"

I alluded to a friend who had promised me work at the Radun electric power station. Indeed, several days ago I had met a person who was the manager of the Radun power station and, "just in case," I had asked him for a "letter of invitation" to come to Radun for work. I could not find the letter but my NKVD officer came to my aid. He very calmly and expertly frisked me: out of my bag poured English books and other things testifying to my peaceful profession as a teacher. Finally, he also shook out the letter that I thought I had lost. He took the letter and advised me to find work in Lida and not to stick my nose into Radun, into which entry was forbidden. That was all.

Three months later, I would not have gotten off so easy. Moreover, I was "lucky" that they detained us not at the border itself but on the road to it. They released our entire group, and we decided not to risk it again in fear of a repeat meeting with the regime; in that case, they would talk to us differently. I again set out for Pinsk.

Some remained; others went to Święcany to try their luck at another border post. Many of the persistent ones managed to cross in January. On January 2, a family whom I knew from Lvov crossed the border near Lida with little children and many suitcases. It cost them all their possessions but it did not save them from death—two years later during the massacre of Vilna's Jews.

I, in any case, had had enough. I was not suited to be a "contrabandist." I was deadly tired and wanted to sleep and rest. On December 31, 1939, with great difficulty, I squeezed into an overcrowded train and traveled back to Pinsk.

At midnight, we arrived at Łuniniec. The train to Pinsk left at 6:00 a.m. I sat for a while, walked around the train station and suddenly recalled that at this moment around the world people were celebrating the New Year and hoping it would bring an end to misfortunes and the advent of happiness. The New Year! Without giving it much thought, I went into town.

The streets of the desolate village were empty and silent; the snow crunched under my feet, and I trudged through the drifts like the Wandering Jew, with my pack on my back. I stopped under a little window. Behind the closed shutters, I heard joyful noise, New Year's cries, and rejoicing. They were welcoming the New Year, and I was standing under the window like a beggar! Taking my chances, I knocked. They opened the door and, like Santa Claus, I stumbled into the warm, lit corridor. It was a lucky choice because the New Year's party was organized by the Teachers' Union of Łuniniec. They took my word that I was a teacher. I put down my pack in the cloakroom and went to the buffet, where there was still some beer.

I thus greeted the New Year 1940 in a crowd of strangers, at an alien table. It was a wretched, ill-omened year, full of blood, sorrow, and the triumph of evil. It brought death and slavery to millions of people and the most fantastic adventure of my life to me.

3

The Story of a Disillusionment

NOW I SHALL briefly recount a story of disillusionment. Not my personal disillusionment. I was never enchanted by the Soviet regime, and I never doubted that its theory was unsustainable and its practice full of cruel human fraud. As an outsider, I personally viewed the Soviet Union without illusions or hostility. There is no doubt, however, that the arrival of the Red Army evoked sincere gratitude and great hopes among the majority of the population of Western Ukraine and Belorussia.[1] Humankind inherently believes in the good will of any new regime until it is proven otherwise. Until it receives a hard blow, it is inclined to optimism, and even afterward, it still hopes that it was a misunderstanding.

The account of how, in the course of one winter, the Soviet regime managed to turn the population of the occupied territories into opponents, without distinction of class, ethnicity, or political affiliation, has a certain timely interest, as it provides an insight into the general methods and techniques of Sovietization.

Experience has taught me that no arguments or evidence can dissuade a person who considers him or herself a communist. Only Soviet reality itself can do this. The same experience has convinced me that communism does not correspond to a Westerner's preconceived ideas about it. "Imagined communism" in a democratic order is the sum of opinions or a political position that harms no one. Ninety out of a hundred people who profess communism in Paris or Rome and have no clear idea of what it is like in practice would reject it if they saw in it action, when it cuts like a knife into the body of its victim.

---

1. Now independent Belarus.

Only the butchers would remain, people for whom brutal violence is not only a means but also the cornerstone of the social order.

I observed the stages of Sovietization in my native city of Pinsk.

First, the representatives of the Polish administration disappeared. No one was disturbed by their removal, and no one pondered their subsequent fate. And yet, in a characteristic Soviet measure, they were not simply removed from their posts but also liquidated as a population group. They no longer were among us. The *osadnicy* [settlers] followed them. During the twenty years of its existence, the government of independent Poland divided up the estates of landowners at the eastern border, allotting the land not to the local population but to Polish settlers. The majority of them were decorated soldiers from the Polish-Soviet war of 1920 who reinforced the ethnic Polish element in the eastern regions and were a power base for the Polish state. During those twenty years, the *osadnicy* became close to the local population; their children spoke the local dialect, and one could predict that they would not Polonize the Belarusians, but the Belarusian peasant element would absorb them just as it had absorbed the Polish gentry before them.

The local people would not have harmed the *osadnicy*, who were farmers just as they were. The new Soviet regime classified them as enemies and deported them the way the Gestapo deported the Jews. The reprisal against the *osadnicy* made a strong impression on the Jewish population of Pinsk. It was severely cold in the depth of winter. By word of mouth, news spread about unheated train cars standing in the station for two days and about the corpses of frozen children, which the mothers threw out the windows of the locked cars. These Nazi-style crimes evoked general horror. The future would reveal that these and similar measures, whose aim was to "purge" the population of unreliable elements, did not accomplish their goal and were unnecessary. The Red Army's retreat from the occupied regions in June 1941, when the war with the Germans broke out, took place with lightning speed despite the absence of *osadnicy*.

A systematic and massive deportation deep into Russia of socially active, popular, and leading individuals from the villages followed the liquidation of the *osadnicy*. Not only the village bourgeoisie and intelligentsia or patriotic Polish element suffered liquidation but also all people with authority— Belarusians and Ukrainians; the more popular they were, the worse it was for them. The majority of these people perished in the Soviet north. Here are two examples. In the spring of 1944, in a camp in the north of Russia, I met a landsman from a village near Pinsk. This person was dying of malnutrition. His manner, style of speech, and education was that of a Polish farmer from the area of Kresy [near the eastern Polish border]. He told me that fourteen men had been taken with him and only two were still alive. He was one of the "living," and he was half-dead. The second encounter was with a Ukrainian, the former mayor of a town in Podolia. A respected lawyer and public figure before his arrest, he had received an eight-year sentence. The petition supporting him, which three hundred workers had signed, severely harmed him. "Now we see that you are a truly dangerous person," they told him. "You have influence among the workers."

The next stage came very quickly in Pinsk—the turn of the urban Jewish population. "The fifth column" of local informers helped compile lists of "non-proletarian elements." This list included merchants, homeowners, lawyers, agents, storekeepers—hundreds of families. All these people faced expulsion from the city. They were sent to small villages and surrounding towns where no one knew them and where they were homeless refugees. Of course, this was better than Nazi ghettos, but at that time, people were far from such comparisons, and they regarded exile as a catastrophe and the collapse of their life. They had to leave their family homes and furniture—which were impossible to move given the ruined state of transport—and travel into the unknown. The very fact of exile, humiliation, and social discrimination deeply shocked these people. The NKVD would round them up at night. I remember the March nights of 1940 when I would wake up and hear bone-chilling sounds in the darkness: the entire street was weeping; the howls and lamentation of the women were carried from afar. "They came to the neighbors!" And I imagined the scene of the nocturnal invasion, armed men, cries, prodding, threats, a two-hour limit to assemble one's belongings. . . . The next morning, the tiny nearby store, where until yesterday one could buy cheese and butter, was empty; the windows were shuttered; the doors were barricaded as after a pogrom. During those nights full of reverberations of weeping, the peaceful residents of Pinsk started to develop a feeling of indignation and outrage at the regime that waits for the darkness of night to break into homes and destroy everyday life.

The next stage was the destruction of cultural institutions and the Sovietization of schools. Newspapers, libraries, and bookstores are closed. In their place, standard Soviet model ones will be established. This "extirpation of culture" is carried out in the crudest mechanical way, as if extracting a healthy tooth in order to replace it with an artificial one. At this point, we lost the right to teach our children anything other than communism, the right to read what we wanted, the right to think for ourselves, and the right to live as we wanted. This process was painful. There was a Jewish gymnasium [academic high school] called Tarbut [Hebrew for culture]. It was the pride of the city: seven hundred students, a large library, the citadel of Zionism, the center of Jewish education, an object of many years of loving care by the Pinsk community. After the arrival of the Bolsheviks, the teachers were ordered to change the language of instruction to Yiddish. The classic Hebrew poets, Bialik and Tchernichovsky, overnight became illegal authors, and books in Hebrew were confiscated. The following scene occurred in one of the classrooms at that time. The teacher turned to his pupils with the words: "Children, today I am addressing you in Hebrew for the last time . . ." and his lips trembled. He started to weep and the entire class cried together with him. The youthful students were persistent. That winter, boys and girls continued secretly to study the forbidden language, vowed not to forget Zion, nor let themselves be severed from the national culture. . . . One should remember that there was no Jewish family in Pinsk that did not have a relative or close friend in Palestine. Of course, this youthful resistance did not last long. It died out by itself or, with the passing of years, was trampled upon in camps and exile, as was any attempt at an independent national—and not just Jewish—movement in the Soviet country.

The destruction of political organizations and centers of public life was completed in the spring of 1940. The leaders of the Bund were arrested and deported; in April came the arrests of the Zionists, who each received eight years in forced labor camps. Systematically and mercilessly, the regime destroyed all active elements that could oppose the "re-education" of the masses—everyone capable of independent thought, all potential organizers of resistance, the brain and nerves of society who just the day before did not suspect that they were doomed to fall into the meat grinder and be reworked into a formless glop in the Soviet kitchen. The only salvation was to dive into the mass, become like everyone else, not to stick out; even this, however, did not help people who in the past had been socially active: in the eyes of the regime, they were branded and doomed. The new Soviet society felt endangered until the last traces of cultural and political "life before September 1939" were extirpated without a vestige. With the help of the NKVD policing apparatus, strangers carried out this operation blindly and indifferently, without hatred or pity, against a society in which there were live, creative traditions, vital strength and youthful pride, whose culture was on an immeasurably higher level than that which sought to destroy it. This society, which in Polish times had become accustomed critically to evaluate each move of the regime and never recognized the ultimate authority of the state, now faced the terror and domination of a dark, unreasonable force that made no distinctions and destroyed everything that did not fit into the framework of Gosplan [state planning]. They say that one cannot slaughter an idea with bayonets, and culture is not a military trophy. In Pinsk, we came to see that bayonets and military seizure, in any case, constitute the first stage in the castration of a live cultural organism. It was insufficient, however, to paralyze the masses by politically disarming them and removing active leaders and prominent figures. In this case, the common person always has a strategy of retreat. He retreats into the fortress of his private existence. Like a snail, he climbs into his shell, withdraws into the circle of family and neighbors, and relies on material resources, on "reserves" or vestiges of the good old times. But the Soviet regime keeps at his heels.

In January 1940, without warning, the Polish zloty was withdrawn from circulation. Until then it had served as the legal and almost sole currency. Workers were paid in zlotys, farmers and the urban lower class kept their savings in zlotys. When the zloty was withdrawn from circulation in January, a maximum of 300 zlotys could be exchanged for rubles. It should be noted that, from the autumn of 1939, the Soviet Gosbank [state bank] had been inviting the population of the occupied regions to entrust their savings to the state as it had been doing previously in Poland. In January, these savings were simply expropriated insofar as they exceeded 300 zlotys. One can easily imagine the effect of this "ingenious" operation on those with meager savings. This move meant that people who had some monetary reserves lost them instantly, and many families now lacked money for bread: in other words, those who until then had avoided working in Soviet institutions had to seek work immediately and had to accept the work offered them by the sole employer—the state. The state brought the little man to his knees. A general proletarization occurred immediately. A salary became the sole source of existence for those who, until the day before, had relied on hidden pennies, on reserves, on family funds. Of course, the zloty did not become worthless right away; for a long time it remained an illegal means of payment. Many preferred speculation and private earnings to Soviet service. They were, however, only the foam on the surface of the Soviet sea, pitiful remnants subject to liquidation.

At the beginning of 1940, all of us, except for the speculators and people with indefinite sources of income, became Soviet employees. Until then we knew that there was a right to work. Now we became acquainted with the system of coercive labor, with the iron obligation of work that one does not choose freely and that lies like a yoke on the neck. The transition was gradual. They did not immediately submit us to the Soviet labor regime. But we already knew what was awaiting us. We knew that in the Soviet Union people were assigned a fixed place of work, that leaving work on one's own volition was severely punished, that it was easier to divorce your wife than quit work that did not suit you. A divorce is granted if one party requests it, but to leave work, you needed the state's consent. Many people equated this situation to serfdom.

The work conditions also surprised the Pinskers. The state is not a private enterprise where you do not have to stand on ceremony and can go home after eight hours of work. The state demands that you respect it. The state expects its new citizens to show loyalty and zeal. The Pinsk residents were not used to working extra hours in the evening, to slaving away on days off, or, instead of going home to dine after work, going to an obligatory meeting, pretending that they enjoyed the speeches—and not receiving their salary on time. Their faces fell. Most were surprised to discover that labor and social welfare conditions in the Soviet Union were worse than in bourgeois Poland.

You would think that nothing could be better than a health clinic and free medical service. The doctors, however, lost the right to a private practice, while they were given a salary of merely 300 rubles a month, with the price of bread at 85 kopecks a kilo. The Pinskers soon felt the difference between paid and free medical treatment. The numerous lawyers who were forbidden to practice were in a worse situation. Only five young people, who had not had the right to practice under Polish rule, were admitted to the bar. This was a tragedy for some. The whole city spoke about lawyer B., a talented jurist who loved his profession, who wept in the office of the Soviet director, pleading with him not to ruin his life. It did not help. Lawyer B. received a job as a petty postal clerk and in a short time was sent deep into Russia. His wife requested that the authorities send her to her husband. A short time later she, too, was sent away, not to her husband but to a backward *kolkhoz* in Kazakhstan, from which she wrote that she "envies Alia." There was nothing else in the letter, but dozens of Pinskers who read it knew that Alia was her sister, who had died the previous year.

The initial enthusiasm gradually began to wane.

The recent past began to appear in a different light. With pathos, the orator at a factory meeting reminded the workers how terribly they had been exploited by the Poles, forced to work for 60 zlotys a month. But at that same time, the Soviet salary was 180 rubles, which was equal to no more than 30 pre-war zloty. The workers' material condition deteriorated sharply; if the Polish salaries had been exploitation, then what should one think of the Soviet wages?

As the smoke of the first weeks and months began to dissipate, it became impossible to comfort oneself with the thought that this was only a temporary phenomenon, a transitional period, and that normal life would return. There were no doubts that living conditions in Soviet Russia were much worse than the present conditions in the occupied regions. This news was brought by workers who voluntarily left for Donbass and other places in the fall of 1939. They told us, in brief, the following: They were greeted in Donbass festively, with speeches and music, and it was clear that the authorities wanted to set them up with the best conditions possible. It soon became clear, however, that a salary of 8 to 12 rubles a day was insufficient to feed oneself, and the living conditions were intolerable for the Poles, who were used to living and dressing normally. Work in the mines was too hard for many, who had not had any idea where they were being taken. For less strenuous work, the salary was halved. Soviet workers knew how to manage without breakfast, without tea or sugar, without meat and fats. Their life consisted of the pursuit of a piece of bread. People from Poland were not prepared for such a life. After some time, they began to quit work en masse. This is a serious crime in the Soviet Union, but they had a special status. Crowds of "Westerners" flocked home, without tickers or funds for the trip. In Minsk, they assembled in front of the city hall and demanded to be sent home. They carried out a street protest: the crowd lay down on the rails and halted the movement of trams. For Soviet people such scenes were unbelievable. The Soviet regime could have dealt with the protesters and those fleeing in the usual manner by sending them to a forced labor camp. But the time for that had not yet come. And they let them return from whence they had come, where their tongues were immediately loosened and they related what they had seen.

Their tales were not needed. Soviet citizens who had wound up in destroyed villages of Western Ukraine and Belorussia were so blatantly happy at their good luck that, without questioning, it was clear what was going on back home. What we considered the depth of devastation was for them the height of abundance. At the Pinsk market, one could still obtain butter and lard at prices that were ten times cheaper than in the Soviet sector of Ukraine. The storekeepers still had reserves of Polish goods hidden away. For those Soviet people, coming to us in Pinsk meant getting clothed, eating one's fill, and stocking up for the children. The Pinskers were taken aback, looking at these people who wore nightclothes during the day, slept without sheets, and ordered ten cups of tea at once in the cafeteria. Why ten? It is very simple: in the old pre-Soviet days, there was enough tea for everyone but now one had to "seize" tea while they were still serving it. After half an hour, there was none for us naïve Pinskers, novices of Soviet daily life, while nearby a person was sitting behind a battery of teacups, smiling happily and treating friends.

The Russians were cautious and circumspect about their everyday Soviet existence. The time would come, however, when after months of neighborly living, the Soviet apartment dweller would cease being shy in front of his landlord, and his tongue would loosen up after drinking. Then we would hear the long-silenced truth.

"Do you understand how good you had it? You lived in paradise! You had everything—and you didn't have fear! And we . . ." and the man would tear open his overcoat: ". . . do you see what I am wearing? Our life is as gray as this overcoat!"

We believed it because our own life became gray and difficult, as if we had been driven into a cellar and the door sealed with a stone.

With growing amazement, we faced this new life. A bottomless, all-encompassing chaos prevailed in Soviet institutions. Pinskers quickly learned to speak about their "work" with irony and derision. When the largest match factory in town increased the number of workers from three hundred to eight hundred, the manager was removed and expelled from Pinsk; fourteen engineers were immediately hired in his place. The manager's salary had been high in Polish times: 4,000 zlotys a month. The fourteen engineers who now did his work cost the state a little less than that one manager, but it may have been more expensive because, to everyone's astonishment, the factory stopped operating because of a shortage of raw material. There was not enough wood in the Polesia forests. We learned about the other side of the planned economy in the Soviet system: elemental disorder and confusion, a natural laxness that could be dealt with only by means of the iron muzzle of bureaucratic regulation.

The elemental disorder was not accidental: it was the logical outcome of a lack of personal interest, of a dislike and indifference to alien, state business. People did not have a feeling of belonging to the enterprise to which they had been assigned: it scorned them and they it. At the factory, people skipped work days. In the cooperative there were no goods; in the cafeteria dirt and discomfort; at the hairdresser's rude treatment; in the workshop slipshod work. To combat this, one needed to supervise each worker and to place a second supervisor over the supervisor, plus the NKVD with a whip. In this system, one can maintain production only by means of harsh coercion, a high production quota, a starvation ration, and the threat of a trial for the slightest tardiness or negligence at work. Had this draconian work regime been introduced in Pinsk immediately, half of the population would have fled the city. They gave us time to become accustomed to this system, especially because the village was more important to them than the city. They needed to purge the former of hostile elements and prepare for the introduction of *kolkhozes*.

The farmers, who had been bringing milk and eggs to my mother's kitchen for a quarter of a century, were not afraid to speak frankly with her. "For twenty years, the Polish lords tried to make Poles out of us," said one of them, "but they did not succeed. In two months, however, the Bolsheviks turned us into Poles."

Such a declaration in the mouth of a Polesian was particularly meaningful. The Belarusian peasant population did not like Poles. Before the war, there had been a considerable number of "communists" among the village youth. Nothing, however, neither the national aspect, nor the division and allocation of the landowners' estates, nor the establishment of schools, nor free medical service could overcome the Belarusian peasantry's antipathy to the newcomers. You could not win the Polesians' trust with a bureaucratic, doctrinaire approach or with a decree or with the demand that they supply bread and submit to compulsory work. You had to help the region stand on its feet without imposing on it and with respect for its authenticity. Such an approach, however, is not in the nature of communism. The upheaval that they forced upon the city and village was not a revolution. Revolution always means overthrowing oppression and violence: new creative forces tear down the obstacles on their path and burst out to freedom. The Bolsheviks, however, introduced pressure from above, a denial of self-determination, and a bureaucratic omnipotence. Living did not become easier for the peasant, but he felt that the new master was more dangerous and merciless than the former one. Among the many paradoxes of life, the Pinskers noticed peasants in the queues in front of the city bakeries—peasants were coming to the city to buy bread, which could not be found in the village.

Taken separately, all this was not so important: thousands of restrictions and deprivations; the absence of communication with the outside world; the disappearance of political parties; and the absence of neighbors who had been taken no one knew where. Very clearly, the Pinskers—those who had not been deported and who continued to live as best they could under the new conditions—in time would get over their own and especially others' misfortune; even the discovery that people were living much worse in the Soviet Union than in Poland would lose its acuity.

When I ask myself why, in the shortest time, not one supporter of the Soviet regime remained in my city, except for a very specific and clearly defined group that stood out among the population like an island in the sea, why no one remained who did not wish for a return to the pre-war situation, the answer is very clear. It was not because the pre-war situation was good and did not need to be changed. Not because it was not possible for us to freeze during the winter or to go without white bread or, ultimately, because we were so backward that we were unable to understood what was good for us. The proclamation about the annexation of Poznan and Łódź to Hitler's Germany spoke of the "high honor and immeasurable good fortune" that was the lot of former Polish cities. "Die hohe Ehre und unermessliches Gluck." This was a lie. What occurred in Pinsk and around it in all of Western Belorussia and Ukraine was exactly the same kind of lie. Someone gagged us and spoke in our name. Someone entered our house and our life and began to run things without our consent. Until September 1939, the Pinskers quarreled among themselves and were unable to reach an agreement on the most basic issues, but this was their internal matter and their internal disagreement. Now there were no disputes or disagreements because everyone saw with his or her own eyes that strangers, uninvited guests whom no one had summoned and no one wanted, had entered our houses with a skeleton key and revolver. From September 17, Poland was torn apart by two predators; we could prefer one to the other but that could not justify seizure and force. We did not quarrel with the communists nor polemicize with them or about them. We simply were choking. Only someone who experienced this personally will understand what it means when people who not so long ago lacked a common language unite in general indignation. Nothing could help the occupiers. The peasants were not grateful for the estate owners' land; the Jews were not grateful for equal rights; the sick for free hospitalization; and the healthy for rations and jobs. All these undoubted benefits evoked not gratitude, but only anxiety and apprehension. We saw them, our masters, and that was enough for us. Those who formerly had sympathized with them and had now spent time in Russia would return confused and say that they had been in a "sanatorium where they had been cured of their disease." We unanimously rejected both the Soviet benefactions and Soviet cruelties. All we wanted was not to see them, to forget about them. At the time, it would have been hard to find one person in a hundred who could have answered the question "What is democracy?," but all of us, learned and unlearned, understood without reasoning or words the difference between democracy and despotism. Everything that was happening occurred independently of us, despite our wishes, our feelings, or our needs. Even the dullest person intuitively felt the inhumanity and barbarity not only in the content but also in the very method, the disdainful attitude

toward people and to everything that humankind had created over the millennial cultural process, as if it were a weed to tear out without looking.

The concept "pogrom" is usually linked to a notion of external force. No
normal society voluntarily carries out a pogrom on itself. The Bolsheviks
entered a peaceful country, which, like many others, or more than many
others, needed social reforms. In a short time, they carried out a total pogrom
in it. One can say that the amount of evil and violence, human suffering and
sorrow that they caused in this short time exceeded everything that the place
had suffered over centuries. Only their successors, the Germans, surpassed
their record in 1941 and the following years. The Soviets' actions did not
derive from the country's needs but were dictated by their soulless, bestial
doctrinarism. The population as a whole was repelled by them. The local
people who joined them and helped them set up the ruling apparatus were
gradually drawn into a process from which they could not free themselves.

The Soviet regime can be imposed on any people and any society, except
the most primitive, only by force. The normal and natural development of
life opposes the totalitarian, one-party, maniacal order. Its implementation
inevitably encounters resistance and no attempt to break or uproot this resistance can succeed, as resistance perpetually arises again, as long as there is a
persistent and healthy life force. Terror thus becomes the necessary condition
not only for the introduction but also for the continued functioning of the
system.

4

The Pinsk Intermezzo

AT THE BEGINNING of 1940, I received an invitation to appear at the OBLONO [Regional Department of Public Education] of the city of Pinsk. They received me with great respect in the library division: "Sit down, comrade doctor! Excuse us for disturbing you!" I was puzzled by such politeness. They offered me unusual work.

Pinsk housed one of the rarest book repositories in Western Belorussia.[1] The local population was unaware of its existence. In the course of the nineteenth century, the tsarist government systematically destroyed Polish Catholic churches and monasteries in the western territory and transported their libraries to Pinsk. As many as 50,000 ancient and new books piled up inside the walls of the ecclesiastical seminary attached to the Catholic church. Built in the Romanesque-Polish style of the late fifteenth century, the church was encircled by a massive garrison wall. In the period of Polish independence, a learned librarian had been sent to Pinsk—the prelate Kantak, a church historian, philologist, and humanist. For many years, he pored over the large tomes, but the catalogue had not been completed by the start of the war. The books, half of which were in Latin, had been arranged in order on the shelves for the use of three hundred young clerics—future priests.

I remember passing by the massive entrance to the church courtyard as a child and timidly glancing into this Catholic oasis amidst the streets of the Jewish city. The courtyard was paved with stones; in the middle stood a small monument to Mickiewicz. On the side was a three-storied white bell tower with a round red roof. In my childhood, it never occurred to me to enter this courtyard. An unconscious centuries-old prohibition, the voice of

---

1. Now independent Belarus.

my ancestors' blood, the discipline of forty generations traced a magic line at this entrance. There was nothing for me to seek or do there. As a child, I would watch the crowd of worshipers decked out in their Sunday best and would look at the young and old faces. As soon as they vanished beyond the entrance, my imagination would not follow them. The two worlds diverged radically, as if it were not a corner of my native city behind the stone barrier but an airless, impenetrable, lifeless space.

This time I entered the courtyard with the inspector of the library division of OBLONO. The taboo of my childhood years was not in effect. The clerics had dispersed and the priest-professor had disappeared in the turmoil of the war. A Red Army military hospital was situated in the seminary building. The books had been scattered and were located in four side rooms; as they had forgotten to lock the doors, the ill Red Army soldiers had been stoking the ovens with the books all winter. OBLONO finally caught on and put locks on the doors.

The key clanked and my eyes beheld an extraordinary sight: in the hall with a vaulted ceiling, the books were piled in a heap, as in a hayloft, up to the ceiling: torn bindings, yellowed pages, book spines gnawed away by mice, the dust of centuries, the overturned cemetery of culture. We walked among the books, raising a cloud of dust with every movement; our feet were trampling on treasures. I bent down and from under my heel, I pulled out a volume with faded gold-embossed lettering and the date 1687. At that moment, I forgot Hitler and all my misfortunes. I felt as if I were in King Solomon's cave full of diamonds. My eyes lit up, and I blessed the fate that granted the Pinsk OBLONO such a cultured inspector of the library sector.

A month later, I discovered the secret of the unusual cultural sensitivity and attentiveness both to the treasures of the monastery's library and to myself. The person who summoned me and, without objections, accepted my work plan and budget estimation and enveloped me with special solic-itude and attention was not a Soviet person. He was simply a Warsaw stu-dent and good Zionist, who, moreover, knew me from several of my pre-war publications. For a whole month, our relations were of an official nature until it turned out that we shared not only a common homeland but also an iden-tical political orientation.

I must acknowledge that never in my life had I held a position that more suited my inclinations. I would not have objected had I been offered similar work at the National Library on Mount Scopus in Jerusalem. My task was to save tens of thousands of books from destruction, look through them, and sort them into separate groupings—books that were suitable for the Soviet reader, books on theology, books with anti-Soviet content, and books of bibliographical value. I contacted the department for recycling raw material, and in the first month I sent 700 kilos of torn pages, old newspapers, and all kinds of scrap paper. With hindsight, I think that it was rash to send so much: it would have been easy for someone to accuse me of wrecking, that is, of intentionally destroying books. One chance denunciation would have sufficed to initiate a criminal investigation. At the time, however, such fears did not occur to me. I began working enthusiastically.

The work plan and budget were sent to the Party regional committee for confirmation—this did not come through until the end of my work. In the meantime, I received authorization that gave us access to the grounds of the military hospital, which were off limits to ordinary mortals, and the right to select a staff of coworkers.

Six people worked in my "brigade." My cousin and roommate Lenya was hired as a helper. A valuable coworker was David, a soldier in the Polish army who had taken part in the September battles against the Germans. A fine carpenter, David built shelves and boxes into which we placed the sorted books.

We donned gray robes that we sewed ourselves to protect us from the dust and started by fixing the roof, through which water had been dripping onto our books. During the initial days, the political director and hospital director dropped in on us to see what we were doing. Having ascertained that nothing suspicious was going on and having borrowed some old English illustrated journals, they left us in peace. A middle-aged military doctor dropped in with a request that we give him something by Sholem Asch.[2] He was a Jew and knew about the existence of the famous Jewish novelist Sholem Asch, but in the Soviet Union it was impossible to obtain his works. This well-meaning admirer of Jewish literature did not want to die without having read at least one work by Asch. We sympathized with him but were unable to help.

We dived into book excavations. Clearing a road forward, we blasted mines, blew up mountains, drowned in books. All the books were examined separately, and in questionable cases, I was called upon to decide. Among the books were scholastics and ancient philosophy, a superb collection of Greek classics in Latin translations, Aristotle in German, and Polish literature of the seventeenth and eighteenth centuries. There were no Russian books, but among the thousands of volumes of Catholic and Protestant theology, Marx's *Das Kapital*, books by Engels, and a set of the Soviet periodical *Atheist* turned

---

2. Sholem [also Shalom] Asch (1880–1957)—Yiddish writer who was born in Poland and moved to the United States in 1938 but spent his last two years in Israel.

up. After a month of excavating, we reached the floor in the first room. This event was celebrated in worthy fashion.

Our digging sometimes turned up unexpected finds. In a far corner of the last room, we found three hundred volumes of detective stories and the complete works of Jack London. Apparently, the seminarians needed a breathing spell now and then. On the other hand, with some excitement, I discovered real treasures: incunabula—books that had been printed before 1501. I held in my hands an enormous tome printed in two columns with red ink illuminations and vignettes, with a wooden cover, encased in half-decomposed pigskin and fastened by a metal lock. It was merely a Latin missal, dated 1493, covered with minute ornamental script of half-erased inscriptions and dedications. No less valuable were massive Belarusian Bibles, printed at the end of the eighteenth and the beginning of the nineteenth centuries, before tsarist policy put an end to the printing of Belarusian books.

I reported to OBLONO about the course of work and prepared to receive visitors from the Belarusian Academy of Sciences. Every few days, the director of the Pinsk OBLLIT,[3] a flaxen-haired Latvian, would drop in on us; he was, in fact, the censor, who was interested in anti-Soviet literature. We set up a large box, into which we threw everything that might prove useful to him: antisemitic literature, of which there was an exceptionally large amount, as one would expect for future shepherds of souls. The director of OBLLIT pounced on material about the persecution of the Catholic clergy in Soviet Russia and on anti-Soviet pamphlets just as a high school student would seize pornographic postcards. With astonishment and an aggrieved look, he would examine brochures (an obvious translation from the German) that sketched the leaders of the Soviet Union with Jewish noses and facial features, and under each picture was a legend in verse in the style of Streicher or Goebbels. The OBLLIT director had never seen such things; he blushed, looked around, and furtively shoved several booklets into a briefcase. "Check them out in my name!" he mumbled. "But, look, don't show it to anyone; don't let anyone in here!"

The months passed, the Germans were preparing to invade Norway,[4] and the Soviet Union helped as best it could. At the city slaughterhouses in Pinsk, three hundred Jews prepared meat for the Germans. Daily transports

---

3. Regional department of the People's Commissariat for Public Education in charge of publications, i.e., censorship.

4. The German occupation of Norway during World War II began on April 9, 1940.

of meat, grain, and provisions passed through Pinsk to the German border. Throughout the town, the Commission for the Evacuation of Germans from the Soviet zone to the German one posted announcements in Russian and German. The German settlers left Volyn. In leaving, they threatened that they would soon return and slaughter all the Jews (a promise they kept). And I was sitting on a ladder under the ceiling among bookshelves and leafing through a monograph by Chesterton on Thomas Aquinas or relics of Polish antiquity from the times of Jan Sobieski and Ladislas IV.

In the evenings, I would dine at my elderly mother's home. Exactly at seven o'clock, we would seat ourselves at the table in the crowded little room with antiquated furniture, where the same clock was ticking and melodically announcing the time as it had when they awaited my birth in the small house at the back of the grass-covered Pinsk courtyard. Now we would listen to the latest news—from Jerusalem! Occasionally we would hear that it had rained in the morning in Tel Aviv or that so many millions of crates of citrus fruit had been shipped abroad, and these meager news items in snowy and stormy Pinsk, cut off from the world, sustained us more than the military communiqués.

Unfortunately, the Jewish radio report from Jerusalem hardly took into consideration the thousands of Jews who were listening in distant snowy Soviet lands. We wanted to know what was happening at home, but instead we heard news from the military theaters in Europe that every radio station broadcast. It is hard to convey with what feeling people cut off from their own, the residents of Pinsk over whom loomed the shadow of destruction, grasped these sounds of native speech.

In the evening, refugees whom the war had flung into Pinsk would gather in my room. A large poster hung on the wall: "It is forbidden to complain." The poster was not superfluous: everyone was depressed, especially my helper and cousin Lenya, a violinist and unlucky fellow, whose wife and child remained on the German side. I must say a few words about these refugees, who, without exception, were all talented, all wanted to live, and all perished senselessly and horribly. May these words be a final tribute to people who were dear to me and whose memory should be sacred to the reader, not because of their deeds (they had none) but simply because they constitute part of the six million European Jews who perished without a trace.

The first was Leon (Lenya) Shafer, an incomparably gentle and kind person. His amazing musical memory astonished me: from the first notes on the radio, he faultlessly identified every piece of classical music; he knew Beethoven and Berlioz the way we know the corners of our room. That winter, while an icy frost reigned on the streets of Pinsk, he taught me to listen to a symphony or piano recital, and, infected by his excitement, I would forget the cold, war, and grief. We extinguished the light in the room. The dial of the radio receiver emitted a weak glow. Lenya's face was childishly happy and full of proud exhilaration, as if all the music belonged to him. He would direct, sing along in a tenor voice, and would signal in advance when a particularly strong part was approaching—the music lived and resonated in him. This person's every movement, smile, and intonations were chastely charming, but in practical life he was weak, needed a strong friend, and he helplessly recoiled in face of the incomprehensible cruelty of the external world. He was not a maestro: he was a person who listened and heard. The millennial wisdom of his ancient people lived in his sensitive refinement and human attentiveness. Women fall in love with such people, and children become attached to them. He himself was amorous in a feminine way and was as affectionate as a child; at the same time, he was a loyal and true friend, delicate and incapable of offending.

Lenya told me that in the town where the Germans overtook him when he was fleeing, for three consecutive mornings he stood in a queue for bread; three times he received bread, and three times a German soldier with a flat, sleepy face accosted him and grabbed the bread, saying, "Ihr Juden verdient kein Brot—ihr seid schuld an dem Kriege!" [The Jews don't deserve any bread; they are responsible for the war!]

When Lenya said that he was a music teacher and not responsible for the war, the German smirked: "Für Juden ist die Musik zu ENDE!" [For the Jews, the music is OVER!] But Lenya did not believe him.

The second person was Lubliner, a person from the depth of Jewish poverty, a child of Łódź. For him, literature was a "temple," which he entered on tiptoe with a devout look. He kept sitting, covering pages with minuscule letters; he would read Manger[5] the way pious Jews read a prayer book. This person introduced me to Yiddish literature; he first brought me *Zajwl rimer* of Mendel Borejsza,[6] *In New York* of Halperin,[7] and the verse of Kulbak.[8] If

---

5. Itsik Manger (1901–1969)—Yiddish poet, born in Czernowitz [now Chernivtsi, Ukraine], lived in France and England, and eventually in Israel.

6. Menachem [Goldberg] Borejsza (1888–1949)—Yiddish poet and journalist; the work is a tale in verse of the persecution of the Jews in Russia after World War I.

7. Moishe-Leib Halperin (1886–1932)—modernist Yiddish poet and prose writer.

8. Moshe Kulbak (1896–1937)—Yiddish poet, who fled from the Nazis to the Soviet Union; he was arrested during the Stalinist purges and executed in October 1937.

any editions of the Warsaw *Folkszeitung* survived somewhere, one can find his translations of Tuwim's verse for children.[9] After fleeing Łódź, Lubliner appeared in Białystok and settled in the Soviet Jewish Writers' House. As he was starving there, he finally moved to Pinsk, where he worked on a tale, *The Hat*. The book was decorated with illustrations of one hundred hats of all times and peoples (starting with the burdock leaves with which children protected their heads from the sun in prehistoric times and ending, of course, with the Red Army helmet with a five-pointed star).

The tale was sent to the Jewish Detizdat [Children's Publishing House] in Moscow and accepted for publication, an event that ultimately reinforced Lubliner's communist sympathies. The three of us lived in one room: I was a Zionist, Lenya a skeptic, and Lubliner a communist. This did not hinder the three of us from agreeing to meet in Palestine, as Lubliner's communist sympathies were not so strong as to warrant his remaining in the Soviet Union of his own will.

In December 1939, a guest from Łódź arrived in Pinsk: Meir Rozenblum. No one expected such heroism from him. He was so weak and frail physically that it seemed as if merely walking down the street exceeded his strength. I, at least, never saw Rozenblum walk quickly or run in the street. And this person decided to cross the border illegally under conditions that required considerable physical stamina and courage. He made his way successfully. In one place, the Germans caught him, handed him a broom and forced him to sweep the square. This would have ended badly because Rozenblum, a learned and very near-sighted person, could not see the garbage on the ground and did not know how to sweep. Fortunately, he was put in the hands of an old Pole, who immediately released him. At the border, when they were trudging in the deep snow and nocturnal darkness, his youthful companions, burdened by their own belongings, not only carried his backpack but also made sure that he did not get lost. He, of course, was unable to keep up with them and remained alone at night in the forest between the SS and the Soviet border guards. The people from his party, however, returned and led him out of the forest.

There are people in whom an epoch is concentrated, who express the spiritual essence and fate of an entire generation. This person was a live embodiment of "Jewishness," of everything that is eternal but even more so of everything ephemeral in it that was connected to the tragic history of the

9. Julian Tuwim (1894–1940)—a famous Polish poet of Jewish origin who was part of the Skamander group.

Jewish diaspora in Poland. The first, sharp impression that he conveyed was of exhaustion: life seemed barely to stir in him. He was that way at birth, on the school bench, and at the age of forty. There was no strong passion or love in his life. He did not remain attached to anyone for a long time; he quickly tired of people and of things. This apathy and sickliness and some kind of general tiredness was not merely a personal characteristic but a specific racial characteristic—a sign of tired Jewish blood. The grandson of rabbis and scholastics, tired even before birth, he carried within himself this refinement, perversion, and hopelessness of a hundred generations of Jewish doctrinarians. He had not done anything in his life—neither evil, nor good, nor bad. I do not even know whether he was intelligent. There was no one more impractical than he was, and every street urchin could mock him when he made his way down the street, half blind and stooped, prematurely gray, awkwardly moving his feet, narrow-chested, with an anemic face.

Our acquaintance began in our school years, when he once came to me in a neighborly fashion and suggested, "I heard that you are a chess player; let's play." We were both around seventeen then. He played chess masterfully, much better than I did. He lacked, however, the interest and power of concentration to become a real chess master; he simply was incapable of making the necessary effort. Our acquaintance continued all our life: in Poland, France, and Palestine. Rozenblum did not rise to the status of a poet, or rather, here, too, he lacked the will. The verses that he wrote in Yiddish were stronger than ninety percent of what was published at that time. I remember his poem "Shtetl," which dazzled me with its deep lyricism and imagery and its natural, unforced, expressive strength, but this poem was never published, and he did not like people to remind him of his poetry.

He earned a living as a teacher. An extraordinary reader, a person organically connected to traditional Jewish everyday life, he seemed to stand at the threshold, ushering out the past epoch yet unable to part with it. He had the opportunity twice: he lived for years in Paris, where he graduated from the Sorbonne (he specialized in French and English languages), but, nevertheless, he returned to Poland, that is, to the Jewish Polish ghetto. He dreamed about Palestine all his life, and he was there in 1936, but after the first six months, he was drawn back to the customary atmosphere of Jewish exile, to Jewish Łódź or Pinsk. This was his true homeland, and his "Zionism" was the same sort—made up of reminiscences and sentiments, far from anything sharp and rugged.

This person's fundamental feature was his passivity, but not the passivity of indifference. He had an integral, uncompromising personality and was true to himself. He never dissimulated or lied. He was a free person, for whom freedom meant not toeing the line. He could not belong to any political party and no need could force him to accept work in an office: that would go against his very essence. For all his laxity and his friends' indignation at his lack of energy and ambition, he was one of those quiet, stubborn people who live their own way and do not let others dictate to them: most implacable in his everyday humanity. The epoch, milieu, and time that he represented lay in the past. He was a living denial of modernity, a walking protest against its regimentation and mass discipline. Life was hard for him. He even taught with visible tension and disgust, with a patent lack of interest in his students. Nevertheless, an atmosphere of sympathy and good will invariably surrounded him although he did nothing to maintain it. He simply was himself, a person with an absolutely independent spirit and a genuine involuntary Jewish zeal and inner conviction.

We all got angry at Rozenblum, criticized Rozenblum, and regarded him as a negative social phenomenon, but we could not do without him. When this fragile, weak man appeared on our threshold in that cursed Soviet-Nazi winter full of falsehood, grief, and evil, of echoes of bloody injustice and massive, bestial stupidity, we took it as a triumph and victory, a challenge tossed to all enemies of mankind: Rozenblum is alive—and he is with us!

At the end of February, a telegram arrived from Mieczysław Braun asking me to come to Lvov[10] on an important matter. Braun was in despair. He was living in the center of the city and working in the planning commission of the Lvov region. He had his own office and excellent relations with the Soviet management. The Polish section of the Writers' Union in Lvov was busy at the time with a collective translation of Mayakovsky's poem "Lenin." The poem was divided into sections and each of the members of the Polish section of poets received an excerpt for translation. Braun was the only one who conscientiously prepared his part on time. Everything seemed in order. But the better things were for the Soviet official Braun, the worse Braun the person and writer felt. The necessity to lie incessantly, to dissemble and conceal his thoughts was doubly torturous for him as a poet and a publicist. "Never before was I in such a humiliating and absurd situation," he said to me, running around the room in agitation. "Every day we have a meeting or assembly. I sit in the first row, and they look at me. I listen to the propaganda, nonsense, and falsehood. As soon as they pronounce the name Stalin, first my boss begins to

---

10. Now Lviv, Ukraine.

clap and, looking at him, the whole auditorium follows. And I do too; I put my hands together and applaud, like a wind-up clown. . . . I do not want to translate Mayakovsky, but I must! I do not want to clap, but I am obligated to do so. I do not want Lvov to be Soviet; yet a hundred times a day, I say the opposite. All my life I was true to myself and was an honest person. Now I am putting on an act. I have become a scoundrel! And among these people who force me to lie, I am becoming a criminal. Sooner or later I shall give myself away. Do you agree that I should not lead such a life? While there is time, I must get out of here!"

"But where could you go? Back to the Germans?"

"I prefer the German ghetto to Soviet employment."

"Think over what you are saying! You saw the Germans and know who they are!"

"I saw both sides. With the Germans there is the threat of physical death but here it is moral death! With the Germans, you don't have to lie or conceal your thoughts! There are more Jews living with the Germans than here! My place is with them!..."

Braun told me of his decision—to flee from Lvov. Perhaps I could have dissuaded him, but I could not muster the arguments. There was a lull then in the Jewish ghettos of Poland. It seemed as if Jewish life was stabilizing at that level. Men who had fled, leaving their families behind in Polish cities, received letters from their wives asking them to return and assuring them that one could live and work there. Braun was tormented by thoughts of his wife, whom he had left in Łódź. The Soviet regime was not interested in the drama of separated families: it did not deal with personal issues. Braun was unable and unwilling to bring his wife to him; consequently, the only thing left was to return to her.

Living conditions under the Soviet regime were such that people agreed to return to the German yoke and wear the yellow patch in order to see their relatives and share their suffering with them. Russia's alliance with Hitler's Germany created the psychological conditions for this return. Finally, people hoped to escape from German rule into neutral Europe, whereas the Russian borders were sealed tight; no one was permitted across the border. The perspective of remaining forever in Stalin's kingdom instilled a panicked horror in the refugees.

It thus happened that Mieczysław Braun willingly returned to Warsaw, to the Jewish ghetto, which he was not destined to leave alive. For 800 rubles, he bought a Polish birth certificate, which guaranteed him safety if he encountered Germans at the border crossing. He wrote me a note from

Warsaw in April, saying that he was "immeasurably happy." The tragedy of Polish Jewry was encapsulated in a situation where some were "immeasurably happy" in saving themselves from the Germans by remaining with the Bolsheviks, whereas others were just as immeasurably happy escaping from the Bolsheviks to the Germans. This situation soon changed. But the fact remains that, as late as the spring of 1940, Jews preferred the German ghetto to the Soviet equality of rights.

Braun ardently tried to persuade me to join him. I refused, however, and at the beginning of March, I went to Białystok to meet people who had arrived recently from Warsaw. It was not easy to get out of Lvov. I stood on line at the railroad station for a day but did not obtain a ticket. The next day, I stood in line from the evening through the night, by the closed ticket office window, and in the morning, I was one of the first to acquire a ticket. At two o'clock in the afternoon, I took my place on the platform among a crowd of departing passengers. The station had been destroyed; we waited in the snow and wind for the train's arrival. Six hours later, the train was dispatched but to a different platform. Freezing, shivering people desperately raced with their suitcases through a tunnel to the other platform. A line formed in front of each car. For a long time they did not let anyone board, and the train stood dark, desolate, empty, and locked. Boarding began after an hour, with the usual commotion, cries, and brawls. At the last minute, it turned out that the car in front of which I was standing in line was defective and would not be leaving. No one even thought of offering us alternative places. Boarding of the other cars had been completed, and a conductress stood on the steps of each car, blocking entry. Those who had not made it onto the train were cursing, thick snow was falling, and some people were hysterical. Ten minutes remained before the train's departure. Tomorrow I would have to start from the beginning.

At that moment, in a state of complete delirium, I resolved upon a desperate move: I approached the representative of the railroad police and told him that I was a surgeon who had been summoned to Białystok for an urgent operation and had to leave on that train.

My words had a magical effect: the guardian of public order merely asked me whether I had a permit for a work trip. When I confirmed it with the courage of desperation, he took me by the hand, the crowd parted, and he solemnly conducted me and even seated me in a car. Upon seeing the man in the cap with the red band, people immediately crowded together, and a place was found; I sat down, not believing my good fortune. It was too good to be true. But the man in the red cap did not leave. He bent over and, smiling good-naturedly from ear to ear, asked to see my work assignment permit. I became

completely flustered and took the only way out: I dropped my glasses under
the bench—and it was a good move. The young people in the car rushed to
pick them up. My intellectual essence, solidity, and affiliation to the class of
intellectual laborers were written on my face. The man in the red cap did not
wait for me to open my suitcase (and the key was lost) and walked to the exit.
The train started and I went to Białystok.

During the entire trip, the passengers touchingly looked after me and
called me "our doctor." The only thing I feared, from inexperience in bluffing,
was that someone would need medical help during the trip.

We were delayed for a full day in Brest. I went to spend the night in the
city; in the morning they did not want to let me onto the train platform despite my ticket and my arguments. Even my appeal to the director of transport
did not help. I tried various legal ways for several hours, but in the end, I left
the station, and, for a small bribe, they let me onto the railroad track by a side
entrance.

The surrounding milieu thus began to exert a negative influence on me,
or—as some will find—a positive one. My mind still operated in terms of
the concepts of easygoing Poland. I did not suspect that in the Soviet Union,
people pay with years of forced labor for misleading the authorities in
such a way.

On March 8, 1940, I was walking on Saint Roch Street in Białystok. It was
International Women's Day, and the loudspeakers on the streets broadcast
a festive speech. I listened and recognized a high-pitched woman's voice: it
was Asya. My distant relative Asya even now, probably, is still thriving in the
Soviet Union. Her story is as follows:

> Asya came from a working-class family. She spent her student years in
> Warsaw; she had a hard time and was often hungry. For some reason,
> she studied geography, not medicine or history; perhaps geography
> was "cheaper and faster." During vacations Asya would often visit us
> in Łódź, but none of the relatives there guessed that Asya was not a
> simple person but a "militant." She was so successful in "concealing
> herself" in the family that we all considered her a pleasant, cheerful,
> but totally insignificant young lady, without secrets or ideas. We were
> surprised, therefore, when Asya surfaced as one of the main defendants
> at the trial of the Białystok communist cell at the Supreme Court. She
> conducted herself heroically and provocatively; she was taken out of
> the courtroom and given a four-year sentence.

Four years later, just out of prison and on her way to her native Białystok, Asya sat at my table in Łódź. It was the same Asya, a bit thinner, with a noisy laugh and brusque student manners; had I not known that she was a hero of the revolution, I would have taken her for a provincial young woman. Her four years in prison, however, had not passed in vain. For Asya it had been a genuine communist academy. In her cell, they organized a kind of party school; the older comrades instructed the younger ones, and Asya left the prison armed with all the wisdom of Leninism-Stalinism. When the conversation came to current political events, Asya would explain to me their meaning briefly with such magnificent assurance that I understood: for this girl, there are no longer any secrets in our poor life; she knows everything and you can't fool her. The Abyssinians who were dying near Addis-Ababa were puppets of British capital; Italian fascism was a clever trap of international bankers; the tragedies of nations and of human passions were fairytales for fools from the petty bourgeoisie. I understood that it was difficult to argue with Asya, and I accompanied her to the railroad station somewhat sadly. Asya returned to her native city and was arrested again a few months later. This time she was already a member of the Central Committee of the Communist Party of Western Belorussia and received seven years.

She did not have to sit in jail very long. In September 1939, the women prisoners in the Fordon women's prison were released, and in Soviet Białystok Asya attained a position that suited her merits. I no longer remember where she was chairwoman. Now it was Asya's turn to settle scores for her years of underground activity and imprisonment. Asya had caused a lot of grief to her parents; she had been the "ugly duckling" in the family, and suddenly, the ugly duckling had turned into a fairy-tale swan! Her mother shyly looked on when her daughter, wearing a luxurious fur coat, would drop by for a half hour, sit down at the table, animated, rosy-cheeked, and talk about her new apartment and furniture. Asya and her husband, a prominent communist, received high salaries, and finally she could permit herself a private life and comforts that until then she had only glanced at from a distance. I started to tell Asya that my family was in Palestine and I was trying to obtain permission to return to Tel Aviv, but I did not know how to go about it.

Asya looked at me with such unfriendly, hostile eyes; she exuded such coldness and distanced herself from me as if I were a leper. I sensed that my very desire to leave, my affiliation with Palestine, hopelessly compromised me in her eyes. I felt this and I became fearful: I understood that not only would she never help me depart or get free from the yoke of the Soviet regime but also that no matter the misfortune, whether a ban on leaving, exile, or imprisonment, she would unconditionally take sides with my persecutors. She was not interested in my personal details. For her I was not a living person with a family, a longing for home, and the right to self-determination but a hostile class element, "the servant of Anglo-imperialism," whom, if possible, one had to "curb." Venomously, almost with malicious joy, she looked at me askance and then stopped looking at me. The wall that incomprehensibly rose and separated me from my family, homeland, and freedom, the heavy hallucination from which I could not escape, the invisible net in which I became more enmeshed every month all took the features of a person who had seemed close to me, knew everyone who was dear to me, and was so infinitely hostile to me. Asya turned aside and was silent.

"You don't think that I can go home soon?" I asked her.

Perhaps the word "home" was inappropriate? What kind of home—Palestine? That's only a counterrevolutionary, clerical-bourgeois enterprise. If all the Białystok Jews would plan to immigrate to Palestine, over whom would she preside as chairperson?

"I don't know, I don't know," said Asya, moving away with vexation, as if I were a superfluous, bothersome person—"a socially dangerous element"—who did not know how to behave in a proletarian society.

I was upset by this meeting which bode no good. I had not asked Asya for protection or expected her help. Her attitude indicated, however, that in the Soviet order, human norms did not obligate anyone to anything—the very norms on the basis of which I should have been allowed to go home without the authorities detaining me. Not a misunderstanding or a temporary delay was holding me back: it was the start of a nasty story. I was like a fly who has landed on a sticky leaf with the inscription "Death to the flies," and although it is illiterate, does not know what glue is, and understands nothing, none of this is necessary—in a split second, it is mortally afraid and bewildered: it is impossible to break away! Something irremediable and terrible has happened.

In the meantime, important events occurred in Pinsk: in March 1940, Polish passports were taken away, and in their place the local population received Soviet ones. With regard to the refugees, that is, nonlocal newcomers, it was not possible simply to give them Soviet passports. The regional Committee for the Care of Refugees was therefore established; in its name, proclamations were posted around the city that offered refugees a choice: either accept Soviet citizenship or register to return to their point of origin, that is, to the German zone of Poland. In the latter case, the Soviet regime promised shortly to offer the possibility of returning, based on the Soviet-German agreement on the exchange of refugees. Whoever accepted Soviet citizenship had to leave the regional city of Pinsk within ten days and settle in the provinces but more than 100 kilometers away from the Soviet-German border.

The refugees thus were given a stark choice: you may either accept Soviet citizenship or you may go back to where you came from. The options were troubling: voluntary acceptance of Soviet citizenship could in the future cut off the path of return. Refusing it meant handing oneself over to the Gestapo.

Two thousand refugees were located in Pinsk; in all of Western Belorussia and Ukraine, they probably numbered up to a million. Approximately half of them accepted Soviet citizenship; the other half rejected it. This did not mean that everyone who rejected a Soviet passport was prepared to return to the Germans. Both prospects were absurd for me. I wanted to go to Palestine, to my home and family, where, on the basis of a certificate and visa, I ought to be able to go at any time. In no way did I want to accept Soviet citizenship, but in March 1940, the only way I could legally avoid receiving a Soviet passport was to register to return to the German-occupied sector of Poland. This is what I did. In March 1940, in addition to my registration at OVIR for departure to Palestine, I registered at the police station to return to Łódź. In registering, I reinforced my right to return to Łódź, but at that moment, I had no thought of returning to the German-occupied city. Had I wanted to do that, I would have followed Braun in March. I wanted to remain on Soviet territory without accepting Soviet citizenship and to wait until it was possible to leave for Palestine.

What fate awaited the refugees who did not accept Soviet citizenship? They numbered about half a million, and from the start, it seemed improbable that the Germans would accept so many, especially because the majority of the refugees were Jews. It was hard to imagine that Hitler's Germany would open its borders to hundreds of thousands of Jews. One thus had to be prepared for the possibility that the Soviet government would place hundreds of thousands of people in internment camps until the end of the war. From March onward, I faced the prospect of internment, but I preferred that to taking Soviet citizenship or returning to the German side.

Not everyone reasoned as I did. My circle of friends with whom I had passed the winter in Pinsk dissolved. Lubliner accepted Soviet citizenship and in ten days moved to the village of Janowo outside of Pinsk. He decided to unite his fate with that of the Soviet Union; it was easier for him because he was single and not tied to anyone. No one was waiting for him in Warsaw or abroad. He settled in a village near Janowo, where he emphasized that he was a Soviet person. He hung a portrait of Lenin that he had made, like an icon, not even inside his room but outside, over the entrance to the house. The village life, work in the Jewish school or for the "House of Culture" pleased him. His fate was death in the Pinsk ghetto a little over a year later at the hands of the Nazis.

Rozenblum hesitated for a long time: the Soviets were alien to him, but most of all, he wanted to avoid upheavals. One illegal border crossing was enough for him. He feared internment but the thought of the Germans terrified him. Finally, he accepted Soviet citizenship, not suspecting that this, too, was a path straight to the Germans. At the beginning of May, he moved to Kremenets in Volhynia and found a job as a French teacher in a high school. His fate was death in the Kremenets ghetto with the liquidation of the Jews.

People who did not believe that the Germans would accept them legally did not wait for the promised re-evacuation and crossed the border illegally, as Mieczysław Braun had done. One of the workers in my library brigade followed that route to Warsaw, where his wife was waiting for him. His wife, a dentist, had begged him to return and had written that one could live and work in Warsaw.

He perished in the Warsaw ghetto.

Leon Shafer did not accept Soviet citizenship and returned legally to Warsaw. Unexpectedly, on May 13, 1940, the Germans organized a train for Jews at the Brest railroad station, and he managed to get on it. About six hundred people traveled on this train. The German lieutenant in charge of the boarding at the Soviet station of Brest went to the crowd of Jews on the platform, shrugged his shoulders, and said to them:

"I don't understand why you are coming to us! Don't you know, after all, that the German government does not like Jews?"

These people, however, were returning to their wives and children and thought that the German "antisemites" were no more terrible that the Soviet "protectors." In this, however, they were mistaken.

At the end of May, I received a letter from Lenya from Warsaw. As Braun had written in his letter, he wrote that he was "immeasurably happy," that the trip from Brest to Warsaw took two days, that they were given food on the way and were treated well. In Warsaw, the police gave him a month to choose a permanent residence. He traveled to acquaintances in Lublin, and for a short time he was under the illusion that he could join his family in Łódź. At that time the border was established between the Polish General Government and Germany, and he did not accomplish the goal of his trip: meeting his family. Leon Shafer perished in the Warsaw ghetto.

At the same time that touching signs of the Committee for the Care of Refugees were posted on the streets of Pinsk, and we felt with satisfaction that we were an object of government concern, in the distant north of Russia, by the White Sea, barracks and camps for Poles were hastily repaired and put in order. These were not camps for internees. They were Soviet corrective labor camps for criminals. The local Pinsk authorities could not have known about this. Our fate was decided in Moscow.

In the regional police department, people who came for a Soviet passport were advised to consider whether it was worth it. Young people of around seventeen to eighteen who initially came to get a Soviet passport ended up registering to return to Poland. They were told that anyone who registered would certainly leave, and soon. The police inquired whether they took into account that in the opposite case they would not see their fathers, brothers, or fiancées for years because at that time, the Soviet regime was unable to bring in their families from the other side of the border. The officials spoke to them good-naturedly, offered fatherly advice, and in the end, they wrote declarations requesting re-evacuation. Several of my acquaintances had this experience. They went to the police for a Soviet passport but were dissuaded. They signed a request for return, which was the equivalent of a sentence to several years of forced labor.

In April and May 1940, a paradoxical situation arose among the refugees in Pinsk. Those who accepted Soviet citizenship had to leave the city quickly and move to a village or shtetl. Those of us—about a thousand—who did not accept the passports, in anticipation of being sent to the Germans, remained in our places and continued to work. In the city from which during the winter thousands of people had been deported against their will, only we remained—the official candidates for departure. On all sides they warned us, shaking their heads, that it would end badly. "We are a thousand people," we replied. "But in all Western Ukraine and Belorussia, there are half a million of us, with children, families, old people. What can they do with us? Send us out? We'll go. Can they put half a million in prison?"

We thus naïvely evaluated the abilities of the Soviet proletarian state. We thought that there were too many of us to put all of us in prison. At this time, word came that a commission had arrived in Lvov from Kiev[11] to review requests to depart abroad! I again rushed to Lvov, arriving there on May 2, 1940.

I could not help wondering at the change in the city since my visit there during the winter. It was a warm sunny day; the streets were decorated for

---

11. Now Kyiv, capital of Ukraine.

May Day, and at little tables on the street corners, people were selling honey cakes and bags of candy. This was not the important thing, however. Lvov was glowing as if a miracle had happened that was possible only under the Soviet system: the city had been switched to a "special regime."

Several large cities such as Moscow, Leningrad, and Kiev had always enjoyed a special status in the Soviet Union. For the sake of foreign propaganda, these cities had been transformed into oases where a European or similar standard of living was maintained. This produces a dual effect: it demonstrates to Soviet citizens what "happy communist life" could look like, and it creates the impression among foreigners, diplomats, and tourists who visit these cities that things are not so bad in the Soviet Union.

In May 1940, Lvov was not simply a "Potemkin village" but a super-Potemkin capital! Thousands of private stores had been opened and along with them sparkling state stores—grocery stores, stores with perfumes and cosmetics, shoes, textiles. Bakeries were overflowing with baked goods and the shop windows were piled high with heaps of products that had been unavailable even in Polish times. It seemed like a dream to me. I was not prepared for such a sharp transition. During the whole winter in Pinsk, Brest, and Białystok, not to mention the peripheral areas, we did not see sugar or white bread; the stores were empty; one had to obtain basic food stuff "under the table"; and we simply forgot about such items as chocolate, cocoa, and preserves. The whole winter we lived in misery, froze in queues, arranged expeditions to the outlying areas for food products, and suddenly I landed in paradise where you did not know where to look first. Seeing sugar in a shop window, I entered and modestly asked for a kilo. They gave it to me for the incredible price of four and a half rubles, that is, for free. In the second store I again asked for a kilo and again received it—without standing in line. In the third store, I took three kilos at once. In Pinsk we paid 50 rubles for sugar; that means, with a normal working salary of 150 to 200 rubles a month, it was unobtainable. You did not buy sugar, you "got hold of it"!

Evidently, being a resident of Lvov at that time was a great privilege; just as for a Soviet *kolkhoznik* or provincial, living in Moscow or Leningrad was a career goal and the summit of success. It was impossible to obtain a registration permit for Lvov; I lived with friends without a permit. I used my stay in this magical city to buy up everything that I lacked: a penknife, a stock of bath soap, books, and food. The visit to Lvov lifted my spirits: here everything looked "normal," and they spoke to me "normally" at the commission on 12 Rozvadovski Street, where there was a long line of people requesting exit visas. They did not tell me, as they did in Pinsk and other places, that it was impossible to stamp a Soviet visa in a Polish passport, and they agreed that I needed to go home. They posed only two little conditions: first, that I return from Lvov to Pinsk, where I was registered, because they only received Lvov residents here, and second, that I immediately extend my Palestinian visa, which had expired in February. I immediately telegraphed my wife in Tel Aviv: "Send an extension" and received the reply: "We shall send an extension." Everything was wonderful. If only I could have remained in Lvov, that marvelous city under a "special regime"! But I could not.

I thus returned to Pinsk, loaded with presents for friends: sugar, chocolate, and high hopes. In Pinsk, however, the illusions ended, and I returned to the former nonsense. No one in the Pinsk office of visas and registration of foreigners had ever heard of the Lvov Commission. They simply mocked me, and my department director hypothesized that in the Commission, they "pulled the wool over my eyes." I remember these words very well. The important thing was not whether they really pulled the wool over my eyes but that a Soviet official could easily imagine that I was not treated properly and that they laughed at me behind my back, because this accorded completely with his work experience.

All May I waited for the visa from Palestine. Had I received it on time, I would have traveled to Lvov, and, perhaps, I would have succeeded in departing before the "liquidation of the refugees" in June. But the British administration in Palestine was in no hurry. The British consul in Moscow received an order not to issue or renew Palestinian visas. The people who were ruling Palestine did everything, at this last menacing hour, to block entry to those for whom it was the sole hope for salvation. In essence, they became accomplices of the butchers of the Jewish people. In the end, they did send me a visa extension. They could not refuse me because I was a permanent resident of Palestine and possessed a certificate from February 1937. They sent me the extension, however, only in September, four months later, when it was too late and I could not use it.

In May, we stopped work on sorting the library in the Pinsk OBLONO. Two of my coworkers had fled to Warsaw; others who had Soviet passports had left Pinsk. A different circumstance, however, forced us to halt our work: not receiving our salary on time. Our accounts with OBLONO were not an easy matter. Having worked a month, we began our ordeal at the department, and after a month's delay, we received not money but a check on the State Bank [Gosbank]. We then began to visit Gosbank, where they paid no attention to the checks from OBLONO. Money was given first for forestry and industry. Education could wait. We stood in line before the door of Gosbank from two o'clock in the morning. Every night, another member of the brigade stood in line. Jack London, which we had found in our library, came in very handy here. While waiting in front of Gosbank's door, I read some dozen stories by this pleasant American. Each morning, reaching the director around ten o'clock, I presented my check and had it returned with the words, "Today we won't be paying." "Then when?" "When there is money." About two weeks later, I found a protector, and in five minutes without waiting in line, I cashed the check with the help of a kind young lady who had entry to the director's office. Finally, around May 1, when OBLONO was in such a difficult situation that we were unable even to receive a check, I proposed halting work until we received money. In the interval, I traveled to Lvov, and upon my return, found other work.

One morning, the flaxen-haired Latvian director of OBLLIT, who was riding his bicycle, caught up with me on the street. "You really walk so quickly," he said, "that I barely caught up with you. Come with me to OBLLIT; there is work." The head of OBLLIT had a high opinion of my abilities. Once when he visited the book repository at the military hospital, he saw me toss a scientific book into the theology box without even opening it. "Excuse me," he said, "this is a useful book, *The Theory of Darwinism*; why did you throw it with the apostles?" I showed him that on the cover, under the author's name were the letters "S.J.," and I explained that this was not a first name and patronymic but stood for the Society of Jesus, a Jesuit order, and the book was not suitable for the Soviet reader. Still distrustful, he asked me to show him an antiscientific passage in the text. I opened the book to the last page and easily found clerical lines that denied that man was descended from the monkeys. The head of OBLLIT was overwhelmed with respect for me: this person was so learned that merely by looking at the cover, he could discern concealed counterrevolutionary material! He needed just that kind of person.

Mountains of confiscated books had piled up at OBLLIT. The Soviet regime confiscated all books from private libraries and bookstores. The director of OBLLIT brought thousands of books to his institution. He had to sort out what should be destroyed and what was permissible to read. As the only language he knew was Russian, he needed a translator. My task was to compile a register of all Polish and Jewish books and to indicate in Russian: the title, year and place of publication, author, and a short description of the contents. If the book contained anti-Soviet material, I had to provide a verbatim translation of at least one passage. The last column in the register was reserved for the director's decision.

I was paid by the piece: a ruble for each book. There were books, however, for which I did not receive anything: books by banned authors. They showed me sheets that were sent systematically from Moscow, listing banned authors. If an author's name appeared on the list, it was forbidden to read any of his books, and they were all removed from circulation. Consequently, if such books were found in the warehouse of the Pinsk OBLLIT, I was not supposed to enter them into the register. They were destroyed immediately. Precise rules governed the technique of destruction: the books were either burned or shredded. In the latter case, each page of the book had to be torn into pieces separately so that no legible pages remained. Until then, I knew about the Catholic papal Index. In the Middle Ages, Jewish books were burned; in the squares of Berlin in 1933, German students danced around bonfires with anti-Hitler books. Now I directly encountered the Soviet inquisition.

First on the list that they showed me was the name of Kaden-Brandowski (1885–1944), the greatest Polish novelist of the Piłsudski epoch. Suddenly I glimpsed the name of Kulbak, a Jewish poet whom I knew as a friend of the Soviet Union living in Moscow. This was the first news of Kulbak in years: his name was on the Index.

The head of OBLLIT, the Soviet inquisitor, was not only semi-literate but also a fool. Should one really have brought an outsider behind the scenes of Soviet censorship? I should not have been shown either these lists or the instructions on how to destroy books.

Each morning for several weeks, I would arrive at the third floor of the building that housed OBLLIT with a little suitcase and choose fifteen to twenty books for my daily review. I would select technical booklets, innocent brochures. Ultimately, I myself did not know what a Soviet reader could read and where counterrevolution begins.

One morning, I found my own book on Zionism in the book pile.[12] I moved it away and decided that I would not remain on this job. The head of OBLLIT offered me a fixed salary instead of piece work. I would have left Pinsk immediately for the south—to Volhynia, the Ukraine, as far away as possible from the inquisitors! In June, however, the ticket offices at the railroad stations stopped selling tickets to refugees. I rejected a fixed salary.

It was June. The city on the River Pina was bathed in the streams of sun and light. The calm and beautiful Polesian summer arrived. It seemed as if nature wanted to compensate the Pinskers for everything that human

---

12. *Idea Zionismu*, translated from Russian into Polish by M. Olkowski (Warsaw- Łódź: Atid, 1938).

beings had spoiled and befouled. The city began to empty out: thousands of residents had been forcefully deported, sent to prisons and exile. The war raged in Europe; France fell; England was on the verge of catastrophe; evil was triumphing, and we in the Soviet Union were on the side of the aggressor. Everyone was dissembling and lying, and a threat hung over everyone. Families, tribes, and people were separated by borders and bans. We lost the freedom of movement, and we felt that the monstrous senselessness in which we were bogged down could and ought to explode at any time. The Poles and the peasants hated the Jews; the Jews feared the Soviets; the Soviets suspected non-Soviets; the locals hated those who had come from afar to rule them; and the newcomers hated those whom they suspected of disloyalty or sabotage. On the surface, everything was smooth and trouble-free, full of official Soviet phraseology; underneath, however, enormous hatred seethed, ready to strike.

During these final days of my normal life, I ceased thinking or worrying about the future. Every morning, having taken a pile of books from my inquisitor, I would leave them until the evening and go to the river, take a boat to the other, low shore, take a kayak, and canoe past the city. Soon the church spires and towers that had been damaged in the September bombing disappeared from view. An imperturbable silence and placid quiet enveloped the river; the verdant reedy banks swept by, and the birds chirped in the thickets.

I would reach a sandy shoal, undress, lie on the hot sand, and gaze at the clear, pristine sky. I was alone, and only the kayak on the shoal connected me to the absurd and terrible world where millions of people were suffocating between the German Gestapo and the Soviet "Mustapo." *Geheime Staatspolizei* on one side and the "wise Stalinist policy" [in abbreviated form in Russian—*Mustapo*] on the other, and in the middle on a sandbank—a naked, defenseless man with no rights or way out, without a homeland or a link to the outside world, who had been lied to, deceived, driven into a corner, and doomed to death.

5

Elijah the Prophet

BEFORE CONTINUING MY story about the events in Pinsk in the summer of 1940, I would like to digress briefly into the realm of the miraculous. Let us imagine the impossible—something fantastic and supernatural: what would have happened in Pinsk, if Elijah the Prophet had appeared in the city at the beginning of the summer of 1940?

Much time has passed since that summer, and although none of us is a prophet, and it is hard to project ourselves into the prophetic mode, in the given case, we can easily imagine how a person in Pinsk would have felt if he were able to see the future.

That person would have seen a city on the verge of destruction. Tens of thousands of people condemned to death. At best, these people had about two years left to live. Many thousands were destined to perish even earlier. The Jews of Pinsk were in a trap with no way out. On one side was the German border and the Gestapo. Anyone who crossed that border would die. On the other side was the Russian border. The "Mustapo" closed this border under lock and key. No resident of the condemned city was able to cross this border separating the Russian occupied zone from the territory of the Soviet Union.

The three thousand Jews of Pinsk—in the entire Soviet-occupied zone there were about 2 million Jews—were in a cul de sac. Unaware of their future, however, they did not take their situation too deeply to heart. First, they did not foresee that very soon they would fall into the Germans' hands. Second, they did not imagine that in such a case they faced total annihilation. Third, they all hoped that normalcy would be restored after the war, and each in his or her way imagined a rosy-colored future: one in Palestine, another in democratic Poland, and yet another in a super-democratic Soviet Union.

Just imagine that Elijah the Prophet would come to this city and say to the poor blinded people: "Here is the truth about your life: those of you who stake your future on the Soviets should know that in a year, the Germans will arrive and lock you in a ghetto. In another year, you will be slaughtered with your wives, children, and elders. And anyone who runs to the Germans runs straight to his death."

Lo and behold, a second miracle would occur: the people of Pinsk, who generally would not listen to prophecy, would believe him.

They would say to him: "What should we do, Prophet Elijah? We don't see a way out. On the right is the Gestapo; on the left is the 'Mustapo.' Beneath us is the earth that soon will become our grave. Above us is the sky. Take us to the heavens, Prophet Elijah, because we see no other way."

And the Prophet Elijah would answer them angrily: "You already have an assured place in heaven. You must find a place on earth where you can remain alive."

And they would say: "We don't know what to do. Show us the path of life."

And the Prophet Elijah would show them the path of life.

In fact, there was a path of life for those millions of Jews. Now we do not need to guess or break our heads over it. No matter how surprising this route was—and, of course, it surpassed their mental and moral capacity—now, with hindsight, it is clear what they should have done. The only thing that Elijah the Prophet could recommend to them was to stop lying and pretending. The teachers in the Zionist Tarbut high school should not ob-sequiously agree to renounce their national language and education. They did so not because they changed overnight from Zionists to communists but because they were mortally afraid and thus hoped to avoid persecution and the loss of students. This was, however, the wrong way; it was simply a base betrayal. The opponents of Zionism always contended that the Jews did not need Hebrew or Palestine. The "newly converted" teachers hastened to agree with them: "Yes, Hebrew and Palestine—that was good before you [the Soviets] arrived, but now we renounce them, and we will do what you tell us to do."

Indeed the sole "path of life" for these teachers and hundreds of their pupils was to declare: "We request that the authorities confirm the rights of our school because its language and educational program conform to our wishes, and we refuse to change."

Thousands of Jews who did not want Soviet citizenship should not have taken part in elections to the Supreme Soviet or have accepted the Soviet passports imposed on them. Instead, they should have said aloud what they all thought at the time: "We don't need your citizenship, and we are asking you to let us leave for Palestine." If there were still non-Zionists among them who preferred to remain in Pinsk, then, they, too, should have declared clearly that they did not accept the Soviet regime. That would have been the sacred truth. Deep in their hearts, they did reject it. Such a campaign of civil disobedience, of course, would have been pure madness. I do not suppose for a second that such a thing was feasible without Elijah the Prophet's direct intervention. I can very clearly picture the deceased inhabitants of Pinsk. For example, there was a Doctor Y., my friend, a very good doctor and a fine person. In his waiting room hung a framed portrait of Maimonides with a long inscription in Hebrew. The blue and white Jewish National Fund charity box stood in the most prominent spot. Doctor Y. never concealed his love for his people and attachment to Palestine. He did not remove Maimonides's portrait even after the Soviets' arrival. Somehow, however, this man of tradition and owner of two stone houses turned into an ardent Soviet patriot within a week. It was as if his eyes had been opened, and he began to deliver welcoming speeches to the Soviet regime. Why? Perhaps he feared losing his houses? Perhaps he considered it necessary. In any case, it was simply *a lie*. In reality, all that Doctor Y. wanted was to be left in peace or given the opportunity to leave, if not for Palestine, then, at least for America. Probably, he did not want the Bolsheviks.

And Elijah the Prophet was not there to tell him, "Stop lying and pretending. It won't save you from death."

A campaign of civil disobedience would have had fatal consequences for the Jews of Pinsk. The Soviet regime does not treat such cases lightly. Of course, at first it would have been surprised because it was not used to Jews directly and openly saying what was in their hearts. Initially, the regime would have snared some leaders. Ultimately, however, it would have forced all the Jews, with their wives and children, with their prayer books and belongings, up to 100 kilos per person, out of the border zone.

They would not have been the first nor the only people in the Soviet Union to suffer such a fate.

In Central Asia or Yakutia, it would have been extremely difficult for them. Many would have perished. Some, however, would not only have survived the war but also their resistance would have created a decisive argument for both Jewish national culture and a national movement. The "wise Stalinist policy" would have taken into account that Hebrew and Zionism have roots among the Jewish people.

The Jews had the opportunity to choose their own path—the path of open and honest struggle. Unfortunately, the Prophet Elijah was not there to explain this to them.

They were all intelligent, practical people. If someone had told them never to compromise with an alien and hostile element, they would not even have bothered to disagree. They would have said, "This adviser is crazy. He is either a fool or a Don Quixote. We, however, have children, homes, and work, and we are responsible for them."

That is what intelligent people would have said. And they would have been right, from their rational point of view. Subsequent events, however, could lead us only to the following conclusion: Common sense is not always a good guide. Especially when the other side of "Reason" is ordinary cowardice.

For two thousand years, Jews have been adapting to the world around them. And for two thousand years, their shrewd calculations invariably turn out to be built on sand, and all their history, as in the case of the Pinsk Jews, is a chain of catastrophes and a road to death. The story of the Pinsk Jews is not an isolated case. We survivors have no guarantee that in the near future we shall not wind up in a similar situation to that of the Pinsk Jews in the summer of 1940. An enemy will arise on our right. And on the left, another enemy. And above us will be an empty sky and a gaping grave at our feet. And the Prophet Elijah will not come to help us in our misfortune, nor will there be a new Moses to part the waves and bring us forth on dry land.

Then—if the lessons of history are worth anything—we shall recall the story of the Pinsk Jews who perished because they lacked the courage to be themselves to the very end.

6

The Pinsk Prison

ON JUNE 19, 1940, at ten o'clock in the evening, a policeman came for me and brought me to the police station. For four days, the police in Pinsk had been arresting refugees who had registered to leave the Soviet Union. These refugees were Pinsk Jews who were fleeing the Nazis. Having arrived from Vienna and other Nazi-occupied lands, they had leaped from the frying pan into the fire. The Red Army occupied Pinsk and the entire eastern part of former Poland. I knew that many people, including acquaintances, had already been taken. It was not clear whether they would take everyone or make exceptions for vitally needed, irreplaceable workers. The fate of the arrestees was unknown. The refugees did not panic at the first arrests, calmly awaiting their turn; they believed that nothing bad would happen to them, and in the worst case, they would be sent into Russia, where they could find work and wait out the war.

On the morning of the 19th, in my absence, a policeman came and asked when I was usually at home. They told him that I would return in the evening around ten o'clock. He warned that he would come then. In the evening, I sat in my room. Everything was ready: I had packed a case with the necessities. On my table was a book that I had not managed to finish reading—*Short Course of the History of the CPSU(b)*.

Exactly at ten o'clock, the CPSU(b) in the form of a pug-nosed fellow with a youthful face entered my room. Seeing my case, the policeman smiled and said, "That's unnecessary. They are summoning you only for a half hour, for a conversation with the commander." I felt relieved. I did not know that this was a standard trap. The policeman is supposed to bring in a number of people every evening, and he does not want to frighten them or wait until they pack their things. Moreover, he does not have an arrest warrant, just an invitation to "drop in at the police station."

My neighbor was taken in a different way. Armed men broke into his place at night. They surrounded the house. The proprietors began to cry, thinking the police had come for them. They searched my neighbor's place but not mine. They took him straight to prison in an overcrowded truck. They also promised him that he "would return soon." This was a lie; none of those who were taken returned, and many perished in exile.

I left the house just as I had been sitting at the table—without any belongings or money. At the door, the policeman said that it would be better to take a coat just in case I had to wait my turn for a long time. I carried my coat. The gate slammed, and we went, conversing peacefully. I crossed the threshold of the police station on Logiszynska Street, not realizing that I had crossed a line that divided two worlds. In a short time, however, I understood that something unbelievable had happened.

I had never sat in prison. At the time of my arrest, I was thirty-nine years old. I was the father of a family, materially and mentally independent, accustomed to the respect of others, and, undoubtedly, a loyal citizen. I had never insulted anyone, had never broken the law, and firmly believed in my right to consideration and defense from the institutions of any state other than the Nazis'. In general, I remained a rather naïve European intellectual, even after nine months of trying to escape from the sticky Soviet spider web, and with my heart and soul, I still considered myself a citizen of splendid Europe, with its Paris, Florence, and the azure expanses of the Mediterranean Sea.

When I crossed the threshold at the police station on Logiszynska Street, I immediately ceased to be a human being. This transition occurred abruptly, without any preparation, as if in broad daylight I had fallen into a deep pit. From literature and various descriptions, from films and stories, I knew what a prison looks like; I understood that they were detaining me, would conduct an investigation, and would lock me up. But I was totally unprepared for what happened. They pushed us—several dozen people—into an empty room. Uniformed men carrying revolvers were darting around. They were not the polite and affable Soviet people that we had known until then. First, they addressed us in the demeaning familiar form of address; second, they laughed in our faces. Our agitation greatly amused them. They relished the effect on us of our first encounter with genuine Soviet reality. The atmosphere was thick with heavy swearing, which we had not heard until then. We thought that cursing had died out in the Soviet Union. It turned out that these people were painfully holding back among "outsiders," but here, behind the walls of the NKVD, they were at home and need not be embarrassed. From their behavior, I understood that they no longer regarded us as witnesses. For them, we were dead people, crossed off the human registers.

We were led, several at a time, into a room where young men in jodhpurs were sitting. They were in an excellent mood as they found this entire procedure simply amusing. While chuckling and joking, they emptied my pockets, took out my fountain pen, documents, watch, and wedding ring. I was unable to take off my wedding ring, which for years had not left my finger.

"It doesn't come off?" laughed the man in jodhpurs. "Come here; we'll do it fast!" Indeed, the agile fellow managed to get the ring to slip off my finger by itself. I never again saw my documents, the ring, or the watch. Everything that they confiscated was gone forever.

"Undress!" In the blink of an eye, I was undressed, placed on all fours, examined in front and behind, like a hardened criminal; they checked the anal passage; shook out my things; ordered me to get dressed; cut off the buttons, took away my belt, and hustled us into the courtyard and into a car.

At midnight, they brought us to the NKVD prison. The NKVD was located at the end of Albrecht Street, in a former Polish army barracks. They pushed us into a tiny storeroom without windows or ventilation. A bright light shone the entire night; it was unbearably stuffy and hot. About fifteen people were lying side by side on the floor. We undressed completely; the sweat poured out; we began to choke and bang on the door. From time to time, they would open it slightly to let in a little air from the corridor.

We endured the entire night without sleep. At noon the following day, they led us into a cell with two-story bunks. (In Polish times, they had kept potatoes in this cellar.) The cell was almost dark except for a square opening near the ceiling. We lay on bare boards along the four walls of the cellar; in the middle, people settled on the bare floor. We were all Jews. A short, rotund man wept incessantly like a child; it was Burko, a pharmacist from the city drugstore from whom I had bought medicine the previous day.

We spent a week in the NKVD potato cellars. They gave us bread and soup, but they did not let us out at all, except to the toilet at the end of the corridor. People were still well fed from before their arrest, and under the shock of the arrest, they lost their appetite. They barely touched the food, leaving a lot of bread. People incessantly asked for water, and the day passed in a struggle for water, of which there was very little. Water was distributed as a reward for good behavior. The cell included turbulent youths; people would converse, sing, and bang on the door for water or to relieve themselves. All day someone would be standing near the door, pleading to be allowed to go to the toilet. Finally the door would open, and the guard, standing at the threshold without entering (this was forbidden according to the rules), would rain curses on the prisoners and slam the door in their faces. Someone said "comrade." An enormous, ape-like giant burst into a rage: "What kind of a comrade am I to you? A wolf in the forest is your friend, not I!" They soon explained to us that arrestees are not permitted to use the term "comrade," and we must address the authorities with the word "citizen."

In the morning, when they led a group of about sixteen to an outhouse, the difference between the faint-hearted intellectuals and men "of the people" immediately became evident. There were people who were painfully embarrassed to relieve themselves in front of everyone for the first time (there was one round hole for sixteen people) while being goaded on by the guards. Someone fainted on the befouled, slippery floor. They carried him outside; the guards cursed roundly, all around people laughed; behind the low, bolted doors, prisoners yelled and drummed with their fists.

Nocturnal interrogations began. A person who had been summoned did not return to the cell. He was taken to another place; after a few hours, they would remove his belongings from the cell, if there were belongings. We all impatiently awaited our turn. If these goons treated us like criminals, it was because "they did not know," "they had not sorted things out." What could one expect of them? From our conversation with the investigator, we expected an explanation of what they wanted from us. After all, we had not committed any crime. We waited expectantly for three to four days. Late at night, they summoned me from the cell. By that time, I was already very filthy, disheveled, unshaven, and savage, as befits a person persecuted by the state. I did not have soap or water for washing, a towel, comb, pillow or other such things. I acutely felt the social inequality when opposite me sat a young, dapper NKVD investigator, shaven, pomaded, well-rested, with an embroidered "sword" on his sleeve (the symbol of workers of the NKVD legal-political apparatus).

It was late at night. The second story of the NKVD was a different world. Below was a cellar, jam-packed with disheveled, frightened people. Above were clean white corridors. Silence. Green lampshades on the tables. In a large empty room, on the investigator's table stood a bottle of lemonade with a package of cigarettes next to it. The two were items in a magical dream. It was impossible to buy lemonade; undoubtedly, it came from a special internal distribution center. I was painfully thirsty, but the lemonade was not for drinking. It was as inaccessible and unreal as my native home and freedom.

The investigator offered me a cigarette. The interrogation of other prisoners started the same way. This must appear in the "instructions." The person who interrogated me had studied in the NKVD's school for investigators, and these interrogations were his careful and finely elaborated specialty. After we established my personal details, the fact of my higher education, and my work in OBLONO, the investigator became very polite. I sat on a chair not near the table but in the middle of the room. I was full of curiosity: what would they charge me with and what would the investigator say? It would be an exaggeration, however, to say that at that moment I felt that I faced a genuine investigator. At the table sat Soviet justice with the shield and sword insignia on his sleeve. A free man of the West sat near the table and attentively took the measure of things.

Indeed, my real crime was this feeling of independence and the unwritten right to judge my judge. Then, however, neither my investigator nor I thought about that. The man with the insignia contemplated how to conduct the interrogation. His colleague proceeded very intelligently that same night when in another room he interrogated my neighbor, a lawyer, N (this person now lives in Israel). He said to him, "You are a cultured person; now you will start proving that you are not guilty of anything. All this is superfluous. You are not going to be freed. We are going to send you to work in Russia. You will work in your specialty (this was a lie). Everything is already decided, and you should understand that I cannot change anything. I am only a state worker. I am not supposed to say this, but I'll tell you frankly: interrogations, a protocol, and your signature are only formalities. Your answers change nothing. So don't make any trouble for me and sign this paper," Later on, hundreds of Russian citizens in camps confirmed the same thing: "It's not worthwhile to quarrel and to be obstinate with the NKVD; that will only make it worse."

A Russian signs what they tell him to, without looking or reading it. And he knows this will save him much unpleasantness. He will receive what is coming to him; otherwise, they will pile on more.

My conduct at the interrogation was (from the Soviet point of view) a mistake, because I attached much too much significance to external appearances. I paid with an extra two years of my sentence for the cheap pleasure of pressing my interlocutor to the wall, for verbal stubbornness. I did not understand that the real trial of myself and of hundreds of thousands of others had ended and the verdict had already been rendered. We were supposed to receive three or five years. They did not permit us to attend this trial and they did not question us. What happened now was only a farce. Had I not persisted, I would have received three years instead of five. But I took my "defense" seriously.

"You are charged with violating the passport regime," the investigator told me. "You are residing on the territory of the Soviet Union without documents." "How can that be? I have a Polish passport."

"The passport of a nonexistent state is not a passport. We do not recognize Poland. Your Polish passport is not valid in our eyes." "But until now, however, you recognized it! After all, I am registered with the Pinsk police on the basis of this passport!" "Which is precisely why we arrested you," said the investigator, looking at me with a smirk, "because you are registered on the basis of that passport! In the Soviet Union you must have a Soviet passport."

"As a citizen of the former Polish state, I cannot have a Soviet passport until they give it to me. Of what am I guilty if I have a Polish document? After all, you did not demand that I exchange or replace it with a Soviet one!"

"I did not say you were guilty!" said the investigator. "You are not guilty, but nevertheless you are violating Soviet law! According to Soviet law, you must have a legal document!"

"For nine months, I have been on the territory of the liberated regions, and not once did any representative of the law tell me this! Perhaps you can tell me exactly when I became a law breaker?"

"I cannot say," the investigator began, in a slightly annoyed tone. "And why do you need this? Now you are breaking the law!"

"Rather, from the day I was arrested! And what am I supposed to receive for 'violation of the passport regime'?"

"Oh, nothing!" said the investigator. "A mere year."

My hair stood on end.

"You're kidding me? A year of prison. For what?"

"A year is the maximum!" said the investigator soothingly, and his eyes sparkled gaily. "Perhaps they will give less!" As he interrogated me, he simultaneously wrote down my answers. In the protocol of our conversation, however, only a little appeared. . . . He noted the history and dates of my escape from Łódź, the fact that I had relatives abroad, and then the question: "Why don't you want to live in the Soviet Union?"

"Because I want to live in Palestine. My family is there and that is my permanent residence. I came to Poland from there for a short time and I want to return there. I never lived in the Soviet Union, and it would be strange if I wanted to live here merely because I wound up here as a refugee. I am a stranger here."

For about an hour, I tried to convince the investigator that my unwillingness to remain in the Soviet Union did not mean that I harbored hostile feelings toward that country.

"But why did you register to return to Łódź? The Germans are there."

"The war caught me in Łódź, and the Germans won't be there forever, and I have the right to return there—now or after the war. The road to Palestine lies via Łódź. While the Germans are there, I would willingly travel to Palestine via Odessa."

"You mean, you don't want to remain with us?"

"No, I don't want to."

The investigator noted briefly: "He does not want to live in the Soviet Union as he has family abroad."

Finally, he entered in the protocol: "Do you acknowledge that you are guilty of being a refugee who is living illegally in the Soviet Union and intends to go abroad?"

I was stunned. None of the preceding questions or replies had implied GUILT. What guilt should I admit?

"No, I do not admit it!"

My interlocutor gave me a look that bode no good.

"Well, should we start from the beginning?"

"You should understand that I cannot accept that way of stating the question! What kind of traveling 'abroad'? For you it is abroad but not for me. For me, abroad is precisely here, in the Soviet Belorussian Republic in the city of Pinsk! Poland is not abroad for me as I have Polish citizenship. Palestine is not abroad for me as I am a Jew and lived there before the war."

The investigator jumped up and went to a side door. He called someone. A tall, swarthy man entered the room.

"I'm fed up," the investigator said morosely. "He's making me sweat. He twists and turns, and you can't catch him. A mean one."

"What is he, a lawyer?" asked the swarthy man. "Surely, a *Pan* lawyer."

"No, I am not a lawyer," I replied, "but I must defend myself when I am accused of the devil knows what—of being a refugee. I am not a lawyer but a doctor of philosophy."

The swarthy man's threatening look turned to astonishment. "Well, so that's it!" he said. "We have not yet seen any doctors of philosophy here. That means that you know *diamat* [dialectical materialism]?"

I confirmed that I knew it as well as the fingers on my hand.

"Do you know who Rosenthal is?"

Rosenthal was the "specialist" who from time to time in *Pravda* gave "consultations for the public at large on questions of dialectical materialism." In the eyes of the swarthy man, this was, evidently, the height of wisdom. The conversation took a somewhat fantastic turn. We calmly spoke about

Rosenthal, Deborin, and Lukacs,[1] and those Leninist academicians, who by now have slipped my mind, weakened by years of Soviet forced labor. The swarthy man was simply excited when he found out that I even had read Luppol[2] in German translation.

"No," he said, "we need someone like that. You'll go work in Russia. They'll find a use for you there."

"Why to Russia?" I said. "I am a Palestinian; my family and work are there."

"We will not let you go to Palestine," said the philosopher from the NKVD. "Forget about Palestine. That's past. And don't worry about your wife. She'll find someone else."

My head was spinning. It was like a nightmare from which you can't awake. The interrogation had been going on for about four hours.

Finally, I signed: "I admit that I am a refugee and I do not have documents aside from those taken away upon my arrest; I want to leave the borders of the Soviet Union, but I do not admit any guilt as I see nothing criminal in the indicated facts."

"Do you have anything else to adduce in your defense?" I felt that I was up against a wall, that I ought to add some special words in my defense so that these people would understand what was so clear to me: my "case" was non-sense from start to finish, unbelievable nonsense. But I did not find any more words. "Nothing."

I signed "nothing" and suddenly remembered that I should indicate something else: the certificate of the Palestinian government . . . and so forth and so forth.

"Well, no!" said the investigator. "Once you signed, that's it; I won't let you write anything more." He added, "At the trial, you can say what you did not include here." He knew very well that there would not be any trial and the protocol was final.

It was turning gray in the corridor when he handed me over to the guard. I asked for water. He ordered the guard to take me to a faucet. I drank insatiably from the tin mug with my eyes closed. My head was burning, as if a nail had been hammered into it: "We won't let you go home. . . . Your wife will find someone else. . . ."

---

1. Mark Moisevich Rosenthal (1906–1975) and Abram Deborin (1892–1963) were official Soviet philosophers. Georg Lukács [György Lukács] (1885–1971) was a prominent Hungarian-born philosopher and Marxist literary critic.

2. Ian Luppol (1896–1943) was another official Soviet philosopher.

They led me into another cell. It was a narrow cell containing sixteen men on two-tiered bunk boards. I spent the entire next day lying down without moving, overwhelmed. Not by the news that the road home was cut off. I did not believe that; I simply could not imagine it. I was amazed at the cynical baseness of this nocturnal interrogation. In nine months, I had become accustomed to the façade of the Soviet edifice; now I saw what lay behind it—a cave of brigands. My first impression was shock. I was ashamed. My feeling of painful, deep shame for mankind increased from the moment that I crossed the threshold of this institution, which is central in the Soviet Union. This burning shame tormented me for many days until it burned out, creating a cold zone, and I developed a calm hatred toward the people deceiving the entire world.

In the new cell, there were Poles, who had already been in prison for half a year. Opposite me lay a sixteen-year-old boy with a dead, expressionless face. He seemed stunned. I was not beaten before or after, but these people had been beaten. An old Jew named Nirenshtein lay next to me. He was one of the most gentle and fearless people whom I met in the camps. He was full of religious faith and groundless optimism. He indeed believed in God, that is, he believed that a miracle could happen at any moment. He had an amazing, perhaps, deserved feeling of moral superiority over other people who were fearful and did not understand that it was all not so terrible. I very much wanted to be like Nirenshtein.

Most of all, I feared being cut off from everyone and forgotten by everyone. To remind myself that I was not alone, I would take out the photograph of my son and pictures from home. I would show them to my neighbors and tell Nirenshtein about life in Palestine.

Three days later, they led both of us to a courtyard where a large group of arrestees had already assembled. It was a spacious courtyard, overgrown with grass such as one finds in the provinces; the chickens were pecking in the hot sand, a young woman, probably from the kitchen, went out with a pail, and at the end of the courtyard, workers dawdled by the storehouse. It was the end of June—a warm, sunny day.

A truck entered the courtyard; we were ordered to climb in and lie on the bottom, and they lifted the green sides of the truck. An armed guard sat above us. The truck turned around and entered the cobblestone street. We were on our way.

While lying there, I thought how often in recent months I had seen on the Pinsk streets this kind of empty truck thundering on the stones, with an indifferent-looking armed man sitting in the corner. This meant that, then, too, those trucks were full of people lying on the bottom, hunkering down so that no passers-by would see them. Perhaps now my acquaintances were passing by, and they were hiding me from them. This regime concealed its deeds within the green sides of the truck. It was a deception. People at large did not know that they were surrounded—and so near to them—by arrestees, prisoners who were forbidden to raise their heads.

Lying there, I promised myself that someday I would describe the green side of this truck so that the whole world would see what it concealed. Lying on the bottom of the truck, according to its turns, I guessed what streets we were passing.

They brought us to the Pinsk prison and divided us up among the cells. Around ten of us were led into an empty cell. We were happy that there was so much room and comfortably settled down between the windows near the wall opposite the entrance. In half an hour, however, the door opened, and a crowd piled into the cell. It immediately became crowded and stuffy. In another half hour, they tossed in another group of prisoners. This was no joke. The room was about seven meters long and five wide. Whitewashed walls, two grated windows, a cracked wooden floor, a slop pail near the door, a barrel with water in the corner, and something like a table in the middle. That was all. Around seventy-five men were settled on the floor. During the day, we barely managed sitting up, but at night there was not enough room on the floor for everyone to stretch out, and people literally lay on top of each other. People slept on the table, under the table, sitting, half lying down, with the most fantastic intertwining of feet, hands, heads, knees, and backs. People who did not find a resting place at the start of the evening squatted on their haunches; later, when sleep flattened out this human mass, they would fall randomly on top of the others, forming a second layer. Waking up at night, a person would not immediately recognize on whose stomach he was lying or who was crushing his feet. A fierce quarrel would ensue when someone's dirty heel struck the face of a sleeping man and woke him up. Gruff curses were drowned out by the neighbors' protests. Finally, "silence" would reign, full of snoring, heavy breathing, muttering, and sleepy cries. Someone would get up and walk over heads and hands to the slop pail. People swarmed and lice and fleas swarmed on them. They did not issue prison underwear, and we had only what was on our body. We were not permitted to receive packages from outside until the end of the investigation. The July heat forced us to undress down to our long johns, turned up above our knees. The cell resembled the antechamber of a bathhouse. From the morning, people who had succeeded in wresting a washbasin and some water would wash their shirts. A heavy, stale odor pervaded the cell; a person from the outside would have had trouble breathing there.

The cell was populated entirely by Jews. People of all generations, classes, ages, starting from fifteen-year-old children, who were guilty of registering to return to their parents, and up to men over seventy. The majority were young: hairdressers, waiters, tailors, bank clerks, teachers, accountants, a proletarianized refugee mass. To my satisfaction, the winner of the Pinsk regional chess tournament was in the cell. We fashioned chess and checker figures out of bread and sketched a chessboard on the floor with chalk. I would spend half the day lying on the floor, moving the chess pieces. Evidently, we were not yet truly starving; a year later, there would have been nothing from which to make the pieces: all the bread would have been eaten in the wink of an eye.

My neighbors on the floor were the Kunin brothers, two accountants, previously merchants (both perished in Soviet captivity); the pharmacist Burko, whom I already mentioned (in the meantime, his tears had dried and he became reconciled to his fate); a young Varsovian Arye Barab, who would sing cheerful couplets about Jewish summer residents on the Otwock train line; and, happily for me, David, a member of my library brigade.

Of course, I would have preferred that he had not been arrested, but insofar as he, too, was subject to elimination, it was very good that he landed precisely in my cell. As David had been arrested a week after me, I found out from him what had happened in the city during that week. The arrest of almost one thousand people disrupted the economic and cultural life, left enterprises without managers, and students without teachers. The residents were depressed and frightened. Such a large round-up had not occurred since March, when the local population and the Jewish politically active element had been purged.

My arrest had produced the strongest impression on old Doctor Margolin. My father, who then was eighty years old, no longer left the house. He was an idiosyncratic person who had his own opinion about everything and did not submit to outside influence. He was the strictest, most uncompromising critic of my writings. He followed my activity in the literary-political field from afar; from time to time, I would receive a severe dressing down from him, but rumors reached me that he did not deny that I had certain abilities. He was very surprised when, in the first days after the Bolsheviks occupied Pinsk, I gathered and destroyed all copies that I found of my book about Zionism.

The old man deeply and childishly grieved. "See where you got to!" he said to me bitterly.

After my disappearance, he fell into a deep reverie. He waited three days, and one fine morning, he quietly dressed, and without saying a word, went outside. The building where I was detained was located not far from our home. Looking out their windows, the neighbors saw him wandering quietly on the sidewalk, leaning on a cane—a small, white-haired old man. "Where is old Doctor Margolin going?" He went up to the massive locked gates in the NKVD courtyard, hoping to speak with the head of the NKVD and to explain to him that I was a good person and he shouldn't detain me in prison. He was a totally diminutive figure against the backdrop of the huge iron gates. Through the windows of their homes, dozens of eyes gazed at the strange behavior of Doctor Margolin: the old man lifted his cane and knocked on the gates. No one heard this knock. He waited and knocked again. He stood for a long time, lowering his head, waiting and listening. Finally, quietly, he sighed and returned home. At home, he did not tell anyone where he had gone or why.

No one, of course, could have heard him sigh. But when David told me about my father's last outing, I seemed to hear that sigh.

The day would start early in the Pinsk prison—either with the distribution of food or a trip to the toilet. When the door lock began to clang, people rushed to the exit, equally prepared to receive bread or go into the corridor. Everyone went out, whether they needed to or not, as people were let out to the toilet only in groups, once or twice a day. The toilet was the center for exchanging news: the walls were covered with inscriptions and messages that were thus conveyed from cell to cell. They included family news, friendly exchanges, prison lyrics, and useful information: "Misha Rappaport is sitting in the fourth [cell]"; "Stefan, answer me! Shimek." "Send me some tobacco, Friedman." "Mama is well, hold up, Witek!" Every few days the inscriptions were erased, and new dialogues would begin the following morning. In addition, there was a "post office box"—a crack in one spot under the board of a seat, where notes were inserted and passed from cell to cell.

For breakfast, we received bread and granulated sugar, which they distributed after measuring it in a matchbox. People ate the bread sprinkled with sugar; some reserved a piece of bread for lunch, which consisted of soup. Between one and three o'clock, a cart with a pot would arrive at the door and the cook would ladle soup into aluminum bowls. This marvelous vessel remained from Polish times, but we did not have spoons. We sat along the walls, our legs crossed, and drank the scalding liquid; then with our fingers we picked out the turnip or piece of potato, while at the same time we were goaded by those who were next in line for the bowls. The prisoner's soup was bad, not at all like at home. By that time, however, we were already sufficiently hungry, and the soup was the sole hot food. One of the fellows in the cell tried a ruse: after eating three-quarters of his soup, he filled the bowl with water, caught a few flies, threw them in the bowl and made a fuss. Once or twice he managed to obtain a new portion of soup until they figured out his trick. Evidently, in 1940, the Pinsk prison was a cultured institution. In a Soviet prison, people would have mocked anyone who complained about a fly.

Around 11:00 a.m., they let us out for a walk. For this occasion, we would put on our trousers, and twenty to thirty people would line up in the corridor. The small courtyard was surrounded by a high wall. Two wardens stood on the side, and in single file or in pairs we walked in a circle with our hands behind our back. "No talking! I'm speaking to you, with the long hair!" We would fall silent as we passed them, but the buzzing would then start again. The sun shone and the sparrows chirped. Some of our cellmates were so weak that they were unable to move, and with the guards' permission they went to the side and sat on the sand.

From time to time they opened a clinic. They placed a small table with bandages and medicine in the corridor. The nurse would call in turn the people with complaints. The cell contained people with high fever and delirious people, but they were never taken to the hospital. "It's nothing," said the warden, looking through the door, "He won't die." Unfortunately, I developed an inflammation of the middle ear and had experienced several nightmarish days. I do not know what drove me crazier—the unbearable pain or being left without any treatment. The nurse was unable to help; she bandaged my head and promised to sign me up for the doctor. I also had an abscess on my arm above the elbow. Half the people in the cell had abscesses and swellings. The nurse did not spare the ichthyol [anti-inflammatory ointment], but she was helpless in serious cases. A few days later, I was summoned to the doctor. He was a Pinsker, so frightened by the presence of the NKVD representative that he was afraid to look us in the eye or speak to us. He did not have a mirror to examine the ear or other medical instruments, and he, too, was unable to help me. The sole ear doctor in the city was Doctor P., my good friend, and I had counted on seeing him, but, of course, that was a naïve hope. For the first time in my life, I survived an illness without medical help, and it passed on its own, but my hearing was impaired for a long time.

The nurse, a young Pinsk girl, looked with tears in her eyes at the shaggy, semi-naked, hungry prisoners covered with sores, whom the wardens had driven into the corridor, like animals from a cage. The arrestees from other cells whom we encountered on our passage were supposed to turn their faces to the wall when we appeared—they did not have the right to look at us. We passed by the rows of people standing with their noses to the wall. No one could recognize us as people who had recently been walking the city streets. A week later, we learned that the nurse had refused to continue working at the prison.

We were covered by hosts of lice. In the morning, after eating our bread, we would sit on our haunches and start the so-called "reading the latest news," that is, killing the lice. The bitten bodies, covered with red spots and abscesses, festered; the green smear protruded in foul stains on the unhealthy leaden gray skin. Lice of all sizes and colors swarmed on the undershirts: chestnut, brown, black, and transparent white lice, brunettes and blondes, and powerful pregnant lice, from which blood spurted when they were crushed under a nail; bright red live dots that with the least touch smeared into a stain— a surprising and unfamiliar abundance of strains. . . . Seventy-five thousand lice for seventy-five people. You did not need to look for them; they simply appeared under one's hands. We picked them off the bread and our faces, off the collar and the pillow of our neighbor, and we crushed them with gloomy satisfaction, as if they were our jailers.

During the six weeks that we spent in prison, they took us to the bathhouse a few times; each time it was a big event. The bathhouse in the Pinsk prison had been equipped by the Poles and consisted of a room with hot showers for about fifteen people. They let the water run for about five minutes, after which we put the same old underwear back on our damp bodies, and marched through the prison courtyard to the cell, where we dried up. The shirts that had been washed under the shower hung over our heads, the bare bodies were steamy and the cell filled with fumes.

People would crowd by the window, but that was prohibited and the guards would drive them away from there. Beyond the window was a high fence with barbed wire on top, and above it, a slice of blue sky: all that remained from the summer. We were cut off not only from nature and people, but also from any news about the external world. For us, the world war had ended.

What did seventy-five people sitting at the bottom of a deep pit in a Soviet prison do? We were not depressed. The shock of the first days had passed. We were in a state of great astonishment and some kind of mocking defiance. We were mostly preoccupied by the scandalous absurdity of our treatment. We felt not like criminals but victims of some idiotic arbitrariness. Everyone related how he had been taken and interrogated. There was a great variety.

Not everyone was interrogated so politely and civilly as I had been. They used intimidation and threats against young Jews who understood Russian poorly. Most of them had illegally crossed the border from the Polish side to escape from the Gestapo. They were treated unceremoniously: "You German spy, f--k your mother!"

"But citizen comrade, I was never in Germany! I don't know the Germans at all!"

"Then where were you? In Romania?" "I was in Romania."

"Excellent: we'll write you down as a Romanian spy!" There were fellows who immediately confessed to all kinds of espionage and then asked whether they needed to confess to anything else. Seeing such willingness, the investigator would wave his hand and give them the protocol to sign. At this point, some would balk: we don't know how to read, we don't understand anything and we won't sign! They would curse them, beat them, drag them nightly to an interrogation and place them in the punishment cell. In the end, they would sign.

Everyone was puzzled. Why did the Soviet regime need this? We, of all people, could not be spies or agents. Those kind of people, of course, all had Soviet passports or were registered for Soviet citizenship. With all their scorn for the investigative farce, people in the cell did not feel guilty and did not understand why it was necessary to make criminals of them.

Two floors of the prison were filled with arrested refugees. The women sat separately. All the arrestees were single. What happened to the families? In Pinsk there were many refugee families with children who registered to return. These families received an order to prepare for resettlement deep inside Russia. They were not arrested, interrogated, or accused of violating passport rules, nor were they charged with espionage or illegal border crossing. They did not look for lawbreakers among them. The thought that each of us would have avoided prison if he had had a wife and child greatly encouraged us and made us think that in the future, in Russian exile, living conditions for families and those without families would even out.

Week followed week, and our condition did not change. When current affairs and political topics had been exhausted, conversations took a different direction. People were stirred up by the heat and inaction. The distance between prison cell and army barracks is not great. A stream of jokes poured over us. Wits and storytellers stepped forth. In the course of several days, I heard more dirty jokes than I had heard all my life. Each bawdy joke evoked a burst of laughter. As soon as one hairy-chested storyteller in upturned long johns became silent, another immediately began. After a few days, this mass delirium subsided. Then came the turn of a "cabaret." This was the term for an improvised entertainment program in which everyone with any talent took part. Among us were comedians, singers, mimes, storytellers. Before lying down for the night, the cell would be entertained this way for an hour or two.

As soon as it became noisy, the door would open, and the duty warden would appear. To punish us for the noise, he would close the window shutters in the cell. As it was, we lacked air. Half an hour after enduring the hermetically sealed room, a deadly silence and talks about capitulation followed. Particularly stubborn disciplinary cases would be removed for several hours. But no means succeeded in imposing silence for a long time. When the repertoire of the cabaret artists was exhausted, choral singing began. All of us, with or without singing voices, sang songs—Yiddish, Polish, and Soviet—about "clouds above the city." These stubborn songs expressed our freedom and obstinacy in face of the enemy. The people in the corridor were our enemies. The regime's behavior could still be a "misunderstanding" or a "mistake," but there were no doubts about the people in the corridor: these were a breed of pit bulls trained to hunt people, a type of "golem" well known to the Jews, an obtuse servant of violence.

"Stop singing!" yelled the duty warden. "I'll teach you now! I don't understand why they are so cheerful. They ought to be crying, and they are singing songs!"

With no less zeal, the prisoners would play a well-known game with an indecent name. We chess players, intellectuals in eyeglasses, did not participate, but we were involuntary spectators. In the game, a participant's eyes would be bound, and he would expose his rear end. Those around would hit him and he would guess who did it. If he guessed correctly, the one who hit would take his place. This crude game gave the participants complete, childish pleasure.

Healthy lads who seemed to have just come from the smithy or the butcher's shop would crowd around. Their bared teeth, the shining whites of their eyes, smirking faces and wide open mouths all expressed the most primitive savagery. At this moment there was no big difference between them and the Cossack-Tatar faces of the NKVD men who guarded us in prison. You had to see the savage animation and joyful anticipation when a person would creep up with a raised hand, shaking his palm, taking aim. When the deafening blow would sound—as if a firecracker had exploded in the cell, the spectators would let out a cry "oof," and electric charges would scatter in all directions. In embryonic form here was the potential for all kinds of torture and murder. These jungle orangutans, however, belonged to the oldest and most cultured nation of the world. This was a demonstration of the duality of the so-called "energy of the masses," that energy of the masses that engenders liberation movements and revolutions equally with SS programs and the exploits of the Soviet security organs.

In our first days in prison, they permitted us to write appeals to the prison director. They gave us pieces of wrapping paper, a pencil for the cell, and we wrote to the prison director about the sums of money owed us from our work places and the things that were left in our apartments that we requested be sent to us. I also requested via the prison administration that my mother send me needed items and informed her that in one of the books in my room she would find money for herself. This letter, however, was not given to her. We did not get the right to meet with our relatives and dear ones whom we were doomed not to see again.

In the middle of July, however, the administration allowed us to receive packages. Our living standard improved immediately. We received blankets, underwear, suits, towels, soap, even pajamas; we received mugs, bowls, food— we became rich, and those who could not expect anything received a share in our riches. Butter, sausage, eggs, and cucumbers appeared in the cell. We did not save any of this and ate it immediately. We did not know that permission to receive packages meant that we would soon leave. The packages were supposed to be for the trip. The day of departure drew near.

Before sending us to our destination, the prison authorities photographed all the arrestees and fingerprinted us. This material went to the NKVD Central Archive along with our "files." It is probably still kept in Moscow to this day. I do not remember the occasion when I saw my photo. It was a nightmarish product not only from the technical but also from the human point of view, and I did not recognize myself in the picture. The six weeks of Soviet prison had corroded all features of comeliness and culture. Looking out from the picture was a gloomy, shaggy and criminal mug of a professional murderer with blue circles under bulging eyes (they ordered me to remove my glasses) and thick swollen lips. One could not give such a person less than five years of forced labor.

7

The Wandering Coffin

AT DAWN ON July 28, 1940, the two floors of Pinsk prison received the command: "Come out with your belongings."

It did not take long to get ready. They brought us to the prison courtyard and ordered us to sit on the ground near the fence. A commission sat at a table in the middle of the courtyard. They summoned prisoners to the table individually and recorded and registered them. Each had to strip naked. A warden carefully checked his clothing, shook out things from his sack, and confiscated forbidden objects: metal mugs, bowls, and penknives. After the search, the people dressed and crossed to the other side. When the entire group finished, they led us to a truck. We turned into a side street and went toward the train station.

In a field outside of the city, far from curious eyes and bustle, a freight train was standing. People with bayonet-tipped rifles encircled the train. The commotion and crush were like those at a train platform. Guards hurried us. The truck turned back for the next group of nonpaying passengers. The sun was high in the sky. David and I approached the closest train car. Suddenly we heard cries from the neighboring car: "Come here, here!" Leaning out of the door, the Kunin brothers waved to us; behind them were little Burko and other prisoners from the potato cellar. We went up the railroad embankment and climbed into the car that would become our home for the following days.

The train had ten cars with about seventy men in each. In the middle of the car was an empty space. To the right and left were two-tier bed boards. On two sides were small barred windows. Opposite the entrance, a hole had been made in the wall, into which a wooden trough of two boards had been inserted. It exited outside and served as a slop pail.

We climbed on top. I lay down in the corner; next to me was David, my faithful companion and friend. On his other side was Doctor Movshovich, a thin, small brown-haired man. Most of the people in the car were new and unfamiliar.

There were around seven hundred people on the train. They cleared out the Pinsk prison that day, making room for others. It is difficult to estimate how many people were sent out before and after us. Not everyone was taken out of our cell. There was one person whom we suspected of being a stool pigeon; he was not with us now, as the administration at the last minute left him in the cell. Our "children"—the two fifteen-year-old boys—also were not with us; nor was the old man, who, evidently, did not have the strength for the journey. We saw this as a humane manifestation: the children belong in school and the old man in a hospice. We were very pleased that they had been left behind, but when we arrived at our destination, we discovered old people and children in Soviet camps.

As many had sisters and relatives who had been arrested, everyone wanted to know whether women were traveling with us. There were a few women on our train; they were put in a special car. Considering that families with children were sent out separately, the total number of refugees deported from Pinsk and its environs probably amounted to between 1,500 and 2,000. Probably around half a million refugees in Western Ukraine and Belorussia[1] were dispatched to camps and exile in the summer of 1941. If one adds the local population—Poles, Belarusians, Ukrainians, and Jews who were deported for political reasons—then the total rises to one and a half to two million people.

The people who carried out this "operation" assumed that they would never have to answer to world public opinion, nor did they think that many of the deportees would return to Europe. They thought that they could treat us as they treated their own population.

The wooden door creaked and the entrance to the car was bolted. We were locked in. It grew dark. The light fell through the square little windows onto the upper bunks. The lower ones were dark as night. Daylight penetrated there only through cracks in the walls. We heard a bustle outside, sounds of a roll call, and the cries of the guards.

Suddenly the car door opened and a hand from below extended a bucket of water. "Look after the water," said a gruff voice. "We won't give any more today." Voices were buzzing in the car; people were quietly conversing, spreading out blankets, and lying down. Someone sighed sadly, like an old person. At the opposite end of the car, a fight broke out; the neighbors

---

1. Now independent state of Belarus.

separated the sides. Gradually, the train fell silent, as if everyone had died. Hours passed. People fell asleep; so did I. We did not hear the train start. It was night. Suddenly I woke up from a sharp jolt. The car jounced; the walls rattled; the train was moving. How long had we been traveling—a half hour or several hours? Where were they taking us and what awaited us? There was no answer.

The human cargo sighed in the darkness. David was sleeping, his arms extended. I turned on my side and put a blanket over my head, but they did not let us sleep. Suddenly, the train stopped. The car door was opened. A flashlight beamed, the tip of a bayonet, and two guards rushed toward the sleeping people.

"Get up!"

A night check. They drove all of us, half dressed, into one corner of the car. We huddled together, sleepy, shivering from the nocturnal cold. Through the open door, the stars shone against the black sky. The guard dived under the bottom bunks and checked that everyone had come down from the upper bunks; he stood in the middle and made everyone pass by him one by one. His companion held a flashlight. Clean-shaven young faces, very tense. Just don't make a mistake. Shadows swept across the car wall.

"One, two, three . . ." speaking with a northern accent, uttering each word carefully, he counted, touching each prisoner with his finger to be extra sure. People quickly flowed by as in an hourglass, past the zone illuminated by the flashlight and then into the shadow. ". . . Seventy . . . seventy-one . . . seventy-two . . ." He finished counting, jumped from the car, and they locked us in again.

The night was uneasy. As soon as the train started to move, we heard a frenzied clatter on the roofs of the cars. They were guarding us from above. The guards banged on the roofs, from the engine to the last car and back without interruption. About two hours passed. Again, we were asleep. "Get up!"

A second inspection! They were already counting. My neighbors shook me; this time I was sleeping soundly. "Get moving, faster!" Again, the door was opened into the night and people were rushing around in the light of the flashlight while I hastily put on my shoes. You couldn't walk barefoot on the floor—it was full of spit and excrement. "Get moving, faster!" The prisoners grouse. "You'll sleep during the day!"

At dawn, they counted us for the third time. It was a difficult, senseless night. "It's a bad business," said David. "If they are guarding us this way, it means they are taking us to a bad place. They are afraid that we'll escape. Where could you escape to from here? This is truly a coffin on wheels."

On the morning of the second day, we began to organize life in the coffin. We elected a *starosta* [elder, leader], who was responsible for maintaining order in the car and distributing bread. We began to look around and get acquainted. Two or three of the seventy people in the car were Poles. Opposite me lay the village teacher Karp. He was a small person with a short beard and the look of a hunted mouse. His eyes expressed horror and incomprehension, and he seemed crazed. This car full of Jews probably seemed like a nightmare to him. He remained supine without getting up for days on end, would avidly eat what he was given, and would look around at each shout, trembling with all his body.

On the other side of the car was a group of young people who called themselves "Theater of the Young." They were youthful Jewish actors from the Warsaw "Teatru Mlodych," students of Weichert's studio,[2] who had also landed in the common mess. Their leader was Wołowczyk, who had traded a tailor's needle for the theatrical stage. In Warsaw, their theater had been avant-garde and performed plays by Soviet authors and Bergelson.[3] The Soviet regime proposed that they perform . . . in Belarusian; when they refused, they arrested them for violating passport rules.

The news spread among the local population at the train stations where we stopped that "they are transporting Jews." A crowd would gather by the train cars, but the guards did not let anyone come close. In Baranowicze,[4] people tried to give us food, but the guard prevented it. They moved us to the side, and we stood opposite a passenger train. Through a little window, we could see what was happening in a compartment of that train. Suddenly Wołowczyk turned pale and started waving at the window.

Directly opposite us, behind the window of the passenger train stood a man who was staring at us and weeping. He did not say a word. The tears flowed uncontrollably down his cheeks. The actors from the "Theater of the Young" waved at him, smiling, but he kept crying, looking at them as if he was

---

2. Michal Weichert (1890–1967) audited lectures of Max Reinhardt in Berlin in 1916–17. Director of Yiddish theater companies, he ran his theater studio in Warsaw until 1939. He survived the Warsaw ghetto and was accused after the war of collaboration with the Nazis but was absolved in a post-war trial in Cracow. He immigrated to Israel in 1958.

3. David Bergelson (1884–1952)—noted Yiddish writer. Born in the Ukraine, he moved to Berlin in 1921. He relocated to the Soviet Union in 1933, where he participated in the Jewish Anti-Fascist Committee during World War II. One of the victims of the Soviet campaign against Jewish cultural figures, he was executed in August 1952.

4. This is the pre-war Polish spelling. In Russian it was referred to as Baranovichi, a town with a large Jewish population. Now Baranovichy in Belarus.

parting from them forever. This was Kamen, one of the best Jewish actors of pre-war Poland, the pillar of the Vilna Troupe, whom I had seen perform several times. Thus, window to window, Wołowczyk and his companions parted from him at the Baranowicze station on the way to Russia.

At the very start of the trip, the guards carried out a careful search in our car, turning everything over and groping everything. They confiscated not only kitchenware, which was prohibited, but also books. Someone had brought into the car books in Polish and Russian, which we were counting on reading. They brusquely threw the confiscated books into the dirt under the wheels of the car. They took away two thermometers from Doctor Movshovich. Protests were useless. They broke the thermometers on the spot. You might have thought that there was an abundance of thermometers where they were taking us.

The wandering coffin traveled eastward, to Eurasia, deep into a foreign continent. We did not know what awaited us. Our European concepts were, evidently, inapplicable to these people—to what they called a judiciary, culture, order, and justice. We were surrounded by ambiguity, doublespeak, and the unspoken. Where were they taking us? There was no answer. Who were the real criminals—we or those who were transporting us? What awaited us—exile, a settlement, *kolkhoz* life? The transport conditions were inhuman. Here, too, however, they maintained an outward appearance of order: each morning, a woman doctor in a stainless white robe entered the befouled, stinking car, where, side by side, people relieved themselves and ate. She would ask whether there were any complaints, and following her instructions, our companion, lice-infected like everyone else, an arrested doctor who was not destined to survive in the land of the *zek*, would distribute medicines and bandage wounds.

This was the appearance of the "social welfare," which cooperated with social evil instead of fighting against it, prettified it, and expressed that same duality of barbaric content in a pseudo-humane wrapping.

They distributed bread once a day. There was no hot food, but on the fifth day, they handed out clay bowls and wooden spoons. Toward evening on the fifth day, we tasted our first "Soviet" soup. Acute hunger tormented us, but we were preoccupied by other thoughts.

We crossed the former Polish border at Stolbtsy. Immediately, the clean white buildings of the Polish railroad stations, covered with red tiles and with a round clock above the central entrance to the platform, disappeared. Old wooden structures from tsarist times—gloomy and squalid, started appearing. Rags or plywood were often stuffed into the broken windowpanes. The villages that we saw through our tiny window were *kolkhozes*. These villages with their darkened huts and straw roofs looked so miserable!

We arrived in Minsk, the capital of Soviet Belorussia. As prisoner trains were not supposed to stop in sight of the population, we were stationed outside of the city. It was an overcast, sunless morning. Through the little window, we saw an unpaved street on the city's outskirts, with little wooden houses and hurrying passers-by. Women in kerchiefs and children passed by without raising their eyes or looking in our direction.

Our stops on the Polish side had looked so different! No matter where our train would stop, a crowd would gather immediately, and the guards would have to drive away the curious onlookers. The children, as if bewitched, looked at the train with its human cargo, at the freight cars packed with prisoners, at the guards' bayonets; they would point with their fingers at the faces looking through the grating. Their mothers would try to give us bread. We saw tears and fright on the faces of the Jewish women, sensed the atmosphere of compassion or at least interest.

On the other side of the Soviet border, we ceased being a sensation. It became clear to us that for Soviet citizens, a train such as ours was the most ordinary spectacle, a part of their daily life, nothing special. They had already seen so many of these trains! Transporting prisoners was an everyday occurrence. Adults would pass by, averting their eyes, to stay out of harm's way. The children—ten-year-old boys and girls—went past, chirping and laughing; for them this entire train was neither interesting nor terrible but simply unremarkable. What was there to look at? Seeing this deep and natural indifference, I recalled my own childhood: playing along the railroad embankment, we, too, would not glance at the flatbeds loaded with lumber, ordinary and boring, seen a hundred times. It was a different matter when an elegant express from the capital went by: multicolored cars, spiffy passengers! A prisoner freight car in Soviet Russia—nothing special! No one bothered to look back at us.

The prisoners followed the schoolchildren with serious eyes, recollecting their own children. And I blessed fate that my son was not living in a country where trains with prisoners are a common phenomenon.

From Minsk, we turned northward. For ten days and nights, we lay in the darkness, and the rhythmic motion lulled us to sleep. Our ears became accustomed to the monotonous clanging of the train and our bodies to the jolts and to the shaking of the car walls.

They kept counting us day and night. New guards entered the car, new stations sailed past us, and, finally, it became cold in the car. We began to freeze at night although it was only the beginning of August. Time moved in a closed circle. It seemed as if we would never arrive.

All this time I had a strange feeling. In the darkness of the wandering coffin and isolation from the external world, I lost the sensation of movement on the earth's surface, and it seemed to me that we were moving downward, continually downward, underground, away from the world of the living. Each day we descended deeper and deeper, and the darkness increased and thickened around us as if we were descending into a bottomless well. With each kilometer, we were farther and farther from the earth's surface where the sun shines and people smile at each other, and one breathes freely, without fear.

It was an unbridled descent; a demonic, invisible force led us into the heart of night, to a subterranean kingdom from which there was no return. With each day, we were farther and farther from our past. It was not an ordinary journey. It was a journey to the other world. And we knew that when it ended, we would leave the coffin, everything around us would be different, and we ourselves would be different.

Our train was not moving in an ordinary human dimension. We left our native places. The European summer was behind us. We had departed from human memory, from history. The very duration of this journey had a hypnotic effect on us; we had become subdued.

We descended interminably. Sometimes, waking up, we would hear savage, hoarse voices outside. A dim, bloody flush lit the sky, and we did not know whether it was sunrise or sunset. Sometimes we would hear a distant thundering and noise, a metallic clanging—semaphores lit up the tracks—and we knew that we were at a large station but they did not tell us which one. Perhaps Novgorod? Perhaps Leningrad? And again, the car would shudder abruptly, and the wandering coffin would travel into the boundless, empty void.

When the evening came and the last slanting rays of the sun fell on the car, we would pull out boards from the bunks and set up a bench near the window. On this bench on the upper bunks, we would sit like roosting chickens, crowding closely together. Accompanied by the train's clatter, we sang for a long time, sad Russian songs with a Polish accent—drawn out songs that filled the heart with longing and a deep chill. . . .

The road is long and distant.
Come out, my beloved!
We shall part at the threshold,
Perhaps, forever. . . .

When it became completely dark, stretched out in the darkness face to face, we would tell each other about our past life, although now there was not much meaning to the diversity in our experience or our recollections.

"Work!" said my neighbor, a typesetter from Warsaw with a thin, nervous face. "I don't fear any work. Let them just give us an opportunity, and we'll show them that we can handle work better than they can. In Pinsk, I was a housepainter. I had not been a painter before that, but it's not difficult. If you have a head on your shoulders, you can understand any work. Well, what harm can they do to us? We'll live together and work together—that's all!"

"What kind of country is this? What strange people. What do they want from us? In Poland, we imagined them differently. Why did they throw us into prison? Why don't they let us return to our family, to our home—to Palestine?"

I told my neighbor what I knew about this mysterious country:

"The country to which we are traveling lies neither in Europe nor in Asia. It is a mistake to regard Russians as Europeans. You saw them in Pinsk and now you know that this is not a European people. But they are not Asians. It is Eurasia—and they are an intermediary people.

"For a thousand years, Eurasians have been living on the border between East and West, between Asia and Europe. European culture finds expression in one great idea—the idea of Man, of individual freedom and dignity.

"We Jews were the first to teach the world that man is created in God's image. The Greeks and Romans praised Man, and the idea of Freedom developed in Europe up to the epoch of the Enlightenment and the Great French Revolution, which proclaimed the rights of Man and the Citizen.

"There was, however, a reverse side to the coin with respect to the European idea of the freedom of man: constant unrest and dissatisfaction, anxiety and greed, which drove Europeans to all corners of the world, to inventions, experiments, and conquests. Asian culture had been cultivated for millennia in India and China. That culture possessed wisdom and tranquility unknown to the Europeans, a feeling of unity with nature, an eternal source of strength. It was, however, a mass culture, and its reverse side was a herd instinct and the all-encompassing despotism of the Tamerlanes and Genghis Khans.

"The Eurasians left Asia but did not reach Europe. They could have taken the great and positive elements from both the European and Asiatic cultures— the idea of civil liberty and human dignity, on the one hand, and the idea of universal life, full of the wisdom of tranquility and self-containment on the other hand.

"Had they combined them, they could have become the greatest people on earth! But just the opposite occurred: they took the negative aspects, the worst from each culture. They combined European anxiety, dualism, and torturous intellectual inquiries with Asiatic despotism and suppression of the personality. This people has neither the modest wisdom of the Indians and Chinese nor the respect for the individual and personal pride of the French and Anglo-Americans. It is eternally dissatisfied and suffering, and those around it perpetually suffer.

"Eurasians are dangerous neighbors because they are never satisfied with their borders and incessantly start quarrels. At times, they go to war against the 'rotten West'; at other times, they need to 'overtake and surpass America.' They lack a European sense of measure and tact. Everything they take from Europe loses its European meaning in their hands. This people perpetually misses the boat; invariably it takes from Europe the cast offs that Europe itself has already discarded. In the tenth century, it took from Europe the Byzantine version of Christianity, which Europe had already rejected. In the time of Tsar Peter the Great, it took the external forms of civilization, technology, and the stupid German military drill. Now they have taken Marxism from Europe. What they did with it, you will soon see with your own eyes.

"Europe is infected with Nazism and fascism; it is her internal illness, Europe's perversion. Eurasia presents an external danger, a threat from without. The Gestapo is the cancer and syphilis of Europe. If it is not eliminated, Europe will putrefy alive.

"The 'Mustapo' is a barbaric misunderstanding. This train stuffed with human cargo, this farce that the NKVD is playing with us, is the form in which the people, breaking away from its Asiatic roots, challenges Europe.

"We are Europeans. This Jewish train is a small piece of Europe. Those of us who survive will return to Palestine, the sole place where the Jewish people can continue its European history.

"And if Europe survives this war and deals with Hitlerism, which threatens it from within, then it will also have the strength to stop Eurasia and, perhaps, bring it closer to its humanistic ideal. This, however, is a difficult and complex task because the Eurasians are not a clean page on which history is only beginning to be written. This people is a thousand years old, and it cannot be reborn within one or two generations."

8

BBK [Baltic-White Sea Canal]

TEN DAYS AFTER our departure from Pinsk, the train with human cargo arrived at the Medvezhegorsk station on the rail line to Murmansk. Here they ordered us to get out of the train. Grasping their packs and bundles, the crowd poured out of the car, stretching legs and blinking in the unaccustomed light.

Standing somewhat to the side, a man in a long military coat, with an imposing "commander's" bearing, met us at the station. We were very surprised to hear him speaking in broken Yiddish. "I myself am from Warsaw," he laughed. "And you see, I still remember something." People surrounded him on all sides.

"Don't come near! Don't get close!" He squeamishly distanced himself from us and took out a gleaming cigarette case. The eyes of the dirty, exhausted travelers immediately fixated on it. "What did you do? And what did you do?" he asked, pointing his finger at one and then another; he merely nodded his head at all the replies and decreed:

"To felling trees! To felling trees!"

A wrinkled old man told him he had been a merchant in Poland and sold spices, pepper, vinegar, and so forth. "Pepper, vinegar," chuckled the man with the cigarette case. "Here, even without pepper, Grandpa, your life will be bitter." He laughed, but his eyes stared intently, without a smile—the eyes of one who acquires merchandise or of an appraiser in a pawnshop.

This man was Levinson, a major in the state security service, head of the BBK camps, that is, camps in the zone of the Baltic–White Sea Canal, with their center in Medvezhegorsk. We were now in the Karelo-Finnish Republic, at the northern tip of Lake Onega, which has a surface of 10,000 square kilometers. Hundreds of corrective labor camps [Russian acronym ITL] subordinate to Levinson[1] extended from here to the White Sea. We did not yet

---

1. As an officer in the NKVD, Levinson was in a privileged position, with more authority than other officials.

know that he had about half a million state slaves under his authority. We had
so little understanding of what was awaiting us that we posed naïve questions
to the "kind uncle" at the Medvezhegorsk station.

"Will you now let us go around town freely?"

"No," smiled Levinson, "How can we let you go free? After all, you are
prisoners."

Here we learned for the first time that we were "prisoners," but we still did
not understand what it meant.

They arranged us in a column. David, a former soldier in the Polish army
and a man of experience, showed me how to tie up my sack: he put a little
stone in the lower corner and with string tied a knot above the stone that
would hold it; he tied the other end at the top of the sack, and I slung it on
my shoulders. We set out in rows of four.

The town of Medvezhegorsk was constructed entirely from wood, like
most of the cities in northern Russia. The houses reminded me either of the
outskirts of Pinsk or of the summer cabins in Poland, with little balconies,
porches, shutters, and small windows. The streets were unpaved. We marched,
raising clouds of dust. The streets were empty; there were no stores or signs.
In one place, a line of old women and barefoot boys waited patiently near a
locked door with the inscription "store."

We walked for a long time. Suddenly, directly out of the sand and knolls, a
three-story stone mansion with a colonnade appeared.

"Well?" our guard asked us, "are there buildings like this in Poland, too?"
With a clear conscience, we answered that there were no such buildings in
Poland. This was the headquarters of the administrative command of the
NKVD Baltic–White Sea Canal [BBK] camps, a model of Soviet culture.

This entire town, of twenty to thirty thousand residents, had been built
by prisoners. The residents were either personnel of the BBK camp administration or released prisoners who had been allowed to settle here, after having
served their term. All these people whom we saw walking in the streets were
not free people! With astonishment, we repeated this news, which sounded
fantastic to us. But it was true. All the people here either were serving their
term, had served out their term, or were part of the penal apparatus. Of
course, those who supervised the prisoners from stone mansions in the center
of Medvezhegorsk were not free people either. They were jailers.

Where was our place here? We walked 5 kilometers, leaving the town behind. We barely moved with our bundles and sacks. The guards drove us with
their rifles at the ready, pushing the laggards, goading us with crude curses.
Finally, we reached gates and sat on the ground. After some time, people came

out with lists and began calling out names singly. Hours passed. Through a narrow door at the side of the gates, they let us into a wide courtyard, surrounded by barracks. A high fence with barbed wire on top encircled the yard. In olden times, this was called an *ostrog* [prison]; now it was a *lagpunkt* [camp sector].

More precisely, we were in a distributional transit camp; from there, all arriving groups of prisoners were sent to the various sectors of the BBK camps. In Medvezhegorsk itself, there was a camp for three thousand people, a specially privileged camp; it was considered good fortune to land there as people lived in "the center," which was better supplied and offered the possibility of urban work. Our "transit courtyard" was separate; no one was there besides us, and the barracks were for our exclusive use. The barracks were sheds without windows, clearly unsuitable for permanent housing.

We spent three days in this place, resting from our journey. After our starvation diet during the transport, the soup and kasha that they gave us seemed unusually tasty. A table with medicines stood outside; one could go there with medical complaints. Here we became acquainted with the basic abbreviated camp term *sanchast* (medical sector).

On the second day, our belongings, which had arrived in the same freight train, were brought from the station. They threw them in a heap near the fence. Many suitcases had been damaged; the bundles fell apart, and when we came to search for our things in the general pile, for some it was already too late—all their possessions had been stolen. My suitcase was lying open but most of the contents remained, including a dozen shirts. I still had so many wearable items that I could consider myself well provided for a long time. In all of Medvezhegorsk, there were not as many treasures and items of European provenance as lay scattered near the fence of the BBK transit point that evening.

Those were the good days. They took us to the bathhouse, and I can confirm that in the following five years, I was never in such a remarkably clean bathhouse. There were no European showers, just Russian basins, benches under the windows and lots of hot water. For two days, we lay in the sun on the grass—hundreds of people—we sat on the earthen mounds by the barracks and under the northern August sun, we "read the latest news," that is, we crushed lice on our shirts.

Wandering around the yard, we made a discovery. People were lying in a spot on the other side of the fence. Although it was forbidden to approach this fence, we nevertheless managed to linger there. Through the cracks between the boards, we saw a clearing that was covered with people who were lying down. It was an unforgettable moment. For the first time, we saw Russian prisoners. It was a gray mass of people in rags, lying motionless with bloodless, pale faces, cropped hair, with a shifty, gloomy look. Some of them got up and furtively approached the fence.

"Who are you?"

"Poles."

"Do you hear, Poles!" they began to shove each other. Lifeless, heavy, cold eyes looked at us through the fence. We asked, "Perhaps you know where they are sending us?"

"What, you don't know?" they laughed from the other side. "You're going to the forest." In pantomime, someone began to show us our fate.

At first, we did not understand the meaning of his motions. He bent his arm and began to move it rhythmically back and forth. It was the motion of sawing. The man sawed and laughed soundlessly, looking at our astonished faces.

"Maybe you have some bread to sell?" Others began to approach. Someone began to sell his shirt. "Let me try it on!" Before the inexperienced seller knew what was happening, his shirt was pulled through the crack in the fence and immediately disappeared. On the other side of the fence, people were laughing: "Look how the Pole sold his shirt!" At that moment, a guard arrived and chased us away from the fence.

On the third day, they assembled us toward evening and under escort led us away from this marvelous place. Soon we were again raising dust on the road, this time on the way back to the city. We turned into a side street and emerged at the Medvezhegorsk harbor.

At the harbor there was a smell of resin and sawed wood; barges stood near the shore. A place had been prepared for us in the hold of an enormous barge into which 650 Pinskers were crowded. In addition, there was a group of about thirty Polish women, several dozen escort guards and BBK employees, and guards with rifles and watchdogs. Huge black canines, trained to guard and hunt people, were settled in the front part of the barge on the deck. Below, in the passage, people squeezed together into one tight mass on the floor so that it was difficult to walk among them. There was no kitchen on the barge. They gave us bread, a herring per person, and a can of peas for four. They said the trip would not be long, but it took around a day and a half.

A small tugboat towed our barge. We sailed from Medvezhegorsk in the afternoon. It was my first journey on Lake Onega. I had no doubt that there would also be a second, in the opposite direction. There was no time to think or grieve: what was happening to us was so extraordinary that we were preoccupied with current impressions. We entered the broad expanse of water. As large as a sea, the lake had a dark azure sheen with a silver shimmer. At first, we sailed in sight of wooded shores, then we reached the middle, and the shores receded and disappeared. . . . Occasionally we saw small islands on the horizon and sailboats and small steamboats sailing in the distance.

We saw all this, however, only furtively, in snatches. The prisoners' barge is not made for enjoying nature's beauties. From the hold where we were situated, nothing was visible except for a narrow strip of sky at the exit. One had to go up to the deck to see what was happening outside, but we were not permitted to stay there and the dogs drove us away. We froze at night, and as the journey dragged on, we would have been starving were it not for a circumstance that turned our thoughts in a different direction.

The combination of half-baked black bread and Onega water that we drew in buckets for drinking had grave consequences. Acute, mass diarrhea broke out on the barge, which had no toilets. En route, they had hammered together on deck a kind of booth from boards that protruded over the side. One place for seven hundred people. From the morning, a great tragicomedy would play out on the Onega barge. The police dogs and armed men guarded the way to the deck. We discovered that among the series of European democratic freedoms that we had not valued, the freedom and ease of attending to physiological needs were not in the last place. A crowd would huddle on the staircase leading upward; people were howling, groaning, and imploring to let them pass through, and ultimately dozens of people could not hold out. The barge turned into a ship of misfortune. Every possible and impossible corner was befouled. A guard stood at the exit to the deck, and every three minutes his booming voice would give an order that I cannot convey here in all its picturesqueness. On the other side was a line of women who watched indescribable scenes.

Poor women! They were situated separately on the barge but treated as roughly as we were. These were girls from Warsaw, who, even in these conditions, retained a shred of some good looks; they behaved courageously and looked presentable. One of them found her brother in our crowd. She was unable to go to him, but from afar, she waved and smiled. Her whole face shone with happiness at the meeting. And many of us were sad that there was no one to smile at us like that and bestow upon us a crumb of warmth in this alien country, among enemies and jailers.

In the corner of the ship, people were singing. Probably, it was the first time such songs sounded on the Onega because suddenly the Soviet lieutenant— "citizen commander"—shuddered as if he had been burned and came close to listen. A young Jew became silent.

"Sing!" the lieutenant told him.

"I won't sing!" and he turned away as if he remembered: "On the Rivers of Babylon."

"Sing!" said the lieutenant. "You are a Jew, and I am a Jew. It is twenty years since I heard these songs. It reminds me of my childhood, it pulls at my heart, and I cannot listen calmly. Let's go upstairs; I'll give you as much as you want to drink, just sing!"

For the price of pure water, the young lad sang a song for him that wandering Jewish musicians would sing in Warsaw courtyards:

Tsu dir—libe—fil ikh!
Mayn Harts is ful mit Frayd!
Nor dokh shtendik fil ikh
Az mir veln zayn tseshaydt.

Ikh halt sikh in ayn Shreken
Mayn Harz iz ful mit Payn
Venn ikh vel sikh oyfveken
Un du vest mer nit sayn!

[My feelings are for you, my beloved! / My heart is full of joy! But I always sense that we are destined to part. / I am always afraid. / My heart is full of pain, / that when I awake, / You will be gone. Trans. from the Yiddish.]

The melancholy melody wafted above the Onega and tore at our heart strings.

Dray kleyne Verter—gedenkn sey git—Ikh bet bay dir—farges mikh nit!

[Three small words—remember them well, / I implore you: Don't forget me!]

The lieutenant looked somber and went to the other end of the barge. He did not approach us again.

The barge anchored in an inlet lined with warehouses of logs and boards on two sides. We began to disembark onto the sandy flat shore. Directly in front of us was a narrow gauge rail line. Immediately after the rails began the damp forest and swampy slough. It was a grim landscape: bog, forest, and piles of logs. Slowly, with the clang of the shock absorbers, the open cargo flat cars approached. We settled down on them with our bundles. The few women among us were seated separately. The camp sector where this occurred was called Ostrech (on the northern shore of Lake Onega). We set off.

The train proceeded slowly through the forest. Illuminated by the August sun, birches, pines, and fir trees sailed by—woodland, glades, swamps, and damp plains alternated. The sad monotony of this landscape somewhat recalled Belarusian nature. Only there were no people, and the shadow of some desert-like bleakness hung over everything. A desolate, godforsaken place. On the turns, our little steam engine whistled deafeningly, and we read an incomprehensible inscription on the wooden signs on the side of the tracks: "Close the blower!" Fresh, pure air entered our lungs, and after our stay in the ship's hold, the road through the dense forest was restful. Blockhouses appeared in the forest—constructed from large logs. We sensed that this was not an ordinary forest nor an ordinary region. Although we had already traveled a considerable distance, we had not encountered stations, signs, or traces of civilian life. At one stop, we saw an old Uzbek with a white beard and desiccated Mongolian face. How had this Uzbek landed in the Karelo-Finnish forest? "Grampa," they yelled to him from our car: "What is the name of this town?" The Uzbek turned and looked with lifeless eyes. "What kind of town?" he said in sorrowful astonishment. "You really think you came to a town? You came to a camp!"

At this moment, I recalled the opening lines of Dante's "Hell":

> *Midway upon the journey of our life*
> *I found myself within a forest dark,*
> *For the straightforward pathway had been lost . . .*[2]

Yes, it was an amazing forest: who was not here?—Uzbeks, Poles, Chinese, Ukrainians and Georgians, Tatars and Germans. . . . In one spot, we passed through a clearing in which a group of about forty people was standing. They were the inhabitants of the forest.

They looked at our train carrying the "newcomers" with curiosity, while we looked at them with no less curiosity. Both sides had something at which to marvel.

We were "foreigners," which was immediately obvious from the yellow and green suitcases, the jackets and overcoats, the shirts of various colors, the European shoes, and the variety of suits. How rich, how variegated,

---

2. http://www.online-literature.com/dante/inferno/1/

and dissimilar we were—we understood this only when we saw the forest inhabitants.

The people were of a gray mousy color. Everything on them was mousy gray: some kind of wadded vests, long rags, formless old footwear on bare feet, mousy gray hats with earflaps that bounced apart and gave the face a savage look. And the faces were also mousy gray, with an earthy hue, as if they were powdered with dust. Everything they wore fit them clownishly—either it was too wide and long or too narrow and short. They all stood in a group; to the side stood an armed man in a military uniform who clearly belonged to "another race."

We finally arrived at our destination. To the left was a tall pine forest. To the right were heaps of logs and firewood; behind them in the distance, a tall camp palisade and gates were visible. A broad road paved with beams led there. We walked on the road, slipping and trying not to get our feet stuck between the beams. On both sides of the wooden planking was a dark swamp. We came up to the gates and read the inscription on the top: "A MERCILESS STRUGGLE AGAINST SLACKERS AND WRECKERS!"

Lower down, a slogan was scrawled on a board in discolored, faded letters:

"KEEP UP WITH SAVCHENKO AND DEMCHENKO"

They were waiting for us. A tall lame man was in charge of our reception. He was the director of the camp. Behind him stood men with rifles: they were the armed guard [Russian acronym—VOKHR]. The commander of the VOKHR platoon and the head of the camp held our fate in their hands. Other people from the camp departments were also present at this meeting: the directors of the financial section and of the medical sector, the inspector of the cultural-educational section (KVCh)—people whose names and functions we could not figure out. The lame camp director became very agitated: "Call the director of the accounting and allotments office!" The director appeared, dressed in a mousy gray suit as befitted a prisoner, but with good boots, which testified to a high position in the camp. The camp commander cursed him loudly and roundly for his tardiness. The director of the accounting office pulled out lists and began to call people one by one. We entered the guardhouse, where the riflemen of VOKHR checked our belongings and let us pass through into the camp territory. Then they assigned us places for the night.

We walked along the street. It grew dark. On both sides, the camp huts looked black. A high-pitched squeaking greeted us: "Look, look!" Enormous camp rats were running under our feet, scurrying in all directions. We had never seen rats of such size and audacity. There was a reason why there were no cats in the camp: the rats would devour them. The barracks smelled of mustiness and dampness. We climbed a rotting staircase into a dark, large entrance hall. The door hung on one hinge. From the hall, four doors led to four rooms, each for about thirty to forty people, with double decker bunks. Nothing but bare boards. Half of the glass in the windowpanes was broken. There was no lighting.

In the courtyard, a line was already forming under the kitchen window, and our leader (we remained together in groups based on our placement in the train cars at Pinsk) ran to find out about food. Bread had been distributed in the morning; now we were supposed to get soup and kasha. The distribution proceeded slowly, as there were not enough bowls for 650 people. We ate when it was already dark and lay down to sleep without undressing.

We still did not believe that this was the end of our journey. The barracks looked like a temporary rest stop, not a human dwelling.

A frantic howl woke us at night. We jumped up: in the neighboring room, on the other side of the wall, people were screaming. We ran there and found the guard on duty with a flashlight and a panicked crowd around him. What had happened?

It was the "rat mutiny."

The newcomers did not know that at night one must not leave bread in sight or even in a bag. At night, the rats pounced, climbing out of every crack, driven by fierce hunger, sensing human warmth, bread, crumbs, leftovers, the smell of food. The rats were not afraid of people and flung themselves on the bunks, and then the people were frightened by the rats. Someone woke up and saw a huge rat on his chest. He yelled wildly like a child, "Mama!" This triggered general hysteria; peoples' nerves were shot. The tension of recent weeks, fears that had built up inside these raw youths over the months in prison and during the transport, burst forth as inhuman, crazed shouting and weeping. Hundreds of people rampaged and shouted: "Rats! Rats! Get us out of here! We don't want to stay here!" The VOKHR armed guards ran up from all over the camp. When the orderly learned that the Poles were afraid of rats, he was astounded. He could not understand it. The riflemen roared with laughter. The orderly tried to calm us like children.

"You'll get used to it!" he said. "Really, it's not dangerous. Didn't you have rats in Poland?"

He was right. We got used to it. After three months, I was so accustomed to rats that they could dance on my head. I would only turn to the other side in my sleep and with my hand brush them away from my body or face.

9

Square 48

THE CAMP THAT will be described in this chapter is not as terrible as those where the Germans annihilated millions of people. It is one of the innumerable Soviet corrective labor camps (ITL) that continue to function in the Soviet Union after the war just as they did before. As you are reading these lines, normal camp life goes on at Square 48. I shall not tell about horrors or exceptional events. My topic is an ordinary Soviet concentration camp.

The people living in the camp are called *zakliuchennye* [prisoners]. The technical and colloquial abbreviation is *z/k*, read *zek*.[1] In the camp under discussion, in mid-August 1940, there were 650 zeks from Pinsk. A few days later, a group of 350 zeks from the town of Złochów,[2] near Lvov,[3] arrived at the same camp. The total number of zeks reached 1,000. They were almost all Polish Jews and a few dozen non-Jewish Poles. Subsequently, about fifty Russian zeks were transferred into the camp for various jobs. The camp thus contained 1,050 zeks, a medium-sized camp. Some are smaller; some are much larger.

About forty riflemen guarded inside and outside the camp. Several dozen free people (the commander of the camp, his deputy in charge of camp property, and other workers with their families) lived in small houses off the camp grounds. Over one hundred free people were working in the camp of 1,050 prisoners, but they were not permitted to live in it or remain after work hours.

---

1. Although Margolin wrote "zeka," this translation will use the more familiar term to English readers, "zek."

2. Now part of Ukraine, it is called Zolochiv.

3. Now Lviv, Ukraine.

Square 48 lies in a forest to the north of Lake Onega and belongs to the Second Onega Division of the BBK. It is a camp sector [Russian—*lagpunkt* or *l/p*]. Several sectors form a "division." Several divisions form a whole, called the BBK Camp. In turn, the BBK Camp is only one of a large number of camp complexes covering the Soviet Union. These camp complexes (officially abbreviated as LAG), are located in all parts of the Soviet Union although they have their own geographical demarcations, that is, the LAG penal-police divisions for imprisoned Russia do not correspond to the administrative *oblasti* [regions] for "free" Russia. No matter where you put your finger on a map, you will always find a LAG—in Novaya Zemlya, Kolyma, Kamchatka, the Caucasus, near Moscow, in the Altai Mountains, or on the shores of the Pacific Ocean. All of Soviet Russia, probably, contains considerably more than one hundred LAGs, in each of which there are hundreds of camp sectors. Thus, 100 times 100 equals 10,000 camp sectors. If each sector, as in our "Square 48," contains about one thousand zeks, then the total number of prisoners in the Soviet Union constitutes 10 million.[4] In certain years, when a wave of terror (a "purge") swept over the Soviet Union, the number of camp inhabitants could reach 15 million or more. Not all LAG are as large as the BBK, but some camp sectors number not one thousand but several thousand zeks. Only the Head Administration of Camps in Moscow, abbreviated as GULAG,[5] knows the exact figure for the camp population, but it does not tell us.

The Gulag is a very taciturn, discreet, and secretive institution. Its representatives do not speak at press conferences or international congresses. Nevertheless, it has something to brag about. Among the greatest achievements of Soviet construction, which the regime does not cease publicizing worldwide, first place actually belongs to the gigantic enterprise of erecting tens of thousands (or more) of settlements of a special type, forming the greatest industrial complex in world history. Regrettably, this complex has been rendered invisible: the government that makes no secret of its records concerning "socialist construction," has thrown a veil of conspiratorial secrecy over it. Probably, however, it knows what it is doing.

I was at Square 48 from mid-August 1940 until June 24, 1941—over ten months. It is a wood felling sector, which produces lumber for the domestic

---

4. Scholarship based on recent archival research suggests a much lower number, perhaps around 2.5 million.

5. The acronym GULAG will henceforth appear in the more familiar English form, Gulag. The term is used commonly to refer to the entire punitive camp system in the Soviet Union.

and foreign markets. If the lumber that the Soviet Union exported to world markets before the war was able to speak, it would have told about a sea of blood and tears that was spilled in Soviet camps.

In addition to the wood felling sectors, there are sectors for agriculture, metal mining, coal mines, factories and workshops, construction of canals, cities, railroads, and highways—in short, all forms of labor, including the highly specialized work of engineers, draftsmen, and research scientists. This entire network of camp sectors, punitive sectors, work colonies, and OLP (separate labor camp sectors) is subject to the same conditions as Square 48, that is, state slavery.

Our division had its center in the village of Pyalma, halfway between Ostrech and Square 48. The "Poles," or "Westerners," as they called us, were placed in a series of camp sectors in our division (for example, the fifth, eighth, Bobrov, and others). It was said that fifty thousand people were brought from eastern Poland that winter to the area of Lake Onega. Places were easily found for them in the hundreds of camps of the BBK complex.

The free population in this region is very sparse, and the further one goes in the direction of the White Sea and Arctic Ocean, the sparser it becomes. In the extreme north of Russia, not a *kolkhoz* but precisely the corrective labor camp is the "normal" type of settlement. There are parts of the country where the majority of the population is imprisoned in camps.

Square 48 occupies an area of three hectares [30,000 square meters]. It is surrounded by a high palisade. On the four corners outside of the palisade are wooden watchtowers, where sentinels stand watch day and night. It is forbidden to approach the palisade. There is a "forbidden zone" encompassing every camp sector both from inside and from outside. At a distance of 3 to 4 meters from the palisade are low pegs driven into the earth with a sign on wooden slabs: "Forbidden zone." The guards have the right to shoot at anyone who enters the forbidden zone. The space inside the fence, aside from the forbidden zone, is the "camp zone," or simply, "the zone." People say that the prisoners work outside the zone and live in the zone. Millions of Soviet people as zeks and hundreds of thousands as guards or NKVD workers spend their lives "in the zone."

One may enter and leave the camp only through the guardhouse. After opening the door, everyone passes by a little window where the armed guard on duty is sitting, and he notes down those who enter and leave. Of the thousand zeks in Square 48, about thirty have a pass with the right to leave the zone. It is not easy to obtain this pass. Generally, it is not given to political prisoners, and "nonpoliticals" receive it only when they have won complete trust. In order to receive a "pass," one must spend many years in camp, be known to everyone, and be serving the last year of one's term. The commander of the guard platoon gives a pass to people whose work requires relative freedom of movement: the work boss, the bosses of the work sectors, workers in the stables and tool sheds located outside the camp zone, and so forth. These are permanent passes; provisional ones are given for a day or two to individual prisoners who are sent on a specific task—courier, accountant, or driver.

Everyone else passes through the guardhouse only as a member of an entire brigade with an armed escort. Entering through the guardhouse, we land on the street. To the right and left are buildings. Here is the camp "construction": the building frames rise up, and round, smooth beams lie nearby. They are building two new barracks: one for arriving zeks, the other as a central punishment cell for the division, that is, a prison inside a prison. Directly across from the guardhouse is the bathhouse, a decrepit, lopsided hut, with a laundry attached to it. Here the street curves. On the right is a bakery and a shed where they cut the bread. On the left is the clothes warehouse with the attached shoemaking and tailor workshops. Further on is a small infirmary with eight to ten beds. On a knoll is a new, clean little house. On one side, it is surrounded by barbed wire. The women, who must be guarded specially because of the nearby male population, are located there. On the other side of this barrack is the provisions warehouse and the *larek* [camp store]. Prisoners sometimes have an opportunity to buy what is available in the store at "commercial" prices, but for the most part, it is empty and it is better not to count on it.

The street turns again. To the right and left are the residential barracks, each for 150 people, and among them a "club" with a cultural-educational sector, a kitchen, and an ATP barrack (for administrative-technical personnel). This barrack is populated by the camp aristocracy—brigade leaders, foremen, and office workers. At the end of the street is the office, which in other camps is sometimes called the headquarters: the accounting office, camp administration, and office of the commander are located there. Opposite the office is the outpatient clinic, that is, the medical sector, a little building with an antechamber and three little rooms, where they receive and treat patients and where the prisoner doctors, nurses, medics, and medical assistants live. Here the camp ends; beyond it is the forbidden zone and the fence. If you descend from the hillock where the clinic stands, then on a path behind it one can reach a little fence with a locked wicket gate: inside is a decrepit shack, which looks like an uninhabited and forsaken ruin. It has a tiny window with dusty glass, dark from dirt and thick cobwebs. This is the SHIZO or simply, punishment cell, where prisoners are incarcerated at the order of the camp commander. In the Arkhangelsk region, the camp inmates have their own name for the SHIZO—a *kur*.[6]

That's it. Past the punishment cell, however, where the swamp begins, stands a little isolated shed. It is the "boiler room," one of the vital centers of the camp. Inside is an oven that contains two or three enormous cauldrons. The boiler heats water day and night, and when the camp is already sleeping, a fire burns in the wasteland where this shed stands, and through the open doors, one can see the half-naked figures of the stokers rushing about. It is an important and responsible task to supply a thousand people with boiling water. At dawn, at five o'clock in the morning—in winter it is still dark—the orderlies[7] stream from all the barracks to the boiler room with heavy wooden pails. Woe to the stoker if, before going to work or upon returning from the forest, frozen and soaking wet, the brigades do not receive boiling water, which Russian people with all seriousness call "tea." Such a careless stoker will be clobbered by his comrades, reprimanded by the administration, fired from the job, placed in the punishment cell, and then sent to "general work."

The last option is the worst for a person who belongs to the camp service staff. The threat "go to the forest" hangs over everyone who had the good fortune to find work in the camp service sector: the better his placement, the more terrible the threat. Social inequality in the Soviet Union is the most blatant precisely in the labor camp, where the difference between kitchen manager or any other manager and the ordinary zek who is driven into the forest every morning is greater than that between a millionaire and a shoeshine boy in New York.

All the above-mentioned buildings are situated on a slope and do not take up much space. The rest of the camp territory is a swampy lowland that smells of decay, where one can hear the toads croaking. No one goes there except the orderlies, who draw water from the low well with a leaky bucket attached by a hook. A large puddle surrounds the well. In the summer after rain and constantly in spring and fall, this entire part of the camp is an impassable swamp. The street, too, drowns in mud.

---

6. Kur is an abbreviation of the Russian for a special regime punishment cell, but it is also a pun, as the term "kur" evokes the Russian word for chicken, "kuritsa."

7. The orderly is a prisoner assigned to take care of the barracks; he or she is responsible for bringing boiling water to his barrack.

Several years ago, a forest stood where the camp is now. The prisoners uprooted it, but to this day, the entire camp is full of ruts, ditches, and stumps. The enormous exposed roots lie around everywhere like monstrous octopuses or dead spiders, lifting their twisted wooden tentacles to the sky. On a rainy autumn day, these torn out roots, strewn across the road, give the camp a look of convulsive, mute despair, resembling those live beings who scurry among them. Alongside stand stumps grounded in the earth, and it seems as if their underground roots still dream about the tall crown and live greenery, just as a person with an amputated leg still feels a tremor in the missing toes.

It was not always so good and comfortable at Square 48. Old-timers told the Westerners how this camp had been built. With their own hands, the prisoners built the places for their imprisonment. In 1937, when a wave of millions of prisoners flowed to the north, there was nothing at this spot. People lived in tents in the forest during the harsh winter, spending nights around the campfire in the snow, without food or medicine. Those who arrived first left their bones here. Square 48, just as other camps, rests on human bones. People here froze and perished from starvation. There was a time when it was impossible to carry bread for distribution for a hundred meters without an armed guard. Half of the group from Georgia and Kazakhstan, people of the torrid south, died during one winter here. Only 250 remained from a group of 500. The person who told this to me, a Georgian from near Batumi, was not an old man, but after three years in the BBK, he was a goner—a feeble invalid destined to die. Not half but one hundred percent of his group eventually perished in the Onega forests. We Poles arrived with everything already prepared, and people congratulated us on "your good fortune that you arrived in 1940 and not in 1937 or 1933."

Relatives and loved ones will not visit the anonymous graves of the prisoners. The families of the deceased are not informed of their deaths, and only many years of silence signal a person's death in camp. While people are alive, they write. In the so-called "open" camps, one may not only receive but also write letters. In special circumstances and after lengthy bothersome efforts, it is possible even to obtain a visit with a prisoner. A zek can write once a month or once every three months; these restrictions are not enforced equally in every camp. "Closed" camps lie in the far north, in the Arctic zone and north of it. Especially "dangerous" elements are sent there. People in those camps do not have the right of correspondence or a meeting with family. Those who wind up there are buried alive and will never return to the circle of the living. If they are ordinary people, they will soon be forgotten.

If they are well known, people will think that they died but will not know the date.

After serving his five, eight, or ten years, the prisoner does not receive permission to return to his former place of residence. Most often, he remains where he is. People know him here, and his past will not compromise him. He becomes a settler, finds work related to some camp, and with time can advance in the service. We were told that almost every camp commander who came to Square 48 from Pyalma or Medvezhegorsk was a former prisoner. Ex-prisoners who leave for Central Russia or other "normal" regions of the Soviet Union receive a mark in their passport indicating their camp stay; this makes it impossible for them ever to receive responsible or well-paid work. Legendary "exceptions to the rule" only confirm the rule. And the rule is that no matter where they settle, they will be entered into the NKVD lists, and at the next opportunity, they will be the first candidates to return to camp.

The Soviet regime with total justification and logic cannot trust someone who spent even a short time in camp and saw the regime's shameful secret. For such people, liberation and return to freedom is only an interlude or vacation that in a few years will be followed by return to camp. Soviet camps are full of people who became resigned to imprisonment as their fate. They were first arrested in the 1920s; since then they have been released and sent back to camp two or three times. In each trainload of prisoners bringing reinforcements to the camp, among the newcomers are "veterans," for whom the camp zone is their home. Passing through the guardhouse, they naturally and instantly enter the familiar and customary routine of camp life.

10

Rabguzhsila [Man/horsepower]

RABGUZHSILA IS A brilliant camp word. The camp is comprised of people—
that is, a [human] work force (Russian abbreviation *rabsila*)[1]—and of horses
(*guzhevaya sila*)—that is, transport. The word man/horsepower [*rabguzhsila*]
joins people and animals together for work tasks and equates them in dignity,
value, and destiny.

The camp boss Petrov, a lanky, lame Civil War veteran and former Red partisan, was thoroughly bewildered when he saw the strange man/horsepower
at Square 48. The horses were typical camp horses: nags, skeletons standing
on shaky feet, hides covered with raw sores, chewing their government ration
of hay. But the people! Never before had there been such people assigned
to felling trees: Westerners, Polish Jews, a scrawny people dressed in elegant
suits, speaking foreign languages, and not understanding anything around
them. The women were wives of Polish officers, proud, aristocratic. Petrov
was even more astonished when 350 Galician Jews from Złoczów[2] arrived at
the camp. These Jews had been taken hastily; there had not been enough time
to interrogate them or confiscate their valuables, and they brought with them
watches and gold rings, walked around in black kaftans and caps, and looked
like clergy of an unknown Judaic denomination. Some brought several thousand rubles, which were confiscated and consigned to the financial sector in
Pyalma.

Petrov began by assembling the group for a conversation and saying:

---

1. *Rabsila* is the shortened form of the Russian for work force—*rabochaia sila*. *Rab*, however, is
Russian for slave; thus, the term might suggest slave labor.

2. Now part of Ukraine, it is called Zolochiv.

"You do not have terms or sentences. You are cultured people, foreigners. But the thing is that you are in a corrective labor camp and, consequently, you must submit to the camp regime. Let us hope that your situation will soon be clarified, but in the meantime, please work. In the Soviet Union, he who does not work does not eat."

The following day, a woman doctor, a prisoner named Vagner, arrived from Pyalma and determined our ability to work. They divided us into three categories: the first and second for heavy labor and the third for lighter work. Next were invalids of the first and second degrees with partial or complete disability. It was incomprehensible what the last category was supposed to do in a corrective labor camp. They received less food than everyone else did, but everybody envied them: they don't have to work.

The female doctor looked at my thick-lensed glasses, asked what I did as a free person, and relegated me to the third category—light work.

In practice, these distinctions made little difference. All categories merged in the forest. Petrov went through the barracks with his assistants and quickly divided people into brigades. The brigade leader does not ask who has been assigned to what category. The difference between weak and strong would become clear anyway. And woe to the weak.

In the course of two to three days, they divided us into three units. The first were the work brigades. There were about thirty brigades at Square 48, twenty to thirty people each. There were brigades of wood fellers, drivers, porters, unloaders, loaders, trawlers, sawyers, road builders, carpenters, stablemen, and tool workers. People had little understanding of what was expected of them. To explain the various tasks, they appointed work bosses, heads of sites, foremen, forestry experts, inspectors, and road building experts—all prisoners, experienced Russian camp inmates except for a few "free men," that is, former zeks or exiled settlers.

Several "Westerners" who seemed more energetic and smarter than others were appointed brigade leaders. Veteran Russian foresters from neighboring camps headed other brigades.

About 120 people were assigned to "camp service work." They were designated as cooks, bakers, shoemakers, tailors, barbers, boiler attendants—there were over thirty orderlies alone. For the last job, they chose the weaker, old people. Some people, however, made careers. A zek named Friedman, a chauffeur by profession, a healthy, sturdy fellow, was appointed head of the punishment cell. Women were assigned to the laundry, as sweepers, or cleaners; from the remaining women they put together a forest brigade for burning the debris from the felling. For this task, they sent a French language teacher, the wife of a colonel, the wife of a pastry chef from Tarnov, and other such types. The old Jew Nirenshtein was placed in charge of them.

The third group, in addition to the workers and camp service staff, were the "trusties" [Russian—*pridurki*], a camp term apparently derived from a word describing those who circled around the authorities, impostors, pretending to work but actually doing nothing while others plodded in the forest. The trusties are an office clan, people of "intellectual labor," which in camp is regarded as a sinecure, an evasion of the burden, not only by the drab prisoner mass but also by the administration itself. Trusties are the camp bureaucracy. Their number is strictly limited to four or five percent of the total number of zeks, and it is controlled from the center. At our Square 48, there were almost twice as many trusties than the norm. This was a result of the unusual conditions at our camp: many of the zeks did not understand Russian; the administration, as usual, without exception, basically illiterate, encountered difficulties at every step and found it difficult to reduce the staff when the appointed trusties were unable to cope with the work because of inexperience and the complexity of the matter.

I was ready to take my place as an economist, when suddenly the chief accountant approached—a young Soviet zek named Mai with a big Adam's apple, thin face, and piercing eyes—and said:

"Drop that work, go to the commander, and you will be a secretary." I did not want to leave my "tranquil" spot but to no avail. Petrov needed a person who knew the Russian language. Learning that I was a person "with an education," he decided that he could not have a better secretary. In this, alas, he was mistaken. In the given case, "an education" was an obstacle. My own stupidity blocked me from a great career in the camp. According to the regulations, the position of the commander's secretary (he is also a record keeper) is to be held by a free hired person; I thus appeared in the camp lists under the heading "substitute for a hired worker." A quick-witted person or veteran camp inmate in this position would quickly have gained the commander's trust, become his right hand, "alter ego," and the scourge of the camp. He would have been well fed, shod, clothed in the best, and would have called the shots for his fellow zeks. I neither understood nor took advantage of all these possibilities. The excellent start of my camp life rapidly deteriorated.

Petrov led me into his office. In the entryway before the office stood a table, a chair, and a simple cabinet—all unembellished camp work—and on the side was a wall telephone. I would receive and dispatch mail, compose letters and orders for the camp, receive and convey telephone messages. Each morning I would submit the "summaries" for the previous day: the condition of the workers, the implementation of work, and the report of the medical sector. At hand was the book of "incoming" and of "outgoing" material, a book of telephone messages, a file of the division and a file of the administration, and a book of orders for the camp. This all sounds impressive, but I had neither ink, pencil, paper, nor glue; the telephone was broken and barely worked, and my "books" consisted of pages of old, used paper that I would write on only crossways and which zeks would steal from me so that they could roll cigarettes for themselves.

Petrov would affix his resolutions on the incoming papers with his large slanted handwriting: "To the educator—for your information"—"To the chief accountant for implementation"—"To the commandant for verification." My job entailed not only bringing these resolutions with the camp boss's instructions to the attention of the designated people but also seeing that they really understood and implemented the matters under discussion.

My assistant was Peterfreund, a tiny dwarf, a fellow of about twenty from Nowi Targ in Poland. His childish figure amused the forestry workers, and he was appointed as an office courier. All day long, Peterfreund, dressed in a pea jacket that reached to his heels and, like a puss in boots, with enormous boots rushed around the camp on errands. The guards at the watchtower knew him and would call him "Sonny"; they used to ask him mainly scabrous questions and would roar with laughter at his replies. When I would go to dinner at seven o'clock in the evening, Peterfreund would replace me at the telephone and in the boss's office.

The work was not difficult but complicated. I would receive all kinds of messages from the zeks for the camp boss. These included complaints, requests for receiving money from a personal account or for a transfer from one brigade to another. Prisoners were not permitted to have more than 50 rubles in their possession. Within that limit, they were able to request each month that the financial department transfer money to them from their accounts. The camp boss would forward their requests along with a "reference" from the Cultural-Educational Sector that stated how the given zek was working and behaving. If the "reference" was good, the department would transfer 20 to 30 rubles. I not only received these requests but also wrote them myself for illiterate zeks so that my table soon turned into a "request bureau." Requests to transfer from one brigade to another were reviewed twice monthly—on the first and fifteenth of the month. Petrov would misplace most of the requests and never read them. A person did not mean much in camp. My reminders annoyed him: "Here's a defender!"

I felt best when Petrov would leave for "production," that is, to the forest, and I would be left alone with my papers. I was hopelessly alien. I did not swear, did not tell jokes, and did not display any zeal for my work. Once, when I arrived for work, I overheard Petrov and Mai discussing me:

"An educated man," said Petrov, "but what good is that: here you need a strong hand, to pressure, to yell: but is he capable of that? He sits like a mouse. Too polite."

"And dissatisfied," said Mai. "He's dissatisfied with the camp and he criticizes it."

"And they are all dissatisfied!" said Petrov angrily. "The scum don't want to work."

That was the truth. We did not know how to work, did not want to work, and complained endlessly.

The complaints were first and foremost about hunger. Our kitchen had four "cauldrons" signifying rations with differing degrees of nourishment. The first one was the penal ration for those who did not fulfill the work norm. Those who did not fulfill the norm one hundred percent received 500 grams of bread and a thin soup in the morning and evening.

Those in the second category, who fulfilled the norm one hundred percent, received 700 grams of bread, soup in the morning, and soup and kasha in the evening. This data applies to 1940, when the Soviet Union was not at war. Subsequently, it became much worse.

The third, "shock troop" ration was for those who surpassed the norm by up to 125 percent.

The fourth food category, called the "Stakhanovite,"[3] was for those who fulfilled 150 percent of the norm or higher. The Stakhanovites received the best food possible: 900 grams of bread or sometimes a kilo, two servings of food in the morning and four in the evening: soup, kasha with butter, a baked dish from macaroni or peas, a roll or a "cutlet." The terms "cutlet" or "goulash" designated rotten horsemeat. The basic nourishment for all four categories was black bread. On paper, one was supposed to receive also fats and sugar but, in fact, there wasn't any or there was almost none. . . . Salted fish was added to the second food ration—a piece of cod, vobla [Caspian roach fish], humpback salmon, or hitherto unfamiliar to us, dolphin.

Only the third and fourth ration categories enabled you to eat enough in 1940. The first and second ones doomed you to death sooner or later. Therefore, the only road to salvation for a person who did not receive packages or other help was to surpass the norm by 125 to 150 percent. The norms were calculated

---

3. A Stakhanovite was an especially productive and industrious worker in the former Soviet Union, named after a legendary coal miner, Aleksey Stakhanov.

for healthy laborers. The law of natural selection operated in the camp: only the physically strong survived. The others died if they were not clever enough to find a cushy job—as the so-called *pridurki* or as technical specialists.

We did not discover all these things right away, but we did begin to starve immediately. The office, including myself, received the second ration, that is, "normal" food. In the morning, I ate half of the bread with soup, and by one in the afternoon, I was beastly hungry. There was no lunch. At one o'clock, Peterfreund and I drank hot water—*kipyatok*. At other places, it was customary to divide the ration into three parts, but at Square 48, they divided it in two. Only the Stakhanovites received kasha at midday. The others worked all day without food, but in the evening, they received more. I was not yet emaciated and was not doing physical work. Nevertheless, I found it hard to endure the daily fast.

At Square 48 the day began in the summer at five o'clock in the morning; in winter it started a half hour or hour later. In winter at that hour, it is completely dark; the moon shines over the camp. The trusty on duty comes out of the office, approaches a scrap of the railroad track that is hanging on a pole in the street, picks up a stone or piece of rusty steel, and forcefully strikes the rail. The muffled, doleful sound resounds in the darkness. The barracks are silent, as if they do not hear. The fellow on duty strikes powerfully several times, until his shoulder aches, and he returns to the office, where a sooty kerosene kitchen lamp has been burning all night. In the dark lairs, people begin to stir on the bed boards. "Get up!" The ominous, gloomy sound, like a tocsin, comes from afar, emerges from the subconscious, and interrupts the soundest sleep. People gradually awaken, sober up, and remain prone for a few minutes with their eyes open. Then a wave passes through the barracks; everyone rises at once, and the orderly yells in a strident voice: "Get up!"

Before the signal, the orderly has already managed to drop by the drying house and the repair shop. He has brought a pile of rags from the drying house and heaped them on the floor by the door. Each person searches for his things that he handed over for drying the previous evening. In a separate pile lie the mended items. Each thing has a tag—that is, a wooden tab with a surname and brigade number. All night in the mending workshop, the prisoners' torn rags are patched and fixed, patches are placed on patches, and decrepit boots are stitched with twine so that the prisoners are able to wear them to work in the morning. People curse and rush around, searching for their belongings. One is missing his rag boots, another has received his padded trousers unmended because it was impossible to fix them anymore, and he curses so that the entire barrack can hear; a third is seeking the person who took his jacket and left him his own short, dirty one. In the meantime, the orderly has brought water for the barrel and placed a pail of boiling water next to it. Not everyone washes. In work barracks, few people have soap and a towel; people are black and dirty; many do not wash between the obligatory visits to the bathhouse. The majority splash themselves with water from a mug and dry themselves with their sleeves. It is not worth smartening up as you'll never get rid of the dirt anyway. And there's no time. An hour and a half—at most two hours—pass from rising until going out to work.

Queues are already forming under the kitchen windows, the Stakhanovites separate from the first and second ration groups. In the winter, in the darkness, with minus thirty degrees frost, the fingers stiffen in the torn mittens, and it is easy to lose one's coupon. Whoever loses it will receive nothing and will go hungry until the next morning. Someone on the other side of the window takes the coupon, tears it in half, and returns the other half—that is for supper. The coupons are made from old tram tickets from Leningrad, homemade tickets with the signature of the clerk and the office stamp; in some puzzling fashion, more slips always arrive in the kitchen than were handed out. Another person mechanically stirs the cauldron and ladles out soup. "Next!" One carefully carries the valuable portion to the barrack, which is sometimes at the other end of the camp. There people are already sitting at the table in a close circle, bundled up and ready to leave for work, and they slurp hastily. Others eat in the depth of the bunks, where their camp property lies: a wooden footlocker and a rolled-up blanket. The barrack is smelly and crowded. The door opens, and the work supervisor appears on the threshold with a list from which he reads the names of those exempt from work for the day. Those who are exempt are lying down amidst the general commotion. The reveille is not for them. They will get up later when the brigades leave, the camp empties out, and there won't be a queue under the kitchen window.

The gong rings again, this time for assembling and marching off to work [razvod]. The brigade leaders assemble and lead people to the guardhouse. On all sides, lines of prisoners stretch out from the barrack doors. Like funeral processions following a coffin, they march slowly, reluctantly, as if it takes a great effort to lift one's feet. All these people are walking against their will. The orderly hurries the laggards: "faster, they are already driving people on the march." The camp inmates do not go: they are "driven out."

It is not easy to assemble five hundred to seven hundred people near the guardhouse. Each brigade lines up separately. Someone is always missing. Cursing, the brigade leaders rush from the guardhouse to the barracks and back. Finally, like mad dogs, people from the second section—work supervisors, assistants to the commandant—race around the barracks. They search the bunks, check whether anyone has curled up in a ball under his jacket, and peep under the bed boards. They are looking for people who are trying to shirk work. Many hide in the outhouses or in nooks and crannies, but it is not easy to hide from the work supervisors. From all sides, with curses and blows, they lead people to the guardhouse. Not everyone is capable of being a work supervisor. It is the most difficult task in the camp, for which you need strong and merciless people. They themselves do not work—their job is to force others to work.

In most cases, the refuser who is caught complains of weakness or illness. An on-duty medic or doctor stands by the guardhouse during the march to work. There is no time for conversations with the refusers. They take their temperature and if it is not above normal, nothing will help: "Go to work, come in the evening." Someone complains of a hernia, a pain in the stomach. The doctor waves his hand dismissively and leaves. The gates open, the entire camp administration and a mass of armed guards stand by in attendance. Official caps, fur hats, rifles with bayonets. The brigades are called out in order. The guard on duty counts each one and makes a mark on a wooden tablet.

"Brigade, attention!"

People stand in pairs. The brigade leader is in the first row. He checks whether all have received an "instrument": saws, axes, shovels, crowbars. The doors of the tool warehouse are open, and tools for each brigade are allocated. The sharpest saws and finest axes are reserved for the Stakhanovites and the best workers.

"Brigade, attention! On the way to your work place, no talking; maintain order; no stepping out of line. In case of disobedience, I shoot without warning. Got it?"

The young guard recites the memorized words in a salvo, as if repeating a lesson, and with such concentration that people start laughing. When he hesitates, they prompt him. Every morning, every zek hears these words. He hears them thousands of times, for five years or ten years, as the refrain of his entire existence. When he leaves the camp, no matter where he will settle, these words will ring in his ears.

When the camp gates close behind the last brigade, the office workers still have an hour before their workday begins. One can get dressed and have breakfast without hurrying.

Again, the gong clangs: it is a roll call. At the signal, people in the barracks come out to the square by the guardhouse and are counted. Everyone comes out, even those who are ill, except the ones in the infirmary. The orderlies

and those engaged in important matters stay behind. An armed guard or assistant to the commandant enters every barrack. Communication between
barracks is halted. Everyone freezes in place. They take a long time counting,
make mistakes, and start counting over again. In the meantime, they push a
group of refusers who were discovered after the assembly for work into the
punishment cell. Now it is too late to send them to work, as there are no
armed guards to conduct them outside the guardhouse to the brigade. In
the punishment cell, they will receive a penal ration: 300 grams of bread and
thin soup. For refusing to go to work, they will receive several days in the
punishment cell although still "going out to work." That means that the next
morning, they will be conveyed directly from the punishment cell to the assembly point, and in the evening after work, directly from the guardhouse,
the head of the punishment cell will return his people to the cell. If the refuser
is stubborn and does not want to go to work on the second day, too, then the
matter becomes serious. An "educator" will come to him at the punishment
cell, that is, a person from the KVCh (cultural-educational sector). Let us
not forget that we are in a corrective labor camp; here people are corrected
and re-educated. The educator tries all means of persuasion and admonition.
A stubborn refuser who is not broken by several days of punishment cell and
hunger has a chance of attaining concessions from the authorities, that is, they
may give him easier work.

The main reason for refusals is backbreaking work. If persuasion does not
help, a "report" will be drawn up about malicious refusal to work. The brigade
leader and commandant or other people compose the report, which must include a note by the doctor that the given zek is healthy enough to work and a
remark by the camp boss that he is satisfactorily shod, clothed, and fed. This
report is transmitted to the third (the political) section. When several such
reports have piled up (ten or more), the third section goes into action and
does its job: they shoot the prisoner.

The list of those shot for multiple refusals to work will be printed in
Medvezhegorsk with copies sent to all camp sectors of the BBK. Such a copy
will also arrive at Square 48. The file clerk, zek Margolin, will assign a number,
register it in the incoming mail, and convey it to the camp boss. The boss
Petrov will add a remark: "Inform the prisoners via the KVCh." And the educator will explain to the slow-witted "Westerners" that no one is forced to
work in camp, but if one refuses to work, one will be tried and sentenced to
capital punishment.

The commandant Panchuk is walking around the camp. The orderlies
tremble. The commandant is a free person with high cheekbones, an unruly

cowlick, and the manners of a Cossack constable. Upon his entering a barrack, the command resounds: "Attention!" and everyone rises. Panchuk's booming curses are heard at a distance. In one of the barracks, he finds disorder: the bunks and the floor are not washed, and there is dirt by the entrance. He looks at the orderly with the greatest scorn and asks, "What are you? Turks or something? Did you live like that at home, too?"

He commands the orderly Kiva, a bent old Jew who does not understand a word of Russian: "This minute, bring water—do you understand? Wash, clean, wipe, sweep—do you understand? Tidy up; clean up under the bed boards, on the boards, outside, inside! Look at me . . . you motherfucker, or else I'll take you out yourself . . . do you understand?" Panchuk dashes into the office and finds the camp boss's door locked.

"Open!"

"It's locked, citizen director!"

Panchuk squints, stares at me, and I feel that his hand is itching to slap me on the ear.

"What was the point of educating you, four eyes! Open it with a nail."

"I don't know how, citizen director."

"You don't know how; come here and learn!"

And Panchuk shows me how to open a locked door without using a key.

When I try to give Panchuk papers addressed to the commandant, he quickly waves his hand and disappears. He is no expert at reading, and every written line arouses his distrust and apprehension. My situation is difficult. If it is written on a piece of paper in Petrov's hand "Give to the commandant," I am obliged to do so, but how can I force the commandant to take the paper and also to sign that he received it? My authority is insufficient for this, all the more so because each received paper means a new bother for Panchuk. My work is full of unforeseen difficulties. There are no office supplies and I have to find everything on my own. An envelope is required for an important report to Medvezhegorsk, but there are no envelopes. I have to make an envelope myself. A scrap of paper is the greatest treasure in the camp. An envelope requires glue. One also has to make glue on one's own. You can't ask for it; that's naïve and annoys the administration. "Get it yourself."

Tables, summaries, and reports are written on plywood in the camp because of the lack of paper. Buttons, shovels, spoons, and bowls are also made of wood. It is the only thing available locally in a sufficient amount. Westerners are so helpless, however, that they are at a loss when they have to scrape off yesterday's note from the plywood. They ask for an eraser. Panchuk is beside himself: "You don't know to erase with glass?"

"There is no glass, citizen commandant."

"What kind of people!" wonders Panchuk. "They can't find glass. Look, here it is—glass."

He goes into the courtyard and, in a minute, finds a piece of broken glass on the ground under the window.

The Westerners do not know how to do anything—neither to open a lock with a nail, scrape off plywood with glass, light a lamp without matches, nor to work on a hungry stomach.

Lamps are also a source of grief. There is no electricity at Square 48. There is so little kerosene that it is not distributed to the workers' barracks. The Westerners do not know how to manage with broken, rusty kerosene lamps where the wick is not a wick, the system does not work, and the glass is cracked. If there is kerosene, then the wick is no good. If there is a wick, then the kerosene does not burn. The burner sleeve falls out of the lamp font, and when Peterfreund puts the glass chimney back on, it bursts and we blanch in horror.

The commandant falls into a rage when he sees the broken glass.

"Five days in the punishment cell for such a deed! You are killing me! Where shall I get glass? Better you should break your head, you damn fascist! We have enough heads but we don't have glass!"

At the last minute, everything is resolved in the simplest manner. In one of the barracks, an orderly has got hold of a lamp, and at night in the dark, Peterfreund, the little gnome, slips in and steals it. We are saved for now: the commandant's office has light.

Seven o'clock in the evening. Having worked for twelve hours, the brigades pass through the guardhouse in a steady stream. But they are far from rest. The tormented, filthy, sweaty people wash off the dirt and sweat and run to stand in line for food. In the open air, they stand in long lines under the kitchen windows in the darkness. In the middle of supper, the signal for the evening roll call erupts. In the winter, they carry out the count in the barracks; in the summer, everyone goes out to the courtyard and stands patiently for a long time. After dinner and roll call, you immediately have to take off the damp, torn clothing; otherwise, the orderly will not collect it for drying and mending. Lights out are at 9:00 or at 9:30. People are sleeping. On a table in the middle of the barrack, an oil lamp glimmers dimly; the night orderly sits at the table with his head on his hands, fighting sleep. If the night round catches him sleeping, he will lose his job and land in the punishment cell.

Only in two places are people bustling around until late in the evening. One place is the clinic. With a camp population of one thousand people, it is normal that from fifty to hundred will come to the reception hours in the evening. Not everyone obtains an exemption from work. It is given with difficulty. The medic is responsible for his actions, and if he exempts too many, then in a few days he will receive an inquiry from the center. The medic risks his position if he is too liberal. He cannot release everyone who deserves it. The first thirty easily obtain exemptions but when the crowd at the door does not thin out, the attitude toward the people changes. No complaints or wounds produce an impression. The doctor, who has already seen sixty people, looks indifferently and says, "Go to work" without looking. You can't have pity on everyone. Too many exemptions have already been given, and people are still breaking down the doors. They carry on and threaten. For this situation, however, there are robust medical orderlies with whom it is better not to fight.

Late at night, the list of exempted zeks goes to the work supervisor. While leaving, the sick person looks suspiciously at the doctor: "Am I released?" The doctor does not tell him his decision. The next morning before dispatch to work, the sick man does not hear his name when the list of the exempted is read out. What a misfortune! He starts to question again, "Comrade supervisor, look again! Is my name really missing? It can't be!" Used to such questions, the work supervisor does not answer them, and the person who stood in line for two hours in vain last night begins to dress, groaning and cursing.

The other place where life begins only in the evening is the office of the camp boss and the brigade leaders' rooms where they draw up the "work reports." After supper, when people have gone to sleep, each brigade leader goes to write up a complete report on his brigade's work. It is not easy. He has to provide a detailed description of the work carried out by each squad[4] and each individual in two categories: the quantity of work and the percentage of the norm that was fulfilled. The sick ones and refusers are listed separately. Work reports are confirmed by the work boss or foreman who received the work; without their signatures, they are not valid. Drawing up the report is not a simple task: the brigade's bread depends on it. Based on this document, the food distribution clerk reckons the amount of bread and the food ration to which each brigade member is entitled. On the third day after the report, the zek receives a coupon and the bread ration that he has "earned."

---

4. Group of three to eight people.

In filling out the report, one has to consider many varied circumstances: you have to know to describe the work without harming anyone. You have to know how to calculate and exaggerate; usually the brigade leader does not compose the report alone but with a trusted person in the brigade. If one person fulfilled sixty percent of the norm and another two hundred percent, they will ascribe one hundred ten percent to the first and one hundred fifty to the other. In any case, the Stakhanovite will receive the fourth ration, and the sixty percenter will gain the second category and an extra piece of bread. You have to feed the brigade with the help of juggling figures on paper. "The pencil will feed" is a camp saying. Every means are used to fudge the missing percentages. The norm for sawing wood is 2.5 cubic meters of wood per person. Hungry, inexperienced people cannot do that. In the report, they then add on "carrying for 40 meters," as if they carried the logs for sawing a distance of 40 meters. The norm setter and the foreman turn a blind eye to this stunt; after all, they, too, are prisoners, and everyone understands that you have to support the hard laborers. If you followed the regulations literally, then everyone would starve.

The work report, prepared after long consultations and efforts, is a fantastic combination of truth and invention. First, the brigade leader gives himself 150 percent and the fourth food ration although he did not work at all. Next, he takes care of his friends and assistants. Then he gives high percentages to those whom he has to: the hard workers who do the work of two people and the bandits whom it is dangerous to antagonize. In contrast, there are those whom the brigade leader wants to squeeze out of the brigade or punish. The first rule of camp wisdom is "be on good terms with the brigade leader." Your bread depends on him, and frequently, in order to feed the brigade, he takes a personal risk, reporting accomplishments that were not and could not be.

At nine o'clock in the evening, the camp boss arrives from outside the zone and his office fills up with people. His office is a bare room, a table with a kerosene lamp; along the walls are stools and benches made in the camp; on the wall is a portrait of Voroshilov[5] and the sign "Do not drink unboiled water" or a huge picture of a louse with the inscription "Carrier of typhus." The work bosses, forestry experts, and other functionaries fill the room. They sit until midnight or later, smoke cheap tobacco [*makhorka*[6]], and drink an enormous

---

5. Kliment Voroshilov (1881–1969) was a member of the Politburo and defense minister of the Soviet Union from 1934–1940.

6. *Makhorka* is the cheapest, most common form of tobacco in camp. It is rolled into cigarettes.

quantity of unboiled water for lack of any other. Peterfreund keeps running to the boiler room to see whether the water has boiled. They discuss orders from the center, yesterday's results, and draw up the most important camp document—the work schedule.

The work schedule for the next day lists the allocation of brigades to work places and the tasks for each brigade. Heavy bargaining begins with various brigade leaders: "Tomorrow your brigade must supply no less than sixty cubic meters of wood. If you give it, you will received ten packages of *makhorka* for the brigade; if you don't, you'll lose your job." The brigade leaders are called into the office in turn; they hem and haw, spread their arms in dismay, make excuses, bargain, and set terms: get rid of the weak people and give us serviceable tools. The brigade leaders are in a touchy position. It is dangerous not to appear zealous, but it is also dangerous to promise 60 cubic meters of wood and not deliver: two or three unfulfilled promises and the angry boss will accuse him of wrecking. If you promise and deliver 60, the next day they will demand 70. The rule of the camp administration is that the zeks can always do more than they are doing now. If they can fulfill the norm, then they also can surpass it. The administration's job is to pressure, which it does with promises or threats. Alternately, peals of laughter, good-natured cursing, thumping on the table or furious swearing come from the office. There is always swearing; camp talk cannot do without it.

From time to time, an order comes from the office: "Summon brigade leader Kunin!" "Summon Doctor German!" "Summon zek so-and-so!" A prisoner summoned to the camp boss—sometimes at midnight, when he is snoring and dreaming his third dream—simply does not want to go. He sends the messenger to the devil, does not want to get dressed, and knows that no good can come from the conversation with the boss: he can expect punishment for poor work or for a mistake in carrying out his job, and it is quite possible that they will take him straight from the office to the punishment cell. Often it is therefore necessary to summon the worker several times, and he does not start dressing until they threaten him with three days of the punishment cell and drag him by the feet off the upper bunks.

Time passes. While the bosses converse in the office, near the door in the small antechamber stands a crowd of those who have been summoned and those who came on their own with grievances. One was robbed, another beaten, and a third came to show his bare body and ask that they allocate him whole trousers for the next day. A dramatic struggle plays out around several blankets that are in the warehouse. In the end, they go to the hero of the day—the brigade leader who produced the best results that day and promised to surpass it tomorrow.

Sitting in the entryway, the "secretary" has to be on the alert; otherwise, in five minutes, he will be left with no pen, pencil, or paper on the table. Grasping hands will pilfer everything, especially paper, which is needed for rolling cigarettes. People sit on the window sill, squat along the walls, and crowd around the table, barefoot, uncombed, bare chested, in open jackets. The telephone rings: from the department they are transmitting a telephone message or calling the camp boss to the phone to berate him for not delivering sufficient lumber and not fulfilling the plan. Nothing is audible in the commotion, and in the end, with savage curses and shoves, they push the entire waiting crowd, together with the agitated zeks who are expecting to be sent to the punishment cell, out into the courtyard.

Finally, the evening session is over, and everyone disperses.

The on-duty clerk sits at the empty table.

Night is the time for sending and receiving telephone messages and summaries from the camp sector to the department and back. During the day, the lines are overloaded and it is impossible to make the connection. The telephone operator and the switchboard are at the guardhouse, and one must call there first to get a line. Barely audible, the orders arrive.

"To the bosses of all camp sectors and OLPs: I order! According to the directive of the people's commissar ... according to order no. . . . speed up the rate of transports. . . . In a week's time liquidate the backlog. . . . I order: fire for not fulfilling the norm . . . Bring charges against . . . For the last time, I warn you . . . Bring to your attention . . . Pass a strict reprimand. . . ."

For the entire long night in the Onega forest, the bosses, chief accountants, commandants, supply chiefs, technical supervisory staff, and guards converse among themselves. The camp is immersed in darkness. A light is burning only in the watchtowers, where the sentries are. The forest rustles, gusts of wind shake the treetops. Murmuring and rumbling, as the sound of the sea surf, emerge from the forest. All night the guard dogs howl savagely. To the man at the table, it all seems like a dream. How did he land here? What is he doing here?

Night rounds. The guards make the rounds of the barracks, glance into the office, and leaf through the papers on the table. "Who's this?" In the adjacent room, the Registration and Distribution Bureau, zeks who work in that office are sleeping on the same tables at which they work during the day.

At two o'clock at night, the telephone rings, and the dispatcher of the department announces the arrival of a train of eighteen cars at such-and-such a sector for loading.

Alarm! This train is arriving with a delay of thirty-six hours; nevertheless, once it arrives it must be loaded immediately because the camp boss is responsible from his own pocket for a delay, and the zek has to answer to the administration. Alarm! The on-duty clerk calls the guardhouse and asks to wake the boss. He then runs to the senior supervisor, Grib, who dresses hastily. In the middle of the night, he has to wake up the brigade of loaders, who returned from work late at night and are sleeping like logs after their twelve or fifteen hours of hard work. Going to them now is like a tamer entering a cage of rapacious beasts. Before entering the barrack, the supervisor secretly crosses himself. The armed guards follow him, just in case.

The awakened zeks snarl and snap, call the gods and devils as witnesses that they have worked their full, they can no longer stand on their feet, and their hands and shoulders are injured. "Go to . . .! Get out of here. Don't push us to sin!" But the supervisor is tougher than steel; you can't wear him down. First, he tries kindness, then threats. The brigade leader comes to his aid. They start to trap the more meek and obedient. When three or four have gotten up, it is easier to talk to the rest. The camp boss enters, upset, angry, sleepy. "Brethren," he says, "fellows, don't let me down." He promises them rewards, unbelievable food, and a minute later, he gnashes his teeth and threatens to drive them to their grave. On both sides, crazed faces show furor and despair. These nocturnal scenes of sending to work people who are enervated, woozy from exhaustion and yearning for sleep are full of explosive tension. A clash between the zek and the administration always ends in the victory of the supervisors and the bosses, who are backed up by the entire apparatus of power: bayonets, revolvers, and the allocation of the meager camp rations.

In an hour or two, they will march out the brigade, but while they are making efforts at persuasion, the entire camp is agitated. People wake up in the neighboring barracks and lift their heads: "What's going on there?" "They're taking out a brigade. Quiet! Or else they'll get us up too!" Loading after work hours at night in the forest, in the rain, snow, or storm—just the thought makes you shudder. "If they only would let us sleep until reveille." The people who are going out now will not return until they finish their job, even if it continues all night and all day. The sole possibility for them to return to the camp to rest is to dispatch that cursed train.

Again, it is quiet in the camp. The hours pass. Finally, the telephone rustles drily in the office. The guardhouse reports that it is time to give the signal for rising: it is 5:30 a.m. The on-duty clerk puts on his jacket and wanders into the street. In a minute, one hears the deep, resonant blows of the stone on the piece of rail: boom-boom-boom!

And a new day begins at Square 48.

II

Conversations

THE PEOPLE WHO sent one thousand Polish Jews to Square 48 gave them three weeks' time to turn into lumbermen and full-fledged workers. They told them: "Your past does not interest us. You must work. That is the basic law of Soviet life. He who does not work does not eat. Your salvation lies in labor. If you are weak, then work will make you strong. If you are ill, work will make you healthy. You have nothing else to do in camp but work, and if you do not work, you will perish."

The merciless work norms in a Soviet camp were calculated on the basis of the complete utilization of the strength of a healthy Russian *muzhik*.[1] The easier the work, the higher the norm that had to be fulfilled. Ultimately, all work was equal and boiled down to the exploitation of the limits of one's physical strength and endurance.

There is no light work in the camps. Weaving brooms or weeding vegetable patches is easier than working in a mine or carrying heavy burdens, but the lightest work turns into torture if the norm exceeds one's strength. We never were strong enough to do what they demanded from us in order to receive enough food. The hungrier we were, the worse we worked. The worse we worked, the more we starved. There was no way out of the vicious circle.

At Square 48, the Soviet method came up against living beings. These people were Jews. We Zionists knew how difficult it was to make a hard laborer or a skilled worker out of a person who grew up in the conditions of a Jewish shtetl. In Europe, we devised a complex system of agricultural education for our youth. We would send them at the age of seventeen to eighteen to *hakhshara*, that is, to places of labor education for a year or two. In Palestine,

---

1. The word literally means peasant, but in this context, it signifies a simple Russian man.

we then provided them with the supervision of our organizations. Moreover, these youths received ideological preparation. They were enthusiastically aware of their historical mission and their role as a national avant-garde.

The Soviet regime sent masses of intellectuals, semi-intellectuals, civil servants, storekeepers, merchants, and petty Jewish artisans to the camps. It told them: "You have three weeks to learn to work. In the first week, it will suffice if you produce twenty-five percent of the norm. In the second week—fifty percent. In the third week—seventy-five percent. At the end of three weeks, you will work under the same conditions as any other zek."

This was the experiment that obtuse doctrinaire bureaucrats conducted on hundreds of thousands of people who had been seized abroad and placed in conditions of forced, hard physical labor. The experiment was supposed to provide an answer to the question: what can be obtained by the use of direct force? The means of coercion was hunger. The guiding principle—every person can do any physical work.

The Moscow experimenters knew, of course, that human casualties were unavoidable. After all, millions of Soviet people perished in the camps to which they sent us.

The Soviet zeks, observing the ineptitude of the Westerners, the majority of whom were taking an axe or saw in hand for the first time, said "You'll get used to it! And if you don't, then you'll croak."

Three weeks passed, however, and the Westerners at Square 48 did not begin to work. It was the beginning of September, and it was warm. In the forest, people felt like carnival actors performing in some absurd farce. They rummaged in the bushes for mushrooms and berries. An atmosphere of "passive resistance" developed. Hunger forced them to think not about Stakhanovite records but about selling things. They had brought enough things with them, and the local "free" workers paid high prices for Polish suits, shirts, and shoes. Trade flourished. After a while, packages from relatives and friends began to arrive in camp. Packages up to 8 kilos were permitted. A person who received 8 kilos of food products did not need the camp "percentages." This led to demoralization: a weak worker who regularly received packages from home would eat better than a Soviet Stakhanovite who busted his gut in order to earn the fourth food ration category.

Particularly farcical were the brigades of Galician Jews in their long frocks. There were cases when a brigade of thirty people together fulfilled ninety percent of one norm, that is, less than a single person was supposed to do. In the evening, the brigade leader divided this ninety percent among thirty people, that is, three percent per person. People received the first ration category, that is, half a kilo of bread and soup. According to their reasoning: "In any case, I can't do one hundred percent, but if for three percent, fifteen percent, or for fifty percent, they will assign the same first food ration, then why make the effort? Three percent is enough. I'll sell a pair of trousers and wait until they send the next package."

In the eyes of a Soviet person, this was a despicable, individualistic, anti-state calculation. Clearly, the relations between the BBK administration and such egoists were bound to deteriorate rapidly. At first, the administration watched the situation and did not undertake strict measures. The very fact that they had settled us "Poles" separately, in a special camp, elevated us, not only in our own opinion, but also in the opinion of the local authorities.

After a month, people arrived from Medvezhegorsk to see what was wrong, why the Westerners were not working. A high-ranking individual summoned several Westerners for a conversation. Among others, he summoned Tenenbaum, a taciturn, gloomy Jew who worked as a bookkeeper. They asked him about the Westerners' attitude toward the Soviet regime—were there fascists? He said that there were no fascists and everyone respected the Soviet regime, but the sole thing that Westerners did not like as an institution and a system was the camp.

They also summoned me. A portly NKVD official with puffy cheeks, wearing a cap with a red band, offered me a seat and asked the date of the Jewish New Year. I told him that I did not know the exact date.

"How can that be?" asked the functionary in astonishment. "I thought that you are from the clergy, a rabbi. Look, you have glasses and strange head gear."

I could not help but laugh. Indeed, my headgear was strange. They arrested me without a cap, and they sent to me in prison, among other things, my landlady's beret, a woman's beret, large and round, which looked like a chaplain's cap.

For the first time in his life, the chief saw such strange people as the Złoczów Hasidim with side locks, beards, and frock coats. I explained to him that among the Jews, this was similar to the Russian Old Believers. He understood that.

"You speak Russian well," he said. "And, in general, you are knowledge-able. Tell me your opinion: do you think these people will work or not?"

"No," I said. "In my opinion, these people will not work."

"Why?"

At this point, I gave him a full lecture. First, I told him, these people are not Russians; they are foreigners. In order to work normally, they must also live and eat normally, which is not the case here. Second, these people are Jews, that is, they are the least suited of all foreigners here for physical labor, which their ancestors have not engaged in for two thousand years. Third, these are refugees of war, victims of a Nazi pogrom, who have been cut off from their families for a year already and are languishing in a foreign land. They are nervous, physically weakened people, who should have been sent to rest and not to corrective labor camps. Fourth, these people are resentful and do not understand why they were sent to prison and deprived of their freedom. This is an important point because it is difficult to force people who feel that way to work enthusiastically. Fifth, these people do not believe that they will remain for a long time in camp. They consider their situation temporary and hope to return home soon.

I told him that because of cultural-historical, sociological, psychological, medical, and political considerations, it would be hard to expect that these Jews could meet the norm for felling trees.

Having heard my report, the high-ranking person became strangely cheerful and began to glance at me with laughing eyes.

"What an oddball," said my interlocutor. "What is your name? This is the first time I am hearing something like that. You can be sure, however, that we shall *force* all these people to work. They will work here like little lambs."

He did not add, "Or else go to hell." That ending was understood. I said those words to myself, having heard them earlier from less highly placed individuals.

A little over a month passed, and lightning struck. Our sentences arrived at the camp. First, they had arrested us and then convicted us. Until that time, we had been living without sentences, and the authorities were not sure whether to regard us as prisoners. Now all doubts were dispelled.

The Special Commission of the NKVD in Moscow,[2] having reviewed our cases, delivered sentences of three to five years of imprisonment for such crimes as the absence of a Soviet passport and presence on the territory of East Poland. They summoned all of us to the "Second Sector" [URB—Registration Distribution Office], and to each one they declared his sentence. I received five years on the basis of an article about a socially dangerous element—for violation of the passport regime. The elder Kunin brother received five years and the younger three, although they conducted themselves identically at

---

2. The Special Board (Russian acronym OSO) operated from the 1920s until 1953. It was a three-man board authorized to convict and sentence people in their absence and without the right of defense.

the interrogation and were equally guilty or innocent. It was totally incomprehensible why some received three years and others five. It seemed as if on several hundred thousand blanks, they placed the numbers three or five at random. I must say that the Westerners reacted to these sentences very insolently. In signing under the statement of the sentence, they laughed, shrugged, and behaved as if they did not take their sentences seriously.

Indeed, had we believed that we would have to spend five years at forced labor, we would have been ready to hang ourselves. It all seemed like a waking bad dream, fantastic nonsense, some kind of misunderstanding.

The surrounding Russians reacted differently: "They gave you childish terms," they said. "Three and five years—that's nothing. We get ten years. And once you get it—have no doubts! You will have to sit out the full term, 'from bell to bell.' Get your Warsaw out of your head. You'll never see Warsaw again any more than you see your ears."

A few days later, the bosses arrived in Square 48 from Pyalma: Drobyshevsky, Shevelev from the cultural-educational sector, and others. They assembled the people and started speaking in a business-like, frank manner. They explained that we had to abandon hopes of returning to Poland. We shall have to spend years in camps. Physical weakness does not exempt one from work. On the contrary, lying on the bed boards is sure death. Everyone to the forest to work!

For a start, Square 48 was supposed to give the Soviet state 15,000 cubic meters of wood a month. The prisoners, however, did not believe assistant commander Drobyshevsky. Something about these people divested their words of seriousness and weight. We saw that they did not understand or sense what was being done to us. We were further repelled by the Russian camp mates and foremen's blatant gloating at our sentences. These people did not hide their satisfaction, and with sadistic delight, they would repeat a hundred times a day that we would not see Poland, just as we would not see our ears. At first, it seemed to us that they were abnormal, that misfortune had poisoned their ability to sympathize with others' sorrow and transformed them into satanically malicious and vicious beings. Months passed until we learned to recognize friends and good people among them. And it took an even longer time until we—or those of us who thought about our camp world—understood the entire profundity of their unprecedented misfortune.

The zeks' first move after the announcement of the convictions was to defend themselves, protest, and appeal. In Soviet camps, prisoners have ample opportunity to write complaints. Alongside the ordinary box for letters that hangs in the office and is emptied once a week or whenever, another special box is hanging; it bears the inscription "for complaints and petitions to the

Commander of the camp, the Presidium of the Supreme Soviet, or the Chief Prosecutor of the USSR." Petitions that are deposited there are, of course, not free of the general censorship. Everything that the zek writes and receives is subject to censorship. If, however, the censorship, the cultural-educational and political sectors, are not opposed, the petition, with an attached character reference of the prisoner, will be dispatched. A month after it is deposited in the box, the zek will receive an official notice that his request is being processed. In another six or nine months, the long-awaited response will arrive from Moscow.

That first autumn and winter, the Westerners at Square 48 wrote an unbelievable number of complaints, appeals, and requests for pardon to Kalinin,[3] Beria, and other officials. The Russian zeks made fun of their contents. Wise from bitter experience, they did not write. Writing petitions is something like the measles—the childhood disease of every camp inmate in his first year of imprisonment. The Soviet regime is sufficiently tolerant and humane to give each prisoner the opportunity to pour out his heart. Moscow archives contain millions of petitions from camps, including mine, which was written in the fall of 1940.

In this petition, I requested a review of my case and liberation. I related my biography as a writer, the history of my arrival from Palestine to Poland in the summer of 1939, and eloquently explained that I was a peaceful, progressive person who never wronged the Soviet Union, never lived in it, and never crossed its borders, either legally or illegally—the Red Army, in liberating Western Belorussia, found me on the territory of the former Polish state. For other Polish refugees, the road home is temporarily closed, but I, as a permanent resident of Palestine, can return there without difficulties. The Soviet regime, to my great regret, considers me a socially dangerous element to the Soviet Union, but there is nothing simpler than allowing me to return home, where I can be a socially useful citizen. This and much else was expressed with great persuasive force and faith in Soviet humanism on two pages of letter paper and handed in to the cultural-educational sector, where because of my job as the camp boss's secretary, my acquaintances wrote a wonderful accompanying character reference.

The answer arrived half a year later. It had been a difficult half year, and when I signed in the Registration and Distribution Office that I had received

---

3. Mikhail Kalinin (1875–1946) was the formal head of the Soviet state from 1919 to 1946. A popular figure, perhaps because of his peasant origins, many appeals were addressed to him, although his power was only nominal.

it, I already was less steady on my feet. The answer arrived on a printed form. Clearly, neither Kalinin nor the Chief Prosecutor of the USSR had read my appeal. It had gone from their offices to a lower one, then to a third, fourth, and it finally arrived in Pinsk, at the office of the very district prosecutor who had been responsible for my arrest. This prosecutor took a printed form, put my name on it, signed, and sent it back. The printed sheet had the standard format:

"Upon a review of the complaint of so-and-so . . . it is noted that the punishment was meted out correctly, in accordance with his deeds."

This "in accordance with his deeds" clashed with the article according to which I was a socially dangerous, suspicious element, but had not yet done anything, as in that case they would have described me as a socially dangerous activist rather than an "element," and I would then not have gotten away with a measly five years. I had not "done" anything and therefore could not be punished "in accordance with my deeds." It was difficult, however, to demand that Soviet justice examine the personal circumstances of every one of the millions of camp inmates. In the course of a year, Kalinin received so many appeals from the camps that neither he nor his staff were able to read them even had they sincerely wished to do so. The Soviet penal system handles millions of people and carries out mass measures. A person who lands in camp and drowns in the mass of zeks cannot, as a rule, extricate himself from it in an individual way.

A few days later, Stepanov, the operative agent of the Third Sector, visited our camp. Such "operatives," who exercise political control and secret surveillance—the eyes and ears of the NKVD—are found in every department and arouse general fear. They are the actual masters in the camps. They gave over the camp commander's office to Stepanov. It was in daytime. My work place was in the passageway to this office, and I took advantage of a moment when he was free. I knocked and entered.

Stepanov was a small, disheveled officer with piercing, malicious eyes. Sitting at the table with the collar of his military tunic unbuttoned, he looked suspiciously at me.

I told him that I had received a five-year sentence and wanted to know whether I could write about that to my wife. Would they allow my letter to be sent abroad?

Stepanov: "I don't understand; why do you have to write to your wife about these things?"

I: "A wife is an intimate person and ought to know her husband's fate. By us in the West things are done that way. Five years is a long term. My family ought to know what happened to me; they should not be left in the dark. Perhaps my wife does not want to wait that long for me."

Stepanov: "Your wife should understand on her own that you will not return to her. What's there to write about? It is all clear."

I: "In the Soviet Union this is clear, but not abroad; by us no one knows anything about the existence of camps. My wife does not know where I am."

Stepanov: "Look, all the time you keep saying 'by us,' 'by you.' 'By us' and 'by you.' A curious division. In view of this, I must ask you, what is your attitude toward Soviet rule?"

I: "My attitude is positive. I am a Jew, and I see that the Soviet government does not persecute Jews as other states do. I am a working intellectual, that is, from a class point of view, I have no reason to be hostile to Soviet rule. Moreover, as a scholar, I am fully aware of the value of Marxism."

Stepanov: "All right. If you yourself are a worker, then why do you say all the time 'by you,' 'by us'? The Soviet Union is the motherland of all workers. That means it is also your motherland."

Here I lost control and forgetting all caution and where I was, I addressed the operative in the tone of a teacher instructing a dull pupil:

"You are wrong, citizen operative. This is simply a misunderstanding. The Soviet Union is the motherland of all workers in the sense of an ideological-political center but not in a geographical sense. You can't ask all the workers of the world to live in the Soviet Union and consider it their fatherland. My motherland is Palestine. I lived there before the war, and I want to live there in the future."

Stepanov flushed with anger. At that moment, one of his assistants entered the office.

"Just look at this one," said Stepanov, pointing to me. "He is sitting and explaining that Germany is his motherland."

Here I realized that the operative was not strong in geography: he thought Palestine was in Germany. But it was too late to teach him geography.

In general, it can be dangerous to get into disputes with representatives of the political police. With NKVD operatives in the forests of the Russian north, it is simply senseless. You can never know what will come of it.

This conversation had disastrous consequences for me. Stepanov ordered that I immediately be removed from the office. "This one," he told Petrov, "is not one of ours. A person who says all the time 'by us' and 'by you' must not remain in the office, where he knows everything that is happening. Send him to the forest, to general work."

My neighbor in the office, Spiegel, also was ejected from his post as a planner. One evening, when he was sitting with his boards on which he would write the percentage of the norms that had been fulfilled, the camp boss entered. At that time, the simple-minded, inept Petrov had already been dismissed, and our boss was a Ukrainian, Abramenko. On the table lay a freshly arrived telephoned message: "I order. . . ." It was an order not to give liberated camp inmates money to purchase a train ticket to their place of residence. They had to buy it from their own funds.

"That's how it should be!" said Abramenko.

"But I think it's wrong!" said Spiegel, deceived by Abramenko's good-natured look. "All over the world, released prisoners customarily are sent home at the government's expense, just as they brought them in at the state's expense. All the more so in the Soviet Union, where there are such distances. Here you need one hundred or two hundred rubles for a ticket. Where could they get such money?"

"What do you mean from where?" said Abramenko. "We give them the opportunity to earn money in the camp."

"How can you say such a thing?" said planner Spiegel in distress. "Don't you know what the workers earn? Here, I have all the figures; take a look. . . ."

And he showed him what Abramenko knew very well without him: the fictitious earnings of the workers boiled down to symbolic payments, to petty change.

"I myself," said Spiegel, digging himself deeper into a pit with every word, "What do I earn here? Ten rubles a month. Tell me, where could I get money to buy a ticket to Warsaw? You probably need five hundred rubles for that."

At that moment, a guard platoon commander entered and, warming his hands by the stove, turned to listen carefully.

"What, you are still thinking about Warsaw?" Abramenko said angrily. "You Poles are stubborn cusses. Now you are Soviet."

"You are all contras," said the platoon commander. "And all your conversations are counterrevolutionary. And you won't go to your Poland. Your Poland doesn't exist anymore."

Here Spiegel realized what he had said and tried to backtrack. But it was too late. As he left, Abramenko told him not to return to the office and ordered him to show up in the morning with the work brigades.

After the conversation with Stepanov, I nevertheless wrote a letter to my wife in Palestine. It was a very laconic notice that I had been sentenced to five years in a labor camp, I am in such-and-such a location, I am grateful for everything that happened in the past, and I beg her not to despair.

She did not receive this letter or any of the following ones.

12

Karelin's Brigade

WHEN THE NEW Western arrivals' total inability and unwillingness to work became clear, the BBK administration took measures to end the isolation of the "Poles." The authorities gradually began to disperse them among the surrounding camp sectors. "Native" brigades were brought into Square 48 to replace them. Soviet zeks were supposed to set an example and teach the novices to work.

The first Soviet brigades at Square 48 were supposed to consist of select, reliable people, capable of carrying out an educational mission. In a secret circular, the BBK administration recommended carefully and cautiously selecting people for dispatch to the Polish camps, paying particular attention not only to their working ability but also to their moral qualities. The circular, however, did not help much. The order was not so much difficult as impossible to obey. The "moral condition" of Soviet prisoners completely matched their slave and captive status. The camp bosses simply could not select ideal partners for us. The idyll at Square 48 ended with the arrival of the Soviet brigades.

The BBK administration had every reason for recommending extreme caution in selecting Soviet zeks. They entered our milieu like wolves into a flock of sheep. The sheep huddled together more closely. The orderlies were directed not to allow outsiders into the barracks and even to lock the doors after roll call and supper. Our new neighbors quickly scouted out the camp— they rapidly toured all the buildings and mentally noted where and what was located everywhere. The Poles' suitcases lay under the bunks and their coats hung on nails. Bold raids and daring thefts on the first night showed us that safe times had ended: the *urki* had arrived!

In the camps *urki* was the term for the criminal bandit element—not according to the criminal code, but in the psychological sense, as a particular camp type. An *urka* is a predatory person who doesn't give a damn whether a few years are added to his term; he is a bandit and a thief, grabbing everything that he can get his hands on, unscrupulously exploiting the other's weakness or stupidity. An *urka* lives in the present and does not think far ahead. He immediately eats everything he gets; he seizes everything that is poorly guarded; and he is always hungry, rancorous, and ready to fight or to steal.

The administration overlooks a lot in the case of the *urki* for, on the one hand, it fears them and on the other, it does not consider them politically dangerous. For minor compensation, the *urki* willingly spy and cooperate with the Third Sector. In Soviet camp conditions, where nonpolitical and political prisoners are mixed together, the nonpoliticals are privileged in all respects, because the regime basically does not regard them as enemies. The hooligan *urki* not only curse their Western companions as "damn fascists" but also, as in the times of tsarist pogroms, they call the Jews "Yids." You can immediately recognize an *urka* by his torn clothing, his insolent, provocative manner, outrageous language, and willingness to start a fight at any moment. Young people who land in camp quickly become savage and turn into *urki*. Even our young "Westerners" did not escape this fate, whatever their social origin or upbringing.

At seven o'clock in the morning after my conversation with the security operative, I went to the forest with Karelin's brigade, a mix of Western and Soviet zeks. Karelin was a robust, crafty, bearded fellow. His brigade was considered easy and calm. I was fortunate to have landed in it.

That morning, I was full of energy and fighting spirit. I wanted to test myself and show that I was suited for physical labor. I took up the matter with extraordinary enthusiasm. We went into the depth of the forest, about 2 kilometers past the camp gates. It smelled of pine needles and dampness; neither buildings nor fences were visible.

The armed guard sat on the side. The prisoners made a bonfire for him. From time to time, he left the bonfire and made the rounds of the scattered work teams in the forest, counting people. He did not let people disperse at too great a distance. If he had any doubts, he whistled, and the brigade members immediately came to him for a roll call.

Karelin entrusted me and others to clear a glade with axes. The people poked around lazily, the work did not advance, and the guard approached several times to prod the people to work. I, however, did not need any prodding; on the contrary. The first thing that I did was to cut down a young fir, the first tree in my life. I lowered it right on the head of my neighbor. His name was Aizenberg.

I will not forget this name to the end of my days. The fir tree was small; otherwise, it would have finished off Aizenberg. He moaned weakly and slumped to the ground. In falling, the fir had grazed him and scratched his head. Nothing serious had happened, but at the sight of blood, Aizenberg started to holler, and I was scared to death. In despair, I bandaged his head with my last handkerchief. Aizenberg did not work for the rest of the day; he sat mournfully on the side with his bandaged head. He then received another two days off from work, so that, in general, he came out all right in this incident. To exculpate my sin, I rushed with my axe at the firs and felled them by myself. The others sat on the grass and looked gloomily at my zeal. "What's your hurry? There's no time? In five years, you'll work plenty!"

I recall dragging the cut firs to the fire, and they were heavy as lead. I simply could not lift them. Not surprising. I was severely short-sighted, and I dragged the trunk with my hands while my foot was on the branches, all Chaplinesque exploits. The behavior of my team irritated me. In the evening, I said to Karelin, "Tomorrow, put me in another team. I want real work."

The next day, I received real work. Karelin's was a "wood rail" brigade. We were building a wood-strip road deep into the forest. After felling, the forest sector is heaped with hundreds of felled tree trunks in the thicket. Ordinary wagons cannot reach them. The trees are carted out with the help of "skidding" and special wood roads. Haulers drag out the trees from the most distant corners. They tie together separate trunks with a hook and chain and drag them with a horse to a place where a wagon can reach them. The wagons penetrate into the depths of the forest along the wood strip road, where instead of iron rails, there are wooden strips.

Three to four people comprise a work team of the wood-strip road brigade. The principal worker uses an ax and drill. He marks out the route of the road, clears it of bushes and brushwood, uproots occasional stumps on the road, and smooths out protuberances. This is easy to write about but very hard to do. In the meantime, the others cut down smallish trees, from which they prepare strips of 10 to 12 meters in length, and thicker ones, from which they cut the railroad ties. The head of the team places the ties at 2-meter intervals; the strips are placed on the ties in the form of wooden rails. The thick end of the strip is called *komel,* the "butt"; with the ax one cuts a cavity in it. In the cavity, one places the thin end of the next strip; under the butt lies the tie. An aperture is drilled at the juncture of the tie and the two strips, and a wedge is driven into the opening; the wedge is tapered downward and is driven deep into the earth. Along this wood-strip road, wagons loaded with lumber travel in any weather and mud. This wood-strip road is built quickly and holds for about a year, that is, just the time it takes to fell a given sector. The work of the team leader is not very difficult but requires the hands of a carpenter, the ability quickly and adroitly to plane the strips and to adjust and secure them. While the team head sits with a hatchet, hews the pegs, and lays down the planks, two or three of his partners continually cut down trees, saw them, and bring strips and ties to the road.

Our work team comprised three people. The head was Skvortsov, from Orlov, a solid-looking, large *muzhik* with a broad chest, who was no longer young. Skvortsov and Karelin were friends. Skvortsov was an excellent, confident worker. His story was as follows. During the great famine of 1931, he was in charge of a grain warehouse. His closest relatives were dying of hunger, and he committed a crime: he gave them several sacks of government flour. He was denounced by an informer and sentenced to capital punishment. In view of his military merits during the Civil War, his sentence was commuted to five years of imprisonment. After serving his five years in camps, Skvortsov was released and chose to live in one of the regions of Central Russia, where he worked in a factory. He did not have the right to leave that district. After some time, they summoned him and proposed that he become an informer at the factory. Skvortsov refused but he was afraid to say "no" categorically. The NKVD began to call him in frequently, to pressure, and to threaten him. When they saw that he was trying to wiggle out, they gave him an ultimatum: by a certain date, he had to give them the names of twenty-five "enemies of the people" at the factory. "If you don't bring a list, you yourself will wind up in camp," they told him.

"Why did it have to be twenty-five names?" I asked Skvortsov. "What if there aren't so many enemies of the people at the factory?"

"Indeed, they, too, have their quota," explained Skvortsov. "They have orders to prepare a contingent of such-and-such a number of people to be sent to camp. According to the plan, there has to be twenty-five 'enemies' at that factory. We have a planned economy everywhere."

As Skvortsov did not present them the requested list of twenty-five people, they took him instead. This time they gave him a second term of ten years and sent him to the BBK as a counterrevolutionary element.

Here he developed an ulcer. This large, imposing person would appear every evening at the clinic to cadge from the doctors some baking soda, without which he could not survive. I had a few packets, which I gave to him, and I promised that I would write to my mother, asking her to send me baking soda in my parcel. This favorably disposed Skvortsov to me, and we met in the forest as friends.

The second person in the team was Batukai, a mute, hook-nosed Chechen, strong, with the face of a child. Batukai was serving time for "banditry," although it was impossible to understand in what kind of band he had participated. Batukai carried enormous logs effortlessly, but in everyday life, he was gentle and meek, like an obedient child. He emitted unintelligible sounds, making himself understood with gestures, or he would pronounce a few words, like a child learning to babble.

It would be difficult to bring together more varied people than the Caucasus mountaineer with steel muscles, the Orlov *muzhik* with an ulcer, and the guest from Europe, raised on Kant and Husserl, with eyeglasses and the look of an astonished sheep.

The norm was 17.5 meters per person. In order to earn the second food ration, we three had to lay 52 meters but we did close to 70. This comprised 140 meters of rail strips. We had to fell a dozen pines just for the strips and another dozen for the ties.

When the first strip was ready, Batukai easily placed the thick end on his shoulder, and with considerable effort, I raised the thin end on my shoulder. We carried it to Skvortsov. I staggered a bit, but managed to carry it. I was wearing a yellow leather jacket, which was excellently suited for autumn work. At that time, I was not wearing government-supplied clothing, as I had my own. The twelve-meter strip weighed heavily on my shoulder. When we arrived, we dropped it on the ground together on command. I wiped the sweat from my brow. Then quietly, I took my mitten and put it on my shoulder under the jacket to reduce the pressure. Batukai cut down pine after pine; I barely managed to cut off the ends and branches. My shoulder became numb, my chest ached, but I gritted my teeth and decided not to give up.

Unfortunately, we were not walking on even ground. We did not have to drag the rails over a long distance—about a hundred meters—but we had to make our way past heaps of dried brush, treacherous potholes, and tree trunks that had to be climbed over. Batukai went in front like a tank, without stopping. I started to become short of breath and my vision blurred. I had to continue carrying my end at any cost! Suddenly I cried out, "Stop, stop!" There was a ditch in front of me. I felt that I was unable simply to jump across it with a 12-meter rail on my shoulder. I needed to stop for a second, to gather my strength. Batukai looked back at me in astonishment and snorted disapprovingly.

I managed to carry that rail, but now I had to rest. Five minutes. I needed nothing else in life. Batukai was already nodding in the distance. I went slowly toward him, resting on the way. Each second of respite counted.

I fell while carrying the last rail; it was a 13-meter strip. Twelve meters was the maximum that I could drag. It was an awkward sensation. I could hold the rail while standing, but on the move, it simply pressed me to the ground.

Mid-way, I stumbled into a ditch; I strained all the muscles in my body. Batukai mercilessly dragged me onward. I lunged, and in order not to lose the rhythm, I made a wrong step. My knees buckled, and I collapsed under my burden.

Fortunately, that was the end as they called us for a "snack." The workers of the brigade assembled from all sides on a hillock where, near a large stump, a man from the kitchen, with a pail of kasha, was standing next to a guard and Karelin. A wagon with a green barrel was visible in the distance; it made the rounds of the brigades, bringing boiled water to the workers at the "production sites." Only the Stakhanovites were entitled to kasha. The others simply drank water and rested. Skvortsov and Batukai had sawed out round pine disks, like trays, and made spoons from wood chips. Each of us received a small ladle of millet kasha. Karelin winked at the cook—and I, too, received a scoop of kasha for the first time, as encouragement.

I no longer, however, took the 13-meter strips. My work comrades saw that it truly was beyond my strength. On the second day, Skvortsov, with his stomach ulcer, silently, pushed me aside and carried the strips with Batukai. I took up the drilling, realizing that I would not continue working in this team.

They transferred me to carrying ties. On the following days, we worked in a swampy hollow, where we had to lay down ties, one after the other as planking. I would take two ties on my shoulder and slowly go 100 to 200 meters into the forest. Water sloshed under my feet. At the start of the day, I chose dry spots but by the end, I didn't care. Soon my pants were torn to shreds, my jacket ripped at the shoulder and turned black from dirt. My hands were full of sores. The worst, however, was that I was unable to overcome my exhaustion. I was forty years old when I landed in the camp. It is difficult for the organism to adapt. I worked all day like a beast of burden and feared that my strength would soon give way. My greatest desire was to sit motionlessly on the end of a log for five minutes. After a few days, I sprained my right hand. It swelled, and I could not move it. This did not free me from portering, but now the work turned into torture. In a short time, I became unrecognizably gaunt.

Returning to the barrack after a day of work, all damp and dirty, I would collapse onto the hard bunk and lay motionless for an hour. When I recovered, I would go to supper. After a day without food, I did not have an appetite, and I did not manage to rest sufficiently at night. They were not yet heating the barracks, there were no dryers, and my shoes and socks did not dry by morning. In the morning, I would put on all the damp items and report to the work lineup in despair. I needed a breathing space, but ten days had already passed, and we did not have a day off. The camp week did not include a Sunday.

Toward the end of that period, I was completely sapped and shattered. One evening, we were detained by work in our sector, and at seven o'clock in the evening, Karelin, with the rest of the brigade, left for camp without us. We lost track of him, and in the dusk, remained alone in the forest. To this day, I do not understand why the guard did not look for us. Apparently, Karelin convinced him that we would join the brigade on the way.

I was totally wiped out, but at that moment, we all experienced a terrible fright. At the guardhouse, our absence was sure to raise an alarm, the immediate dispatch of guards with dogs, and upon our return, the punishment cell in the best case. If they also accused us of trying to escape, we risked a trial and additional years of imprisonment. We started running through the forest in the direction of the camp. Soon I lost sight of Skvortsov and the others. They were running like the devil. It became dark, and in the darkness, I soon ceased hearing their voices. . . .

Fortunately, I ran to the rail line. Along the rail bed, out of breath, I ran up to the guardhouse at the last minute, when they were already letting our brigade through. I paid dearly, however, for this desperate effort. I began to feel ill after supper. I felt a weakness and pain all though my body. Then I began to vomit.

Everyone was sleeping soundly and no one came to my aid. At dawn, they found me unconscious. Everyone rushed to the lineup for work and no one had time for me. All the same, someone took an interest in me: anonymous hands stole the galoshes in which I used to go to work. They took away my wallet, towel, and scarf, as if I were already dead. The wallet contained pictures from home, which were dear to me. They left me only torn shoes, which were no longer suitable in the autumn mud.

The work coordinator waved his hand in resignation when he saw the vomit-filled boards on which I had been lying, and at eleven o'clock, he took me to the infirmary. This was my first real rest in the three and a half months since my arrest. I was happy. No sanatoriums or European resorts that I had visited in my former life could compare to this divine place.

The infirmary consisted of a kitchen, where the doctor slept on a bed, and of a room with cots, real wooden cots with straw mattresses, pillows, and military blankets. It was clean and quiet. The work coordinators did not come here to drive one to work. I undressed and lay down in the hospital gown. The doctor, nurse, and medic were our people—Westerners. True, they could not give me the diet that I needed, but they did bring the food to the bed. There were eight patients. One of them, a young actor from the Warsaw Teatr Młodych, recited poems and told jokes. In the corner was Heissler, a well-known Warsaw pedagogue.

The only unpleasant part was when, wrapped in a blanket, we had to go out into the courtyard to take care of our needs, in the nasty October mud. Then the feet would give way and slide in the mud and the head would turn. The medic accompanied the weakest patients.

The rest in the infirmary did not last long. A volume of Shakespeare turned up and I reread *Hamlet* and *King Lear*. At Square 48, there were no books, newspapers, or radio, and from the time of our arrest, we had been cut off from the outside world. I spent time conversing with Heissler. In the summer of 1939, on the eve of the war, I had read in a Warsaw journal a long article of his about the unpublished works of Gabriela Zapolska.[1] Heissler was a distinguished pedagogue with a lengthy career, well known in Polish literary circles, a critic and literary historian, a nonpolitical person. This delicate and fragile, infirm person yearned endlessly for his homeland, his home, and his family. He had a wife and five-year-old daughter in Warsaw. He constantly thought about her, wondering whether he would see his little girl again. I assured him that the evil times would soon pass and together we would celebrate our return. . . .

These lines now provide the sole memory of this man. Not only his family, including his beloved daughter, perished, but also the Germans murdered, evidently, the entire circle of people who read and knew Heissler. There is no one in the new Poland to remember him. Heissler himself was killed in the corrective labor camp. Someone needed to "reform" him through labor. This man's death in camp can only be termed murder. Despite his severe asthma, they drove him mercilessly into the forest. There, in the Polish brigades, his fellow prisoners had so much respect for him that they allowed him to sit, almost not participating in the work. At the end of the workday, the Polish brigade leader would attribute a norm of thirty percent to him in the work report—an insufficient norm to survive, but necessary in order to avoid being sent to the punishment cell. How long could this continue? . . .

---

1. Gabriela Zapolska (1857–1921), a Polish writer and actress.

They kept me in the infirmary for five days, and then came the "banishment from paradise." I had rested, the pains had passed, and someone else needed my place. Before returning to the forest, I managed stay in the camp for another four days doing "special work" as a translator for a judicial investigator.

I earlier mentioned the presence in the camp of a transport of Złoczów[2] Jews, who had been brought in without interrogation or investigation. Now an investigatory commission arrived from Złoczów to conduct interrogations in the camp itself. The investigators were two young "lawyers"—polite, correct, the type that I had met in the Pinsk prison. As the Złoczów Jews did not understand Russian, a translator with knowledge of Yiddish, Polish, and Russian was needed. They assigned me to assist the commission. The interrogations went on morning and night. Each evening I would receive a list of fifty names of people whom the work coordinator had to remove from morning muster for work. The line formed in the corridor of the Second Sector; men and women were agitated, as if this interrogation could change their fate. It was not worth getting excited; the scenes of interrogations were boringly similar. They would begin with the investigator offering the prisoner a cigarette. I was already familiar with this gesture, which meant: "Don't be afraid! We are cultured people and we do everything honorably, according to the law." Then the stereotypical questions followed: name, place of birth, residence, occupation, party affiliation. You weren't in the Bund? You weren't a Zionist? He would mark down "non-party" and continue. Do you have relatives abroad? How did you become a refugee? Why did you refuse to accept a Soviet passport? Many complained that they had submitted an application for Soviet citizenship but had not received a reply; others said they had "received a passport and lost it." In addition to the Jews, there was a group of Silesians, that is, Silesian Poles, coal miners, who, even as refugees, had been mining coal in the area of Złoczów. Rough workers' faces, blue eyes, a characteristic dialect and a quiet, intractable stubbornness of people who are waiting to be sent home to their native Silesia. Each one would take a cigarette and ask for another upon leaving, but then the "citizen boss" would not give one: you cannot satisfy everyone. As all these people had already been placed in the camp, all these post factum interrogations had no significance for them or for the investigator. Each one would sign the protocol, first glancing at me inquisitively: Is this some kind of deception?

---

2. Now part of Ukraine, it is called Zolochiv.

These people did not receive "sentences," nor was this necessary. Soviet zeks sometimes sit for years without a declared sentence, not knowing "for what" or "for how long." Two years later, they summon them to the Second Sector and read a document that says they have eight years remaining; they ask them to sign, but do not hand over any document. They see neither their judges, their denouncers, nor their prosecutors, and they are not entitled to a defense.

13

Dehumanization

IN THE WINTER of 1940–1941, a thousand people in the camp subsector Square 48 were dehumanized. Not all of them were from the West; some were Soviet people. The ratio of Westerners to Soviets changed continually. As the number of Westerners diminished, Soviets increased, and eventually, three hundred Westerners remained out of a thousand prisoners. We were an island surrounded by a variegated mix of peoples of the USSR: Russians, Ukrainians, Uzbeks, Turkmens, Kazakhs, gypsies, Georgians, Finns, and Germans. An exceptionally large number of people from Central Asia, the so-called "national minorities," were interned in the camps of the second Onega section of the BBK.

The Asiatic brigades, vestiges of generations that had perished in the camps, inspired horror: monstrously dirty, bestial-looking people with heads encircled by dirty rags, with incomprehensible speech, savages who had descended to some cave-like condition. They worked ferociously, neither mingling with anyone else, nor permitting anyone to approach them. A Westerner who was sent to work with them was finished. They did not recognize his right to own anything and would unceremoniously strip him of all his possessions. At work, they would egg him on with a wooden stake, hitting and kicking him like a dog. A Westerner faced mortal danger among them. On the Russian side, however, the *urki* were lying in wait. Bandits given to cynical humiliation, theft, even an ax blow, the *urki* were no better than the Asiatics. These thoroughly dehumanized groups revealed to us, as in a mirror, our own future.

Westerners were soon assigned a minimum norm of thirty percent of the Soviet inmates' work quota. A person who did less was sent to the punishment cell in the evening. You could no longer lie low or slowly dawdle at work. A daily war was waged in the forestry sectors. From morning to evening, the guards' rifles drove people away from the bonfires; the foremen and camp bosses circled through the forest, vigilantly checking that work did not stop for a second. The hungry prisoners would snarl; the guards would threaten them with clubs, or the foreman, emerging from the bushes, would catch people by surprise near the fire, grab a bludgeon and cursing, drive the circle of resting men away from the fire. The punishment would follow in the evening. Each brigade leader would submit a report listing those who had not fulfilled the thirty percent, and the convoy's armed guard would sign: "We, so-and-so, wrote up the present report because the here-named zeks of brigade such and such, on day such and such, maliciously shirked work, about which they had been warned. Despite the warning, they did not begin working and did not carry out the brigade leader's assignment."

Without verifying, the camp boss would append a terse order to the report: "five days" or "ten days." In the course of the evening, about forty to fifty people would be locked in the punishment cell, and the next evening, about the same amount would be added. Understandably, there was no room for them in the punishment cell, and the warden of the penalty isolator was unable to carry out the director's order. Quickly a waiting list for the punishment cell would be drawn up. Consequently, many did not even land in the punishment cell, especially if they belonged to the camp aristocracy—the trusties [*pridurki*]. Every evening, Panchuk and the penalty isolator warden would make the rounds of the barracks, exercising their own judgment about whom to select from the long list for the punishment cell. Savage beatings would ensue in the barracks when people did not go voluntarily, and sometimes it was necessary to summon help from the armed escorts or the warden's assistants.

For the vast majority of Westerners, even a thirty percent "refugee norm" was unattainable, not because of a will to resist but for perfectly objective reasons. I was never capable of fulfilling thirty percent at tree felling, and at much easier work such as sawing wood, I managed thirty percent with extreme effort, working all day without a break and to the very limit of my strength. Perhaps I could have achieved thirty percent of the norm at unloading train cars or with a wheelbarrow at land works, but to do that, I would have had to eat differently and to rest normally after work.

When the entire Soviet Union was working eight hours a day, camp inmates put in ten hours. At the beginning of the World War, when a ten-hour working day was introduced in the Soviet Union, our camp working day became twelve. In reality, however, our torments lasted much longer. Delays at work, lines by the kitchen windows upon our return, hours of standing in line during roll calls or when we assembled and were dispatched to work all demanded physical exertion and came out of our rest time.

Nominally, a zek has three free days a month, once every ten days. If, however, the camp administration does not issue an order confirming the vacation day, it does not happen. At Square 48, we never knew until the last minute whether we would rest, and in most cases, we did not. The day off was simply canceled because the plan had not been fulfilled. In the bitterest frosts of the winter of 1940–1941, we labored at the most difficult forestry work for sixty days in a row, that is, two full months, without one day of rest.

This seems improbable because it exceeds normal human endurance. Yet this was one of the stages of our dehumanization. We had no guaranteed normal rest, and each free day was a gift and favor from the administration. Soviet holidays—May 1 and the anniversary of the October Revolution— were not observed in the camps. Nothing was added to the ordinary ration on that day, and the prisoners were taken out to work in order to emphasize that the Soviet citizens' holiday had no relevance for the zek.

Prisoners do not receive a salary. They are not entitled to it because their work is part of their punishment. Instead, they are given a "prize-compensation." The difference between a "salary" and "prize-compensation" is that the money received is not gauged by the work performed; it is a prize that the state grants as an incentive, without being obligated to do so. This "prize-compensation" amounts to measly pennies. For the job of secretary to the camp boss, a position that is supposed to be filled by a "free" worker, I received 15 rubles a month. The orderlies, who have to wash the floors, bunks, and windows, carry water, stoke, guard, and serve crowded barracks, receive 5 rubles. The monthly wage of a "workhorse" at the most difficult work, fulfilling the norm by one hundred percent or exceeding it, is 5, 7, or 9 rubles.

In the war years, when a kilo of bread in the camps of the Arkhangelsk region cost 100 rubles and an egg was 5 rubles, "prize-compensation" was a fiction even at the highest salaries: doctors receive 40, 60, and sometimes 100 rubles. In a separate category are the "workhorses," who receive a few hundred rubles, and the legendary cases when a zek who has served out a ten-year term, walks out with 3,000 rubles. We shall say more about these camp Croesuses later.

Backbreaking work and destitution were thus two methods of dehumanizing the *Homo sapiens* who landed in a Soviet camp. Millions of people are forced to work outside of their professions. Despite the frequent questionnaires, registrations, and accounting, it is impossible to place the people who wind up in this colossal human dump in positions that suit them.

In Soviet camps, as in any forced labor in any country, the work is not adapted to the people but the people to the available work. Cooks, hairdressers, shoemakers, and tailors have a slim chance of finding appropriate work, but there are too few such places to suffice for all the candidates. Clearly, the chief accountant of the camp is always an experienced accountant, but not every experienced accountant lands in an office. The vast, overwhelming majority, ninety percent, go to menial hard labor. The camps, which are designed to "reform by labor"—as if one could reform someone by turning him or her into a slave—in reality constitute a savage profanation of labor and complete lack of respect for human talent and ability. People who have worked for decades in beloved professions become convinced in camp that all their life's efforts were in vain. In camp, teachers carry water, technical workers saw wood, merchants dig up earth, good shoemakers become bad mowers and good mowers become bad shoemakers. In order to squeeze the maximum out of the weak, they are sent to work with the strong and experienced: in such conditions, physical labor becomes not only physical torture but also deep humiliation. Yet, not even strong people can escape such a fate. The camp system dehumanizes free people, turns them into "man/horsepower," and the slaves are transformed into cattle by methodically pressuring them to increase the tempo and the productivity of work.

According to the stories of old Russian zeks with whom I served time, the history of Soviet camps is divided into three periods.

In the first, there were so-called "special purpose isolators." Political prisoners were not mixed with the nonpolitical ones and lived in better conditions. The regime regarded its seeming opponents not as criminals but as some kind of infectious sick individuals who had to be isolated from the Soviet people. A person who had served time in the Solovetsky [Solovki] Camp[1] in 1924 told me that the prisoners there—people from different political parties, officers of the tsarist army, gentry, intelligentsia, representatives of free professions—were not forced to work, had enough to eat, and received significant financial support from relatives. As in a normal prison, the state, having deprived them of freedom, took responsibility for their upkeep. The

---

1. In 1923, the Bolshevik regime opened the Solovetsky camp of Special Destination, known as SLON, on the site of a former monastery and tsarist prison (the Solovetsky islands, or Solovki, form an archipelago in the Onega Bay of the White Sea). Tens of thousands of people were imprisoned, tortured, and killed there between 1923 and 1939. In *The Gulag Archipelago*, Solzhenitsyn terms it the mother of the Gulag system.

camp had a library of three thousand books and its own theatrical troupe consisting of professional actors.

The second stage in the development of the camps commenced when the prisoners began to work to supply the needs of their own camps; for example, they sawed the wood for the winter, prepared the forest for the construction of living quarters, and worked in the fields and vegetable gardens. When Soviet construction requirements necessitated sending millions of people to camps, political isolation turned into a means of colonizing the country's out-lying areas. The camps turned into a sector of the Soviet economy, existing on autarchic principles, on self-sufficiency. The prisoners had to work for their keep.

This second stage with tragic logic slipped into the third; the camp inmates' work, it turned out, created value, that is, they were not only paying their way but were bringing in a profit. The income of working people belongs to working people. Camp workers, however, were prisoners. They, with all their revenue, belong to the state that "organized" them for work. The slave driver placed his heavy paw on them. The camps were supposed to generate revenue for the Soviet government.

The penal system—as part of the planned economy of the USSR—was assigned a specific production goal. Henceforth, each camp had to fulfill an annual plan. It was not enough, however, to fulfill the annual plan. The penal administration, which wanted to curry favor and receive a reward, made every effort to surpass the plan.

Stakhanovites surpass the plan, but Stakahanovites do not appear from out of thin air. In order to produce them, one must submit people who are fulfilling only one hundred percent of the plan to conditions of un-bearable starvation. There is nothing easier; after all, these are prisoners, people without freedom of speech or the right to protest. And that's the least of it.

A method of "labor competition" is established. In freedom, this is called "socialist competition."

In the office of Square 48, a poster was displayed, from which we knew that our BBK camp had concluded an agreement with the camps of the Arkhangelsk region concerning labor competition. We had taken on the ob-ligation to surpass our plan and overtake the Arkhangelsk camps. Completely voluntarily, the administration of the BBK assumed this obligation in our name.

In order to meet this obligation, the BBK administration organized labor competition among the divisions within the camp. In turn, in each division, separate camp subsectors competed against each other and, in each camp subsector, separate brigades attempted to outdo each other.

It went like this: In the evening, they would summon the weary brigade members, staggering from exhaustion, to the KVCh (the cultural-educational sector), which organizes the labor competition. At the KVCh, an "educator," a paid state worker, would deliver an ardent speech about the need for the brigade "to prove itself."

Our neighbors had already committed to surpassing the plan by 140 percent, to reducing spoilage, and to raising work discipline. What about us—would we do any less?

But we were silent. Some people in the barrack, upon hearing what the meeting was about, simply shrugged it off, and lay down to sleep. We who could not wriggle out, who were in the administration's "sights," had come to the meeting. The educator stared relentlessly at the brigade boss. The latter began to hem and haw, gagging:

"Well . . . yeah, right . . . comrades! They are one hundred forty percent but we'll give one hundred fifty! We'll do it, what do you think?"

It was more than clear to everyone present, including the educator, what we thought. His presence was meaningless; after all, he was only doing his job, for which he was paid 400 rubles a month. No one wished to come out "against." And, thus, our life became even more precarious: they may delay giving you padded pants or transfer you to a national minority brigade—and it's curtains! We thus all signed an obligation scripted according to the rules of Soviet eloquence. It began thus: "Desiring to aid the Motherland and the valiant Red Army, which is protecting us from the vile enemy . . .," and it ended with the obligation to surpass the plan by one hundred fifty percent and not only to reduce waste but also in the course of a month not to permit one instance of dodging work.

No one took these obligations seriously—except for the administration. It needed them in order to pressure and demand, to detain us for extra time after the end of work, to threaten, and to harass us. We always owed something to the Soviet state; we always were behind. . . . We always let them down and were deplorable. In the camps and beyond their limits, this system of standing with a whip over one's head constituted the most merciless and shameless abuse of power over slaves. No exertion of ours could satisfy them. If the brigade would perform at one hundred fifty percent, the administration would nod and say: "We knew that you could give one hundred fifty percent," and it showed that earlier we were deceiving them when we gave only one hundred percent, and now we had better make every effort to surpass this one hundred fifty percent because yesterday's record was no longer impressive. "You must work even better!" "You must give even more to the state." The limit to this break-neck race was reached when a person broke down. Then the inmate was moved to the list of incapacitated and sent to one of the camp subsectors where live wrecks, "camp veterans," were withering on invalids' starvation rations.

Like night, the degrading camp destitution inevitably descended upon us. After several months, all our European possessions and trinkets were sold, or were used up, or had been stolen from us. The cleverest among us had immediately sold everything possible to the camp bosses, the work supervisors, and the free workers, who, in return, would provide an easier job, some bread, or an extra meal ticket. The rest were quickly looted when the *urki*, from whom there was no escape, flooded the camp or when the administration sent the inmates on transports from camp to camp. In transit, bandits who had nothing to lose surrounded every Westerner and everyone who possessed something edible or of some value. The administration abetted the robberies—the commandants and armed guards facilitated the *urkis'* task and received their share of the loot. Before going out to work, the Westerners would tie their footlockers and suitcases with rope to the bunk boards, but it did not help: upon their return in the evening, their things were gone. Often the owner of some overcoat would receive friendly advice: give it willingly for a few rubles. It's still better than nothing: they'll take it anyway. The fall overcoat that I wore to the camp attracted general attention. At night, when, covered by the coat, I was sleeping on the upper planks of an overcrowded barrack, someone took it from me. I woke up at four o'clock at night because I felt light and cold. The coat had disappeared, the barrack was sleeping, and the orderly had not seen anything. The coat was brought beyond the guardhouse, and around two weeks later, it was sold to a free worker at another camp. I knew about it and knew the price it had fetched, who sold it and who bought it, but I couldn't do a thing. The camp authorities do not protect the prisoners' property. The camp law is simple: whatever you have—guard it, and if you don't, it's your fault. In camp, everyone tries to save him or herself as best one can. One foreign overcoat among a thousand unclothed is an exception; it bothers everyone and their sympathy will always be on the side of the thief, not the victim.

We gradually were liberated from the weight of possessions. No lost item could be restored. The last piece of soap. The last box of matches. The last shirt is stolen. The last shoelace: there would be no more strings for the shoes. Levandovsky's yellow boots were, ultimately, stolen. It's simply impudent to

wear such boots in camp. Now he, like everyone else, wrapped his feet in a bag
and walked in the snow in *bast* shoes. The last handkerchief. The zek Margolin
tried for a while longer to wipe his nose with his sleeve but even that was impractical as the sleeve would not suffice for long. You must learn to clear your
nose the camp way, pressing your finger on one nostril while blowing strongly
through the other.

The moment arrives when we no longer have anything of our own. The state
dresses and undresses us as it pleases. In the morning, as teams are being sent
out to work, the clothing warehouse stands wide open. An enormous heap of
stinking rags is laid out for the barefoot and unclothed. If you have nothing
to wear, the brigade leader takes you to the "clothing clerk," who checks in the
clothing record book what was given to the supplicant and when, and whether
he sold or lost something, which entails punishment. If everything is in order,
with a note from the work boss or the head of the Special Supply Unit, the brigade leader gives a note to the supply clerk, and the supply clerk offers you a
choice of worn-out footwear and rags that dozens have worn before you.

The dehumanized zek looks like a scarecrow. On his feet are *cheteze*
[ChTZ]: these letters are an acronym for "Chelyabinsk tractor factory," that
is, something reminiscent of a tractor in its bulkiness and clumsiness. ChTZ
is camp footwear made without size or form as a receptacle for the feet, from
the rubber of old tractor tires. This footwear lets in water: it is tied with string
or pieces of cloth that are threaded through slits in the rubber. In summer,
the zek wears tarpaulin ankle boots. In the winter, the colossal sized *cheteze*
are worn over padded stockings that are damp, torn, and black from dirt.
The padded stockings are tied with string around the padded trousers, which
are bound around with string instead of a belt. The trousers have one or no
pockets, but they have variegated patches in the front and back. On his upper
body, when it's not freezing, the zek wears a padded jacket [*telogreika*, literally body warmer] and in winter a *bushlat*, which differs from the former in
that it is longer and has more padding. In the absence of a collar that could be
raised, the zek wraps a towel around his neck if he has one, if not, some rag.
On his head is a hat with earflaps [*ushanka*], from which clumps of padding
stick out. All these masquerade items are first-, second-, or third-hand. First-
hand is new or almost new. You can obtain it only if you are a Stakhanovite
or have special pull, and there never are enough of such things. You can spend
five years in a camp and not receive one first-hand item. The majority wear
"second-hand" rags—rust color, torn, fantastically patched, and muddied.
There is even third-hand: that is when a *bushlat* unravels, the sleeves are
coming apart, one's body sticks out of the holes, and the item is about to be

"decommissioned." Ultimately, as is the case with people, things are subject to "decommissioning." The time comes when a thing or person is officially recognized as unsuitable for further use. For things, a minimal period is a year. People often hold out longer: irreversible damage takes long years of torment and deprivation.

Our camp inmate stands before us, with a hungry glimmer in his eyes, impoverished, dressed in clownish rags. And these rags do not even belong to him. If he falls ill and stays in the barrack, the work supervisor will take his jacket and toss it to a neighbor: "Put it on, he doesn't need it today." A brigade leader's first threat to a brigade that hasn't met his expectations is: "I'll undress you, I'll take everything away, and you'll go around in third-hand clothing." This, however, is all external. One must take a lot more from a person in order to turn him into a "trembling creature."

First, family ties are liquidated. The camp inmate has no right to be a father, brother, husband, or friend. He abandons all that when he enters the camp. It is incompatible with his being a zek. Families are, therefore, separated inside the camp as in the period of serfdom in prerevolutionary Russia, or, as we read in childhood, in *Uncle Tom's Cabin*: Brothers are sent to different camps, fathers are torn away from their sons, wives from husbands. It's not always on purpose; simply no attention is paid to family ties when it's a matter of "man/ horsepower." There were Polish women in Square 48 who were later sent to Kem, on the shores of the White Sea, where special women's camps were set up. These women had husbands, brothers, and children at Square 48, but this did not interest the BBK administration. I remember one of them, a cousin of the famous Polish writer Wiech (pen name for Stefan Wiechnecki). She was a tall woman with a proud bearing, but all her pride and self-possession left her when she had to part with her eighteen-year-old son as their paths separated, perhaps forever. Many times in those years, I witnessed a father weeping as he embraced his son and a brother his brother as they separated under guard and went in different directions. In camp, I myself invariably lost everyone with whom fate brought me together and whom I regarded as a friend. It is not worth getting close to people in camp because no one knows where he will be tomorrow; at any moment, the work supervisor can enter and give the order: "With your things to the guardhouse." Transfers are systematically carried out; one purpose is to prevent people from becoming accustomed to a place and to each other and to prevent them from forgetting that they are only "robots"—impersonal objects of the state's work force.

Dehumanization, consequently, entails not only exploitation with the aid of material pressure and harassment but also depersonalization. We

Westerners resisted this depersonalization for a long time. We used to call each other "Doctor" and "Lawyer," maintaining the comic and ceremonially polite forms although each of us was like a truncated tree whose roots dream of a nonexistent crown. Calling someone "Doctor" who is in tatters, dragging a barrow loaded with earth and sleeping at night without undressing on bare planks, is an expression of stubborn protest. These distinctions did not exist for the camp administration or for the enormous mass of Soviet zeks into which we gradually and hopelessly dissolved. And we gradually forgot about our own past. If, at first, the present seemed like an impossible nightmare, within a short time, our entire former life seemed like a dream. European culture, the ideas to which we had dedicated our life, people whom we loved and who accompanied us—all that world where we had been full-fledged, proud people—were all a distant dream.

Gradually, even the camp inmate's normal human feelings disappear or become deformed. Let's start with love and relations between the sexes. Cohabitation is forbidden in camp. In some camps, there are no women or almost none, and there are women's camps where there are no men or very few. In a normal camp, women comprise a small minority and live separately. The many years spent in a camp are a greater tragedy for a woman than a man because, while serving her ten-year sentence, her florescence fades, and she loses not only her health but also her youth, attractiveness, and the possibility of finding a man who will love her. The camps, in which ten to fifteen million people in their physical prime spend long years, condemn them to infertility and to surrogate passions—the men to depravity and the women to prostitution. Under normal conditions, these people would have annually brought hundreds of thousands of children into the world. The greatest infanticide in the world takes place in the camps.

You might think that people in the camps suffer from the curse of every prison in the world—sexual deprivation. There is a small library on this theme with respect to places of confinement. Yet it is a mistake to think that this phenomenon exists in Soviet camps. My book knowledge of this topic had to be revised when I landed in camp. In West European prisons, forced sexual abstinence gives rise to mass phenomena of pederasty and masturbation; there were cases of arrestees in solitary cells fashioning a likeness of female sexual organs from bread. Before my imprisonment, that had seemed terrible to me, but later I realized that if people could waste bread on such matters, it meant that they were not hungry. Such a thing is impossible in a Soviet camp, where the smallest crumb is seized. Every Soviet zek would say that whoever could think about a woman must have been sated. In the camp, sexual deprivation yielded to food deprivation. Worn down by many years of malnutrition, people became impotent. Their way of life simply left no room for sexual attraction. Working, eating, resting—that was it. A camp inmate would re- nounce all the temptations in the world for an extra piece of bread. In all the camps where I spent time, there were hardly thirty or forty out of a thou- sand who felt like men. Such people existed, of course—the relatively well-fed camp aristocracy, who wore good shoes and first-hand jackets, who not only ate enough themselves, but also could "support" others. Doctors and medics, who had the magic power to free people from work, kitchen managers, in- spectors of the special supply unit, and work bosses needed women. And the entire population of the women's barracks was at their disposal.

During my work as secretary, I read "decrees" sent to Square 48 from Medvezhegorsk, disgraceful reports of disciplinary punishments imposed on zeks caught in forbidden sexual relations. I could not help but think that these men and women who "were caught," exposed, publicly shamed, and placed in the punishment cell, might sincerely love each other, be attached to each other, and be the sole source of mutual support and comfort. Later, I observed in the camp instances of intense human love and tenderness, which under these conditions have a tragic value. No Shakespeare, however, could dream up this camp variant of Romeo and Juliet, in which the authorities drive the pair apart with a stick, like coupling dogs, place them in punish- ment cells, list their full name in the administration's decree and scatter them among various camps to prevent further violations of camp rules.

For women, who are few in number in comparison to the men and thus will always find a stalker, the labor camp, even though ninety percent of the men become impotent, is a school of prostitution. The only means of survival for a young woman, often a seventeen- to eighteen-year-old girl sent to camp for an incautious word or because of her origin, is to sell herself for bread, clothing, easy work, or the protection of the boss. Young girls who land in camp, in a milieu of prostitutes, thieves, bandits, and professional criminals, are defenseless, and the best they can do is to find a tolerable protector as soon as possible. They have nothing to lose. After ten years in a camp, in any case, they will turn into wrecks, worn-out human rags.

Pregnant women are sent to special camps where they receive better food and are freed from work for some time before and after birth. The state takes the children from them. The "book of norms" that lists the nutri- tional standards for adolescents and children, for record-setting workers and penalized ones, also has rations for pregnant women and infants in camps. These rations—milk, better food, and rest—impel women to seek pregnancy in order to escape, at least briefly, the severe camp conditions. Their driving motive is not sexual but material need. As a result, in women's camps, where thousands of women are crowded together, a man cannot appear without an armed guard. The shrews surround him and are ready to use force to extract what they need. The child will be taken from them in any case, and their sexual desire is suppressed. All they seek is rest from work and better food in one of the special camps.

The camp inmate's feeling of self-worth—that fragile and recent product of European culture—is destroyed and trampled upon even before he is brought to camp. A person cannot preserve his self-dignity when he is subjected to cynical and crude violence and cannot find any justification for his suffering, even in the thought that the punishment is deserved. The state, with all the enormous force and authority of organized society, has crushed him without any reason and for no purpose; it did not punish him or expel him because of a crime but simply abused him. Everything is suppressed in an ordinary camp inmate: his logic and feeling of justice and his personal right to attention to his most elementary bodily and spiritual needs. The only thing left is resignation and the recognition of his absolute worthlessness and lack of rights. Even a Western person, who by nature prizes individual willfulness and personal pride, cannot preserve the feeling of his own self-worth if he remains in camp. The surest way to make a person ludicrous and contemptible is to force him systematically to do work that he is incapable of doing, in the company of hostile people who are superior to him in strength and skill. In the camp, I saw an old and respected public figure, a lawyer from Western Ukraine, who was unable to light a bonfire quickly; healthy fellows, illiterate, but infinitely more skillful in the forest, egged him on and mocked his clumsiness. The old man had tears in his eyes. When someone cannot keep up with the others and gradually gets used to the idea that he is worse than everyone else because he cannot do what is repugnant to him—even that tragedy seems ludicrous. This is another, important stage in dehumanization. The time comes when a person hates himself, hates everything that constitutes his essence, and hates his own abilities. He aspires only to fade into the common mass, to be as obedient as possible, an industrious instrument of another's will. He forgets today what he did yesterday and does not know what they will order him to do tomorrow. He has learned not to have his own desires and knows how dangerous it is to show his unwillingness. He differs from the beast only in that he can be used in a wider variety of ways: in the forest and field, at a desk or a machine. He does not differ from a beast in his obedience and complete dependence on those feeding him and leading him to the work assignment.

For years, the zek is kept in a state that is neither satiety nor that acute hunger that might drive a person to rebellion, to madness, or to a speedy death. His condition is only malnutrition, a minor, humiliating feeling that weakening a person physically and mentally, imperceptibly and gradually, renders his body more fragile and directs all his thoughts, feelings, and appraisals in one direction. Like a hunted animal, the camp inmate is driven into an impasse, the ring around him is tightened, and the circle of his human manifestations and interests becomes more and more constricted. If a person doesn't get enough air and water, the thought of air and water will drive away everything else in his mind. If he does not get enough to eat, one can bring him—not immediately, but in two to three years—to a bestial condition when the moment of satiety becomes the culmination point of every day, the sole stimulator of all his actions. Being sated, lying down and resting, feeling beneficial warmth, living in the present without entertaining any memories of the past or thoughts about the future—that is the limit of desires and the degree of dehumanization that every prisoner reaches sooner or later.

As long as he still feels sorrow and pain, longing and regret, he has not been properly dehumanized. The ability to suffer is a basic human quality. A time will come, however, when, ultimately, he is indifferent to everything that happens to him, when he is dulled to complete insensitivity to everything that is not tied to the base functions of his organism: In the eyes of the KVCh (cultural and educational sector), he then becomes a person "worthy of trust," and, after they have dehumanized him, he can be made into a trusty and allowed to move unguarded, as they know he will not try to escape.

Soviet camps differ from all other places of imprisonment on earth not only by their astonishingly gigantic scale and murderous living conditions but also by the need to lie to save your life. You have to lie incessantly, wear a mask for years, and not say what you are thinking. Of course, in Soviet conditions "free" people are also forced to lie from fear of the regime. In camp, however, where he is constantly and intently watched for years, the inmate's behavior determines whether he will ever get out, and, in this case, pretense and lying are necessary conditions for self-defense. You must obediently echo the regime. You must suppress the inner voice of protest and conscience once and for all. You can never be yourself: that is the most terrible and torturous thing for people with a free spirit. People in camp, even if they formerly were friends of the Soviet regime or did not have an opinion about it, cannot help but be its enemies now. No one who knows the camps from the inside can remain a supporter of the system that created them. Nevertheless, millions of prisoners do not give themselves away by a word or gesture. Does the Soviet regime believe them? Of course not. But both the administration and the cultural and educational sector maintain the fiction, pretend that all prisoners are as good and devoted offspring of the Soviet country as they themselves are. They are isolated only temporarily, for a check-up. The meetings and assemblies, conversations, and wall newspapers for the zek are all full of saccharine official phraseology in which there is not one word of truth. It is difficult for a person who has grown up in the West to understand what this means—for five or ten years to have no rights nor the possibility to express oneself, to suppress the least "illegal" thought and to preserve funereal silence. A person's inner essence becomes deformed and disintegrates under such unheard-of pressure. In artificial camp conditions, it is impossible for any length of time to hide the contraband of impermissible thoughts and convictions from peeping Toms. In the course of time, the hidden invariably is discovered and revealed. Therefore the instinct of self-preservation forces millions of simple, unedu-cated people not merely to lie but also inwardly to conform to the fiction, "to play" at Soviet patriotism and behave according to the rules of this game. This is the grounds for "re-education" in the camps.

Camp "re-education" is based on the idea that years of suppressing out-ward signs of human convictions and feelings will cause them to die within a person, too. The intelligentsia, which is incapable of completing this process, die off at a rate of ninety percent. The remaining ones experience general atrophy of their consciousness and "puppetization" of the spirit. There are no longer lies and truth: this difference exists only for a robust and free consciousness. Dehumanized zeks retain something unexpressed in their subconscious, but their consciousness becomes steady, thick, and gray—absolutely passive and dead. No one demands that a zek "believe" in the wisdom and justice of everything around him. Even his executioners do not believe in that. It is sufficient simply to accept the known thought process—as an external sequence of things—and carry it out as a kind of camp ritual and uniform. It's enough to behave obediently, as if this entire sinister theater were truth.

A person who has spent five or ten years in camp can be released without worries that somehow he would get in the way of the Soviet regime. He is "educated," and this education will suffice for a long time. A dark foundation of fear has been implanted in his soul. I have mentioned the subconscious vestige that cannot be completely destroyed. The presence of the suppressed, deeply hidden subconscious vestiges in the zek's puppet-like existence leads to particular forms of what might be called "a camp neurosis," which I shall discuss in greater detail later.

How is it possible that the methods that I have tried to outline do not arouse mass protests in the camp itself and beyond? Although rare, there are cases of sudden, unconditional protest in camp. They always, however, come from exceptional people. Exceptional either in the sense of absolute ideological intransigence and faith, or, on the contrary, in the sense of having nothing to lose and not giving a damn. Here are examples of each.

At Square 48 and later, I met fanatic Christian martyrs. The camp people called them "little Christs." They were the last remnants of the crushed "Holy Rus"—the religious hermits, holy fools, and self-immolators of the eighteenth and nineteenth centuries. They regarded the Soviet regime as the work of the Antichrist, and they simply refused to serve the Antichrist. Old women and young girls—whether former nuns or simply profound and unflinching believers—refused to work on Sundays and holidays. A group of ten to twelve men, "little Christs," at Square 48, refused to work altogether. The authorities tried to keep them in the punishment cell or in the barracks on a punishment ration of 300 grams of bread but it turned out that the "little Christs" were receiving sufficient bread and food from the surrounding zeks who sympathized with them. Such support and the conduct of the "little Christs" could not, of course, be tolerated in camp. They tried for a long time to persuade them before bringing a charge of malicious refusal. In my presence, the director of the KVCh, a Komsomol woman, summoned a refuser-nun for a conversation. This was a "light case" because she refused to work only on Sundays. A woman entered, enveloped in a scarf to her eyebrows; she made a deep bow and stood by the threshold. Her face was stony, alien, not of this world. Perhaps this was a saint in a Soviet camp. The Komsomol woman looked at her with annoyance and some fear, as if at a mentally ill person. They had no common language. To me, the snub-nosed interrogator—some kind of Maria Ivanna[2] in a colorful blouse and ankle boots, who addressed the prisoner in the familiar form [*ty*] whereas the latter called her "citizen director"—was many times more disagreeable, repulsive, and disgusting than the unfortunate woman who faced either execution or a second ten-year term. They soon shot the "little Christs," and everyone forgot about them.

Suddenly, we Westerners at Square 48 had our own protester; he soon became so notorious that the district bosses and very nearly Levinson himself came to have a look at him.

---

2. Term for a simple peasant type.

This was Met, to whom I send a greeting if he is still alive somewhere and is continuing his barefoot, nonchalant existence.

Met was a round-faced, healthy Jewish fellow from the *Unterwelt* [under-world]. In any case, that's how he described himself. When they registered our trades, he did not allude to any proletarian virtues but told them to write briefly and to the point: "thief." To this day, I don't know whether he was indeed as thick-witted as he pretended to be or simply was much more intelligent and inventive than the rest of us. Met did not let them dehumanize him: from the first day, he dehumanized himself so radically that the authorities gaped in astonishment. Met demanded that first they feed him properly.

"Why don't you want to work?"—the prosecutor asked gloomily—I was present in my capacity as secretary.

"What good will it do me?" Met shouted happily in reply, with his Good Soldier Shweik–like idiotically grinning mug, his hair strewn with straw, and wearing an unbelievable rag from which his bare body protruded. "This isn't food, citizen chief! I won't work for such food."

"Where should I send you after this?" asked the prosecutor.

"To Hitler," barked Met.

"What?! Are you praising the German government?"

"The government doesn't interest me," answered Met guilelessly. "I am talking only about sausage; they have good sausage!" And he said that the Germans gave him sausage at work, but here they don't give it.

You can be sure that the interrogating authorities, deep in their hearts, enjoyed Met's frank answers and the audacity with which he said what they themselves knew but could not say. They put Met in the punishment cell, first taking off all his clothes. After being locked up, Met immediately began to yell savagely and horribly. He howled as if they were slaughtering him, and he yelled for hours on end. Who knows where he found the strength. At times, the screaming became particularly frightful, and then in the barracks people said: "Now they surely are beating him." As luck would have it, the punishment cell was right next to the fence, and in a separate little house on the other side of the camp fence lived the camp boss. Met howled inhumanly in his very ears and did not let him sleep at night. They used to release him in the morning. To our amazement, he would come out dressed like a prince, in all the best to be found in the camp: a new jacket and pants and shoes in good condition. The authorities thus were trying to win over Met and show him that if he worked, they would spare nothing for him. Met's appearance, dressed impeccably, with a broad smile on his foolish face, caused a sensation. For one day, he puttered around at production and graciously did thirty percent of the norm. That was enough from him, and the next day he did not agree to do anything. In the evening, they would take away his new jacket and trousers and again send him to the punishment cell. At night, we would lift our heads from the boards and hear a bestial low howl emanating from the little house in the wasteland. It was the protesting Met, screaming furiously.

"They will shoot him," some said.

"They won't!" said others. "He knows what he is doing. He is pretending to be a fool. No doubt he thinks that they will take him to the hospital or someplace else."

In fact, they did not shoot Met. Despite his counterrevolutionary speeches and praise of Hitler's sausage—or, perhaps, precisely because he was able to create an impression of lunacy and foolishness, the authorities backed away from him, and he was one of the first to benefit from the amnesty in the winter of 1941.

14

Wood Felling

AN HOUR BEFORE sunrise, in the half-light of the moon, the forest brigades go out along the snow-covered paths, along frozen icy roads. They leave
behind them the noise and commotion of the dispatch to work. The brigades
have stood for an hour, waiting for the gates to open and for the names to be
called; then, on the other side of the gates, the crush begins under the window
of the tool storehouse. Brigade leader Wroczynski takes an armful of axes,
straight saws, and bow saws, distributing them to the group leaders, who hand
them out to their men. On the right shoulder a bow saw, under the arm or on
the belt, an ax. "Let's go!" And the brigades are drawn into the thick of the
forest. We walk silently and morosely for about half an hour, accompanied
by the clanging of the pots where some have saved their morning soup. There
is no danger of its spilling; it froze immediately in the cold air. The drowsy
men feel weak; their bones ache, and their step is heavy. In an hour or two,
however, the feet will adjust, and the arms will gain strength. The work will
imperceptibly draw them in.

The groups disperse throughout the forest, about 100 meters apart from
each other. Upon arriving, we begin to rake through the remains of yesterday's
bonfire. The silvery heap of ashes is still warm. Underneath, at the bottom,
coals are smoldering; often it is just one little piece of coal, as small as a cigarette butt. Then, with the greatest patience and art, on our knees in the ashes
and snow, blowing on the little coal, we ignite it with a scrap of paper or rag
or padding ripped from our own jackets. Dry sticks about the size of a match
are placed on the small fire; next, we add larger chips from that valuable piece
of dry wood that we purposely hid yesterday evening. Large dry branches,
then resinous firs and pine branches, whole small saplings crosswise on them,
and finally, crushing everything, a 4-meter heavy log is placed on top. The fire
bursts forth; the pine needles crackle and scatter sparks around.

A large block is placed in front of the bonfire, and members of the unit sit down to rest. It is still dark. People sit motionlessly, focusing on the feeling of warmth, calm, and the final minutes before the start of work.

The sky turns gray and the brigade leader, emerging from behind the trees, rouses the men: "You've sat enough!" The guard makes the rounds of the units, counting people. A separate fire is prepared for him, where he can sit and doze until dusk. Finally, the feller rises first. Choosing a tree, unhurriedly, plodding through the snow up to his knees, he clears away the snow around the tree, laying bare the base of the trunk. Then, with the ax, he chops, but not deeply, on the side where the tree is supposed to fall. Straddling his legs, he bends over with the saw. Now he resembles an enormous mousy-gray ugly spider who latched onto his victim and will not let it go until he "drains its blood" and topples it onto the snow. The dry, grating noise of the saw disturbs the silence of the forest. The blade moves back and forth with a hissing and grating, and each time a stream of wood dust flies out of the transverse notch, like the tree's white blood.

Before 1940, the Westerners did not know anything about a bow saw. In Poland, they sawed trees the old way: two men with a straight saw. The Americans invented the bow saw. It is a Canadian saw with a fine blade on a frame. The teeth of the saw face in three directions alternately: one is bent to the right, the second to the left, and the third is straight: this is called "tooth setting." If the saw is properly taut, well sharpened, and the teeth have the proper setting, then in the hands of a master feller, it moves like a bow in the hands of a virtuoso violinist. The fine, fragile blade passes through the powerful trunks as if through butter. Every fifteen minutes, a 20-meter column of wood falls with a thunderous crash, breaking the branches of neighboring trees in its path. The feller straightens up, and then one sees that this is difficult work. His face is red from exertion and his heartbeat is strong and fast.

Four men work in the group. The first, the feller, kills the tree. The second, the limb stripper, disrobes the tree. He rushes at it with an ax, cuts off the crown, and then the transversal branches and boughs, which sometimes are rather thick. The bough burner follows him. He collects an armload of the cut boughs, brings them to the bonfire, and turns them into fire. According to the regulations, by evening there must be no remains at the location of the felling. The fourth person is the cutter. He is equipped with a 2-meter pole that he has measured and marked with the necessary divisions. His task is to determine the wood's use and to saw the bare trunks in accordance with size and tree type. There are many sorts of trees. The aspen is used for firewood; the pines go for "plank timber" and to the sawmill; the birches for "balance" and paper manufacture, the substandard for pallets and props, and "shipbuilding" wood for masts. The firewood is cut into 2 or 4-meter lengths, the "balance" into 2.25-meter pieces; the construction material and masts have their own measure. Improperly cut wood is considered defective, and the foreman will not accept it in the evening. Cutting wood that is suitable for "balance" to the length of firewood or substandard means a loss for the state. A cutter who makes such mistakes is incompetent or a wrecker.

"Watch out!" yells the feller, without looking around when he feels the tree starting to tremble and give way under his shoulder. Press harder, and the cracking tree starts slowly to fall. One must never saw the tree all the way through as it will lose its equilibrium at the base, turning into a terrible murder weapon. It is impossible to guess where it will fall, and it could suddenly crush the feller himself. Even if it does fall in the right direction, often some side branch gets stuck on the way, and the trunk changes direction. Wood felling has its victims. Each season at the camp people fall victim to lack of caution or inexperience.

Don't think that the work of the one who does the stripping or of the bough burner is easy. They used to send the weak Westerners to do this work, and they lost their last strength there.

Throwing fir needles into a brightly burning fire seems like a very pleasant task. In fact, no bough burner manages to handle the enormous weight and volume of fir boughs that a good feller will amass for him. The nightmarish aspect of this work is that it is never-ending. The feller cuts down a tree and, without looking around, saws the next one. Immediately one has to cut off and carry away a mass of branches; otherwise, in a few minutes, another tree will lie across or next to it, and then a third on the second. The branches of the lower lying tree will be crushed, and it will be impossible to reach them. You should see how a narrow-chested worker of the third category with a typical intellectual's face, the Viennese Jew Muller, in the past a merchant or accountant, drags enormous bundles of branches to the fire—for an hour, two, or three. He no longer has any strength, but the more he drags, the more they pile up. He is drowning in this flood of pine and fir, and in the meantime, his bonfire is dying out. Either the water from the snowy boughs extinguishes the fire, or everything burns up in the ten minutes it takes him to drag the fresh boughs. The fire plays hide and seek with Muller: now it appears and now it hides; now it burns clearly and now it dies down. So much tension and strain on the nerves! A thick, acrid smoke rises from the bonfire. Muller's face is black and scorched, everything on him is torn, wet, and dirty; he is covered in soot and grime, but he cannot sit down: trees are falling behind him with a crash, and the feller yells angrily, "Are you sitting again, you Yid's mug?"

One good thing about this work: having made our way into the depth of the forest and lit our bonfire, we, in Glatman's unit, can forget about the camp for some time. We are our own masters. No one breathes down our necks, no one hurries us, curses, or harasses, and the bosses—in the person of the foreman or work supervisor—drop in on us no more than twice a day. Our group boss Glatman, a driver by profession, seeing in the distance that someone is coming, warns us: "He's coming," and with redoubled zeal we grasp our saws and axes. In the presence of the bosses, you won't sit down to rest. Taking advantage of their absence, however, from time to time we sit down for a so-called "smoking break." The flame from the bonfire scorches the face, while simultaneously, at 30 degrees below zero, the back of the neck freezes. At midday, whoever has a piece of dirty, matted bread takes it out of his pocket. The Westerners have their own way of enjoying it; they stick the bread on a long bough and hold it above the burning coals until the bread becomes golden and hot and is covered with a bronze crust, and when you break it, it is all steamy and aromatic. . . .

At around ten to eleven o'clock, the first wagon arrives. By that time, we have gathered enough for the first load. Huge tree trunks, like carcasses of forest animals, lie on the smoky glade, chopped into pieces by the cutter. Not one but two or three bonfires blaze in the clearing. The bough cutter, following in the tracks of the feller, transfers the fire from place to place in order not to drag the branches too far. The glade is full of smoke, and in the heat of the work, people have thrown off their jackets. The difficult task of loading begins. Everyone participates along with the driver. The wagon can hold from 1 to 2 cubic meters of wood. Armed with stakes, people begin to roll the logs to the wagon: "One! Two!" Sometimes the efforts of five men are insufficient to move an enormous log that has gotten stuck in the mud. You need to plant the stake, apply the shoulder, and press until your eyes pop out of their sockets. The long, sharpened stake bends and cracks. Our bones also crack. The most difficult part is to load the logs onto the wagon. With the aid of the stakes, they place them above the poles that have been arranged below. Often at the last second, someone lets go, and the log, almost on the wagon, slides and slips down, to general despair. When the wagon is loaded, all efforts are directed at the unfortunate nag, who is no condition to drag the wagon on the difficult, slippery road. Finally, the wagon starts to move, and the entire group accompanies it, helping the horse pull, supporting with their shoulders on the dangerous turn where the wagon leans on its side. The wagon disappears from view; all are enervated, their feet are trembling, and they are out of breath. We need to rest, but in fifteen minutes, the brigade leader appears with the news that the wagon overturned halfway. And all of us, with poles on our shoulders, go to load it again.

Is it surprising that under these conditions, we never were able to dispatch more than two or three wagons? And I never exceeded thirty percent of the work norm, while busting my guts.

During that first winter, we were still dressed warmly. I had felt boots and wool socks sent from Pinsk. Despite that, on the first day that I went to wood felling in the forest, my big toes got frost-bitten. The Belarusian soft, black felt boots that my mother had sent were not suited for Karelia. In the north, people wore thick, heavy gray felt boots, but only the select received them. The masses wore *bast* shoes and leg wrappers, torn footwear into which they stuffed straw, and we all had frozen fingers and toes. At midday, a nurse would make the rounds of the brigades with Vaseline, just in case.

Our unit leader Glatman was one of the few Jews whom the administration presented as an example and proof to others that Westerners are capable of all kinds of work. To further this goal, they flattered and praised Glatman, and in the evening, they added on the missing percentage to give him a Stakhanovite ration. Glatman, a tenacious and healthy man, set himself the goal of staying in the first ranks of wood felling. He succeeded for some time, and, possibly, under normal conditions he would have become an excellent wood feller. At Square 48, he overtaxed himself. Soon he would toss away the saw in the middle, without sawing through, straighten up with a contorted face, no longer red, but pale, convulsed with a spasm. He became irritable, began to clutch his chest, and quarreled with the foreman. I was unable to remain in his group, as he unambiguously let me know that he needed a better worker. By the spring, Glatman was a goner; he was drawn and thin and barely moved his feet. They removed him from wood felling.

Sooner or later, wood felling kills everyone who makes an ephemeral career of a camp record-setter. Each one ends as a cardiac case and invalid. The camps are full of "former stars," people who walk with a cane and tell what bear-like strength they used to have and what miracles they accomplished not long ago. Here is a typical story.

People who spent that winter at Square 48 remember the name Zakrjevski. He was a Russian, despite the Polish surname, a youngish person who made a name for himself throughout the BBK. Zek Zakrjevski was earning 800 rubles a month at wood felling. His unit was super-Stakhanovite. It produced 80 cubic meters daily, i.e., three times more than Wroczynski's entire brigade of thirty Westerners. This unit alone was served by an entire brigade of wagon drivers, who worked from morning to evening and did not manage to transport all the wood felled by this thin, dark, young zek with the eyes of a doomed man. Zakrjevski's fame reached all the camp sectors. He was our celebrity and pride, the ornament of Square 48 and its number one man. Even the camp boss, when speaking with him, would fawn over him and pat his hand. There were no food norms for him. When in the evening, Zakrjevski's unit—the camp elite—returned from work, the kitchen manager himself would come to ask what they would like to eat, and they would bring them bowls full of macaroni, cutlets, and rolls—the fanciest that there were and without limits. For them, they got hold of forbidden alcohol at 100 rubles a liter, and the zek Zakrjevski lived at the camp like a feudal prince—in separate premises with his unit.

Zakrjevski was needed to show the gray mass what "the aristocracy of labor" is, to urge on the masses, and to give them a goal. They spurred us with Zakrjevski, goaded the masses with Zakrjevski, as one drives a lagging nag with a whip. Of course, he was a strong and skillful worker, moreover, obsessed by his record, like one possessed. All this, however, does not explain 80 cubic meters a day. Zakrjevski's record was a bluff. The administration needed it for publicity, and it was achieved in the following way: Zakrjevski was assigned to an exclusive sector of the forest, given the best instruments, and exempted from the obligation to cut down everything in succession; he felled only selected trees, ignoring the unsuitable small ones; he was also released from burning the leftover cuttings. Others cleaned up after him. Nor did he take part in the loading. On the contrary, every arriving wagon driver was obliged to take a saw and fell a couple of trees before leaving. Finally, if you divide 80 cubic meters equally by four, it would not be such a sensational record. Therefore, they ascribed fifty percent of the norm to Zakrjevski's coworkers and concentrated all the production results on him alone; this yielded that enormous wage, which he divided among his group's workers.

Zakrjevski did not impress those who witnessed up close how his super record was achieved. He made waves and shone at Square 48 like a falling star. He squeezed all his remaining strength and blood out of himself and burned up in three months. People soon stopped speaking about Zakrjevski. He became ill with tuberculosis. They moved him to another camp to die. Invalids of forced labor do not get credit for their former records. Like a squeezed lemon, they toss them to the farthest corner of the enormous garbage dump where millions of "goners" swarm.

The word "goner" [*dokhodyaga* in Russian] requires an explanation. When a zek loses the physical and moral minimum necessary to remain on "the surface" of camp life, when in the process of dehumanization, he crosses the fatal boundary beyond which unrestrained collapse begins—in short, when he loses his human image, then in camp slang, people say that he has reached the bottom. In Russian, this is generally said about someone lying on his or her deathbed, in final agony. "Hitting the bottom" in camp means no longer washing in the morning, not undressing at night, and ceasing to pay attention to your appearance and to what people say about it. Hitting the bottom means becoming completely demoralized, sinking into complete despondence, begging for an extra scrap under the kitchen window, finishing off other peoples' leftovers, and drowning without resisting.

A goner is a person with a broken spine, a pitiful and repulsive phenomenon, in rags, with lifeless eyes, not only without physical strength but without the strength to protest.

The *urka* is the camp wolf, a dangerous being, ready at any moment to bite and bare his teeth.

The worker is the one who somehow manages to hold on and knows his worth; the administration protects him because the camp economy rests on him.

The goner is the camp mangy dog or hyena. Everyone has given up on him, including the administration, which no longer expects any benefit from him and leaves him to his fate: "Let him croak and the hell with him."

When the camp carries out a periodic check of the weakened and exhausted people, they send primarily those who are still worth feeding to the "weak groups" and the "resting groups" in the hopes of returning them to the regular work force. They do not take the goners, as it is a failed business; they are written off the accounts. It is not worth wasting time, attention, or meager material resources on a goner.

That winter was savagely cold; the trees in the forest cracked, lips turned blue, and the blood stopped in one's veins. The ethnic minority brigades from steamy Central Asia were released from work at 25 degrees below zero centigrade. For us, the limit was 30 degrees. But they did not stick to this limit. The sole thermometer hung at the guardhouse. Often, going out in the morning to the work lineup, we saw the thermometer removed so as not to upset people. When we remained in the barracks because of the cold, the day would be entered into the calculation of future days off. The number of goners at the camp grew daily. The wind blew snow into the barracks through the cracks in the logs and windows. We slept on bare boards, putting down the jackets in which we worked during the day. I was happier than others: I had a blanket from home in which I wrapped myself with my head inside it. Under my head was a bag with my things; on a ledge affixed by my friend Arye Barab was a small, rusty metal pan and a blue mug. Waking up in the morning, I would see the head of my sleeping neighbor covered with snow: the snow covered the bed board and was on the hat with ear flaps in which he slept. There were 350 goners in the camp. The experiment with Westerners was drawing to an end: half had fallen off their feet.

At Medvezhegorsk, they sounded the alarm. In order to get people back on their feet, they assigned them to the "weak team" for two weeks. They released them from the obligation to fulfill the norm and gave them Stakhanovite rations. Then people completely stopped working. They set ful-filling thirty percent of the norm as the condition for inclusion in the weak working force. That meant that they awarded Stakhanovite nourishment to those who were still capable of working but left the others to croak. We skidded lower and lower but tenaciously clung to life: packages would arrive; we still had a few items; the official ration was not the sole anchor of our life. In the neighboring sector, a former bank director committed suicide; in our camp there was a case of insanity, but these were isolated cases. Hospital deaths, however, became more frequent. The Westerners died most frequently from pneumonia—the result of poorly dressed, weakened people doing hard work in the winter forest.

One of the first to die at Square 48 was the young feller Timberg. He kept waiting for letters from his sister and grieved that they had forgotten him and did not write. He never got the letters, but after his death, suddenly let-ters began to arrive frequently. By then, however, there was no one to read or answer them.

One of the earliest symptoms of exhaustion is a weakening of the bladder. This is a burdensome misfortune, when people have to get up five or six times during the night. You have to picture the upper bunks which one can reach or descend from only with a little stepstool, with great effort, the foul-smelling lamp on the table—spindly legs of a semi-skeleton dangle in the flickering light of the burner, groping for the edge of the lower bunk and the floor, a person in his underpants, wrapped in a blanket or jacket, wandering to the exit in minus 30 degrees centigrade. Relieving oneself next to the barrack in daytime can lead to being sent to the punishment cell, but at night, no one goes more than a step away from the door. Then, from the sharp, piercing cold, straight to the stove. At night in the barrack, the stove is plastered with thin figures in blankets who stand immobile, hugging the stove, clinging with their entire bodies, leaning their foreheads against the hot wall. There are goners who stand that way for hours, until they are driven away. People who have to interrupt their sleep every hour and run outside cannot sleep enough or rest during the night. It is not surprising that during the day they fall asleep at work.

The first signs of self-mutilation appeared at work. One of the Westerners slashed his hand with an ax, cutting off two fingers. People who froze their fingers were not sure that they would be released from work. The person without fingers did not fare well: the authorities expertly checked how this occurred and the wretch who preferred mutilation to forced forestry labor was brought to trial on a charge of intentional self-wrecking. They took him away.

The Westerners held on as best they could. Fantastic things would happen in the Onega forests. Once, sitting in a circle around a bonfire, which was shooting out red-gold sparks in all directions, a brigade of hapless lumbermen started to argue: What is the theory of relativity and can ordinary human reason comprehend it? It was midday, the time for a cigarette break. I audaciously took up the challenge to explicate clearly and intelligibly for everyone what Einstein did. It was an audience of socially dangerous Jews; they sat sticking their feet clad in the rubber *chetezes* directly into the fire; the rubber stank; the jackets were burning, and agape they listened in the snowy forest, watched by an armed guard, to a story about Ptolemy, Newton, and Michaelson's experiment, an illicit tale forbidden by the KVCh educator and not envisioned by the Plan.

The jackets, indeed, would catch fire. From time to time, someone would sniff the air and say to his neighbor, "Friend, you are burning." "Where?" the neighbor would ask, and he would start turning in all directions until he found the place where the spark had fallen. From the cotton-wool socks and quilted trousers to the jacket and hat, each of us was dressed in cotton wool, wearing an entire quilted blanket. It was impossible to protect yourself in the bonfire's smoke and flame. A spark, landing on the jacket, would immediately burn a hole in the thin cotton cloth, and, from within, the cotton wool would imperceptibly begin to smolder, smoke, and burn. After five to ten minutes, smoke would start to seep through the holes. A zek who noticed this in time would gather a handful of snow and stuff the hole, suppressing the spark. If that did not help, you had to throw off the jacket and stuff the burning spot into a snowdrift. It is hard to extinguish burning cotton wool. Sometimes it seems as if the fire is extinguished, but somewhere a burning fiber remains, and half an hour later, smoke will appear again from the same hole. Sometimes at work, a person would suddenly feel that he is hot in one spot—it burns; that means that the jacket has burnt through and the fire has reached his bare body. One must act radically and decisively—tear out not only the reddish-burning spot but also, unsparingly, all of the cotton wool around it. It is easy to spot a lumberman by the gaping holes in his clothing from which strands of burnt brown cotton stick out on all sides.

As a professional bough burner and near-sighted person, I frequently dueled heroically with a burning jacket that refused to be extinguished. I would snuff it out on the back, and the sleeves would start to burn. I would extinguish the sleeves, and the back would start smoking again. In the end, I would tear out almost all the stuffing and bury it in the snow. I can still sense in my nostrils the odor of the frozen and burnt, sooty and rotted cotton wool. For a long time, I would dry the damp jacket in front of the fire; then, finally, after I donned what remained of it, no matter what, in half an hour, again it would emit choking, rancid smoke. As a prisoner is allotted a jacket and quilted pants once a year, you can imagine how picturesque we looked in a short time.

The hoary forests on the shores of the Onega are majestically beautiful. In the winter, it is a gleaming, white kingdom of rainbow-like, opalescent iridescence, a Niagara of snow, and such amber, rosy and dark azure water-color radiance on high, as if an Italian sky had opened over Karelia. The forest depths are undisturbed by wind, and the flames from the bonfires rise directly to the sky. Nature is beautiful and virginally pure so long as there are no people. The people in this forest and everything that they have set up are so monstrously ugly, so absurdly terrible, that it seems like a nightmare. Who thought up this agony, who needed slaves, guards, punishment cells, dirt, hunger, and torture?

Behold the zek from the road brigade walking along the forest track. Today, I, too, am with them. They are on the move all day, from darkness to darkness. They cover 15 to 20 kilometers, checking the roads, fixing holes, putting logs down in the ditches, planing the roads for the sledges. It is difficult to be in the freezing cold all day without a fire. And, yet, how good it is to walk by yourself with a group of friends through the forest, forgetting what is before and behind us. Here at the turn, we see a "Karelian match"; this is a hollow, rotting tree, beaten down by a storm, which has ignited on its own and is smoking—somewhere deep inside the hollow, a small flame glows for more than a day or two. Driving past, the driver stops the sledge and lights a cigarette. He will do it again on the return trip. For kilometers around, no one has a match or flame, and only a few camp veterans have flint and steel for striking, and instead of the old-fashioned tinder—a cotton-wool wick in a small metal case.

The road brigade enters the forest with axes and shovels. They are not permitted to deviate from their route, and an armed guard is waiting at the end of the road. Alongside passes a driver with a valuable cargo, the "aviation birch"—the most valuable tree in the local forests. The famous "Karelian birch," which is used for expensive furniture, is found not in the forests near Pyalma but somewhat to the south. The so-called "aviation birch" is an impeccably straight and smooth, undamaged trunk, a flawless one that will be used to make blades for airplane propellers. A wood feller is very lucky if he finds such a trunk—one in a thousand—as the norm in this case is lower than a cubic meter: if he finds one or two trees, he has exceeded the norm. "Hunters" seek the "aviation tree" in the forest like a rare beast; they wander in the snow up to their waist, scrutinizing the thick forest in search of the miraculous tree, and an armed guard trudges, sinking, through the snow after them, cursing his fate. When Westerners encounter something that seems like an aviation birch, a commotion begins: they call the foreman, consult, and examine it for a long time. If, indeed, it is an aviation birch, Glatman's gloomy gaze softens, and his dark-browed still handsome gaunt face expresses satisfaction. Today is a success, everyone will receive a Stakhanovite ration: there will be bread and kasha and a "baked dish"! More often, however, looking over the round white marble tree column with his vigilant eye, the foreman will point to a barely noticeable defect, and then everyone is disappointed and feels betrayed.

The road brigade proceeds from one work brigade to another. Now we are again at a place that needs work. A cloud of ferocious cursing hangs over the forest, not the naïve pre-revolutionary kind but a new type in which the sexual expertise of the village is interwoven with unheard of variations; instead of the devil, which has been irrevocably tossed out of the communist vocabulary, a certain blatant and unclerical means of reproduction figures most prominently in all expressions. The trees crash down, the loaders yell, the axes clatter. Groaning hangs above the forest, which has turned into a hell not only for humans but also for suffering animals. The camp horses, like the people, receive a ration and are perpetually hungry. The men beat them mercilessly with sticks on their sides, rump, and head and swear at them as if they were people. The horses suffer from thirst. Camp horses with protruding ribs drink dirty water from puddles, which normally a horse never does.

The last sledges have hurried past with the savagely howling driver, and the brigade that has finished the day's work assembles in the glade. It is dusk. The groups come together in one spot where a central, especially important group was working. The expert forester is already sitting there and smoking, the brigade leader bustles around, calling the workers, but the guard does not let them go on their way; it is too early. Where the groups had been working, the abandoned fires are burning out. They pour water on the flame while trying to keep coals under the ashes, so it will not be extinguished before tomorrow. Otherwise in the morning, you need to send someone to the neighboring group to request a favor, a firebrand, and then run with it through the forest, waving it so it does not burn out.

Before leaving, each group quickly saws a tree—a selected dry log—for the barrack orderly. Each one carries a little log. In the darkness, an especially bright flame burns in the clearing where the brigade has gathered. They have ignited a gigantic bonfire of such height and heat that you cannot approach it. People form a wall around it, drying themselves. They wash their hands in the snow; they have hung up their jackets around the fire. Backs smoke, jackets, quilted pants, worn over clothes from home all give off steam; in front of one's eyes it becomes dry, and then, gets darker, and bronze colored—you must pay attention that it does not start to burn, but at the edges, where it was damp, it remains that way. The brigade leader, cursing, collects the saws broken during the day and counts the axes. One is missing; someone flung it away. We must look for it; we cannot return without the axe. Finally, the long awaited: "Let's go, guys!"

The brigade has stretched out along the forest path, walking in pairs along the road, meeting and passing other brigades. All stream toward the guard-house; there they receive them while taking count. One says calmly to the other: "Your nose froze! Rub it fast!"

The little logs have to be hidden: they are stolen. They turn a blind eye to the logs that the wood fellers bring from the state forest: "It is against the rules, but the hell with it." However, the sawyers, road workers, and others, who did not fell trees themselves, have picked up their logs along the road from the piles prepared for dispatching—those had better be hidden under one's jacket. "Drop the logs!" the guard yells threateningly. And he holds up the brigade until they fling him enough wood to stoke an iron stove at the guardhouse for two weeks. Let them freeze in the barracks; that's not our problem. Some people are sent straight from the guardhouse to the punish-ment cells but the rest, clanging their pots, go to wait in line under the kitchen window.

15

The Medical Sector

IN THE FALL of 1939, a considerable number of Viennese Jews arrived in Lvov,[1] which was occupied by Soviet troops. The Germans had taken them to the Soviet border, and SS troops had transferred them at night to the Soviet side. They forced them to run through the forest at night along a narrow path; the SS men ran along to the right and left with their rifles atilt, making sure that no one fell behind. After Vienna, Soviet Lvov, thronging with refugees, seemed like a very sad and unpleasant stage in their wanderings. "The war will end soon; they'll defeat Hitler, and we shall leave this place," the guests from Vienna consoled themselves. But the war did not end. In the summer of 1940, the Austrian Jews were still in the way. The Soviet regime arrested them, sentenced them to forced labor camps for illegally crossing the border, and dispatched them to "BeBeKa" [BBK].

The Viennese musician and violinist Leo Winer thus arrived at Square 48. His name is not important. He could have been called Chopin, Schubert, or Mozart. His talent made no difference. He could have been the composer of the Unfinished Symphony, which would have made him world famous. At Square 48, however, no one pays attention to such things. He was in poor health, very nervous, and very naïve. An artistic bohemian type. He had spent his entire life in Viennese cafes, at a marble table on the Ring[2] or in the vicinity of Saint Stephen's Cathedral.

From the time of his arrest, this little man had been in a total daze. His wide open child-like eyes registered perpetual astonishment. "How could this be?" Over a cup of black coffee everything had been clear on Kärnterstrasse: "From

---

1. Now Lviv, Ukraine.

2. Ring—the main boulevard that encircles central Vienna.

each according to his abilities, to each according to his needs."—That is socialism. Leo Winer never thought about the hidden poison of this formula: in the future ideal society, who will assume the right to judge a person's abilities and needs? After all, the individual will not be the one to decree what his abilities are or dictate his needs. Who knows what he might decide he wants? Leo Winer regarded himself as a genius awaiting recognition and capable of great things. Leo Winer's needs always exceeded what was at hand. In this, he differed from a normal person.

When they brought him with his goggle eyes to Square 48, to a corrective labor camp for Soviet people, he finally understood. He understood that Soviet people's abilities and needs are not determined by personal caprice. It is an objective measure that is established by the recognized organs of the people's power. In the given case, these organs were the Gulag and the administration of the camp sector.

Leo Winer's capabilities were determined by the medical sector and the camp administration: a worker in the third category can be a bough burner at wood felling. Leo Winer's needs were boundless and unrealizable. A socially conscious and disciplined bough burner, however, cannot want more than what Soviet society at a given stage of development of its productive forces can give him: once a year, a marinated second-hand jacket, bare bed boards, and the first category of rations for those fulfilling thirty percent of the norm, that is, fish soup without kasha. For one hundred percent—kasha, and for one hundred fifty percent—other supplements. But what percent must you fulfill in order to attain freedom and the right to live in Europe and engage in musical activity?

Looking at Leo Winer, from whom they had taken his violin, I recalled another musician, my friend Leon Shafer, to whom a Nazi soldier had said: "The music is over for you Jews." They did not, of course, say that to Leo Winer. They simply put him in a train car and brought him to Square 48 to serve his term.

At camp he immediately developed myocardia, an inflammation of the heart muscle, and he was sent to the infirmary. In this forest hospital, however, there were no medicines for his illness. They decided to move Winer to Pyalma, to a real hospital. Discussions began. Little Doctor G., who had not yet been removed from his position of director of the medical sector at Square 48, would come into the office and yell with frustration into the telephone receiver in his peculiar Russian-Polish dialect, "Permit me to say![3] Permit me to say, citizen boss, he is dying here, and we cannot help him."

---

3. The doctor uses a similar sounding but incorrect word in Russian and what he actually says is, "Destroy me to say."

After protracted efforts, the order came to transfer the zek Winer to the central division hospital. Just then, however, misfortune struck: precisely, the sole locomotive on the Pyalma–Square 48 route broke down. Communication was discontinued. We were cut off from the world. Neither packages nor letters. The head of the Pyalma medical division Tsypodai categorically demanded that the sick man be transferred. The camp sector boss Petrov added a resolution: "To the commandant for implementation." Commandant Panchuk scratched behind his ear: "A wagon?"

The sick man's condition made it dangerous to transport him in a jolting wagon through the forest. There was, however, nothing to lose. There was no treatment here, and there, after all, was treatment and a hospital. They agreed upon a wagon, but there was no horse. All the wagons and horses were at work in the forest. How could one take a horse from the work site at such a critical time, when the plan is not being fulfilled anyway?! The work boss began to drag things out, to procrastinate.

Then the director of the medical sector Doctor G. phoned the head of the medical division in Pyalma, Tsypodai, and the latter phoned the boss at Square 48, who had a meeting with the work boss. And they ordered a driver with a horse. But there was no armed guard. The zek Winer could not be sent out without a guard. The commander of the guard unit, however, categorically refused to allocate a person to guard one sick man. It would have been a different matter if there were a few sick people, but one sick man could wait until a group formed.

Then Doctor Wasserman, the head of our infirmary, ran to the head of the medical sector, Doctor G., who, "permit me/destroy to say," phoned Tsypodai at Pyalma. Tsypodai, however, was too unimportant to speak with the commander of the guard unit; Tsypodai spoke with the head of the division, who then addressed the request to the commander of the guard unit.

They allocated a guard, but at that time the wagon broke down. Petrov summoned Panchuk and cursed him roundly. Panchuk, leaving the office, crimson with anger, showered curses on the people who arrived from Vienna to die in the Onega forest.

The next day they fixed the wagon. A day later, they attached a horse to it. In the meantime, the guard who had been assigned had left with an entire group of prisoners. They waited for his return. They waited two days. During that time, Winer died. Nevertheless, they sent him to Pyalma. It was a dank, foggy morning. The coffin lay in the dirt on the mound behind the infirmary in the open air. Finally, the long-awaited wagon with driver, horse, and guard arrived. Panchuk personally organized the dispatch. Everyone felt relief that this incident had finally ended. In such cases, they say in the camp, "He was released before the end of his term."

Theoretically, one must not force invalids and sick people to work. In practice, in camp conditions, it takes considerable time to determine who is sick and who is an invalid. They take no one at his word. When a prisoner feels that he is getting weak, is coming to the end of his strength and feels worse every day, that does not release him from the duty of rising at 5:00 a.m. and standing in the lineup with the brigade. Each goner goes through a critical and tragic period until he succeeds in convincing those who decide his fate that he is not faking, that, indeed, he needs a rest, that, in fact, something is wrong with his heart and his feet are shaking. In the meantime, he must work equally with everyone else.

At Square 48 there was a Polish national, Oczkowski, who would come to the infirmary every evening seeking a release from work. For some unfathomable reason—either he did not look sufficiently miserable, or, in the usual evening crush of patients, the doctor did not have enough time to examine him properly. Every evening, they would drive him away in contumely from • the clinic. In the evening, he would bicker with the doctor; in the morning, he quarreled with the brigade leader. Every evening, they reported that he had not fulfilled the minimum thirty percent of the norm, but the medical sector asserted that there were no grounds for dismissing him from work. And every evening, they would put Oczkowski in the punishment cell with instructions "to take him out to work." Oczkowski's existence turned into a nightmare: nights in the punishment cell, a penal starvation ration during the day, and from morning to evening, backbreaking work in the forest amidst shouting and harassment.

"Again, that Oczkowski!" said the doctor in the waiting room. "To hell with him."

"Again, that refuser," the brigade leader said in annoyance, catching sight of him at the lineup.

"Again, that slacker Oczkowski," said the camp boss, and he ordered him to spend five days in the penalty isolator.

And suddenly, after an entire week in the punishment cell while going out to work, Oczkowski proved incontrovertibly to everyone that he truly was ill: returning from the work site with his brigade (7 kilometers away), he tottered, fell, and died.

The evening of that same day, looking over yesterday's statements on refusers, the camp boss decreed another five days of the punishment cell for Oczkowski, who thus was sentenced post mortem to a penalty. Camp mechanisms operate with difficulty. I was then again sitting in the office, replacing the ill secretary. Seeing the deceased on the list of those designated to be sent to the punishment cell, I exceeded my authority and crossed his name off the list. That was, however, not the end of the case of Oczkowski. Learning that he had died, the medical sector took fright. This was no joking matter: a person had let himself die, although that morning and the entire preceding week, they had refused to release him from work. Of course, in the dispute between Oczkowski and the medical sector, he could not be right. They summoned the brigade leader, discussed the circumstances of the case, and composed a report that found that Oczkowski's death occurred completely accidentally and with no connection to the minor ailment that he had alluded to and which he did not have. The medical sector had acted properly, and the deceased would have been healthy if he had not died.

This report was brought to me in the office, and I sent it to the central division administration with a report of the death that contained not one word of truth. For now, it was not a matter of Oczkowski; now it was necessary to exonerate living beings who could be charged with criminal negligence that had deprived the state of a useful work force.

This incident had an epilogue in the boss' office. Our chief accountant, the zek Mai, with a thin neck and large Adam's apple, was going to travel to the Central Division to hand in the accounts for the camp sector, and another two office workers were accompanying him. "That's excellent!" the camp boss told them. "So you won't be bored, Oczkowski's coffin will ride with you." The office workers grimaced.

"Indeed!" said the boss, "Oczkowski should be accompanied to his final resting place."

As the boss Abramenko was a Ukrainian with a sense of humor, he pantomimed how Mai and his comrades, with heads hanging, walk after the wagon in which the coffin lies and sing a dirge. Bursts of healthy laughter reached me. That is how people with a clean conscience laugh. Boy, did these people laugh! Until tears, doubling over. It did not even occur to them that Oczkowski did not simply die but was murdered, tortured to death at the camp. Or that this Ukrainian with a sense of humor was complicit in his death—that for a full week, he sent a half-dead person to the punishment cell.

If you were to say that to his face, perhaps he would have been even more amused. Can the boss of a camp sector really answer for each incidence of death? And can the doctor in the medical sector really discern who is truly ill and who is faking? Who is to blame? Who, in fact, is to blame if people such as Oczkowski die, if they put them in the punishment cell after death and make merry over their graves?

I do not think that it was so difficult to answer that question. The answer was simple and clear. No allusions to so-called "historical necessity" can justify the deaths of millions of Oczkowskis. The Soviet regime's crime is not justified but, on the contrary, aggravated and accentuated if it turns out that there is no other way of reinforcing the power of those in the Kremlin other than the monstrous camp system of contemporary slavery and millions of anonymous deaths. The people who sent Oczkowski to the camp, the people who established the camps and the deadly grip of collective compulsion are guilty of his death.

There is no point in blaming the medical sector. In camp conditions, it inevitably becomes an accomplice in crime. The people who treat us are the same unfree prisoners as we are. I heard Doctor G., a prisoner-doctor at Square 48 say: "If in Poland, I had sent people to work in that state of health, they would have spat in my face." We are talking about Poland before 1939, but one can say that, not only the free world, but also the slave-owning America that we read about in childhood in *Uncle Tom's Cabin* did not carry out such systematic abuse of human beings. Why did Doctor G. act differently in camp than he would have in other conditions? Because he had been instructed not to let the number of those released from work for medical reasons exceed three percent of the total number of prisoners. One can excuse three out of a hundred, but the fourth and the fifth will arouse the anger of the Medical Division. Why are there so many sick people?—because the doctor is no good; the doctor answers for the number of sick people; therefore, he must be removed from the position. The medical sector sends reports to Moscow, and it is interested in showing a minimal number of sick people. How can you decrease the incidence of disease if every evening, crazed, half-unclothed and tormented people storm the door of the camp clinic, and they constitute not three but ten or fifteen percent? No doctor is capable of examining properly one hundred or more people in one evening, and it is not in his power to extend genuine aid without medications, bandages, or medical instruments. You cannot release all of them from work. That winter, the Western doctors fought with their own conscience; many became psychopaths, lost their mental equilibrium, cursed the sick, and kicked them out of the waiting room. When, however, a genuine *urka* arrived, a bandit with a bestial mug, and in answer to the question "What hurts?" would open his jacket on his chest, the doctor wordlessly would release him from work for three days. They did so with good reason: across his chest under the jacket hung an ax, a very convincing argument in camp life. The camp doctors were terrorized from two directions: by the *urka*'s ax and the perpetual threat of losing their job because of excessive leniency. As the percentage of those released was always higher among Western doctors than among Russian medical attendants, they very quickly were removed from responsible and managerial posts, and the authorities appointed "their own people" above them. They appointed a young Soviet zek-medic named Polonsky as the new director of the medical sector above Doctor G., and immediately the number of ill persons declined by half.

Of course, the prisoner-doctor's magical power of releasing his comrades from work was not unsupervised. A comparatively easy form of supervision is the sudden arrival of a doctor from the center, who is present during the evening clinic hours. The medical personnel immediately close ranks; the sick people know there will be no mercy for them today, and many immediately leave the line. It is a more serious matter when the inspector from the medical division arrives in the morning after the work brigades have left for work, and he orders an examination of all those who had been released the previous evening. They thus catch all those who had been released with insufficient reason, through acquaintance or pull, and the result of such a review can sometimes prove fatal for the doctor.

In my years spent in camp, frequently I saw the following scenes: the camp boss, who was missing workers to fulfill the plan, would order all those released for the day to appear in his office. The barrack orderlies wake up the sleeping zeks (each person who is released for reasons of illness does not, of course, get off the bunk but sleeps all day): "Go to the boss." This is an extreme nuisance. A crowd of bandaged and nonbandaged stand next to the door. Each one tries to flaunt *his* wound, hobbles demonstratively, and suffers excessively. The boss looks over each one critically, feels the bandages, and asks, "Hey, what's the matter with you? Don't fake it, I know you, you lazy-bones! Go, go to work, don't play the sufferer!" They immediately force the selected ones to go to the guardhouse, without letting them stop at the barrack lest they scatter. This is arbitrary conduct, but you will rarely find a doctor who dares to protest against this interference in the medical sector's rights. The camp boss is, after all, the physician's master: he addresses him familiarly, has the right to send him to the punishment cell at any time—and it is better not to argue with him, especially as complaints and denunciations against the doctors incessantly go to the Division anyway. Those who do not receive a release from work write vindictive denunciations against those who, in their opinion, were unjustly released. Every doctor has enemies, and in every clinic, an informer sits observing unofficially, and they send "special" sick people to every hospital and infirmary—from the third sector [the intelligence sector]—to spy on those who are suspected of machinations and collusion with the doctor.

Imprisoned doctors are better off than the ordinary zek. They have a circle of patients outside of the camp among the free workers. When free workers— whether the guard's wife with a child or someone from the settlement—arrive during reception hours at the camp clinic, they are always received out of turn. The doctor is frequently summoned to the guardhouse at night or in the middle of the day. The zek doctors often are very qualified and are the sole specialists in the district. Many have a renowned past, have attended universities in London, Vienna, or Italy. They are fortunate that in their Soviet imprisonment they are working in their specialty. If they had had a different specialty such as literature or philosophy, no learned works would have saved them from physical labor. In exchange for treatment, the free workers give the doctors a bag of potatoes, bread, or some other payment in kind that enables them to live and survive in camp. The kitchen also feeds them (semi-officially) better than the other prisoners, taking into account that they hold the keys to a prisoner's life. The cook who fills their bowls knows that the next day he may need their help if he loses his job. Moreover, he meets with them twice a day in the kitchen. The on-duty member of the medical sector arrives before breakfast and dinner are distributed, and he "tests" the food. The food is not distributed without his approval, and the "test" boils down to the doctor's eating a generous portion from the Stakhanovite ration.

In large camps where there are many sick people in the infirmary, the general kitchen and the infirmary kitchen are separate, and they cook separately for the sick. In fact, of course, the medics and medical personnel get extra food from the sick people's pot. The dead feed the living: if a sick person dies in the morning, they report his death to the food sector after two o'clock in the afternoon, when it is already too late to remove his name from tomorrow's meal list. The next day the kitchen will give bread and food for the deceased. It will not go to waste: someone will eat it.

During the five years that I spent in camps, I witnessed the stubborn and daily struggle that the medical sector workers conducted on behalf of the prisoners' health in hopeless conditions of a forced labor regime. It is a hopeless struggle, as the only means of saving the life and health of millions of people in camps consists of opening the gates wide, letting them free, and burning down those foul, shameful places where they are imprisoned. Truly, ninety percent of the camp population never committed a crime, and the entire one hundred percent do not deserve the many years of imprisonment in the hell created for them. One should distinguish between the individual good will of the medical personnel and the medical sector as a state institution whose task is not to defend the prisoners from the regime's arbitrariness but to guard the supply of workers in the interests of that regime. The significance of the medical sector is that it prevents epidemics, whose results would be horrible in the overcrowded and filthy camp. In my five years, there were no epidemics in the camps. The medical sector successfully fought against lice. We Westerners laughed when the order came from the medical division to Square 48 to liquidate lice infestation within a week. It seemed to us that instead of sending an order, they should have sent some soap and clean linen. However, we were wrong. Every camp has a "disinfector" who carries out an incessant struggle against lice, fumigates the barracks with sulfur, and sees to it that the camp linen—even if it is unwashed and unchanged—passes invariably through the "disinfection room," otherwise known as the "lice slaughterhouse." In this war, sometimes the lice and sometimes the people are victorious, but without it, the situation in the camp would be catastrophic. Understandably, these measures, carried out with barbaric zeal and threats of harsh punishment, can neither feed the hungry nor halt the elemental process of the weak dying. In some documents, former camp inmates evaluated the camp's annual mortality rate at thirty percent. This is a patently, absurdly exaggerated figure. In the course of a year at Square 48, the deaths among the thousand prisoners did not reach three hundred. I can state, however, with full confidence, that if they remained in the camp to the end of their three- or five-year terms, half of these thousand would not survive. For me, who spent five years in camp, that is, a full term, the end approached at the beginning of 1943, that is, after two and a half years. In 1943, and a year later, in 1944, I stood on the threshold of death from malnutrition. In both cases, only a "miracle," i.e., illegal outside help, saved me from a wretched camp death.

The medical sector's work reminds me of the work in the camp vegetable warehouse. At the end of 1941, I worked there sorting potatoes. This was not in Square 48 but in a different place. Generally, they send women to this work, but for two weeks, I sorted potatoes with a brigade of Poles. A 3-meter long wire netting stood in the basement, where the temperature was never lower than 0 degrees centigrade nor above 4 degrees so that the potatoes would neither freeze nor sprout. People with wooden spades stood to the right and left. Bags of potatoes would be emptied onto the netting, and the people would shovel and sort the potato stream: small potatoes would fall through the net but large ones would fall into big boxes at the lower end. They would place the potatoes in various sized bins: the large ones separately, the little ones separately, and the rotten ones, which they picked out by hand—separately. They winnowed potatoes incessantly. The state took the large ones and left the little ones and rotten ones for the camp kitchen. Standing with the spade above the stream of potatoes, I thought that there was a similarity between the work of the medical sector and that in the basement: the medical sector tirelessly winnows us—the healthy ones separately, the weak ones separately, and the rotten ones separately. The sieve of the medical sector is as full of holes and as unsuitable as the one above which I was standing, and it, too, lets through the rotten and petty elements and mixes together the dregs with the choicest material. The sole difference is that the potato lies where it was placed, whereas the human potato incessantly changes, transforms itself, shrivels and grows smaller in front of one's eyes. They shovel it with large spades without paying attention. They have just managed to put it into bins: first category, second, and third, invalids, the sick ones—and you already have to repeat the work from the beginning. Human potatoes are dumped into the machine in tons; the NKVD works, pours in more, and incessantly tops it off. Train after train unloads in the Onega forests, in the Pechora tundra, in the coal mines of Karaganda, the metal mines of Vorkuta, in thousands of Ural and Siberian camps, in the icy Arctic wastes. There are not enough doctors in white frocks, not enough medics, not enough working hands, nor the nerves and strength to sift and stir this mass. The human meat stinks and rots as it decays. Its lot is to be utilized to the end, to lie in the earth, and be forgotten. Yet this will enrich the Soviet land with the White Sea Canals and Turkestan-Siberian railways, steamships sailing from Moscow down the Volga, and the smoky furnaces of Magnitogorsk. Proletarian poets in wonderful France or South America will compose stirring songs about the Soviet country, and the entire world will repeat the words of the famous song: "I do not know another such country where a man breathes so freely."

16

My Enemy, Labanov

IN THE COURSE of ten months, there were three different camp bosses at Square 48. Petrov, given to foul curses, but good-natured and simple, was unable to maintain order in the camp. He quickly became dejected and lost any air of authority. On the final morning before his departure, Petrov was completely depressed; he went out to the carpenters who were putting up a fence around the women's barrack, joined them, and began nailing boards together and banging with an axe. He took off his official shirt and old cap and became absorbed in the task. Working together with the prisoners, he seemed to feel more of a man and more at ease than facing official papers in the office. His thin, nervous, and tired face assumed a peaceful and calm expression.

Petrov was a man of the older generation. Such people remember the romanticism of the Civil War and a past without camps. They preserve their cherished feelings and thoughts of Russia and silently harbor their sorrows and regrets that they do not talk about to anyone. It is unlikely that he dreamed in his youth, when he was a Red partisan and fought against the enemies of the revolution, that in his old age, fate would put him in charge of a concentration camp.

Petrov's successor, Labanov, was so incredibly young that when he first entered the office, it did not occur to anyone that this was the new boss. He owed his position to pull in Medvezhegorsk. Labanov wore a tight short jacket; he had a snub nose, and the look of a pen-pusher; he resembled, like two drops of water, the janitor Stanisław in Łódź, who swept the floor and opened the doors at the office where I had been working.

Labanov arrived during one of my periodic returns to the office. After Stepanov, the operative of the Third Sector, forbade them from keeping me in the office, I still returned there briefly several times. The office trusties were on my side. Sometimes, the time clerk Tenenbaum would toss me a food coupon, or the accountant Kunin would think up some work for a couple of days. Once, when I was diligently penning some report, Stepanov unexpectedly entered the office. Passing by, he barely squinted at me and said nothing, but the chief accountant Mai grunted with annoyance and ordered me to return to the barrack as quickly as possible—to get me out of his sight.

As Stepanov was living in Pyalma, he could not systematically harass me. Labanov, however, soon became a threat to me. I could not understand why, but it became clear later. In the first days, I indiscreetly had said to someone that Labanov was unsuited to be a boss, and in Łódź he could have been a doorkeeper in an office, at best. The walls have ears, and Labanov found out about those words. He never forgave me for that, and he bullied me according to all the rules of that art.

Labanov was so illiterate that he could barely read. Every day I had to read aloud to him and explain the contents of all the official papers. However, he mercilessly rejected every paper that I wrote, forcing me to redo and recopy it several times. With particular passion, he would send me on errands around the camp until late at night.

Dark days began for me. It was late fall, when the camp was drowning in impassable mud. I did not have footgear, and Labanov did not give me any. "You are not a worker," he said, "and you can run around the way you are." I went around the camp practically barefoot. Wounds and abscesses developed on my feet, but Labanov did not release me from racing about. I did not have the strength of character to decline this work; I feared that it would be even more difficult in the forest. The work supervisor Grib, whom I once gave some lard from my package, wanted to do me a favor and included me in a transport, that is, in a group that was being sent to another camp sector. At the last minute, however, Labanov ran into the barrack, saw that I was packing a bag for the road, and said in his squeaky tenor voice: "I won't permit it! He won't go!" and he crossed me off the list.

The first time that they ordered me to the punishment cell was when the dwarf Peterfreund, who remained in the empty office while I went to supper, did not immediately answer the phone. Because I was not near the phone when he called, Labanov penalized me with two days of the punishment cell. I myself wrote out the sentence, and Labanov signed it with pleasure. We then were sending so many people to the punishment cell that my turn did not come so fast. Now I can confess that I never did sit there. The head of the penalty isolator, Fridman, wrote my name down in the punishment cell register, and I spent my two days (that is, two nights) there only on paper.

Labanov forced me to read out his daily orders for the camp at the lineup before dispatch to work. I had to get up with reveille, go to the guardhouse, and, standing in front of the assembled brigades, read his orders for the camp, which included disciplinary measures. Writing these orders for the camp was part of my obligations as "secretary." It afforded him unbelievable pleasure that I thus had to compose and publicly announce the order for my own dispatch to the punishment cell. "Well," he asked, "Did you read about you yourself?" and he snickered.

Although Labanov committed me to the punishment cell three times, I did not sit there any of those times because the person in charge was "one of ours," a Westerner. Labanov soon got bored with torturing me, and he sent me to the forest. They chose a Russian as my replacement. My successor was a quiet, polite, sickly person, who was more skillful than I at utilizing the advantages of his secretarial position. His pockets were full of Stakhanovite food coupons, and each time that I would drop in on him at the office, without my asking, he would give me a coupon. In exchange, when I would receive a package, I would invariably bring him a pack of Ukrainian tobacco.

Under Labanov, half of the Westerners collapsed from exhaustion; the plan was not being met; and in the end, they soon transferred him elsewhere. In his place, they sent Abramenko, a former worker in the Third (political) Sector—the "Ukrainian with a sense of humor" whom I mentioned earlier. Abramenko fixed the "production" with the help of several hundred Russian zeks. The "Westerners" remained useless until the end of their stay at camp.

One winter morning when we had already been working for three hours in Glatman's unit, a wagon drove up to us. The approach was difficult, and it was not easy to position the sled in the right place. The horse balked, and the driver was unable to control him. The driver's movements were so awkward, and everything that he did so encumbered our loading that Glatman became furious. The driver kept doing the opposite of what Glatman ordered. Finally, Glatman swung his arm and hit the driver in the face.

I thought that a fight would start, but instead, the driver dropped his hands and broke into tears like a little child.

Glatman spit and walked away. "Why are you hitting him?" I said reproachfully, catching sight, under the cap with earpieces, of the very young face of a seventeen-year-old boy. "Everyone beats him! As usual it is Salek!"

"Why does he creep in where he shouldn't!" Glatman said angrily. "Does he really have the strength to be a driver? Is this really work for him? He cannot even turn the sled. Here he gets away with it, but if this were a Russian group, they would have broken his bones!"

Salek continued to cry, leaning on the shaft without wiping away his large tears. I went up to him and began to console him like a child.

Salek, indeed, thrust himself into the wrong places. He resembled a curious and naïve puppy, who sticks his nose everywhere and endures undeserved insults from all sides. His mother, no doubt, spoiled him at home. Salek told me about his parental home and his father's bakery in a Galician shtetl—what rolls they baked and what down bedding his mother prepared at night. He was healthy; his face was round and childish, and he had an amazing capacity to get under everyone's feet. In descending from the upper bunk, he invariably would kick the person sitting underneath. When he went to the stove in order to help (he was, moreover, complaisant, as a well-bred boy), to hand someone his mug from the fire, he invariably would turn it over and spill it. When they kindled the stove in the barrack, he would stir the wood until the fire went out although no one asked him to help.

Everyone, therefore, beat him mercilessly and fiercely. No day would pass without his uncontrollable sobbing, without his pitiful, childish wail ringing out, without his tear-stained face annoying us in the barrack. When someone wanted to warm himself at the stove and there was no room, he would kick Salek away like a puppy. "But I came first!" Salek would sob, stung by the injustice. When they asked who wanted to work with the horses, he responded without thinking. He was still unable to estimate his strength. His bones were still soft, but he had a wolfish appetite. Salek could never get enough to eat, and wagon drivers were well fed.

My sympathy or pity could not feed him or ease his work. The camp, however, educated him mercilessly—it taught him about the right of the strong and the laws of the struggle for existence. Salek turned out to be a quick learner.

I soon noticed him beating those who were weaker than he was. He learned how to get out of the way of the strong and to grab the weak by the throat. He developed a hoarse, bass voice, and he began to curse grandiosely and with virtuosity like a genuine *urka*. At the end of the winter, again someone was weeping pitifully in our barrack. But this was no longer Salek. Salek was the person who did the beating—in the chest, the teeth, the mug, just as they beat him; and then he walked away and spit, just as Glatman had done that morning. "Why are you doing this?" I wanted to ask but I did not dare. Salek looked at me scornfully, as if I was nothing. He had a wolfish look. A wolf cub! He already was able to bite painfully, he had learned to steal, was not embarrassed openly to take someone else's property, like a genuine *urka*, insolently looking one in the eyes: "Just dare to say anything!" People already feared Salek in the barrack, and there were rumors that he reported to the Third Sector what the Westerners were talking about. For a long time, they had trampled on Salek, until he learned to trample on others.

How could it be otherwise? The regime itself—infallible and omnipotent— taught him the lesson of cynical and crude violence. No one pitied him; no one taught him to respect others. In the camp itself, people respected only force. Salek soon learned to scorn the goners, people who were sinking to the bottom without resisting and did not know how to trip up an enemy. Salek's enemy was the whole world.

The seventeen- to eighteen-year-olds who landed in camp either became goners or quickly turned savage, rapidly adopting the outlook and ways of the bandits. Not all became wolves like Salek. Others, ultimately, like hyenas and jackals, lived off carrion; they trailed after the rich and powerful in the camp, gathering the left-overs; they would sit near the kitchen, waiting for the slops and potato peels to be thrown to them—they would stand guard, and when a wagon with cabbage would drive up to the food warehouse, they would fall upon it in a pack, despite the blows of the whip, to steal a head of cabbage and escape with it.

"Youth in camp" is a matter not only of prisoners. Vanya, an adolescent of about sixteen, was a free worker in the office of Square 48; he had a round head, closely cropped hair, and intelligent eyes. He was the son of exiles who were restricted to living in the region. He was a capable young fellow who had finished accounting courses and worked in the accounting office. At an age when he ought to have still been studying, he was completely independent and had started a career as a Soviet civil servant. The camp did not surprise or disturb him; he could not even imagine a world without camps. He was unusually solid and reserved for his age. Vanya lived in poverty: he ate little better than we did, wore a mouse-gray jacket and shirt just like a prisoner; he did not have his own room and found shelter in a corner of the room of one of the guards. I looked at him with curiosity: what did this youth know about life; what were his prospects for the future?

From a European point of view, Vanya was a semi-savage: never in his life had he been away from the Onega forests; he had no concept of urban comfort; he was amused at the sight of hats and ties in photographs of Westerners; he knew about apples or pears only from hearsay; he had never traveled on a tram; he had never eaten or slept in European style (he knew nothing about blanket covers).

Vanya had a very vague idea about Christianity—he had never seen the Old or New Testament. For him, all the wisdom of the world was contained in political education. He was spiritually castrated: he did not know that one could have differing opinions about various things, that one could doubt something written in a book published by the state, or that one could have one's own opinion about something.

Vanya, of course, cursed like an adult, without realizing that he was saying anything cynical or dirty. It was an ordinary means of expression for him. He willingly drank vodka with adults and spoke crudely about women.

The romanticism, elevated reveries, exaggerated youthful idealism—the rapturous communism that in the West operated with such concepts as "the struggle for freedom," "uprising of the enslaved," or "humankind" simply did not apply to him. He was an accountant at a camp and saw life as it is. At school they had taught him that this is the very best life, whereas abroad, there is capitalism, exploitation, and everything is much worse.

Once he asked me to tell him about the fruits in Palestine. I described oranges, bananas, grapefruits. "Yes," said Vanya, "interesting fruits. Only the exploitation there, that's what's bad!"

With all that, Vanya was a kid: it was hard for him to get up early and spend all day until late at night plugging away over numbers and papers, and he often was late to work. The guard would mark down all the free workers who worked in the camp as they passed through the guardhouse, and precisely at nine o'clock, I would take the list from the guard and report the tardy ones to the camp boss.

Vanya was warned once, twice. Finally, they wrote up a charge and sent it to the appropriate place. Vanya received a summons to the People's Tribunal. At that time, such cases did not have serious consequences. He was given between four and six months of forced labor at the same job and a salary cut of twenty-five percent. Vanya, however, became morose and even more docile. Life did not spoil him; it taught him iron discipline. Soon they took him from us and sent him to a neighboring camp.

As the son of exiles, Vanya grew up with a feeling of social guilt and stigma. In the vicinity of the camp, however, there were also many children from the families of camp bosses and guards. This was especially true of the camp where I spent three years after Square 48. These children frequently came to the office of the camp repair workshops (outside the camp gates), and when we were working beyond the guardhouse near the settlement, they would run up to us and play near us. They grew up in our sight, and we grew old before their eyes. The camp favorite was five-year-old Vova, the son of the head of the workshops; he was always surrounded by a mob of children older and younger than he was. When the brigades lined up on the road during the midday break and in the evening in order to go "home," the kids would crowd around them. The prisoners joked with them, lifted them onto their shoulders, and thus carried them up to the guardhouse. Vova and his friends would then attempt to sneak inside the camp gates, but that was forbidden, and the children were pushed aside. The guards would laugh: "You'll get to sit there when you grow up!" The children would stand in a group on the side and look with curiosity as the guard came out with keys and opened the door while another one counted the pairs as they passed by. Sometimes it was more interesting as the guards would search those coming from the field or vegetable storehouse to check whether they stole something. They would also search those who had just been joking with the children and carrying them on their shoulders. This was all right. Vova knew that there are two categories of people: some are counted and conducted under guard; they must behave and do the work that they are sent to do. That is the reason for the zeks' existence. They are poorly dressed, and when Papa arrives, they stand up and fear him. Papa can yell at them, but can they yell at Papa or Vova? It is ridiculous even to consider this. Papa, or Vova himself, or the people in the village, are entirely different from these zeks.

Vova grew up with camp inmates, just as the son of a landowner used to grow up with serfs, not asking why some carry arms, give orders, and live in separate houses while others live behind barbed wire, where outsiders are not permitted to enter. From childhood, he considered this natural, just as we urban children took it for granted in our childhood that villages surround the cities, and in them live alien, dirty, and poor peasants who perform hard physical labor and live entirely differently than we do.

The entire region was strewn with camps, and the zeks were not "criminals" but a normal, basic part of the population. Not "criminals" but simply outcasts. Seeing Soviet children growing up among prisoners, in an atmosphere of lawlessness and human degradation, getting used to prisoners as a most normal phenomenon, I thought that the adults ought to move the children away from here, as if from a brothel, and not allow children's eyes to see what they are doing. What kind of adults could develop from these children other than jailors—or slaves? I felt sorry for Vova, who from childhood grew accustomed to the sight of state-regulated slavery. He had clear blue eyes and was an inveterate mischief-maker. At five years, however, he already accepted the fact that these hundreds of "uncles" do not and cannot have families, children like him, that they do not have the right to go where they want to and are creatures midway between people and a herd of cows who are driven along the street and locked up at night. One need not fear them: if they dared to offend him, Vova, then immediately Papa or some "uncle" with a gun would lead them to the punishment cell, to that mysterious little house outside the camp, surrounded by a double fence and always tightly locked.

Often, encountering children with a carrot or piece of bread in hand, the famished zeks would stretch out a hand and ask "to have a taste." The children, however, would not fall for that bait. These were special children. No one taught them to give hand-outs, and I never saw a child give anything to a prisoner. It is true that they never had leftovers. When some ragged scarecrow would raise his head from a half-sawed log and look at them with longing eyes, you could not understand what the object of his longing was—the child or the carrot that he was holding in his little fist. And the chubby little seven-year-old, noting the persistent look, would shout to him from afar: "Hey you, go work! Or else I'll tell the guard!"

There was a direct link between Labanov, Vanya, and Vova. These kids would eventually grow into Vanyas and from the Vanyas would come Labanovs. Little was needed for themselves to land in camp. Up until 1945, I did not encounter children in camps, but in the fifth year of my imprisonment, at the Kotlas transit point, I ran into a children's brigade. There must have been some kind of "work colony" to which they were being sent. Children from ten to fifteen lived in a special building. They had their own "educator," an old Western zek named Pick, a Jew who before the war had worked in some commercial firm somewhere in Lithuania or Latvia. The children, just as the adults, went to work daily, dragged wooden boards or dug ditches. With the permission of the local educational sector, Pick invited me to give them daily readings for an hour after supper. In exchange, he gave me a bowl of kasha. Not for anything in the world would I agree to hold a discussion with them, and they would not allow me to, but I agreed to read stories from a book for older children. By good luck, I got hold of a suitable book, a very patriotic one. I went to them several times in June 1945. At that time, I had withered, my hair had turned gray, I moved with difficulty, and the children called me "Grandpa." I had grown wiser from experience and did not impose my reading on the young zeks as that would immediately have produced an opposite reaction. I would take a seat in a corner and, choosing one or two listeners, begin to read to them quietly. After a short time, a circle of ten to fifteen people would gather, and the children themselves would begin to hush those who were not listening: "Quiet, don't bother us!" Around us other children would continue to play with self-made cards, do their own thing, and converse. The judges who had sent these juvenile criminals to camps with two- and three-year terms must not have read Makarenko's *Pedagogical*

Poem.[1] When Makarenko wrote this book, he himself probably was unaware of what was happening in the camps, otherwise he would have lost the desire to write. All these children and adolescents were serving time for petty theft, hooliganism, and vagrancy. One received two years for stealing a kilo of potatoes from a private kitchen garden. The Kotlas transit point, where they were located, was a nightmarish assemblage of scoundrels, dying people, and hags in the last stage of human degradation. There is nothing more terrible and repugnant than a female goner who has not yet turned into a skeleton but no longer finds anyone who wants her body. The presence of children in this place was a double crime. What judges sent them here? I asked some twelve-year-old children, who told me that a woman had sentenced them. In my fifth year of imprisonment, this no longer surprised me.

Let us return to the camp by Lake Onega. I could not avoid the punishment cell after all. No zek can forget his first night in the "cooler." My first night came after a very unfortunate and difficult day. It all began very well. We went to the wood felling in a good mood: the snow glistened in the sun; it was a windless cold morning. We found a remarkable sector. Immediately, however, I sensed that something was wrong: the forest was too good—all pines equally perfect. This kind of forest was for record breakers, not for sickly Westerners with blunt axes. We lit a fire, sat down for a moment, and had just felled our first pine when the foreman ran up with a shriek: "You must not fell here!" The pine, however, was already lying there, and there was a fierce quarrel over it between the foreman and the brigade leader and then the brigade leader with our group leader. The trouble started with this quarrel. In revenge, the brigade leader sent the group to an open field to collect scattered trunks from under the snow, carry, and load them. We wasted a lot of time, and until the evening, we froze in the open field without a fire. We barely managed to gather enough for one wagon. A second was ready toward the evening, but the brigade leader did not send us a driver, and the wood was not hauled away. In such cases, it was customary to write down an "advance" for the wood that had not been hauled away. In this case, however, the brigade leader not only did not credit us with the remaining wagon but even wrote a report against us for not fulfilling thirty percent of the norm.

In the evening, we barely dragged ourselves to the barrack, starving and shivering after an entire day wandering in the open field. We were soaked through from carrying the snowy trunks. Before we could dry ourselves or

---

1. Anton Makarenko (1888–1939) was a Soviet educator and writer, who wrote about his experience in reforming juvenile delinquents.

receive our supper, they summoned the four of us with the group leader to the camp boss.

An unfamiliar person was sitting at the boss's table, a guest from the Department. Labanov, sitting on the side, was smiling insidiously.

"Wha--at's going on?" the visiting boss asked us severely. "Four healthy guys—they feed you, dress you—and how do you work? Against whom is this report?"

"Against us, citizen boss. Let us explain. . . ."

"Be quiet! No talking! I see what is going on! Laggards! Immediately to the punishment cell! Labanov! Give the order!"

My enemy Labanov gave the order with evident pleasure. They led us straight from the boss's office, without food for the whole day, in clothing bloated with water, to the hut near the fence. They brought in others, too, about ten people altogether. Letting people pass by him through the fence into the cell, the commandant Panchuk lifted up the lantern and lit up my face.

"And Margolin is going there too," he said with ironic surprise. "What's the matter with you, Margolin, you didn't make an effort today?"

At the entrance to the punishment cell, they searched us, removed belts, and everything that was in our pockets. In addition, they took away my glasses, without which I am blind. Then they pushed me into the moldy, stinking hole.

It was dark and cold in the cell. It was a square cage with plank bunk beds opposite the door. A jumble of humanity was lying on the bare boards. I groped with my hand—somebody's feet, doubled over bodies. There was no room. A latrine bucket stood near the door. A fetid puddle overflowed onto the floor. There was no place to lie down. I stood in a corner, leaning against the wall. I was trembling and feverish. I was standing for a long time. . . . Suddenly from the other side of the door, I heard the voice of the head of the punishment cell: "Margolin!"

"I'm here!" I replied.

"They brought you bread from the barrack. . . . Will you take it?"

"Give it to me!" I said and stepped forward in the darkness. Above the door was a small opening through which it was easy to push a ration. My comrades in the brigade had received bread for me, and someone brought it to the punishment cell, knowing that I had not eaten since the morning.

At that moment, in the darkness, a fist delivered a strong blow to my chest. Someone pushed me aside and without saying a word, stood in my place by the door.

"Fridman!" I cried desperately. "I don't need bread! Take it back!"

"You don't want bread?" the voice on the other side of the door said incredulously.

"Take it back!"

The voices on the other side became silent, the steps receded.

"What a bastard, damned Yid!" a hoarse voice wheezed near me. "He gave back bread! Just wait, I'll teach you!"

"Give it to him, give it!" responded a bass from the bunk boards. "That's the secretary. He sits in the office and writes reports against us!"

"Leave me alone," I said quietly. "I am not the one who writes; they write against me."

It is a very unpleasant feeling before a beating: not the fear of physical pain, but a humiliating sensation of impotence, complete hopelessness—in a pit, in the gloom, at the bottom—a mindless animal horror in the face of another's hatred and of one's own doom.

I screamed in a choked voice and called my friends from the group. They were nearby, but no one stirred or responded.

What happiness it is to fight, to resist, to roll in a heap of bodies! But that winter my deformed arthritic fingers could no longer bend, and I was unable to form a fist! I raised these unfortunate, useless stumps and screamed savagely into the darkness, as if I were alone in the entire world.

I screamed so loudly that the cry was heard throughout the camp. I fell on the floor near the latrine bucket, and someone whom I could not see found my head and started to kick it with his foot, clad in the shapeless camp footgear.

My cry came not from pain or fear. Long after he stopped kicking, I continued to yell. It was an attack of helpless fury, as if this cry could bring down the walls of the punishment cell, the walls of the camps, the foundations of all the prisons in the world!—People! People! People! Why must it be this way!

I then sat on the floor near the wall but was unable to sleep the whole night. The cold seeped through the walls, blew up from under the floor, an icy cold that shoots through the body to the bones, from which you cannot hide. Someone sat next to me; perhaps it was my enemy, but now the cold enveloped us and pressed us together. Freezing, we warmed each other, sitting with our mittens and caps tied under the chin, tucking in our feet to keep warmer, and trying to warm our hands in the jacket pockets or under the armpits.

Finally, we became indifferent, and we simply sat; when the dawn broke, I saw sitting next to me some old man with a wrinkled, red face, who continuously whispered and rocked his head, as if that made things easier. I was hungry. Then I wanted as fast as possible to be in the forest by a large bonfire.

When they rang the wake-up gong, the zeks in the punishment cell began to stir. The *urki* arose and began calmly and efficiently to break the boards on which they had been lying all night. They broke the boards with the focused look of people doing something understandable and necessary. In ten minutes, the punishment cell was broken up. They collected the broken boards and started to burn them. They did not, however, manage to set them alight, although pieces of cotton wadding torn out of the jackets had already started to smolder. The doors opened, the head of the prison and the commandant drove everyone out with a shriek. In the melee, people pulled out belts and things that were heaped on the floor. I found my glasses, which was the main thing. I grabbed the first belt that I found and ran to the barrack. My bread was intact! But I firmly resolved not to return to the brigade where the brigade leader brought a charge against me, and the people in my group watched indifferently when I was beaten. I was unable to live or work with them anymore. That morning I left for work in Gardenberg's brigade of railroad workers.

17

Gardenberg's Brigade

ON JANUARY 1, 1941, inventory was taken at Square 48. This important event occurs annually in camp and is always scheduled on a nonworking day. The state thus loses nothing, but the prisoners are deprived of a day of rest. Taking inventory demands a maximal effort for all camp inhabitants without exception—the zeks, administration, and the guards.

The first day of the new year in camp began early in the morning with the alarm: "Get out of the barracks!" We began to pack as if for departure. They had warned us that no items must remain in the barracks. The only exceptions were the clinic and infirmary, where the inspection took place on the spot. Barrack after barrack emptied out. People exited, burdened down with their belongings, dragging sacks, boxes, suitcases, with a pot tied to the belt and a bowl inside the shirt. The guards and work supervisors hurried them, urging on the laggards; the brigade leaders organized their people in columns on the street. The camp was enveloped in noise and shouting. Finally, everyone moved to the guardhouse, and the great exodus of a thousand zeks to the open field outside the gates was completed.

When the camp emptied out, the commandant's assistants and office workers carefully searched the barracks. They did not leave anything untouched; they emptied everything, picked up everything that had been jettisoned or concealed in hiding places, under the floor, in all places where the prisoners contrived to hide surplus items and all kinds of contraband.

In the meantime, we stood in the open field—a crowd of one thousand, like a grotesque wagon train. A snowstorm swirled above and among us; the numb figures blackened in the snowy mist. People hid behind their comrades' backs, sat patiently on their belongings at the edge of the road, while the snow covered their jackets, shoulders, and heads.

They placed tables in front of the guardhouse and began to call brigade after brigade. This was the tested camp method of checking whether the government-issued items in the zeks' possession corresponded to the record in the registry books. Each person was summoned to the table as if for an exam. Each one showed everything that he had, including the underwear on his body. Then, right there in the snow, the armed guard rummaged through the contents of the sack or suitcase, shaking up all the junk down to the bottom, and every illegal item of government property that was discovered was immediately confiscated.

Here it became clear who sold his government-issue shirt for a piece of bread, and who has two of them; who was wearing two pairs of padded pants or stolen footwear—all the improprieties, machinations, and thefts— especially thefts—over the year. Without further ado, whatever was illegal or excess was confiscated, and on this occasion, all the prisoner's property was examined publicly down to the slightest detail: every hidden scrap of paper, every item from home, every photograph or memento.

Hours passed. The search dragged on unbearably. People stamped in the snow; the weaker ones fell into apathy and sat immobile on their little trunks. It was three o'clock in the afternoon when our turn came, and a crowd still stood behind us. First, they let women and invalids pass through, also selected camp brigades who had to be shown esteem. They did not yet let those who had been checked return to camp but instead herded them to the other side of the road, where a cordon of guards separated them from those awaiting their turn. The snowstorm soon abated. Through the snowdrifts one could see only the camp palisade and above it, the signs that we knew by heart: "Don't smoke at work," and "Struggle mercilessly against slackers and wreckers."

The short winter day finally ended. It was already dusk when we stumbled through the camp gates in a hungry, frozen mob. In the barracks, there had been a pogrom: it was unheated, boards had been removed from the bunks and we had to get to work to restore the dwelling to its normal state. The orderlies split wood and searched for kindling, the workers again nailed down the torn-out shelves above the bunks and put back the blankets.

The kitchen had not been working all day; they started to cook only after the inventory had been completed. Late in the evening, in the darkness, cursing, people crowded by the kitchen windows; distribution of supper lasted until eleven o'clock. The *urki* grabbed bowls out of peoples' hands, taking advantage of the crush and darkness. We thus passed our "nonworking" day. The New Year did not begin very festively. What holidays does a zek have anyway?

Here and there in our barrack, one could still see the green fir boughs that the Poles had placed at the head of the bunk boards to celebrate Christmas. In my new brigade—Gardenberg's—there were many Poles.

Karpowicz, an engineer from Warsaw, with a thin, friendly face, was my friend. We exchanged addresses. I gave him mine in Tel Aviv, and he gave me the address of his wife in Warsaw—1 Freta Street. We agreed that whichever one of us survives the camp and returns home will seek out the other's family and convey greetings. Upon returning to Warsaw, I remembered my promise but was unable to carry it out: among the sea of ruins in postwar Warsaw there was neither Freta Street, building number 1, nor the wife of the late Karpowicz, who did not survive the Soviet camp.

The old railroad worker Gakh was my work partner in Gardenberg's brigade. That winter we built a narrow-gauge rail line at a distance of eight kilometers from the camp. In comparison to wood felling, where people were broken, this was easy work.

We went out when it was still dark. Ready, dressed and bundled up, we remained sitting in the barrack, delaying our departure until the last moment, when the foreman would run in: "Gardenberg, why don't you bring out your people?" Or the work supervisor ironically asked, "What's the matter; you're waiting for an invitation?" Passing the guardhouse, we plunged right into the cold, into the icy expanse, and we began the day with a two-hour march to the work site. "Attention, brigade!" When we reached the railroad track, we formed a chain and went along the ties. Behind us, in front of us, and on the side paths walked other brigades, creeping like worms to the right and left. The nocturnal movement of the brigades, in absolute silence, was a sinister spectacle, terrifying in its unnaturalness and tension.

Each brigade was like a taut spring that had to unwind all day, and then the guard would drag it back to the starting point in the evening, like an inert, useless body that has lost is elasticity. We walked ahead and soon were drawn into a deep, narrow, dark ravine. On both sides loomed steep walls of the tall forest, in the snow, in the night fog, and moon glow. The night procession hypnotized us. We walked slowly, like a file of ghosts, bobbing with a heavy step from tie to tie. Each of us was immersed in his thoughts, his bodily sensations, was gathering strength, checking his feet, hands, heart, and muscles. Suddenly a locomotive overtook us from behind, and we descended into the snow drift up to our knees, waiting for the train to pass. We were silent. The lower part of our faces was wrapped up; our moustaches and eyebrows were covered by hoarfrost. The brigade leader and foreman walked ahead of us; behind us, the guard urged on the laggards. The cook Pantel carried the pot. As our site was too far away from the camp to deliver the Stakhanovite kasha to us during the day, they gave it to us together with the pot. This was a great advantage: through "pull" in the kitchen, they gave us enough kasha to cook for the entire brigade.

When we arrived at the work site, we sat down to rest. On the side, one bonfire was lit for the guard and another for the cook, who immediately got started on his sacred task. He hung the pot above the fire on two sticks and boiled water. Pantel was small, round as a ball, with a large Jewish nose, a member of the left Poalei Tsion Zionist party from Mława. He was fired up with energy and a will to live, highly conscious of the importance of his task. Our brigade leader was a very young apprentice lawyer from Warsaw. Novak, the foreman and protector of our brigade, was a former Soviet prosecutor who had received a three-year sentence for an imprudent act (he incautiously helped compose a petition for a person with whom a Soviet prosecutor should not have been acquainted). Novak was the first Soviet person in the camp who treated the Westerners humanely, tried to help them, and got close to them. Novak took care of us, kept the spirits up in the brigade, generously assigned us excess work percentages, and obtained extra kasha for us in the kitchen. He was a broad-shouldered Ukrainian with an open, naïve face. Upon arriving at the work site, he and Gardenberg went into the bushes and dug up the brigades' tools that had been hidden under the snow: crowbars and picks, pickaxes, and boxes with steel. This was too heavy a load for us to drag daily to the camp and back. The work began.

Old, wrinkled Gakh, the only "genuine" railroad worker in the brigade, from near Katowice, fastened the rails together where they met. I followed him, carrying the box with nuts and elongated separators. Gakh would put down the separators and continue on; I would add the nuts and tighten them with a wrench. For this simple work, I fulfilled, or rather, Novak allotted me from fifty to seventy percent of the norm so that I "earned" the "first ration" and from 500 to 700 grams of bread.

This sufficed as long as the packages from Pinsk gave me the missing fats and sugar; it enabled me to walk sixteen kilometers daily in addition to working six hours at the site.

We did not do too much work. The walking alone took four hours a day. We started work at ten o'clock, and at four we already lined up on the road in order to reach the guardhouse on time. During the day, we had a half-hour break for "lunch." Then the brigade would sit festively around the pot, and Pantel, his face shiny and red from the frost, would pour his kasha into the mugs and tin cans. We ate it slowly, and then would drink the hot water and

converse civilly, warming our hands and feet by the fire, until Gardenberg
arrived with a humble request not to set a bad example but to get up and return to work. It was a downright miracle that we built a railroad: it seemed as
if the road was building itself. Nevertheless, over the winter, we constructed
one and a half kilometers of rail, although the quality of our work was more
than dubious, and the entire branch ultimately turned out to be unnecessary.

The work began with leveling the route and preparing the embankment
upon which the ties and tracks would be placed. After Gakh and I screwed,
unscrewed, and again screwed on all the nuts of the track, I had to attend to
the trolley. I worked in a foursome with the engineer Karpowicz, the actor
from the Warsaw Młodych Theater Wołowczyk and Grinfeld, a Czech citizen and refugee from Brno. In the open pit, we struck the earth with picks
and crowbars. When the crowbars were unable to pierce the frozen earth,
we lit a fire to defrost the clumps of earth and loaded them onto the trolley.
Wołowczyk and I leaned with our chests against the wagon and pushed it
along the rails to the very end of the construction site. There we emptied it,
flattened out the earth, and having rested a minute, trotted back with the
empty trolley to the pit, where it was again filled up. Now and then the trolley
would slip off the rails. We all gathered to put it back, applying pressure with
shoulders and cudgels, straining while Novak directed:

> One, two—the girls are coming,
> One, two—they are singing songs.

With the word "girls" and "songs," together we lifted the wagon into the air
and lowered the wheels onto the tracks. Above us, the pure blue Karelian
sky shone, the rosy dawn glowed in the east and was reflected in the west,
the forests looked like lace, and our voices resonated in the distance. "What
number wagon are you up to?" Novak would ask. And we lied, sometimes
moderately and sometimes beyond measure. Two of us managed to load fifteen wagons a day but such work would lead only to the punishment cell in
the evening. The brigade, in fact, fulfilled eight hundred percent of the norm;
in the evening Novak "rounded it" to 2,000 to 2,500, and we were about
thirty people!

Once I did, however, earn a shock troop ration in this brigade.

In the middle of the day, we had to bring rails that were lying about 3
kilometers from the main road. It was not easy to find volunteers. I joined
them. The walk in the winter forest would have been completely wondrous
and would have given us the illusion of freedom were it not for the two wagons

that we pushed along. The wagons rolled easily, and we followed them, lost in the silence of the forest. For us, however, it was not silent. We knew that it is divided into squares, full of brigades and guards, the smoke of bonfires, and the screeching of saws. Somewhere in the west was the Finnish border, but we were separated from it by swamps and roadless forest and the impossibility of finding bread and shelter on the way: bread was to be got only with a ration card and shelter was only in the camp. Several people ran away from the camp that winter, but after wandering in the forest, they returned on their own.

Having loaded the rails, we turned back. Now it became difficult. We frequently stopped in order to catch our breath. The road went up and down the hills. The load of iron rails would sometimes break away from us and sometimes, going up the slope, would press on our chest. The four zeks moving the wagon were drenched in sweat. The snow piled up, but we unbuttoned our jackets and pushed, lowering our heads, and tensing our bodies. We had to hurry; it was already getting dark. What if a train would come our way? We would have to remove the wagon and the load from the rails. But we managed to turn off in time to our branch. From the distance we saw that the brigade was already lined up on the road, waiting for us. "Hurry up!" yelled the guard. Without resting, we got in line and marched the 8 kilometers home.

On the way, we met other brigades—not ours but from the neighboring camp—and, while walking, we managed to exchange questions and answers. Westerners were working everywhere; everywhere one heard people speaking in Polish and Yiddish.

For delivering the rails, I was listed for 125 percent of the norm and received the shock workers' 900 grams of bread and pea kasha with oil. I ate it with proper respect and the awareness that I did not deserve it. In fact, in order to earn the shock workers' ration, one had to do more than push a wagon with iron for 3 kilometers. Even so, this kasha with oil and extra bread did not recoup the calories expended for the three-hour exertion with the wagon.

Our brigade was soon disbanded when it became clear that it was not earning what it was eating. But I did not make it to the end of the idyll in Gardenberg's brigade. When the security officer Stepanov learned that I was working with the railroad group, he ordered that I be moved elsewhere. Apparently, dangerous people such as I was could not be entrusted with screwing on nuts. I again returned to the forest and began to work with the bowsaw, preparing meter-length logs. It was work that entailed picking up leftovers in sectors where other brigades had already carried out the main sawing.

Again, the scene changed. This time I worked alone. I was satisfied to fulfill three-quarters of a cubic meter, that is, thirty percent of the norm. I was on the go all day. I had to pile forty to fifty logs, carry each one on my shoulder, while sinking into the snow. But there were no ready logs. I had to cut them from the trees growing around or from the abandoned trunks left over from the summer and buried in the snow.

At that time, I began to drag my feet and feel that particular weakness and heaviness throughout my body that marks the start of a physical catastrophe. I deeply hated the forest: it was a murder weapon, a place that executed prisoners. At a glance, I could tell how many logs one could cut from each tree and how many measured pieces there were in an aspen of 28 centimeters diameter. For me, the forest smelled of sweat and blood. I knew that I could never again see a forest with the eyes of a summer vacationer or a poet.

Upon arriving in the forest, I would cut down two branches and pound them into the earth: that was the support for the stockpile that I was assembling. Between them, I placed another two branches on the snow and laid the logs crosswise on them. I knew that the birch is heavy and difficult to saw; the easiest to saw is the rotting aspen, which the bowsaw cuts through as if through butter. I also learned to pile the logs in such a way that there was a lot of free space between them, giving the appearance of a greater quantity.

I had to watch vigilantly: the zeks would steal the wood, trying surreptitiously to carry away a neighbor's log. We recognized each log of ours so well, however, as if it were our own child, and we were able to stick up for our goods. Gradually, the camp instilled this ability in us. Whoever was unable to react forcefully became a victim of the camp wolves and hyenas. A camp inmate who cannot fight perishes. I knew this but still was unable to fight. It was, therefore, not dangerous to steal from me. Ultimately, in the barrack, they stole all my possessions.

The "incident with the bottle" is a minor example of camp morals. A bottle with oil remained from my package. Actually, it might have been honey. In any case, the bottle's contents froze, and I had to defrost it.

Naturally, I did not keep this bottle out in the open; otherwise, they would have stolen it immediately. I hid it with the doctor in the clinic. Finally, when everything else had been consumed, the turn came for this secret bottle. I brought it to the barrack and hid it until midnight.

What was in it, oil or honey, and which is better, oil or honey?

At midnight, when the entire barrack was sleeping, I woke up and pulled out the precious bottle from under the headboard. From the upper bunk, I had an excellent view of the entire dwelling: rows of sleeping bodies, a table with a wick lamp in the middle. Kiva, the orderly, had dozed off. The large stove with the attached metal plate on top was covered with worn out footwear, boots, "Cheteze," and with leg wrappings and padded socks hanging all over. All this was drying and giving off vapor. I descended from the bunk and placed the prized bottle on the stove so that it would defrost in the warmth.

Then I drowsed off and had a terrible nightmare: GAK UBBLAG NKVD came to me.

It was hairy, terrifying, like the demonic character Vii in Gogol's story, like a giant hedgehog with steel quills, and it stood above me and thundered like a rock avalanche: Gak ublak! Gak ublak! Gak ublak enkavede! I woke up in a sweat: the devil knows what frightened me. GAK UBBLAG is simply the acronym for the words Main Review Commission of the Administration of the Baltic–White Sea Camps of the People's Commissariat of Internal Affairs. But the nocturnal, panicked cry still rang in my ears: Gak ublak! Gak ublak!...

I glanced down below. Two zeks were sitting by the stove. Both were thieves; one from our barrack and the other from another. He came to visit. What were they discussing at one o'clock at night?

They smoked and whispered, and my bottle was standing on the stove. Gak ublak! It was already their bottle.

I climbed down from the bunk and went to the stove. I yawned, sat down briefly, and as I left, inconspicuously as possible, snatched the bottle away from them. I felt that if they had noticed it, it was already their bottle.

I went to the bunk and tossed the bottle up above, far away. I heard it gently hit the jacket. Then I went to a corner of the barrack where there was a small pitcher of water. I drank from my mug and went back to my place.

Not more than ten seconds passed while I drank water with my back to the stove. Both zeks were still sitting in the same pose, head to head and whispering. The barrack was soundly asleep; no one stirred.

When I climbed on top, however, my bottle was not there. Where had it disappeared? My neighbors were sleeping soundly and sonorously. They were my kind of people; they would not steal anything from me.

I lay down with astonishment and pictured how, in those ten seconds that I drank water, one of the urki in cat-like movements dashed to the bunk. . . . Gak! Ublak! He could not reach the bottle with his hand. But he managed to jump up to the upper bunk. He climbed down, returned to the stove, and sat at his former place.

He stole it, and now he calmly is getting up and going to the exit. My bottle is in his shirt. What to do! Jump down, stop him, search?

I shall never, ever know what was in that bottle—honey or oil.

Really, should you create a commotion at night because of a bottle?
Nevertheless, even I once raised a hullabaloo.

A camp hyena attached himself to me—a person with fused black eyebrows, a gypsy type with darting eyes and a soft, moist mouth. In his former life, he had been a respected forwarding agent, the owner of an enterprise in Lublin. In the camp, however, he changed completely, perhaps unexpectedly even to himself. What do we know about ourselves, without having been tested?

He relentlessly followed me, pursued me, and used every occasion to pilfer something from me. He understood that I presented no danger: even if I catch him with the evidence, what will I do to him? He did unbelievable things to me: once, without asking, he took someone else's padded socks, sold them to me for bread, then immediately stole them from me, and returned them to the original owner.

He did not fear me, but he was afraid of the original owner. I saw my things with him—now a belt, then a towel, then soap—and I kept silent. Finally, however, he began to close in on my bread.

One morning, I hung my jacket on a branch near a forest bonfire. For half an hour, without straightening out my back, I sawed. Midday arrived, I straightened up, and went to my jacket. There was a slice of bread in the pocket, the only food until the evening. But the bread had disappeared from the pocket. I reacted painfully to such matters. The loss of possessions or money is not felt as strongly as the disappearance of bread about which you are thinking since morning. Patiently you wait until noon; you barely make it to the designated moment, and when you extend your hand—there is no bread; they stole it! The cold penetrates the heart. Tears welled in my eyes, as if I were a child, and I was speechless.

My neighbor pointed with his eyes to the gypsy, who sat indifferently by the fire. He not only ate my bread, but he also scorned me, smiling derisively, looking to the side. . . .

A few days later, the orderly Kiva, who after the dispatch to work remained alone in the barrack with those released from work, heard strange noises from the upper bunk where I slept. Something clinked. He looked up and saw the Lublin gypsy sitting among my possessions as if he were the owner, having spread out my belongings. He had pulled out the box where I kept my provisions, but all the tins that he took out were empty. Finally, he found a piece of sausage at the bottom, the remains of a package, and stuck it in his mouth. Seeing the gypsy with the sausage in his mouth, Kiva, although an old man, dragged him by the foot from the bunk and thrashed him on the neck. In the evening, after Kiva's tale, I went to the gypsy and asked him, "Was the sausage tasty?" But my refined irony made no impression on him. He morosely lay in his place and did not even turn his face toward me.

What should I do? I always disliked nonresistance to evil, but my methods of nonresistance were intellectual ones. I took out ink and pen and with Ciceronian eloquence, I asked the commandant of the camp to remove from the barrack this person who . . . The brigade leader, orderly, and fourteen idealists signed onto this petition.

At this, my torturer grew anxious, as he did know what could happen as a result of such an unusual protest. The next morning, at the work dispatch, he came up to me and offered to make peace. I would not submit the petition, and he would leave me in peace and henceforth would not even come near the place where I was. Hearing such mild words from the mouth of the Lublin dispatcher, I rejoiced at my victory and sent him to the devil without even hearing him out.

The paper remained in my pocket; why destroy a person who apologizes? For a whole week, his behavior was exemplary. Suddenly, late one evening, when I returned from the clinic, people told me that again he came up and rummaged through my things: in front of everyone, openly and insolently, until they drove him away.

I made an immediate decision . . . and lay down to sleep. I was furious at myself. Even now, when this man made me the laughingstock of the barrack, I did not harbor any malice against him, any of that blind and irrational fury with which a beast snarls when you take away his bone or a zek, when you take away his ration—his blood and life. People kill for a ration in camp; they pick up a board from the ground and beat someone on the head. I, however, made my decision coldly, rationally. I was unable to hate this scoundrel; I even put off the necessary reprisal until the morning. Why? Because people were sleeping all around, and he himself was sleeping, and I should not wake him and ruin his sleep.

The next morning, I awoke like a person who is about to plunge into icy water. I felt bad, but I had to do what was necessary. I approached the man with the black fused brows. He was lying below, near the window on the right side. He was lying on a pile of rags, and he looked at me expressionlessly, like at a fly on the wall. I came up to him as if in my sleep and asked:

"Yesterday did you climb up to my place?"

Without waiting for an answer, I struck him on the temple with my fist. For the first time in my life, not counting childhood fights, I struck a person. For the first—and if fate spares me a return to places like Square 48—the last time. One should never hit a person. When I struck him, he was terrified. He did not think that I could hit him. He was bigger and stronger than me, but now he had lost his bearings, his eyes showed genuine fear, and for me, after the first blow, it burst open the dam. I was carried away, as if I had crossed some line, and with all my being, I felt strength, desire, right, and an unexpected ease with which one could hit. I pounced on him and showered him with blows. He covered his face with his hands, turned sideways, and if they had not dragged me away from him, I would have beat him to a pulp, until he lost consciousness. There was a big commotion in the barrack. When I returned to my place, my neighbors began to congratulate me. The entire day, like a birthday celebrant, I kept receiving congratulations from people who approached me with laughing faces and said:

"Is it really true? Finally, you did it! Well done! Now he will leave you alone! But how did you dare? To tell the truth, we did not think you were capable of such heroism."

But I was not happy; I was full of shame, humiliation, and grief. On that day, I underwent another stage of dehumanization. I did something that was against my very essence. Among the tribulations for which I shall never forgive the camp or its grim creators—all my life, my memory retains that blow in the face, which for one short minute made me their accomplice, follower, and pupil.

18

Evening in the Barrack

THE BARRACK IS full of people. The bed boards are crowded with zeks who are sitting or lying down. The air is heavy and filled with the incessant buzz and noise of conversations. Suddenly there is silence, and all heads turn to the person entering—letters!

A man from the Cultural-Educational Sector (KVCh) goes to the table with a bundle in his hands. Immediately, a crowd gathers round him; someone tries to look over his shoulder; those lying on the upper bunks sit up and watch him, clasping their knees.

The man from the KVCh reads all the names of the addressees in order. Everyone listens attentively.

"Odynets! Lenga! Prais!"

"Prais is here!"

"Vilensky, Eiger, Kosyarsky!"

"Kosyarsky was sent to Camp 5!" they call out from the bunks. "And Eiger is sick; he's in the infirmary."

The man from the KVCh makes a note and continues:

"Margolin! Timberg! Again Margolin! Winer!"

"Timberg died! Winer died!"

Having finished reading the names and handing out some of the letters, the man from the KVCh with the pack of letters goes to the next barrack and starts over again:

"Odynets! Lenga!" until the only remaining letters are to unknown addressees, who have not been in the camp for years or, perhaps, are no longer among the living.

One can easily identify letters to camp by their address: there is no street number or house number, but there is a post office box: "Pyalma Station, Post Office Box 233/2, to so-and-so." The first number "233" is the number of the camp; the number after the slash, "2," is the number of the camp sector. The camp is thus never mentioned by name. There is method to this camouflage. Similarly, the newspaper bulletins that are put out in some camp centers for zeks, with the note "for internal circulation only," are produced without stating for whom they are written, and one does not encounter such indelicate words as "camp," "prisoners," "forced labor," or "punishment cell" in the text. It is as if there is nothing, as in a room where they sweep all the dirt under the bed so that it is not visible.

In order to answer a letter, a prisoner must first get hold of a piece of clean paper. This is not so simple. There are no stationery shops in camps. Having written his letter, the zek folds the paper into a triangle and writes the address on the other side. You do not need a stamp; the addressee will pay. On the letter, you must indicate the so-called identifying data. These are required for internal censorship. My identifying data were as follows:

"SDE [socially dangerous element], term 5 years, lib. date 20/6/45."

This inscription is written in the corner of the envelope in pencil; from this inscription, which was not erased by the censor, my mother first learned what had become of me after my arrest. Incidentally, in my fifth year of internment, in Kotlas, they accepted letters to mail even without the identifying data. In the Kotlas KVCh, however, they kept a card file of those who wrote, and they noted down every dispatched letter. Those sentenced to "hard labor" are allowed to write once every three months; the others once a month, and in some cases, a zek could be deprived of the right to correspondence. The stamp of the camp censorship appears on every page of a received letter. In the war years, the stamp of the general military censorship was added.

One drops the letter into the mailbox at the camp sector, and when the opportunity presents itself, it is sent to the Central Division. They are not too careful with prisoners' letters. Sometimes when they are looking for paper to roll for cigarettes, camp *urki* break open the mailbox and seize the letters. In my five years in camp, I did not receive one letter from abroad. My family in Palestine knew my address in the BBK in the first year of my imprisonment. My mother in Pinsk reported the address to Tel Aviv. Many letters were sent to my address from Palestine, but not one was given to me. Similarly, none of the letters that I wrote home to Palestine from camp were mailed. Zeks have every right to send correspondence abroad. This right is not disputed. Their letters land in the third sector as "material," but camp authorities do not feel obligated to dispatch them to their destination.

One of the reasons why zeks' letters cannot be sent abroad is that the handmade triangles used throughout Russia were not allowed to be mailed outside the Soviet Union. They were not sufficiently "representative."

In the camp, however, we did not know this, and we also did not know that letters destined for abroad are not dropped into the mailbox but are transmitted at the post office by hand. As camp inmates, we were unable to satisfy this condition. Our correspondence was taken and dispatched by our jailers.

That winter I did not suffer from a lack of letters. When I arrived at camp, I informed my elderly mother of my camp address and asked her to write me every five days. "Don't worry if you have nothing to write about," I wrote to her. "The important thing is not the contents, but simply the greeting, the piece of paper from home." My mother did more than I asked; she wrote every three days and always found something about which to write. Thanks to her letters and postcards, written in the familiar, large hand, that winter I retained a connection with the external world and even with my family in Palestine. My wife wrote to my mother in Pinsk, and my mother served as a link between us. Until the summer of 1941, we knew about each other, but then the link was severed for many long years. Because of the will and law of the state that had seized me, I was unable to convey news about myself to those at home, and I was buried alive in the camp.

Not understanding that in the eyes of the Soviet regime, I was a criminal serving my term, my mother sent me in camp a visa for entry into Palestine that had come from the British embassy in Moscow. This visa was not only useless, but also it turned into evidence against me, a circumstance aggravating my guilt. They gave me my mother's accompanying letter, and on the margin, they made a note: "The document was confiscated and affixed to the charges." A year later, already far from Karelia, I was speaking to one of the heads of the third sector, who said to me: "We know that you are corresponding with a foreign consulate, and you even receive documents from there." In his eyes, this demonstrated guilt. For "contact with a foreign consulate," Soviet citizens are buried in camps for ten years.

My mother's letters were full of worry, love, and naïve incomprehension of my situation. "Where are you working?" she wrote. "And what kind of room do you have?"

When I informed her that rats had bitten through the suitcase where I kept the lard from her package, I received in reply not only the news that is she sending a new suitcase but also kind advice not to hide the lard in the suitcase but to hang it up under the ceiling. It was hard for me to explain to my elderly mother that in my living conditions, it was impossible not only to hang lard in the barrack, but even to eat it openly in the presence of others. The fortunate person who received a package would hide it, treat his closest friends and neighbors to something and eat the rest inconspicuously, in order not to attract attention or arouse envy. We ate furtively, turning toward the wall, like criminals.

Of course, we did not act that way immediately. You need camp experience for that. The neighbor with whom you do not share contents from a package becomes an enemy. And there are many neighbors—in the barracks a hundred men live together. As soon as a zek pulls out his treasure and cuts off a piece, dozens of people around him, some of whom had not seen such things in years, suddenly become serious, stop their conversations, and silence reigns. You have to be a veteran, hardened zek not to choke up when all eyes are turned in your direction or not to sense the saliva in the other's mouth, feel the insult and sorrow of the deprived ones. The weak-willed ones come up to beg for something. They are answered roughly and angrily driven away like dogs. Others do not ask but follow with eagle eyes to see where the remainder is hidden. A third type, who pretends not to be interested in others' goods, becomes gloomy and, in a bad mood, turns away, not only from the sight of the lard but also because the person who is savoring it so obnoxiously gets on his nerves.

The days when packages were distributed at Square 48 were full of electric tension. A day or two in advance, the word already spread that packages had arrived. There usually were forty to fifty packages for a thousand prisoners, but sometimes there were only eight or ten. They arrived irregularly, sometimes with an interval of a week but sometimes two months apart—packages from Western Ukraine and Belorussia[1] with their lard as thick as one's palm, white refined sugar, and excellent Grodno tobacco were a sensation for our Russian companions. They received rye rusks, dried potatoes, and formless lumps of sugar. The contents of those packages testified to *kolkhoz* poverty. The packages arrived at the provisions warehouse, a list of the lucky ones was compiled, and in the evening, after work, they were summoned "with a bag."

In the administrative and technical barrack, there was a "room of brigade leaders," where "work reports" were written up in the evening. We brought the packages there from the warehouse for distribution. Not everyone, only the most solid and reliable among the receivers were admitted to the distribution.

---

1. Now independent state of Belarus.

Carrying the valuable packages wrapped in rope and canvas, we marched in a festive procession in the snow. The packages were placed in the corner and watched by the guards. The camp boss, the guard on duty, work supervisors, and the commandant all sit at the table. On the other side of the table is a crowd of prisoners—not only the receivers but also spectators, *urki*, bandits, and simply the curious. Vanya is here, too, looking with his round, astonished eyes at the riches of the Westerners. The summoned zek must answer the question: "From whom do you expect a package?" This is for verification, to avoid any mistakes. They open the plywood box, and the orderly or work supervisor takes out tin cans, jars, and paper bags, one by one. Everything is carefully checked. Sealed jars are opened; the butter is tested with a knitting needle to make sure nothing else is inside. Alcohol, cutting objects (razors, penknives), and marking pencils are confiscated. Medicines are given to the medical sector for verification. The happy beneficiary is in ecstasy. He offers cigarettes and candy to the bosses. The camp boss refuses: it does not befit him, but the others unceremoniously help themselves, especially Vanya, a great lover of candy.

The box is emptied. The zek hastily shovels what he has received into the bag and leaves. He has put something in his pocket, but the rest, under cover of the dark night, he brings, not to his place, but to another barrack, to a friend whom no one will suspect of having a hidden treasure. This is a necessary precaution. Otherwise, he faces the risk that they will steal his package that very night and sometimes in the first half hour, when he is still walking in a happy fog.

In the evening, transactions, purchases, and exchanges take place in the barracks; people who in the morning had looked with hungry eyes at another's bowl are now rich, glow with happiness, and treat the brigade leaders. They receive congratulations: "Best wishes on your package!" It is customary to respond with a sour look and say, "a miserable package . . . a little barley and some . . ." They do not say what the "some" is in order not to provoke others or lead them to temptation.

The significance of packages lay not only in their nutritive value. They were not merely food products and things! Sometimes arriving from a distance of thousands of kilometers, the package was a greeting from home, a sign of love and evidence of fidelity. Each carefully packaged, tied, and wrapped item radiated warmth and affection. We again felt like human beings and found new reserves of resistance. In one package, I found an old tin box for English tea that had been standing on a shelf in my mother's kitchen for twenty years. I rejoiced at the sight of this red lacquered box with geishas and a toy boat as if it were my best friend. An enamel blue mug with a handle. Socks with a monogram! In what hothouse atmosphere of warmth and love had we spent our life until chance thrust us into the power of people for whom our life had no value. Was it truly chance? Or on the contrary, were the camps the real school of human "values" and the climate in which we had lived previously an exception?

That winter I barely ate from the official rations. The disgusting, rotten odor of the "fish soup" poisoned the air in the barracks. Then we began to receive "cabbage soup"—sour water in which a few black leaves of last year's cabbage were floating. They fed us soy kasha, from the soy husks, which stuck in my throat. Grabbing a fistful of salted cod, we went to the barrack, where the table was covered with fish bones. The "goners" would sift through them and gnaw the bones that had already been in someone else's mouth. Sometimes, when they finished distributing the camp "soup," the so-called *balanda*, a drowned rat would show up at the bottom of the pot. The zeks, however, were not fastidious.

We would be gripped by real despair when, having passed through the guardhouse, knocked out by a twelve-hour workday and march, dropping from exhaustion, hungry and frazzled, we would heard the word "bathhouse." The evening was lost; there would be no rest! The compulsory bath was torture at Square 48. "This minute to the bathhouse!" They would not distribute supper until after we returned from the bath. An assault begins in the barrack. The exhausted zeks do not go voluntarily. The bath attendant personally checks the bunks, forcibly dragging out those who are lying down: either to the bath or to the punishment cell! Nevertheless, they never succeed in bathing the entire brigade: someone always hides. Two hours are spent on the bath. You have to unload quickly every little thing from your pockets—the supper coupon, a pencil, penknife—and hide them somewhere until your return. Then you wait in the courtyard by the door to the bathhouse until the entire group assembles—about thirty people—and until the previous group leaves the dressing room and they let us into the room, covered with liquid dirt and half-illuminated by a kerosene lamp. When they bring the rings, a complicated operation begins of stringing on the ring all the incredible rags, which the zeks wear in winter. If there is no ring, you have to make a bundle of all your things and tie it with your underpants twisted into a rope.

The disinfection room worker loads up our bundles, and in a few rounds drags them to the "lice slaughterhouse" where they are thoroughly heated. In the meantime, about thirty people are sitting and standing naked, waiting to be let in to wash. They shiver from the cold, as every minute the doors open to the frost, the tardy ones enter, and, in their damp jackets, force their way through the nude bodies. At the opposite end, they try to force their way through the locked bath door, and in the middle, in a chorus, they sing the famous soldiers' song "Katerina." In the dressing room are the disinfector (we know him; it is our little Burko, the Pinsk pharmacist) and a barber. The obligatory shaving of the armpits and pubic area is carried out. Each one soaps up with a common brush from the common, disgusting dirty yellow soap dish and then submits to the Chinese torture of being shaved with a dull blade. The zek-barber is impatient and rough. He wipes his blade on the prisoner's shoulder or knee and, when finished, pushes him aside.

Finally, they let us into the bath. We enter, each one holding his shoes in his hands—they do not take them into the lice-roaster, and it is dangerous to leave them in the dressing room. Feet slip on the floor, covered with soapy water (that winter we still had soap)—in the steam, bare backs, torsos, feet are thrashing about; a line with bucket-tubs is waiting by the faucet of a wooden water tank. The bath attendant, with rolled up pants, pours each one his allotted measure. After having doused themselves with the hot water, the zeks proceed to their laundry. The bath is an important opportunity to wash your shirt, leg wrappings, or towel. There is no time to lose. They wash diligently, in a close line above the bench where the buckets stand. Whoever is not doing laundry, hurries to take a place by the stove and dry himself, waiting for the signal to leave.

No outsider is supposed to be present when the people exit to the cold dressing room. Outsiders are thieves. It's true that in one's own crowd there are thieves, too, but you know them, and you watch them when necessary. The critical moment arrives when the outside door opens and from the courtyard, with frost and wind, the person from the disinfection room bursts in with our things. The door behind him remains open until one of the naked jumps up to close it. Here one must be on guard. Everyone's things are piled in a heap on the floor; the pressure and pushing begins. In the feeble light of the kerosene lamp, one must find one's own things in this pile of steaming rags, where everything is mixed together, torn from the rings, separated, and jumbled. People get in each other's way, rummage through for the tenth time, toss away what is not theirs, and scream: "My jacket disappeared! My shirt is missing!" The bath attendants go back to check whether something was left in the disinfection room or dropped on the way.

After each bath, invariably there are victims and people who have nothing to wear back to the barracks because everything was stolen.

One is supposed to get clean underwear after the bath. That means a new queue, but for the most part, there is no underwear, and, donning the hot jacket on his bare body, the zek carries what he just washed back to the barrack to dry. The zeks wade through the pitch-black darkness and deep mud; the rotten steps fall apart underfoot, and passing through the knee-high muddy swamp around the bathhouse, a zek may sometimes return to the barrack even dirtier than when he left. This procedure is not easy for a person who is fresh and rested, but for starving prisoners, who have worked all day in the forest and have barely made it to the guardhouse after a march of several kilometers, this is a new torture.

Only now is it time for food, for the "fish soup," the ration card, and bread.

After eating, we immediately fall asleep. It is good to lie down, stretching out on the upper bunk in the close row of bodies. Your jacket is underneath you, and the rolled up padded pants and everything else are placed under your head. What separates you from the others—your home and shelter—is the blanket, the large half-wool blanket brought from Pinsk. This blanket, an object of the zeks' envy, will, of course, soon be stolen from you. In the meantime, however, you can wrap yourself in it completely and, falling asleep to the noise and talking of the crowd in the barrack, feel that you are not among alien people but among your own, people like you, Westerners: Karpowicz, Grinfeld, and Wołowczyk.

Soon we are sleeping the sleep of the dead, as only people with a clean conscience after a full day of work in the frost and two hours of "bath," who will be awakened by reveille before dawn, can sleep. Suddenly something tells the sleeping person that he must wake up.

He lifts his head. It is the middle of the night. In the barrack, one hears quiet whispers, that elusive anxiety that wordlessly warns of approaching danger. The enemy is near! The neighbor is already sitting up. His face is calm, and moving his lips without turning his face, he says, "A search!"

A night search in the barrack! This does not surprise us; night frisking is an ordinary matter. They unfailingly occur in camp on the eve of holidays—October and the first of May. It is not clear why this is necessary but such is the custom in camp. The first search in October 1940 caught me by surprise. I was then living in the barrack of the technical and administrative personnel and was the only person who suffered from the frisk: from my pants' pocket they pulled out and confiscated my marvelous "genuine" penknife from home. Since then I got used to night raids and daytime inspections; I would stand with spread out hands while alien fingers grope under my jacket and along my feet, and watch as they leaf through the pages of books found on the bunk or, sneaking up from behind, take an unfinished letter out of my hands and read what, in any case, would go to the censorship.

The first thing that I do is hide the penknife. Quietly, I put it in the crack between two bunk boards. I do not have any money (they take away anything over 50 rubles). I also must hide papers and letters. I take a little package from the suitcase, and at the last minute, I manage to stick it into the padded socks in which I sleep.

In a search, either they drive everyone to the middle of the barrack and rummage through the empty bunks or, as now, the guard jumps up to the bunk (four guards check at the same time from above and below from both sides; a fifth watches in the center of the barrack). Reclining on the bunk, with feet hanging down, I hear the guard's command: "Get up!"

I feign awakening and astonishment. I am lying at the end of the row and the guard is already tired. He is bored. Having emptied out my bag and shaken out the blanket, he is hurrying on. "Hand over the penknife!"

"But I don't have one, citizen boss" (for us all guards are bosses).

"And where is this bowl from?"

I bought the bowl from another zek, but, of course, it comes from the kitchen, government property.

The bowl flies downward. It is unpleasant when they take away books. Once a book has been taken (for examination), it is rarely returned to the owner and is used to roll cigarettes at the guardhouse. This time, however, they need kitchenware—bowls, tins, jars.

Although the search is conducted at night, in the neighboring barracks, they already know what is happening in ours. The guards therefore will not find anything; it is useless to go there. A simultaneous search of everyone in the camp is conducted only once a year, when they do inventory. In normal times, the guards' strength suffices only for partial searches and night raids, for searching incoming and outgoing brigades, and for individual inspections.

Over the years, every zek becomes accustomed to the humiliating police ritual of searches and inspections, to the vigilant eye and unremitting observation, to the state's rummaging in his underwear, his thoughts, his possessions, and his soul, as if it were a desk drawer, always open for police control. This is part of camp "re-education." In camp, there is neither solitude nor opportunity to keep secrets for a long time. It is better for a camp inmate that he is living in a crowd—it is easier to bear joint misfortune. As to secrets—whether it is a matter of a penknife or a forbidden thought—of course, it is impossible to keep them concealed for years. If the guard had wanted to spend the time, he would have found both my penknife in the crack of the bunk board and discovered my faith in the crevice of my heart. In the course of a day, or a year, or five years, all forbidden penknives or thoughts invariably come to the surface—and if they are not always noticed and confiscated, that is explained not so much by the imperfection of the camp system as by the lack of well-trained personnel capable of implementing the instructions. The camp system is the ultimate expression of Stalinism. But people qualified to carry out the task do not yet exist. It is the ideal instrument of communism, although generations will pass before Soviet people learn to carry out searches properly. We can assume, however, that they will master this difficult art as the regime's existence depends on it.

In addition to the searches, there is another operation in camp that the anarchistic and undisciplined Russian nature finds difficult to implement. This is the roll-call [*poverka*]. Prisoners are supposed to be counted twice a day in camp. In reality, they are counted constantly, incessantly; mistakes are made in the counting and it starts over again and never stops. The brigade leader counts. The guardhouse counts. The chief planner counts. The guard at the work site moves his lips in making the rounds of the groups. In the infirmary, they count the sick in the beds. In the bathhouse, they count the naked people washing. The administration counts. And the numbers never add up. Until it gets very cold, they count in the open air. A half hour after the last brigade has returned from work, the signal booms, summoning the camp population out to the street. Distribution of supper is halted and whoever has received his portion tosses it in the barrack and runs to line up. A thousand zeks grouped by their barracks stand in two rows, with the brigade leader on the right flank of each brigade.

It is an unforgettable sight for which a newsreel photographer would pay a handsome sum. The sun sets on the scene of grimy people in fantastic tatters with a rope for a belt, in torn jackets from which the red padding protrudes. A mosaic of Mongol, Slavic, Jewish, and Chinese masks, where everything is intermingled—thievish mugs, rabbinic beards, aged grimaces of hungry patriarchs, intelligent faces of professors with battered butts, faces on which the story of their suffering or a complete stupor is written, crooked jaws and flattened heads, adolescents with the look of tubercular monkeys and men who resemble adolescents, half of their normal size. One person runs past along the front, counting, and a second runs behind him for verification, and both poke each chest with their fingers and count aloud. It is forbidden to disperse when the counting is over: you stand for a long time, sometimes in the rain, in the mud. If someone leaves the line to sit down by the barrack, he is driven back. And everything starts again. The count did not match. One time, two are missing; another time, there are two extra. It is not clear for whom it is more difficult—for the counted or the counters. Sometimes the second and third counts do not yield the proper results.

In winter, they count in the barracks. Everything dies down after the signal, the orderlies are inside and guards watch outside to make sure that no one enters or exits. In each barrack, the zeks line up in the middle in two rows and count themselves. When the guard runs in, he merely checks the number given him.

For more than an hour, huddling together in the barracks, they wait for the all clear signal—the end of the count. And suddenly, a zek is discovered between the barracks, walking with an innocent face from a "certain place." His appearance evokes panic: who let him out and when? Was he counted or not? Like a rabbit running from hunters, the zek tries to hide from the counters: if they catch him, they'll take him to the punishment cell! He tries to dive into the first door, but there, where all the people have been counted, they drive him out. The count could continue for an extra hour because of such a bastard who was not counted or counted twice!

In the administrative office, they add up the figures and are perplexed: it does not come out right! What if someone has really run away? The administrative director, striking his forehead, remembers that he, too, is a zek and forgot to count himself.

Everything comes out right on paper—and almost never works in reality. The numbers drive the people, and the people chase after the numbers. A statistical tragedy, like a bad dream, harries the camp and the higher administration. Man stubbornly resists being contained in a number. Nevertheless, people add, subtract, multiply, and divide him. It is bad enough when you relate to a person solely by means of arithmetic, but it is much worse when this arithmetic is applied by people who, although ignorant of the four basic arithmetic operations, try to re-educate mankind and reform society.

19

People at Square 48

THE POLISH GROUP of Grzymała was sitting around a bonfire in a forest glade; it looked like a print of Grottger[1] from the series "1863." When they got up to return to work, one person remained. As I approached from behind the trees, I saw him praying silently with hands clasped. Although he looked youthful, the men in his group treated him with the respect accorded to an elder.

The young man was a Catholic priest who was hidden among the Poles. That winter, we all "concealed" something in camp: one hid his Zionism; another, his social origin, and some—even their nationality. There were Poles who made themselves out to be Belarusians or even Germans, thinking it was more expedient. A silver-haired man of noble appearance stood out among the Poles. He walked around in a long peasant tunic, which suited him well. He had a soft, pleasant manner of speaking and a good-natured, round face. He was Lewandowski, the conductor of the Polish radio orchestra in Warsaw. Indeed, I did not recall his name, but the presence of a musician among us was officially recognized: Lewandowski was entrusted with two balalaikas and a guitar, which were kept at the "club," and at first, they even permitted him to sleep in a warm corner of the KVCh. When I entered the club, I would find Lewandowski stoking the small iron stove or I would watch as he played on the balalaika, with a serious face and laughing eyes, while our "educator" performed the heart-rending romantic song "Oh, Why This Night. . . ." It was not easy for this man of almost sixty, but he never complained, was always calm and imperturbable, and full of quiet gaiety. In conversing with him,

1. Arthur Grottger (1837–1867)—prominent Polish Romantic painter and graphic artist, whose series depicted the difficulties of life under Russian occupation.

I became convinced that he was not the person he claimed to be; he did not show a professional approach to music.

His wife was an Englishwoman who was in Egypt at the outbreak of the war. Lewandowski told me in great secrecy that he had lived in Kresy [the eastern regions of Poland that belonged to the Austro-Hungarian empire before World War I] in a house with twenty-eight rooms. I probably was not his sole confidante: soon, people in the camp began to say that a Polish aristocrat was hiding under the name Lewandowski. He died tragically in the camp. People who survived told me that his real name was Count Waszczyc; my informants must bear responsibility for this information.

As for me,[2] the fact that I presented myself as a "non-party Palestinian" was no help. They labeled me a "Jewish nationalist," although doubts about my identity persisted. Mai, the chief accountant, would say: "Margolin is neither a Jew nor a Pole; he is rather a Russian. He speaks just like a Russian!"

There were many religious people at Square 48. It is worth noting that religious Jews conducted themselves with great moral strength and fortitude in camp. Young yeshiva students, young Hasidim held out better than former Komsomol and socialist youth. When the latter landed in camp and convinced themselves that this was neither a bad dream nor bourgeois slander (some of them had already spent time in Polish prisons for communism), they suffered a real shock. I remember that on May 1, 1940, when they forced us zeks to work, one of the Komsomol fellows burst out crying from shame and vexation: it was the first time in his life that he had been forced to work on the first of May.[3]

Our religious Jews refused to be coerced into working on Yom Kippur. A group of Jews received permission from the administration not to work on that day on condition that they would make it up by working on the next day off. They received a place to pray, and a "hazan" [cantor] was found. About fifty to sixty people prayed on Rosh Hashanah and Yom Kippur. The camp boss and commandant Panchuk came to look at this unusual and unfamiliar spectacle. The Poles in the camp did not organize prayer services, and the Jews' zeal for prayer soon cooled, too: they did not mark Passover at all. The camp clipped their wings.

Among us was a youngish junior rabbi, a calm, quiet person. Old man Nirenshtein was another religious devotee. Nirenshtein was a work foreman

2. This paragraph is found in the French, but not in the published Russian version.

3. May Day is the traditional workers' holiday in socialist and communist countries.

in charge of a brigade of Polish Catholic and Galician Jewish women, who were dressed in men's jackets and sent to the depths of the forest to burn the debris from the felling. With a serious mien, leaning on a gnarled stick, he would lead into the forest Polish colonels' wives, teachers, deathly frightened aunties, Warsaw refugees, and Jewish storekeepers, who had lost their husbands during the transport. Old man Nirenshtein did not join in political conversations. "All your calculations," he said, "are meaningless. If God is willing, everything will change in a day."

With the young rabbi, I would converse on philosophical topics: "What is freedom?"

"Freedom," he and two believing Jews from Stolin responded in unison, "is following God's commandments." I asked why the Book of Job, which relates that God returned all his losses to the sufferer and restored his good fortune, says nothing about his children who perished? How is it possible that the fate of these children has no independent significance, and they died only in order to test Job? The junior rabbi smirked when he heard that remark. He was always freezing, and he went to work in Gardenberg's brigade that winter wrapped in a black military blanket as if it were a skirt. With regard to Job, he informed me that the whole story is only a "parable," a tale, not something that actually happened, and one need not take Job's children's fate to heart— they could not die as they never lived.

In the office of Square 48 and later at the most difficult work in wood felling, I also met a [Protestant] pastor, a rare phenomenon in the Soviet Union. The pastor, a broad-shouldered, thickset man (narrow-shouldered pastors had already died by that time), spoke to me in German. That winter of 1940–1941, Germans did not yet lower their voices when speaking German in the camps. I asked him to tell me the history of the Lutheran church in Russia after the October Revolution. It was a sad story, which cannot be recounted in detail here. One of the two elderly bishops who guided the Protestants in Russia died, and the other was sent to Germany. The Soviet government then gave permission to open a school for pastors—thirty to forty students for the entire Soviet Union. My interlocutor graduated from this school. Sometime after completing his studies, he and the remaining alumni of this school were sent to the camps.

He related this calmly, without a shade of pathos or indignation. Recalling Niemöller[4] and the pastors who had been shot in Poland by the Nazis, I looked

---

4. Martin Niemöller (1892–1984)—anti-Nazi German Protestant pastor, who was interned in Nazi concentration camps until his release by the Allies in 1945.

with sympathy at this man, who did not have much chance of ever returning to his calling. Two months later, leaving the forest with a brigade, I saw the pastor in a wood feller's jacket, with an ax and bow saw, at work. I marveled at his strength and agile movements. Non-Jews, even if they were intellectuals, still showed their heredity—their peasant or worker origins. It was easier for them to adjust: their ancestors helped them, whereas in my case, sixty generations of scholars and individualists, who had not been serfs, hindered me from resigning myself and submitting my neck to the camp yoke.

There were also many Russian Orthodox priests among us. I shall tell about only one of them, the orderly in our barrack of administrative and technical personnel, a short but strong person, with a Mediterranean appearance. In the past, he had been an assistant head of a diocese. We conversed at length. He was good looking, with a sonorous church tenor voice and deep, dark eyes. He was not a "Soviet person"; despite many years in camp, he still gave off the aroma of incense and loved to chant phrases from the liturgy in a low voice, blinking sweetly like a cat. The mass of Russian prisoners did not manifest religiosity except that old people would often cross themselves before eating. The reverend father crossed himself both before and after eating, but that did not hinder him from being a faultless orderly, keeping the barrack clean, and bringing food from the kitchen for the office workers and foremen. And he would receive the leftovers of this barrack of camp dignitaries. He had an assistant—a young Polish lad of about seventeen, whom he treated tenderly, giving him cleaning work, for which he fed him and cooingly called him "Adam, my boy."

A closer look, however, revealed that this priest was painfully depraved and corrupt. Upon learning that I was from Palestine, he evinced unctuous curiosity and often would sit with me, tilting his head sideways, and glancing askance with his dark eyes. He was terribly interested in the "Sanhedrin" and "Jewish elders of Zion." It seemed that the revered father fervently believed in "The Protocols of the Elders of Zion" and probably also in the blood libel....

They had arrested him for attempting to escape abroad, and at his interrogation, the NKVD showed him pictures of his entering the building of a foreign consulate in Moscow. The two sides in the interrogation were quite a match. In the camp, they treated him with cruel irony, considered him dishonest (snatching what he could in the barrack), and at every occasion cursed him not only as a "priest" with an added obscenity but also with the Russian term signifying a pederast. He gave them back in kind, and soon they drove him away from the ATP, from a good spot, not because of thefts in the barrack but because of the abominable, hysterical scandals that he created. During one such "clash," I caught sight of him, and my heart stopped: what happened to the honeyed, cooing voice and calm look, dignified church decorum and sweetness of movements? His lips spouted coarse, blasphemous curses, which were unheard of even in camp; he was foaming with anger, jutting forward, fists clenched, not like a mad dog but like a mad cat ready to scratch out your eyes . . . and then, sitting in a corner in the orderly's place, he kept shaking and weeping impotent pathetic tears of a broken and ridiculed person—a priest in camp, nothing more. What could be more ludicrous? A priest who cannot rid himself of an invisible cassock, although his sole salvation comes from his and other people's forgetting his past as quickly as possible.

At the other end of the camp spectrum were Party[5] workers, former secretaries of Party committees and regional committees who had been purged while serving zealously but had not yet lost hope of returning sometime to that marvelous world of power and privileges. These people, like failed students, waited impatiently to retake the exam, and they looked at us aliens from the West as at some kind of smart alecks. We did not respect the unjust tyranny of the camp, but they did: they were like Gogol's sergeant's widow, said to have flogged herself. These people were voluntary assistants, the support of the administration, collaborators, something like Kapos in the German concentration camps. After five to six years, their fervor, too, flagged along with the vestiges of physical strength.

In the camp, there was a commissar, in the past a member of the government somewhere in Uzbekistan or Turkmenistan, with a name that ended in -baev.[6] He had a Mongolian face, dried like yellow parchment, a bald skull and goatee, wrinkled and mummy-like. He was incapable of climbing an incline: his heart was failing—he was a second-category invalid. It was unbelievable to hear that just a year ago, he used to fell eighteen cubic meters in the forest. His life was ending. All that remained was a dream about a marvelous time of his life when he had maintained a European standard of living and even had a Russian wife—a doctor in a white frock. His wife—a doctor in a white frock. . . .

Suddenly the dentist Dyatlovitskaya arrived at Square 48 for three days with a special group from Medvezhegorsk. Although there was no resident dentist in the camp, we all had our teeth checked once every three months

---

5. Of the Communist party—the only political party in the USSR. Only its members could hold leading positions in government, industry, army, arts, etc.

6. The ending of the surname indicates that he came from a Central Asian republic.

when a specialist made the rounds of the forest sectors. They set up a little office for Dyatlovitskaya at the KVCh and installed an especially strong lamp; she set out her instruments, medicines, and a line formed by the door. She had a very short sentence, just three years, and I immediately recognized a familiar type: a Jewess from Bobruisk. Her assistant was the beautiful Natasha, also a prisoner. Both women were dressed in white; everything around them was so unlike the usual in camp—clean and nice as in freedom. The commissar from Central Asia did not want to leave. . . . As if enchanted, he stood, watching as the two females moved in the circle of light from the lamp and a soft, gentle voice was heard. They had already attended to him, but he continued to stand, staring, searching for words . . . and his eyes express a yearning, a longing for the civilized other life, where everything is so clean and beautiful . . . if you have a cut, there is iodine; if it is cold, you stoke the stove . . . if you are hungry, come sit at the table. . . . Suddenly, Dyatlovitskaya guessed what he wanted (although she did not know that this was a former people's commissar[7]) and said to him, "It probably is not very pleasant for you in the barrack. . . . So, Grandpa, sit here for a while and warm yourself up. . . . Natasha, bring a stool. . . ." And he sat and waited while they filled my tooth. He reveled in the human kindness, in this improbable oasis, like a puppy let in from the street to warm up.

In the little side room where ten people were living, a circle of Jews would come to listen to Pappenheimer, the orderly. Hiding behind this Schilleresque name[8] was an ill individual, a young German Jew, crippled, dragging his foot, a stutterer with a morbidly pale face. Pappenheimer would tell us about the Nazi concentration camp Dachau, where he had spent seven months. His stories implied that he was interned there among the Aryans, which did not accord with his Semitic appearance. "Then I was still healthy!" related Pappenheimer. "Life in Dachau was enchanting before the war. No work norms. You work for forty-five minutes and you rest for fifteen. You get thirteen hundred grams of bread, sausage, marmalade, goulash for dinner—real goulash! And each person has his own bed! After work, everyone had to wash up, take off the work clothes, and put on felt slippers that were under the bed. Everyone could spend seventy marks monthly in the camp canteen, and you could find everything there...."

---

7. Soviet equivalent of government minister.

8. In Friedrich Schiller's drama *The Death of Wallenstein*, the hero alludes to the heroism of Count Pappenheim's soldiers.

The cripple would talk for hours, shaking and biting his lips, about the good times in Dachau. The Jews eagerly listened to him and believed in the German paradise in Dachau! Each one of them yearned not for freedom— that was too much—but for a European concentration camp where there are beds, a canteen, and 1300 grams of bread. Jews yearned for Dachau! The macabre grotesqueness of this scene was engraved in my memory. Each of them was ready, at any time, to exchange Square 48 for the Nazi camp of 1937. Although I was unable to share their rapture about Dachau, I, too, would then willingly have exchanged the Soviet camp for the good old Polish prison where they kept political prisoners separately, did not force them to do slave labor, where there was not only books and food but also the possibility of studying and where one did not have to conceal one's opinions.

Among the several intellectuals living in the shack where Pappenheimer was the orderly was Farber, a young man with a foppish mustache and an exceptionally elegant green jacket. Farber worked in the office and stood out not only because of the green jacket but also because of his wit and markedly "refined" manner. Farber was from Lvov.[9] Nature endowed him with the ability to capture female hearts and to shine on the dance floor. He was a poseur, of the type who never forget the "impression" that they make. He had an uncle in Lvov upon whom he placed his hopes; he wrote to him about a package, but the uncle did not reply. At that time, Farber was full of self-confidence, would tell jokes, and to everyone's amusement, comically would drill Pappenheimer, instructing him how a model orderly should conduct himself: "Pappenheimer! Come here!" the dictator Farber would command in a cockish tenor. "Stand in line with chest out in front of the chief! Why isn't the floor swept under the bunk?"

"Me-me-me-melde gehorsamst,"[10] replied poor Pappenheimer, in whose head Dachau and Square 48 were completely fused.

Suddenly, they drove Farber out of the office. Expulsion from the office automatically entailed a transfer to a worker's barrack. Farber was unable to withstand the work and hunger. First, he sold the green jacket. Next, he stopped washing and lost his sense of humor. Then they caught him stealing a piece of bread and beat him up in the forest. Finally, they sent him to the boiler room. In that wasteland, eye to eye with a semi-savage Asiatic who did not understand Russian, he became completely wild. He began to have fits of

---

9. Now Lviv, Ukraine.

10. German: I have the honor to report.

madness during which he yelled fiercely at his fellow worker. Yelling in camp is a common phenomenon, but his cries were somewhat louder than necessary. Once I saw him at midnight running out of the boiler room, clasping his head in his hands in frenzied despair. One stormy evening, we heard this savage howl from the boiler room, and suddenly someone said, "Listen! Surely he simply went crazy!" They removed insane Farber from the boiler room but continued to send him to work. He then began to urinate without going out of the barrack. They put him separately, in the worst, coldest, and befouled spot near the door. He was separated by a space from his nearest neighbor, as no one wanted to lie next to him. When cleaning the barrack, they skipped his place.

He would smile a shy, pinched, lost smile. Although he was not dangerous, he had to be watched when the brigade washed in the bathhouse: he would take everything that he saw from the disrobed people and put on someone else's clean shirt or shoes. Then when someone in the barrack could not find his things, he would go straight to the corner where the unfortunate invalid was lying.

None of the people from his group of office trusties, who had embarked upon camp life with him and lived with the help of received packages, made the least effort to help him, feed him, or look after him when there still was time. In camp no one either wanted or was able to save those who were perishing. Each was preoccupied with himself. The rarest exceptions in no way changed the camp atmosphere. Philanthropy in camp is just like eau de cologne in a slaughterhouse.

In that first camp winter, Jews and Poles lived side by side without friction. The Poles were in the minority among us; the Russian zeks and the administration both called us "Westerners." A common misfortune, common language, and common nonacceptance of our surroundings brought us together. Sometimes, this astonished the Russians. Russian Jews were surprised by the Polish ones: "Where did you get this Polish patriotism?" they asked. "You yourselves tell us about Polish antisemitism, yet you defend them!" The Russians did not like the Poles and related to them ironically, with instinctive hostility. They understood neither their Catholicism nor their cultural insularity. "Pany, shliakhta!" [gentry], they would say about each one and shrug their shoulders, seeing how ardently we defended everything Polish. Among the hundreds of Jews were dozens of Poles and, of course, we were closer to them than to others in the camp. Among the Poles were former judges and policemen, engineers and civil servants, workers and peasants, people of all parties, former national democrats [Polish acronym: Endeks][11] and future

---

11. "Narodowa Demokracja" [abbrev. Endeks]—ultra-right Polish party in the first half of the twentieth century with a pronounced antisemitic bias.

Anders' Army men . . . but then, under the influence of the terrible national catastrophe, all the divisions and differences were forgotten and suppressed, and in particular, the Polish and Jewish intelligentsia easily got along in the camp.

We did not, however, trust the closed and silent Polish youths; we knew and sensed their recent Hitlerism, remembering how, in pre-war Poland, they went en masse in the direction of cannibalistic chauvinism. The camp was not a school that could counteract those inchoate tendencies. On the contrary. The camp cultivated a wolfish malice, the feeling that everything is possible and permissible with regard to the regime that had created this ignominy. The camp instilled hatred. We had no doubt that these young people would take from the camp not respect for democracy and human dignity but counter-communism, that is, fascism. The camp made an impression on some of them: they learned how to deal with enemies. They would have liked to introduce such camps throughout the world—but intern other people in them. They wanted not to destroy the camp system but to appropriate it. Among us was a young Pole with a typical student's face, a pointed beard, and a square cap of the Confederation worn at an angle. He acted in an independent, provocative manner and would look at his surroundings with gray, mocking eyes; while he felt healthier and stronger than others, he would strut around. His name was Jacko. Once when we happened to be neighbors on the bunk boards, he confided what was seething inside him. Just once it burst forth: he told me that the Germans are right to use force in Poland, and whoever does not utilize his physical superiority is a fool!

"Crush the weak!" he said, his bright eyes shining feverishly, and I thought then that he himself must not be very healthy. "And we will crush, we shall certainly crush! Piłsudski is a dolt! Is that how Poland should have prepared for battle! Just you wait, our time will come!" But it was already too late for Jacko to crush the weak. His number was up. Many people in camp dreamed of crushing the weak but wound up groveling before the strong.

Our feelings about Polish antisemitism were effaced when we encountered the more massive and elemental Russian antisemitism. We did not expect the open and mass hostility toward Jews that we encountered in the camp. Twenty-five years of Soviet rule had changed nothing in this regard. Invariably, in every brigade, every barrack, every column there were people who hated me only because I was a Jew. There were enough of them to poison the atmosphere in every place where we lived. Although they knew nothing about Hitler, at times they created a Hitlerite atmosphere around us when they addressed us impersonally: "Hey you, Yid!" "Who has the shovel?" "The Yid." These were people from the city or *kolkhoz*, who had been raised in the Soviet period, and their attitude had all the features of a natural and common phenomenon. At that time, I learned the nickname which in the Soviet Union often replaced the term "Yid": "abram," with a guttural "r." At liberty these people were more cautious, but in camp, they had no scruples. Once the fact of our Jewishness was established, it was used against us in everyday relations or at work—in daily discrimination, in minor quibbles, venomous remarks, in a thousand ways of poisoning one's life. If the bonfire dies out and you have to get embers from a neighbor, he will not give it to you because you are a Jew, which is precisely why your fire is not burning—you counted on using his fire and neglected yours. If you do not fulfill the norms, it is because the Jews do not want to work. If a Jew is taken to work in the office, the office trusties try to get rid of him. Distrust of the Jew is prevalent everywhere and you must overcome it in order to establish some kind of personal relationship with people.

In camp, there is only one position that is filled primarily by Jews—that is storekeepers. The kiosk [*larek*] is next to the food warehouse from where food is sent out to the kitchen and guards. The kiosk contains the surplus products that are "dumped" on the camp sector for sale to the zeks on a commercial basis as a kind of prize. When I was there, the kiosk at Square 48 was usually empty, but sometimes two things would arrive there: herring and the worst quality bryndza cheese. They also sold wooden spoons made in camp (by the "consumer products" brigade) and bread as an addition to the ration. All store and food warehouse managers whom I knew in the camps were Jews because this position required the ability to handle goods, calculate, weigh, and give service in a way that satisfies everyone, including the administration. Russians in that job immediately start stealing and receive an additional term. A store or warehouse manager cannot be an absolutely honest person nor one without restraint. Both extremes do not suit the administrators, who need the storekeeper to feed them but not to get caught. Most often storekeepers are thus old Jews with considerable experience in commerce.

Russian Jews got along well with their fellow zeks only when they were able to impress them with their ability to carry on with daring or strength, when they were more Russians than Jews. Except for his dark features and hooked nose, the Jew Sashka was not different from his neighbors in the brigade of mowers. Just like them, he sang Russian songs and cursed and similarly

could throw a shoe at his neighbor or threaten him with a knife, pilfer what
was left unattended, and give his last drop of energy at hard work. When
Sashka saw the Polish Jews, suddenly it plucked some chord, and to his and
the general astonishment, he began to speak to them in something resembling
Yiddish. . . .

A Jew also turned up among the Georgians. Usually, they did not immediately admit their Jewishness; first, they circled around, looked us over, and
then cautiously, as in an intimate confession, "opened up" to us, as Joseph
did to his brothers. The Georgian Jew was still a boy, with a delicate face and
limbs. He told us that he had visited his grandmother in Tbilisi and lost his
identity papers. As he was a passportless individual without a profession, they
attached him to the nearest group and sent him to camp "so that he would not
be in the way." He called to mind his grandfather the rabbi and fragments of
Hebrew. He would repeat certain Hebrew words like a talisman. The Polish
Jews, hearing him say "Shma Yisrael" [Hear, O Israel], would smile, clap him
on the shoulder, and treat him to sugar.

Whereas Russians knew nothing about life and work abroad, the sight of
Russian Jews, withering like weeds, cut off from a live connection with their
people, was doubly painful to us. From 1937, the Soviet regime "recommended"
that they and all other Soviet citizens cease all correspondence with relatives
abroad. Long before that, the regime had suffocated Russian Jewry and detached it from national Jewish life throughout the world. Such is the condition of the children of those who once were the vanguard of the Jewish
people, who founded Zionism and laid the foundations of the new Palestine.
Their children and grandchildren never heard about Palestine, were unfamiliar with the Bible, and had no knowledge of Jewish national culture or of
the names that every Jew revered: it was as if they were from a different planet.
When we told them about Tel Aviv or the Jezreel Valley, they would listen
as blacks from Central Africa would listen to the white man's tales of the
miracles of Europe—with astonishment but without special interest, as about
something too remote to be real. And I recalled May 1 banners on the streets
of Tel Aviv with greetings to Stalin (that is, to our camp boss) and to the Red
Army (that is, to the head of our army unit), and I thought: we Jews are such
a generous people that we easily forget about our own flesh and blood. "You
can stay in the camp, Sashka, we won't quarrel because of you. . . ."

In line with Hitler's successes, antisemitism intensified in the camp. One
could observe here how the German racist side won hearts and attracted
sympathies, how it created the psychological prerequisites for political rapprochement. The rare Soviet newspapers that landed in the camp at that time

were full of pro-German publicity. Later on, the Soviet press never carried Churchill's speeches the way they did Hitler's before the big rupture: they would take up half a page. All the arrows of irony and criticism were directed at the rapacious Anglo-American imperialism. This cynical campaign was conducted very consistently. When the Italians invaded Greece at the beginning of 1941, at Square 48, the political instructor explained condescendingly that the guilty party was . . . Greece, and that Italy was only defending the Greek coast from seizure by the English. This doubled as an indirect defense of the Soviet Union's policy in Finland. The camp riffraff reached their own conclusions: Hitler is right, and you should beat the Yids. A few months later, under the influence of Hitler's initial successes at the Soviet front, the atmosphere in camp was such that the Jews had no doubt what fate would await them if the camp fell into the hands of the Germans or the Finns. They would slaughter us on the first day. The other zeks threatened us openly, and when we crowded together by the kitchen window, they would direct glances full of hate at the Jews and one could hear: "They should all be killed! Not one should remain!"

In December 1940 in the barrack in the evening, there was a heated dispute between me and the "intelligentsia" from the administrative-technical barrack. In the large hut there stood a stove, on top of which water was boiling round the clock, with mugs and kettles placed around. Here there were no rusty, bent metal kettles or bowls picked up from the dump. The bowls were metallic and clean; the tin plate kettles were in good shape, with handles. Instead of bunk beds there were wooden cots with straw mattresses. At the back of the room stood a table on a trestle; by the light of a kerosene lamp, people would sit there in the evening to eat and write reports. There, on a winter evening in 1940, I got drawn into an unpleasant conversation.

The people among whom I was sitting had a high school technical education and some even had a higher education. All were raised in the Soviet Union, were of proletarian origin, and had come together in the camp from all parts of Russia with the most disparate life experiences. Some had been arrested for embezzlement, some for an everyday crime, others for an incautious word, but even those who were sitting for Article 58, "counterrevolution," were not really political conspirators and represented the average citizenry. These people belonged to the mass of fifteen million Soviet zeks, and this mass, in turn, was representative of ninety percent of the population of Russia. One could free all these millions and arrest other millions in their stead, with the same justification.

The conversation started with Hitler—"Why does he dislike the Jews?" and "What did the Jews do to the Germans?"—and moved on to the Jewish people. I was talking with only one person, but within ten minutes, the entire barrack heatedly joined the conversation. I tried to tell these people— who had never stepped outside the borders of Russia or gone beyond Soviet information—about the historical martyrology of my people, its contributions to humankind, and creative ability to work wherever given an opportunity.

With equal success, I could have preached this to the German SA [Nazi brown shirts] or the Polish middle class. So much concentrated malice, poison, and seething hatred was dumped on me that I suddenly felt as if I were at a meeting of Endeks[12] in Poland. People who had been quietly lying on the cots, their shoes off, and resting their head on their hands, suddenly could not restrain themselves, jumped up and turned on me as if I were responsible for all their misfortunes. Without knowing it, I had touched a sore spot. Jews were not to be spoken well of in their presence. "Your nation!" resounded from all sides. "Don't make up tales; we know for ourselves; you are a cunning people!" Each was able to speak about the Jews without embarrassment, knowing that the bosses and guards and all free workers were on his side. Antisemitic outbursts were never punished in camp; the administration smoothed them over, as it never occurred to them to hurt "their own" Russian person because he "couldn't restrain himself."

On that evening, too, things would have gone badly for me, but in the end, everyone's darling, the blond Vaska, the receptionist at the forestry market exchange, a joker and clown, entered and stood up for the Jews. "Come on, what are you talking about, guys!" he said. "There are all kinds of Jews. Look, I was at a Jewish *kolkhoz* in the Ukraine . . .," and he began to describe the Jewish *kolkhoz*, and then the conversation effortlessly turned to another topic.

I went to the stove where my cot stood, undressed in the darkness and lay down. Vaska's voice reached me, carefree, familiar, and all of them had already forgotten the conversation that had upset me. Vasya was one of their own, and everything was fine among them. Once more, I saw that it is possible to drive antisemitism underground but not to eliminate it as long as the Jewish masses remain, as previously, a markedly foreign body in the social organism of other peoples.

---

12. National Democrats—see note 11.

20

Spring 1941

SPRING ARRIVED AT Square 48. The snow swelled with water, gave way underfoot, and did not support the sleds. We walked to our site through the glades, where the snow still was smooth and even. At each step, however, we sunk above our knees, trudging as if crossing a stream, sinking in, then lifting our feet, with the water gurgling under us. The forest brigades worked in the water; the delimbers reached the chopped branches with difficulty. Finally, they changed the work hours.

At night, the sleigh roads were still passable because of the frost, but in the daytime, they melted. Consequently, we went to work at midnight and returned at midday, sleeping until the evening. At night, the forests were full of bonfires and shouting as if it were daytime. The snow looked green in the moonlight, and the people, with thin, dark faces and sunken eyes, looked like aliens.

In early spring, I went to work at Depot No. 5. The forest depot is a square that stretches for a kilometer on both sides of the railroad tracks, filled with warehouses, woodpiles, and reserves of wood ready for loading. The stacks are piled higher than a man's height. All day the wood arrives by wagons from the felling site. The arriving shipments are piled up and taken down, and the wood is brought to a certain distance near the railroad bed. Sawhorses stand next to the piles, and people saw the wood. Bonfires are not permitted at the depot, and all day guards and brigade leaders are busy extinguishing fires that the zeks contrive to light for at least half an hour in the shadow of the stacks.

We worked in a team of three: Margolin, the Georgian Chikavani, and the Westerner, the Pinsk Jew Kleiman. We placed several logs at a time on the saw-horse and sawed together at meter intervals. Two men saw together, side by side. Kleiman piled the wood, but he had one more special task. Everywhere under the snow and in the ditches lay half-rotting, buried stacks of sawed wood that had been left behind. Finding such a stack under the snow, for-gotten from the past year, Kleiman, awaiting a favorable moment, would drag some ten cut blocks and add them to our pile. Sometimes the depot manager would yell to him from afar: "Where are you dragging the wood from! Drop it immediately!" Then Kleiman, with his small, foxy face, wearing a beautiful fur coat that he never parted from for a moment, would drop the wood and wait until the depot manager went past. Meanwhile, Chikavani and I sawed all day, without leaving the spot.

The camp instilled in me a feeling of respect for the Georgian people. The Georgians were distinguished among the general mass of zeks by some innate gentleness and calm; they knew how to behave with dignity, without savagery, with the pride of an ancient, cultured race. These traits were all characteristic of my friend and brother Chikavani, one of the unknown martyrs of that na-tion, whose contribution to the camps' mass grave is one of the most valuable in the Soviet Union. I became close to Chikavani in his declining years. He had been in the camp for three years already, and he had more time to serve than he could endure. His whole being was toned down and softened by the premonition of his end. Chikavani was just a Georgian farmer, but he had the delicacy, the largesse in everyday details, and nobility that an English lord would have envied. I loved this person. Being with him, sawing, and standing alongside him alleviated the work. And I loved to hear his stories, which brought to life the distant, bright world of that southern Caucasus country, the valleys and mountains of Kartveli,[1] the white, rustic house of his mother, the sun, vineyards, and streets of Batumi on the Black Sea.

Chikavani's stories could fill an entire book. We both yearned for our homeland and lived only in thoughts about it. I dreamt about traveling some-time to my land, Palestine, via Batumi, and then we would both be free. But it turned out differently. And I forgot the Georgian words that he taught me, "Megobaro Chikavani," my friend Chikavani. . . .

We would return to camp at midday, walking about 3 kilometers, passing by places where they were uprooting stumps. That is very difficult work; sometimes a team had to waste half a day on a particularly stubborn, giant, deep-seated root. The *ukazchiki* swarmed around the stumps. You dig just a little, and the pit fills with water. You have to dig under the water, find and cut off the offshoots of the roots, free the stump, and finally put long poles under the root in one or several places as levers. The end of the pole, like a shaft,

---

1. Georgian language designation of Georgia.

would stick out on top, and the group would lift it, turning it around, pulling up and overturning the root. Sometimes, however, no efforts help: that means somewhere down below under the root where you can't reach with an ax or pick is the last unnoticed spur, and you have to dig deeper and deeper until people are up to their waist in the swampy water.

The *ukazchiki* who were uprooting stumps at Square 48 that spring were young people around seventeen to twenty years old who had been sent to camps in the summer of 1940 on the basis of a notorious decree (*ukaz* in Russian) directed at getting rid of undisciplined youths. At that time, throughout vast Russia, courts were tasked with ruthlessly combing through Soviet youth and eliminating hooliganism in the shortest possible time. The method of police operations here corresponded exactly to the method of "liquidating lice in a week" at our camp. Then, itinerant brigades would liquidate the lice, making the rounds of the barracks and checking the zeks' shirts. If a louse was found on someone, he was immediately dispatched to the bathhouse. Similarly, the peoples' courts liquidated hooliganism by dispatching to camps a mass of people who at that time had the misfortune to be rounded up. On the eve of the war, about a million young people were thus sent to camps for terms of one, two, or three years.

The *ukazchiki* stood out among the mass of Soviet zeks not only because they had "kiddy" sentences but also because they were a different type—confused, frightened youths who had been brought to the camp straight from the classroom or from the boulevards of a large city where they had committed their crime. One got drunk and carried on in a public place. Another accosted a girl in the evening, and she called the police. A third cursed on the street. Many fit the latter category. Of course, petty delinquency of this kind is no rarity in the Soviet Union, before or after the decree. In order to wean the youth from the swearing that they had learned from adults, they thus sent them to labor camps, where they were exposed to a coarse vocabulary that far exceeded everything they had heard at home, and they could see that not one free worker, not one camp boss, including the "educator," could do without the unsurpassable profanity that penetrated one's thoughts and consciousness at all times. In the "corrective labor camp," their life was truly crushed with ruthless and savage cruelty. They were terrorized for life, and their camp stay was marked in their identity documents, which eliminated the possibility of leading a normal life in the future. For what? Each one of them was guilty of a petty act, which was the result of the education he had received on the Soviet street. Talking to them, I was struck by how young and lightheaded they were, still recalling the atmosphere of their parental home, speaking of "mommy" or saying "at home we have a rocking chair on the porch." In the camp, they mixed them with criminals, recidivists, with *urki* and prostitutes, and even worse—with completely innocent masses perishing for no reason, driven there from all sides of the enormous country—at the age when this experience and these impressions would become decisive for them. I saw them sitting in the melting snow by the bonfire, shivering from cold, in rags that did not cover their bodies, in an indescribable condition: their mothers would wring their hands in despair if they could see them. The hunger and the camp turned them into true *bezprizornye*.[2] One midday, passing by, I saw Vitya, the son of an urban architect in a regional city in the Northern Caucasus, an eighteen-year old, half-naked, in smelly, filthy rags with black hands and an unwashed face, put in the pocket of his jacket rotten herring heads from the garbage of the camp kitchen. One of the senior zeks saw this rot and forced him to throw into the mud those things that even a pig would not eat. But no sooner did he turn away than a fight broke out behind his back: all the *ukazchiki* rushed pell mell to pick up the herring heads, cursing and fighting as they tore them from each other's hands.

Spring came, the roads were flooded, and we were cut off from normal communication with Medvezhegorsk and Pyalma. The delivery of packages ceased in March, and in May, in order to eat, I sold my last pair of pants from home. I went around in government-issued padded pants and also slept in them, without undressing. In May, they transferred us to work in the "quarry." We worked as if on an island surrounded by swampy water. We made our way to work over boards, and losing our balance, would fall into the water.

The "quarry" was the most suitable place for the Westerners. On both sides rose steep, yellow clay walls the height of a man. With shovels, crowbars, and picks we broke up the sand and loaded it onto wooden wheelbarrows. As the barrows were unable to move in the damp dirt, passageways of boards were laid down. There was a lot to do. Some would carry the boards on their shoulders for half a kilometer; others would put together the planks; some would shovel the sand, and others would bring it in the wheelbarrow to the embankment; others would even out the embankment and bring the sand farther along the depression. We literally filled the swamp with sand. The quarry was unusually lively; the low area swarmed with people. Behind us, they drove piles into the water with heavy blocks that four people lifted with difficulty. Ahead of us, where the embankment broke off, was a narrow,

---

2. *Bezprizornye*—term used to designate abandoned or orphaned children, a social phenomenon which became widespread in the 1920s after the Civil War.

swampy ravine, from which the water had to be diverted. Canals were dug on both sides to do this. Each zek had his task of fulfilling a certain work norm. I pushed wheelbarrows unceasingly, work during which one could have one's own hidden thoughts.

While Grinfeld loaded my wheelbarrow, I stood by the side and watched his spade rise and fall as the damp sand filled the barrow. When large rocks landed in the sand, I would toss them out. "Enough!" Grinfeld flattened the sand with the spade; with my gloved hands, I took the two handles of the wheelbarrow and carefully rolled the load along the boards to the embankment. Logs and uprooted stumps lay around everywhere, the water gurgled, and far away, in the open field, white snow was still lying, all eroded, turning rosy in the sun.

Grinfeld possessed the special talent of guessing the time without a watch within fifteen minutes of accuracy. None of us had a watch and, therefore, we would ask Grinfeld when necessary. The living clock of the brigade, he would look at the sky and say confidently: twelve-thirty. Then the four of us would sit down and on overturned wheelbarrows, a session would begin by the quarry wall: a Georgian, a Pole, a Palestinian, and a Czech. Batumi and Tel Aviv, Warsaw and Brno would meet in the Karelian-Finnish forest. Each day during the work breaks, one of us in turn would tell a story. The stories comprised a camp Decameron: one hundred stories on the margins of our own wretched history.

Before the war, Grinfeld was the representative for a Czech firm and often traveled by car along the Danube.[3] He knew the Balkans up to Greece. Now he would stretch out his thin legs in gray pants with blue patches. His pointed red nose protruded from under his peaked Budennyi[4] cap. He rolled a cigarette and said, "In Hungary, there is a beautiful city, Varaždin. Have you heard of Varaždin? Once upon a time in Varaždin. . . .

A fantastic story would begin: ducks purchased at the market at half price, a sunny market full of light and colors, peasant women in black corsets with multicolored ribbons and white skirts. In Czech, a potato is called *brambori*. Varaždin, *brambori*, freedom!

---

3. This paragraph and the following one are taken from the French translation that was published in 1949 under the title *La condition inhumaine*. The Russian original of this excerpt was not found.

4. Cap named after Semyon Budennyi, the Red Army hero of the southwestern front during the Civil War who figured prominently in Isaac Babel's stories *Red Cavalry*.

A railroad was located a kilometer from the quarry. They often would bring us there to unload cars with sand or to load cars with wood. On the way, we would not know what they wanted from us or what awaited us at the end of the road. It did not matter to us at all. The important thing was to make it to the end of the day. Sometimes they would bring us to a train loaded with heavy rails, and then grumbling and indignation would begin: "Where do we have the strength for this!" Somehow, we would drop the rails from the flat car down to the ground by the train wheels. The next day, they would bring us back to the same place to move the rails away from the train in order not to hinder the train's movement.

On June 10, 1941, a snowstorm struck the camp. The area was covered by a thin layer of snow, and as we walked, we did not know where our feet would land. The Onega June did not pamper the Westerners. In these spots, summer, in essence, is limited to one month—July. Snow still lay on the ground in May; June was capricious; and in August, the cold nights would start again. A sharp wind and snow made work impossible on June 10. We started bonfires as in winter. There was no place to take shelter. People sat numbly and froze, drawing in their necks and sulking, looking like frozen nags under hopsack. As there was not enough room by the fire, a second row stood, extending their hands in tattered gloves above those sitting by the fire. We, the new fire worshippers, prayed over the fire as our mothers had over the Sabbath candles. The wind changed direction every minute, and smoke blew into our faces. The snow fell on us, on our shoulders, on our round ugly caps; snow covered our padded jackets and knees in a feathery armor. We could do nothing but wait. The snow will pass, and we shall remain. And the day will pass, but we shall remain. The entire camp will pass. . . .

"Panie," Karpowicz said, leaning over. "I don't feel well. . . . What in the world did they do to us? Why?"

"We have to stick it out," I said to him with blue lips. "The winter in June is not long. It's like a tunnel."

And I told him a story about a tunnel. It was in Italy, in Genoa. There were two of us; we were young. Our first time on the Italian Riviera.

We sat in a quaint, overcrowded third-class train car. The Italians laughed and joked with us. One old man, lively and quick like mercury, asked: "Is that your wife? How long have you been married?" I signaled: a week ago. The Italian poked me with his finger and jumped back with a comic grimace: "It's hot! It's on fire! It's burning!"

Everyone started to laugh, and we, finally, could not sit any longer and went to the open platform at the end of the car.

The train traveled along the Ligurian coast, hovering like a bird above the calm Mediterranean Sea, in a flood of light and sun, in radiance and space. The bays, full of colored sails and masts, peaceful towns and green groves lay before us. In the distance, bells were ringing; it was Sunday.

Suddenly, with no transition, we dived into a tunnel that cut through a hill. It was as if someone had sneaked up from behind and thrown a bag on your head. It became dark and stuffy, and standing on the open platform amidst the car's sharp jolting, blinded and choking, we grabbed hold of each other, and the acrid soot and fumes enveloped us. While the train thundered, we stood, holding hands, patiently waiting—seconds, minutes—a dark passage from light to light.

Suddenly, just as precipitously as the train had entered the tunnel, it burst out of it. And again, the train flew forward, like a bird, and the same panorama of Ligurian spring, the same sea and same sky and sunny glare. Only the two of us were black and sooty, like two chimney sweeps.

It's nothing! In life, too, one encounters a tunnel, as in a mountain. A mountain of evil, a mountain of misfortune and sorrow. You can't break it or circumvent it; you have to pass through.

They officially recognized June 10, 1941, as a nonworking day. The food ration was based on what we had earned the previous day.

In thick fog, we walked along the railroad ties toward the watchtower and palisade, and suddenly I saw a zek. He was lying, resting straight on the damp earth, legs bent, and hands extended, his head resting on a stone; he was as soaked as the earth on which he was lying.

He was not afraid of the dampness. He knew that all the summer and fall rains would fall on him. And we, the entire brigade, did not trouble his rest and did not say a word to him but simply stepped over him in turn, as if stepping over a log, and continued on.

Everyone stepped over; no one tripped. The guard, with his rifle on his belt, passed last.

We lived in the kingdom of the Dragon, where everything was topsy-turvy.

Hungry invalids loaded rotten potatoes into torn bags.

Here the wagons did not transport the people, but the people were harnessed to the wagons.

Here the illiterate educated the literate.

The criminals gave orders to the innocent.

Healthy people sent the sick ones to work. Liars and cretins checked every word and thought.

Snow fell in June. Women swore like men. Lenin's works were not taken out of the closet in the KVCh so that the paper would not be rolled for cigarettes. We smoked ordinary books.

Letters arrived for dead people, but the living did not have the right to indicate that they were alive.

They guarded millions of people with guard dogs so that they would not escape.

No one lived where he wanted to, or spoke what he thought, or worked as he knew how.

They brought foreigners here from occupied territories, considering them socially dangerous in the Soviet country.

You did not need to commit a crime to land here; a stay in this place turned everyone into a criminal.

Boiled water was called "tea" here; a barrack—a residence; the torture of forced labor—work.

In the morning, commenced a mad masquerade of people who no longer resembled themselves. They scattered busily to their places: drivers to fell trees, violinists to peel potatoes, bakers to cut hair, hairdressers to pump water, and intellectuals to dig ditches.

In the evening, the authorities would check what had been accomplished. It was bad. And everything was changed around: the next day, the violinists felled trees, the intellectuals carried water, the drivers were used as medics, and the cooks went to general work.

In the evening, however, it still did not come out right until they arrested the camp boss himself and appointed a replacement who had not yet served a term or had already served a term and was just as mistreated by fate as we had been.

The camp was called a "corrective labor" camp, but the people who spent time there detested the labor process for the rest of their lives and developed a virtuoso ability to evade conscientious work.

An enormous squandering of labor and human resources took place in the camps that covered the body of Russia like a monstrous rash. The people who were there were overwhelmed by their unbelievable, nightmarish fate—the fate of millions, of generations, tribes, who were reprocessed here into wood for export, minerals, gold, material goods, and simply human chaff doomed to annihilation.

I spent one of my last days at Square 48 apart from the brigade, "on the hillock." This was a tall hill; my work partner and I gathered dry branches and uprooted stumps, lit a fire on top, and lay there for half a day, resting.

The work was a bluff, contrived by a Russian highway engineer, in order for us to be able to sit together without peeping eyes. Our task was to study the composition of the soil and to find a place suitable for digging up sand for construction.

We dug two pits at a depth of a meter and did nothing else. The engineer arrived at noon, and we sat on the slope of the hill. In the distance, one could see the dismal, swampy ravine with well-trodden footprints, remains of snow, and the damp edge of the forest, beyond which lay the quarry and the road to the camp.

The engineer, like every Russian *intelligent*,[5] was interested in facts. I was supposed to tell him what had happened abroad during the past decade, which he knew about only from Soviet sources. We did not say a word about the Soviet press, the camps, or life in the Soviet Union, just as in the room of someone who is deathly ill, no one speaks about his patent illness.

"Are there camps abroad like ours?"

"No," I responded, "there are not and there cannot be."

"But Hitler?"

"You can't compare Nazi camps with yours. Neither in scale or in essence. There is a thorn there that Europe will soon tear out of its body. Your camps are a durable system, the logically, well organized culmination of the regime. Europe can exist without Hitler and his camps. But the Soviet regime cannot exist without camps."

"Do they write a lot about the camps abroad?"

"They do not write, they do not know, and they don't want to know. I heard something about the camps before the war, but I did not believe it. First, your camps are a well-kept secret. Second, the more that no one tries to uncover these secrets, the easier it is to keep them."

"Hmm . . ." said the engineer, engrossed in his thoughts. "Are there many communists abroad?"

"How should I say it? There are many who place their hopes on you, but few who know you."

"Yes," said the engineer. "You can't figure us out right away. And you think that you know the camps because you spent a year there? No, so far you have seen little suffering. You have more to learn."

"I still managed to learn something during this year," I said, and I recalled the intelligence officer Stepanov's question about my attitude toward the

---

5. An *intelligent* is an individual member of the intelligentsia (see Glossary).

Soviet regime. "To you I can tell the truth about my attitude toward the Soviet regime. In the past, I had many different thoughts, both positive and critical evaluations and approaches—like the rest of the European progressive and humanist intelligentsia to which I belong by education and, so to say, by birth. Now, however, all that is not important. My attitude toward the Soviet regime now is completely defined: fear. Until I arrived in this country, I did not really fear people. Soviet Russia taught me to fear man.

The engineer began to laugh: "You mean that in Europe, people were not afraid?"

"Look, it's like this. In Europe, there are frightening things and fearful people. But people there are ashamed of their fear. There people dare not to fear. There is no abomination that people would not fight. If the Soviet government wanted to terrorize me in sending me here, then it achieved its goal. Everything here is unspeakably terrifying. I feel fear and I am not ashamed of it. I am afraid of what is being done and of how it is done. I never saw anything more terrible in my life than the good-natured face of Molotov, and the front of thousands of poets and writers singing praises, and the fatherly smile of that one,[6] among children . . . and alongside those bodies tortured by that one and the claws, which lightly and unnoticeably, among velvety touches, sink into the live flesh."

"Well," said the engineer, "it is evident that you have been in the camp for only a year. Stay for five and you will stop being afraid. And you will become a Soviet person. You'll get used to it. Fear hinders one from getting accustomed to it. That is why ninety percent of those like you—intellectuals—die off. And for those who survive—it's nothing! They get used to it, they work, and they are not afraid."

----

6. Clear reference to Stalin.

21

Etap [Transfer]

RETURNING FROM WORK on June 22, 1941, struggling past the stable through the mud and horse manure, we heard words that made us tremble and break ranks: "War against Germany!"

All day something had been brewing. From the morning, the bosses were running around with distressed looks, not paying attention to our work. At two o'clock, along with the Stakhanovite kasha, they brought strange news to the work site, which no one believed.

Around six o'clock, even before we reached the guardhouse, we already knew that the Germans had attacked the Soviet Union.

In the evening, despite the absence of a radio, everyone already knew about the bombing of Soviet cities and the order to the Red Army to advance and wipe fascism off the face of the earth.

Everyone was gripped by an inexpressible agitation. What would be now? Some kind of gigantic abscess broke open and now rivers of blood and pus would flow. . . .

Knowing about [Rudolf] Hess's[1] visit to England, we feared only one thing: that a pact with England was concealed behind the German attack. An agreement between Hitler and the democratic West would be an even greater catastrophe than his pact with Stalin. The Russian zeks were silent, but some—perhaps provocateurs—expressed an opinion that the Soviet Union would not last more than a month. I invariably replied to those people

---

1. Rudolf Hess (1894–1987)—loyal follower of Hitler and deputy leader of the Nazi party in the 1930s. In hopes of bringing World War II to an end, on his own initiative, Hess parachuted into Scotland in May 1941. Hitler disassociated himself from Hess's proposals and the British government treated him as a prisoner of war. At the post-war Nuremberg war crimes trials, Hess was convicted and served a life sentence.

that they underestimated the strength of the Red Army. To myself, however, I thought that the Soviet Union would not survive this war.

For Westerners buried in the camps and deprived of the hope of ever escaping from the Soviet Union, this war was the sole chance of reaching freedom. We had nothing to lose in this war between two enemies of European democracy, and we sincerely wished both of them a speedy destruction. The role of tertius gaudens[2] now passed from Stalin to the Anglo-Americans.

Two days passed. At the evening roll call, the camp boss Abramenko delivered a speech to the assembled brigades of zeks. He announced the start of the war and immediately proceeded to threats.

"We know what you are whispering to each other! You are waiting for the Soviet Union to be torn to pieces! But first we shall tear your bodies to pieces! We'll spill a sea of blood, but we won't give up our power. . . ."

That day, several men from the barracks were arrested. The authorities had to set an example. Among those who were shot was Lewandowski, the supposed Warsaw choirmaster. He paid with his life for a few incautious words that were reported to the administration.

The Westerners stopped talking politics with each other.

In another two days they sent us on an *etap*.[3] The Karelo-Finnish SSR was declared a frontal zone, and the camps had to be evacuated. A small group of prisoners who remained at Square 48 were evacuated later in the winter in tragic circumstances. We were more fortunate. We were dispatched to the east with the mass of other BBK prisoners. When the war seethed around Lake Onega, the Finns occupied Petrozavodsk, the capital of the Karelo-Finnish SSR, and Medvezhegorsk, the center of the BBK camps. The Baltic–White Sea Canal and the Murmansk railroad were subject to air bombardments and were partially destroyed. Square 48, however, did not fall into Finnish hands and the front remained several kilometers away.

The first stop of our *etap* was Bobrovoe, a small agricultural labor camp, 8 or 10 kilometers from Square 48. We stayed there until July 1. We lived outside history and knew nothing of the catastrophe at the front. From there they moved us to Ostrech by Lake Onega.

---

2. Tertius gaudens: third party that rejoices from the benefits of a conflict between its two enemies.

3. The Russian word *etap* refers to a transfer from one camp or prison to another, often by rail and/or ship. In this chapter, however, the zeks covered a considerable part of the journey on foot.

We walked part of the way along the difficult forest road. We immediately broke ranks; the elderly and sick fell behind, and the guards became furious. Several times they commanded us to "lie down," and the entire crowd fell to the ground where they were standing. It was a way of restraining the prisoners when they became disorderly. Karpowicz began to lag behind.

"Get moving!" "I can't go any faster!" said Karpowicz, with a deathly pale face. "I have a heart problem." "I don't care about your illness! I'm not a doctor!" At the tail of the column, a disturbance arose. The guard was yelling fiercely at someone: "Get out of the line! Go to the forest!" The prisoner, of course, refused to "go to the forest," as doing so was the equivalent of an attempted escape, which gave the guard the right to shoot.

In the forest, they put us on flatbeds and brought us to Ostrech by the same road on which we had arrived the preceding August. We spent several difficult days in Ostrech. It was a large camp, much larger than our Square 48. It had large barracks, electricity, and a crowd of people. They put us in an empty building with numerous small rooms, and we lay down on the floor, without undressing; we filled up the entryway and corridor in a solid mass, and in the morning, we went to work at the lake.

A strong wind blew from the lake; the temperature here was always lower than in the depths of the forest. For two or three days, we worked at rafting the wood. The shore was a labyrinth of woodpiles and lumber warehouses. We unloaded the woodpile into the water, placing hefty round beams on both sides. Along them we pushed tree trunks. Using poles as levers, we lowered the woodpile, layer by layer, until only the last one remained, an untouchable base. The guard sat nearby, watching our every movement. One would approach him at the legally permitted distance and say: "Please allow me to relieve myself, citizen guard!" to which he replied, "Go," and pointed in the direction behind the pile. The logs thunderously toppled down from on high, bobbing or settling down heavily. The bay was full of floating logs, which were then joined together into rafts.

After taking off our shoes and pulling up our pants, we entered the water and with long poles we split the logjams by the shore that hindered the movement of the logs. Every minute someone would fall from the slippery logs that were dancing in the water and would crawl to the shore to dry. It was gloomy and cold as the clouds sailed above Lake Onega. When it was raining, we would crowd under the woodpile, between the boards, and we were pleased that we had a brief respite. The day by the lake dragged on endlessly. Toward the end, we lay exhausted on the logs. At night, they forbade us to go outdoors in the alien, overcrowded camp. If someone barely stirred, they would yell out in the darkness: "Stop! Where are you going?"

Again, the barge, crowded with Poles, Jews, and Russian zeks, sailed across the endless expanse of the Onega. We crossed Lake Onega and arrived at Podporozhe. We saw a panorama of an important water transport center. Dozens of barges and steamships plowed through the water; factory chimneys emitted smoke on the shore next to rows of grain elevators and large wooden structures. The lively, populated spot differed sharply from the deserted northern places from which we had arrived.

On the shore, they lined us up in rows of four and marched us forward. The Westerners with their suitcases and bundles were in the middle of the large column. The others were in front and behind us. I carried my backpack on my back and my suitcase in my hand. I asked a companion, a strong, robust man from Lvov,[4] to carry another suitcase. While we lined up, we sensed that the *urki* were watching us on all sides, attracted by our baggage. They tried to draw the people with suitcases into their rows.

"Stand here!" the *urki* shouted to them, forcefully pushing and pointing: "Here there are three in the row, you'll be the fourth." Seeing the alien faces, however, the Westerner would back away and quickly leave, as mocking cries flew at his back:

"Abram,[5] what are you afraid of?"

"It's a bad deal," said our leader, a man from Lvov. "In the barrack, it will be rough. I know this riff-raff. If you want to hold on to your things, stay together in a group and don't let anyone near."

They put us in an enormous empty silo. Hundreds of people were lying on the floor. We passed through as if running the gauntlet. Our appearance aroused everyone. The *urki*, teeth bared, rose to meet us from all sides, mixing into our group, brushed against us, and before I knew what was happening, they pushed me away from my companions, and I felt a knife cutting the strap of my backpack. Someone ripped the suitcase from my hand. But I did not surrender either. Someone in front yelled piercingly: "Help!" My Lvov companion arrived in time to save the backpack, which had been taken half way off my shoulder. We oriented ourselves in a flash. A group of about thirty broke through to a corner of the silo. We put all our belongings together and covered them with our jackets. We tied all the suitcases with rope so that it

---

4. Now Lviv, Ukraine.

5. Abram—a derisive term for a Jew.

was impossible to move one separately. The strongest and sturdiest sat on top, covering the suitcases with their feet. Others sat on the floor with their backs to them on all four sides. And the rest, lying down, leaned against them. Thus, a wall of human bodies formed around our things. In ten minutes, everything was ready.

The recently constructed enormous silo, still smelling of fresh boards, was full of prisoners, noise, and buzzing. The rays of the setting sun entered through the large door. Suddenly they closed the door. We were alone in the semi-darkness, full of grumbling, an island among the Russian zeks. The Westerners were interspersed in islands of thirty to forty people among a hostile element. A year ago, they would have taken us like little children, but now we were prepared to resist.

The *urki* attacked from four sides in chains of five to six people. They moved in single file; they looked alike: pointy-nose emaciated apaches, stony-eyed, with bare necks and muscular chests. They formed one group of their own. Without saying a word, an unfamiliar fellow with a gangster-like mug and burning eyes, like a pike among small fry, went after the most vulnerable spot, where old man Nirenshtein was lying.

"Where are you going!" yelled old man Nirenshtein. "There is no free space here! You're going to sit on my feet?"

The fellow mumbled, "Don't get excited, Grandpa . . . Just a minute . . . I just . . ." And suddenly, with an unexpected, agile movement, like a swimmer diving into the water, he stretched out his body, and before we realized it, his hand groped among three rows of bodies to the jackets, threw them off, and in a split second, he checked what we had hidden. "Here are the suitcases!" He jumped up and rushed off. He was the reconnaissance man. The storm troopers followed him. Unhurriedly, a skinny, high-cheek-boned *urka*, his shirt flapping, said in a no-nonsense tone, "Move off," and, pushing aside the intimidated Nirenshtein with his shoulder, stepped in the middle. Several more followed him, and they made a wedge into our emplacement.

At this moment, the man from Lvov got up and forcefully pushed back the first attacker. In another second, a fight would have started, during which behind the back of the brawlers, they would have ransacked all the Westerners' belongings. But something other than a brawl occurred. All thirty Westerners began to yell at the top of their lungs.

The effect was impressive. Immediately, other groups of Westerners responded. There were about two hundred people in the silo. Our collective, thunderous roar resounded far. We shouted: "Fire!" The attackers, covering their ears, retreated. The doors burst open and armed guards ran in.

The guards, a seasoned bunch, immediately caught on. "They're robbing?" They did not even ask "who?" We were not interested in squealing; we just wanted to be left in peace. The guards waited until silence was established, and they left. This did not presage anything good because, at night, in the darkness, they would have attacked us again, and then we would have been unable to repel them. It was impossible to remain in the same place with the *urki*.

After fifteen minutes, we again began to yell "Fire!" This time we shouted so fiercely that the commander of the guards himself ran up. Half an hour later, they took us out of the silo. The doors opened, they gave the order: "Only Poles, come out!" We moved over to a large, empty barn nearby, where we had plenty of room; no one else was there, and the entire building was at our service. We spread out, undressed, and spent a quiet night.

For two days, we lived under lock and key. All day we stood in line "for water" or to "take a leak." It was impossible to continue the trip with two suitcases. I kept my backpack and small suitcase. I gave my excellent blanket to the man from Lvov and threw away the other suitcase with all kinds of camp "junk." I saw that others more practical than I picked up the worthless abandoned suitcase and extracted all the metal parts, locks, and clamps that a carpenter could use, which could be exchanged on occasion for a piece of bread.

On the third day, we left Podporozhe. Guards lined the route so that no one would escape from the ranks. Arriving prisoner transports went past us. It was a monotonous picture; everyone was the same. Suddenly, however, there was a stirring on the road. Everyone pointed in one direction. They pushed a new transport into the barn that we had just left, and it was, truly, a fantastic spectacle.

It was a group of Lithuanians straight from Kovno: in the last days before the German invasion, they drove away tens of thousands of political prisoners, all the Lithuanian elite—the bourgeoisie, intelligentsia, bureaucrats, and simply "suspicious people." It was immediately evident that these were "newcomers," people who had no notion where they were going or why they had been taken. They still had a respectable and frightened look—a procession from the other world. Patricians and senators were walking—rabbis with fur hats, lawyers and bankers, majestic pot bellies, Jews and non-Jews, in indescribable coats, furs, hats, and they dragged behind them ludicrous trunks, fancy leather suitcases, as if they were traveling to a resort on the Riviera.

Their appearance created a sensation: the guards and *urki* and crowds of zeks looked at them and spread the word: "The Lithuanians have arrived! Infinitely wealthy! Never have there been such people! Look at the one with the beard, a minister!" We looked at the well-groomed beards, the golden pince-nez, at the mountain of baggage, and we imagined what would happen to all this tomorrow, when they would force them to go by foot for hundreds of kilometers. What infantile naiveté led them to appear that way in Podporozhe! Later, we heard that only a few of these people survived the camp. The Dutch and Belgian Jews who were transported in passenger trains to the gas chambers of Auschwitz must have looked just like these Lithuanians. In Auschwitz, their agony ended on the very day of their arrival. These people waited years in camp. Whose death was easier; who knows? And we started on our way.

Our group numbered eight hundred people. Half of them were Westerners. People from Square 48 were mixed together with zeks from other camps and divisions. We walked five in a row, in two columns, about 100 to 200 meters apart. In front was the commander of the *etap*, a NKVD officer in a reddish-brown coat who was responsible for our sleeping arrangements and food. On the sides and behind were guards with rifles cocked, about twelve men. A wagon for the sick ones plodded in the rear. It soon fell behind, and we saw it from time to time at major stops. Sometimes they gave us a cart for our things, but we never knew until the last minute whether there would be one. When the order "get up!" resounded and there was no cart, panic ensued. Then some would toss away their things while others would lift their bundles and suitcases onto their shoulders, only to drop them in another hour or two, or they took turns carrying with others, giving up part of their things. Half of the items loaded onto the cart were lost. Upon arriving at a stop, they threw them on the road, and the cart, taken from a *kolkhoz* for a day, went back. When the zeks collected their possessions, some would not find their things, and others would find opened suitcases and untied bundles. After a week, people were less burdened. The baggage had melted, the road behind us was dotted with abandoned jackets and the prisoners' wooden chests.

We were going East. We were part of the Soviet landscape and of the ancient Russian tradition. We went in a large mass, as they had gone in the time of Nicholas I, a hundred years before us, and we asked ourselves, how is it possible that such an enslavement of hundreds of thousands of foreigners and millions of their own citizens did not evoke a protest or reaction abroad, as if we had fallen into the hands of savages in Central Africa or slave traders in the seventeenth century.

We covered 30 to 40 kilometers a day, through forests and plains, towns and villages, past a sparsely inhabited area where there were no railroads and where, probably, there had been no war since the time of Vaska Buslaev.[6] This place never witnessed foreign troops or foreign visitors. We passed through the Karelo-Finnish villages, where tall, unwieldy huts stood on the hills.

It was the first weeks of the war, and in passing, we occasionally noted posters addressed to the population. The villages appeared abandoned. Young children, women, and the elderly pottered around the huts, and we very rarely saw a man. The barefoot, ragged *kolkhoznik* looked as if he had escaped from our ranks. The bleak Karelian *kolkhozes* were the image of desolation and devastation, as after a fire or pogrom. There were many ruined, uninhabited houses where the windows and doors were boarded up. There were no fences between the huts. We would stop at the entrance or exit of the village, and immediately, urchins would begin to prowl around us. The guards would not let anyone near us, but sometimes we received permission to buy food. The peasants, however, would not take money for food products. They offered us eggs and milk—the only things they had—in exchange for bread! The peasants went out on the road to beg for bread from prisoners! They knew that we received 500 grams of bread daily, an *etap* ration. For this bread, they offered us eggs and milk. One did not need to ask what their life was like. It was sufficient to pass through dozens of villages to gain a picture of dark and bitter poverty such as Russia had probably not seen since the Middle Ages. We did not ask ourselves what had happened to their bread, the fruit of difficult and coerced labor. Their bread was distributed to us every morning—and in the hands of the state this bread turned into a means of upholding the political and military apparatus of the dictatorship.

For hundreds of kilometers—a monotonous spectacle of human need, misery, and suffering. We soon left Karelia, and the funny-looking small houses with an added story were replaced by Russian huts with attempts at decorations: sometimes carved shutters, sometimes a carved cornice. We were in the Arkhangelsk region. Someone once had free time for these decorations, which remained as a reminder of earlier days. They were a ludicrous and pitiful contrast to the sagging walls and sunken roofs.

We passed through the town of Pudozh, little provincial alleys, one-story wooden houses, unpaved streets, and no stores. A sign "warehouse of the industrial cooperative" . . . and a familiar picture: a locked door and a patient line of peasant women and young children with bottles for kerosene. A young woman passed by, probably a teacher and a Party member: a nice Slavic face, freshly scrubbed rosy cheeks. A bright-colored blouse, city shoes, and braids

6. Russian thirteenth-century folk hero from Novgorod.

encircling her head. She glanced at the crowd that was raising dust, at the
guards, and for a second our eyes met. Walking in the line is a strange bespecta-
cled man with the clearly non-Russian face of an intelligent. "A prisoner." She
turned away, obstinately clenching her lips as if a tooth was hurting: there are
too many at once; let them pass already. Suddenly I recalled: "the Fourteenth
Pudozh division of the BBK." In this little town is a division of the BBK
camps—and the fourteenth no less!

We continued. It was July, the best time of the northern summer. They
woke us up before dawn in order to utilize the cool early hours for the march.
It was best to walk until 10:00 a.m. When it started to heat up, we were
drenched in sweat and were exhausted from the weight of our luggage. We
walked until sunset, about 6:00 p.m. when we camped out at the edge of a
forest or in a meadow under the open sky. Sometimes they drove us into old
sheds, where the roof leaked when it rained. One night I slept in the attic
of a half-destroyed house, amidst dust and chicken droppings. Mosquitoes
swarmed all over us in a thick cloud. At night I got up, unable to get comfortable, wandered around the attic among the sleeping bodies like a specter
and went down the rickety steps—everywhere dozens of bodies were lying,
clothed, and only the shoes stood near everyone's head. The mosquitoes drove
us crazy. The blood streamed down our faces, and our hands were smeared
with blood. We walked through the Arkhangelsk forests along shady paths,
and the lilies of the valley blossomed under our feet; I never saw so many
of them.

We rarely encountered people. Occasionally a wagon would pass by; the
peasant would look at us sullenly from under his cap. Her legs tucked under,
a pale peasant girl with a kerchief sat in the straw, or some important barrel
belonging to the state was in the wagon. Sometimes a truck would overtake
us, full of household possessions, beds, tables, with women and children piled
on. This was the evacuation of the civilian population from the frontal zone.
The prisoners yielded the right of way, they descended to the side until the
truck rushed past, rattling over the pits in the road. Sometime a *kolkhoz* herd
would be driven by. The thin cows jingled with bells as in the Tyrol. During
the entire march, the melodic jingling of the bells accompanied us. The
cowbells were all identical—large and clumsy, a standard product, probably
from one factory for the entire Soviet Union—and the bells rang the same
everywhere, here and in the Altai region, in the ears of the prisoners, walking
for long days from camp to camp.

We walked for twelve hours a day, from six to six, and sometimes, we began
our march even earlier. It was savagely cold at night. I no longer had a blanket.

I lay on the damp, soggy ground; the dampness penetrated the body, made the feet ache. I would shiver from the cold and pull my jacket alternately over my chest and face to protect myself from the mosquitoes or onto my freezing feet. We slept little and poorly, suffering, and at dawn, when the pale stars still hung over the field full of prone bodies, someone sat up and the guard immediately shouted from the edge of the field, "Lie down this minute!"

"Let me relieve myself, kind guard!"

"Stay where you are!" Finally, at the signal, the entire mass rose. There was not much time. If there was water nearby, a stream or pool of water, we washed with cupped hands. Then long rows formed for bread. They distributed half a kilo of bread, a ladle of gruel. The zeks would eat the bread instantly, but I would keep half of it for midday. The others did not eat anything until the evening.

The order comes: "Get in line!" The first rows are already on their way. They wade through the deep, dark mud, marching up and down, through hills and valleys, raising clouds of dust, rhythmically and quietly swaying, silently, with downcast eyes. As soon as the column becomes noisy: "Stop talking!" I walked in my jacket and old padded pants, tugging at the straps of my backpack, which weighed down on my tail bone, and now and then, stretching, I would raise the burden to my shoulders. I carried my small suitcase, changing hands every kilometer. Along the route, road markers indicated the kilometers we had passed. Immediately, dirt and pebbles penetrated the torn shoes with an almost detached sole. It became painful to walk and, on the march, we had to clean out the footgear. Someone was already limping, and the adolescents and sick people would lag behind. The thin body was on the alert, getting set: these feet, these shoulders, heart, and lungs; they are your only allies. They won't betray you, they will hold up, they will carry you today, as they did yesterday! You can do what the others can! When 5 kilometers had been covered, the suitcase became leaden. The backpack was forgotten as if it didn't exist. All attention focused on the suitcase. The hand does not manage to rest. I had to change hands more frequently, inserting my hand under the rope that encircled the suitcase.

We rested every 8 to 10 kilometers, depending on the presence of water. They would halt us when we reached a river or stream. When there was no water, we went extra kilometers. The time would come when we had no more strength. The shoulders smarted, feet tripped, the body was bathed in sticky sweat, and the hands convulsed in a painful shudder. Only the movement of the column, through inertia, advanced the clump of human sludge. Soon, another ten minutes, another quarter of an hour.... And now in the distance, we can see: a stream under a hill, bushes, willows. The first column is already lying down, like a gray caterpillar, at the edge of the road. The command: "Lie down, rest!"

Hundreds of people toppled onto the ground, still strapped into the backpacks in order not to waste time later putting them back on. When the pack stops dragging one's shoulders down, it turns into a support. The body gratefully leans on it. A moment of such blessed complete physical relief ensues as if we had separated from our flesh and entered heaven while alive. The eyes close and the hands drop. The half hour rest flows like a smooth, slow cool stream. The pots clang around us. We draw up a lot of water, drinking in turn, passing it from hand to hand. Sometimes it seems as if the guards forgot about time. They sit away from the prisoners. They march as we do and tire as we do, but they are not as hungry. . . .

"Get up!" Immediately there is movement throughout the mown human field. During these few minutes, many managed to fall asleep, but they slept lightly—just touch a shoulder and they hastily get up.

Now you can't even think about weariness; a two or three-hour march lies ahead. The sun scorches. In order to make walking easier, we would think about something else. We thought about food. The feeling of hunger that stunned us along with the July heat and dust from the road was not personal but collective, an all-zek feeling. We marched in a cloud of hunger. Everything in us was burning, agitated, taut like a string. I secretly rejoiced: in my pack I had 200 grams of bread that I had not eaten in the morning. . . .

In two hours, I shall eat. Who wrote about hunger? Hamsun. "Ilayali."[7] This is so ridiculous, so literary. . . . What kind of hunger can there be in a city where everyone is satiated, where there is such varied food, and the shop windows are full of every good thing? This is a pose, hunger from pride. Every garbage heap contains so much that is edible, just bend down. . . . The city is full of the scent of bread, which indifferent nostrils do not even perceive. The city is full of immeasurable, squandered, unnoticed riches; there at the markets, people step on food, crush it, dogs and birds do not manage to gather the crumbs.

Years before: A pole in a balustrade . . . I walked like a drunk. At the seaside promenade in Tel Aviv, on a pole of the balustrade, a child on his way to school had left a piece of a white roll, an uneaten piece with cherry jam. On my way to swim in the sea early in the morning, I saw this piece of a roll.

7. The hero in Knut Hamsun's 1890 novel, an impoverished, hungry writer, wanders around Norway's capital Christiania, imagining a Persian princess who has everything.

White with cherry—a reddish spot and nothing more. It never occurred to me that it could be eaten. In the evening, I was at the same place. A long, full, happy summer day passed in that city where so many people are happy to the extent that they do not sense their fortune. Thousands of people passed by that pole, and the morning piece of a white roll with cherry jam was still there—untouched! The birds did not peck at it, and there were no starving people in that city. . . . "Ilayali." . . . The store windows are full of light; the trams clang. . . . Here there is hunger in the wilderness, hunger on the road, prisoners' hunger. There is nothing and there won't be anything. Just seeing food is half of satiety. Is it really hunger—not to have money to buy food? Is it really hunger to be embarrassed to ask for it? "Ilayali."

And suddenly, in place of Ilayali, I had a vision that made me stumble and brought a lump to my throat: a piece of finely ground bread. Bread so fresh that a knife can't cut it; on one side it is all white flour, and the flour crumbles in the fingers; the polished, smooth golden crust had cracked. You had to spread honey on this fragrant enormous piece of bread. But I did not succeed. My hands trembled from greed. The honey was at hand on the table. But I didn't get to pick it up. . . .

A mouthful of bread. I walked with my backpack, opening my parched mouth like a fish. . . .

On the horizon arose a small church with a green cupola. From afar it looked respectable and peaceful, but an hour later, when we finally wandered past along the village street, we saw a ruin without a cross, doors torn off the hinge, broken windows.

No, I would not be defeated! When the dried lips became black and the leaden burden began to fall from my hands, I called for help. And a white figure, whom only I saw, entered into this crowd of convicts. I moved to the side, leaving room, and lifted my head. We walked together, side by side, as we had been doing all our life. How strong I was! This was not delirium; it was the truth! Thousands of kilometers separated us, but I erased them that minute. I was conversing with someone, turning my head and smiling. I tried not to show how hard it was for me so as not to frighten the bright shadow walking alongside.

"You see what's going on!" I said. "But it's nothing. Don't worry. I'll make it."

And I cheered up enough to bend down and lift up a dark blue, woolen pea jacket from the ground. It was Kunin's good jacket, that same Kunin who in the office of Square 48 used to assign ration levels. Now he was walking in front of me, and he had just thrown this jacket onto the dusty road. I lifted it and tossed it over my arm. People in the row looked at me in astonishment.

I'll carry it! And I'll have something to cover myself with at night. . . . The next day, however, I gave my suitcase to Met to carry; he walked in the first rows, happy, grinning, and healthier than ever. For one day of carrying, I gave him a pair of shoes, which I still had. I thus went lighter handed, with one backpack and the blue pea jacket on my arm. Without the suitcase, the weight on my back seemed heavier.

On the fifth or sixth day of our march, we arrived at the shore of a large lake. Here we spent a blissful day. The lake slumbered in all its expanse, the opposite shore was barely visible in the haze, thousands of people lay on the sandy shore. Here several transports of prisoners met. The traces of yesterday's bonfires indicated that we were not the first ones at the place where we settled down. In the morning, we bathed in the lake, and amidst the splashing and horseplay, we felt as if we were at the beach. We then dried ourselves in the sun and slept. When I woke up, I realized that while I was sleeping, someone lifted my glasses off my nose. This immediately changed my situation very drastically. I did not immediately understand how I could continue. I do not see anything without glasses. I went to the head of the *etap* to ask him to put me on the wagon with the sick people. There was no room there, however, and when the columns moved, I discovered that it was possible to walk without seeing. People and objects merged into a foggy cloud, the earth under my feet swirled, but I did not have to suffer for long. On the second day, I bought back my eyeglasses from the thief for a towel and a pair of socks. At the moment that I put them on, I was happy and completely reconciled with life.

In the evening of the seventh day, we beheld Kargopol, the ancient city of the Arkhangelsk north, in all the beauty of its cupolas and bell towers, its five-domed cathedral, and white-walled monasteries. The city shone and gleamed in the rays of the setting sun, like a vision of the fabled past. We spent the night near the town. Here, as by the lakeshore, thousands of prisoners lay on the adjacent fields, separated by armed guards. We were able to move around only on our section of the field. Noise hovered above the camp as at a gypsy bazaar. I could not take my eyes off the panorama of the city. While I was gazing, the inevitable happened: they stole my suitcase. I found it open and empty, about fifty meters away. The underwear, shirts, and other riches from Pinsk had disappeared. Now I did not need to fear a long journey. It did not take long to find the thieves. A band of *urki* nearby were dividing up my things. I entered into negotiations with them, as a result of which one of them magnanimously threw me a photograph in a frame, the only possession of mine that they did not need. I still tried to ask for one spare shirt. A pockmarked, goggle-eyed fellow on whom my sweater was stretched, rose threateningly "Go away, go," he warned, "or else I'll smack you on the head." I nevertheless went to complain to the guard, which was completely stupid. The guard was walking back and forth on the edge of the field and did not even let me get near him. On hearing about the matter, he waved his hand dismissively, "It's not my business." The guard was responsible to the authorities for the number of zeks but not for their property. The surprising thing was not that they stole my suitcase, but that I had managed to drag it all the way to Kargopol.

By the walls of the legendary city of Kargopol, they removed from our ranks all those who were ill or unable to continue working, and here I parted with one of the Kunin brothers with whom I had served time together from the first day in Pinsk prison. They hospitalized the older Kunin in the Kargopol camp hospital, where he ended his life. The younger one, from whom I inherited the blue pea jacket, died upon release from a camp somewhere in Central Asia. The total of six million Jewish victims of the war thus includes victims of German and Soviet camps.

We did not know then that Kargopol was the center of Kargopolag (the Kargopol region camp system) and owed its livelihood, to a considerable degree, to the army of slaves concentrated in enterprises and camp sectors of the area. However, in connection with the war, the administration of Kargopolag moved to Ertsevo, along the northern railroad line, and we had to continue on our way to Ertsevo.

On the morning of the following day, they led us through the streets of Kargopol. Up close, the town turned out to be, like Pudozh, a devastated and poor backwater, with dilapidated little wooden houses, a Lenin street, and a squalid little municipal garden where barefoot children were playing skittles. We raised dust along Lenin Street, under the bored glances of the Kargopol citizens, with whom I would not want to exchange places even while I was in the prisoners' ranks, and we arrived at the dock.

At dusk, after hours of standing in line, we were loaded onto a steamship and sailed down the river. We lay down on the sloping deck, stretched out, and rested. It was good to lie on one's back at night, with hands under the head, and to look at the dark, starless sky. It was good in the daytime in the sun, watching from the deck as the low shores and green dewy meadows floated by. We felt like tourists; it was our genuine "journey into the unknown." We had been on the march for ten days.

Around two o'clock on the following day, the steamship suddenly docked at a low, sandy bank near an open field, and again, to our great disappointment, we proceeded on foot. Again, we encountered an eroded road with deep ruts. And again, we passed by road markers and sparse villages with boarded up homes of mobilized soldiers and exiles. On the next to last day, we were supposed to cover 40 kilometers, but we lost our way and went 7 kilometers in the wrong direction and then the same 7 kilometers back. Our record journey was thus 54 kilometers in one day.

It was morning, a dewy July morning with the chirping and fluttering of birds and the pecking of a woodpecker in the forest thicket, when we reached the guardhouse in the forest, where some business-like free workers in caps were waiting for us. The guards rejoiced when they saw them, and we understood that our journey was over. They directed us into the depth of the forest, and we went, stumbling along the wooden planks. The cuckoo bird promised me 120 years of life so I stopped counting. It smelled of resin, and one sensed a work place nearby. We were staggering from exhaustion but kept our spirits up, as we understood that this was our final effort. We had covered 500 kilometers on our journey. The forest ended and we came out on a broad double railroad track.

It was not a narrow-gauge line as above Lake Onega, but a broad, well-built line, straight as an arrow. We walked in disorderly fashion along the railroad ties, and suddenly to the right a large camp was revealed. There were barracks behind a barbed wire fence, guard towers at the corners, a broad road led to the guardhouse, and on both sides of it were many buildings "outside of the [camp] zone." We did not reach the guardhouse. At the end of the day, they left us for the night in an open field outside the zone. This was Ertsevo, along the northern railroad line, the center of the Kargopol camps.

In honor of ending the *etap*, I took a cherished treasure out from the bottom of my sack—the remains of my mother's packages—Soviet "noodles," a product of the Odessa canning factory. I boiled water in a mug on the coals of the bonfire, crushed the compressed slab with a stone and poured it into the boiling water. In fifteen minutes, the mush was ready. For the last time for many years, I ate non-camp food; sated, I fell asleep by the dying embers.

In the morning, they loaded us on flatbeds, and in 40 minutes, we arrived at our destination. A column of about three hundred men were disembarked from the flatbed at the crossing point, beyond which stretched a broad street. We walked, staring at the little buildings on both sides.

"Is there long to go, citizen commander?"

"Twenty-six kilometers," answered the officer in charge of the trip, giving us a threatening look.

We sighed, pulled at the straps of our bags and prepared to walk until the evening. We had hardly gone one hundred meters, however, when a high fence arose on the left, the familiar gates with the inscription "Long live the wise Stalinist policy!" and a booming command resounded: "Stop!"

We had arrived.

22

Amnesty

THE MEDICAL SETTLEMENT Kruglitsa extended over about 30,000 square meters. Each square meter inside the fence was utilized. In contrast to Square 48, there was no rotting swamp or uncollected stumps lying around. Wooden pathways were laid alongside the barracks. By the kitchen windows where they handed out food, there was an awning so those waiting would not get wet. When we saw a flowerbed and bench in front of the infirmary, we felt as if we were in a sanitarium. To complete the effect, the punishment cell was beyond the fence and was not an eyesore for the zeks.

The medical town Kruglitsa was, indeed, a kind of sanitarium, where the medical center of Ertsevo camps was situated. It contained two pulmonary barracks, a surgical one, several ordinary infirmaries, a pharmacy, dentist's office, and x-ray room. About 300 to 350 patients and the same number of workers and personnel were located here. Not only the hospital barracks but also the workers' barracks were equipped with electricity and radios.[1] A loudspeaker was placed outdoors near the guardhouse, where the roll call took place. To the left of the guardhouse was an open square with benches and a stage in the shape of a shell such as one for an orchestra in a municipal garden. In the summer, movies were screened there and performances staged.

On the other side of the camp fence was a row of small houses—the village of Kruglitsa. About three hundred free workers lived there. They were all feeding off the camp, either in the administration, in the medical sector, or as guards. To the right of the guardhouse, in the direction of the crossing were located the camp's "central technical repair workshops" [acronym TsTRM in Russian, or so-called "tseterem"]. Here there were lathes, and they repaired

---

1. The radio was, in effect, a loudspeaker, which broadcast programs of the state radio.

tractors and agricultural machinery. A brigade of forty prisoner metal workers worked there; there was also an engineering design office and an electric power station. Farther on, near the railroad track was a petroleum depot, tall cylinders protruded, reservoirs colored in black and red. To the left of the guardhouse, along the village street was a fenced cattle yard, which also belonged to the camp: a stable, a pigsty, and about thirty cows.

Walking along the village street, which was impassable mud for ten months of the year, in five minutes you reached the *selkhoz* [agricultural farm]. Beyond the fence was an extensive vegetable garden and hothouses where they raised tomatoes and tobacco. In the war years, when the Ukrainian *makhorka* (tobacco for rolling) was unavailable, this planted tobacco was the only thing available in the entire region. The tomatoes here did not ripen; the camp kitchen pickled them when green. Up to sixty hectares were planted with onion, carrot, cabbage, and turnip (meant for cattle but fed to prisoners), but mainly with potatoes. In the far corner of the *selkhoz* was a shack where the prisoner poultry maid Anisya tended white chickens. The chickens laid eggs, but, of course, not for the prisoners. In Kruglitsa, the zeks took care of cows and pigs, but they did not own them. A very insignificant percentage of all the agricultural products was allotted to the camp's needs. The state took the rest.

I spent three years of my life in this marvelous camp, where there was no wood felling or hard labor. It was great luck; few Westerners managed to remain in the medical settlement.

They brought us here not to stay but for a medical examination and distribution to work camps. The medical commission selected those who needed rehabilitation and assigned them to a team of weak workers, and the others were sent away from Kruglitsa in two days.

On the second day, I went to the medical sector, located in a small building to the left of the guardhouse. Three steps, a hallway and a waiting room, from which four doors led to four tiny rooms: a dental office, an administrative office, and two outpatient reception rooms. Everything was sparse but clean. The waiting room had a barrel with drinking water covered with a board, a bench for those waiting, and a radio loudspeaker.

I complained of extreme weakness and strong pains when breathing. The doctor's movements were precipitous, his eyes flashed truculently, his accent was clearly Polish. He was a young Warsaw surgeon, Doctor Spicnagel. Without hesitating, he dispatched me to the tuberculosis infirmary. The director of the medical sector sat alongside, looking suspiciously at both of us, but kept quiet. I went out, overwhelmed at my success. Was I really suffering from the start of tuberculosis? That would enable me to remain in the medical town for a long time, perhaps for months. . . . My imagination did not extend beyond months. Conditions in the infirmary exceeded all my expectations. I was lying in a long white ward on a clean cot. I had a night table near the bed, slippers, and a robe. In fact, the felt slippers and robe were common property and wandered from patient to patient but even asking "Where are the slippers?" was pleasant. They brought me a mug, spoon, and towel. They fed us three times a day. I was astonished when at midday they brought me some fried potato and a real meat cutlet. I forgot about my hunger and was deeply moved by the humane aspect of this attitude toward the sick. In the forest we did not have a midday meal, and I had not seen fried potatoes for a year. . . . Oh, what happiness to have a pulmonary disease! This was worth walking the hundreds of kilometers of the *etap*.

My neighbor was called Ivan Nikolaevich. He was an office worker who had grown thin like a splinter of wood, gloomy and waspish. He looked me over carefully, recognized a Jew and immediately scowled. This did not surprise me. I was so excited by the magnificence of the infirmary that I was ready to embrace all Soviet antisemites.

The following morning, Ivan Nikolaevich looked at my bed for a long time. The blanket was spread unevenly. "Jewish nature," Ivan Nikolaevich pronounced quietly but distinctly. From the first glance, immediately and irreconcilably, he hated me, my looks, words, movements, and even the book and eyeglasses that were lying on the night table. Ivan Nikolaevich was a veteran camp inmate; he had reached the eighth year of his term and shortly was preparing to go free. Tuberculosis and freedom raced in competition for his life. A half year later, when I asked, "But where is Ivan Nikolaevich? I don't see him around . . .," I was told, "Don't you know? He was released." And I pictured Ivan Nikolaevich at liberty, charged up with antisemitism, hate, and bitterness deeply ensconced in his heart, with his consumptive cough and his hump of eight camp years—one of the million mass of Soviet Ivan Nikolaevichs.

On the second day, to my horror, the pain in my chest had passed. I breathed in all different ways and it didn't hurt! It would be good in the hospital were it not for the doctors! The head of the tubercular ward was Valentina Vasilievna, a plump, pleasant individual with large eyes and cherry lips. She was the one I had to fear: chief doctor and also a free worker! Valentina Vasilievna sent me for an x-ray, and my imposture was revealed. In three days, I was expelled from paradise. Ivan Nikolaevich rejoiced and snickered. All I had was a simple muscle pull in my chest.

Spicnagel smirked when he saw me again in a prisoner's jacket.

"I knew that you did not have anything dangerous, but in the meantime your *etap* was sent away from Kruglitsa, and you stayed. Now I shall prescribe two weeks of light work for you."

The light-work team meant that we worked every other day, did not work much, and ate even less. On my free days, I walked around the camp, dropped in at the office and offered my services to the work assigner: wasn't there a need to calculate, write up things? The Kruglitsa barracks were large; each one held one hundred or more zeks. When an *etap* such as ours made a stop-over, the barracks would be stuffed; people would sleep on the floor and on benches. Then afterwards, it was again spacious. At the entrance to each barrack was a reserved area. There, behind a board partition, lodged the notables of the given barrack: the assistant work supervisor, the commandant, and so forth. Two rows of double-decker bed boards stretched on the sides of the barrack; they were dark from dirt and full of bedbugs; in the middle was a plain table and two benches. Behind the partition, in contrast, the bed boards had clean bedding (the ordinary zeks did not have any bedding), clean kitchenware stood to the side of the stove, and people from the barrack were forbidden to step in there without a good reason.

In one such little room, I wrote reports for an assistant work supervisor, and I hoped to keep this job, but things turned out differently.

At the end of July, an issue of *Pravda Severa* [Pravda of the north] was posted on the bulletin board of the KVCh with news about the concluding of a Polish-Soviet pact: an amnesty for imprisoned Poles! The first consequence of the war, a new course! We experienced days of uplifted spirits and happiness, going around in a blessed fog, excited and proud. Those who had prophesied death for the Poles in an alien land were wrong! We had been right, when a year ago, we laughed on receiving three- or five-year sentences and refused to take them seriously. In Moscow they had been too hasty to wipe Poland off the geographical map.

Having seized Poland, Hitler turned it into the "General Government,"[2] but he did not call it Germany. The Soviet regime went further. On Soviet maps of that time, there was no Poland, but there was, to the West of the rivers Bug and San, "The region of German state interests." In the camp, only one of the four words remained. When they interrogated Polish zeks, they would write for place of birth "Warsaw," with Germany in parentheses. July 1941 was the month of the Red Army's retreat and the month of a reversal of this wise

2. "Generalgouvernement für die besetzten Polnischen Gebiete" [German for the General government for the conquered Polish territory].

Stalinist policy. Yesterday's allies became enemies; the enemies became allies. The despair of those Poles in the camp who pusillanimously had passed themselves off as Belarusians or even Germans was indescribable, but we Polish citizens rejoiced and prepared to go free.

We thought that the "amnesty" would take just a few days: once said, it's a done deal. If people are amnestied, they have to be released. The word "amnesty" meant that one had to unscrew the meat grinder and take out the human meat that was bound for grinding. The word "amnesty" politely designated an act of returning captured human booty. It restored our standing and our human dignity. A terrible impatience came over Poles and Polish Jews.

Whereas yesterday the camp authorities had abused us like working cattle, now we were guests in the camp. Soviet zeks regarded us with envy and bitterness. "The Poles have raised their heads," the zeks said, sneering wryly. We who had raised our heads were embarrassed to look at those without hope.

From the moment that I read the report of the amnesty, I was in a state of feverish expectation. It simply did not occur to me that I could be excluded from the amnesty. I do not know whether there was any other Westerner who awaited freedom with such passionate impatience as I did. I already pictured myself in the uniform of the Polish army, imagined detachments of Polish Jews fighting in the front line, and I thanked the fate that finally gave me the opportunity to participate in the war against Hitler. Never before had I felt the absurdity and humiliation of my forced passivity so acutely.

Week after week passed, and we remained in the camp. Finally, at the end of August, the first small group of Poles was released. I was bitterly disappointed that I did not land in that group. Among those released was Koren, a Jewish Polish officer from a Belostok industrial family, who had completed an officers' course in Vilna.[3] He had been a commandant of one of the camps in the neighborhood, and he had been "overzealous" in that position, arousing the hatred of Polish zeks. They threatened him, "Just you wait, sometime in Poland, we shall settle accounts with you." The train with Poles had barely left Ertsevo, when they took revenge on Koren. They beat him to death and threw the corpse out of the train.

On September 1, they brought all the Poles in Kruglitsa beyond the guardhouse. Instead of liberation, something unexpected happened: they transferred all of us to the penal camp Osinovka, some 15 kilometers from Kruglitsa.

---

3. Now Vilnius, capital of Lithuania.

On the first day in Osinovka, I worked as a water carrier. I remember very well the overcast, cloudy day of northern autumn. In the morning they gave me two heavy wooden buckets. I drew the water from the well in a bucket tied to a rope and dragged it 200 meters to the boiler room. I carried a total of thirty-five pairs of buckets back and forth. I thus covered seven kilometers with full buckets and seven with empty ones. Along the way, I climbed up a wooden path, crossed a ditch beyond which was total mud, where I clambered on wooden boards laid over the mud, jumping from board to board; in some places I would stop to figure out how to get through. During the day, my wadded pants—the very ones with which I had left Square 48—and my jacket were thoroughly drenched.

Moving slowly so as not to splash the water, stopping once or twice on the way, I recalled the old Pinsk water carrier named Herschl. Every morning for several years, this Jew would bring two buckets of water to my mother's kitchen. Herschl, disheveled, with a stubbly, grayish chin, red eyes, red nose, thin as a scarecrow, seemed to me the personification of Jewish poverty. I looked at him with a feeling of guilt and fastidious pity, not foreseeing that a time would come when I would envy him. Now Herschl appeared to me in a new light. I was now doing his work. My rags were much worse than his clothing. I wore worn out shoes that let in water. Dirty, damp rags served as leg wrappings. The camp buckets were much heavier than my mother's. Herschl received ten groszy[4] for a couple of buckets. At the time, those groszy seemed like alms to a beggar. Now, slowly swinging my buckets, I amused myself by calculating how much I would have earned if they paid me at the rate of the Pinsk water carrier.

Ten pairs of buckets. And I already earned a zloty. What could I buy for that money? First, I would buy a kilo of bread. In Pinsk, a kilo of bread cost 15 groszy. Then I would buy ten eggs. That would cost 50 groszy. With the remaining 35 groszy, I would buy 200 grams of lard. What a gigantic omelet I would make from all this!

Thinking about the omelet, I stepped up my pace. The buckets banged my knees and the water spilled over, splashing my feet. But one zloty is not enough. One has to carry another ten pairs of water buckets! With the second zloty I would buy half a kilo of sugar and ten packets of tea. Then also a liter of milk for 15 groszy. And I would have enough left for a kilo of barley!

---

4. The Polish zloty is divided into 100 groszy.

I calculated and calculated, and from thirty-five pairs of water buckets, I still had lots of money left. Now I understood that Herschl could feed not only himself but also a wife and child. This money was enough for meat and fish for the Sabbath. That Herschl was a rich man in comparison to me! Moreover, he had that supreme, divine right to toss those two buckets to hell any time that he wanted to! I did not have that right, and all they gave me in camp for fulfilling one hundred percent of the norm was 700 grams of bread (in the best case), which in terms of Polish money in 1939 equaled 30 groszy. Six buckets! And I carried thirty-five!

At five o'clock, the commandant allowed me to finish working. I brought the buckets to the boiler room and headed to the barrack to rest. Another two hours remained before the arrival of the brigades. Wonderful work! I willingly would have remained working as a water carrier, but I did not have sufficient pull for that. . . . Anyhow, these were my last days in camp! It was not worth it to make a special effort. . . .

The following day, I was assigned to a Russian haying brigade. Again, good luck! After intense summer work, this brigade was "marking time" in September, that is, with the administration's knowledge, it pretended that it was working, gathered uncollected hay in the meadows and finished mowing parts they had missed. For its past merits, the brigade was allotted a ration of 125 percent of the work norm, the shock troop ration. For the additional food, they deducted from one's "wage," so that my "reward" for a "shock troop" September was 3 rubles and 25 kopecks. At dawn we went out, hiding in the foggy, muddy lowlands. No one paid attention to us. Perhaps, the calamity at the front was reflected in a lack of supervision and in demoralization of the camp authorities? Having sluggishly wandered through the damp reddish-brown glades and fields, a cluster of people climbed a mound, started a bonfire and dozed until around eleven o' clock. A guard sat above us on the hill, like a guard dog, and also dozed. Then we would suddenly remember the time and someone would say, taking hold of the rake, "Shouldn't we get going, guys?" and for an hour or two, we would rake and again sit down. Before leaving, we would again walk with the rakes for an hour or two. We barely fulfilled a quarter of the norm, but in the evening, the brigade leader would write up a fantastic "work report" for which we were allotted supper from the special window, the "shock troop" one, with a piece of dolphin or dried fish.

Time passed and we remained, as if there were no amnesty. The woods near Osinovka were full of rowanberries. The red clusters of rowanberries irritated us because they were inedible. Beggars can't be choosers. In the end, we began to eat the rowanberry. It drizzled all the time in the first half of September. In the light rain we would gather damp, shiny clusters of rowanberries, break off the rustling flaming branches, bring armfuls to the fire, and start to roast the berries. The crimson bunch blackened, the burning berries burst open, and a tart, viscous juice flowed out. We thus consumed rowanberries in enormous quantities, filling our empty stomachs and deceiving our hunger. By then we already were feeling the absence of packages, which we had stopped receiving from the start of the war. We also felt the effects of the *etap* and the preceding camp year along with a sharp reduction in camp food. This was just the first reduction; a series of others followed. Even at the early stage, however, the "shock troop" ration was insufficient for us, and we fell asleep hungry.

The first half of September was colored by the bright rowanberry; the second half passed under the sign of the potato. I worked in the Polish brigade, where an atmosphere of irritation, strife, quarrels, and daily conflicts reigned. A hornets' nest! These people were at their wits' end: either let us go free or we'll go crazy. The brigade leader, Wiktor Brandes, a Warsaw journalist and ardent Polish patriot, had difficulty keeping his people in order. His intelligence and energy made him the leader of the Poles in Osinovka.

With hoes, we dug up potatoes in deep dark furrows. Others carried them in boxes to the brigade leader. We were not permitted to light a fire and cook the potatoes. Brandes negotiated with the guard, and state potatoes were illegally cooked in the ashes of his bonfire. The brigade leader, furtively looking around, would throw a baked potato to each of his men, right into the open furrows. Having eaten our potato, we waited a half hour or an hour until Brandes, the pockets of his Polish jacket bulging, would run again across the field, distributing "one large or two little" ones.

Cabbage was growing in the neighboring field. The bold ones stole large white cabbage heads and immediately divided them up, as the head had to be eaten in a flash. I then discovered that the rabbit is not stupid: it does not even matter whether the fleshy white leaves are spotted with dirt and were lying in the mud. The moment when the white spot of a cabbage head gleams in a crowd of crouching zeks and someone whispers: "Whoever has a knife, quickly get to it. . . ." that is a moment of triumph. Just then, the guards and people with maliciously distorted faces run up from beyond the fence: they noticed us. . . . Shouts, cursing, threats. . . . And finally, they get us up and lead us to work farther away from the dangerous site. . . .

Those who participated in the theft of state potatoes and cabbage had never in their past life stolen someone else's property: they were lawyers, teachers, judges. Here theft was an act of self-defense against the state's blatant violence against us and its revival of slavery. Without philosophizing, we knew that morality is one and indivisible, and the laws of communal living do not obligate the victim more than they obligate the executioner.

As September wore on, anxiety increased among the Poles in Osinovka. The second month after the declaration of the amnesty was coming to an end, and we still remained imprisoned. As before, we were cut off from the outside world. We feared that we would be forgotten or deliberately detained in camp. The local administration was unable to answer our inquiries; it also knew nothing. We began to solicit a meeting with representatives of the camp administration in Ertsevo. No one, however, was in a hurry to talk with us. We then decided to organize a protest demonstration. This was not easy. No collective unauthorized acts are permitted in camp. Saying "we" means inciting a revolt. When Wiktor Brandes and other "Westerners" turned to the administration, they did so in their own name as for their own matter; saying "we" meant taking responsibility for a counterrevolutionary act because in the Soviet Union only the party and its organs of power have the right to organize the masses and to speak in their name. Russian zeks had often told us about incidents of hunger strikes and riots and outrage of despairing masses, suppressed by bloodshed or by an extra bread handout, but those outbursts never had the nature of an organized political action. Our undertaking was a dangerous innovation, a protest against injustice, against our illegal detention in camp.

On the evening of September 28, in great secrecy several people went through the barracks and collected the Westerners' food tickets that had been distributed in the evening for the following day. All handed in their tickets. At dawn on the 29th, as soon as reveille sounded, 120 people gathered in one barrack. This was the entire Polish population of Osinovka 1. Everyone was in an uplifted and solemn mood. As if reciting a prayer before battle, the Poles and Jews stood up and sang an ancient choral song: "Kiedy ranne wstaja zorze" [Polish: When the sun rises early]. Then they gave the camp boss a package of 120 food tickets. We resolved not to take food or go to work until we attained our release.

"The Poles are striking!" Word spread around the camp. If the Russian zeks tried something like that, the authorities would not handle them with kid gloves. The very daring of this action testified to the Poles' feeling of their strength. The administration was flustered. First, the work supervisor, whose job was to bring people to the guardhouse, ran up, and was nonplussed. He tried force, cursed, began to threaten, but the overcrowded barrack did not fear him. Curious neighbors began to glance into the barrack. Our orderlies did not let outsiders in. The KVCh inspector ran up in fear, asking remonstratively: "Have you gone out of your mind? Don't you know what you will get for such a thing?" But we did not listen to him. In the meantime, the other zeks went to work and the camp emptied out. Only one barrack, the new "Battleship Potemkin,"[5] was full of rebels.

Finally, the camp boss appeared. He slowly walked into the thick of the crowd, stood in the middle of the barrack, looked at the bed boards where the prisoners were lounging, was silent for a moment, and asked in a voice as sharp as a bayonet:

"So, what's this? Not working?" A dead silence ensued. Suddenly voices spilled forth from the back rows:

"Why are you detaining us? You don't have the right according to the amnesty. We are starving!"

"What do you want?" asked the boss. The camp administration was frightened more by our refusal to eat than by our refusal to work. A hunger strike is a serious weapon of the prisoners, as the camp authority is obligated to give the zek food. It dares not withhold it. It is held responsible for not feeding people, and in the given case, our breach of discipline did not intimidate it, but withholding food for 120 people could lead to the most unpleasant consequences. The administration was afraid for itself.

Brandes spoke first and calmly laid out the Poles' demands: the immediate summoning of the prosecutor from Ertsevo for negotiations. Our detention is against the amnesty and the law, and no one has the right to force us to work after we have been amnestied.

Doctor Spicnagel and the young Pole Nowak, who, if I am not mistaken, was a relative of one of the Polish ministers, also spoke. Finally, I spoke too, to explain to the camp boss, in as calm and conciliatory a way as possible, that we were not enemies of the Soviet regime, that we were citizens of an allied state, and our place was in the ranks of the Polish army fighting against the common enemy.

"If you are friends of the Soviet Union, you should help us!" said the camp boss, looking at me attentively. "Why are you refusing to work?"

"Work in the camp," I answered, "is punishment from which we are released according to the amnesty. We shall not work in camp."

"We won't! We won't!" all those assembled shouted in chorus.

---

5. A reference to a mutiny on the battleship *Potemkin* during the Revolution of 1905, which was immortalized in the 1935 film of that name by Sergei Eisenstein.

The boss silently turned and left. Fifteen minutes later, the commandant entered and summoned all four who had spoken to the camp boss. They brought us over, and one by one, they led us into his office.

When my turn came, I saw an entire tribunal in front of me; behind a table sat a commission that included, in addition to the camp boss, the directors of the KVCh and of the medical sector, and other camp directors.

They interrogated me for three and a half hours. They were trying to find out who had collected the food tickets yesterday evening, to whom I had given my ticket. I said that I did not remember. Then I was ashamed of my irresoluteness, and I said that they should not ask me such questions.

"Why?" inquired the camp boss.

"Because even if I remembered, I still would not tell you those names. I understand that you are looking for people to blame, but the people who collected the tickets were not our 'leaders'; they collected them simply by chance."

"Then why don't you tell us their names?"

"It would be dishonest. You would be the first not to respect me if I squealed on my comrades."

"Do you hear what he is saying?" sighed the camp boss. "That's how he is!"

My answer was naïve, as every one of the people sitting behind the table was himself an informer and worked for the NKVD.

They took me to the adjacent room, stripped me, searched me, found and took away my little knife for the nth time, and within ten minutes I was installed in the punishment cell, where Brandes, Nowak, and Spicnagel were already sitting.

The administration followed the classic formula: it first removed the representatives of the "rebels"—and thus "beheaded" the masses. We were prepared for a heroic defense, felt an influx of strength and courage. We had shaken off our slavish torpor, and the awareness of a common struggle immediately united us. All of us in the cell immediately began to address each other with the intimate form of "you."

We did not, however, have to suffer. The door of the punishment cell opened three hours later, and the prosecutor of Kargopolag entered, the very person whom we had been trying in vain to reach for an entire month, and after a brief interrogation, he ordered us to be released. We were met with general rejoicing in the barrack. In our absence, all the central authorities had arrived from Ertsevo: the head of Kargopolag, the heads of the KVCh and medical sectors, the security head, and the prosecutor. At a meeting in the barrack, they promised the Westerners that within a month they all would be released, and when they complained about being kept in a penal camp, they were promised an immediate transfer to other "normal" camps.

Thus, a victory on all counts! Brandes stepped forward and, in a short speech, congratulated the Westerners with the success of the demonstration and their model discipline; he particularly thanked his three comrades of the punishment cell. In the name of all the strike participants, I expressed our gratitude to Brandes, and both speeches were greeted with applause. A long line of Westerners formed under the kitchen window to receive breakfast.

The next morning, they moved us out of Osinovka 1. Part of the group was sent to Osinovka 2, and the part that included me went to Kruglitsa. I thus again wound up in the medical settlement on October 1, 1941. In the first half of October, a large group of Westerners was released. This was sufficient to appease the remaining ones. We awaited our turn with faith and hope.

Brandes, the main organizer of the resistance, was sent to Ertsevo, where he continued to rebel. He demanded permission to send a telegram to the Polish mission in the capital. They permitted him to write a letter, to which he did not receive an answer. Not one of the flood of letters that were dispatched that winter from the camp to the Polish embassy was answered. We could not imagine that the Polish embassy did not respond to the letters of Polish citizens in distress, and we thought that either our letters were not delivered or that answers were not allowed into the camp. Either way, the fact remained, that after the "amnesty," we were deprived just as before of contact with Polish authorities, and we depended entirely on the arbitrariness of the NKVD organs.

Brandes then again—this time individually—refused to work. This time he sat in the punishment cell for nine days, refusing food. After that, they transferred him to the hospital. After his discharge, he again refused to work. Then he officially was released from work "for reasons of health," that is, they legalized his protest. Finally, in January 1942, he and Nowak were released. Spicnagel and I remained in camp.

The winter of 1941–1942 was the most difficult trial of my life. Hunger sapped my strength, but that was not the worst thing. Until then, I had related to the camp as an outside observer, a writer, a person who in the future would write a book about it. The camp seemed like a very rare, secret document about Soviet reality to which I had accidentally obtained access, an engrossing panoramic document. That winter, I understood that it was easier to enter a camp than leave it. The camp was no longer an object of observation. I ceased observing and began to die in camp. I felt that my exclusion from the amnesty meant a death sentence.

I was cut off from the entire world, from family, relatives, and friends. My letters abroad were not dispatched. I had no one in the Soviet Union. There was no one to give me material or moral support. Pinsk, where I had left my elderly mother and devoted friends, had been occupied by the Germans, and Soviet newspapers reported the murder there of 10,000 Jews. Now I know that my poor mother was still alive at that time. The Pinsk ghetto was destroyed in October 1942.

Ignorance of the future weighed heavily on us. For us, the Soviet-German war was a war of gorillas and cannibals. Both sides were an inhuman distortion of everything we held dear and sacred. The "amnesty" turned into a weapon of six-months' torture and endless torments. Every two to three weeks during that time, five to six people would be released from Kruglitsa— sometimes just one—and it was incomprehensible why those and not others. Our hair stood on end from horror: what if they didn't release us? Being excluded from the amnesty was much worse than not having one at all: it took away hope for the future, too. We had long ago ceased trying to find sense or logic in the way we were treated. Notorious fascists, dyed-in-the-wool antisemites, opponents of Sikorski's government[6] were free to join Ander's army. We Jewish democrats, whose families were perishing in the ghettos, were detained without explanations. We had no idea how or against what to defend ourselves. No one explained any secret motives behind our detention. At first, we ascribed the delay in liberation to transport difficulties: there were no train cars. Months passed and this explanation was eliminated. Finally, the very "we" began to melt away. Every month the circle of Westerners grew smaller. We were hundreds, then dozens remained; finally, in March 1942, half a year after the strike in Osinovka, only a few people remained. The "amnesty" sucked the blood out of us drop by drop, drove us to hysteria and a nervous breakdown. Only when we were the last ones, and ninety percent of the Westerners had left the camp, did we understand what they ought to have told us at the very beginning in order to spare us the inhuman torture of expectation: we were not being released, the Soviet regime was not applying the amnesty to everyone who was eligible, and to us, a small bunch of those remaining, it would not be applied.

For several months, we lived in indescribable nervous tension. We would wait for weeks until the list of those to be released would arrive. In the evening, after work, we would learn that a list of seven people was lying in the

6. The Polish government in exile during World War II was headed by Władysław Sikorski (1881–1943).

camp registration bureau. "Who are they?" Everyone was agitated but pretended that he was calm: "If not this time, then I'll be in the next. . . ." But inside, everything seethed and quivered: "So many people have left already, and I have been waiting so many months—why should I be the last?"

And now the seven are named, including your neighbor on the bed boards or someone whom you know for a long time. Your happiness for them is mixed with personal despair. The faces of those summoned by the work assigner are transformed and focused, serious and full of hidden agitation. Some are summoned from work in the middle of the day: "Stop working, go immediately to the camp to carry out the procedures for release."

It is a complicated procedure. You have to hand in all your camp belongings and exchange some. According to instructions, a released zek who does not have his own things is given second hand clothing, not new but neat and decent looking. A bath is obligatory before release. People are stunned and try not to betray their happiness, but the majority "don't believe it"—"until I travel one hundred kilometers from here, I won't believe it."

We, however, already feel some kind of border that separates the living from the dead. At the last minute, we foist on them little notes with the addresses of relatives abroad—"Some time tell about us, remember us!" Everyone promises, but most very quickly forget the camp, like a nightmare, along with all those who remain there. And if someone remembers and writes to the camp where he once served time, his letter will not be delivered to us.

All the months when the release of small groups continued, we feared to remind the authorities of our presence, to hasten matters, or press inquiries so as not to betray our unease and not to show that in general we consider it possible that we would be excluded from the amnesty. Then, when the misfortune became a fact, it was already too late. We wrote complaints to the Polish representatives, but there was no answer. We turned orally to the prosecutor from Ertsevo when he was in Kruglitsa: "Why don't they release us?" The prosecutor laughed and replied: "You are Jews; Sikorski doesn't want you." We considered that reply a bad joke. We were not all Jews. I wrote complaints for myself and a dozen comrades to the Kargopolag boss. An answer arrived a month later: they replied to my friends that they were detained "until a special order," incomprehensible words that explained nothing. I received a reply in a letter, and I had to sign on the other side that I had read it: "In answer to the inquiry of zek Margolin, Yu. B., it is explained to him that he does not fall under the amnesty for Polish citizens as a person of non-Polish nationality."

I replied to this "explanation" with a vehement protest. I wrote that the amnesty was intended for all Polish citizens regardless of ethnicity and religion.

That Jewish Polish citizens en masse had been released according to the amnesty, and I, therefore, do not accept an explanation that I was detained as a Jew, and I request that I be informed of the true reason for my detention. As long as they do not inform me on what basis I was excluded from the amnesty, I shall consider my imprisonment illegal. That imprisonment threatens my life, ruins me materially, and subjects my family to suffering and deprivation, and I lay the blame for all this on the government of the Soviet Union. That the London Polish government of Sikorski is a democratic government, free of antisemitism, and I refuse to believe that excluding a Polish Jew from the amnesty for Polish citizens occurs with his knowledge and consent.

I did not receive an answer to this letter. There was no one to talk to, to appeal to, no one to pin hopes on except those abroad—free people in the West, my friends and relatives who could intervene on my behalf. I placed my hopes on them, not suspecting that neither then, nor later, nor to this day, do people in the West whose close ones disappeared without a trace in the Soviet Union raise a finger to save them. And it is a good thing that we did not know that.

I could do nothing to save myself from this monstrous, senseless misfortune that struck me. I hoped, however, that the war would still clarify many things and that my lengthy and unexplained disappearance in the Soviet Union, as well as that of many other people from Europe, would attract the attention of broad public circles.

I did not utterly lose hope nor did I despair. In the spring of 1942, however, I experienced a shock that rendered me temporarily a deranged, abnormal being. I turned gray in those months. I had been young when they arrested me in Pinsk. Suddenly, I was astonished to hear people at work called me "Dad," and soon they began to call me "Grandpa."

Hunger had shriveled up my body; work beyond my strength had bent my back, my knees shook, my face became wrinkled, and my hands trembled. My hearing declined and my eyes dimmed. My nearsightedness increased considerably, and the glasses that I had brought with me to the camp were no longer strong enough. The camp boss refused to free me from general work. I went to the security operative to ask for help. The operative—no longer Stepanov but a round-faced person, said to me, "Yes, indeed, I know you: you correspond with foreign consulates." This was an allusion to the copy of a visa to Palestine that had been sent to me at the end of 1940. When I asked him to help me find work in the office because of my poor vision, he replied: "The trees in the forest are large, and if you have trouble seeing them, then what will you do in the office? The letters on the papers, after all, are very small!" And I did not know whether he was making fun of me or speaking seriously.

My body was falling apart and everything in me was crushed and dislocated. The only thing remaining was an animal terror of the freezing cold and physical pain. I would go out in the morning to the field; the snow fell on my rags, and I stood in a stupor, as if asleep, until the others, cursing, would force me to move a beam, to drag something, lift up something, help someone. But I was unable to do anything. Around me were alien faces. What I had feared most of all had happened: the Westerners had left, and in the entire camp about fifteen to twenty people like me were scattered among hairy, hungry, brutalized beings. Not one brigade wanted me. The day came when I stole a little knife from a neighbor.

I did not need that knife; I do not know why I did that. The pitiful hand-made camp knife was lying at the edge of the bed board—it fell out of the neighbor's jacket. I hid it in my pocket. Then the neighbor began to search for his knife, cursing high and low. I lay in the deep shadow, not responding, and I felt a sullen satisfaction from the fact that it did not occur to anyone in the barrack to look in my pocket. . . .

23

"One Must Work"

IN THE WINTER of 1941, we—the last Poles awaiting an amnesty—went out with knives and sickles into the forests around Kruglitsa. We were preparing forage for the cattle. We cut thin birch and alder twigs and fashioned them into clusters; the norm was one hundred per person. We made between thirty to seventy. All day we wandered in the snow among the trees; every so often, the guard would call to check on us. On my right, was Elektrowicz, an elderly Pole with a sullen face, taciturn and unsociable. Like me, he had been excluded from the amnesty, and that winter he died in camp. When we found a young birch shoot, we mercilessly destroyed it, leaving only stalks in the ground. On my left worked the former burgomaster of the town of Kopiczyncy in western Ukraine. He was an elderly lawyer with a flabby, puffy face, very similar to Molotov's; he had miraculously managed to retain his long black overcoat from home. With a concentrated effort, he bent a tall branch, pressed it under his arm and then cleaned off the side branches with his sickle; when he released the branch, it sprang back noisily, and the snow cascaded from the tree onto the old man's shoulders and head.

Even at such simple work, the common norm for everyone was barbaric. Some of us, particularly the sharp-eyed youth, would quickly find a suitable tree, cut dexterously and quickly, with one well-aimed blow of the knife separating the shoots from the trunk; others in the same situation lost several seconds getting their bearings and would strike with the knife once, twice, or three times and then tear off the branch by hand with a strip of the bark—those were never able to fulfill even half of the norm. Under normal working conditions, the norm is a means of selection—it winnows out those who are not suitable for the given work but are suitable for something else. Elektrowicz, the old burgomaster, and I no doubt were able to do many things well, but we were incompetent when it came to preparing clusters, and, therefore, for us the norm of forced slave labor was a norm of starvation and an inevitable death sentence. My clusters did not hold up—either they fell apart or fell from the stand on which I hung them. Passing by, the brigade leader would look at them critically and doubtfully shake his head. While cutting the branches, I thought about how terrible it is to combine a fixed norm that did not take individual differences into account with forced attachment to the place of work and the impossibility of changing it as one wished. I knew that even "free" Soviet workers operate in conditions similar to our camp ones. I recalled my friend, who had arrived in Palestine and began working in vegetable gardens. He was unsuccessful in raising tomatoes and quickly left tending vegetable patches. He turned out, however, to be an excellent bee keeper and could raise chickens. In a labor camp, if they had sent him to work in a vegetable garden, he would have suffered endlessly without fulfilling the norm and would have died on a penal ration. In dictatorial conditions, the Soviet formula, "Work is a matter of honor!" conceals imposed occupations and absolute, slavish dependence on the employer, which is not easier, but rather considerably more difficult when the employer is the police state.

My gums deteriorated and started bleeding, and two gold bridges fell out of my mouth. Before I managed to think about what to do with them, one of them was stolen. A blue-eyed Carpatho-Russian fellow lay next to me on the bunk boards. His oblique acknowledgement of the theft was expressed in his bringing me the following evening an entire cooked calf's tongue! From such a tongue they could slice twenty portions for the second level rations!

"Eat!" he said to me magnanimously, and he explained that he filched two tongues from the kitchen, one for himself and one for me. He used to help voluntarily in the kitchen after work—he would wash, tidy up, clean vegetables, for which they would feed him a little, and on occasion, he was able to steal some leftovers, but two tongues! So much meat! I didn't believe him and understood that my neighbor simply shared his proceeds from the gold bridge with me. Without any hesitation, I ate the entire calf's tongue without bread.

I gave the second large bridge to the chief cook Vaska. This Vaska was a sleek, foppish young man, and I had complete trust in him. I decided that I should make a friend in the kitchen, and I refused to take money from Vaska. I played the magnanimous role. How could I translate into monetary terms such a thing as friendship with the chief cook? "Take, Vasya, I don't need money—feed me when you have a chance."

In fact, in the camp kitchen, which served hundreds of people, some extra soup or kasha always remained. The administration, which understands that the cook must be sated and, incidentally, feeds itself from that same camp pot, watches vigilantly that a certain bound is not trespassed, that the cook neither deprives some zeks nor feeds others at his own discretion. But it is difficult to monitor the kitchen. In the morning, the representative of the medical sector checks the quality of the food. Often, he will forbid serving some rotted fish or bread from moldy flour (but that does not mean that we receive something else instead). An armed guard is present when the food is distributed and— in Kruglitsa—a representative of the prisoners. These "supervisors" primarily stuff themselves and regard their supervisory duty as a chance to eat to satiety. In the conditions of mass and chronic hunger, abuses are inevitable. Everyone who has access to material goods steals. The prisoners never receive what they are entitled to by law. People steal from the central warehouses, they steal during hauling of goods, they steal in the supply depot; the accountants of the products warehouse take whatever they please, they steal in the kitchen and hand less out the window to the prisoners. When the cook sees that he is being watched, he demonstratively stirs the pot vigorously and ladles out the "thick" part from the bottom. The worker in the line has to follow the cook's hand attentively, but he cannot interfere; if the cook is angry at him, he can dip the ladle so that nothing but water will come out. Therefore, and to show professional solidarity with all kitchen workers, one should never quarrel with them.

I approached the window where Vaska was standing, choosing a time when there was no line, knocked on the window and wordlessly handed over my metal mess tin with the ticket. Vasya, indifferently, without looking at me, gave me a full bowl of kasha, and poured some liquid soup above, so that it was not visible, and silently returned the meal ticket. This meant that I could receive another meal with this ticket.

One should never importune for additional food. Only the camp goners do that, the camp beggars. If you're going to do it, then do so with a barely noticeable movement of the eye or corner of the mouth. You must not forget that, although you cannot see him, a supervisor, the on-duty guard, may be standing behind the window on the other side. Sometimes Gordeeva, the head of the special supply unit, an energetic woman, not old despite her gray hair, would stand like a shadow on the side and watch, arms crossed. At her word, you could receive an extra ladle or, on the contrary, be sent to the punishment cell. If at such a time someone under the window would make inappropriate friendly signs: "Please feed me, Vasya!" the cook stonily would pour the correct amount and command in an official, strained voice: "Next!" You have to take your half liter of gruel, a ladle of 200 grams of liquid kasha and clear away fast.

Vasya fed me royally for an entire week, generously filling up my mess-tin. On account of this, in exchange for 200 grams of bread, I ordered a cover for the tin from the camp tinsmith Charnegi so that others would not see my riches. Here, however, misfortune struck: Vasya was diagnosed with tuberculosis and put in the pulmonary infirmary. He did not return to the kitchen. I remained toothless and hungrier than before.

At that time, I developed an enormous boil on my shoulder, and I was unable to dress or undress myself or go to work. Previously, I had had boils on my neck or other places that did not hinder me from working. When I fell ill, I first tried to persuade the brigade leader to write me down for one hundred percent of the work norm for the last work day. Seeing the boil, the brigade leader immediately understood my situation. A sick person who is excused from work but does not need to be in the infirmary receives the ration that he earned on his last working day. Everyone therefore first tries in every way possible to get listed for the full norm or the Stakhanovite one and only afterwards goes to the doctor. In our Kruglitsa, they later instituted a procedure to avoid machinations: the prisoner exempt from work was assigned a ration based on the last three days before his illness. In the evening, I went to the clinic and received the requested release from work from the kindest and most loyal doctor in the world, Maxik. I stood for two hours in the crowded line until they called my name. A hard, red growth the size of a plum swelled on my shoulder. They smeared it with ichtyol ointment, bandaged it, and I was free until the next evening.

Dozens of camp prisoners suffered from boils because of malnutrition. My boil, however, surpassed all records. It was impossible to get rid of it. Evening after evening, I received a release from work, and every time, Maxik found a new boil in a new place. Finally, when the number of boils on my body reached sixteen, Maxik lost his patience and decided to put me in the infirmary.

You have to imagine the uplifted spirits of a zek who leaves the clinic, calm and satisfied, knowing that tomorrow they will hospitalize him. A burden falls from his shoulders. He no longer cares about what is happening in the barrack. Early in the morning, when after reveille the person from the second sector arrives with the list of those released from work, he no longer rests on his elbow, listening anxiously whether his name appears. As of today, he is not simply "released" but also is taken off the brigade lists and transferred to the infirmary list. He can now sleep calmly, while the barrack goes through the ordinary bustle of rising, preparations, and departure for work. Between seven and eight o'clock, he can listen to the radio broadcast in the barrack— a communiqué from the front, a march of the wind orchestra, and a young

Pioneers reveille[1]; then he goes for soup and whiles away the inspection and morning cleaning of the barrack. The orderlies wash the floor, during which time those released from work or those on the night shift are forbidden to descend from the bunk beds. After nine o'clock, the zek who is assigned to the hospital goes to the medical sector. There, in the administrative office, they send him to the bathhouse. All those on the hospitalized list drift in a pack over to Sergei Ivanovich, who is in charge of the bathhouse. This is an unavoidable formality. In the morning, the bathhouse is unheated and cold. "Do you have lice?" asks Sergei Ivanovich, a dark-eyed, thin Armenian with a ten-year sentence. We swear that we don't have lice, but, nevertheless, the procedure calls for undressing, entering the empty bathhouse, dousing oneself with the barely warm water, and returning. Now, with a paper that certifies we have undergone "sanitary processing," we are able to "be hospitalized." We are not entitled, however, to hospital food until the following day; therefore, we wait in the barrack until the evening and, only after having received supper, do we begin to pack for the move.

The surgical barrack is situated at the very end of the camp. Burdened with all my possessions, my backpack and wooden chest, I reach the low door and knock; they let me into a tiny hallway. To the right is the distribution room, to the left, the doctor's office: that is where Maxik resides—Doctor Max Albertovich Rosenberg—an excellent surgeon and a well-educated person. Stumbling into the ward, where the patients are lying on cots on two sides, I wait patiently by the door until the "superintendent" enters, a janitor in charge of the barrack property. "Undress!" He collects my backpack and chest for keeping, takes my camp clothing and hands me coarse calico hospital linen with the stamp of the medical sector. It is important to get a cot close to the stove, as in the winter it is cold in the infirmary, and the patients mercilessly freeze under thin flannelette blankets. It is a triumphal moment when a person lies down on the straw mattress covered with a sheet and stretches out full length, smiling happily. He faces the prospect of several peaceful days until the boils are healed. The food is not as good as it was in July, but there is quiet and freedom from the camp clothing; there is cleanliness and protection from the camp. Over "there," beyond the walls of the low, whitewashed hospital barrack is a dark hell of stinking lairs crowded with a tattered and savage horde—there are robberies and quarrels, groans and weeping, lines in the frost under the kitchen windows, lines in the morning

---

1. Pioneers—the Soviet children's (ages 7–14) organization, the only one allowed in the USSR. *Pioneer's Dawn* was the daily morning broadcast for Pioneers, 1934–1991.

dispatch to work, punishment cell and slave labor. Here the work supervisor won't come to force me to go to work. Here one can lie down, collect one's thoughts, return to oneself.

I spent eleven days in the surgical infirmary. After two and a half years in a state of uninterrupted stupefaction, I finally had the opportunity to rest and contemplate what had happened to me and mankind from the time of the German invasion of Poland, when an enormous wave swooped me up and transported me from the customary and normal world and brought me to the "other side of life," where fortunate Europeans are not supposed to look.

I was half dead—a mixture of despair and fear, stubbornness and hope, but emotional reactions of that sort could not help me at the brink of death. I needed to restore a normal sense of self. Then I remembered Aristotle's ancient theory of catharsis and began to cure myself with special methods.

I regained the ability and need for logical thought. For hours I lay motionless, thinking resolutely. Then I began to write—not in a stream of consciousness but only the final conclusions and formulations. Thus, in the course of eleven days, I wrote a work that was small but important for me in my condition at the time—"The Theory of Falsehood."

While the kind Maxik treated my boils with a lancet and ointments, I countered the incipient process of mental decline by turning the surrounding reality into an object of calm, dispassionate investigation. This was my revenge: *non ridere, non lugere, sed intelligere* [Latin: (Spinoza) do not laugh, do not grieve, but understand]. It was falsehood that surrounded me, pressed on my head, was suffocating me and my generation. The logical and psychological nature of falsehood, its cultural-historical manifestation, was my topic at the end of the winter of 1942.

Falsehood has always existed. From the mimicry of primitive organisms to diplomatic communications and government declarations, one can construct a ladder of falsehood analogous to the ladder that appeared to Jacob in his dream. . . . On Jacob's ladder, however, angels ascended to heaven, whereas my ladder led to hell, and weak, unfortunate sinners were going down it. I distinguished between the "sacred lie" and the "Wallenrod lie," glorified by Mickiewicz, the poet in the enemy's camp.[2] I made my way through the lineup of individual and collective falsehood, the verbal and conscious lie, and the kind that penetrates into the depth of the subconscious and subordinates a person's reason and feeling to itself. I sought a way out of the vicious circle of

---

2. Reference to the poem "Konrad Wallenrod," by Adam Mickiewicz (1798–1855), the Polish national poet, who spent the period from 1824 to 1829 in exile in the "enemy camp" of Russia.

falsehood and recounted to myself the history of hundreds of disappointments on this path. I assembled all the arguments in favor of falsehood advanced in our time in order to counter them with the truth of the dauntless heart, the truth of suffering and sacrificial exploit. I knew firmly that "the light shines in the darkness and the darkness does not engulf it."[3] Finally, I wrote a telegraphically compressed sketch, "The Theory of Falsehood," and even tried giving it to Maxik to read. An author needs an audience, but Maxik, the best of surgeons, was a weak philosopher. He did not understand a thing and returned the manuscript to me with the remark that it was too complex for his purely medical mind. We worked with dissimilar lancets.

Maxik cured my boils, and I detached myself from my persecutors with the work about falsehood. I left the hospital intending to live and not yield to my enemies.

Around this time, I became acquainted with Semivolos, not the famous Aleksei Semivolos, laureate of the Stalin prize, a Soviet hero and leading Stakhanovite of the Donbass, one of the most popular Soviet personalities, but a considerably more modest figure: his cousin, who perished in a Soviet camp in 1943. He was a tall man with a powerful build, a Kiev[4] journalist or student at the Institute of Red Journalism, a Soviet person with a Ukrainian accent, sense of humor, and curiosity. The latter was evident in his endless conversations with me about the countries where I had been and the cities that I had seen. Semivolos condescendingly took me under his wing, but I had already learned not to take too seriously either the friendship or enmity of Soviet people. I was no longer insulted by cursing that would be completely forgotten the next day, and I was not deceived by closeness that at any minute could turn into betrayal. Their words did not obligate them and carried no weight, and their feelings were insubstantial and fleeting. These people seemed to lack an inner compass: the dictatorial regime had taught them to wind themselves like ivy around an external iron rod. I was very cautious with Semivolos, not certain whether he might inform on me to the administration. Even in the camp, Semivolos remained a potential party member, one of those who was expiating his guilt or mistake by imprisonment and was trying to dispel suspicions and show his wholehearted loyalty. That is who Nikolai Semivolos was—a brigade leader and Stakhanovite, a work leader who in January 1942 was even nominated for a reduced term.

---

3. From the Russian text of the Gospels according to John.

4. Now Kyiv, capital of Ukraine.

Winter in the camp is always a difficult time. The beginning of the year always coincides with general depression, when it is necessary to use skillful propaganda in order to support and encourage the weakened, despairing people to work. The new year is the time when the administration spreads rumors about an "approaching amnesty" or a "reconsideration of the case," or "reducing the term by half," or rumors that prisoners who have less than three years to serve will be sent home. Of course, not everyone, but the Stakhanovites, the deserving workers. In every camp they prepare lists of model workers and tell them that the Camp Administration considers it possible in their case to appeal for an early release. An electric agitation passes through the camps. . . . The "veterans," however, laugh cynically and explain to the "youths" that this is an old trick, repeated year after year. The list of candidates will go to the Gulag Administration in Moscow, and the matter will end there. In fact, if people work well in camps as organizers or conscientious "doers," then the Soviet regime will be happy to leave them in their place until the end of time. The regime needs camps and the camps need the "doers." The regime is totally uninterested in releasing the very pillars of the camp. Invariably, the mountain of propaganda and rumors about an early release gives birth to a mouse. In rare cases, people who have served five years and have that many more to go receive a discount of ten months or half a year. That still does not mean that the camp has given up on them. They liberate them without the right to leave the region, and if they are specialists, they remain at their former work as "free" workers.

Semivolos, too, was designated for an early release, but he did not make it. At the height of his successes, suddenly some petty embezzlement was discovered: they caught him selling some camp property on the side, and they immediately removed him from his post, sent him to another camp, transferred the case to the prosecutor, and his shining camp work record was of no help. In the period that I am describing here, however, Semivolos was the lion of Kruglitsa. Working tirelessly and energetically, he still found time to read a school textbook, *Ancient History*, which lay under his pillow. His proximity was not always pleasant for me because of the enormous extra-large portions that he obtained by his pull in the kitchen. I was lying next to him but was not invited to participate in the extra food. I was constantly hungry, and this neatly covered aluminum mess-tin standing on the shelf just above my head annoyed me. Around eleven o'clock in the evening, Semivolos would return from the office and begin to clatter the tin, having taken off his shoes and settled eastern style on the upper bunk.

He read the history textbook not out of an interest in ancient Greece or Rome but simply because no other book was available. His interest in me was similar. He did not finish reading the history book, and I did not remain long in his brigade. For some time, Semivolos took an interest in me as he might in an entertaining picture book in a foreign language; he quickly looked over the pictures and tossed away the book. In any case, during the two weeks that I worked in his leading brigade, which received preferential treatment from the bosses, he got some things for me, including a straw mattress, the first one since June 1940. For a year and a half, I had been sleeping on bare boards; now, as befits an old camp inmate, I began to acquire "property."

Our brigade supplied Kruglitsa with firewood, advancing far in the deep snow. Then I discovered a dispiriting circumstance: I was unable to keep up with the brigade. I started out in the first pair. We stretched out in a chain, and soon I was in the middle and then at the tail end of the brigade. I zealously and hastily trampled the snow with my feet, trying to step in the footsteps of those ahead of me, but my feet were not obedient. In three months' time, this became a general phenomenon: by springtime everyone had become weak, and the majority had difficulty moving their feet. At that time, however, people were still surprised—the very same people who would themselves reach the end of the road of hunger depletion. They were surprised and admonished me: "One must work! Must work!"

I did not need their telling me that one had to work in order to survive in camp. I already saw, however, that no effort guaranteed saving our life. I hated that eternal camp refrain, that sole commandment of the Soviet Sinai, that grim camp wisdom that day and night was drummed into the brains and souls of millions of slaves until it became their only spiritual possession. "Don't reason! Others have already done that for you! Your job is to work!" I, a Western person, knew that first one must be a human being. Only a free person knows the joy of free labor, and for him this labor is meaningful because it serves a goal that he chooses and in which he believes. In the opposite case, slogans such as "one must work," which millions of dulled people in the Soviet Union repeat piously and blindly as fate and mission, as the irrevocable fate of their pitiful existence, is brute wisdom, applicable in equal measure to people and animals. This wisdom treated the horse and the cart driver in camp as equal in worth, melding them into the body of the centaur, into one concept Man/horsepower [*rabguzhsila*]! I myself was not worth anything; my right to life was measured by the percentage of the work norm I fulfilled.

"Whoever does not work, does not eat!" That was the second threat that hung over us. I recalled their hanging signs with that inscription on the streets and boulevards of occupied Lvov[5] in September 1939, and it had seemed like a revelation of supreme justice. Not true! Labor under threat of a rod, forced labor, does not save humankind. It is sufficient if we proclaim the slogan: "He who works, eats." How I yearned in Kruglitsa for my homeland, for the country where every worker is sated and where, therefore, you do not have to keep track of the bread given to those dependent on family and society! Here, even the one who worked was not sated. The difference between me, a weak worker, and Semivolos, a Stakhanovite, was only the degree of deprivation.

Indisputably, as they lost their physical strength, the mass of camp prisoners lost the will to work. That was not surprising—the surprising thing was that one would meet people who still felt the need to work. Such a need is the normal result of health, accumulated strength, and normal work capacity. Enjoyment of work is familiar to everyone who knows how to do something—to do it like an expert in his or her field. They forced us to do things that we did not know how to do, and then they accused us of not being able to do them because we did not want to. In reality, our unwillingness meant only that we had no strength or ability to work. Just as it is unthinkable that a violinist would give up his violin, so it is unthinkable that a physically healthy and strong person would not be attracted to work. We lived in the camps in an atmosphere of crime. The crime, however, was not that people who were so feeble that they could barely drag their legs detested and feared work: the crime was the social system that turned the right to work into the coercion of forced labor, a camp system that first acquainted me with the phenomenon of wrecking (sabotage). I was never a wrecker in camp, but I understood how people full of deadly hatred toward the yoke and harness forced on them against their will would develop a cynical and destructive attitude toward work.

Of course, I did not speak about all this with Semivolos. He was too primitively healthy to be my friend. Suddenly, one evening, having eaten his brigade leader's supper on the bunk, he handed me his mess tin and said casually and lazily, thinking about something else: "Margolin, wash my tin."

I did not understand that there was no equality between us and that I should do such menial services for him in order to justify my existence in his magnificent brigade, and I answered naively, "No, I already washed mine and I am not going off the bunk again. . . ." A day later, without saying anything to me, Semivolos wrote me down on the workers' report for the punishment

5. Now Lviv, Ukraine.

portion and for 400 grams of bread. The entire brigade received 600 grams. When this was repeated on the second and third day, I went to the work boss and asked him to assign me to other work.

Our work boss Aleksandr Ivanovich was a tall, thin Russian Pole with sunken cheeks and a small Chekhov-style beard, a gentle and compassionate person who would never raise his voice and was respected by everyone. Although he never spoke with us in Polish and perhaps had already forgotten how to speak that language, he was especially considerate to Westerners, to the point of pity. I explained to Aleksandr Ivanovich that it was difficult for me to walk several kilometers into the forest. He nodded, thought for a minute, and said: "Tomorrow, go out with the fifth brigade to the *selkhoz*, to the potting factory." I thus became a potter.

There were about forty people in the fifth brigade. Half were women who worked in the hothouses of the *sovkhoz*, the vegetable gardens, preparing for the planting of seedlings of cabbage and other vegetables. These women spent their working day in the hothouse warmth, wore clean new jackets and shoes and men's hats with earflaps, but they wore the men's clothing more neatly than the men did, and their faces, prematurely faded and tired, still showed traces of their urban origin. I was not permitted to enter the large hothouse where a clock hung—the familiar standard Soviet clock with a green square dial and two weights suspended on a chain—but I often peeked inside to check the time. If I did not run into a guard, then Tasya, an older woman who looked like a teacher, with measured, gentle movements and dark, sad eyes, would not drive me away, and I could stand in the warmth for a minute. While I was a potter, however, I did not need that.

After exiting the camp gates, we would cross the village street and walk past the scattered houses—in one was a store for the free workers, in another lived Valentina Vasilievna, head doctor of the Kruglitsa medical city. Circumventing the firehouse, passing the repair warehouse on the right, we crossed the field and entered the *selkhoz* through the partially opened gate. The entire brigade, followed by an armed guard, went to the central yard, and from there dispersed in groups to various jobs. We potters turned before reaching the end of the yard and marched in single file for about 300 meters to the end of the *selkhoz*. It was still dark when we reached the door of the wretched, broken-down shack where the guard used to sleep at night. He was supposed to stoke the stove in advance of our arrival, but when we entered, stumbling in the darkness and groping our way, a cold wind greeted us. This tiny ramshackle hut, with a broken little window and uneven dirt floor, had become cold. The guard had already burned all the wood chunks prepared the previous evening. We sat silently in the darkness on the overturned wooden boxes until the gray dawn came through the window. We then went out into the courtyard to look for a piece of wood for the stove; someone went with a sled to the central courtyard to gather some wood, to filch it if necessary. The low clay stove stood in the middle of the hut. Having stoked the stove, we stood by the production trays.

We made earthen planting pots for cabbage seedlings. Along the walls at chest level were shelves, laden with soil. Near the shelves stood four to five broken old installations. They looked like narrow wooden mortar tubs,[6] and a metal cup was mounted in each one. With our hands, we would stuff the soil from the shelves into that cup; then we inserted into the mixture a massive metallic canister with a handle and, pressing on the handle, we would turn the canister firmly several times in both directions. A neat little pot would be formed between the canister and the walls of the cup. At the bottom of the cup was a pin. The canister, which had an opening on the bottom in the center, was fitted onto the pin. Carefully removing the pot, we smoothed its edges with our palm. The result was a smooth sturdy little planting pot for a cabbage seedling, with a round hole below.

The norm for these little pots was enormous, but with our discount from the medical sector, we had to yield only five hundred pieces per person. Working for ten hours a day, we were supposed to make fifty pieces an hour in order to fulfill our norm. Near each of us were flat wooden boxes where one by one we placed our planting pots like children playing with dough. Every hour, Ninka, the girl from the drying room, would come with a sled to take our pots to the drying room where they calculated how many pieces were taken from each and rejected the unsuitable ones.

While four to five people shaped the planting pots, two others prepared the soil. The mixture used to mold the planting pots consisted of three parts: garden soil, peat, and horse and cow manure. On the floor on the other side of the stove lay an enormous pile of the latter "materials," while under the ceiling on a bunk lay the garden soil and the peat, which "defrosted" during the night. The one-eyed Pole Ganko was considered an expert at preparing the mixture. He would begin the day by taking a wooden shovel and knocking down everything from the boards to the floor. Around nine o'clock, a wagon would bring the manure from the cattle yard. By then the stove was already sputtering, smoke escaped through the cracks, and we were all working,

---

6. Shallow trough-like boxes.

having thrown off our jackets. This was considered excellent work—in a warm, closed building—the envy of all. We were satisfied. Behind our back, water gurgled in kettles. On the other side of the stove, Ganko, stripped to the waist, was stirring the manure with a spade. If Ganko's mixture was not good, or if the soil was too moist, or there was too little of it in the cup, or we did not press the canister firmly enough, the earthen planting pot would not hold up and would fall apart in the hand. The sides would crack, pieces of straw would stick out, and Ninka, returning from the drying room, would say: "Galina Mikhailovna is angry: half of the cups were no good!"

Galina Mikhailovna, a thin Polish prisoner from the Lvov area, appeared behind her on the threshold with a worried look: "I don't know what's happening to you today—the pots are falling apart!"

Along with me worked the burgomaster from Kopiczyncy and Jatscko, the same snooty young Pole who had behaved so arrogantly last winter in Onega at the wood felling. Now he had grown thin and his face had changed terribly; he was a shadow of his former self. He, too, had been excluded from the amnesty. We worked quickly, not straightening up from morning to evening, and we barely managed to make the norm. Sometimes the brigade had already lined up at the gate when we were finishing the last dozen, and we would run to the road, barely having washed our hands, without resting. The two women who worked with us, however, would finish their five hundred by 4:30 and they would sit, resting in the warmth until six o'clock. One was an elderly, short prostitute with a hoarse masculine voice, stocky, light-fingered, with rotting teeth; she was the best worker in our group, the quickest to obtain a rolled cigarette and to grab the best installation and the best place between the stove and the window. It did not pay to quarrel with Lizaveta Ivanovna: her tongue was sharper than a razor blade, and she was not shy in her choice of words. She lacked only a broom to look like Baba Yaga in a mortar tub.[7] Her favorite was the one-eyed Ganko. She treated all the others with total scorn, would send us for wood, for a bucket of snow to put on the range, or would shove an old broom into our hands, "Sweep a bit, meanwhile!"

Ninka, despite her youth, had quite a story. A homeless child from the Ukraine, born at the dawn of the NEP period,[8] she was raised in the home of a priest, then in a Jewish family, and went through a Soviet orphanage. In 1939,

---

7. Baba Yaga—a supernatural, deformed-looking witch in Slavic folklore who rides a broom or flies in a mortar tub, wielding a pestle, and lives deep in the forest.

8. NEP—New Economic Policy instituted by Lenin in 1921 to revive the flagging Soviet economy; it ended in 1928 with Stalin's introduction of the first Five Year Plan.

she wound up with the Red Army in Lvov, which was the high point of her biography. She found a patron in Kozyrev, the chairman of the Lvov municipal
committee, the ruler of the city. What could be better? In some mysterious
way, however, this led to three years in a corrective labor camp.

The entire camp knew that Ninka had a powerful patron outside, that
the camp was a misunderstanding, and that Ninka, in fact, was an ardent
daughter of the working class. Ninka looked at us potters suspiciously with
her shining brown eyes and would pry: "Did you just speak in Polish? You
think I don't understand?" And she would threaten: "I'm going to go today to
the security officer and inform him about all your gossip! He respects me very
much!" And that was true. Ninka often visited the security officer, and in her
presence, therefore, we all sensed a breath of authority, and we tried to speak
loyally and patriotically. Ninka checked the quality of our work, and every
unusable pot aroused her suspicion: "Maybe there's sabotage?" Fearfully
trying to win her favor, I therefore lied to her and said that in Lvov, I knew
that very Kozyrev and that he was as good as gold. I asked Ninka upon her
release to convey my respects to Kozyrev: "He'll probably remember me!"
Ninka glowed, and I immediately became trustworthy in her eyes.

Lizaveta Ivanovna and Ninka were friends. In addition to their common
Soviet origin, they were united by their professional affinity—the incomparable speed with which they made pots. The burgomaster from Kopiczyncy
with the puffy face and round feline head enjoyed their good will and they
often gave him their snack: "Eat, old man!" In the work break, Lizaveta
Ivanovna, a robust broad despite her age, would lean against Ganko, poke him
on the shoulder, chuckle, and they would exchange a series of salty male jokes.

Workers changed frequently. For several days, a girl with a delicate,
nervous face and dark Jewish eyes worked at molding the pots. I recalled
seeing her in the infirmary. She used to come there to wash the floors. At
the time, I took note of her face: familiar, one of ours—I used to see such
girls in the kibbutzim of Palestine, wearing blue blouses and kerchiefs—or
in the halls of the Sorbonne and Liege. What brought her here? We became
acquainted in the infirmary: her name was Agronskaya; she was a Kiev student from a Soviet Jewish family. She was amused and astonished—unable
to understand—when I told her that I preferred the fate of a shoe shiner in
Tel Aviv to the good fortune of a commissar in the Kremlin. . . . I sat with her
during the lunch break. Ganko brought the meal to the potters in a bucket.
They gave us 250 grams of soup each. Agronskaya took out a piece of bread.
"Where is your bread?" I did not have any; that day I had again received 400
grams and there was none left.

The Kievan "girl from the kibbutz" calmly broke her piece of bread in two and offered me half. I did not understand at first what she was doing. What a way of doing it! So naturally and simply, as if "by the way," as if this was merely the ordinary execution of some generally accepted act of politeness that one does not speak about or think about in particular, as if we were sitting at a tea table in her parents' home, and she moved the sugar bowl toward me. But this was a camp where people grabbed each other by the throat for one hundred grams of bread. I took the bread; I was too hungry to refuse, and I looked at her. Suddenly my lips started to tremble.

Agronskaya will not read this book and she will never know how solemnly and devotedly I remember that piece of bread that she shared with me in camp. With one move of her hand, she firmly supported me. The word "comrade" had lost all meaning in the Soviet Union. But in every normal— and in every abnormal human life there are particular moments, sometimes so insignificant and unnoticeable as the head of a pin—that radiate energy and an unceasing light that shines for years in the depths of our being. From the way that she handed me the bread, I knew that Agronskaya was an excellent person, and because I knew, moreover, that she was the most ordinary, commonplace person, I again believed in humankind and in the concealed meaning of its existence.

Two years later, I was told that Agronskaya became pregnant and was sent to a special camp for pregnant women. The fragile figure with the large dark Jewish eyes again appeared before my eyes and my heart sank: what had the camp done to her? Fortunately, the father of her child was neither a *urka*, nor the camp barber, nor the camp commandant. It was a person worthy of her, and in the bounds of the camp, they both could not have made a better choice.

As making the pots was considered a too easy, female occupation, I soon had to yield my warm spot by the stove and go work as an assistant to one-eyed Ganko. I remained at this work for a month until we made more pots than the camp needed and they closed the factory.

In March, Ganko was sent to Square 54, the camp where they sent the Poles included in the amnesty. Ganko's sister was in a "free settlement" in the Altai region, and the old man, all spiffy in a new suit and cap, prepared for the trip to distant Altai, where, according to rumors, there was food. I wished him a good trip. At Square 54, however, there were no train cars. While waiting for the cars, Ganko died, on the eve of liberation.

That month I did not work that much with him but we worked hard. In the morning, we would clear out the snow by the hothouse ditches, where there were layers of so-called "garden soil." Then we would break up the frozen earth with a pick and crowbar. I was already unable, however, to work with a crowbar; it was hard for me to raise the massive iron pick, and my blow lacked force. After half an hour of work, I was unable to function. Ganko worked better than I with the crowbar. After many bitter remarks and protest on his part, we divided the work: he broke apart the earth, and I carried it in a sled around 300 meters to our workshop. We loaded the enormous round basket on the sled, and I, tensing up my entire body, pulled like a work horse. Ganko helped from the back and the sled moved, creaking in the snow. Every day we made five trips. I knew every meter of the way, every ascent and turn, descent and ditch. All sweaty, straining in the rope harness, with a last burst of strength, I would drag our burden to the door of our hut. I still had the strength to take off the enormous basket and drag it to the threshold. Then the potters would come out to help me toss the basket across the threshold.

There was one uphill section on the route where my strength failed me. For a quarter of an hour, I would suffer at this place, dragging my burden up the hill, knowing that there was no other way. At such moments, when the bright winter sun was playing on the pure snow, and I was hopelessly lost in this deserted, strange world, transformed into a beast of burden, I experienced real paroxysms of humiliation and rage. No one would hear me as I loudly cursed fate, people, my inhuman work, and the deadly burden, which did not move no matter how much I tugged at the harness straps. It was even worse when a wagoner would appear at a turn. Then I immediately had to move the sled off the road to give him the right of way; my sled would fly into a ditch in the deep snow, turning on its side, and then I had to drag them separately back onto the road—the sled and the basket with soil.

This work continued until one o'clock. After a rest, the two of us began to crush with spades the peat and manure on the floor of the hut. We shoveled the frozen earth onto the upper board so that it would defrost during the night. Then we stretched out a "sifter," a rusty wire screen in a wooden frame and pushed our mixture through it, throwing away the straw, pebbles, and frozen clumps. Then I took away the screen and the prepared mixture would lie on the floor. I carried it in a wooden box near the machines and poured a supply of soil for every potter.

This work left us all dirty, covered with soil, and smeared with manure, but every day from one to three o'clock, we had complete rest and we would lie down to sleep on the dirt floor by the stove, placing a block of wood under our heads.

At dusk, they called us to line up for the road back. We washed up with water from the stove and exited one at a time. The brigade was already standing by the gates and waiting impatiently for us. They yelled at us: "Hurry up!" But we went very slowly. A deadly exhaustion shackled our limbs. Exhausted, we walked, moving our feet with difficulty and maintaining a sullen silence.

24

Ivan Aleksandrovich Kuznetsov

IN 1942, THREE Kuznetsovs lived in the medical settlement of Kruglitsa, and all three had the first name of Ivan. I shall tell about just one of them. He was my dear friend. And my tale will not harm him in the other world.

Ivan Aleksandrovich was much older than I; in 1942, he was fifty-nine. In another year he would reach sixty, and they would classify him as a second-degree invalid.

People over sixty are not forced to work; they work if they choose to. Ivan Aleksandrovich was rather strong. One's outward appearance at that age is deceptive, and balance is unstable. The body no longer has reserves of strength; one shove and the zek is gone.

I met Ivan Aleksandrovich in Barrack 9. Our closeness had a professional basis: two bibliophiles, two lovers of the word. I had graduated from Berlin University and was a Westerner; Ivan Aleksandrovich graduated from the Pedagogical Institute of Voronezh, and back in tsarist times, he had taught Russian language and literature. After the revolution, he settled in the Ryazan oblast, in one of the villages where there was a secondary school or "ten-year school." Such schools, which correspond to our gymnasia [high schools], are located not only in cities. Ivan Aleksandrovich taught in the gymnasium in the village. He had a brother who was a doctor and a sister in a *kolkhoz*. He did not like to talk about his son and never mentioned him, as if he did not exist.

The village where he had lived uninterruptedly for twenty years was in Ryazan *oblast*, in the district of Lebedyan, sixteen kilometers from the small town of Lebedyan, which had a railroad station of that name. It was a most provincial area in the very heart of central Russia. During his entire village life, Kuznetsov traveled to Moscow just once, for some supplementary summer teachers' courses. He was a peaceful, provincial, undemanding person: 400 rubles a month and a modest room in a village house satisfied him perfectly well. The windows of his room faced the front garden. His sister the *kol-khoz* worker cooked for him. She kept chickens and sheep in her courtyard; sunflowers grew under the window. I asked Ivan Aleksandrovich for details about the value of the sheep—how much wool, how much meat they yielded, and what kind of care they required. In camp all such things become interesting. Ivan Aleksandrovich explained comprehensively.

In the summer, Ivan Aleksandrovich would often go shopping in Lebedyan. Of course, he would take off his shoes, sling them over his shoulder and walk barefoot; on the outskirts of the town he would again put on his shoes city style.

"You take bread, cucumbers in a knapsack, a bottle of milk and about 400 grams of ham with you to town," related Ivan Aleksandrovich, "and you walk without hurrying; it's very pleasant!" He had a way of pronouncing "plea—sant!" blinking sweetly and smacking his fleshy lips to sing the word distinctly with a particular intonation from his very heart.

It is not hard to understand why such a person had to land in a corrective labor camp. He was a man of the older generation, and his specialty, as luck would have it, was ideological: Russian literature. Of course, Ivan Aleksandrovich taught loyally and precisely according to the textbooks of the People's Commissariat of Education, where there is Bagritsky and Mayakovsky,[1] but all the same, he was an old teacher who under Tsar Nicholas had taught using the textbooks of Sipovsky and Savodnik. When I told him that I had also used those textbooks in school, the old man rejoiced: "You can say what you want," he remarked, "but then the textbooks were solid—serious!" Indeed, only in a village near Lebedyan could such a literature teacher last for twenty years. His time came, however, and the communist school director suggested that Comrade Kuznetsov switch to teaching physics. Ivan Aleksandrovich was insulted and refused outright. But it is not acceptable to refuse. A conflict arose, and they began to glare daggers at Ivan Aleksandrovich. They spoke about him to the appropriate person. They reported Ivan Aleksandrovich to the appropriate quarters; he drew attention. One cannot tolerate such a person as an educator of Stalinist youth. And one fine day, exactly five years before our meeting, they came to him to conduct a search. They rummaged through his books and took, among other things, Renan's *Life of Jesus* as evidence of a clerical mode of thought: a Soviet pedagogue and look at his proclivities! They sentenced him to ten years.

1. Eduard Bagritsky (1895-1934) and Vladimir Mayakovsky (1893-1930), popular Soviet-era poets.

In the first year, he occasionally was still sent packages. When I met him, however, he no longer received any. We starved together in the fatal year 1942. I, however, was twenty years younger. I had survived just two years of Soviet hard labor, and he had done five. Finally, I found ways of secretly getting food in the camp above the legal ration, but no one fed Ivan Aleksandrovich. He held out as long as he could, but in the spring of 1943, he died of hunger.

There is nothing remarkable in this case. Anonymous zeks, whom no one mourns and no one remembers, die that way in camp after suffering several years. No one organizes show trials because of this or delivers emotional speeches. Ivan Aleksandrovich did not die in Bergen Belsen or in Mauthausen. Countless hordes died in the year 1943 in NKVD camps. No one counts these millions, and merely mentioning them is considered a crude, tactless act and a sign of disrespect for the Soviet regime.

Ivan Aleksandrovich's story is a pure paradox, an irony of fate: he lived all his life in the backwoods, died in a camp, but after his death, I am telling his tale as if he were an important person. For me, however, Ivan Aleksandrovich was a very important person. This man is not fictitious; he is a real person, and others like him perished and will still perish in Soviet and non-Soviet camps, but primarily Soviet ones—countless millions of them. The UN, the League in Defense of Human Rights, and international monitoring do not deal with such trifles, which are supervised entirely by the Soviet NKVD. "Man, that word has a proud sound"; Maxim Gorky's eloquent words alluded to man with a capital "M."[2] Ivan Aleksandrovich, however, was a man with a lower-case letter; his story deserves to be told not to arouse the reader's pity but in order to make one aware of the price of lofty words and propaganda posters, even when they are signed by world-famous names.

Kuznetsov's friendship with me had one unpleasant consequence for him. Everyone began to think he was a Jew. With his prominent ears and bald pate, large nose and thick lips, he, indeed, resembled a Jew, but no one would have noticed this until he began to climb up to visit me on the upper bunk. We were two peas in a pod, both scrawny, wearing eyeglasses tied with string, both shaved every three weeks, both "academics," both represented the type of impotent intellectual so despised in camp, both never cursed. Not surprisingly, they got the two of us mixed up, and Kuznetsov soon was considered a Jew, at which he merely smiled, dismissed it with a wave of his hand, but never disputed it.

---

2. Line from Maxim Gorky's play *In the Depths*, which premiered in 1902.

Despite the external similarity, only Russians without a flair for racial af-filiation could consider Kuznetsov a Jew. No Jew would see anything Semitic in his bony, knobby face or in his bearing and manner of speech. I valued Kuznetsov's gentle nature, archaic politeness and equanimity; he never lost his temper, and I never heard him say a coarse word. This forgotten and abandoned old man combined pedantry with the need to attach himself to someone and discuss unusual topics. His meticulous camp pedantry was expressed in several ways: he always had a reserve of all kinds of string, and each one was in its place, and every little hole was immediately mended; in-numerable little nails hung above his bunk, and rags for various tasks hung on each—one rag to wipe his glasses, another for his nose, a third for a towel, a fourth to dust, and a fifth to tie around his neck. Separately he had a little bag with needle and thread and buttons separately. He did not refuse me the needle, but I refrained from borrowing it because I saw that this was a great bother for him and disturbed his order. The one time I borrowed it from him, I lost it, and he was very upset until I obtained another needle for him from Galina Mikhailovna.

It was already hard for him to read, but we would converse. In the eve-ning after work or in the morning of a nonworking day, Ivan Aleksandrovich would signal to me from his place on the upper bunk on the opposite wall, waving his hand and questioning in sign language: "May I come to visit?" He would then climb up, settle into a semi-reclining position and the conversa-tion would begin. Ivan Aleksandrovich had an original intellect, and I could never foresee what question he would pose. "Yuli Borisovich," he would begin in his bass voice with the look of a co-conspirator, "I need your en-lightened opinion on an important question: Is mysticism compatible with Christianity?" One time we discussed patristics, and in order to satisfy his curiosity, I had to search every corner of my memory to recall the scraps of my student knowledge about the fathers of the Church. Another time he asked me what I thought about the saying: "Vengeance is mine and I shall repay."[3]

All these conversations had the form of monologues. Whereas before my arrest and stay in Russia, I had been a rather taciturn person, in camp I began to feel a painful need to speak out loud, a need that remained until the end of my imprisonment. I fear that this book, too, is nothing other than the final phase and conclusion of that camp need. Ivan Aleksandrovich would listen solemnly, like an old music lover to whom one presented . . . Beethoven's

---

3. Paul's Epistle to the Romans, 12:19. It is also the epigraph to Tolstoy's *Anna Karenina*.

Tenth Symphony. In his library near Lebedyan, he kept an edition of the full collected works of Dmitry Merezhkovsky,[4] whom he respected deeply. He was his teacher and spiritual leader. As I, too, had read a considerable amount of Merezhkovsky's works in my high school years, we had much to talk about. Then we would discuss the news about the war. I always asked Ivan Aleksandrovich to be extremely cautious about political matters. We referred to the Soviet government by the coded term the "Vatican." "Our Vatican," the old teacher would say with dismay, "never changes. Do you think that they will let us breathe a little after the war?" Like all other Russians, Kuznetsov did not doubt that they would defeat Hitler. The question "Will the Vatican hold its own?" related exclusively to the dictatorial domestic regime. I comforted him, saying that after the war many things would change for the better. Ivan Aleksandrovich, however, was not given to illusions. "It's unlikely that we shall survive," he said, "and it is hard to believe when you look at our porcupines. . . ." I looked at him reproachfully, and he corrected himself: "Excuse me, I meant to say 'Vatican.'"

I tried to encourage him and sketched a marvelous picture. The war has ended. Democracy won. Peoples and kingdoms return to their borders. Having liberated Poles, Lithuanians, Latvians, Estonians, Romanians, French, and others, the Red Army gloriously returns to its borders without desiring to keep any foreign lands. Peoples of the entire world are grateful. The Soviet Union opens a new era of peace in international relations. Now, Soviet citizens, particularly senior citizens such as Ivan Aleksandrovich, will be able to travel abroad. I invite Ivan Aleksandrovich to visit me in Palestine. "But where will I get the money from?" he asks me fearfully and distrustfully. "You have to travel by sea and pass through Constantinople and Greece—that is a pile of money!" But with a wave of the hand, I dismissed this obstacle as insignificant and promised to send him a ticket and money for the journey. At that point, the old man gave in and was moved, and I depicted heaven on earth for him: Jerusalem and Bethlehem and orange groves in the coastal valleys.

From there we would proceed to discussions of gastronomic and other everyday topics. Ivan Aleksandrovich, for example, asked me, "What is schnitzel?" He knew about this dish only from books. This did not surprise me. The Soviet people with whom we lived in camp—and all the prisoners there were, of course, Soviet people, and it did not change matters that the

---

4. Dmitry Merezhkovsky (1865–1941) was a Russian poet, novelist, literary critic, and religious thinker of the Silver Age of Russian literature. Like numerous other intellectuals who did not accept the Bolshevik Revolution, he immigrated to France in 1921.

police disqualified them—were all interested not in Western democratic free-doms or political ideas but in how much people in the West earn, how they dress, and what they eat. I had to tell Ivan Aleksandrovich how the table was set in the morning, what we prepared for breakfast, what we ate for dinner, and my former modest existence in a three-room city apartment turned into a magic epic. Milk that appeared by the door in the morning, a telephone call that arranged the delivery of goods from the grocery store in the same building to our kitchen—without standing in line—or the miracle of a gas heater in the bathroom were things that my interlocutor heard with excitement and a sigh: "If I could live that way at least for a month." Ivan Aleksandrovich and I got to the point where we yearned, like children, not for better times "when people, having forgotten their quarrels would unite in a great family," but very simply for the warm bathroom off the corridor where the walls are tiled, and on the side hangs that funny roll of paper with a little mirror. Hearing about the mirror, Ivan Aleksandrovich laughed heartily, opening his toothless mouth, and his face strangely resembled a camel's. Outsiders, of course, were not privy to these secret conversations.

With outsiders, we were never sure where a conversation would lead. When I told the Leningrad cook Ivanov, a serious and solid person, that abroad, after dinner they serve coffee, liqueur, and cheese, the cook suddenly became very angry. "Cheese!" he said huffily, "Cheese? What do you take me for—a fool?" Ivan Aleksandrovich, in contrast, trusted me completely and listened avidly, no matter what I was saying.

If, however, during our conversation—whether about Gnosticism or schnitzel—word went through the barrack that they were handing out extra food under the kitchen window, Ivan Aleksandrovich immediately would stop listening, interrupt the conversation in the middle of a word, hastily mutter "Excuse me, I now . . ." and rush off the bunk. Words could not compete with soup. He, of course, would forego without hesitating all our conversations and the wisdom of centuries, our friendship and cordiality, for a bowl of soup. There was no comparison. I once asked Ivan Aleksandrovich to get my break-fast for me before he went to work. This was a common practice: neighbors would take turns standing in line to receive meals for two so that both would not have to stand outside in the cold. Ivan Aleksandrovich willingly took my mess-tin and food ticket and stood on line. Alas! He could not withstand the temptation. On the way he allegedly "slipped" and poured out half of my soup. All the thick part spilled and only the watery liquid remained. I was taken aback, but I did not get angry: we were in a camp. I did not entrust him to get soup for me again.

Here is Maria Frantsevna leaving the kitchen window. She is a Russian-German, an old woman with a handsome, severe face that inspires respect, an intelligent, highly cultured individual. At liberty she has grandchildren, and she had a lovely, good life. It is a pleasure to speak with her, and we all are very respectful of Maria Frantsevna. She lives in the infirmary, where she cleans and helps with housekeeping, serving the women doctors who "support" her. Now she is carrying mess tins with the midday meal to those doctors. She is carrying them carefully, with a short, elderly gait so as not to spill anything. She has turned the corner of the barrack, but she does not know that I am watching her. She stops and takes out a wooden spoon. Fearfully looking around, she takes the cover off someone else's tin . . . and I turn away so as not to see. Poor old granny! Hunger is stronger than human dignity. Not she, but the people who brought her to such a condition ought to be ashamed.

Camp gluttony takes a very specific form; when the body is broken, food provides the sole sexual pleasure. Hunger quickly brought us to a state in which we artificially began to drag out the process of eating. Normally one could eat in five minutes. We would eat for an hour or two. We put the tins on coals in the barrack stove (what a line and crush in front of the stove!) and then would take out the burning red tin with a glove and bring it to the table in the middle of the barrack. Everything was mixed together in the tin: a liter of camp gruel, a ladleful of kasha, a "hint" of meat or piece of fish. We would crumble a piece of bread into it, which would yield a thick white concoction. If there was an anti-scurvy addition in the form of 200 grams of some vegetable (turnip or cabbage) seasoned with vegetable oil, that went in, too, and still it was insufficient. We would pour in water until the two-liter pot was full.

You had to see how Ivan Aleksandrovich approached this sacred act centered on the pot. At that moment, his face was not that of a normal person: it was diffused with a focused, dim fire; it trembled from painful agitation. He would try to extend the enjoyment of food as long as possible. He did not eat but played with the food; he would stroke the surface of the brew with a spoon, take out pieces with the spoon and drop them back in, take a spoonful and pour out half so as not to eat it all at once and return too quickly to the hopelessly hungry condition in which we remain in the intervals between one meal and the next. He was simply reluctant to destroy this wealth; his hands trembled. It was hard to look at this elderly lasciviousness, the moist, sensuous lips, the eyes shrouded with a senseless fog. Now one must not talk to him! He did not hear, did not answer, and got angry that he was being distracted at such a time. As the pot began to empty out, he clearly began to yearn and lament . . . now it is already finishing. Having eaten, he still could not calm down; he would pour hot water into the tin and crush the last bread crumb into it and then sit for a while, overwhelmed, with a look of sorrowful astonishment on his thin, bony face.

I needed Ivan Aleksandrovich. In his welcoming and cordial old-mannish company, I would rest, recall the old days and, exploiting his mildness, I would even turn into a tyrant, order him around, and impose my thoughts and attitudes on him. As I said, we were two peas in a pod. Naturally, therefore, in the *selkhoz* where we met in a brigade in the spring, we began to work together, hauling stretchers with soil to dump into the ditches in the greenhouses. It was placid work; we shuffled in the mud and the earth fell off the flat stretchers. We would take turns loading: five stretchers each. Having carried twenty stretchers, we would sit down to rest, choosing a corner where the bosses could not see us. We thus lived peacefully, until we quarreled.

It happened in the following way: I would not eat all my bread at once but divided it into two parts. I would hide the main, evening part in a little chest on the bunk by my head. The chest did not have a lock, but I wrapped string around it so no one could open it quickly. At some point, I noticed that my portion of bread strangely changed shape from morning to evening. In the morning, it looked rather square, weighing, as it was supposed to, 300 grams, but in the evening when I ate it, it seemed oddly light, dry, and thinner. I simply did not recognize it. It was difficult to suspect Ivan Aleksandrovich of stealing part of my bread, particularly because his bunk was one away from mine. Ultimately, a neighbor informed me what Ivan Aleksandrovich was doing in my absence: with a deft hand he would take my bread ration and neatly cut off a piece with a knife, not a very thick one so that it would not be noticeable.

I was deeply offended by Ivan Aleksandrovich, but I kept putting off a confrontation with him until a most unpleasant incident happened: Ivan Aleksandrovich could not restrain himself, and he ate my whole bread ration.

You have to understand: first he cut a thin piece from the top. He ate it, lying on his side, in the semi-darkness of the upper bunk. He ate with pangs of conscience and a heavy heart. Then he gathered up the crumbs on the pillow. In the meantime, the bread is lying there and Ivan Aleksandrovich sees clearly that he was too noble and had cut a small piece; it is possible to cut off a little more. He cuts off another piece, and, oh, horrors! This time he cut off too much. You can't help noticing it. Now inevitably Margolin will make a fuss: "who touched my bread ration?" Saliva gathers in the mouth of the sinner, and suddenly, he does not care: just eat what remains, come what may! As the saying goes, if you sin seven times, you'll be punished just once. In any case, the ration is deformed. One dizzying moment, one movement of the hand and—a jump into the abyss, come what may. Every gram of extra bread acquired illegally, in addition to the eternal hunger ration, is doubly tasty. How good it is: an entire 300 grams! Not simply good, but as Ivan Aleksandrovich says, "plea-sant!"

The next day at work, when we had carried the fifteenth stretcher, I growled to my companion's back: "Ivan Aleksandrovich, admit it; did you eat the bread?" Ivan Aleksandrovich shrugged his shoulders and walked faster. We carried the stretchers, turned them over into the ditch, and I saw his guilty, confused face. Not bothering with reproach (it is, after all, a regular camp matter), I demanded that he pay me back the stolen bread. He knew how to steal—learn to give it back. And the schedule: one hundred grams a day.

I was unreasonably cruel. As if Ivan Aleksandrovich was able, with his own hand, to give over part of his starvation ration. It would have been easier for him to cut off a piece of his body. The next day he received a large shock troop ration of 700 grams. He ate it immediately, as soon as he received it, from fear that I would come to claim my debt. . . .

On the third day, I waited until he sat down at the table above his steaming mess tin; the bread ration lay in front of him like the cake of Easter Sunday. I was boiling with anger. I was ready to devour him.

"Ivan Aleksandrovich! Will you hand over the bread?"

He turned pale, but he said resolutely and conclusively: "No way! I can't hand over the bread . . . not at all. . . ."

Without much hesitation, I took the bread, but he immediately grabbed it back and held on firmly. We began to tear the bread from each other's hands. Everyone crowded around, laughing, but they did not interfere. Let the friends fight! I felt that this unfortunate ration was turning into a formless mush, crumbling, and disappearing in our hands, but Ivan Aleksandrovich, with a frenzied look, silently latched onto it with all ten fingers. Suddenly I felt his dumb despair and let go of the bread. I was beside myself with anger, and I shamed him in front of the entire barrack—I called him a thief and other derogatory words, even Judas Golovliev.[5]

That was the end of our friendship. I stopped looking at him or speaking to him. I was insulted not because he ate my bread but because of his subsequent behavior, his unwillingness to settle accounts with me. I would have

5. Traitorous figure in the novel *The Golovliev Family* by Mikhail Saltykov-Shchedrin, published in 1880. The name carries associations with Judas of the New Testament.

been less strict with poor Ivan Aleksandrovich had I known that he was already dying; he had reached that extreme state when people cannot control themselves at the sight of bread, but I thought only of myself.

I, too, was becoming savage at that time, declining both physically and morally. Later I was lucky that they transferred me to live in the barrack of the administrative and technical personnel (ATP), among camp aristocracy. In the winter, Ivan Aleksandrovich again began to speak to me, offered to make up, and, gradually, we again became close.

Sometimes, he would drop in the ATP barrack in the evening. In comparison to the workers' barracks, this barrack seemed like the residence of the gods. The orderly would shout roughly from the threshold: "Where do you think you're going?" The old man would point timidly in my direction and make his way to my bunk, by the stove in a corner. He would stand, holding on to a post, and look up, while I would look down, bending my head and speaking with him. It was already too difficult for me to get down from the upper bunk for a guest. We both had become terribly weak. Ivan Aleksandrovich had become very pinched and gray; he looked like a bobtailed hare. Everyone snorted at him and at me, too—why did all kinds of riff-raff crawl to me, in dirty bast shoes and rags?

In January 1943, Kuznetsov refused to go to work. He had reached the end of his rope. They kept him in the punishment cell for three days; then they looked more closely and put him in the hospital. There, finally, he was deactivated, that is, they officially acknowledged he was not fit to work. After leaving the hospital, he lay on the bunk with his invalid's ration of 400 grams, which was not enough to live on; he stopped getting up—enjoyed his "rest." For ten days he lay there, resting so radically that he even stopped getting up for food. His neighbors brought him bread and soup and then informed the medical sector. They again put him in the infirmary, which he was not destined to leave alive.

An extra ladle of kasha and piece of bread would have sustained him, but if the Soviet state fed prisoners according to the prisoners' needs and not according to the state's calculations, it would go bankrupt; it would have to release millions of zeks. In order to enable the existence of the Soviet Union, the Moskva Hotel, the most luxurious metro in the world, the Palace of the Soviets, and the most enormous army of forced labor in history, Ivan Aleksandrovich Kuznetsov, in the sixth year of his stay in camp, thus had to die silently and discreetly, from depletion caused by lengthy malnutrition. At that time, I was lying in the neighboring infirmary, in a state very close to that of Kuznetsov before his death. When I left the infirmary and learned of his death, I recalled that I had written down his address: Ryazan *oblast*, Lebedyan region, such and such *selsoviet*. I wanted to write to his family, but I was told that such notices are not permitted. A camp is not an active army, from which reports of losses arrive at private addresses. The lists of those who die in camps are not published, and statistics on this matter constitute a state secret.

They brought Kuznetsov to "72." That was the name of the camp cemetery at Square 72, 2 or 3 kilometers from Kruglitsa. We did not say, "You will croak," but "You will go to '72.'" On one autumn day, I do not remember which year, I also wound up at "72."

It was necessary to dig a grave in a hurry for several people. At the dispatch for work, the commandant selected a squad of four but did not say for what purpose; he just promised "easy work" for two hours. We then sat for another hour on the rampart by the guardhouse. Then the commandant's assistant arrived, tossed a spade to each of us, and we started walking, but he led us in the opposite direction from the place where the prisoners usually worked. We walked without a guard. We barely managed to keep up with him on the melting forest road. In some places it was flooded with water; in others, he jumped across wide ditches, but we were no longer able to jump as the healthy commandant's aide could. By the time we arrived, we were soaked and exhausted.

The dreary gray rain fell on the clearing, which was surrounded by trembling aspens and damp birches, and in the middle was yellow, slippery mud. This was Square 72, the place of eternal rest. In one corner, he ordered us to dig a pit to the depth of a meter. He stood briefly, rolled a cigarette from newspaper, and left. We remained alone.

The earth around us was grooved, but there were no mounds, crosses, or markers. Here and there some crooked sticks, carelessly pressed into the ground, stuck out. Onto the sticks were affixed little wooden signboards with numbers written in chemical ink. That was all that remained of the deceased: an anonymous grave with a number for the use of the camp administration. Several sticks stuck out from the ground; the others had fallen onto the earth and drowned in the mud along with the signboards and numbers. At Kruglitsa there was only one coffin for transporting the bodies. The corpses were buried nude, several in one grave, and the coffin was brought back. One grave overlapped with another, and after some time, the bones mixed together fraternally.

The thought that I, too, would lie here—and no one would ever know about the location or circumstances of my death—struck me with clarity. Of the four zeks who were digging the grave, by the end of the year, three were laid in that ground. As we were digging, the pit filled up with water. The spades were inadequate for the task; the soil was too hard. We took turns, digging two at a time. I could barely stand on my feet. After several minutes of work, my heart would stop. We who were digging were half-dead, and it was hard for me to believe that I was digging someone else's grave and not the other way round. I recalled those healthy, strapping people who had been buried here over the past months, and I failed to understand how I had survived them and was standing over their bones with a dull spade, shivering from cold, under a dreary autumnal rain, in shoes made from tires, so thickly covered with mud that I could not raise my feet.

The commandant's assistant arrived at four o'clock in the afternoon and spit, seeing that the work had not been finished. The grave was not ready. He watched for five minutes as we poked the ground with the spade and ordered us resolutely: "Get ready to go." After passing through the guardhouse, the assistant commandant conducted us to the infirmary to the doctor. At first, we did not understand what was happening. He asked the doctor for notes saying that we were physically unfit to dig graves. Either such a note or get sent to the punishment cell for not fulfilling a task.

Fortunately, the doctor on duty was Maxik. Seeing me in the role of grave-digger, he opened wide his bulging eyes under pale eyebrows. Then with an official look, he examined all four "refusers." For two, he wrote the necessary note. I and one more were released to the barrack. Two others were sent to the punishment cell. Were it not for Maxik's intervention, I would not have gotten off so easily from this work.

25

A Letter to Ilya Ehrenburg

IN THE SPRING of 1942, the Kruglitsa camp faced hunger depletion. That year for the first time we heard the words "alimentary dystrophy."

They gradually cut our rations. Our strength declined steadily and irreversibly. Even the hospital food became insufficient. The camp's gradated dietary system became meaningless as the mass of prisoners fell into two basic groups—those who still worked somewhat and those who merely pretended that they were working, and there was a minimal difference in the food allotted to the two categories. Whoever performed particularly heavy work received microscopic additions in the form of "supplementary," "reinforced," "restorative," and other rations. This nomenclature was a fancy term for a ladle of liquid kasha or a carrot bun or a potato pancake, items that any of us could have eaten in the dozens with no difficulty. Food thus annoyed us more than it sated us. We fell into apathy, a sleepy stupor, like flies in autumn. I was constantly sleepy. When I was not working, I lay down and spent entire hours motionless. During that time, I did not want to eat. I could remain without food for an entire day, and several additional hours of waiting made no difference. When I finally received my portion, my hunger would awaken, and after eating, I was considerably hungrier than I had been in anticipation of food. The first half hour after receiving food was torturous. I was very irritable, and only later would I fall imperceptibly into my earlier state of apathy from which the food had awakened me.

We were willing to eat anything at all. Sometimes, inexplicably, the kitchen handed out mustard. Although they distributed it late in the evening, after supper, when everyone had already eaten the last crumb of bread, everyone ran excitedly to the kitchen window. Whoever did not have a dish, would put out a finger, onto which the cook would smear the mustard, and everyone ate it as if a gift from heaven. We ate black bread that was so damp it stuck to one's hand, bread with bran siftings and straw, bread mixed with corn flour, which, when it dried, fell apart. Only two years later did American flour and American egg powder arrive in the camps of Arkhangelsk *oblast*. By that time, however, our ranks had thinned significantly: the camp population was dying, and in those years, there were no new zeks.

The latter circumstance inspired hope. It seemed as if the camps were in a state of natural liquidation. The population decreased before our eyes, and we gradually grew accustomed to the reassuring thought that as a result of the war and rapprochement with Western democracy, the Soviet regime gradually would abandon this infamous and shameful form of contemporary slavery.

Around me, zeks were falling like mown grass. The regime, which was unable to keep them alive in camp, blocked their way to freedom, to conditions under which each would be able to struggle for his life. Many of them had left family and children without help and were tormented more by the thought of those dear ones than about themselves. At that time, the camps were not an economically feasible proposition. The vast majority of them consisted of pseudo-workers, goners, and camp service workers; the nonproductive elements included not only zeks but also free workers employed in guarding and administration: they did not pay their way and weighed like dead ballast on the camp economy. Maintaining an army of millions of goners was clearly unprofitable. The regime kept them imprisoned from fear, for considerations of state security. The state needed them to die off more than they needed their "work." Able-bodied zeks yielded only a fraction of the benefit that they could supply as free men. This was especially evident with regard to highly qualified specialists: engineers, doctors, teachers and professors, economists and managers. These valuable, exceptional people, trampled into the camp mud, either lost their human likeness or performed absurd, useless work that was incommensurate with their abilities.

From pottery production, I was sent to the barnyard. They did not permit me to tend the cows or pigs. At that work, I would have been able to get additional food, as the cows were milked, and the pigs and piglets received potatoes and oats with milk—that is, they were fed well enough for the workers to grab something for themselves. But we had no access to the pigsty—like the beggars whom the doorkeeper drives away from the rich man's door. We worked in an unlit, half-empty cowshed, in whose cold, deserted corner stood a forage cutter, a machine that cut forage from the twig clusters that I had gathered the previous fall.

In the morning, they would bring us several loads of these twigs. One person would put the twigs in the machine and the second turned the wheel.

The forage cutter worked on horsepower but there was no horse. Instead of a horse they utilized a writer, seized beyond the borders of the Soviet Union on the territory of another state and forced into slavery by the right of the victor as a "socially dangerous element."

This wheel, which was not designed for a man, was so large that when I turned the handle, it would either bend me toward the ground or thrust me into the air; I turned with this wheel and on the wheel. My eyes dimmed and I was short of breath. In order not to despair, I counted the turns: fifty to one hundred, and I watched my coworker, who turned the same wheel by a handle on the other side. I would press the handle down and immediately let go—the wheel would turn half way around—and then my coworker would press on the other side. This dance of the wheel continued until the rhythm was broken and one of us would slow down. Then we abandoned the wheel and sat down for a minute.

My coworker Zhukov was a jowly, hard-working fellow from Siberia, from a family of Old Believers.[1] At first, he was very hostile toward me and showered me with antisemitic curses. I responded instantly by threatening to go to the security officer: "One term isn't enough? You'll get another!" He calmed down immediately, and by the next day we were friends. Zhukov told me about Siberian customs and their way of life, about his grandfather, who ruled absolutely over a family of twenty-eight people including adult and married children. Before the establishment of *kolkhozes*, Siberian peasants raised cattle; they had hundreds of horses on their farms; now an entire *kolkhoz* possessed no more horses than his grandfather alone once had. He told me that they did not know how to make sausage—"that's a German thing"—and they do not want to know; they simply pickle the pig for future use. The venerable Old Believer was engraved in the grandson's memory as the embodiment of moral authority. Zhukov the grandson rarely cursed—he was trained not to do this in childhood—and he told me how the old man would curse when he was angry: "Oh you, chicken, you wet frog!"—instead of real obscenities. I immediately adopted this Siberian idiom and remembered it; when I saw Zhukov a year later, I shouted to him in a friendly way: "Hey you, flying chicken! Wet frog!!" Zhukov immediately lit up from those words and smiled broadly.

It was cold and dark in the morning in the cowshed. At the far end, behind a partition was a little stove. We would go furtively to the yard when it

---

1. Dissident group within the Russian Orthodox Church that did not accept the reforms introduced by the Moscow Patriarch Nikon in the mid-seventeenth century.

was still dark, to steal, wherever possible, some boards or a log. I staggered like a drunk under the burden of the log and had difficulty moving my legs. We quickly sawed the wood with a borrowed saw and finally lit a little fire in the stove.

During the work break, my coworkers would disappear somewhere in search of food. In the cowshed it smelled of manure and rotten hay; the thin cows stood placidly in the stalls (on the silage diet they gave no more than three to four liters of milk a day). The pale zek cow-maid would pass by; with a kerchief on her head, she resembled a nun. I did not want to go anywhere, but after a few days, hunger drove me outside. At the end of the yard was a low shed. Toward evening we brought a vat with the silage chaff on a sled to the shed and placed it in a large vat on a fire. In addition, a small tank with hot water was embedded in a slab. In the corner of this hut, we discovered a barrel where the pig keepers would pour the dregs of the pig feed—a rotten liquid mass of spoiled potatoes that gave off an unbearable odor of a garbage pit. From this barrel of refuse, my coworkers would collect the rotten scraps of potatoes—a mess-tin full. With endless patience they would wash each shred several times in hot water, cut out the darkened mush, and obtain a tiny healthy vestige the size of a thimble. This work would take an hour, during which time the wheel stood still, abandoned by everyone.

At first, I watched these manipulations at a fastidious distance, but when the time for the midday meal arrived, I drank only hot water while they each had a mess tin of potatoes on the stove, and it did not smell like a garbage dump but smelled like any healthy potato, or almost like one. The water in which it was cooked became brownish, and the potato crackled in the teeth, but they ate it! Not one of them thought for a minute to give me a taste; my heart skipped a beat and I suffered from this sight and smell. On the third day, I made up my mind and joined them. I, too, stuck my hand into the rotten swill in the garbage barrel because now I knew what a treasure resided there. In truth, I lacked the ability to select enough for a full tin, but when the time came for the meal, I had a full mug of potato scraps, and that was enough for me. It was not just a matter of calories but also of the psychological effect: I was not an exception and I, too, was able to obtain food when we were not given any.

We would extract food literally from underground. For entire days we would dig in the canal by the outhouse and would retrieve something that I would have taken for dried excrement but that turned out to be a clump of potato starch, the remains of a potato that had frozen and been thrown away months ago. Like hungry dogs we would sniff the air all day, carefully watching the kitchen where they cooked food for the calves and piglets. Finally, one of us broke in and grabbed something. They punished us by transferring us from the barnyard to the oil depot.

There was nothing edible in the oil depot. We unloaded heavy storage tanks from flatbeds, transferred fuel and machine oil from some storage tanks into others. We saw inscriptions of American companies on the tanks: it was foreign oil. The English inscription was like a greeting from the West, a reminder that not everything was lost for us. I looked at it with excitement, like Robinson Crusoe who finds a trace left by cultured people on an uninhabited island. Within several days, my jacket became saturated with machine oil and fuel and remained that way for many months.

Then came the time for peeling off bark. With an axe and knife, we would strip the bark from the tree trunk until it was glossy white, and the sticky wood liquid flowed into our hands. At this time, the first sun shone on us, the streams were running under our feet, and it smelled of wood. Twice a day a little motorized car would run along the track carrying the bosses from Ertsevo, who rode around, checking on the work. We would calculate the time on the basis of the train's passage. At eight o'clock in the morning, the train passed in one direction and at five o'clock it returned—an old locomotive and two antediluvian cars from tsarist times. Prisoners worked on both sides of the railroad, building a large warehouse and laying down a wooden access road to it.

In May the first green grass broke through and everyone rushed to gather it. Along with us, kids from the settlement of free workers would look for saltbush and nettle. We saw that those at liberty were no more sated than the people in camp. I knew from my reading that in times of famine people eat saltbush. Now I learned to identify its fresh green leaves. Russians taught me that young nettle is a substitute for spinach and sorrel. Incidentally, few of them had even heard about spinach (except for the Ukrainians). I, however, had never heard of a plant called *ivan-chai*. They tried to make soup from that for the zeks, but even those dying of hunger could not swallow that bitter, nauseating infusion, and on the days when they cooked it, more than half remained in the cauldrons in the kitchen.

Some zeks did not acknowledge a difference between edible and inedible grass. In their opinion, any May grass was suitable food. "Whatever a cow can eat, so can I," said Stetsin, a tall, thin blonde with sunken blue eyes who had been a photographer at liberty. He was wrong, and he ended his days before the end of the year. People would sit everywhere by bonfires, busy cooking. They would gather a heap of grass, cut it finely with a small knife, add water from the stream and cook the grass for a long time, boiling, adding water, and mixing. They did not have any salt to flavor this tasteless, unsavory grassy mass, let alone other spices. Once I tasted this concoction. It made me nauseous. Evidently, I was not yet sufficiently hungry. Some would bring along their breakfast—the camp gruel—and mix in the grass to increase the volume. They thus filled their stomachs and deceived themselves. The medical sector intervened and forbade cooking grass. The guards and brigade leaders began to turn over tins and pour out the contents. Scrawny, ghastly people would cook the grass in secret, hiding from the administrators; every day fights would break out when the authorities tried to take away a mess tin with grass. They thus did not succeed in weaning them from scavenged food. Only summer, friend of the hungry, with berries and mushrooms, brought relief. Of course, we prisoners were able to utilize the forest wealth only to a small degree—illegally and occasionally.

People from the BBK camp region arrived at the medical settlement in the spring—the last group evacuated from the Medvezhegorsk district. Acquaintances from Square 48 who arrived in the *etap* told me about winter in those areas. Medvezhegorsk and Petrozavodsk were occupied by the Finns, and there were casualties among the camp population from aerial bombardments. Starvation decimated the *etaps* that left in the winter and spring. My interlocutor, Ukrainian Jew G., told me that on the way, his group was cut off from supplies and wound up in a cul de sac for several weeks. They gave them 100 grams of bread daily, then 50. Potatoes were only for the guards; instead of soup, the zeks on the *etap* received salted water in which the potatoes for the free workers had been boiled. About thirty people died every day from cold and starvation. Very few survived. G. described the following scene: a guard shot into the bushes and came out laughing: "Go, I killed a hare." G. ran into the bushes and saw the carcass of a dog with a crushed head. "I ran up first," he related, "and I managed to suck out the brain before the others arrived. . . ."

From G. I learned a recipe for preparing rawhide straps. On their way, the zeks on *etap* ate all the leather belts and boot tops. G. convinced me that a strap cut into small pieces and cooked well did not differ in taste from goose cracklings. This person, with whom I spent several days in the Kruglitsa infirmary, had been in the Red Army that invaded western Ukraine in 1939. From him I learned of the Red Army soldiers' impressions from their first contact with the West. These stories were particularly instructive for me: they revealed clearly that the Soviet people with whom we had conversed at the time of the invasion were lying to us and concealing their true feelings. They lied not only to us but also in reports and journalists' travel notes, which described the poverty and neglect of the population in "Pans' Poland,"[2] as if it were a region that was two hundred years behind the Soviet Union, whereas in reality they were struck by the well-being, low cost, and variety of life in that country, and they consciously tried to hide from us what was happening in their own terrible country. Here in camp, we finally were able to speak openly. When I told this Ukrainian Jew about Palestine, tears appeared in his eyes: would the time ever come when the hand grasping us by the throat would be unclenched?

The moment came when everything ended together: my strength, hopes, energy; my last possessions wore out, the old footwear fell off my feet, and my last shirt was stolen. At that time, they ordered me to live in Barrack 9, which then was a den of thieves and where *etaps* passing through Kruglitsa would spend the night. A group of zeks that are brought to spend the night and know that they will be sent away in a day or two fly into an area like a swarm of locusts and seize and pilfer whatever they get their hands on, figuring that there will be no one to question the next day. On entering such a barrack, you look for someone to attach yourself to: some pleasant face, an older person inspiring trust. This time, too, I chose "good neighbors," but in the evening they disappeared: one was sent on an *etap* and the other to the hospital. In their place, on one side lay the swarthy thief Yashka, who had been beaten many times for stealing, and on the other side was a fellow with such a bestial mug and Tatar slits of eyes that I felt a chill just looking at him. I raced to the commandant's assistant, the zek Pavlov: "Save me, take me to a decent barrack! These people will strip me!" But in response Pavlov merely sniffed my oil-soaked jacket, looked at my rags and smirked. That meant: "Where could I put you in such a condition?"

When I woke up the next morning at reveille, I saw that the job had been done: my green wooden chest had been removed from under my head, turned over, and was lying on the floor between the bunks, but the main thing was that my sole treasure, my bread ration, was gone. I was less upset by the loss of all my "property" than by the absence of my bread at the moment when I extended my hand toward them. Which one of them took my bread—Yashka the thief or the Tatar? First, I had to run to the commandant Pavlov to report the loss of my things. Descending from the upper bunk in the midst of the clamor and bustle, among the noisy people busy with their own affairs, I suddenly saw a fresh ration, 300 grams of bread, in the place of the fellow with the

---

2. Derogatory reference implying Poland was still a country under the thumb of landlords from the nobility.

bestial mug. They all had their own bread, untouched; only I was supposed to starve? Without thinking for a second, I climbed down from the bunk and put my enemy's bread ration in my pocket. On my way to the commandant's office, I ran into some dark corner and quickly ate those 300 grams. I ate triumphantly, with the feeling of a person who had the last word.

Upon returning to the barrack, I witnessed a fight: two bodies were rolling on my bunk, and the fellow with the bestial mug was pummeling Yashka the thief: "Where is my bread? Give it to me this minute!" "I didn't take it; I didn't take your bread!" howled Yashka plaintively. He was right, but it was difficult for him to prove his innocence when his two adjacent neighbors had been robbed. I do not know which of those two clinging to each other in a fierce fight stole from me. I did not care; both were punished: one lost 300 grams of bread and the other was beaten. With gloomy satisfaction and without the least pangs of conscience, I watched the fight.

Glancing around me, I saw a world in comparison with which Gorky's play *The Lower Depths* and his essay "Former People" were cloying and literarily coquettish. Those people about whom Gorky wrote—like the young author himself—were so in love with themselves and so full of their own singularity and picturesqueness! Here in the camp only unbounded humiliation and demoralization prevailed; here people did not play at ostentatious rebellion, did not dare to consider themselves protesters, did not dare to pose as some Sledgehammer or baron.[3] The Soviet regime had taught them to lick their plates: when the meager meal was over in the barrack, the majority of zeks licked their bowls clean, like dogs, while others would use the side of their index finger to clean the bowl carefully and then would lick their finger; this was considered "more cultured."

I was not a hero or an exception. I, too, like those around me, cleaned the bowl with my finger. My misfortune, however, was crueler, more absurd and senseless, because I knew another life; I was a stranger who had arrived from the West, about which these people had no clue. Their families and past had been destroyed, they had nothing left, just charred ruins; they had nothing to lament about! Falling asleep hungry every evening on my bunk, with the penetrating electric bulb above that burned all night in the Kruglitsa barracks, I would close my eyes and could not help thinking about what was happening at home at the very same hour.

---

3. Sledgehammer and Baron (nicknames)—homeless tramps in Gorky's play.

Nine o'clock Moscow time. That means seven o'clock Warsaw time and eight o'clock in Tel Aviv. The street leading to the sea. The round table is set in the dining room. Everything is in place. Family members and friends are sitting at the table. In Palestine there is no war; people and things look the same as they did when I had not disappeared from that world. How beautifully the table is set! A snowy white tablecloth and butter in the form of rose petals. I don't need butter. If only I could enter quietly, invisible to all, and behind the shoulder of the woman who is waiting for me, extend my hand and take one single piece of bread from the plate. One piece of bread! I am dying of hunger at forced labor, in hell, and no one in the world knows about it!

For what? Were I in the hands of the Nazis, I would know it is because I am a Jew. What right did the Moscow regime have to take away from me the best creative years of my life, deprive me of my personality, trample and torture me, turn me into a slave, drive my family to need and despair, put an end to my writing? Indeed, I was not even their person, not a Soviet citizen, but only a captive, from whom they could not demand Soviet patriotism or enthusiasm or a Soviet passport or a desire to remain in their country. Yet they sent me as if I were a criminal to a "corrective labor" camp because I did not have a Soviet passport and wanted to return home!

If I had fallen into the hands of Chinese bandits or black *niam-niam*,"[4] I would have had hope of being ransomed for money, but I was in the hands of a great power that no one dared challenge, which had established ten thousand camps and let people rot there secretly, in the deepest secrecy from the entire world! I choked from the monstrous implausibility, the nightmarish absurdity, the inhuman infamy of what happened to me and millions like me. I foresaw that it was too terrible for anyone in the world to believe afterward what had happened. It was too distant from them, from the well-off Americans and innocent Swiss, from democrats of all classes, peoples and parties who decided lightheadedly that fascism and Hitler were the sole cause of all misfortunes in the world.

It was not permitted to pose the question "What for?" That question already contained a challenge to a terrible force, acknowledgment of one's right, one's particular value and equality vis-à-vis the state. This regime dealt with us without any superfluous conversations, without explaining their real motives, and without looking us in the face. The stone crushed into gravel over which a heavy steamroller passes can no longer ask "what for?" We were no longer

---

4. Name used earlier by foreigners to refer to the Azande people of North Central Africa.

people with an individual appearance or special fate. We were ciphers in a mass, one like the other, and all together—a petrified, ice-covered surface over which the Soviet tank trod, over heads and necks, backs, bodies: human beings crushed into gravel.

Millions of people perish in Soviet camps. They are too numerous for the question "what for?" So many guilty people do not exist in the entire world. But the question still remains: for what purpose? Why does the Soviet state have a system that splits the population of the country into two categories and creates an invisible Russia, like a terrible cellar to which, aside from the victims, only the initiated participants, "their own" people, have the right of entry.

For what purpose?

If this cellar is needed to isolate and destroy the dissatisfied or the potential opponents among their own population, then what mistake, what mental eclipse induced the Politburo to send half a million Polish citizens there in 1940? What was their calculation? That they would all die there? Or that they would leave as friends of the Soviet regime? These people, after all, had several million relatives in Poland and the rest of the world—fathers, mothers, wives, children, brothers, sisters who could not forget or renounce them and who to the end of their days would not stop trying to obtain from the Soviet government an answer to the question "What did you do with them?"

No doubt, when the Soviet government sent hundreds of thousands of Polish citizens to labor camps in the summer of 1940, they did not expect Poland would ever re-emerge as an independent polity. They did not give a damn not only about us or our relatives but also about the rest of the Polish people. Who could hold them responsible? Poland had been divided between Russia and Germany, and there was no one to demand an answer for the infamy of the camps. They were mistaken: a year later the situation changed radically, and they had to declare an "amnesty" for Polish zeks. The camps were no longer a secret to the rest of the world. When the Poles returned and began to tell about their experiences, however, people said: "They're fascists; don't listen to them." It is true that many Poles who were imprisoned in the camps fell under fascist influence. In other circumstances, they would have become friends of Russia. In these conditions, however, they took out from the camps not only a deadly hatred of the Soviet regime but also a crude and criminal chauvinism, about which I, as a Polish Jew, have some notion.

In Russia, they know the real feelings of Poles toward the Soviet Union. The martyrology of Polish citizens in the Soviet Union during the war years, which started with Stalin and Hitler's division of Poland in September 1939,

thus buttressed the Soviet Union's need to strengthen by any means its control over Poland. In the summer of 1942, we Polish citizens in the camps
learned of a new conflict between Poles and Russians, and we understood
that we would not be freed until that conflict was settled. We also understood
that it could be settled only if a Poland would be created where it would be
taboo to criticize the Soviet Union. Of all the countries in the world, it is in
Poland that the Soviet government can least tolerate the freedom to speak the
truth about the USSR; in Poland, the stones cry out about insult, violence,
and treachery—not only from the West but also from the East.

In the spring of 1942, the question of a shirt on my body became acute.
I had not had a shirt for three months. Everything had been stolen, and on
my bare body, I wore a torn jacket and above it the camp-issued duffle jacket
soaked in oil. In the spring, I had to get a shirt. I recalled the children's story
about an ill princess who was told that she would be cured should she don
the shirt of a happy person. They searched all over the kingdom for a happy
person and finally found one—a shepherd. They asked for his shirt, and it
turned out that this happy person did not have a shirt to his name. The moral
of the story is that one can grieve in the royal palace but be happy in a shack.
Money is not what matters. In the camp, however, I understood that the mere
lack of a shirt does not make a person happy.

In my semi-deranged state in the spring of 1942, a shirt became a turning
point. I think that if I had not succeeded in obtaining one, I would have gone
completely insane. I was on the brink of a mental breakdown. Everything focused on one point: obtaining a shirt. I suppose that this was a healthy approach. Had I continued to despair about things that I was unable to change,
I would have gone crazy. Instead, I focused all my fierce despair on the sole
matter that I did not have a shirt! How could I live without a shirt?

I utilized the sole weapon that I had in camp: the power of the word.
I wrote a petition to the head of the General Supply Unit Gordeeva. I brought
to her attention that I needed immediate help: I had been brought to total exhaustion; I did not have even a shirt on my back. How can I live? There is a
limit below which a person dares not descend!

Gordeeva was a woman with a very energetic, thin face of a schoolmarm,
completely gray hair (she was around forty years old), strict, serious, and
business-like, never smiling or uttering a superfluous word. She was a typical
bureaucrat. In the past, she had been the head of a camp sector. After listening
to me, she pondered: the petitioner looks like a scarecrow but he is a learned
person, a "doctor of philosophy" and a Westerner. He writes smoothly but it
is well known: the more educated a person is, the worse he works. And in the

entire camp there are only five new shirts, which are reserved for special cases. But what to do with a person who uses such strong words: "a limit below which a person dare not descend." She allotted me a new shirt.

The person in charge of the clothing warehouse could not believe his eyes: for whom is the shirt? But when Pavel Ivanovich, the inspector of the General Supply Unit, confirmed "Her Majesty's Order," they gave me a brand new, unworn shirt of thick weave with wooden buttons, long, the color of butter, clothing of the gods. I could exchange such a shirt at any time for bread. But I had no intention of selling it! I enveloped myself in it as in miraculous armor. In this shirt I could survive for another year in the camp.

Such was the power of the word! I decided to go further. I wrote a letter to Ilya Ehrenburg. Obviously, I did not count on Ilya Ehrenburg's receiving it. Even were he to receive it, this Soviet laureate and classic would not permit himself to answer letters coming from a camp! Soviet writers well know with whom they may or may not correspond. They are law abiding and cautious award winners. I did not pin any hopes whatsoever on Ehrenburg, with whom, in times long past, I had mutual acquaintances but who never knew me personally. With the aid of this letter, I wanted merely to reinforce my personal connection with Gordeeva, the head of the General Supply Unit.

This is my letter to Ehrenburg:

". . . I am not a Soviet citizen. We are united by literature. In my eyes you are an ambassador of Russian literature abroad, one of those people who represent the Soviet Union to public opinion in the West. You cannot remember me or those times when we met in the Berlin House of Culture and the Prager Diele café. I, however, know you well from your first poems:

> *In the clothing of a proud señor*
> *I waited my entry onto the stage,*
> *But because of the director's mistake*
> *I was five centuries late. . . .*[5]

"And I remember later on, when you energetically corrected the director's mistake—up to *The Fall of Paris*, the last of your works that I held in my hands.

"Now I need your immediate help. Fate brought me to the far north of Russia. The world is full of my friends, but I am cut off from them, and in the entire Soviet Union there is no other person to whom I could turn with such

---

5. As Margolin cited this text from memory, there are a few minor mistakes. The Jewish Soviet writer Ilya Ehrenburg (1901–1967) spent many years in Europe.

a request. Help me as one writer can help another. Send me several books (if possible, in English) and several words (if possible, friendly). Contact with you has great significance for me. If you are busy, let someone else answer. . . . "A quatrain of yours remains in my head (it seems, from 'Animal Warmth'):

I beg you, oh hatred, stand guard,
Among the stones and Rubenesque bodies.
Send to me, too, an unprecedented burden,
So that I would not want a second earth. . . .

"I repeat these lines frequently although my surroundings are very far from Rubens' and are more reminiscent of Goya's apparitions."

The original was a little different, and I took the word "hatred" out of the last quote in order not to bother the censor with the need to guess what kind of hatred and to whom, and why the unprecedented burden is sent. . . .

I brought this absurd letter, like that of the boy in Chekhov's story who sent a letter to "Grandpa in the village," to Gordeeva. First, I thanked her for the shirt and for her "humane sympathy" (how clever!), and second, I asked her advice: Look, I wrote a letter to Ehrenburg. What does she think—should I send it?

I wanted to break the wall that separated the administration from the zek, to win Gordeeva's interest, force her to see me as a person and not an imprisoned "unit of a labor force." I knew ordinary female psychology (curiosity, instinct of protective care, an interest in the obscure), but I did not know the psychology of a Soviet woman. The letter frightened Gordeeva, and her first move was to get as far away as possible from trouble. She did not offer me any advice; she grabbed the letter and, as soon as I left her office, brought it to Bogrov, head of the Division, which was then in Kruglitsa. Neither I nor she spoke to the other again about anything.

The next day I was summoned to Bogrov. The head of the Central Division (that is, the series of camps around Kruglitsa) took an interest in the strange letter and its author. The letter contained a clear "cry for help sent into space." Puffy-cheeked, heavy-set Bogrov dealt with me very kindly, sat me down, treated me from his tobacco pouch, and our three-hour conversation flew by like a minute. Bogrov, of course, had read Ehrenburg, but there were incomprehensible places in my letter that he asked me to explain. "What is Prager Diele? And who is Goya?" We talked as equals, as if I had come to pay him a visit. The conversation first dealt with Ehrenburg, then with how I had landed in a Soviet corrective labor camp, and finally about life in Europe and Poland. Our talk confirmed how little our administration knew about the circumstances that brought so many foreign "Westerners" into their charge. Genuine astonishment was reflected in Bogrov's eyes when he heard the story how they registered half a million refugees "for return" and then transported them in the opposite direction, to the camps. If Marxist theory asserts that the average person in the capitalist world is doomed to a fatal lack of understanding of the whole and that therefore the world seems to him irrational and beyond understanding, then here, sitting in front of me, was the *Massenmensch* [average man] of the Soviet system, who did not understand even what was happening under his nose.

Our conversation quickly meandered, and Bogrov began with naïve curiosity to ask me about totally extraneous matters. Before the war I had worked in a stock company—what was that? The clever mechanism of that capitalist institution simply captivated him. Thus, we wandered from topic to topic, completely forgetting where we were. Finally, Bogrov took control of himself. I asked about the letter. He hid it in his pocket. "Well, you know, in any case, they won't really send it." And he asked how I was doing. There was no need to ask: my looks, indeed, said everything. Bogrov consoled me: "It will be easier in the summer," and he sent me away, in an elevated mood. That was the end of my correspondence with Ehrenburg. I do not know whether it was a coincidence, but it seemed to me that after my conversation with Bogrov, the Kruglitsa administration's attitude toward me improved, and my work became lighter. There was, however, a follow up to this conversation, which I shall tell about later.

26

KVCh [Cultural-Educational Sector]

THE SMOOTH OPERATION of the camp depends on a half dozen people. The camp boss and the head of the armed guard are at the summit of the power pyramid. The latter is not subordinate to the camp boss; he commands a parallel structure, and often there are disputes and friction between them. The camp boss is the fully empowered master within the four walls of his camp, but the keys to the kingdom are given to someone else. The platoon commander is responsible for the guarding, and at any moment he can send a brigade of zeks back to the camp if it does not suit him to have them remain outside of it.

The camp boss has a series of subordinates: first, the work boss, whose job is to fulfill and surpass the work plan by exploiting the available work force to the limit. His function is to deliver the zeks to work every morning and to deliver concrete results to the state.

His activity, understandably, requires a counterweight. The head of the medical sector provides this. His job is to see that people maintain their ability to work and do not become sick and thus unprofitable for the state. The medical sector is not a humanitarian institution. No one in the camp engages in philanthropy or charity. Unlike the Christian teaching *res sacra miser* [the unfortunate is holy], the view is *res utilis miser* [the unfortunate is useful]: the zeks work and benefit the state that incarcerates them.

The medical sector is the necessary brake in this merciless exploitation. Were it not for the medical sector, the bosses would drive the zeks to death or they would die in epidemics. Within its limits, the medical sector maintains the work force in a condition suitable for exploitation. It has two means at its disposal: medical treatment and rest—both to an inadequate degree. The medical sector, after all, is not treating free people for the patients' sake. It is treating slaves in the interests of the employer, and if the incidence of sickness in camp increases, the head of the medical sector and the medical staff must answer not for peoples' suffering and death but for squandering the state's workforce.

The General Supply Section [Russian acronym OOC]—with the corresponding General Supply Unit [ChOS] in each camp—deals with feeding and clothing the zek. If the head of ChOS is an energetic person, the camp will succeed in receiving another barrel of cabbage, extra barley, or vegetable oil or tobacco tossed in as an extra. If the camp surpasses the plan, it will receive, in the form of an incentive, more food products. If the zeks work poorly, the camp boss will be fired and the prisoners will not receive even what they are entitled to by law. Camps are supplied irregularly, and generally they receive the lowest quality products.

The camp scheme is not complete, however, without describing the KVCh—the Cultural-Educational Sector, the expression of Soviet humanism. Tsarist hard labor prisons did not have a cultural-educational sector; they neither educated people nor used elevated words. Similar to the effort of the medical sector to counteract the zeks' physical decline, the KVCh must counteract their spiritual decline. The day when the camps will be destroyed along with their medical sector and KVCh will mark the victory of genuine humanism, but as long as the camps exist, the KVCh fulfills the role of a kiosk with refreshing drinks in a brothel.

Back at Square 48 we had an "educator," but the work there was too hard, the educator too illiterate, and the human material (Westerners) too difficult to influence. The effect of camp culture was expressed chiefly in the mastering of a Russian "lexicon," which the Westerners easily adopted. In the Kruglitsa medical settlement, however, the KVCh was excellently organized. This was noticeable upon entering the camp grounds: a loudspeaker in the open air, a newspaper on the wall, posters, slogans, inscriptions!

In the morning during the dispatch to work, a prisoner plays the accordion, seated on a step of the guard house, closing his suffering, aged eyes—he is a Hungarian brought to Poland by the war—and he plays the waltz "On the Hills of Manchuria." The accordion emits a thin sound, the zeks are shivering from cold, no one is happy, least of all the musician, who fears that this whim of the administration will pass, and he again will have to go out to general work.

They built a podium by the guardhouse gates, and they detain brigades there for an extra quarter of an hour before dispatching them to work. Every morning the head of the KVCh—a dim-witted fellow, incapable of putting two words together—climbs up to the podium, and stuttering, delivers a speech about the need to raise the tempo of the spring sowing. Where do they get such thick-witted people for the KVCh? The answer is simple: the cleverer man will find better work; camp jobs in general are for losers, and the worst of all are in the cultural-educational sector: there are no pickings—it is neither a kitchen nor production site. During my five years in camp, I never met an intellectual among the free workers in the KVCh. The prisoners are a different matter—they willingly take shelter in the KVCh rather than do heavy physical work.

In the war years, free women from the village worked in the Kruglitsa KVCh. Young, ignorant, and intimidated, all they could think of were their children, left at home without supervision. Their life was difficult, only a little better than ours.... Their husbands were at the front and there was not enough bread. Each one of them willingly would have exchanged cultural-educational work in the camp for a warm place in the canteen or warehouse. In the entire settlement of Kruglitsa, one could hardly find a dozen people able to write or express themselves properly in Russian. Among the zeks there was no lack of highly educated people, but the more educated they were, the more suspicious the administration was of them, and, understandably, there was no question of trusting them with a responsible position in the KVCh. At Square 48, Russians advised me to conceal my knowledge of foreign languages. "For every foreign language, they will add another year!" they said. The camp administration, however, was not bright enough even to be consistent in distancing the imprisoned intelligentsia from work in the KVCh. Normally, political prisoners were excluded from the lists of "readers," that is, people who read given issues of newspapers aloud in the barracks. At Square 48, they deprived me of the right to read a newspaper aloud, but in May 1943 in Kruglitsa, this did not prevent me from being . . . a KVCh inspector for several weeks. I ran away from this work only after they imposed an impossible burden on me: during the dispatch to work, while the musician tuned his instrument and the KVCh boss delivered a speech from the podium, I was supposed to go out with a red banner in my hands and stand by the podium as a live decoration.

The accordionist, the speech from the podium, the KVCh inspector with the red banner were all free theater for the zeks. Most importantly, it delayed the departure for work by a few minutes; it also broke up the usual procedure and provided entertainment. The crowd of zeks listened to the talk with stony seriousness, in no way revealing their feelings; no one clapped at the end or laughed when the orator, getting confused in the middle, talked nonsense. They listened and left for work. The habit of many years in camp creates a particular indifference and immunity to any words: it is useless to propagandize a zek. They know everything. To them, a well-spoken or bumbling speech are all the same.

Kruglitsa is a center of camp culture. One can study its highest manifestation here. From time to time, the KVCh issues a wall newspaper. It is called "For a [faster] Tempo," or "Raise the Banner" or "Stakhanovite," and it is written by hand by the camp's best draftsman. On top is a colored picture: a field, above which the sun is rising, a plowman is walking behind a plow, powerful, broad-shouldered like the legendary hero Mikula. From the side, a girl with long braids and children admire him. The lead article follows: "We will surpass the spring sowing schedule!" Next is correspondence about disorders in the tenth brigade: a sketch depicts a work refuser sleeping under a bush during work hours. Then a disparaging remark about people who do not follow the rules of hygiene and relieve themselves around the corner of the barrack. Next is a graph by the KVCh about the results of the work competition in the camp. Then in large letters: "Honor and glory to the outstanding workers!" with the names of five people who fulfilled the norm by 150 to 200 percent at mowing and construction. A prisoner was caught stealing several potatoes in the *selkhoz*. A sketch depicts the zek in the form of the clown Petrushka while the hand of justice takes the stolen potato from his pocket. An inscription reads: "The fan of baked potatoes will have time in the punishment cell to think about the results of his actions."

The wall newspaper is hung by the guardhouse on a board protected by a wire screen. Also, behind a wire screen one can see once a week or every two weeks an issue of *Pravda of the North*, the newspaper that is published in Arkhangelsk, or even an issue of *Pravda* or *Izvestiya* of ten days back. The wire screens are a must; otherwise the newspapers would be torn off immediately and used for rolling cigarettes.

The KVCh building consists of two little rooms: the director's office, always locked in his absence, and a room that contains a bookcase with books, a table, and benches along the walls. A large map of the Soviet Union hangs on the wall. This is very valuable and is not found in every camp. The prisoners are not permitted to keep maps, and we Westerners had difficulty understanding to where we had been taken. I studied this map by heart during my three years at Kruglitsa. It dated from an earlier time when the Baltic States were beyond the Soviet borders, and half of Poland was in Germany. This map wandered: sometimes they brought it to the director's office and other times it hung in the zeks' canteen, shining its red color on half of Asia and Europe.

The library consisted of random booklets and brochures such as *A Course on Pig Breeding*, or *Molotov's Speech at the 18ᵗʰ Congress of the Soviets*. There was nothing to read, and what was available was given only to especially reliable people who would not use them to roll cigarettes. There were about twenty "readers" in the camp from among the chronically ill in the infirmary, and they acquired books via the free workers from the village. Books were a rarity among the free workers, too. Every book brought into Kruglitsa made the rounds of a circle of readers, and sometimes we awaited our turn for months. In a separate place in the bookcase were Stalin's *Problems of Leninism* in three different editions, the second volume of the popular edition of Marx's works, and twenty volumes from the complete works of Lenin. These books were not shown to anyone, and I was their sole reader in Kruglitsa. I do not recall one person taking an interest in them during that time. In the barrack, I carefully hid these thick volumes so my smoking neighbors would not tear out pages. They gave them to me unofficially and unwillingly. At one time, the security officer totally forbade giving them to me. Why? The KVCh in camp does not engage in the prisoners' political education, and it reacts suspiciously to any interest on the zeks' part in the theory and the classics of Marxism. The books of Lenin and Stalin are very sacred but they are not a subject for critical study. The ordinary Soviet mortal relates to them with a certain trepidation. One needs preparation for them; they are read in circles with party instructors. For the masses there is a minimum reading requirement and canonic guidebooks; breaching those bounds is a sign of unhealthy curiosity.

Some fragile prisoner incapable of physical labor is usually employed in the KVCh, doing the work for his semi-literate "free" bosses. Everything falls on him: the library, distributing and dispatching letters, distributing newspapers to read in the barracks, monitoring the percentage of the plan fulfilled by individual brigades, a card catalogue of disciplinary charges, that is, a record of who, when, and for what sat in the punishment cell, compilation of the references attached to every claim or petition by a zek, composing the newspaper, hanging posters, compiling reports filled with fantastic information about the cultural life of the camp. He is not only a postmaster, editor, and cultural organizer but also the orderly in the KVCh building, as he sleeps in it, stokes the stove, washes, and sweeps the floor. In between sweeping and delivering letters, he writes "references" such as: "zek so and so, term and article such and such, has been working as a wagoner for six months; he fulfills the norm by seventy percent, his daily conduct is good, and he has not received any reprimands." The head of the KVCh signs this reference, which often determines the fate of the petition sent to the camp administration or the Division headquarters.

Two or three sign painters, equipped with brushes and paint, work at the table in the KVCh preparing endless posters and slogans. They write on wooden boards and then hang them everywhere possible. The camp is so plastered with slogans that people no longer notice them: if they were to remove them, the zeks would notice the change. The slogans arrive already formulated from the center. It is forbidden to change even a letter, but it is possible to select from several dozen slogans: they choose the shortest so that they have less to write. Actually, however, the KVCh artists are not interested in finishing their work quickly. On the contrary, it is in their interest to drag things out, as their work is not subject to a norm and is paid at the standard rate for work without quotas—the second category rations and 500 grams of bread daily.

The posters are patriotic: "The motherland calls!" or "All united in the struggle against the fascist invaders!" The motherland counts on the patriotism of imprisoned people, who are isolated and deprived of the right to use the word "comrade." These people participate in Russia's liberation war while sitting in forced labor camps under guard! Up to the summer of 1941, the motherland regarded them as working cattle and a danger to the state. Now, after the military catastrophe, when the Germans had penetrated deep into Russia, the motherland still keeps them in camps but expects them to be patriotic! And we, of course, are all great patriots.

After the start of the war, a stream of requests flowed from camps, asking for release and dispatch to the front. Even during the most difficult moments of the war, however, the Soviet regime did not risk enlisting prisoners in the army ranks.

Other posters related to production: "Let us raise the tempo!" "We shall mercilessly liquidate [work] refusers and bunglers!" "Work well today—and tomorrow even better!" Other posters hung in the barracks: "Keep clean and see to your neighbor's cleanliness!" "Behave in a cultured way!"[1] "Don't drink unboiled water!" It is impossible to hide from the posters. You fall asleep in the overcrowded barrack reading the inscription on the opposite wall: "Whoever does not work does not eat!" The first thing that you see upon awakening is the slogan: "Long live the brotherhood of peoples of the USSR!"

The best illustration of this brotherhood was our bunk, where five people slept pressed closely together: Hassan Ogly Khudai Berdy, Julius Margolin, the Ukrainian fisherman Belovchenko, the Finnish artist Kotro, and the

---

1. A polite way of saying defecate only where you are supposed to.

Chinaman Van Chan-lu, who mispronounced the word "shirt" [*rubashka*] as "lubashka."

The basic cultural-educational entertainment in Kruglitsa was film and radio. Kruglitsa could serve as a model in this respect. I spent my first and fifth year of internment in camp without these conveniences. The three Kruglitsa years, however, were abundantly spiced with music and film screenings.

Films were screened for prisoners outdoors in the summer and in the winter in the canteen built in 1943 (and in one of the barracks before that). From time to time they organized screenings for the patients, who comprised half of the population of the medical settlement. Then they would bring benches into the corridor of the first infirmary; those who were still capable would start to shuffle in from the surrounding hospital barracks, in their gray hospital robes, moving their feet with difficulty. For the sick, who had been lying on cots for months, this was a great event. Around fifty people would gather for such screenings. Around one hundred people, including the camp administration, would come to the screening for the healthy. In total there were up to seven hundred zeks in Kruglitsa. The regular workers or invalids preferred to go to sleep after eating; they were not up to movies.

Screenings were irregular, sometimes once a week, other times once a month. From the morning, the news would spread that a movie operator had arrived (under guard), and if he succeeded in fixing the projector by evening, there would be a film. For some reason, the machine always needed to be fixed. After supper, the audience begins to gather in the canteen. The tables are moved to the side, benches and stools are brought from the barracks, and a white sheet is stretched on the wall. An hour or two passes in waiting for the start of the film. Gradually everyone arrives: the trusties and the cooks, the nurses in clean kerchiefs, the foppish Nastya Pechonkina in a striped skirt sewn from Polish pajamas, the hairdresser Grisha with Sanya the office worker, who is madly in love with him, Semivolos and Agronskaya, Ninka and Lizaveta Ivanovna, the camp intelligentsia, the brigade leaders and the youth, the metal workers from the central machine repair shop with their perpetually black-stained faces, and in the very middle, the beaming and happy Maxik, Doctor Max Albertovich Rosenberg, unbelievably kindhearted and a great movie fan. The small premises are overcrowded; people are sitting on the tables at the side and thronging at the doors. In a separate side niche, as if in a box seat, Gordeeva and several "free" guests are sitting. I come with my stool and, lifting it above my head, I push my way into the first row, where I sit down by the window.

Finally, the light is turned off, and the movie operator, surrounded by people, begins to turn the handle. Immediately on the screen one sees the shadows of the heads of people sitting too close; they are reseated further away and the action begins.

Camp cinema is not at all like what goes by that name in competitive capitalist countries. Something glimmers darkly and hazily; some spot or hook stubbornly shows up on the sheet-screen. Now and then, the old, worn out film tears. As in the old days, there is an intermission after every part of the film. The sound is poor, and in the middle of the showing, the projector inevitably breaks, and the audience waits patiently until it is fixed. In the meantime, latecomers are pressing at the doors, but the guard does not admit them. The latecomers do not leave but wait until the arrival of some important member of the camp administration, who has to be let in, and then they pile in after him through the half open door. They push in more from principle, as those standing in the back rows won't see anything anyhow. The important thing is not the film, which usually is boring, drawn out, and incomprehensible, but the opportunity to stand in the darkness, stretch your neck, hear the crackling and the shrill noises, and groan with anticipation—"When is the end, already?"—and to enjoy the feeling of participating in a cultural event. A diversion occurs with the appearance of the orderly from headquarters, who calls out loudly in the darkness: "Zek so-and-so! Brigade leader so-and-so! Go immediately to the camp director!" Then movement begins in the thick of those seated and pushing starts among the close rows.

Among all the films shown in camp, I particularly remember one, named, I think, *A Day of the World*. One August day in 1940, an army of movie operators filmed this movie in dozens of places in the Soviet Union; the goal was to show a cross section of the ordinary working day of the great country. We see people rising to work at dawn in the *kolkhozes* of Kamchatka and the Caucasus mountains; how the millions in Moscow awaken, children go to school and Mikhail Ivanovich Kalinin[2] goes to the building of the Supreme Soviet; how tractors come off the assembly line of factories and ships from holding docks; how scientists work in laboratories, the crowds cheer in stadiums; a theater curtain rises, and Ulanova[3] is standing on the stage. An excellent survey of a day on one-sixth of the earth, a symphonic and dynamic film. . . .

---

2. Mikhail Kalinin (1875–1946) was the chairman of the Supreme Soviet from 1919 to 1946.

3. Galina Ulanova (1909–1998) was the prima ballerina of the Bolshoi Ballet for fourteen years.

Sitting on a stool in the corner, I recalled what did not go into that film as I spent that August day in 1940 in Square 48. I recalled the Onega division of the BBK corrective labor camp network, and goose pimples crawled along my back. How did the millions of prisoners in thousands of forced labor camps in the Soviet Union spend that day?

Newspapers, books, movies all had a rather symbolic significance in the prisoners' life, as a reminder of the world from which they had disappeared: a random greeting, crumbs from the table from which we had been driven away. The real link with the external world (in the Soviet sense) was radio. In Kruglitsa, the radio was part of our daily life. On the days when the radio was not working in the barrack, we felt bereft and despondent. The radio distracted us from thoughts about food, helped us forget our misfortune. The prisoners heard radio broadcasts from seven to nine o'clock in the morning and in the evening from seven to midnight. We did not hear the morning broadcasts, as we went out to work—it was a privilege of the sick and service personnel. It was impossible, however, to imagine evening in the Kruglitsa barracks without the radio.

One need not picture an idyllic situation here, either. Soviet radio is nothing like that which the Western reader has in his or her room. There is no radio set. The vast majority of Soviet people first saw one abroad during the war years. At home, radio receivers are the privilege of reliable insiders—the Soviet aristocracy. Of the thousands of Soviet people with whom I conversed in camps, only one had had a genuine radio set in his apartment before his arrest: he had been the director of the Dnepropetrovsk food industry factory and a party member. The gray masses listen to radio loudspeakers, both in camps and at liberty.

In the depths of the barracks under the ceiling or attached to a column is a loudspeaker disc made from wax paper. You cannot turn off or regulate the broadcast. This is "Zwangsradio" [German: forced radio]—a funnel placed in our ears. Like it or not, the radio speaks. Those who dislike radio broadcasts lie further away; the radio is clearly audible and understandable only in the immediate vicinity. In the evening, therefore, when a hundred or more men are making noise in the barrack, eating, rummaging around their things, arguing, undressing, looking for lice, playing cards, smoking, cooking, when the orderly is cutting wood at one end, and, at the other, people are standing in line with mugs by the water barrel, the humming and throbbing from the ether mixes into this commotion; it does not particularly bother anyone and is perceived as part of the ordinary camp noise. Only when they broadcast communiqués from the front do people hush others and yell: "Let us listen!"

Whoever really wants to hear goes right up to the disc and turns his ear to it. Then they will tell others what they heard. The majority do not listen, and if they do, they do not understand. In every barrack there are one or two people to whom everyone turns and asks: what did they report today? As to music, one does not have to listen to it; it enters your ears by itself. And what music!

Hearing something like that at home, we would quickly turn off the radio and call the repairman to see what was broken. Here, however, it is a normal phenomenon. That is precisely how a radio monopolized by the state is supposed to sound. A free person can turn it off but cannot tune to something better. We zeks cannot turn it off. If asked for their opinion, half of the barracks in Kruglitsa would reject this falsification, which is as similar to a normal radio as the camp gruel is to normal food, the camp barrack to a normal residence, or Soviet democracy to free human life. Those same barracks loudly express their satisfaction when the loudspeaker is out of order, and for weeks do not bother the KVCh with a request to fix it. Not everyone, however, is so insensitive and uncultured! We radio fans gradually got used to its wheezing and screeches, learned to discern musicality in its cacophony: we know whether it is Beethoven or Glinka, with a correction for the imperfection of the broadcast. We were tolerant and patient. Sometimes the radio roared like a thousand buffalos, but suddenly a pure lyrical melody played by Oistrakh would emerge from it, and we would listen to it devoutly, although in this foul den the voice of the violin sounded almost like counterrevolution.

Over the years, I grew accustomed to falling asleep to the sound of waves on the beach, the murmur and noise of the radio. My place was always on the upper bunk. There it was not only warmer but also farther from other people. Above my head was the ceiling, gloomy beams with spider webs and cracks. The barrack with its pushing and shoving was somewhere below—invisible. The radio is by the feet or very close. The day is over and the bread set aside for the evening has been eaten; what remains is to listen to the low voice of Ruslanova[4] (that Soviet Plevitskaya[5]) or the choir of Pyatnitsky[6] with

---

4. Lidia Ruslanova (1900–1973), Soviet singer known for singing Russian folk songs. During the war, she toured the front to help lift soldiers' morale. She was arrested in 1948 for "anti-Soviet propaganda"; she was released in 1953.

5. Nadezhda Plevitskaya (1884–1940), Russian singer who emigrated to the West. She and her husband Nikolai Skoblin were recruited by the Soviet secret service. She was arrested in France for her involvement in the abduction of a White Army general Yevgeny Miller from Paris to Moscow in 1937. She died in a French jail in 1940.

6. Popular choir of Russian folk music led by Mitrofan Pyatnitsky (1864–1927).

the twangy-bouncy refrain of a song: "And who knows why he blinks . . ." and again Tchaikovsky, who is played to excess on Soviet radio just as Chopin was by Polish radio before the war.

I would fall asleep while listening and open my eyes only at 11:30 p.m. to listen to the last news broadcast. The last five minutes are devoted to news from abroad; then I strain to listen and sit up on the bunk, not missing a word. The entire barrack has been sleeping since ten o'clock: wagon drivers, earth diggers, living skeletons, hungry Russian peasants. Above them like an apparition, an absurdity, floats a melody: Debussy for forced labor prisoners. At least Debussy does not hinder them from sleeping. Sometimes, however, in our barrack full of snoring, lice, foot cloths without shoes, and zeks who have not undressed because of the cold or extreme weakness, the voice of a coloratura soprano rings out. You have to picture the combination of the frantic female squealing with trills and grace notes of Soviet radio technology and hardened male ears at the late hour of general deathly exhaustion. This combination is unthinkable in the West: you need Soviet camps and the KVCh to produce it. Suddenly, three places away from me, the gardener Havrylo from Kuban wakes up violently from his sleep. Havrylo, about sixty years old, who transports manure in the camp, wears a red, loose fitting cloak made of burlap and sleeps in it too. His disheveled head with a pointy beard, with eyes drunk from sleep, looks for half a minute in the direction of the inhuman, piercing staccato and says distinctly and quietly: "She's lllaughing, the mare!"

These two words conveyed so much deadly hatred, so much impotence in face of this nocturnal hallucination and outrage that I am amused and sorry for him. The radio is a marvelous thing, an Italian aria all the more so, and the gardener Havrylo is no less a master in his trade than Verdi in his. It is a pity that Yosif Vissarionovich, who inspired and created the KVCh, does not hear this music or that commentary in his large office in the Kremlin palace, where there is an excellent foreign-made radio instrument. Perhaps, had he heard it, he would have eliminated—if not the camps, at least coloratura exercises in camps. . . .

The radio program ends at midnight with the "International." During the war, they introduced a new state anthem,[7] and the word that seemingly had

---

7. In March 1944, the USSR replaced the "International" with an anthem written by Sergey Mikhalkov to the music of Aleksandr Aleksandrov.

been forgotten was revived: "The union of Soviet republics is indestructible / The Great Rus[8] consolidated forever. . . ."

The melody of this hymn, slow-ponderous, swirling, and mighty, like a rumbling, powerful tank—so simple that even those without a voice could sing it—has been engraved in my memory forever. I heard the old and the new Soviet hymn a thousand times in camp. For me it is linked forever with memories about bodies stretched out on bunks, plunged into a stupor, or with the sight of a brigade assembled by the guardhouse at dawn. "Arise, the damned of the earth! / Arise, the world of hungry and enslaved."[9] We understood this literally, as a reveille. Five years later, I was with a friend from the camp at a gathering in Tel Aviv that ended with singing of the "International." When those first familiar words rang out, I glanced at my friend and saw he was not well. His face became pale and his eyes were roving. . . . He must have felt as if he were in the old mouse trap again. He turned and began to make his way furtively to the exit, but young people blocked his way and forced him to listen to the "International" until the end. He closed his eyes and immediately calmed down. Later, on the street, I asked him: "Where were you running to?" He replied: "You know, as soon as they forced me to listen, I immediately returned to the old, customary condition of a camp inmate. I closed my eyes, and it seemed as if another two hundred million Soviet citizens were standing alongside of me. That way it is normal, as it is supposed to be: to listen to the 'International' under compulsion. . . . I no longer can listen to it any other way."

Soviet radio undoubtedly is the nastiest, the dullest, and most boring in the entire world—it is overloaded with monotonous propaganda; it is not obligated to be interesting, and it is designed for the most primitive listeners. By means of persistent and monotonous repetitions, it accustoms the masses to certain standards that have been approved from above by the all-Union KVCh. I liked Ruslanova's songs the first time but on the thousandth time they annoyed me like a bothersome fly. The sweet lyricism of Tchaikovsky is burdensome and insulting in such conditions. Nevertheless, all this together—Tchaikovsky and Ruslanova, the headlines of *Pravda*, and the slogan "Kill the German" were solidly drummed into my brain and subconscious. There is no slogan or nonsense or lie that cannot be forced into a person's consciousness

8. Rus, an archaic word that precedes the term "Russia," refers to the medieval kingdom of Kievan Rus. It accents Slavic nationalism as opposed to the previous Soviet appeal to internationalism.

9. The opening lines of the Russian version of the "International."

by means of thousand-fold repetitions over many years. This mechanical approach forms the basis for the colossal work of Soviet radio in the service of the Kremlin dictatorship. Millions of Soviet people, who from childhood hear the same thing over and over again and never hear any other radio than the Soviet, are defenseless against its systematic influence. You do not need to convince; it suffices to repeat.

If the radio repeated three times a day for twenty-five years that two times two equals five, this, too, would become the ordinary conviction of Soviet citizens. This is the terrible danger of stultification that contemporary technology creates in countries with a totalitarian regime. In camp we did not have enough bread, but precisely because of that, we had more than enough radio, "opium for the masses" according to the Politburo's recipe. Only in camp did I understand the meaning of "freedom of choice," and I think that a short stay there would give every Western skeptic a better understanding of the meaning of the political freedom that he enjoys and of democratic liberties that spoil him to snobbish surfeit.

Two phenomena derive with iron logic from the camp system of education:

1. The purely urban intellectual word "culture," which was entirely foreign to the average person before the Soviet regime, is now used by and familiar to every camp inmate, along with such words as "plan," "norm," and "100 grams." In camp the concept of culture is equal to the concept of "hygiene." In the mind of the ordinary Russian person, it is associated with soap and a toothbrush. Being cultured means washing oneself, being clean, and not spitting on the floor. The greatest crime against culture is to skip a bath. The achievement of the Soviet regime is that the word "culture," which formerly belonged to the select few, has now entered the philistine vocabulary. A pitiful ersatz, however, masquerades under this term. Every self-respecting Soviet man-in-the-street feels he is lacking in culture if his shoes are not sparkling clean and he does not have a sheet on his bed. All too often, in the barrack one can hear the commandant shower the men with crude, dirty curses because of their lack of culture, that is, because after inhuman labor, people lay down on the bunks without undressing. He does not understand that in addition to bodily cleanliness, there is another kind of purity, and his swearing is at least as uncultured as an unswept floor or dirty bunks. He is even less capable of understanding that camp bunks, even washed clean by the zeks' hands, are incompatible with culture and represent the deepest disgrace and humiliation of a person. In order to turn the zeks into cultured people, one must first take them out of the camps.

The Soviet regime, however, does the opposite: it puts millions of people in camps, and then organizes for these people who have been deprived of their human likeness a "cultural-educational sector." It does not deny culture; it merely puts it in the hands of gendarmes and arranges it so that every cad and jailer can consider himself its representative and instructor.

2. Aside from cultural hygiene and external propriety, every cultural value is compromised in the eyes of the mass of zeks; their respect for culture is undermined by the form in which it is monopolized and represented by the KVCh workers. It is impossible to teach a camp inmate to respect a book or scientific thought or music. On the contrary, all these things for him clearly comprise part of the yoke foisted on his neck, an instrument of a hostile force. The KVCh periodically selects capable camp youth and sends them to special courses for norm setters, receivers of goods, and office workers adapted to camp needs. The people who complete these courses acquire credentials, but they do not develop respect for knowledge, which, they see, is placed in the service of the NKVD. They form a dangerous link in their minds between cultural values and the form of enslavement existing in camps and managed from the outside.

Here is a typical picture: I go to evening office hours at the clinic with a book, knowing that I shall have to await my turn for more than an hour. A person with a book, however, annoys those around him: seeing a person reading a book gets on their nerves. I seem to be sitting quietly, not bothering anyone, but around me an antagonistic atmosphere gradually builds up, as if I started to smoke a cigarette on the Sabbath among observant Jews. . . . Hostile looks. . . . Finally, a lanky, disheveled worker, covered with bandaged boils, cannot hold back and turns to me: "Listen!" he says, "Kindly close that book. . . . I can't watch you burying yourself in it. . . . What is this going around with books all the time about . . . such highbrows. . . ." This person feels some kind of link between my book and his misfortune. Hatred of the regime, which does not take a political form, is expressed in hatred of the intelligentsia in general, which is the source of all misfortune. The dark masses in Russia do not know any other intelligentsia, or any other book, or other science, or ideology than the communist one. Blind, elemental repulsion toward ideology, indifference and scorn of any ideology, have seized all strata of the population, have flooded one-sixth of the earth.

The Russian people are remarkably talented, and there is no camp where you cannot find singers, dancers, and storytellers among the thousands of zeks. Under the direction of professional artists imprisoned in camps, these people entertain themselves and others as best they can. The widow of the Polish communist poet Wandurski, who was shot in the Soviet Union, was imprisoned in Kruglitsa. She was a Polish operetta singer from Kiev.[10] As the wife of an executed person, she landed in camp in 1937, several years after he had been shot. She rapidly faded and aged, but she retained the airs and manner of a "star." She worked in the sewing workshop, and all of Kargopolag knew "Wanda." I saw one of her performances on the outdoor stage in the medical settlement. Heavily made up and dressed in a colorful cotton print, she sang coquettishly, smiling and fluttering her shoulders: "Mirandolina! Mirand-o-lina!" while hundreds of prisoners sat around on benches. It was in July, during the short northern summer. Armed guards stood on four watch towers at four corners of the camp fence; the camp palisade with high barbed wire separated us from liberty, and the "performance" took place in the square inside. The men performed a sketch wearing suit jackets, which had been obtained with difficulty from the free workers of the village. The sight of prisoners in those jackets evoked peals of laughter. Then there were dances. To the sounds of an accordion, they danced a waltz and polka: female zeks in men's jackets and skirts with frayed hems circled around with cavaliers in patched pants and second hand shirts, with deadly pale, pitted faces and sunken cheeks, with missing teeth and shaven heads. To the right was the punishment cell, to the left the delousing station, behind was the guardhouse, and in front the forbidden zone. Each of these people had experienced prison and hunger, a destroyed life, the death of loved ones and separation from kin. This was a camp idyll, a camp holiday. The camp prostitute danced with the camp work supervisor, Wanda with the cook, Ninka with Semivolos, the pharmacist with the charwoman, the Ossetian with the Latvian, the Chinaman with the thief, the hairdresser Grisha with the office worker Sanya; two squat, snub nosed laundry women for whom no cavaliers were found danced with each other like wooden mannequins. On the side, the KVCh director stood in an army overcoat and crumpled cap and watched with satisfaction. The office worker Sanya was happy, not suspecting that the next morning they would send her on an *etap* to another camp, and she would never again see her Grisha nor the office nor the medical settlement of Kruglitsa, where the KVCh was so wonderful.

---

10. Now Kyiv, capital of Ukraine.

27

Isaac the Fifth

OVER TIME, LIFE in camp acquired the features of quiet, steady madness, an experimental bedlam or a movie that is screened upside down through a crooked mirror. Sometimes we would go to the *selkhoz* to remove caterpillars, sometimes we picked up stones from the field, built fences with uprooted stumps, or stripped the needles from pine branches. Each of these activities was needed in that peculiar world where we lived.

I picture myself crawling along the damp furrow of the cabbage patch. Acres of young cabbage have been eaten by worms. The green leaves of the heads are covered with fat, green worms and large caterpillars or barely visible small ones. One can remove twenty to forty of them from one head of cabbage, depending on one's industriousness. Each of us is equipped with a small board and a wooden needle with which he picks off the worms. Soon we discard these inconvenient needles and begin to crush the caterpillars with our hands. At first this seems disgusting, but after half an hour, we do not care. Fifteen zeks, themselves resembling enormous gray caterpillars, walk along fifteen furrows. They alternately squat down, then rush forward when they see that their neighbors have overtaken them. This is no work for the fastidious or nervous. No matter how many caterpillars you remove, plenty still remain, and no one has the patience or the time to bother for a long time with one head of cabbage. The heads are sprayed with something poisonous and bitter, and the green leaves are inedible. Nevertheless, everyone stuffs them into his mouth, and the next morning, half the brigade will suffer from stomach trouble. How long can one pluck caterpillars from cabbage? Half of us have become cretinous semi-idiots, the other half are severe bundles of nerves, but after a few hours, both types only pretend to be working. They are easily caught and accused of criminal negligence (wrecking!), that is, the furrows that have been covered still teem with caterpillars—and they force the zeks to start their work anew.

Meanwhile, the warehouse in the *selkhoz* holds pickled cabbage, and one only has to find the right moment, while the guard is dozing, to make your way to the warehouse, which is 200 meters to the side. The doors are open, the workers roll enormous empty barrels outside. It is impossible to break into the interior of the warehouse; it is guarded by the warehouse manager, the prisoner Anisim Petrovich, an ill-tempered, bearded peasant with wolfish eyes and massive fists. A barrel of cabbage, however, has got stuck in the entrance to the warehouse. This news spreads like lighting throughout the *selkhoz*. Daredevils approach from all sides, peering through the door. Anisim Petrovich is busy with something deep inside the warehouse. Someone screws up his courage, jumps in and removes the heavy cover from the barrel. He sticks in his hand, still full of the whitish-green ooze from the cabbage worms—and grabs a handful of cabbage, then a second one. Where does it go? Into his jacket pocket. The teeth ache from the freezing cold cabbage. One succeeded, a second and third follow. Suddenly, Anisim Petrovich jumps outside with a face distorted with malice and fury. People hurriedly run away but one fellow (from Berlin) with a delicate mouth and sad Semitic eyes, holds his ground. He continues hastily to stuff his pockets until Anisim swoops upon him, tears the cabbage out of his hands, turns him by the shoulders to the exit, and hits him with all his might on the back and neck: "Swine, thief!"

The cabbage is ours, nevertheless. We fill the pot with cabbage—the fellow from Berlin and I—and put it on the stove in the hothouse. In two hours, we shall have cabbage soup. Unfortunately, someone saw us put the pot on the stove. The Berliner runs over in half an hour, his face white as a sheet. Someone filched the pot along with the cabbage. Isaac is on the verge of tears: the blows he received from Anisim Petrovich were in vain.

There were five Isaacs in my life; this one was the fifth. All five were different from each other. The first Isaac was my uncle, my mother's oldest brother. He lived in Pinsk, and I was raised in his house when I was ten years old. He was a gentle, kind, weak-natured person. Thanks to him, I have been playing chess since the age of ten. At that age I both admired and was chagrined by his chess skill, but by the age of fifteen, I was already able to beat him. Uncle Isaac went bankrupt the very year I came to live in his house. His creditors gathered noisily under his windows to create a scandal. Everyone in the house was unhappy, but nothing could shatter Uncle Isaac's innate good nature. Before the bankruptcy, Uncle Isaac was well off, but afterward his children became communists and participated in the October revolution in the Ukraine. Uncle Isaac died in the home of his communist daughter somewhere in Soviet Penza.

The second Isaac was my beloved older cousin, a proletarian and revolutionary. He fought against the tsarist autocracy, spent time in prisons, and from him I first learned that one can love "freedom" and that nothing is tastier than a piece of bread with garlic. He was a red-haired fellow with gray, merry eyes, a "Bundist." In 1920, my cousin Isaac took part in the Red Army invasion of Poland and the capture of his native city of Pinsk, and he became a member of the city's revolutionary committee. Upon the retreat from the city, he was killed, or rather went missing. He was the last to leave the city, and he disappeared without a trace. No one ever saw cousin Isaac again.

The third Isaac played tennis very well; he graduated from medical school in Zurich, and when he returned to Poland, it turned out that with the name Isaac, it was impossible to obtain even unpaid work. This Isaac was neither a Jew nor a Pole nor a Russian; therefore, he became an American. He left Poland in time, that is, in 1938, for America. At first, he worked there as a photographer but, ultimately, the Americans permitted him to practice medicine. My brother-in-law Isaac named his daughter "Frances Carol" and bought himself a good car on installment.

The fourth Isaac was not a relative, just a friend. His parents' home and his inheritance of feather beds were in Poland, but when his father did not want to let him go to Palestine (his father in Częstochowa decided to wait for the coming of the Messiah), young Isaac abandoned his paternal home, slept in Warsaw for a year and a half on the table of the "Irgun" and then left for Israel illegally. The illegal ship with about three hundred people sailed past the Dalmatian and Albanian coast, past Zara and Corfu and many islands to the Jewish shores. This was in 1938. In the motherland, Isaac suffered from hunger. History records his merits: he fought heroically to transfer the transport of sewage disposal barrels in Tel Aviv, from Arab into Jewish hands. He was one of the first to ride with the barrels; yet, after a year, Isaac was seen doing more specialized work, but the chronicles are silent about his further transformations (for the meantime).

I told the fifth Isaac about the four Isaacs in greater detail than is presented here because in camp we were not interested in brevity. Our camp sentences were long, and we killed our spare time with our stories, in which we left the present for the past in order to reach the future more quickly. We greeted each month as an enemy and we let it pass without regret. We believed that someday a month would come that would be our friend.

The fifth Isaac attached himself to me in the Kruglitsa medical settlement when we both were in a poor state. We both had been excluded from the amnesty. He could not be amnestied because he had not been sentenced. He sat in camp "without a term," that is, he was waiting for the administration to remember him and give him some kind of sentence. He was the son of a Berlin homeowner by the name of Knopf. His parents were Polish Jews who had settled in Berlin before the murder of Rathenau.[1] His father owned a small haberdashery shop in the vicinity of Uhlandstrasse, saved money for twenty years, and bought a house in Charlottenburg. Isaac was born in Berlin and spent the first seventeen years of his life there. He was a genuine "Berlinerjunge" with all the mannerisms and dialect of a Berliner; an only child, he was a mama's boy, with wide eyes and a delicate face. After Hitler seized power, the family remained in Berlin for another five years. The Germans took away the house and the store but, apparently, Berlin Jews did not yet live so badly if 80,000 of them stubbornly remained in their old location. Finally, in 1938, the Germans forced them back to Poland, and at the age of seventeen, young Isaac landed in Galicia, which he strongly disliked after Berlin. In the course of a year, he somewhat learned Polish, but then the war broke out and split the family. The parents remained in "German" Cracow, but young Isaac stayed with an aunt in Soviet Lvov.[2] He became a waiter in a restaurant, but in the spring of 1940, he made a mistake and registered to return to his parents in Cracow. The Soviets arrested him in June and without sentencing him, they brought him to Kargopolag. Now, two years later, he stood in front of me, an emaciated, gangly, weak youth seeking protection and explanations—what is happening in the world?

The fact that he had grown up in Berlin and spoke German like a real Nazi compromised him in the eyes of the Soviet regime. To play it safe, as it were, they left him in camp "until a new order," which, perhaps, has still not arrived. I do not know about the fifth Isaac's later fate. But at Kruglitsa, we were great friends. We lived together, worked together, and studied together. Isaac the fifth became my spiritual son. Our acquaintance began when he approached me and asked for a book to read. When conversing, he would smile shyly, and lowering his eyelashes, look "into himself," as if it was not worth looking at everything around. He spoke German in a well-bred way and was oddly

---

1. Walter Rathenau (1867–1922), a Jewish industrialist and politician, who served as foreign minister in Weimar, Germany. He was assassinated in June 1922 by ultra-right nationalists who were opposed to the Treaty of Versailles.

2. Now Lviv, Ukraine.

unlike the camp type of youth. Neither a wolf cub nor jackal, but a gentle, domestic puppy who got lost on the street, became infested with lice, and discovered for the first time that animal abusers exist in this world.

I tried to explain to him that he was only the fifth, not the first nor the last, but one of those with whom fate plays with as with a ball and that he must try to defend himself from misfortune by mobilizing his inner resources, but he lacked such resources because of his youth. His sweet German childhood was replaced by rabbit-like fear and shame; then came alien Poland with strange and unpleasant Jews in kaftans and side-locks; then "Soviet humanism," which could baffle even people seasoned by experience. What kept this little Jewish German above water was his knowledge of another life: he knew and remembered a Europe of divine beauty, entirely different from this camp quagmire, but something had happened to it and to him that he could not understand. Here I began to tell him about people, about things, events, and ideas, about everything that I hoped could support and strengthen him. I taught him; I wanted to make him a "strong person" in camp. At first, he took an interest, but stories are not enough in camp. Then began a process that I tried in vain to stem, the process of "sinking." A person splutters in camp like a drowning man in the salty sea water. For some time, he stays on the surface—on a plank, a life preserver, but in the end, if he is not pulled out of the water, he sinks to the bottom.

In the *selkhoz* they were planting potatoes. Under armed guard, they brought the potato seedlings, placed them in the field and the armed guards protected the bags from the zeks, who circled around all day. The guards' own pockets were full of stolen potatoes and vegetables: they had hungry children at home. Isaac the fifth and I also tried to filch potatoes, but we failed shamefully. When we arrived, none of the guards were visible, and our spirits rose from such success: we quickly stole up and each put ten small potatoes in his pocket. The guard, however, was sitting in an ambush behind empty crates and saw everything. He let us walk away a few steps, then he jumped out and forced us to return. Returning unwillingly under the barrel of the rifle, we tossed the potatoes out of our pockets along the road. When we reached the guard, our pockets were empty, but a trail of little potatoes on the ground betrayed us. Other zeks ran over to collect them, and while the guard tore the potatoes away from them, we managed to flee.

They did not let us near the potatoes again. Isaac and I found another specialty as "markers." They were planting green onions. Women would bring green onion seedlings in little baskets from the hothouse. We walked in front of them with a heavy board on which there were ten "teeth" in two rows. We placed the board across the seedbed and then stepped on it, pressing with our feet on two sides and performing an Indian dance. The teeth went into the crumbly earth and left ten little holes in two rows. We moved the board and thus covered the entire bed with even rows of holes. The women with the onions walked behind us, inserting a seedling in every hole and covering it with dirt. This work, not hard for a healthy person, made us sweat. After finishing an onion bed that was 80 meters long, we lay down on the ground and rested, without saying a word.

When a woman with seedlings approached from the hothouse, we watched carefully and attentively followed her movements. We could not approach her but we begged with our eyes. Surreptitiously, she threw several bunches of onions into the furrow. When she left—not earlier—we collected those onions. Unfortunately, one cannot eat too many green onions. We grew weaker by the day.

In the midst of this work, they summoned me to "headquarters." This was a sequel to my conversation with Bogrov. This time a person from the administration of Kargopolag sat in the office—an investigator or senior security officer. He began to question me very cordially, but suddenly I saw that he was writing down my answers. I began to feel bad. I cursed my unfortunate stupidity with the letter to Ehrenburg, which had drawn the attention of the NKVD to me. I finally understood that in a Soviet camp it is best to hide like a mouse and not enter into any superfluous conversations with the regime. Gordeeva had handed me over to Bogrov, and Bogrov to this man. I decided that my relations with officials would now end.

"You are a doctor of philosophy," he said, "you studied abroad. So, you are a bourgeois philosopher. Correct?"

"No," I said, "I am not a bourgeois philosopher. In my views I am even close to dialectical materialism."

"What do you call your school?"

I pondered and said resolutely: "Dialectical realism." My interlocutor quickly wrote down this term.

"What is the difference between dialectical realism and dialectical materialism?"

"Well, almost none," I smiled. "You know, Lenin used the word 'materialism' interchangeably with the word 'realism.'"

"Hm!" he said and began to recall something. "And what do you think of Hegel?"

"Hegel," I said firmly, "has great historical significance. Marx was the first to set him on his feet; before that he was standing on his head. We took from

Hegel his dialectical method but discarded the outmoded content of his idealistic system."

Here my investigator gave up. He put the pencil aside and laughed. "Well, what shall I write?" he asked. "I'll say it straight: I am weak in philosophy. Tell me, the camp, no doubt, made a strong impression on you. You will remember, perhaps you will write about it?"

"Oh, yes," I said ardently, "a very strong impression. I have reason to be grateful to the camp. We bookish people learned new things in the camp; we are re-educated. Only here did I truly understand what Soviet humanism is. I consider that my stay in camp revitalized me, was useful. It's a pity, of course, that it is somewhat . . . drawn out. With regard to writing, of course I shall write. Not about camps, understandably, but in my specialty: I think that I can develop a theory of dialectics, move it forward . . . in the spirit of the Marxist classics."

"You are a valuable person!" said the investigator with conviction. "One absolutely must help people such as you. It would be a pity if such a highly cultured person died in camp. Incidentally, do you speak to anyone here on philosophical topics?"

"No," I said sadly. "There are no philosophers here. And I cannot speak with anyone about philosophy. You are the first person. . . ."

"You know, you could help us a lot here as an intelligent person. There are many hidden enemies of the Soviet Union here. You often hear them express their opinions and you, of course, more than some dull person, more easily can understand what they are saying. We would value it greatly if from time to time you could inform us. . . ."

Such a proposal is made to almost every zek, and it does not mean that they consider you "one of theirs." It is possible to turn every timid and hungry person into an informer if you draw him gradually onto the path of friendly conversations and personal contact. At first, they ask how you feel, about impressions, then about individual people, then they invite you another time, then they meet you like an old friend, then they exert pressure and switch to threats. One has to know how to wiggle out of this net without annoying your kind, polite interlocutors.

I began to laugh heartily. "At Kruglitsa everyone knows me very well. If I, citizen director, would offer you my services as an informer, you yourself would have to brush me aside. I am not suited for that work: everyone sees me but I myself am partially blind. I cannot deal with people, only with books. . . ."

"You didn't understand me," said the director, "I did not mean systematic reports. But if you hear something, it is your direct duty to tell us!"

"Oh, of course! You don't need even to mention that; it's obvious! It is not only the duty; it is the pleasure of every decent person. Of every zek without exception. I just cannot take anything special on myself."

We parted amicably. The conversation with the senior official was in private; later, the local bosses asked me with concern what and who interested him. I had nothing to tell them, and I calmed them down with a clean conscience, saying that our conversation did not deal with people from Kruglitsa.

In the meantime, Isaac the fifth began to upset me. His case helped me to understand what one could call a "camp neurosis." A prisoner is not supposed to have nerves. No one cries in camp; yet not one person there has not undergone his or her crises. There are no normal people in camp; this is merely a consequence of the fact that the camp itself is not a normal institution. None of my coprisoners was a normal person. Isaac the fifth was relatively sane when we became friendly; he just was very intimidated. In front of my eyes this fear began to assume hysterical forms.

Isaac the fifth's fear focused on one thing: he was afraid of hunger. As soon as we returned from work, he would run to the office to check the work report. A register there gave information about each brigade: the specific ration and amount of bread allotted to each for the day. Sometimes we received the lowest-category ration. Then he was beside himself with grief. His face darkened. He wrung his hands. He could not bear such misfortune, such bad luck. I, too, was upset on such occasions. His reaction, however, was unusual, as if a black cloud enveloped his soul, and the deep despair into which he fell was incommensurate with the cause.

On the bunk next to me, he would sigh so deeply and heavily that I began to get angry, but I was no longer able to console him. On the contrary, he became furious when I wanted to draw him out of this state of frenzied sorrow. He accused me of not wanting to see how terrible this was, how disastrous that they had again taken 200 grams of bread from us. Trembling from this insult and injustice and from my criminal lightheadedness, he would turn away from me.

Why did others not react as furiously as he did? Isaac the fifth was a cowardly Jewish boy, neurotic, delicate, timid by nature. From childhood he was afraid to enter a dark room; then he was afraid of dogs, afraid of life because he grew up in Nazi Berlin, and because at his age fear arises without reason out of the inability to adapt to life's dangerous curves. And Kruglitsa was not simply a sharp curve, it was a pit. And he could react to one abnormality only with another one.

What I saw in Isaac the fifth was not yet a neurosis. It was the psychological starting point of all neuroses: defeat that a person cannot cope with—grief that floods the soul as a salty wave floods the nostrils of a drowning person.

I could not bother with him for long because neuroses in camp generally are incurable. They are cured not by analysis but by a blow to the head, that is, by a shock that is so rough that it instantly straightens out the mental disorder or ultimately destroys the person.

One summer morning, they took seven of us to the railroad track to unload sacks of grain. The open flatbed car with the cargo was standing opposite a wooden walkway on poles. Behind it was a warehouse. From the flatbed we offloaded sacks with barley and oats along a ramp to the walkway.

The warehouse floor was swept clean, but little kernels of grain got stuck everywhere between the floor boards and by the walls. While carrying the sacks, the prisoners would cut them open with little knives and steal the grain. The grain spilled out, leaving traces everywhere. This was not the first time that we were working at this place, and the first thing we did in the morning was to survey the area to see whether any spilled grain remained. The guard Titov, an old zek with a bald head like Socrates, whose pockets were full of stolen grain (a guard was permitted to steal), watched vigilantly that we did not steal openly. The amount of grain we collected from underfoot was too little to cook; we ate it raw or grilled it on a metal sheet over the coals of the bonfire until it turned brown, like coffee grains.

That morning I discovered a whole handful of barley under the warehouse door. I was surprised, however, that no one else was looking for grain. Even Stetsin, that walking skeleton, former photographer, who cooked grass indiscriminately and assured us that one could eat anything that a cow eats, was not paying attention to the grain. I could not understand what was going on. "Stetsin, over here!" He did not come! They ordered me to put the sacks on the scales. The supervisor of the warehouse was circulating on the site.

The general indifference to the grain gave me no rest. I sensed something in the air. People were crowding around the flatcar, and they were lingering too long. Something was there. I finally could not hold out, sneaked away, and looked from behind.

I caught my breath: it was a humpback salmon, a beautiful salted fish with rosy flesh, the Arkhangelsk "salmon" of prisoners. Sometimes they would give us a little piece. Behind the sacks of grain were flat, long boxes with fish, and one of them had already been forced open. They removed the side board. The zeks held a silvery fish, one, then another, each a good kilo in weight.

On the other side of the track was a slope and a green meadow. The silvery birds flew from the platform to the grass. We threw several fish onto the grass. In the meantime, they sent me back to the scales to keep the inspector off guard.

We worked until midday. Then we went down the slope and gathered the fish. We moved them to the side and covered them with a jacket. The group was excited. We still had to divide the fish and bring them to the barrack.

Only Stetsin, the grass eater with blue eyes, persisted: he would not wait, and he did not need a whole fish, just give him half, but right now. They cut him a piece and he disappeared. "Where is Stetsin?" the guard shouted from the embankment. "He went to take a leak, citizen guard!"

Stetsin went behind some firewood and in a flash gobbled up half a kilo of salted fish.

The supervisor caught on accidentally. The zeks had closed the opened box and put it on the very bottom, but something told him that this box needed to be reweighed. Over 6 kilos were missing. The supervisor did not say a word, hid behind the train car, and began to observe us.

The whole work group was lying by the bonfire. We had a rest break from midday to one o'clock, but we were uneasy. We kept whispering. Only Stetsin was lying on the side with his stomach up, dozing. One of us could not hold out and began to circle around the jacket, peeping at it. The supervisor jumped out from the ambush, went straight to the jacket, and lifted it: all the fish lay under it. He called the guard for help. "Whose jacket?"

Such an incident in camp is sufficient to warrant a second term, that is, another five or ten years. They searched us and found another fish in the shirt of a zek, who had hidden it from his comrades. He and the jacket owner were caught with the goods. The rest could wriggle out. They immediately dismissed us from work, led us to the guardhouse, and wrote a charge against us.

While we were sitting in the guardhouse, Gordeeva, the head of the General Supply Unit, passed by, walking energetically and tossing her cropped gray hair. They reported to her, and she gazed at us coldly. "Margolin, did you also steal fish?" "I personally did not take fish and did not eat it. . . . I didn't have the time. . . ." Gordeeva walked inside and in passing said, "Send all of them to the punishment cell."

In Kruglitsa, the punishment cell was outside the camp, in a separate little building, behind a separate fence. The warden was Goshka, a pleasant, handsome fellow with a military bearing, a former policeman; he had been sent to camp on a drunkenness charge. He told us his story: once he had to arrest a friend. Duty is duty: he arrested the friend and was bringing him to the station, but on the way, their throats got dry—"Let's drink for the last time." They went to a third friend and arranged a farewell party for the arrestee, that is, the three of them drank themselves unconscious. Then the arrestee and the other friend brought Goshka to the police, supporting him from two sides under the arms. They gave him four years and, as a former policeman, they put him in charge of the camp punishment cell.

The punishment cell supervised by Goshka was clean; there were separate premises for men and women. It was the best punishment cell in which I sat during all those years, and in winter it was even better there than in the workers' barracks of Kruglitsa. Goshka searched us, not roughly but very adroitly, undressed each one, took away various little items, pulled out the little knife that I had hidden in the sole of my shoe (for the nth time!) and proposed that I sign in the "journal." I glanced at it: it was written "for the theft of fish," and I refused to sign.

"I did not steal fish and I did not eat any!" I said. "They put the whole group in the punishment cell! They could have sent the entire brigade! I refuse to sign and I declare a hunger strike until I am released from the cell!"

This was unpleasant for Goshka, and he was angry with me. He was obliged to report a hunger strike to the camp boss, but he had to take food for me from the kitchen. At six o'clock, he brought a bucket of soup for the arrestees, unlocked the door, and across the threshold, handed each one his soup and bread. Goshka was friends with everyone, and in the kitchen, they gave him a bucket with an addition, more soup than allotted by the norm. He placed a cup of soup and bread for me on the bunk. I did not touch them.

The situation was particularly problematic because the surrounding zeks were not accustomed to looking at another's bread and soup while their stomachs were rumbling. The sight of food irritated them. Hungry people began to approach my supper; someone began to cajole: "Give it to me, if you won't eat it yourself." That would be nonsensical because were I to give it away, the camp administration would not care who ate my meal. Once it is taken and eaten, then there is no hunger strike, and my actual hunger does not interest anyone. Goshka had to bring this meal back untouched. I had to take this bread and soup to my place on the upper berth and guard it carefully lest it be stolen.

I do not know how long I could have maintained the hunger strike in such conditions, but on the morning of the following day, Goshka clanged the keys and said to me: "You won! Get dressed, go to the camp!"

I left triumphantly, but my joy faded immediately when in the barrack they informed me that I had to collect my things this minute and go to the guardhouse: they are sending me on an *etap* to Onufrievka! An *etap*! The news struck me like a thunder clap. I had got accustomed to the medical settlement, they knew me here, there was the *selkhoz*, where it was possible to get a little more food. Onufrievka, 20 kilometers away, was a lumber camp like Square 48, with hard work in the forest, and they were sending me precisely to wood felling. The group numbered thirty, and we went as a "work supplement."

With all my might, I had been holding on at Kruglitsa; only here could I hope to survive! Until then I had wriggled out of all *etaps* thanks to Maxik's help: in the medical sector he found out about all *etaps* a day in advance, and, if I was on the list, he would put me in the infirmary for two or three days until the *etap* left. Now, however, it was too late: the *etap* was leaving in half an hour. I still could hide as many others did. But if I showed so openly that I was afraid of an *etap*, then they would purposely include me in the next one. . . . I was unwilling to lie somewhere in some attic or under the bunk in a different barrack and listen while they searched for me throughout the camp.

Maxik was the only person to whom I managed to say good-bye. He gave me a note of recommendation to the doctor at Onufrievka, as a first toehold in the new place. In an hour, carrying a sack, I was already walking on the bumpy road. Good-bye, Kruglitsa! In the evening, Isaac the fifth will return from work and won't find me.

We went half of the way on foot. It was not a good group. Always, when they transfer a group of workers from one camp to another, they use the opportunity to get rid of undesirable people. Onufrievka needed healthy workers, but the head of the Kruglitsa camp was not so foolish as to give away healthy workers: he himself needed them. The group included goners, shirkers, troublemakers, hooligans, and restless elements. Margolin declared a hunger strike?—send him on an *etap*! Let him starve in another camp.

At the tenth kilometer, in Medvedevka, otherwise known as the Third Camp, a place with a concentration of invalids, we made a stop. From here we were supposed to go by train. While waiting for the train, the prisoners took their sacks off their shoulders and lay down on a slope. I went past and found myself a spot on some boards, where there was more room. I had barely lay down when a dark-bearded peasant darted around me like one stung by a bee.

"Go away!" he said, "Get out of here fast!"

"What's the matter, there's not enough room?"

The *urka* rose impassively, lifted the chipped white board on which he had been lying, and with a swing, with all his might, as if at an insentient object, hit me on the chest with the board. I could not breathe and my eyes dimmed. I was choking. All my feelings left me except the physiological effect of that blow. I writhed, felt nauseous from the unbearable pain.... Were it not for my quilted jacket, he would have broken my rib cage.

The *urka* lifted the board a second time, but they had already dragged me to the side.

"Do you know who you started up with? That's Afanasiev." Afanasiev was a famous bandit in Kruglitsa—a mad dog who attacked prisoners and guards. Hearing that name, I immediately backed off.

A few minutes later, I felt tears streaming from my eyes. I was not crying, but I was helpless: crying came from inside me. I had no strength for anger or insult.... I felt only how terrible it was to be weak among strangers and enemies.

Around five o'clock they brought us to Onufrievka. Again, the palisade stretched out, the pointed stakes, and the same guardhouse and the same slogans: "Long live ... Long live ... Long live ..." "Let us give the motherland even more lumber!" The camp boss came out of the guardhouse to inspect the goods they sent him, and at the sight of the men lying on the ground, he gasped: "What is this?! What kind of invalids, monsters! I won't take them. I don't need people like that! To the medical inspection!" Straight from the guardhouse they led us to the bathhouse, where the doctors were already sitting at a separate table in the dressing room. I undressed with difficulty. I did not have the strength to pull off the rags, my worn shoes, the torn jacket, to undo the strings that tied everything together. But I did not have to go into the bathhouse. A miracle happened.

There was an unusual mixture of nationalities in Onufrievka. Already on the way to the bathhouse, I noticed a thin, wiry, dark-complexioned French-speaking person with an enormous nose. He was an Alsace Jew named Levy. I did not manage to find out how he landed in a Soviet labor camp. In the bathhouse, I gave Maxik's note to a Russian medical assistant, but immediately, another doctor at the medical sector table attracted my attention: he evidently was a member of a national minority, undoubtedly so, but he was neither a Kazakh, an Uzbek, nor a Turkmen but some other national minority, with a strangely familiar face. I could have sworn that I had already seen such faces somewhere, but not in Russia. And this face smiled at me, like the face of a friend. I sensed sympathy in his expression.

"Margolin from Kruglitsa, yes, we heard about you. . . ." said the strange man. "Pleased to meet you. You are a Palestinian! Stay and live with us in Onufrievka. We'll prescribe medicine against scurvy for you, we'll find easier work.... Stay with us." This was Dr. Selyam, an Alexandrian Arab who, probably, had visited neighboring Palestine. Here was a place where, finally, Arabs and Jews were friends: in Onufrievka. Hearing that they were asking me what I wanted, I lit up. Back, back to Kruglitsa! No persuasion helped. Selyam wrote a note, an official certification that I was not suited for physical work, only to "sort biscuits." He repeated this familiar camp witticism three times, with an amusing Russian accent and a blinding white-toothed smile. They thus sent me back, along with another fifteen people, half of the *etap*, as un-suitable for heavy work. They immediately led us past the guardhouse and hurried us along the railroad ties, retracing the route back.

It was already eleven o'clock when I entered the sleeping barrack in Kruglitsa. I was very pleased that I had returned to my old place. I was not yet able to rest; my place on the bunk was already occupied. I settled on the floor of the overcrowded barrack. Then I went to the general supply unit office, where the clerk gave us tickets for bread and supper. In the kitchen they gave us leftover soup.

I was most astonished, however, by Isaac the fifth. His face was all flushed and he was beside himself. The work supervisor had just told him that an order had come from Ertsevo, and tomorrow morning they would send him to the Directorate of Ertsevo Camps. As he did not have a "sentence," he im-mediately imagined that this individual summons signified a notice of his lib-eration. Everyone around believed instantly that this was liberation, and he himself was on fire, on edge from excitement; he could not sleep and did not understand what was said to him.

I listened to this unusual news and lay down to sleep on the floor, but Isaac sat for a long time on the bunk, turning his head in all directions, overwhelmed and frightened by his good fortune.

In the morning, I told him that we had to speak seriously before his de-parture. I thought that sometime in the future, this youth would convey news about me to my family if I was fated to die. I was very attached to him and regarded him as a member of my family. To my surprise and dismay, however, this final conversation did not take place. Isaac the fifth, my camp friend and spiritual son, with whom I spent many hours in soulful conversation, with whom we shared hopes and dreams, forgot me even before he left Kruglitsa. On the threshold of freedom, he immediately lost interest in anything that I could say to him. I was deeply hurt and insulted; I could not understand this terrible capacity to forget or inability to remember that is a feature of a weak heart. Times heals all wounds, but here it did not take much time: one day was enough, one hour, one turn of fate, to erase without a trace that which we had lived by, what had seemed important to us, our sorrows and joys, our intentions, decisions, and pledges. I felt deceived. Isaac ran to the exit, barely nodding to me. I did not manage even to give him my family's address.

I leaned over the upper bunk—I inherited his place—and I shouted fiercely after him: "Be a human being! Remember, be a human being!" But these words did not reach him.

They did not release Isaac, and his dream of freedom dissipated in Ertsevo. He spent another year there and then drowned in the sea of labor-camp Russia. To this day, I do not know whether he survived or perished or how he lived through the disappointment of his supposed liberation.

28

Camp Neurosis

A PERSON'S INITIAL acute reaction to the surrounding camp abnormality gradually diminishes during his years of imprisonment as he witnesses a Niagara of misfortune, a countless number of camp fates. At first, everything astonishes and overwhelms him, but this ceases. He no longer notices the abnormality of the abnormal. On the contrary, he is struck by the abnormality of the normal.

One winter day, when our brigade was returning from work, we suddenly saw a sled drawn by a magnificent horse fly by on a side road. The horse's strong neck was handsomely arched, his tail and mane floated in the wind, the sled was not large but elegantly made, and a man dressed warmly in European style sat in the sled. He even had a muffler.

We were astounded. It seemed to us like a dream, a hallucination. The man, horse, and sled all looked nothing like the people, the animals, and things in camp. We had grown unaccustomed to the sight of normal things. We burst into silly laughter, as if what we had just seen was somewhat funny.

In camp, all people and things without exception were deformed. The same Russian words that people used at liberty meant something else in camp. In camp, they say the words: *man, culture, home, work, radio, dinner, cutlet,* but not one of these words means what it normally signifies in freedom.

Under the terrible influence of camp conditions, no one retains his original form. Observation is difficult because the observer himself is deformed. He, too, is abnormal. In order properly to evaluate what is occurring, he should first take into account his own abnormality. No one is unscathed. All are victims; the government-issue jacket cloaks not only bodies but also souls.

Nevertheless, some people in camp live well and are satisfied. At least that is what they say. These people particularly interested me because they exemplified the realization of one of the camp's purposes. The camp system exists to crush spiritual resistance—and either to destroy the person or to make him conform ideally. The first sign of adaptation is when the camp becomes home, a natural form of existence.

"What's so bad here?" said several former *kolkhozniks*. "Every day the food ration is ready, they take care of you: they dress you, give you shoes, medical treatment, feed you. Just work. At liberty I did not live better."

The mass of zeks regarded such camp enthusiasts with ridicule, with some scornful undertone of their own superiority. It was impossible to know, however, whether they were speaking seriously or not. Moreover, it seemed to me that, in fact, these were the healthiest element in the camp population, completely obedient and totally submissive: they did not need anything, and they felt fine in camp. These are the ideal Soviet zeks: their thoughts and desires, their actions and reactions are determined externally. They could be freed—the Soviet regime can completely rely on such people. Even when they are free, an invisible camp wall will surround them.

All the others suffer from camp neurosis to a greater or lesser degree. Given that dozens of millions have passed through the camps during the existence of the Soviet regime, it means that never before has there been such a colossal psychological process, such a deep fissure carved through the soul and character of a nation of the world.

Dozens of scientific expeditions from all corners of the world ought to visit Soviet camps. Regrettably, entrance is totally barred to all free observers, as if the masters of Russia feared that the "discovery" of the camps by independent Science and Democracy, like Columbus's discovery of America, could lead to an invasion by hostile forces of their carefully guarded territory.

By the term camp neurosis, I mean the painful deformation of the human psyche caused by a long stay in camp conditions. Camp "isolation" is completely artificial, contrary to human nature, and imposed by force. One has to be either monstrously dim-witted or a superman not to change in these conditions. For an ordinary person, the sharper the wound and the more profound the suppression of his protest, the greater the pain. Camp inmates suffer not only the known deprivations—hunger, separation from family and homeland, deprivation of material and all other needs to a degree that brings them to a subhuman condition, but also, they are spiritually wounded and troubled, each in his or her own way.

Although the camps developed in the twentieth century, the classic example of a "camp neurosis" dates to the nineteenth century. The famous example is Fedor Mikhailovich Dostoevsky, who spent four years in a tsarist prison and never was able to overcome the trauma of those years. Dostoevsky arrived at the prison as a young person of progressive views, a typical Russian *intelligent*; he left a broken, severe neurotic. Those four years broke him, overturned all his previous notions about society and humankind. What he saw and experienced there was beyond his strength. His "Petersburg ideas" cracked and broke like a piece of glass on encountering this mass of evil. All his subsequent development was the monstrous effort of a former prisoner to overcome his neurosis. Most importantly, he never freed himself internally from his captivity: he accepted the prison, resigned himself to it, and even sent his Raskolnikov[1] there. This experience left him not with hatred toward his tormentors but rather with the conviction that executions and suffering are part of the essence of the world. In his later life, he became a mystical ally of those who were in charge of the Russian prison system. Dostoevsky's work *Notes from the House of the Dead* records his camp neurosis.

Let the readers of this present work, which is not merely about a Dead House but about an entire Dead Kingdom, reread that book. The scale of tsarist and Soviet prisons is so different! Dostoevsky's prison held 250 people, and that is all that he saw. He spent four years in conditions that every Soviet zek would envy. Suffice it to say that in prison he had his own servant, who for 30 kopecks a month cooked for him, heated up the samovar, and took care of his needs. For the entire four years, Dostoevsky did not eat prison food; he was able to obtain his food at his own expense. "Generally, I would buy about a pound of beef a day. . . ." "For several years, Osip would prepare the same piece of fried beef for me." Things like bread, kasha, and cakes are not mentioned; there was plenty of that in prison. There was no work quota, no one collapsed at work, and everyone got the same rations. In the tsarist prison there were whips and rods. A hundred years passed, and they replaced them with execution for refusal to work. The humiliation of corporal punishment was not worse than that to which we were subjected in Soviet camps, where they forced us to lie, to dissemble, and to reject what was sacred to us. Every person who went through the school of depersonalization in Soviet camps will confirm that disrespect for a person there far exceeded anything that existed in tsarist prison. One sees this in the very numbers of the camp population. Millions occupied the place of thousands during Dostoevsky's time.

In my fourth year of imprisonment, I got hold of Dostoevsky's *Notes from the House of the Dead* and read it, comparing the evolution of imprisonment from the time of Nicholas I. The comparison did not favor the Soviet regime.

---

1. The protagonist of *Crime and Punishment*.

I read excerpts from that book to my neighboring zeks: they laughed and were jealous. In a description of a holiday from the *Notes* (we did not have any holidays), when I reached the words, "Toward evening, the invalids, who had gone to the market for the prisoners' errands, brought back a lot of all kinds of food: beef, suckling pig, even goose . . . " laughter resounded: "What a prison! They went to the market!..." "Akim Akimych's suckling pig was roasted excellently." It is surprising what details attracted the zeks' attention during the reading. The description of the hospital: "A sick prisoner usually brought along as much money as he could and also bread (because on that day, he could not expect hospital food), a small pipe, and a bag with tobacco, flint, and a tinder box. These last items were carefully hidden in the boots. . . ." Here the listeners interrupted me: "There was tobacco!" said one with envy—"and they hid it in their boots. . . ." And everyone laughed, because in a Soviet camp only very few have boots. It was obvious to everyone that in the prison described by Dostoevsky (and this was the most severe of the various kinds of tsarist prisons), people were fed to satiety and not tortured at work. From the point of view of a Soviet zek-goner, all the rest was not so important.

Ultimately, in the tsarist prisons, they were confident that at the end of their term they would exit to freedom, whereas the most awful feature of Soviet camps was the absence of this certitude until the very last moment. Precisely in such a prison, however, which seemed so unthreatening to us, Dostoevsky broke down. Every person who reads his book will see immediately what is going on, will see the "painful spot"—descriptions of scenes of torment, detailed descriptions of punishments by whips and rods (which the author himself did not suffer), the lascivious and brilliant exploration of the psychology of executioner and victim, the unbounded horror of a person forced against the wall and not knowing the way out. So that you should not think that all this derives from goodness and concern for mankind, in stunning contrast, Dostoevsky evinces a lack of humanity in his famous portrayal of the "Yid" and the "little Poles"—with no desire or ability to penetrate sympathetically into their alien life that existed alongside his own, as if they were beings from another planet or only flat pictures on a wall rather than live people.

Dostoevsky's camp neurosis, which would distort his entire perception of the world and cast a shadow on all his work, is, of course, not the result of special "sensitivity" but of a severe burn, flayed skin, an exposed wound. In camp, people lose their delicacy and become coarse. There are no tender people in camp, and teeth are extracted without an anesthetic. The phenomena that upset the equilibrium of supersensitive Western people are viewed in a different light by those of us behind the camp fence. In camp, I managed to read John Steinbeck's novel *The Grapes of Wrath*, which was very popular in the Soviet Union. It describes the process of pauperization of American farmers, but in the strongest places, I felt neither empathy nor particular horror at their predicament. I saw only that their "hunger" was better than our "satiety" and that they were free to move around the country, to protest, and to struggle. They had Steinbeck's pen at their service, whereas our mouths were gagged. If Steinbeck had lived for a little while in our camp, he would have been less upset by American injustices. No, we were not weak-nerved people. The "camp neurosis" was not a consequence of our "sensitivity" or "nervousness" but a necessary, sometimes fantastic grimace, a stratagem or a defense mechanism of the soul.

Our dreams reflected the degree of our inner resistance and rejection of camp life. During the entire first year of my imprisonment, invariably, I saw myself free every night. My aversion to the camp was so great that my subconscious, as it were, repelled any trace of camp. Nothing related to camp infiltrated my dreams even in the form of joy that I was no longer a zek. I simply did not recall anything about camp, as if it never existed in the world or in my life. I was proud that I remained free in the depth of my subconscious, and I waited impatiently for night in order to leave the camp at least in my dreams. I imagined that it would always remain that way and saw it as proof of my mental stamina.

Gradually, however, the camp began to gain the upper hand. A year passed, and I had sailed so far from freedom's shore that, even in a dream vision, I was no longer able to bridge the gap that separated me from it. Now the camp began to mix into everything I dreamed, and my dreams became a continuation of the daily camp life. In my dreams, I even wore the prisoner's jacket, glanced around cautiously, and was full of fear or other camp emotions. My soul was unable to leave the camp. Sometimes I dreamed that I was in a distant country, among friends and family, but while speaking with them, I was full of inexplicable sorrow, which did not derive from the content of the dream. In my dream, I had a strange feeling that something separated me from them, and I was like a dog tied by an invisible chain.

Then hunger dreams began. These are typical and identical among all zeks. Every night in every dream, at completely unexpected moments, one dreams of food in all forms and variations. One dreams of gastronomic palaces and sumptuous receptions; bags dropped by someone; bread is lying on the road; something is lying on the table, and suddenly in the middle of a dream about something else, you hold your breath: what has been lying on the table from the beginning of the dream is chocolate, unnoticed, and you can simply take it. . . .

I remember one of the dreams very distinctly: I was on the street, a colorful, lively commercial street in Łódź, but the stores on the street were majestic, from the time of my student years in Berlin. I had run out into the street, as if trying to escape pursuit, and I knew that I had very little time. I had to hurry, but I got confused among the store displays and did not know where to turn: to the dairy store, where there was butter and cheese? Or to the butcher shop, where there was so much ham that even in my dream, I could smell the fresh odor? Or to the bakery, where there were cookies? I went crazy in my dream and rushed around the street, not knowing which door to enter first.

All these dreams inevitably ended in catastrophe. No matter how many times I gathered large handfuls of all kinds of food, not once did I succeed in tasting it. Something always happened, something hindered me, and I would awake disappointed and annoyed. Even in sleep, I was unable to experience illusory satiety. The implacable censor in my subconscious disrupted all hunger ecstasies at the last minute, not permitting their realization. Why? Here the "prohibition" was dictated by an evident refusal of the exhausted nervous system to permit—even in the imagination—the realization of something so beyond real possibilities. People dream of flight, and those who cannot play the piano dream that they are performing like virtuosi. In normal dreams, those who cannot swim are swimming, and those who never tried to mount a horse are riding. In camp, however, I never was able to put in my mouth those wonderful things that I dreamt about, and I kept on delaying and delaying, preparing, and procrastinating until I woke up.

Then came the shameless thieving dreams. Not one of us failed to dream that he was stealing, as this was the only way in camp of deceiving fate, and all restraints collapsed in dreams even earlier than in reality. In dreams, we stole enthusiastically and triumphantly. These were vivid dreams, and I heard a hundred accounts of such dreams from zeks of all ages and situations, and I myself had the same dreams. We stole in our sleep because we had occasion to steal also in the daytime.

These hungry, eccentric dreams passed with time, when hunger became such a norm that we no longer reacted but simply grew feebler and died from it. A hungry dream means that something in us is rebelling, longing, twitching, striving for satisfaction. People dying from alimentary dystrophy, however, no longer have hungry dreams. They lie quietly.

Our struggle against fate then took another form: we began to develop manic eccentricities in handling food—a massive unwillingness to eat food in the form that it was served. We had to manipulate it, deal with it in some special way. We could not simply eat food that was prepared by some alien, indifferent hands. We did not trust that it was prepared in the best manner for us. We had to improve it, redo it. This "mania for improvement" took on various odd forms. We did not eat anything without heating it to a boil; we would add water, cook salted fish on the stove. We fussed endlessly and wasted valuable rest hours. These zeks were martyrs to their neuroses; I know, as I was one of them. Now it is strange for me to recall what I did.

Instead of eating quickly and lying down to sleep, I would rush around the camp in search of a stove where they would permit me to heat my food. It would take an hour or two in the summer until I found a place to put my mess-tin on the fire somewhere in the boiler room, the disinfection room, or some other place where a stove was stoked. The thought of eating something as it was received horrified me. It would have been a misfortune, catastrophe, a shameful failure. They knew about me and others like me, and where ever I went to shove in my rusty tin, I had enemies who drove me away from the fire. As soon as a "food warmer" appears in another barrack, a cry arises: "don't let him in!" In the winter there is a fire in every barrack, but then a war commences with the orderly, who mercilessly tosses the tins away because they extinguish his fire and do not let the firewood burn properly. In the summer, it is forbidden to light a fire in the barracks. It takes much inventiveness and special relationships to gain access to another's fire or at least to find a friend who will place your tin where you do not have access as if it were his.

In the course of time, this heating, adding water, boiling became a morbid obsession for me. The tension was resolved the moment that I attained my goal. My stubbornness in insisting on my way of eating was no longer normal. With a full, steaming mess-tin, I would climb to the upper bunk, and there, hidden from others' sight, like a beast that has crawled into his lair, I ate my fill. The threads of the entire day led to this minute. I did not eat at midday in order to have more in the evening. I left almost all the bread for the evening. My habit of eating while lying on the bunk and not at the table turned my neighbors against me, but I had lost self-control. I pathologically detested "communal" eating.

In 1944, they built a mess hall in Kruglitsa and stopped serving food through a kitchen window. Until then, we used to stand in the yard by the window, receive the food in our dishes, bring it to the barrack, and eat there.

Now the procedure changed: on entering the mess hall, each one handed over his ticket and received his supper. This was "cultured." In reality, it meant that we ate hurriedly, jostled and crowded, in damp jackets; this was instead of being able to undress slowly in the barrack, dry up, and, unhurriedly, slurp up something hot. For maniacs like me, this was a misfortune, the end of all manipulations! Eat what they give you, get up, and leave.

We did not give in, however, and a war started. Everyone smuggled a tin into supper under his jacket. Then, under the table, at the right moment, one would pour the soup from the clay bowl into the tin. At the doors, however, a guard stood, watching lest anyone carry out a tin. One had to slip by him unnoticed. Sometimes an armed guard stood by the door, and we waited patiently until he left. People used all kinds of unbelievable subterfuges in order to bring food out of the mess hall. For example, they poured it into mugs and thrust the mugs in their pockets so they were not visible, and when they had crossed the threshold of the mess hall, their pockets were damp from spilled soup.

Another abnormality was not to eat fresh bread but to dry it. For the last two years in camp, I almost never ate bread except in the form of rusks. In camp conditions, this painfully complicated life. It is not easy for a prisoner to dry bread.

When I was hospitalized, Maxik or another doctor immediately prescribed rusks for me (according to the calculation that 400 grams of bread equals 200 grams of rusks) in order not to annoy me and sometimes because the underbaked bread was, indeed, hard on me. If they did not do this, then I myself dried the bread illegally, in secret, fearing that it might be stolen or I might be scolded. I did not touch the bread until it was dried. Two hundred grams, brought in the morning from the hospital kitchen, represented seven to eight rusks. I ate one in the morning, two at lunch, and the rest at night. You can chew a rye rusk, hard as a rock, slowly and for a long time, unlike a fresh ration, which melts so quickly in the mouth that it is gone before you know it. This is a logical explanation of the rusk mania, but it does not explain the savage obstinacy with which we insisted on it, nor the art involved in cutting a ration of 380 grams into forty-four parts. By this hysterical and absurd procedure, we were defending something else: our individuality, our right to arrange things as we please, and to exert control over our bread. The more they squeezed us in the pincers of camp regulations, the more ridiculous the forms of our "individual" protests became.

A camp inmate who has spent years in imprisonment—and there are prisoners who serve time from youth to death—can be quiet, submissive, and calm as you please, but he has some secret "hidden" spot that reveals it-self from time to time. For example, a good worker, suddenly, for no reason, refuses to work. "Today I won't do anything!" "Why?" "I don't want to, and that's it!" It is best to leave him alone. Otherwise it will be worse. At liberty a person in this condition will get drunk, but in a camp, there is no vodka or money for vodka. A drunk zek is a great rarity, but even without vodka, he is always half drunk, stupefied, and not completely compos mentis. Zeks are like trained animals—but once in a while they will snarl.

My neighbor was the most inoffensive and quiet person who served time in camps from the Transbaikal to the White Sea. Once he was sitting at supper when they came to rush us to the bathhouse—after a workday, when we were hungry and had not rested. He became obstinate, insisting on eating first. At this point, Maria Ivanna, a snub-nosed free worker from the KVCh in a print blouse, butted in: "You go this minute to the bathhouse!" Suddenly the old man turned crimson and roared like a madman: "Don't get familiar with me![2] To you, I am not *ty* but *vy*"! For so many years, he had heard everyone address him in the familiar *ty*—and with the addition of some coarser words—but suddenly he could not stand this precisely from Maria Ivanna. She became flustered and intimidated. Right then the "master's watchdog," the work su-pervisor Laskin, jumped from behind the partition with a contorted face. Pouncing like an animal, he tore the tin and bowl from the old man's hands and took it to lock it up. "That's how you talk to the administration?[3] You won't receive supper until you return from the bath!"

The people in the barrack reacted in various ways. Some approved of the outburst: "Good for you, that you didn't let them address you with *ty*." Others took the side of the work supervisor in addressing the old man. "Oh, you camp louse! So now they can't address you with *ty*? You became an important gentleman . . . you are just like we are, crap!" The old man came to his senses, went to Maria Ivanna, apologized, and went to the bathhouse in the middle of dinner.

The cases when camp neurosis expressed itself in eccentricities such as fussing with pots and rusks were trivial and unimportant. These people remained untouched inside, their disorder was not deep and did not touch their psychic base. There were other people, however—serious, polite,

---

2. She used the familiar form of second person address in Russian, "*ty*," instead of the more respectful and formal "*vy*."

3. Laskin rejects the complaint, emphatically addressing the old man in the familiar second person.

and disciplined. They behaved in an exemplary manner, did not cause any disturbances, and did not act strangely. One had been a high-ranking officer in his former life, a military attaché abroad. Another was an engineering specialist, who for seven years in the camp had been compiling a book of mathematical problems. A third was a defector who came from Poland in 1932. Two of them worked in the office, the third in the kitchen. Outwardly, they looked like normal people. One had to get very close to them to smell the odor of a corpse. In reality, they were deeply unhappy, hopelessly mutilated people. But their decomposition was totally internal. It was as if the ability for normal human self-consciousness had been burned out of them. Their faith in mankind, logic, and a reasonable world order had been obliterated.

In their veins flowed a concentrate of bile and sulfuric acid. They had once all started with faith in abstract, bookish communism, with mental vigor, and expansive plans. One of them told me how he had crossed the border illegally in 1932, how the border guard wrote the detention warrant on a piece of wallpaper torn off the wall—this piece of wallpaper astonished him—and afterwards, how he was horrified by the Minsk prison. The main thing I remember was not what he said, but *how* he said it: with a cynical, creepy sneer, with a foggy, dull, unfocused look—at the age of thirty, he was a living wreck, a finished person. It was no accident that they all were withdrawn and unsociable: they emanated rot and the poison of decay. Dostoevsky at least was saved through Christ, but these people had nothing other than hopeless despair and the feeling of some kind of universal filth.

These people were sick. Their remarks were a form of neurosis. Might is right; everyone lies; everyone is a scoundrel; fools must be taught a lesson. Their minds became confused the moment they were accused of something that had not occurred, overturning their faith in what they themselves had invented. They had nothing to counterbalance this shock. Inside it was empty. They did not stick pots in the oven like some of us, but I had the impression that morally these people had befouled themselves.

What happens to a person who is mentally depressed to the point of a complete loss of resistance? Soviet theoreticians of violence invented the concept of "reforging." Characteristically, this concept is related to an inorganic, dead substance. One can reforge steel, but first one must transform it into a fiery, flowing mass. A man, however, is not made of steel, and if you crush him to the point of losing some of the basic features of his individuality, then it is impossible to restore him to a state of former firmness and integrity. As a result of the crude, mechanical action ("like a hammer on the soul"), some

"former experiences" disappear from the zek's consciousness, forming a fissure, a crack in the foundation. But all the forgotten and the almost forgotten,
the elusive and buried—which turned into fear and grief—continue to afflict
the zek, depriving his "new life" of stability and creating that dissatisfaction
and uncertainty and anger at himself and the surroundings by which one can
easily recognize the camp neurotic.

I learned to discern expertly the status of this camp neurosis after two to
three years in camp. The zeks from Western Europe yearned for their motherland and freedom. For the Russian zeks, the words "motherland" and
"freedom" were also drawn into a neurotic process; that is, these words made
them feel not better but worse.

A camp neurosis is a unique phenomenon. Before I landed in camps and
ever since I got out of there, I never saw anything at all like it. There were
plenty of clowns and jokers and simply polite, obliging people in the camps.
Nevertheless, a sour smell wafted from them, and in the midst of the funniest
witticisms, one could catch an alien, frightened, and completely abnormal
look askance. Their real essence was concealed inside them—gloominess and
grief, which saturated all their psychic pores. Everything was poisoned to
such a degree that they lost all respect for their own reason. "Humanism" was
almost a swear word to these unfortunate people. Someone spit on their soul
and this spittle remained there forever.

In the German death camps, they separated a daughter from a mother and
shot her on the spot. The mother went on, only there was a smile on her lips,
but not of this world, the smile of a crazy person.

Those horrors do not occur in Soviet camps, but the camps themselves
are a total horror, something unbelievable in their businesslike manner, their
solid management and organization of state crimes against the common man.
Soviet camps are full of people who outwardly are all right, follow the main-
stream, hold up better than others but are not alive inside. They do not weep
or protest. If they wept or protested, they would be healthy. These people,
however, are no longer able to understand anything in the world, in the camp,
or in their own unhinged soul. Their entire being is distorted by a mocking
grimace of cynicism, and they cannot rely on anything in the world. Say to
them: "Stalin, humankind, socialism, democracy." They smile, like the mother
whose child was shot in front of her eyes.

They are neither criminals nor counterrevolutionaries but sick people who
ought to be transferred to a country where there are neither camps nor a total
lie. There, perhaps, they would return to themselves.

It must be stated clearly: an unprecedented carnage is occurring on the other side of the Soviet border, inaccessible to world public opinion; it is an unparalleled pogrom of the spirit and execution of human hearts. You cannot even call what happens to the people who undergo this a tragedy, as it lacks any meaning or justification. All this might not have existed if the Soviet regime did not rest on a system of violence based on false theoretical premises. The camp neurosis, which one could also call "Stalin's neurosis" after its propagator, derives from the senselessness of human suffering in camp, in comparison with which the German genocide was the ideal of logical consistency. Neither a person nor a society can remain psychically healthy that is the victim or witness of monstrous crimes that have been turned into a norm, concealed just as a toilet is concealed in a respectable home—crimes known to all but mentioned by none—which do not evoke a protest in the world and are simply noted and even justified by people who claim high integrity. Many crimes have been committed in the history of humankind, and each of them aroused the voice of outrage. People who died in the Nazi gas chambers knew, when dying, that the world had risen against their executioners, and that was their consolation. People in the camps, however, do not have even this consolation—the thought that the world is responding to their fate—which could lower their terrible inner anxiety. A person is capable of remaining mentally healthy in the midst of unlimited suffering only if he understands the reason for his suffering. Without that understanding, one sooner or later loses one's reason or mental equilibrium. Soviet corrective labor camps are a gigantic and unique factory producing spiritual cripples and psychopaths. The border between normal and insane was obliterated in this Kingdom of the Dead.

I shall explain by example. In the last year of my imprisonment, I lay in a hospital bed next to a mentally ill person. For half a year he was my neighbor in Barrack 5 of the Kotlas transit point. They called him Alesha. He was a twenty-year-old fellow from a village in Yaroslavl *oblast*. He had flaxen hair and blue eyes–a real cherub. He had been taken to the front at the age of eighteen.

Near Novgorod he was captured by the Germans and taken to a German school for turncoat infiltrators. That means that he was then fully cognizant, or else the Germans did not look closely at whom they chose. They trained them for three months, "fed them well," and once even took them on a trip to the capital of Germany, Berlin. Alesha did not remember anything about Berlin except that they took them to a movie (he forgot which) and again "they fed them well." After three months, a plane took Alesha's group across the front lines, and on a dark night, they parachuted onto Soviet territory. The entire group with all their equipment immediately went to the nearest police station and handed themselves over to Soviet authorities. Alesha did not remember what happened next. The result was clear to see: a crazy person in camp with a term of five or eight years.

Alesha's derangement was not dangerous: his mind was fogged, he spoke unusually slowly, attentively looking into his interlocutor's eyes; he clearly had trouble finding words to reply and sometimes stopped altogether in confusion. He was a meek, holy fool; he never started a conversation with anyone and never asked anyone for anything. If, accidentally, they skipped over him in distributing food, he never objected and he lay there hungry. He never bothered anyone and everyone loved him. But suddenly—about once every three weeks—he was gripped by anxiety. Then he would get up and walk directly to the guardhouse, to the gates. "Where are you going?" "I am going home," Alesha explained seriously, "to Masha and Nyura." "Who are Masha and Nyura?" They were his sisters with whom he had lived in a Yaroslavl *kolkhoz* before the start of the war. Ignoring the guards, Alesha would head straight toward the camp gates just as a magnetic needle points toward the north. They would drive him away, but he would not leave. It ended with their bringing the tormented Alesha to the medical sector, and the doctor on duty would put him on a cot in the infirmary.

They had to keep a close watch on him in the infirmary because he would get up in just his underwear and in the middle of winter would set out for the guardhouse—"to go home," if they did not manage to catch him at the infirmary door. The on-duty nurse, Maria Maximovna, would then receive the punishment cell for negligence. If they succeeded in detaining Alesha at the door, he did not go back to his bed peacefully. A fight would break out; the medics would rush in and Alesha would become savage. The medics would put a straitjacket on him and tie him to his bed. Then Alesha would begin to struggle and yell. For twelve hours, during which he foamed at the mouth, he carried on madly, and unceasingly yelled the same thing in a strange voice: "Get away from me! Get away from me! Get away from me!"

During that time, no one in the ward, which included people dying of dystrophy and other serious illnesses, was able to sleep. Were it not for these fits, when Alesha showed unusual strength and fury, the zeks would not believe that he was unhinged. In the camp, they suspect everyone of faking, but Alesha was not pretending; this was clear not only from the fits but also because he did not react when they forgot to give him his portion of food.

However, he was frightfully hungry, and as soon as Sonya came to distribute the food, he would beg her for "bones."

The bones belonged to Alesha. They would bring him a bowl of bones from the kitchen, and he chewed on them for hours, like a dog. I was his neighbor and got used to the crunch of bones, chewed by strong white teeth. We all openly envied Alesha, and if they had given the bones to someone else, there would have been protests, but Alesha was a special case. After an attack, two or three weeks would pass. Alesha would feel stronger and again begin to prepare for the road. Then the doctor would come to him, sit on the bed, and begin to explain to him: he is imprisoned, he cannot go to Masha and Nyura. "Why not?" Alesha would ask very seriously. "I didn't do anything. I didn't harm anyone and I want to go home!" The doctor explained: everyone here is the same and all are prisoners, and everyone wants to go home but they cannot. "Why?" asked Alesha, and then for a minute there was silence in the ward, and it seemed to everyone that we, not Alesha, were crazy—all of us— who could not explain to him why he could not go home and only required him to remain with us because we all, like him, were detained and trampled in the mud. Turning to me, the doctor would stretch out his hands and say: "Yes, indeed, he is right! He, the crazy one, is completely right, and I cannot explain anything to him!"

Alesha was destined to lie in the infirmary for years, chew bones, and suffer hunger, although Masha and Nyura were somewhere, and his dying in camp served no one. At night he yelled in a frenzy: "Get away from me! Get away from me!" He would stretch and writhe; the ropes that bound him would grow taut and cut into his flesh; the cot would creak. Lying next to him, I looked at the possessed one's flaxen head, all sweaty and fevered, and I thought that every one of us, trapped in the net of Soviet "justice," each one, enmeshed and padlocked in the enormous dungeon of people called the Soviet Union, could repeat this crazed victim's cry to his executioners.

29

The Bathhouse

UNLIKE THE CAMP bathhouse, the bathhouse for the free workers, where I was assigned, was beyond the camp gates, about 300 meters to the right, on the same side of the only street of the Kruglitsa settlement. At the dispatch to work, we would go out of the gate together with the brigade of the TsTRM (central repair workshop), walk past the camp fence with the guard watchtower at the corner (around the corner was the path to the punishment cell), and then cross the railroad track. Beyond that was a large camp vegetable warehouse. We walked, our tins clattering. Sergey Yulich, the bathhouse supervisor, stepped first on the ramshackle porch, unlocked the door, and entered. I followed. We entered the first room of the bathhouse, with a tiny window, bench, and little table. One door led to a pantry, the other to the dressing room, which contained only benches along the walls; from there was the entry to the bath. The bath smelled of perennial dampness; on a bench under the window, fourteen small tubs stood in a row; almost all leaked. In the corner, on a platform stood a pot-bellied wooden vat that held seventy buckets; alongside were two supplementary barrels each for thirty buckets.

Finally, deep inside was a small door leading to a steam bath room with shelves. My first task was to take an iron sheet and head obliquely across the street to the foundry of the TsTRM, for coal. In the meantime, Sergey Yulich would stoke the two main stoves with firewood: for hot water and for steam—and a third small stove in the first room. Sergey Yulich did not allow me to stoke these three stoves: regulating the fire was his specialty, and he, the one in charge, was responsible for readying the bath exactly on time. While he was stoking, I would pour fifty buckets into the vat. My job was water. I drew the water from a well in the yard with a long pole with a hook at the end. Pulling up the pole, I unhooked the suspended bucket, with a broad movement shifted the full, splashing bucket across the edge of the wooden well, filled a second bucket and carried both buckets down the walkway in the middle of an enormous puddle to the bathhouse. It was not far, but in the bathhouse, I had to climb a stairway. I climbed the six steps with difficulty, my heart pounding, and on top, I poured both buckets into a wooden trough that protruded from the wall. The water flowed along the trough into the wooden vat. The iron pipes from the stove went into the same vat. On bath days, I had to lift around three hundred buckets of water up this narrow, steep flight of stairs. There were three bath days a week for free workers: on Fridays, the men bathed; on Saturdays, the armed guards, and on Sundays the women. On those days we worked hard. The last visitors left the bathhouse around nine o'clock in the evening, and we would return to the barrack no earlier than ten, when the guard escorted the night shift of metal workers, and on his way back took us "home." On the days when there were no bathers, we prepared the firewood. By the wall of the bathhouse there was always a lengthy stack of logs—a week's reserve. From time to time, they brought us several wagonloads of tree trunks, and we sawed them into meter-long logs. The bathhouse swallowed up so much wood that we were always fearful: "and what if they won't bring us any? And what if we don't have enough?"

My boss, Sergey Yulevich Knauer, or "Yulich," as everyone called him, was a neat sixty-year-old, with a round, gentle face, which still showed a trace of his former trouble-free life. For many years, he had been the manager of a wire and nail factory in Moscow, a native Russian-German, who had been living in Moscow for thirty years; previously he had lived somewhere along the western border of Russia, near Białystok. Sergey Yulich was a German and Muscovite in his soul, a great pedant in running the bathhouse, which was for him a shrine and the focus of his life. He maintained it in a state of non-Russian cleanliness, washed the bathhouse floor himself, prepared the besoms for the bathers, and would accompany each one from the bath, bowing and asking, "How is the bath today, is it good?" The guards and civilians, upon leaving, would reward him for his service with tobacco for a cigarette. Yulich rarely smoked but he collected the tobacco and exchanged it in the camp for bread.

Yulich was pleased to receive an educated person for a helper, someone with whom he could speak heart to heart, in German, and, in addition, recall good old mother Moscow. He was familiar with pre-revolutionary Moscow with its close-knit German colony; he graphically described the "Martyanich" and other famous Moscow taverns and restaurants, and explained to me about special pies and soups, and the technique of drinking tea to "the seventh round of sweat with a towel around the neck." According to Yulich's stories, he was an exemplary factory director, surpassed the plan, received prizes, and kept out of politics. That turned out to be his undoing. Careerists with a Party card in the factory brought charges against him, sat him out, and inherited his place. Yulich experienced a great shock at the very first interrogation in the NKVD office, when they addressed him familiarly (with *ty*), cursed him roundly, beat him, and brought a monstrously absurd charge against him. I was familiar with all this (except for the beating) from my own experience and had heard thousands of such stories. I was unable to verify them, but Yulich's entire mental make-up, his old-fashioned, work-loving, bourgeois and loyal mentality excluded the thought of any kind of sabotage or political danger. This was yet another example of senseless cruelty, a principled lack of respect for a human being. The old man had grown children and grandchildren. His wife had been evacuated to Central Asia, where she had nothing to live on, and in vain sought permission to live with her children. He had already been in camp for three or four years, and the main event during this time was the arrival—on the eve of the war—of his wife for a meeting. Here, in Kruglitsa, his wife was able to tell him what she could not entrust to a letter: how after the misfortune, she went to Mikhail Ivanovich Kalinin himself to plead on her husband's behalf. She and her husband thought that "it can't be," that it was some kind of misunderstanding or mistake. It was not easy to obtain an audience with the "all-Russian elder," the chairman of the Presidium of the Supreme Soviet of the USSR, a person who embodied Soviet humanism and love of humankind. A weeping, trembling woman entered the office of this humanitarian. After the first words, Kalinin jumped up from his seat. The Soviet apostle of humanism in golden glasses and with a gray goatee hastily asked the woman: "Where is your husband?" "In the Ertsevo camps." "Aha," rejoiced Kalinin, "that's really marvelous! Those are our best camps! A real sanitarium! How happy I am for your husband! He'll be fine there! Marvelous! Marvelous! Marvelous!" And grabbing the dumbfounded woman by the shoulder, without letting her say a word, he pushed her to the door and led her out in the wink of an eye, repeating, "Marvelous, marvelous, marvelous!" The entire "audience" lasted three minutes.

Since then I have seen Kalinin on the screen and in photos many times, read saccharine-unctuous reports of this preacher of proletarian culture, and this refrain always rang in my ears: "Marvelous, marvelous, marvelous!"

Those were lovely summer days, and I was happy that I had landed one of the best jobs in Kruglitsa. Many envied me. The two bath attendants—senior and junior—lived in an "aristocratic" barrack, the ATP, which housed, in addition to the administrative-technical personnel, the cook and all those whose work required living in a cleaner building. The bath attendants for the prisoners' bathhouse lived at the bathhouse, but we, who dealt with free workers, were in the ATP barrack, which, in fact, was marvelous: a clock with a pendulum hung on the wall, and the bunks were arranged according to a "wagon system," that is, not as a continuous platform but with spaces in between.

The free workers' bathhouse was an idyll. Having first carried fifty buckets to the vat upon arrival, I still managed to run to the neighboring building that housed the TsTRM office and had a radio receiver. To a damp water carrier like me, the office where prisoners sat at tables with papers seemed like the dwelling place of the gods. I meekly stood by the door and listened to the communiqué from the front. If, suddenly, some camp administrator or convoy guard entered, I immediately left, as I did not have the right to leave my work place. Upon my return, I reported the latest radio news to Yulich. Then I went to saw wood, while Sergey Yulich stoked, cleaned, and prepared the bath for two o'clock in the afternoon. We chopped the sawed wood together: we would stand a round log of about 40 centimeters in diameter; I held the wood axe; and Yulich struck the head of the axe with a club until the log split into two and then into four pieces.

Between one and two o'clock, they called us to the road, where the brigade from the TsTRM already stood in pairs. We went to the camp for lunch. We received 300 grams of water in which a few grains were floating. After passing through the gates, the zeks ran immediately to the line under the kitchen window, but I did not take lunch (so that there would be more in the evening), and I went straight to the barrack to sleep. At 1:55, I was already at the guardhouse, where the brigade gradually assembled. People sat on an embankment or on the guardhouse steps until the guard came out, gave the order to "line up," counted that all were present, and escorted us to work.

As we approached the bathhouse, Yulich and I saw from afar that people with bundles were already sitting on the porch. The women's day was the most difficult. Men use no more than two tubs of water, wash quickly, and when leaving, treat you to a cigarette butt or tobacco from a pouch. Women, on the other hand, bring their family with them, drag bowls and tin bathtubs, wash their children, wash their hair, wash clothing, and use incalculable amounts of water. It does not occur to them that I must immediately refill every bucket that is poured out. Two women with a brood of children can drain half a vat. Each new set of five woman on the road sets off an alarm for me. Sergey Yulich, with a dignified and complaisant look, sits at a table in the first room, collects 50 kopecks per person, and lists the clients' names, while I run to the well and drag the buckets. It is a serious matter: if the water in the vat goes below the level of the red-hot pipes, the wooden vat will dry up. Repeatedly, the bath supervisor goes out to the yard and shouts to me with a worried look: "This minute, twenty buckets!" or "Another thirty buckets, in a jiffy!" The vat empties out quickly, and the added water does not have time to heat up. After a while, a cry resounds from the bathhouse: "The water is cold!" Then Yulich opens the reserve of hot water in the two barrels, which we filled separately for this occasion. Both bath attendants rush around like crazy. Yulich handles the cash, hands out tickets, writes everything down, watches that no one steals the clothing, and incessantly stokes both stoves, for which he has to go out of the bathhouse, because the stoves are stoked from outside. The most important thing—he must accompany those who are leaving and ask whether they were satisfied—and receive a little tobacco for this or a promise to send a little soup in the evening.

In the meantime, I rush between the well and the bathhouse. Sometimes a vigorous cry emerges from the bathhouse (it is heard through the wall): "Stop pouring, it is overflowing!" More often, however, I have to see for myself what is happening. At first, I was embarrassed to enter the women's bath, but I quickly got used to the fact that bath attendants, like doctors, are sexless. Gray and skinny, at the beginning of my third year of imprisonment, I was shriveled like Gandhi, and everyone called me "Grandpa," like the genuine grandfather, Yulich. The crowded bathhouse swam in clouds of steam, a lake formed on the wooden floor. The young girls turned around at the sight of the bath attendant, but the adult female population was so oblivious of my presence that I quickly stopped being embarrassed about fulfilling my work obligations. When I saw that the water in the vat was dangerously low and would not heat up quickly, I declared "Sperre" for half an hour, that is, a ban on taking water. Everyone then sat on the benches and platform on which the vat stood and waited patiently. I turned, in my old rubber boots over bare feet and upturned pants, and went to draw water, while Yulich saw to it that no one took water. Understandably, when Gordeeva or the wife of the camp boss was washing in the bathhouse, we bent over backwards to make sure there were no hitches. If they were dissatisfied, we risked our job: one word of theirs would have sufficed to remove us. Often large families of free workers, upon coming to the bathhouse and learning that "Gordeeva is washing," departed in order to help us: not to create congestion in the bathhouse in the presence of the bosses.

Men's days, in contrast, were a delight. Exiting the steam room (they steam, pouring water on heated stones), ruddy-faced and satisfied, the guards and other free workers would get dressed and sit for a while, smoking cigarettes of "self-grown" tobacco. We had something like pincers to bring them a little coal to light up. I learned to grasp a little piece of coal adroitly from the stove with the pincers and bring it to the dressing room. Everyone in Kruglitsa knew Yulich, and he was the basic beneficiary. I, too, occasionally acquired a half dozen cigarette butts and a small amount of tobacco or the homemade kind, which I could exchange for a food ticket or a piece of bread in the camp.

The bath attendants' main profits came from the neighboring housewives. We worked in the settlement among the free workers. Now and then, they would run to us to ask for hot water to wash clothing. We were not stingy, we gave them government water, and in return, a day later, snub nosed, bare-foot Glashka or Mashka would appear in the bathhouse with a pot: "Soup for Grandpa." Sergey Yulich would take it with gratitude, pour it into his bowl and sit down to eat. Fifteen minutes later, the same girl would appear again: "Soup for the worker!" That was my portion. They gave us the soup which they themselves did not eat—from the state cafeteria. We in the camp knew well that the food prepared in the cafeteria for the free workers was just as bad as that for the prisoners. The difference was only in ration-card products—every month they were allotted five kilos of potatoes, meat, and fat, whereas we were dying from the lack of those things. Not those handouts but their "individual vegetable gardens" saved the free workers: they grew their own potatoes and vegetables. They cooked their own soup and they would sometimes give the state gruel to the bath attendants. For us, each spoonful of this brew was important. Sometimes they would send us a little potato, carrot, turnip, or mushrooms. From all this, Sergey Yulich made a wonderful soup.

At six o'clock, the TsTRM brigade returned to camp; I would gather dishes for two and go to get dinner. Yulich was unable to get away, but I would take the meal to the guardhouse, and there, against the rules, they permitted me to go with the tins to the bathhouse.

Once a week, the zek-hairdresser Grisha would exit the camp with me. At our bathhouse, he served the free population of Kruglitsa on a weekly basis. On other days, the free workers would go to the camp hairdresser, where they jumped the line, were shaved and had their hair cut.

Sometimes the guard would be stubborn and not let me back to the bath-house. Yulich would remain without supper or an assistant. Some catastrophe would happen in the bathhouse within half an hour, and one of the clients would run to the guardhouse, yelling: "Let out the water carrier, there's no water for the bath." I sat patiently with the mess-tins by the guardhouse and waited until they called me: "The one in glasses from the bathhouse, pass through!" We did not have time to eat supper until around nine o'clock, when

everyone left the bathhouse. Before leaving, we had to wash and straighten
out the bathhouse. Finally, by the light of a kerosene lamp (the bathhouse was
connected to the electric grid, but there were not enough lightbulbs), we lay
down on the benches and dozed until the guard's call rang out in the darkness
near the porch: "Bath attendants, come out!" At that time, the last group of
zeks from the TsTRM returned to camp. In step, we walked through the inky
darkness of the autumn evening. The street was drowning in the impassable
mud, ahead of us the camp fence was darkly visible, and from the watchtower,
the guard's voice challenged us: "Who's there?"

The guards on watch were members of national minorities: undersized
Kazakhs or Udmurts, with physical defects that kept them from being taken
to the front, and they spoke little Russian. "Who's there? We'll shoot!" one
of them shouted from the watchtower in a frightened voice, and the zeks
laughed when they walked by. Those guards were not convincing as representatives of the regime. Soon they, too, were sent to the front, and women began
to guard us. Many of them were already widows; by summer 1944, eleven of
the forty mobilized in Kruglitsa had been killed.

Free workers did not discuss "dangerous" topics with prisoners. Once,
however, I overheard a conversation not meant for my ears. Two of our last
guests in the bathhouse were whispering to each other late in the evening.
They were speaking about what all Russia was discussing secretly in the fall of
1942—the situation in the occupied areas. An officer who had returned from
the Finnish front was talking about three days that he had spent in a region
occupied by the Finns. One could gather that he had wanted to remain there,
but first he wanted to assess the situation. He saw starvation, slavery, and the
gallows. The Finns did not have bread or warm clothing; the Finns were not
liberators but merciless conquerors. After three days, the officer returned to
his unit.

This story provided a clear answer to the question why impoverished
kolkhoz Russia held the front and was dying for the Politburo. Not because
these people wanted communism and dictatorship. They wanted it as much
as during the first Patriotic War, in 1812, the Russian peasants wanted the tsar
and the continuation of serfdom. And not because all the dissatisfied people
were sitting in labor camps. Dissatisfaction in the Soviet Union stemmed
from objective conditions and could not be eliminated by repressions.
Imprisoning the dissatisfied in camps is just like cutting nails and hair, which
always grow back on a living organism. Note that for a quarter of a century,
the regime told these people frightening things about capitalism abroad.
What they finally saw—Europe of the Nazi cannibals—turned out to be

even worse than what they had been told. Hitler's greatest crime was compromising Europe in the eyes of the Soviet people and not leaving the Russian people any other way than defending themselves against cannibalism. What he showed in the occupied territory with a population of seventy million was in no way better but much worse than the Soviet regime. This was not clear at once. In the first months, the Red Army vacillated. Entire divisions and army corps surrendered; millions laid down their arms. If then they had given the Russian people—one of the greatest although politically backward peoples of the world—bread, freedom, and respect for national and human rights, this people itself would have liquidated the monstrous regime that had been imposed by Party usurpation.

The officer from Kruglitsa first took a look at what was happening beyond the front line and then returned. He chose the lesser of two evils. At Stalingrad and Kursk, he defended not camps and NKVD terror, of course; he defended his country from the Germans. Every one of us, while rejecting Stalinism, would have done the same. The system of cynical lies and violence that exists in Russia cannot be overturned by impure hands. The population of the camps, which is separated from the rest of Russia, and all the rest of Russia, separated by the Iron Curtain from Western democracy, needs help from outside—not from fascism but from the uplift and ideological support of Western democracy, which could convince the Russian people that it is worthwhile to exchange its inhuman regime for Western-type democracy. It clearly was not worth exchanging it for Hitlerism. Communism was introduced in Russia by a civil war and only an internal revolution can destroy it, provided Soviet society clearly understands for the sake of what it is rising up. Evidently, Western democracy has a long way to go in development and self-determination for it to be understood and attractive to a Soviet person. People in Kruglitsa are not familiar with Western democracy and see it in the distorted mirror of Soviet propaganda. They know about all the hideous things occurring in the West, but they are unfamiliar with the foundation of civil liberty, the power of individuality, and the multicolored brightness of life in the West.

Going out to the bathhouse porch, we saw children and women from the settlement coming from the forest with full baskets of berries and buckets of mushrooms. They did not want to sell anything, and we were unable to make an exchange for bread. Nevertheless, that summer, we bath attendants also utilized "unrationed" gifts of nature. As we were outside camp bounds and not with a brigade, a guard could not keep an eye on us. The guard had to monitor around fifty workers scattered among the workshops and buildings of the TsTRM on both sides of the street: there were warehouses, a smithy, and a machine shop, a power station, a carpentry shop, a supply room, and office. The guard rarely looked in on us during work hours. There was an invisible line drawn around these buildings, which the prisoners were forbidden to cross. Our "forbidden zone" was fifty steps away from the bathhouse; burdocks grew there, beyond which was a little hut where a poor widow lived with her children. A swampy meadow lay beyond the hut, but the meadow was already off bounds. The meadow, however, was close by and overgrown with bushes behind which it was easy to hide. I soon began to run into the forest, the blessed forest, which nourished the people of Kruglitsa without a ration card.

Sergey Yulich let me go for an hour to an hour and a half, immediately after lunch, on non-bath days. Then the guard would lie down to nap. I would take two glass jars and leave the yard. There was a narrow path beyond the burdocks where there was a fading inscription on a wooden board: "FORBIDDEN ZONE." I walked in a business-like manner, absorbed in my task. This was not a stroll for pleasure. I did not look back at the camp, which stood out against the background of the clear sky. An airplane flew very low toward the north in the direction of Arkhangelsk. No doubt, from the airplane, the white barracks and watchtowers of Kruglitsa must look picturesque. I, however, had memorized this view and surrounding fields, where brigades of mowers spent days at work. Golden wheatgrass lay underfoot; sometimes one came across shiny black bird cherries, which were highly valued. In the meadow, rosehips were scattered; their purple seed cases were especially tasty in the first frosts in September. We ate a lot of rosehips, when we went with scythes and rakes to work. Now, I went farther and farther away from the bathhouse. I came across blackberries and bilberries on the muddy meadow, but I did not stop.

I rarely encountered passers-by; I would hide from them in the bushes. I was easily recognizable as a zek and as a stranger: in the settlement of Kruglitsa, all the free workers knew each other. If a guard sounded an alarm or I ran into a camp boss beyond the zone, that would be a disaster: they could accuse me of attempting to escape. It was not difficult to escape from camp. In any other country, there would be many cases of escape, but in the Soviet Union, there are special conditions. Here every person and every piece of bread is numbered. There is no place to escape to and nowhere to hide.

Raspberries were growing right by the road. Never in my life had I seen such an abundance of wild raspberries. Pale green leaves with a silvery underside now and then could be seen in the meadows and in the shade of the forest. The bushes bent down under the weight of the ripe, ruby berries; raspberries were everywhere. I left a bush that I had not finished picking and went to another, where the branches simply broke from the drooping berries. And in the grass, on delicate, thin stems were wild strawberries. Soon my fingers were red from juice. I ate and filled the jars with raspberries. I brought Yulich a half liter and left another half-liter for myself for dinner. In two years, these were the first berries I tasted. In the camp, they would give 200 grams of bread for half a liter of raspberries, but I never exchanged them for bread.

I hurried; there was little time. The little boys whom I met in the thick of the forest were all used to the sight of a zek and could think that my brigade was working nearby. There were enough raspberries for everyone. Children in the settlement did not starve in summer. And the zeks would starve less if they let them gather berries, but no one thought of that. Several invalids in Kruglitsa would gather berries and mushrooms. They would give the berries to the pharmacy administration, and they dried the mushrooms for the winter. The mushrooms, composed ninety percent of water, were the least nutritious product of the forest. Invalids had to fulfill a quota for gathering both items. Upon their return from the forest, they were searched to check whether they hid something for themselves.

Our days were filled with hunting for food. We had successes and defeats in this struggle for existence. For several days, Havrylyuk the wagoner, a good-natured Ukrainian who had been sent to camp for his dislike of the *kolkhoz*, drove past the bathhouse with a load of cabbage. Yulich and Havrylyuk struck a deal, and once, when Havrylyuk drove past, Yulich sent me to him. I went up to the wagon and Havrylyuk, checking all around, threw a cabbage head from the wagon. I instantly tossed it into a bucket and brought it to the bathhouse. We barely managed to hide it in the pantry when the guard entered. It seems that he was hiding around the corner and saw the entire operation. "Where did you hide the cabbage?" We had to hand it over. That was a big disappointment. Havrylyuk and I faced the threat of the punishment cell. I was already preparing for a night in Goshka's little house, but this time it all ended well: instead of handing in the cabbage at the guardhouse and writing a report against us, the guard brought it home to his wife and hushed the matter up.

Another time, I went to the neighboring vegetable warehouse for a bucket that we had loaned them. They brought me to a special cellar where even their own workers are not allowed to enter. Only the manager entered there, and a guard sat by the treasure. I stood by the wall and suddenly I saw by the table a basket with something rosy and white. In the half-light, I could not discern what it was. The manager went out for the bucket, and the guard turned his back to me. He immediately sensed something, turned around quickly and looked suspiciously at me. I stood innocently by the wall. In the second that the guard turned his back to me, I had managed to thrust my hand into the basket, grab a handful of something sticky and slippery, and put it in my jacket pocket. Returning to the bathhouse, I discovered that my pocket held pieces of fresh beef fat: an unheard-of treasure. I gave the booty to Sergey Yulich, and on that day, we ate an extraordinary soup of mushrooms and fat, with salt that Sergey Yulich found for the occasion.

On November 1, 1942, there was a sharp reduction in the supply of food to the camps. This was not the first time, but never before had they reduced our portions of bread and kasha so sharply. Even the portion of camp soup was reduced from 800 to 500 grams. The gruel for those who fulfilled the norm was cut fourfold. The second winter of the war began in the camps, where even before the war, starvation was the usual condition. Simultaneously, my work in the bathhouse became much harder with the start of the cold weather. The stoves swallowed more firewood; I had to saw and carry water in the freezing cold; and as it was dark already at four o'clock in the afternoon, I had to draw water and drag buckets when it was pitch dark. Fall downpours and storms began. The rain gushed for hours. Now people were more willing to go from their cold homes to the bathhouse, and they sat there as if at a club. In the pouring rain in my damp and torn garb, I rushed in the dark autumnal evenings from the well and up the steps with a pair of buckets. In the morning, the water in the well froze, and I had to break up the ice. The buckets slipped off the hooks and fell into the well; I had to crawl into the well to get them. The theft of firewood started. Every day, arriving in the morning, we saw that the neighbors had dragged away the wood that we had sawed—there was not enough fuel in the settlement. We did not manage to saw enough. Work in the bathhouse turned into a nightmare for me. In just one month, November 1942, I lost my strength and turned into a living corpse. In front of my eyes, Sergey Yulich began to melt; his cheeks became sunken and his eyes dimmed. He had become accustomed to me over five months, and he understood that if they sent me to other heavy labor, I would not survive, but he had to think about his own survival. With me as a helper, he could not handle the work. He needed a young and healthy worker. After long hesitation, he finally made up his mind; one evening he went to the work boss and asked that they assign him a different worker. At the end of November, without warning, they removed me from work in the bathhouse. It is difficult to convey the horror I felt at this news. This was the end. I did not know where to go or where to hide. The next day, they were supposed to drive me to the open field in the frost, among brutalized, vicious people to whom I meant nothing and who, at the least sign of weakness, or wrong movement, would crush me. In the morning, at the dispatch to work, I asked for one last day at the bathhouse under the pretext that I had to pick up my remaining things. Aleksandr Ivanovich, the work boss, allowed me to go as a third. Another water carrier was already working in my place. I went to the TsTRM office nearby, where over the five months they had become accustomed to my coming every morning to listen to the radio. There were two or three people there who knew me well and saw that it was necessary to save me. They whispered together and offered me work as a draftsman starting the next day.

30

In the Office

I HAD NO clue about the work of a draftsman. The position of a draftsman was open in the TsTRM office, and therefore, with the consent of the senior accountant and the head of the workshops, they assigned me to this job in order to enable me to rest for a few days and see whether they could find some use for me in the future. I spent a full five weeks in this office.

At this time, January 1943, when there was a turning point in the war at Stalingrad, I was undergoing a physical catastrophe. Office work no longer could save me. I knew that I was dying, but I did not dare show this to the people around me for fear that they would throw me out. With all my might, I clung to my place in the office. I soon realized how oppressive a stranger's mercy can be and how difficult it is for a drowning man to stay above water.

I was like someone who had fallen off a ship into the sea. The ship sailed on. Its last lights drowned in the dark night. One is left alone in the middle of the ocean. One's muscles grow numb, and one knows that these are one's last minutes.

I envied people who died in a dignified way, tranquilly, in the comfort of home, in a snow-white bed, or heroes who died, holding their weapon, for a just cause, whose memory the nation then reverently preserves. Finally, I envied the dog who crawled into his kennel before his death. Our deaths were many times more hideous and agonizing.

At that time, alimentary dystrophy, or the collapse of the organism as a re-sult of starvation, had already become a mass phenomenon in the camps. As always, however, the first victims, the avant-garde of a procession of millions of corpses, were surrounded by distrust, annoyance, and the indifference of those who still had several months' reserve of strength. We were the pioneers of camp death: feeble intellectuals, mentally and physically unsuited, who had been dragged into the very thick of the camp whirlpool, into the anonymous heap of working camp fodder.

I was now living in the TsTRM barrack, where I was surrounded by special people: smiths, locksmiths, metal workers, welders, electricians, tractor drivers, mechanics, and carpenters—all experts, in better physical condition than others because they secretly traded their products with the free workers: keys, locks, pots, bowls, metal parts. They were better fed. I was lucky to land among them, but I had no right to be there, and this mistake would become clear quickly. The five weeks in the TsTRM did not save me, but it slowed down the tempo of the catastrophe, as if I did not fall down precipitously but slid to the bottom down a slope.

Two years later, confined to bed, I observed alimentary dystrophy in the final stage. Death attacks the destroyed organism, which is incapable of resistance, in a specific place. People die of heart disease, tuberculosis of the throat, most often of edema. By that time, they are no longer able to move, and without the medic's help they cannot take care of their basic needs. Like infants, they are seated and carried from place to place. In their reports, the doctors would indicate alimentary dystrophy as the cause of death. In May 1945, however, an order arrived from the Moscow Gulag: stop listing alimentary dystrophy (AD) as the cause of death: instead, indicate heart failure, pulmonary disease, etc. An order from on high thus wiped out death by starvation in Soviet camps. It would seem that the statistics of mortality in innumerable thousands of camps, with the single monotonous refrain "AD," ultimately bored the people who were killing us but considered it necessary to maintain formalities while doing so. Starting in May 1945, not one more person died from starvation in Soviet imprisonment. The fact that this order was marked top secret indicates its authors' awareness of its shameful meaning.

At the beginning of 1943, I entered upon the path of death but passed through only the first stages of alimentary dystrophy. My pre-war weight of 80 kilos dropped to 45. I began to experience difficulties in walking. I covered the 300 meters that I had to walk every morning to the TsTRM office with the greatest strain, covered with sweat. I moved my feet with an effort. I had a sense of their presence, but when I tried to lift my foot, it seemed alien, as if instead of feet I had prostheses or lead blocks. It was a strange feeling when my old legs, which had served me and been part of my body for forty-two years, suddenly stopped obeying me or following my orders. When I approached the three steps of the front porch, I first placed one foot on the lower step, then dragged up the other. Then with a look of concentration, as if solving a difficult problem, I tackled the second step. I was walking like a decrepit eighty-year-old. The process of walking became a dramatic experience for me. I was not, however, an exception; every day more and more people became like me.

The second symptom was a rash on the elbows, knees, and sacrum, bright red on the dried skin that lacked a fatty lining. My bones protruded outside, the collar bone and ribs stuck out; our flesh melted away and the skeleton emerged. A medical examination of dystrophy sufferers consisted of ordering us to lower our pants and turn around. One cursory glance at the place where once there had been buttocks replaced an entire check-up. We no longer had anything on which to sit. When I went to the office, I brought along a little cushion for the chair, but it was already difficult even to sit. I needed to lie down.

I did not have the right to lie down, however, because they did not release me from work. In a state of deep, geriatric exhaustion, when a person is drawn to rest, when one's hands drop on their own and one's heart sinks, when one's feet ache incessantly as after a long journey, when one's temperature drops a degree below normal, and one is dying out like a glowing ember dropped into snow—from morning to evening, I circulated among people while ful-filling my duties. They gave me orders, sent me somewhere, got me up from my place, rushed me—and I was not simply dying but dying on the go, at work, in a crowd, a crush, in fear and eternal apprehension—from which di-rection is disaster coming?

Zeks usually say, "we are not living, we are existing," meaning that for them life boils down to maintaining the organism's physiological functions. Now, even this "existence" turned into an unbearable torment, interminable corporal suffering. When I fell asleep in the barrack, I sincerely wished that I would not wake up the next morning.

In the office I was a scribe. They had me copy over records, reports, ac-counts; my job was to check whether everyone came to work. Before the camp dispatch to work, I would get a list from the medical sector—who in our bri-gade was released from work because of illness. Then I made the rounds of the workshops and all work places to verify that everyone was present. In addition, I swept the floor, brought coal for the stove, carried firewood, and when it got dark, closed the shutters. All day they would send me on various errands. I did all this very poorly, very slowly, with a visible effort, which made those around me uneasy. Very quickly the camp aristocracy had enough of me—they had allowed me to take shelter from general work in the office on the condition that I would be an alert, cheerful, and obliging companion. A conflict arose as early as the first day, however, when it turned out that I was in no condition to chop firewood. They did not give us firewood for the office; we would steal it from the abandoned site near the power station. I went with everyone to this lot, carried a log on my shoulders, but I sawed very feebly and slowly, and I refused to chop altogether. My companions could not forgive me for this refusal. I, who had been taken in out of kindness as a pseudo-draftsman, did not have the right to refuse the job that they ordered me to do.

Possibly, this was not as terrible as it seemed to me, but I reacted tragically to the general hostility toward me. I felt like a superfluous, unnecessary person in the office. One of the symptoms of alimentary dystrophy is a weakening of memory and mental capacity to the degree of feeble-mindedness. I forgot the addresses of my closest friends. I forgot the names of my favorite writers, the titles of Plato's dialogues. After some time, it turned out that I was unable to write any document without mistakes, and there were errors in all my accounts and computations. Everyone around me was clicking with bullet-like speed on their abaci. The dry clack of the beads sounded in the office from morning to evening, and only I was unable to calculate quickly on the abacus and would work faster on paper.

I did not have my own place in the office. There was a table for the accountants, a table for the engineering-design office, and a table for the supply and maintenance manager of the brigade, and I sat in the place of whoever was absent at the given moment. I did not dare, however, to sit in the place of the senior accountant even when he was absent. Nor was I granted a pen or ink. There were no writing implements; each person who was "allowed" into the office got hold of them wherever he could, guarded them, locked them up, and never let anyone touch them. They made ink themselves from an indelible pencil, which they bought secretly for bread because they were prohibited in the camp. I had my own pen. I left it in an unlocked drawer of the table, and it was stolen by the next morning. I obtained another pen, dipped it into an inkpot, and received a stern rebuke: "Don't mess around with someone else's inkpot; bring your own." Everyone sat with impassive faces by their own inkpots, and I was unable to copy an order for the boss because I did not have ink. This was more than malevolence—it was their cold fury at my lack of strength, ink, memory, resourcefulness, and warm gloves. The TsTRM had its own clothing warehouse, and in the office they all received gloves and footgear for the winter. I, however, was a temporary guest, a stranger, and they did not include me on the list. These were Soviet people, with no mercy for a stranger's need, who fiercely clung to their own possessions and hated the weak who burdened the "collective."

Gradually, they stopped giving me work. There was nothing for me to do in the office. My feet were freezing. From time to time, I would get up from the table and go to the stove to warm up, but I should not have done that! I sensed the intensification of hostility toward me in the room. Finally, someone who was better disposed toward me than the others could not hold back and told me directly that I do the least work and warm up the most, and this gets on his nerves. He, however, was wearing felt boots, while I had only thin, torn old rubber shoes, the *cheteze*.

I had to be wary of provocative questions at all times. Once the senior accountant Petrov asked me: "What is fascism?" Before I managed to collect my thoughts for an answer, I saw that behind his back, people were making furious signs that I remain silent. I had to avoid such conversations, which could harm not only me but also those present.

The head of the brigade was the engineer Morgunov, a person who did not look at all like a Jew: a tall, dark-complexioned, strong person. The zek Morgunov had spent many years in China and he spoke English. This is what brought him to the camps: he belonged to that group of employees of the Far East railroad in Manchuria which, after this railroad was ceded to Japan, returned to Russia; they were all sent to camp because they allegedly had been infected by contact with foreign countries. Morgunov did not despair; he was a Soviet-style camp "Nietzschean," who once told me directly that there was no place in camp for the weak: "let them die." He applied this principle of "push the falling" to me with complete consistency. When Morgunov entered the office, I knew that now they would send me somewhere, get me up from my place, think up something for me to do. Morgunov would send me to find some person, and I would crawl, like a dog with a broken leg, from workshop to workshop, from building to building, falling in the snow drifts as if asleep, and I myself was surprised if suddenly I would come across this person, who, incidentally, would pay no attention to the summons. Morgunov would send me to the field to bring logs, knowing full well that I was unable to lift them. I struggled with them until someone would come out of the office to help me.

The people in the office were frequently summoned to do physical work when it was necessary to clear the snow promptly off the railroad tracks or unload some train car. Although my participation was completely useless, I also went, because physical work earned one or two hundred extra grams of bread. I toyed with a shovel or assisted somewhere and then openly and shamelessly sat somewhere on the side. Others still tried to pretend that they were working, but I was no longer suited even for that.

The maximum physical effort came in the evening when we returned to camp. Each one took a thick block of wood or log with him to the barrack, carrying it under the arm, or on the shoulder, with his head leaning against the frozen bark of the wood. This block gave one the right to warm up by the stove. Whoever did not bring anything was driven away from the stove.

It was hard for me to climb up to the upper bunk. Once up there, I would not descend except for extreme necessity. I even stopped getting undressed for the night. The physical effort required for taking off the padded pants and everything that was tied around me was too much for me. I only took the *cheteze* off my feet, removed the jacket, covered myself from the head down with the camp flannelette blanket and fell asleep to the noise of conversations and the buzzing of the radio.

The population of Kruglitsa did not decrease. Sick prisoners continuously arrived at the medical settlement from surrounding camps; when they were discharged from the hospital, they remained to work in the brigades. In the neighboring regular working camps, however, a decrease was noticeable from the beginning of 1943. The camp population was diminishing. The decrease derived from people dying off rather than from releases at the end of terms. As they did not send in new zeks in the first two years of the war, those already imprisoned had the illusion that the end of the war would mark the natural end of the camps. Frequently, looking at the dirty barrack walls, at the barbed wire fence, at the faces of the guards, I said to myself: "All this will soon disappear, it will pass like a bad dream, will melt like snow in the sun . . . and they won't find the places where these things were. . . ." I rejoiced when I heard that the two neighboring camps, where the population had thinned out considerably, were united into one. We harbored this illusion about the end of the camps until the second half of 1944, when a new, powerful wave of prisoners flowed into the camps from the areas retaken from the Germans.

In the beginning of 1943, that is, the third camp winter, Jacko died. I remembered him as a sprightly, self-confident sawyer; when they excluded him from the amnesty for Poles, he became an embittered admirer of Hitler, full of hatred toward his executioners. In pre-war Poland, Jacko was a nationalist and probably would not have conversed with me, a Jew. In Kruglitsa, however, where he was dying from consumption, I was one of the few with whom he could speak in Polish. Once or twice a month, I would visit him in the hospital for tuberculosis patients—the same one where I had spent three good days in July 1941.

The hospital was full of dying people, and Jacko had grown quiet: he knew that he would not leave the place alive. He had a plan: to request a talk with the security officer. He wanted to make an "important statement" to him—to reveal a secret. I tried my utmost to dissuade him from this idea.

It was not worth revealing any secrets to the security officer. Jacko was very afraid of death among strangers, death that was doubly anonymous because he was in camp under a false name. Jacko was not Jacko but someone else, and he had something important that he absolutely wanted to save from oblivion, to convey to trustworthy hands. Finally, he hinted to me that he had to speak with me apart about an important matter, but he did not manage to do so. During his last days, I myself was lying in the hospital, and in vain Jacko asked the medic to find me and tell me to come to him. Only after his death, I learned that he had called for me.

It thus remains a secret who was hiding behind the name Jacko and what unfinished, important business he had in the world. While he was healthy, this person seemed to me insignificant and unpleasant (as I probably seemed to him)—his thoughts and feelings were alien and hostile to me, and in other circumstances, he easily could have been my executioner. But I saw clearly and incontrovertibly that all this no longer mattered. The root of evil was elsewhere. Jacko was neither better nor worse than others. Jacko was my fellow human being.

It was clear to me that people cannot overcome the differences— natural, historical, social, and personal—that separate them, but that is not the source of evil. In camp, everyone died equally: fascists and democrats, Jews and antisemites, Russians and Poles, good and bad. Individuals, just like entire societies and peoples, should be left in peace with their weakness and imperfections, and one must remember that every person is capable of committing a crime under certain conditions. Evil—genuine evil that deserves deadly hatred—is only that which wipes out the living human being in the name of a fetish, a number, a plan or calculation, in the name of "Cheops' pyramid," no matter what it was called in the language of politicians and conquerors. Everyone understands the difference between a human being—even the most hostile—and a soulless machine that sows death and multiplies suffering in the world. The crime that cannot be forgiven is the rejection of our shared humanity and turning a person into a soulless instrument of murder and enslavement.

In the camp, I learned to see the flip side of things, the flip side of every word. A word such as "fascist" signified unconditional evil, and this same word served as a pretext for executioners to break and crush living life in the name of something that was just as evil as fascism.

At approximately the same time, Semivolos died. This solid, powerful man crashed down like an oak in a storm. A chance disease, pneumonia, felled him. Then it became clear how deeply the years in camp had eaten him away from within. This man taught me, a newcomer, how to live in camp, how to take care of oneself, how to start a bonfire in the forest, how one should and should not eat. And, lo and behold, it turned out that I, the incapable weakling, outlived him, the hero and Stakhanovite. The strength of my resistance was greater, and there is a simple explanation for this. In the camp, Semivolos was a leading worker and distinguished personage, whereas I, a normal-looking person outside of the camp, was a formless, pitiful clump of living protoplasm in the camp. I had no ambitions in camp, and I utilized any crack, any hole in the ground to hide. If all the people in camp were like me, the camps would have to be liquidated. Camps rested on people like Semivolos, who wanted to be "worthy camp inmates," on industrious slaves who worked themselves to the bone and from whom the unscrupulous camp regime drew out the last drop of strength. Semivolos's death in camp amounts, of course, to murder. We, human dust, died in the millions from illnesses and starvation, but occasionally we outlived the strongmen, because we succumbed less easily to exploitation and more easily found illegal loopholes in a difficult situation.

At the beginning of February, my good fortune ended. They expelled me from paradise. Late in the evening, the female work supervisor woke me up in the barrack, tapped me on the shoulder, and drily informed me: "Tomorrow to another brigade." I was mortally insulted that Morgunov and Petrov did not consider it necessary to warn me or give me time to prepare myself. Now nothing remained but fatalism: What will be, will be. . . .

There is a gap of several days in my memory: I do not know how I spent the following days. Only the date February 8, 1943, is firmly etched in my memory. On that day, they brought me unconscious to the clinic, and I then lay in the hospital for a long time, until April 20. Again I was in the surgical ward, my usual refuge, where I found protection and salvation every time when the waves already were closing over my head. The first two days I lay in Maxik's ward like a dead person. I sat up only for food, and the rest of the time I lay immobile, rested with all my being, dozed, slept, thinking about nothing, and experiencing the happiness of a person whom the waves tossed onto soft sand after a shipwreck. My imagination did not extend to anything beyond lying here for another week or two.

On the morning of February 15, the ward became alarmed: they began summoning the patients for an examination.

The door from the ward opened to a side corridor from which another four doors led to the storage room of the manager, to the examination room, the medic's room, and the operating room. A line of sick people stood by the entrance to the examination room. All were panicked. Some unfamiliar doctor sat there. We were all acquainted with such monitoring forays, with a one-minute check-up and a brief order: "Discharge immediately."

I was in despair when Maxik, in his white robe, ran into the ward, glanced over the row of cots and pointed his finger at me: "To an examination!" Tears formed in my eyes. Why don't they leave me in peace?

"Max Albertovich!" I gave him a pleading look. I wanted to say to him that one week is too little, that my feet do not support me. But Maxik hurriedly turned away, pretending that he did not hear, and he left. I thought bitterly, "Traitors, cowards." The patients went out to the corridor in turn, while I remained lying down. "The later, the better," I thought. "Maybe they will forget about me." But Karakhan, our Turkmen medic, came to me and sternly reminded me: "Margolin, get up; after all, you were already called."

In the examination room, in the presence of the head of the medical sector, a free worker with little understanding of medical matters, a doctor whom I had never seen before ordered me to undress and began to take notes:

"Scurvy," he dictated, "extreme exhaustion, keratosis, dilation of the heart by two fingers, noise in the upper right lung. Was there pleurisy? Write that there was. Damp, dry? Write damp. What, an ulcer? Very good. Vision: near-sightedness, eleven diopters. Frequent headaches? Write, write everything. . . . Dystrophy, pellagra, boils. . . . Max Albertovich, what else should I write?"

I saw that one can complain to this man, one ought to complain, and it is worth complaining, and I opened my mouth and poured out my soul. I described my condition to him with such details that even a stone would have melted. I saw that today they would not yet throw me out of the hospital, not today in any case.

I left and lay down on the cot. I was very far from the thought that at that minute my fate was being decided. Imperceptibly, I fell asleep. I fell asleep as a third-category worker ("light work") and woke up as a second-group invalid. They "decommissioned" me. The unbelievable, dizzying news fluttered through the ward, transmitted from cot to cot. Everyone looked at me with envy. The medic Karakhan Shalakhaev was the first to congratulate me, but I did not believe it until Maxik himself came, sat on the edge of the cot, and said, rubbing his hands: "Well, comrade Margolin, we have decommissioned you. You working exploits are over. Are you pleased?"

Was I pleased? I was delirious with happiness; I did not know what to do with myself, this was my happiest, most festive day in camp. Decommissioning is more than being an invalid of the second group. Decommissioning a prisoner means official confirmation that not only is he unfit for physical labor but also that he cannot restore his health under camp conditions. This for-mulation "in camp conditions" is very important. Under normal conditions, he still may be able to restore his work ability, but in a camp, the medical sector lays down its arms. In 1943, they released many invalids on the basis of "decommissioning." This document provided a formal basis for my release. My situation in camp changed radically, and this change was sudden. I was overwhelmed.

Just a few days earlier, Morgunov had pushed me around like a dog, and my evident weakness only irritated all those around me. That I had been brought to the condition of an invalid was not enough on its own. Had it not been for the intervention of Maxik, who hospitalized me and then presented me to the visitor—had it not been for "influence" and personal acquaintance, I would have continued to go to work, like others who were in no better con-dition than I and were decommissioned two weeks before dying.

In the hospital, I helped keep the records. Karakhan took me to the exami-nation room, seated me at a table, gave me pen and ink, and I copied fifteen or-ders in two copies each, fifteen documents of decommissioning, including my own. The amusing thing was that this document, which for me was a life saver at the last minute, was a hoax. The document attributed twenty-four diseases to me because simply writing the truth, that after two and a half years in camp, I was no longer able to stand on my feet, would have been insufficient.

I spent the following days in joyful excitement, in a festive fog. First, it was clear that on the basis of the decommissioning, they would let me lie in the hospital for a long time. Decommissioning documents were sent to Ertsevo for confirmation. Half of them were lost there, including mine. Before the end of the year, therefore, they called me twice for a re-examination. My ap-pearance saved me every time—gray hair at the age of forty-two, extraordi-nary emaciation, pitiful weakness, and exhaustion.

The work supervisor's power over me ended on the day of my decommissioning. From that time, I worked only voluntarily and at my own choice—so as not to die of hunger on an invalid's ration. My well-being improved. The camp inmate whom the administration does not have the right to drive to work every morning at its discretion continues to be a zek, but he is already half-way out of the camp—he is no longer a camp inmate in the specific hard labor sense of this word, signifying slavery. He can choose, he can drop work that is too hard for him and not work at all if he prefers to die of starvation.

The first days after my decommissioning, I lay in bed like a happy child, smiling at the whole world and reconciled with everyone. I had not received a religious upbringing, and before the camp I never troubled God with my prayers. In camp, where my fate turned into the plaything of the elements and chance, for the first time I felt the need to express in words a stubborn faith in the miracle of salvation, in universal Reason, invisible but present behind the universal senselessness. Then I learned to end the day with the words: "Lord, take me away from the dirt and return me to my Homeland." Only now did I begin to feel that this happy ending was truly possible.

I had a need to share my happiness with someone. I wrote a letter to Palestine, a letter home to my wife, addressing it to myself: Doctor Julius Margolin. Just as I was finishing it, the security officer entered the ward and saw from afar that I was writing something. It was in the evening, the dim electric bulb was burning opposite my cot, and I did not notice the hostile guest. He came up to me, took away the letter, carried out a search in my night table and found the invariable *Questions of Leninism* by Stalin. Inside was a photograph of my son, the only thing that I still had from my former life. He took the photo, too.

Any other time I would have been upset, but now nothing could darken my mood or bring me out of a state of blessed happiness.

Thank God, I was an invalid!

30a

Three

[MARGOLIN WROTE THIS section separately from *Journey to the Land of the Zek*, but it was included by the editor of the full Russian text as Chapter 30a.]

In January 1943, misfortune befell three people in the TsTRM office. Fate touched each of them in very different ways, and I, an involuntary witness of human misery, was occasionally distracted from my own misfortune by the unusual spectacle of what was happening all around. Our "dead kingdom" was full of bizarre "subterranean" tragedies, which do not occur on the surface of the earth. The tangle of human bodies in which I was enmeshed moved unceasingly, and I involuntarily bumped into others' misfortunes, like a fish trapped in a net that cannot move without colliding with other such fish.

One January morning, we were listening to a radio broadcast about German atrocities. In one of the villages in Voronezh *oblast*, the Germans murdered ten children because one of them filched a cigarette from a German lieutenant. They tortured the children before their deaths, and the radio reported the first and last names: Kolya Kostrov, age twelve, Shura Kostrov, age ten. . . . The abaci were clicking all around and people were not paying much attention. Suddenly, the senior accountant raised his head: "Kostrov, Voronezh *oblast* . . . Our Vasily Nikolaevich—where is he from?"

The supply manager of the TsTRM brigade, Vasily Nikolaevich Kostrov, was a Don Cossack, around thirty years old, short, energetic, lively, and a good friend to everyone.

"No," said another: "Kostrov is from Rostov. But the village fits: Aleksandrov."

We began to listen to the radio broadcast: they flogged them half to death, threw them into a cellar for a day in the winter, and finally shot them. The zeks were silent. We lived behind the fence, and those were accounts of people in the open field. Kostrov came in from the cold and began to shake off the snow from his boots in the corner.

"Vasya," asked the accountant Petrov, "is your village really Aleksandrov?"

"Aleksandrov."

"What *oblast*?"

"Voronezh *oblast*," said Kostrov. "It was Rostov but later became Voronezh."

"You have children there?"

"Two," said Kostrov. "Boys. Now they must be eleven and ten."

A sudden silence fell in the office. Everyone looked around, and the clicking of the abacus ceased.

Kostrov had already served five years of his term in the camp, and he had that many more to go. In such conditions, a father's attachment fades and its nature changes. Children are a matter of the past, a memory. Should they meet, Kostrov would not recognize his children nor they him. All the same— a father! He had to be told; perhaps it was a mistake. . . .

Petrov's cheekbones moved, and we saw that he was very upset that he might be the first to tell him such sensational news. Seeing a calm, unsuspecting person, and knowing that he is in your power, and from one word of yours, he will now bend like birch bark in a fire—that is an extraordinary feeling!

He spoke very weightily and distinctly, looking straight at little Kostrov:

"The radio broadcast this very minute: in the village of Aleksandrov, in Voronezh *oblast*, the Germans killed the Kostrov children, Kolya and Shura."

Kostrov turned white as a sheet and sat down. Interrupting each other, the zeks retold the contents of the broadcast.

"For one hundred kilometers around," he said, "there are no other Kostrovs in the region besides us. . . ."

He looked around inquisitively, as if expecting someone to argue with him, but no one disagreed or tried to dissuade him. He waited a minute and went out to the yard. The voice over the radio was the only information that reached him. Everyone listened to the radio that day in the hope that the report would be repeated. Indeed, several other people heard that report, and each one conveyed his version: each heard the *oblast* and age of the children differently.

Kostrov, however, no longer had any doubts. A few days later, we got hold of a newspaper with all the details. He did not speak to anyone about this matter and for a long time stopped smiling or joking. He then submitted a patriotic request to the Supreme Soviet of the USSR, asking them to send him to the front and to give him the opportunity to avenge the death of his children, which the entire Soviet country had read about.

The KVCh affixed a reference praising his behavior in camp, but nothing helped. Half a year later, Kostrov was still imprisoned in Kruglitsa. The Germans murdered too many Soviet children for the Soviet government to allow itself to free all their fathers imprisoned in camps. Or to put it another way: too many fathers of families are in camps for the fate of their children to have an effect on their terms. The case of Kostrov's children was exploited on the radio for propaganda purposes: "Death to the enemy!" Only we, however, imprisoned in the Kruglitsa camp were able to view this incident in its entirety and to know that the pogrom against the Kostrov family began long before the Germans' arrival in their village.

On the other hand, they released Raevsky, a young Moscow engineer who not only was educated and well-mannered but also possessed self-control. Raevsky was taciturn, unbelievably polite, restrained to the degree of an English phlegmatic; he parted his hair with a comb, smiled pleasantly, and had several French books, which he willingly lent to others. I also borrowed from him a story by Pierre Loti, "Ramuntcho."

We all rejoiced when the order arrived to release Raevsky. In December 1942, he finished his five-year term. God knows with what tension this reserved and correct person waited for that day, with what concealed agitation he counted his last days in camp. He worked in the engineering-design office of the TsTRM. All the technicians of the repair workshops lived together in a separate "clean" partition of a common barrack; they held up well, looked good, and even resembled each other. One had French stories, another had a guitar, a third had clipped pictures from illustrated journals and hung them above the bunk. Upon his release, Raevsky was not permitted to leave the district. He remained in Kruglitsa and received an assignment as head of the very same engineering-design office where he had worked as a prisoner. This was the "freedom" that he had awaited for five years. Now he no longer was escorted under guard to work, but life presented other problems.

First, he could not find a room in the settlement. There was no place to live. Finally, he found a small room three kilometers from Kruglitsa, but it was empty, and he had to obtain a bed and table. Not only was there no one to care for him, to wash his clothing, cook, and mend. Worse, there was no fuel for the stove. In the evening, there was no electricity or radio as in the camp barrack, and they even took away his camp blanket upon his release. In peace time, he would have written to his mother in Moscow, who would have sent a blanket and so forth, but now no packages were sent from Moscow.

Even more important was the issue of solitude. Without being aware of it, over five years, Raevsky had become accustomed to being with people in the barrack, in the noise of shared quarters. The only way for a camp inmate to be alone was to cover his head with a blanket. For sensitive people, the absence of solitude could be agonizing but for unhappy people, it is very supportive. As they say, "Misery loves company." You can imagine Raevsky's state when he returned after a day's work to his cold, empty, dark digs.

Raevsky was unable to handle his long-awaited "freedom." We soon noticed that he changed greatly. Had they allowed him, he willingly would have returned to the camp barrack, to his old, habitual place. But he had been released. In a short time, Raevsky deteriorated; he became drawn, gloomy, and slovenly, stopped shaving, and started to miss work days under various pretexts.

Everyone noticed his mental distress. Something clearly was wrong with Raevsky. He became so absent-minded that he did not hear what was said to him, he answered inappropriately, fell into a deep reverie, and in that state, would sit for half an hour, staring at the wall in our office, as if something invisible to the rest of us was written there.

The most difficult thing for him, of course, was to walk the three kilometers to and from his home in the winter snowstorms. There was no road. He had to walk along the railroad track. One evening in January, there was a disaster. In a snowstorm, a locomotive overtook the distracted Raevsky at a turn, wrapped in the impenetrable white cloud of the storm. Raevsky's mind was again elsewhere. He was walking with his head down, his ears covered with the earflaps of his padded cap. When the locomotive, smoking and shining its lights, approached him, it was already too late. Raevsky jumped aside into a snowdrift, tripped on the rails, and remained there. His leg was cut off.

He thus returned to the camp after all, to the surgical ward. He left there after four months, without a foot, but also without a trace of his mental illness. In the camp hospital, as a free worker, of course, he could not lie together with the zeks. That would have been insulting to his status as a free Soviet citizen. They therefore placed him in a separate little room next to the treatment room, where the medic Karakhan Shalakhaev was stationed. In truth, Shalakhaev, a member of a national minority, was also a zek, but as a medic and cultured person, he was very useful to the patient. Raevsky left the hospital on crutches, but reconciled to life and, as before, polite and restrained, like an English phlegmatic, with a pleasant smile, and with the absolute self-possession that is so necessary to a Soviet citizen at all stages of life.

The nastiest incident happened to a third member of our group. He was the most pleasant of all, a live wire, and he was the one most annoyed by my frequently warming myself by the stove. Grigory Ivanovich Novosadov held the job of accountant in the TsTRM office; he was no longer young, the hair at his temples was silver-colored, but the cowlick on his forehead was combative and playful. His entire short, lean figure was unusually assertive and pugnacious. Although there was something of an officer in his bearing, he was a natural-born accountant by inheritance and a typical Soviet civil servant from Vladimir on the Klyazma River. On the outskirts of Vladimir, he had a wood house with a vegetable garden and a yard with chickens, and in a sty, he raised a pig, which he himself slaughtered for Easter. All this was long ago—ten years back. Novosadov had been imprisoned since the start of 1933. He survived ten years in a camp, but he was saturated with grief, reeked of tobacco, was prickly like a porcupine, and became unbelievably foul-mouthed. Novosadov swore with gusto, with savage energy and inspiration. He garnished each phrase with elaborate grace notes that could surprise even a virtuoso in this field. Novosadov swore with talent; in Russia, an inability to swear or drink is a sign of puny mediocrity. The very juiciness of his language testified that he was a hearty person.

In his youth, Novosadov had one trauma: he had spent time during World War I in Austrian captivity and almost died in a camp for prisoners of war. A German benefactor, an engineer, saved him by taking him to work in a factory in Vienna. Grigory Ivanovich retained bits of German from his stay in Vienna along with very good memories, which he did not hide. This is what doomed him. He tried to speak German with me, too, as he recalled imperial-monarchic Vienna.

Aside from that, he mercilessly pushed me around, considering me beyond help and worthless. As I mentioned, he did not let me stand by the stove, but when there was no work for me in the office in the morning, and the senior accountant Petrov would stare at me with a leaden gaze as if I were something deserving liquidation, Novosadov was the one who would find some work for me, hand me something to copy. . . .

Grigory Ivanovich's two sons were at the front, where they were promoted in rank and earned medals, but neither of them wrote to their father in camp, which filled Novosadov with grief and indignation. "They forgot their father!" he said. "What's a father to them? They are making their careers! Instead of demanding from the regime—yes, demanding—their father's return, pounding on the table, they just remain silent! Just wait, I shall return home, we'll meet, I'll tell them what I think of them. . . ."

The entire TsTRM office and the entire ATP barrack knew the exact day when Grigory Ivanovich was supposed to be released. He had already prepared a suitcase and outfit for freedom: wool pants, a shirt purchased from a Polish zek, a jacket and cap—all new and festive.

"Sixty days," he said triumphantly. A month passed. "Now only thirty days remain!" He counted the remaining days; he beamed and rejoiced, looking like a groom before his wedding. "Chop us a little firewood before leaving!" His colleagues in the office said to him, "In a month you will forget us." On the wall, he hung a handmade calendar on which he circled the precious day when the gates of the guardhouse were supposed to open for him. Even his eyes were brighter and clearer, eyes that ordinarily were covered by a film, as if ten endless, bleak camp years had left a patina on them.

A week before the longed-for day, Grigory Ivanovich was already not living: he stopped working, or rather, he was in no condition to do anything or concentrate on anything.

Suddenly . . .

Suddenly Grigory Ivanovich was summoned to the security officer. After that conversation, he did not return to the office. He returned to his place in the barrack, lay down, and froze. He looked like a ghost. A disaster happened—one of those camp stories which occurs regularly and does not surprise anyone.

Grigory Ivanovich had been living for so many years without knowing that someone was trailing him, recording every incautious word—about Vienna, where he had wandered as a prisoner, about adult sons who don't feel like interceding for their father, and more and more. . . . The material piled up, the reports arrived for years, one after the other. On the eve of his scheduled release, the Third Sector sent his "personal file" to the prosecutor in Ertsevo, who quickly issued an order: "Detain him and investigate." That kind of resolution predetermines a prisoner's fate. First, they ordered him to remain in the barrack and not go to the office any more. Then they summoned the senior accountant Petrov to the security officer: "What do you know about Novosadov? Did he speak about the Germans? Did he criticize Soviet power?" After him, they summoned others, warning that if they hid anything, they would be held responsible along with him. Out of nothing, they started to create a "case." Each summoned person mortally feared for himself and tried to show his loyalty so as not to become entangled.

The last evening that I saw Novosadov, he was like a dead man. No one would talk to him or go near the place where he was lying. Suddenly, he quietly called me. I sat next to him on the bunk, and he whispered: "In a few days, they may summon you to an interrogation; they will ask about me ... so look, don't say anything extra, don't bury me!"

"Of course not, Grigory Ivanovich, what do you think? Do I seem like a squealer? We never spoke about any such things. I know that you are a good person. I'll tell the truth, that you hate the Germans and are proud of your heroic sons."

"Petrov informed on me! Watch out for him!"

"Why are you trembling, Grigory Ivanovich, nothing will happen, they'll check, and that's all. After all, everyone here knows you. You'll be an accountant in Vladimir until your death." They did not summon me to the security officer. The following day they transferred Novosadov to the punishment cell, and from there they sent him to the Ertsevo central prison. In Ertsevo, they gave him a second term—another ten years—and sent him to another camp. He never returned to Ertsevo.

The only reminder of him in the TsTRM office was the small handmade calendar on the wall with the circled date: "the longed-for day."

In January 1943, the fates of Kostrov, Raevsky, and Novosadov caught my imagination only because I happened to be their neighbor in the office. Had I worked in another place, lived in a different barrack, I would have witnessed other sorrow, and there would have been more of it rather than less. Indeed, the TsTRM was still one of the most fortunate places in camp, an oasis of quiet.

31

Maxik

LET US REVIEW the facts: Dr. Julius Margolin, an independent journalist, a healthy person and father of a family, a Polish citizen with his permanent residence in Palestine, who has nothing to do with the Soviet Union and did nothing against it, was seized by the Red Army on the territory of Poland in September 1939 when he was returning to his home in Tel Aviv. His documents, passport, and visas were all in order. What should have happened?

Evidently, upon checking his documents and clarifying that the given person is neither a spy, thief, nor murderer, he should have been allowed to continue on his way to his home. In that case, this book would not have been written, and until his final days, Dr. Julius Margolin would have retained the pleasant conviction that the Soviet Union is a state in the avant-garde of revolutionary democracy. What happened?

Dr. Margolin was detained for nine months, after which he was arrested and, on the basis of an implausible, absurd charge that he lacked legal documents (as if the possession of a Polish passport by a Polish citizen violates the laws of the Soviet Union), sent to a corrective labor camp for five years. There the world lost track of him. After two and a half years, he was turned into a cripple, a pitiful and perpetually hungry being, whose closest friends would not recognize him. At first, Doctor Margolin was, of course, astounded, overwhelmed by such treatment. It seemed to him that this was a mistake or his personal bad luck. In camp, however, his eyes were opened, and he saw, to his horror, millions of people around him, Soviet and non-Soviet, who were in the exact same situation. He made an astonishing discovery that took his breath away: this was not a mistake but a *system*—a singular method of running a state taking up one sixth of the planet and of controlling a nation that could be kept in submission only in this way. Camps arise out of historical necessity, an inevitable consequence of the system of forced labor introduced in Soviet Russia. The system of forced labor itself derives, with logical necessity, from communism. Communism on a national scale cannot exist without a harsh central regime that implements an economic plan by means of sharply coercive measures. There is no communism without state planning of production, and there is no planned production without forced labor. And there is no forced labor without camps. All this, evidently, with the population's consent. Securing this consent is child's play for a regime that has unlimited and monopolistic control over the sweat, blood, and every hidden thought of all of its subjects. An election system is dangerous only for weak rulers; it obediently serves the strong, just as a dog servilely stands on its hind legs for its master.

The purpose of the camps is to isolate from Soviet society all elements who do not fit into the above communist scheme harmoniously and voluntarily, or "as if" voluntarily. Understandably, in this system, human life has no meaning. In sending people to camps, mistakes are not only possible but also unavoidable: "You can't make an omelet without breaking the eggs." Is it really possible, with a camp population of ten or fifteen million people, to track each individual injustice? But that is not what matters. A Soviet citizen, if truly loyal, should not be upset by a mistake that affects him personally or his neighbors. He must understand that the re-education of society cannot take place without such—even if massive—mistakes, and even if he is in camp through no fault of his own, he is obliged to work conscientiously for the state in accordance with the plan because *this*, rather than his personal dreams and desires, constitutes the objective purpose of his existence. If he wants to be completely loyal, then he must not simply suppress his protest or personal feelings (which amount to concealed counterrevolution), but he also must bring himself into harmony with the system. He must desire the same thing that the Politburo desires; he must not simply obey, but *love* the Party, love the NKVD, love the camp, love his camp lot and his camp death, on which this beautiful, first, and sole proletarian democracy in the world is founded.

Having understood this, Dr. Margolin ceased to be amazed but did not become a friend of the Soviet regime. It became clear to him that this regime had, from its point of view, the right to send him to camps because in the system of contemporary slavery, every person potentially joins the great family of workers, whether he is a Pole, an American, or Chinaman. One cannot yet utilize the Americans for the good of the organized communist world, however, as they have protection from consulates and everything related to them. With the Chinese, you can be less polite; there are many Chinese in Soviet camps. As to the Poles, in the summer of 1940 and the following years, they had no protection and no power that was worth taking into account. The Soviet regime therefore sent them to camps and exiled them indiscriminately and without restraint in every case when the unified repressive production plan required this. It was entirely superfluous to send Dr. Margolin to his wife and children abroad or even simply to review his particular case, because no one abroad raised a hullabaloo about his fate, and here he could bring some benefit to the Soviet state as a digger, sawyer, or loader.

The previous chapters have told the story of my first two and a half years behind the scenes of the Soviet system. As a hopelessly decommissioned invalid, I had hoped that they would release me, but I hoped in vain. That was my second disappointment in camp. The first time, they arbitrarily excluded me from the amnesty for Polish citizens in the winter of 1941. In 1943, they kept me in camp despite my decommissioning. They released many ordinary prisoners, but all those who were "suspicious" in a political sense were left in camp despite their decommissioning. I shall describe the second half of my camp imprisonment as briefly as possible. The specific difficulty of my telling my tale is that I am forced to omit many events and details, many names of people who remain in the power of the Soviet government, in order not to harm them. Consequently, I must omit several basic moments from my story. The Soviet camp kingdom is not only an institution; it is millions of live people, millions of puny existences in conditions that a European cannot imagine. The important thing is not only *what* is told about them but also the very fact that something is said about them despite the will and decision of the Soviet dictatorship, which has isolated them from the world. Whoever hears these two words, *Soviet camps*, should know that this is not only a method, not only a banner and symbol of the regime. It is something that goes beyond the borders of political debates, propaganda, and counterpropaganda: it is *people* in *bondage*.

To this day, Doctor Max Albertovich Rosenberg—a person with whom I lived for three years in Kruglitsa—is alive and well in the Soviet Union. He served out a ten-year term there. They arrested him in 1937 on Article 58, for counterrevolution. Max Albertovich came from Przemyśl in Galicia, from an Orthodox Jewish family. His father was a Hasid; the son, however, could not read or write in Hebrew. In 1915, during World War I, after a long siege, the tsarist army conquered the Austrian fortress of Przemyśl, taking General Kusmanek and 120,000 prisoners. Among the prisoners was a young Austrian medical student, Max Rosenberg. He spent two years in Russian captivity, in the city of Shuya in the province of Kostroma. Maxik's main feature, both then and afterward, was a loving heart. He fell in love with a Russian girl. The Russian Revolution took place in 1917, and in 1918, he returned to Przemyśl and set out for Vienna to finish his medical education. In 1921, Maxik graduated from Vienna University. By that time, Przemyśl was already a Polish city. The young doctor, however, did not like Poland, just as Poles did not like Maxik's large Jewish nose. He did not receive a license to practice; he encountered difficulties at every step—and his beloved girl was waiting in Shuya. Max did not hesitate, and in 1922 he crossed the border.

Those were romantic times of much confusion and disorder. Max was reminded of his [illegal] border crossing only fifteen years later. Max Albertovich lived in the Soviet Union for fifteen years in complete satisfaction. He became an excellent surgeon and a solid, law-abiding citizen. Max Albertovich always emphasized that he had lived very well before his arrest, and he wanted nothing better than returning to that time in his life when he was a free Soviet citizen. Unlike many others, he did not regret having crossed the Soviet border. His life was in the Soviet Union. He could not imagine that he might return to Europe sometime, and it did not have a place in his heart. He was a Soviet Russian doctor. He spoke Russian fluently, and only a few peculiarities in pronunciation betrayed his Western origin. As one of his mispronunciations came from German and the other from Polish, one would have to know Max Albertovich's biography in order to understand them. Later, I discovered that Max Albertovich could read in Polish but neither liked nor valued that language, whereas he not only loved other European languages, but they were his entertainment, his hobby.

Max Albertovich had an excellent nature—imperturbable and full of calm goodwill toward people. He was one of the best people that I ever met. The fact that he—with his most sincere, genuine loyalty toward the Soviet regime—was serving time in camp and could visit a patient in the settlement only accompanied by an armed guard with his rifle at the ready was one of the Soviet absurdities that did not surprise anyone in camp except Maxik himself. He was not offended, but he was extremely surprised by the incomprehensibility of what had happened. You had to see the expression of dismayed disbelief when he told the truly grotesque story of his "investigation and trial." In 1937, they isolated all those who had arrived from abroad, including Maxik. His fifteen years of irreproachable work did not help. As Maxik was a genuine and sincere patriot of the Soviet motherland, who would reject the least criticism of the regime, I amused myself by "explaining" to him the profound meaning of his imprisonment and showed that he, as a Soviet patriot, ought to accept and approve of his presence in camp. Maxik, however, was not a dialectician; I felt that in the depth of his soul, something, all the same, remained incomprehensible. He could neither understand nor justify his misfortune, but he became reconciled to it because of his good nature, meekness, and inexhaustible vitality.

In 1943, he was fifty-four years old. He was round-shouldered, with the energetic face of a sailor; his clear, lively, youthful eyes shone under his light brows. He went around in his own short fur coat and wool cap, his body tilting forward, walking quickly, as if afraid to be late. In conversation he would listen to his interlocutor as if soaking up what was being said to him, and then he would respond decisively, enveloping the interlocutor with his conviction and determination. He had a doctor's manner, as if instructing his dull, uncomprehending patients how they should take their medicine. With all that, Maxik was a gentle person, a lyrical one. I never heard him raise his voice, yell, or scold anyone. He was in charge of a fifty-bed surgical ward and a clinic, but in both he handed over the administrative side to more energetic aides and dealt only with treatment. The patients related to him with that special respect mixed with apprehension that is always evoked in simple people (incidentally, not only in simple ones) by a surgeon, a person who cuts the body. The calmer and more peaceful Maxik was in his white medical coat with his firm, shaved chin, large plebian mouth, and solid, massive nose and transparent gaze from under the pale brows, the more fantastic did his profession seem: opening up stomachs and sawing human bones. Maxik trepanned skulls, amputated limbs, sewed up intestines, applied stitches, wielded a knife.

Such skill could not but inspire respect in the most hardened scoundrel. When he came in from the corridor to the middle of the ward and, clasping his hands behind his back, stopped to listen under the column where the radio loudspeaker was, the patients would lower their voices and there would be relative quiet.

The surgical ward was at the end of the first line of barracks in the medical settlement, in a corner of the camp rectangle. Walking on the narrow path alongside the "forbidden zone," one had to circumvent the Special Supply Unit, two workers' barracks and one hospital barrack, and then turn the corner. A low door opened to a small entryway. From there, one directly entered the ward; to the right was the "kitchen" and to the left—Max's residence. His room, which measured three by one and a half meters, contained a small stove for heating and cooking and across from it, an iron bed. Under the small window with a yellow chintz curtain stood a wooden dresser-table; on the side was a little bookshelf. Above the door was another shelf. Under the bed was a suitcase with linen. Two stools. On nails driven into the door hung a sheepskin jacket, the doctor's medical coat, and other items.

Normally, doctors and medics were housed two in a room. Maxik's room was so small, however, that it could not hold two, and they allowed him to live there alone. In camp, this was an exceptional luxury, but Maxik was valued by the administration as an outstanding doctor. He also earned money from treating the free workers. Of course, this well-being was relative, but, nevertheless, the locked dresser under the window had a few things not found in a general barrack—a few potatoes, carrots, onions, occasionally a glass of rendered fat, sometimes an extra piece of bread. Government rules allotted the doctor second-category rations, but in Kruglitsa, the hospital kitchen was separate from the general one and, of course, the cooks here did not adhere to the norms, adding food to the doctors' and medics' tins. None of the medical personnel was starving, although the hospital food at that time was insufficient to feed the patients properly.

Max Albertovich's room had luxurious items: a table lamp made in the camp, with a chintz lampshade sewn by a female hand. There was a radio loudspeaker—not a government one but his own. The KVCh tried several times to take it from the doctor when one was missing someplace else, but Max Albertovich always proved that it was his personal property, and they left it with him. The most striking feature of Maxik's abode was the pictures. The entire wall above the bed up to the ceiling was covered with small pictures—watercolors and oil paintings. They were the work of the camp artist, the Finn Kotro, a tall, gloomy person whom Maxik, out of love for art, appointed as a medic in his ward. Kotro spoke Russian poorly and painted even worse, but Maxik was pleased with his paintings. "How do you like it?" he would ask with the air of a patron of the arts, and he enjoyed Kotro's new works: a light blue northern landscape or a still life of crimson roses. Maxik's enjoyment of these scenes was so evident, that I did not have the heart to criticize them. It was awful kitsch. On the whitewashed wall above the prisoner's iron bed, however, these colorful blotches signified something, and they satisfied Maxik's aesthetic need. Moreover, it was touching that he had such a need, that he respected art, even in the form of Kotro's works. The medic and artist Kotro, who once taught me Finnish in camp, has died since then, and Maxik left Kruglitsa long ago. Objects, however, outlive people, and "Kotro's collection," no doubt, is preserved in the hospital by the prisoners, in whose pitiful and gray life, every colorful postcard, every trace of life outside the camp is a reminder of something unlike their present life, something beautiful and enchanted.

I spent many hours in this room conversing with its occupant, and I even had the right to drop in there in his absence. I would flee from the general barrack, and here I felt like a human being. At five o'clock, the time of the roll call, when there was a knock on the door, Max Albertovich would answer "two," and everyone knew that I was the second person behind the door. Max and I shared a passion for linguistics. He would spend his free time at the table reading French and English books—a rare aristocratic passion for a camp inmate. Stubbornly, assiduously, and persistently, Maxik would study these languages; he read French decently, but English was hard for him. He contrived to get hold of any books that landed in the Kruglitsa backwoods; whenever a Kruglitsa free worker went on a work trip to Moscow, he invariably brought some textbook back for Maxik. Over six years in camp, he thus collected a dozen books.

In 1944, he acquired a treasure: at that time, they brought two English sailors from Arkhangelsk to Ertsevo—when intoxicated, they had behaved disgracefully in the port. The Englishmen did not stay long in camp. The administration did not know what to do with them: they housed them separately, gave them easy work at the flour mill and released them in two weeks. The prosecutor himself arrived from Arkhangelsk to settle the "misunderstanding." When the Englishmen departed, they left a treasure: half a dozen cheap detective stories in English. Maxik bought them second-hand for 50 rubles a book. We read all these books together. I taught Maxik English, or rather, studied together with him. Even though I began to study the language later than he did, I understood the text more easily. Soon Maxik got used to reading several pages in English with me every evening. This was his sole opportunity to find a teacher, and for me, a pupil. For a year and a half in Kruglitsa, every evening, I would come to his window, knock, and he would open the locked hospital door for me. The book that we used to study the English language, "chewing over" and discussing every word, was *Elmer Gantry* by Sinclair Lewis.

I read the book three times in camp, and I am sure that Sinclair Lewis never had more grateful and faithful readers than Maxik and I. In the winter, it was warm in his room in the evenings. Max Albertovich would stoke the stove himself, at nine o'clock, upon his return from reception hours in the clinic. Upon entering, I first would eye the stove, where a bowl of hospital soup awaited me. This was my reward. The hospital soup was considered better than the regular one: it was cooked with oil. Sometimes Maxik also saved something else for me—a piece of salted fish or slice of bread. He would apologize if there was nothing, but I was pleased simply to be in the warmth and cleanliness, with a lamp and a book. This regular bowl of soup for a year and a half and this little corner in the camp where I felt like a human being, of course, were a great help to me in staying alive in 1943–1944.

The topics of our conversations were inexhaustible. I related to him what he did not know about Western literature or about film, and I mentioned writers and directors. Maxik wrote down such names as Roger Martin du Gard, author of *Les Thibaults* or René Clair, who was unknown in Russia. It was touching how he loved everything from which he was cut off in camp: good books, good music, and good cinema. He did not miss one film screening in camp, and seeing the enjoyment with which he reacted to everything that he read or watched, I wished with all my heart that someday he would be in a real movie house and read the best books in the world. Max was sincerely able to enjoy books and art, and precisely this person was condemned to pitiful surrogates all his life—in camp and the deep Soviet backwoods, the most desolate in the world.

He was an excellent storyteller. One evening, we recalled German films from the start of the 1920s, his and my student days: Henny Porten and Lil Dagover, Olga Chekhov and Ksenya Desni. On another evening, he told about his travels around the Soviet Union. Maxik sailed on the icebreaker *Sibiryakov* and for two years served in Spitzbergen. You could put together an entire book from those stories. Once there was an article about him in the newspaper *Vechernyaya Moskva* during his stay in Spitzbergen. Russians have a concession to work two coal mines there; they live apart, barely coming in contact with the Norwegians, the island's proprietors. One stormy night, Maxik was called to the Norwegian side across the gulf by a young doctor colleague, who was afraid to perform some complicated operation without the aid of his senior friend. There was no time to travel by land around the gulf, and Max Albertovich bravely set off in the storm to cross the gulf in a rowboat. This was an exploit. He was received with honor in the Norwegian doctor's European five-room apartment; he performed the operation and left the next morning, refusing to accept an honorarium. They drove him back in a sled alongside the gulf, and as a parting gift, the Norwegians give him fur gloves for the road; they remained with Max Albertovich as a memento of his trip to Norway.

The account of the night trip across the stormy gulf and a photo of Max then appeared in *Vechernyaya Moskva*. Such stories and listening to the radio frequently distracted us from our English reading. Of course, we subjected the radio news to a thorough analysis. This was my specialty. I was a "professional radio commentator." Maxik was a one hundred percent ardent Soviet patriot. He naturally thought in Soviet categories—the result of a twenty-year habit.

He proudly and excitedly received news of Soviet victories. If the radio reported some sensation in my absence while I was lying in the hospital, he would run to my cot to convey the news and listen to my opinion. Of course, our hearts and souls were with the Red Army, but sometimes I was struck by the enthusiasm of this person sentenced to ten years on a political charge. I rejoiced at Hitler's defeat, but he, beyond that, rejoiced in the glory of Soviet arms. I did not, however, disclose this "nuance" to him, and we rejoiced together, not thinking about the distant future.

Contact with his family had been cut off long ago. His wife wrote him once a year, and his daughter never wrote. His daughter inherited his linguistic proclivities and graduated from the Institute of Foreign Languages. He recalled his family with a tinge of resignation and sorrow, as he did all those whom he had met in life and who no longer remembered him—people whose life he had saved in camp and who had promised him gratitude until the grave but forgot him as soon as they were freed. Max was absolutely sure that I, too, would forget him as soon as our paths diverged, and he just laughed when I assured him that I have a good memory. This does not mean that he was a misanthrope, not at all. But he knew life and had his own experience.

This person conquered my heart with one distinctive feature. I must acknowledge my guilt: I shamelessly stole from Maxik. This matter took place among zeks in the subterranean kingdom, which has its own customs and rules of behavior. Having been decommissioned as an invalid, I continued to be savagely hungry, and the thought of food never left me. Maxik supported me with a little something, but it was too little for me. Remaining alone in his room, I would open the cupboard, and if I found some onions or potatoes, I would take one; if I found a bowl with kasha, I would eat two or three spoonsful. Only people who have spent several years in a Soviet camp can judge this behavior. Of course, Max soon realized that it was somewhat dangerous to leave me alone. . . . He began to lock the food cupboard, but this did not help. In my fourth year of imprisonment, I was already able to make my way inside locked cupboards. Once, on a shelf, I found a stitched-up pouch with rusks. An old woman who worked in the hospital had given the pouch to Max to keep for her. I did not know this, however, and I thought that Maxik had obtained the rusks somewhere from a free patient. There were about two kilos of rusks. I broke into this pouch, cut it along the seam, took out a rusk, and a second one a day later, and then a third. . . . After a few days, the old woman came for her treasure and raised an outcry. Only a few people had access to Maxik's room. We both were extremely confused. Maxik looked at me with mute reproach, but even then, he did not say anything to me. Everything was clear without words. Neither then, nor later did he speak roughly to me, recall the incident even by a hint, embarrass me, or close his door to me, and he did not deny me his respect, which was so necessary to me in that bitter time of humiliation and decline. That was truly spiritual beauty. This person acted like a perfect gentleman toward me.

Maxik could not bear solitude. Here I am coming to a delicate point. May one touch on the intimate life of a person who is alive and your contemporary? An impenetrable barrier, an iron curtain, however, has been lowered between me and this person by the world's greatest despotic regime. This book will never fall into his hands or into the hands of those around him as long as Stalinism exists. It is as if he were an inhabitant of another planet. Speaking about him, *We* do not violate the laws of coexistence because there is *no* bridge and no link between him and us. It is indiscreet to read other people's mail or to peek into another person's life. For us, however, the life of Doctor Max Rosenberg in the subterranean kingdom, of which a guest from the daytime world was an accidental witness, is not an ordinary private life! He is not our peer. He is a Soviet prisoner, whom the world has turned away from, and whose fate interests us as a terrible portent and example. How, indeed, do these people spend their lives in conditions that, in truth, have no precedent in world history but hang like a living threat over the life of Europe?

I have already said that Maxik's basic feature was a loving heart. This sensitive, solid, older man could not do without a woman, whom he needed both physically and spiritually, and his social position as a doctor afforded him the most opportunities in camp. As far as I remember, Maxik was always entangled in a romantic "story." And the very nickname "Maxik," an intimate, endearing term, came from female lips. There was, however, little poetry in this. He expressed his view of women to me—the view of an old bachelor: each woman strives mercilessly to exploit, demands things, food, release from work—everything boils down to that. Each thinks only of her personal benefit, and from the first day, one must take a firm position and not let oneself be exploited. I was surprised by the bitterness and sharpness in his tone, but I understood that this was not cynicism but only the sediment of camp experience; in reality, Maxik deeply needs a genuine female attachment, warmth, and affection, which he had been deprived of for so many years.

Women in camp, indeed, generally are much more brusque and "prosaic" than men. They do not indulge in "feelings" but just work hard to survive. The explanation lies not only in the Soviet demystification of relations between the sexes but also in the entire camp set-up, where male prisoners are so far from the ideal and so reduced to the ridiculous, each in his own way. . . . It is difficult to love a slave. A woman's love in camp always has an admixture of self-irony and the harsh absence of illusions. After many meetings and disappointments, however, fortune smiled on Max.

A simple, good Russian woman fell in love with him—one of those quiet, meek creatures who are created in order to become attached and who know how to be faithful all their lives. I remember her very well, a round Russian face, not beautiful but pleasant, very calm, very quiet, with a meek smile. She not only did not ask Max Albertovich for anything but she even brought him potatoes from the *selkhoz* where she worked; she cleaned his room, sewed for him, and put everything in order as only a woman knows how to do. And she behaved in a dignified way, without being pushy, came and left silently, and Max adored her. He beamed not only in her presence but even when awaiting her arrival.

When she cautiously knocked on the window at nine o'clock, I would immediately leave through a door in the corridor in order to avoid her. She was about twenty-five years old, that is, she was half his age, pleasant-looking, with light-brown hair, wearing a clean kerchief; her large eyes already had seen much in life. Once, when she came to Maxik in the daytime, she encountered a woman in his empty room—the one with whom Max had been friendly before her. Now she was located in another camp and by chance landed in Kruglitsa for a day or two "on assignment." She, understandably, visited Maxik. The two women conversed without a trace of embarrassment or jealousy. In camp, there is no family life or family ties; everything there is shackled and only love is free. But this love, like a blade of grass under a wheel, can be trampled and crushed at any moment.

Maxik's happiness ended when they sent his friend on an *etap* to another camp. The evening when he learned that she would be sent away from Kruglitsa on the next day, he was stunned and grief-stricken. He learned about it when it was too late to change anything. That evening, I did not study with him, and they sat together until late at night in the little room. Max Albertovich, like a nanny, supplied her for the road, obtained everything necessary, and she sat in tears, and kept repeating: "I don't need anything; I don't need anything. . . ."

After some time, Maxik arranged for her to be brought back to Kruglitsa, but then came the genuine separation: her term ended. She had a short term—three or five years, and they permitted her to settle in Central Russia, in Tambov *oblast*. When she left, she promised to wait for Maxik, even for years, to send packages and books; she was happy that now she would be able to care for him "from freedom." Maxik sent many letters to Tambov *oblast*.

She sent two letters full of care and affection from the road—two good letters. Then silence.

It is not known what happened. The letters from the road suggested such devotion, such ardent impatience to arrive more quickly at her place and from there to let him know about everything and do everything, even to obtain English books for Maxik. And suddenly—nothing. Two weeks, a month. Three months. We were all sure that she had not forgotten Maxik. Perhaps she fell ill, did not receive Maxik's letters, or they did not give him her letters. What happened to the promised package, to memory, to tenderness, to firm determination never to part in life?

A year passed and we ceased even to recall her. Is this not understandable? It was not the sole incomprehensibility in Maxik's life. Everything around was incomprehensible. Strangers passed through his life. It was impossible to predict anything, to calculate anything in advance. An alien hand rearranged, changed, cavalierly overturned everything. A person could not know what awaited him at the next curve of the road. Why, in fact, could these two not be together and get to know each other better? Why did people from the south die in the north and people from the north die in the south in the camps of Karaganda? Why did people die apart, in imprisonment, who not only needed each other but also were needed by society, which was prepared to surround them with love? Why was the pen snatched from the hand of the writer and the thoughts of the scientist and philosopher blocked? Why is it impossible to send Maxik books in camp that he and others need so much? Why thirty years after the revolution, does human life in this country resemble a garden where at any moment an iron harrow can abruptly pass through the patch, uproot flowers, and not leave room for a new planting? In the upturned soil they sow hatred and lies. They drive millions behind a barbed wire fence, and in the place where free life could have developed, a camp arises, a place of forced labor and cold despair.

32

The Doctrine of Hate

AFTER MY RELEASE from Maxik's hospital, having had an opportunity to rest, and armed with certification as an invalid, I returned to the camp regime. In Kruglitsa, a certified invalid with a higher education has a wealth of possibilities. You can choose: assist the work supervisor in compiling the lists of personnel in the brigades; work in the Cultural-Educational Sector (KVCh); or be an orderly in the barrack. Until a prisoner is taken off the official work register, he will not be sent to such unproductive work. The place for a healthy, able person is in the forest or field, where hands and shoulders are needed. The work boss will not allow an able-bodied worker to have an office or service job. An invalid is another matter. Whatever he is able and willing to do without being obliged to do so is pure gain for the state.

At first, I was amused at the accessibility of work from which I had been barred as a third category worker. When they found out that Margolin had been deactivated, people immediately invited me to work in various places, and I succumbed to temptation. An invalid is allotted the first level food ration and 400 grams of bread. By working, I received the second level and 500 grams.

For an entire month, I tried various places. After a ten-week stay in the hospital, it was pleasant to be occupied and to be listed in a job. After a month, however, I came to feel that I had been deactivated for a reason. I lacked strength. The job with the work supervisor dragged on until late at night. Work at the KVCh entailed being in motion all day, making the rounds of the barracks, rising before reveille. As a worker in the Cultural-Educational Sector, I had to get up an hour before everyone else: by the time the brigades went out to work, I had to list on the huge board at the gate the percentage of the norm that each brigade had fulfilled the previous day. A worker calculated these norms in the headquarters at night and, before going to sleep, he left the list for me in a desk drawer in the office. The camp was still sleeping, the dawn reddened behind the barracks, and the guards were dozing on the corner watchtowers, when I would climb with difficulty onto a stool that I had placed in front of the giant chart and begin writing in chalk on the blackened board the figures for the twenty brigades.

This work bored me. The thought that as an invalid I was not obliged to endure this misery gave me no rest. I had been an invalid for an entire month and had not yet utilized the blessed right to do nothing; I had not taken advantage of my marvelous, unbelievable freedom. Of course, working is an entirely different matter when a person knows that it depends on his good will and that the next day he does not have to go to work if he does not feel like it. Ultimately, I had to try out this carefree camp freedom of the Soviet invalid.

In the middle of the summer in 1943, I finally made up my mind and declared a grand vacation. At the same time, it represented a great fast: 400 grams of bread and a watery soup. It was June. Blue and yellow flowers bloomed in the flowerbeds in front of the headquarters; under the windows of the infirmary, the medical workers had planted potatoes and tobacco. In the morning, the patients crawled out to the sun and lay on the grass in their underwear or sunned themselves in the area around the barracks. When I went by, barefoot, in my mousy gray jacket without a belt, fastened by one wooden button near the collar, they shouted to me:

"Margolin, you're still alive? We thought you were gone already!"

Without stopping, I went on to the farthest corner of the camp territory. I had a blanket, a little pencil, and paper. There was lots of paper: in the past month, I had hoarded a respectable amount. I even had a little bottle of ink from my work in the KVCh. I would take a rest from people, the camp, work, and eternal fear. I lay on my back, watching the clouds float above Kruglitsa. A year earlier, I had worked in the bathhouse and ran into the forest for raspberries. Amazingly, then I was able to carry three hundred buckets of water a day. That year depleted me. Now there were no raspberries but neither did I have to drag water buckets. I was satisfied; it was a profound rest.

In the summer of 1943, a storm raged over Kursk, and Soviet communiqués spoke of gigantic battles, as if all the blood receded from this great country and flowed to the single effort in that one spot. One hardly saw healthy males in Kruglitsa. Women guarded the prisoners and conducted the brigades to work. Havrylyuk, who the past summer had been a Stakhanovite wagoner, now, like me, had been retired from work, and women prisoners worked as wagon drivers in camp. Women, like reservists, went to the first line of work.

We knew from the newspapers that, throughout the country, women were working as tractor drivers, in factories, and in the fields. The free men held the battle front while the male prisoners in the camp melted like snow in the spring sun and descended under the ground. I knew that in another year I would be weaker than I was at present. If the war dragged on, I would die and not even know how it ends. Out of pure curiosity, I wanted to make it to the end of the war.

That summer, my first grand interlude as an invalid, I wrote "The Doctrine of Hate." In the years of my imprisonment, I contrived to write three works. I already mentioned the first; this was the second; the third was entitled "The Doctrine of Freedom." That summer I was preoccupied with thoughts about hate. Lying in the grass behind the last infirmary, I returned to the topic from day to day and turned out chapter after chapter. I experienced a profound and pure enjoyment from the very process of thought and from the aware-ness that this thinking was outside-the-camp, normal, free thought, despite my current conditions and despite the barbed wire fence and guards. This was "pure art." There was no one to whom I could show it or who could read what I was writing, and I felt pleasure from the very activity of formulating my thoughts, and, as the work advanced, I also felt proud that to a certain de-gree, I was prevailing over hatred, was able to grasp it, and to subject it to the court of Reason.

This subject was dictated by my life. What I had endured and seen around me was a true revelation of hate. In my previous life, I only had heard or read about it, but I never encountered it personally. Neither racial nor party ha-tred had crossed the threshold of my peaceful home. In camp, for the first time, I heard the word "kike" directed at me, felt that someone wanted me to perish, saw victims of hate around me, and witnessed its organized apparatus. In camp, I, too, for the first time learned to hate.

Now it was time for me to elaborate all this material theoretically. How simple it would be to go away from the haters to that bright kingdom of warmth and humanity in which I, unawares, lived before the Holocaust. It is natural for a person to live among those who love and are loved by him, not among enemies and haters. But this was not my fate. Nor was I able to resist hatred actively. The only thing that remained free in me was thought; only by thought could I respond. There was nothing else I could do but try to under-stand the force that wanted to destroy me.

I was less interested in the psychology of individual hatred than in its so-cial function, its spiritual and historical meaning. I saw hatred as a weapon or as a fact of contemporary culture.

The most important thing, with which I began, was the dialectic of hate. Hatred is what unites people while dividing them. The link via hate is one of the strongest in history. Souls come together in hate like the bodies of wrestlers—they seek each other like wrestlers in a fight. You cannot understand hate as pure negation because if we merely do not love or do not want something, we simply walk away from it and try to eliminate the unnecessary and unpleasant from our life. There was something in my hatred of the camp system that forced me to think about it, and I knew that my hatred would not let me forget it even when I got out of here. Hate arises in conditions when we cannot escape. Hate is a matter of proximity. Personal, class, or national hatred—it is always between cohabitants, between neighbors, between Montague and Capulet, over borderline and frontier.

The paradox of hate is that it leaves us in spiritual proximity to that which we hate until, ultimately, there arises rapprochement and similarity. Sometimes, the hate itself turns out to be merely concealed fear of what attracts us, as in Catullus's poem, *Odi et amo* [Latin: I hate and I love], as in Hamsun's "duel of the sexes,"[1] as in a lackey's hatred for the lord, and finally, in antisemitism of the maniacal type, when people cannot do without the Jews. Here is an acute example. Adolf Nowaczyński, a talented Polish writer, was a malicious hater of everything Jewish.[2] When he approached old age, he took off for Palestine to see things with his own eyes, and it turned out that he felt quite good in Tel Aviv. This man's life would have been empty without Jews. If they had not existed, he would have had to invent them, and ultimately that is what he did all his life. There is hatred toward fascism and even hatred of communism that derives from a certain moral closeness and, in any case, leads toward it over time. We cannot hate what is absolutely incomprehensible and alien. The incomprehensible arouses fear. Hatred, however, needs an intimate knowledge and multiplies it, and it endlessly forces us to take an interest in what we detest.

This was the paradox of hatred that I examined from all sides while lying in the sun in the corner of the camp yard. Hatred was not only before me—it was also inside me. In me, however, it was *different* from that against which my entire being rebelled. It thus was necessary to differentiate the various

---

1. Knut Hamsun's novel *Pan*, which appeared in 1894, dealt with the war of the sexes.

2. Adolf Nowaczyński (1876–1944), son of a Catholic aristocrat and of a Jewess, who used the pen name Neuwert. Originally an ideological adherent of the Endeks (National Democratic Party of Poland), Nowaczyński was one of the most virulent antisemitic Polish journalists. An opponent of fascism, affected by the suffering in the Warsaw ghetto, he helped organize aid, was arrested and tortured by the Nazis, and was killed in 1944 during the Warsaw uprising. Margolin was not aware of this later development in Nowaczyński's life.

forms of hatred, in order to distinguish between the hatred that was inside me and what to me was an odious and evil hatred.

First, I distinguished some bogus and altered forms, the pseudo-hatred that only obscures the essence of the matter. I saw that an inapt item or something with an external resemblance paraded under the label of hatred. Away with counterfeits!

First: juvenile hatred, *odium infantile*. Children are capable of the most fierce, frantic hatred, but that is only "ersatz," not serious. Juvenile hatred is a momentary reaction, an acting out. It boils up in an instant and passes without leaving a trace; it rises and bursts like a soap bubble. In essence, it is an outburst, a fit of emotional distress. This is precisely the reason why, in its mass manifestation, by virtue of its qualities of easy arousal, easy manageability, and evanescence, it is particularly suitable for the purposes of cold-blooded producers of this hatred and inciters, who always mobilize it in the masses when it is necessary to stimulate them to an extraordinary effort, to struggle in the name of changing goals. Hatred goes to the masses, flows along the channels of calculated propaganda, but it is all on the surface; it has neither depth nor stability. Left to itself, it dies out or unexpectedly changes direction, as in 1917, when the masses, filled by tsarist governments with pogromist and front-line hatred, turned against the government itself. The savage hatred of the incited mass, like fuel in a car, turns the wheels of the military machine, but the ones at the steering wheel are calm and cool.

Ripe, mature hatred does not have the nature of a momentary reaction; it is a person's automatic, internally determined and stable position. It does not exhaust itself in one ferocious outburst but gnaws at a person's entire life and lurks behind all his manifestations and deeds. Psychologically it is manifested in a thousand ways. From open hostility to blind nonrecognition, all shades of dislike, malice, vengefulness, cunning and envy, mockery, lies, and slander form the vestments of hatred, but it is not linked exclusively with any one of them. There is no specific feeling of hatred; in its extreme form, it ceases to need any kind of "expression." A child's hatred is expressed in screaming, foot stamping, and biting. The hatred of a savage, which is the same as a child's hatred, elementary, bestial fury, is expressed in a pogrom, in broken skulls and bloodletting. There is, however, mature hatred that is expressed only in a polite smile and courteous bow.

Perfect hatred is Ribbentrop in Moscow, kissing the hands of commissars' wives, or Molotov, smiling at the press conference. We adults have learned to suppress and regulate manifestations of our hatred like a radio receiver, turning it off and on like a light switch. Our hatred is a potential force;

therefore, it can be polite and calm, without external manifestations, but woe to the one who shakes an enemy's extended hand and walks along with him.

The second form of pseudo-hatred is *odium intellectuale*: the hatred of scientists, philosophers, and humanists—it is the hatred of those incapable of hating, the academic hatred of intellectuals, which was introduced as an antidote and placed as a lightning rod against barbarism. This vegetarian, literary hatred would have us hate abstract concepts—not an evil person but the evil in man, not the sinner, but sin. This hatred unceasingly exposes vices and fallacies, mistakes and deviations against which we are ordered to fight. This theoretical hatred completely fences itself off from the practical. Unfortunately, the street does not understand these fine distinctions: mass hatred recognizes only that enemy whose head one can break.

Humanism in its essence cannot oppose hatred. We know of two attempts in the history of culture to eliminate hatred from human relations: "nonresistance to evil" and the view that the end does not justify immoral means. Passive resistance to evil, however, invariably switches to active resistance against the bearers of evil, and the question of "ends and means," with its artificial division of the indivisible, remains intractable so long as we do not know what specific means are being used for precisely what goals. Historically, butchers and murderers invariably used abstract, theoretical hatred for their own purposes, expertly contriving to turn every intellectual product into a weapon of mass murder and unlimited slaughter.

Christ drove the money lenders out of the Temple. His successors excommunicated the heretics from the church and lit the bonfires of the Inquisition, up to Torquemada and that papal legate who, upon suppressing the Albigensian heresy, said, "Kill all of them; God will recognize his own." The Encyclopédistes and Rousseau hated vice and believed in the triumph of virtue. The French Revolution introduced the guillotine. Marx started with the liquidation of classes and of exploitation in human relations. His followers turned Marxism into a formula of mass terror, when a "class" is destroyed not as an economic category but as millions of living, innocent people. "Kill them all; history itself will revive what it needs." The process contains a tragically inevitable progression, and, unavoidably, the warrior-humanist becomes a captive of an alien element, as in the case of Maxim Gorky in the role of a Kremlin dignitary. The teachers either capitulate in the face of the conclusions that the pupils derive from their lessons or perish in prison or on the scaffold.

Odium intellectuale, the theoretical scholarly hatred, thus either fails to achieve its goal or leads to results that are diametrically opposite to the original intention. Luther throws an inkpot at the devil. The devil turns the philosopher's ink into blood and a sea of tears.

The third form of hate that I isolated in my analysis is *odium nationale*, the well-meaning hatred of those who take up arms in order to halt the force of evil. Evidently, there was never a dark force that did not try to pass itself off as just and worthy. Evidently, we have no other means of distinguishing between good and evil than by Reason and Experience, which teach us to recognize the essence of phenomena from their manifestations and consequences. There is, thus, a hatred that is rational and transparent in all its manifestations. It is clear to us why and when it arises. Its logical basis is at the same time the reason for its conditional nature, as it disappears along with the causes that evoked it. This hatred is so secondary and reactive that we can easily designate it as counter-hatred [*Gegenhass*]. We do not need it intrinsically, but when an enemy imposes it upon us, we do not fear to take up the challenge, and we know that there are things in the world that are worth fighting against—the passion and force of survival which do not yield to the enemy's force and passion but have nothing in common with them in their inner essence.

Having thus carefully differentiated the historically present forms of pseudo-hatred—mass-juvenile and intellectual-abstract—and the rational counter-hatred of the warrior—I approached the eyeless monster that at the time of my imprisonment had spread over all of Europe.

Unlike the superficially emotional, infantile hatred of the crowd, the theorizing hatred of the intellectual, and the sober, clear conviction of the defenders of humankind, there is a force of primal and pure hatred, proactive despite its blindness, and blind despite its initiative, and the more active the less causally provoked. It fears only the light of day. Reason is its natural enemy. Haters of the world are united in their negation of freedom of the intellect. The mark of Cain by which one can recognize genuine hate is scorn of free thought, rejection of the intellect. For Hitlerism, free thought is "a Jewish invention"; for the Inquisition, it is a mortal sin; for the ideologues of communism, it is counterrevolution and bourgeois prejudice. Every basis for such hate is imaginary and pseudo-rational. It is therefore natural that the people who established forced-labor camps in Russia simultaneously eradicated freedom of discussion and the right of independent investigation there. In a pure, undiluted form, hatred is self-affirmation via another's suffering. People become haters not because their surrounding reality forces them to that. There is no sufficient basis for hatred in the external world. There is nothing in the world that could justify the annihilation of flourishing life and proud freedom undertaken by Hitler, the fires of the Inquisition, or the prisons and pogroms and the camp hell of the Gestapo and the NKVD.

There is a pyramid of hate, higher than the Palace [of the Soviets],[3] which is being constructed in Moscow at the cost of hundreds of millions while people are dying of starvation in the camps. At the base of this pyramid are people similar to children, wild savages, like the one who hit me with a board on the road to Onufrievka, or the SS man who shot my elderly mother on the day the Pinsk ghetto was liquidated. These people rape, destroy, and murder, but tomorrow they themselves will be the most mild and obedient and will serve the new masters or believe the opposite of what they believed yesterday, and others—just like them—will come to their homes to murder and rape. Above these people stand others who teach them and entrust them to do what they do. Above them are still others, who engage in ideology and theoretical generalizations, and those embellishers, who service the hatred, deck it out, put it to music, and dress it in beautiful words. Ultimately, however, at the very top of the pyramid stands a person who needs all this: the incarnation of hatred. This is the organizer, the mastermind, the engineer and the chief mechanic. He has assembled all the threads in his hands, all the subterranean streams and scattered drops of hatred; he gave it direction, a historic impetus and scope. At his signal, armies cross borders, party congresses adopt resolutions, entire peoples are exterminated, and thousands of camps are erected. And he may be kind and sweet: he may have six children as Goebbels did or a "golden heart" like Dzerzhinsky's, an artistic nature like Nero's or Hitler's, and the Gorkys and Barbusses will not stop slobbering over him. He, however, decreed that somewhere people must suffer. He executed them in his mind when no one yet knew about his existence. Even then he needed this.

This brings up a central question in the doctrine of hate: "What is the makeup of a person, a society, an epoch if naked hatred has become such a necessity for them, if senseless tormenting of their victims becomes a necessary condition of their own existence?" It is not at all easy to answer this question if one does not adduce the familiar so-called arguments that the German people "were defending themselves against the Jews," that the Inquisition was "saving souls," or that Stalin is re-educating and reforming "backward and criminal elements" with the help of the camps. This is obvious nonsense. Of course, I in no way harmed the Germans nor needed a Stalinist re-education,

---

3. An enormous edifice that was supposed to replace the Church of Christ the Savior in Moscow, which the Soviets demolished in 1931. The project, however, was never realized, and in 1958, a swimming pool was built in the area. In the post-Soviet era, the church was rebuilt.

but even if that had been the case, it would not justify the gas chambers or
turning millions of people into slaves. Germany did not need the gas chambers; the Russian people did not need the camps. But they are truly necessary
for the big and little Hitlers and Himmlers, Lenins and Stalins of the world.
What, indeed, is going on?

One must clearly recognize that the people holding the keys of power are
fully aware of and admire the extent of the avalanche of human and inhuman
suffering that seems like an elemental misfortune to us little people. Those
people are responsible for its existence every minute and second. They have
started it and control it, and it exists not because of their ignorance or impotence but precisely because they well know what they are doing, and they are
doing precisely what meets their needs. Only a dull, wooden German lacking
imagination, such as Himmler, needed to visit Auschwitz in person in order
to look through a little window of the gas chamber to see how hundreds of
young Jewish girls choked to death, girls who had been specially dispatched
to execution that day for that purpose. People of the Kremlin do not need to
observe personally; they have statistics about the camp death toll. There is no
answer to why this is necessary other than to analyze the known pathological
peculiarities of human nature. There is no rational, "economic," or other explanation of hatred. The logic of hatred is the logic of madness.

That man hates[4]: He cannot do without this attitude to people; without
it, he suffocates. Hate is the oxygen that he breathes. Taking hatred away from
him would leave him destitute.

That man hates, which means that some kind of inner weakness develops
into hate, the result of some organic problem. Some kind of lack, defect, or
unhappiness may remain within the bounds of his sense of self, but it may
also spread to his social milieu and be transmitted to other people. There are
wounded people, vulnerable classes, ready to turn into breeding grounds of
collective hate. There are situations when people, groups, or societies are unable or unwilling to look truth in the face.

In Vienna, young Hitler discovered that the Jews are responsible for
depriving him and the German people of their deserved place in the sun.
This is preposterous but, indisputably, this man started with some feeling of
pain; he was deeply hurt. Had he wanted the truth, he would have found a
real cause, but the truth was too much for him to bear. He therefore began
to search for external guilty parties. Here the mechanism of hate begins to

---

4. Margolin is referring to Stalin.

operate. The real pain turns into an imagined insult. An enemy and offender must be found. The need for an enemy is radically different from the need for a struggle that is characteristic of every strong person. Strong people seek an arena, an outlet for strength. The hater seeks offenders to accuse. On the one hand, the need for a struggle engenders courage and initiative. On the other, the need to deal with a cunning enemy engenders aggressiveness and malice. The offender is always nearby. If he is not visible, that means he is in disguise and must be unmasked.

All haters are great unmaskers. Instead of a mask, however, they tear off live skin, the true nature, and they replace reality with a creation of their inflamed fantasy. Hatred starts with an imaginary unmasking and ends with real flaying, not in theory but in practice.

The analysis of our epoch given by Marx and developed by Lenin crossed all bounds of reasonable interpretation of reality. Pseudo-rational theory turned into a Procrustean bed that did not accommodate real life. It is sufficient to compare the tirades of *Mein Kampf* with Lenin's passionate polemics and his thunderous charges against capitalism to sense their psychological affinity. It is the language of hate, not of objective research. We can learn as much about reality from Marxist-Leninist scholastics as we can from the *Protocols of the Elders of Zion.*

Every hatred that reworks pain into insult carries out "transference" (*Uebertragung*) in the language of modern psychoanalysis. The source of the pain is internal but we transfer it to the outside. Others are to blame when things go wrong for us, when our plans do not succeed and our hopes are crushed. We thus find an outlet, relief, but only an illusory one. Hate acquires an address—a false one. Revenge, dictated by hate, misses the mark, like a letter sent to an incorrect address. Hatred engenders a constantly hungry vengefulness.

An imagined or real hatred becomes a pretext for hateful acts if a person has a need and desire to hate. Sooner or later, this need will be expressed in aggression. Even if there is a real cause at the basis of the hatred, it is always incommensurable with the repression; and vengeance born of hate far exceeds what is acceptable to reason and normal human psychology. Genuine revenge, as we know from history, entails a search and attainment of expiation. The act of revenge is a final one, closing the account. Blood is washed away by blood, and the insult is compensated by insult. The need for another's suffering, which forms the essence of hate, derives from the illusion that, in this way, one's suffering will be suppressed and mental equilibrium will be restored.

Because the connection between one's own misfortune and another's guilt is, however, imaginary, no acts that derive from hatred stifle it, and it turns into abiding, eternal mental anguish. There no longer are Jews in German and Polish cities, but things did not become easier because of this. Millions of people have been destroyed in Soviet camps, and the world gradually realizes that hatred of capitalism does not derive from its criminality because the crimes of communism are just as great. There is neither benefit nor satisfaction from the crimes that are carried out, nor is there a way out as long as hatred spins in a vicious circle.

The people who wrecked my life and turned me into a slave in the summer of 1940 did not know me, and I did not know them. But hatred formed between us. It was not their personal hatred but the collective creation of the epoch, a Leninist-Stalinist concoction, an abstract poison that penetrated the flesh and blood of the generation. Indifferently, calmly, and with bureaucratic dispassion, they carried out their deeds. The important thing was not a psychological expression of hate. The same people would have been capable of torturing me. Indifference to human life and dignity, as if it were a matter of an animal at a slaughter house, is the highest measure of concentrated hate. It is a violent, monstrous but completely *objective* murderous force, that derives from a hopeless attempt to build one's own cursed existence on the misfortune and death of those around.

In order to find support in the external world, this deadly force needs to falsify it. The world is not suitable as is. It is literally true that Streicher and Goebbels could not hate Jews because they did not know them at all. If they had known this people with true, live knowledge, this hatred could not have developed. Their hatred related to that distorted, deformed notion of the Jewish people that they themselves had created and that was dictated by their need to hate. In the institutions of the National Socialist Party, in the Erfurt Institute, there were enormous piles of material about the Jewish people, but the thousands of pieces served them only to create a monstrous mosaic of slander. In the same way, the people who sent me to camp did not know me. Their hatred consisted precisely of their not wanting to know me and not having hesitated to turn my life and face into a screen onto which to project a NKVD film: "A threat to society, a lawbreaker. Henceforth this person will be not what he thought he was but what we want him to be and what we shall make of him." In order to erase my existence as they did, one had to harbor a great, formidable hatred of humanity.

Until we uproot this hatred, it will not stop slandering people and their real impulses, will not cease circling around us, seeking out our every weakness, mistake and sin, which are numerous, not in order to understand us better or help us but in order to blame us for its own thirst for cruelty and blood.

Pathological hate reflects the primal instinct of the rapacious beast who knows that he can appease his agonizing hunger by the warm blood of another. Millennia of cultural development infinitely distanced and complicated this instinct by pseudo-rational sophistry and self-deception. Human rapaciousness exceeded that of the beasts, differing from it in that it manifested itself under senseless pretexts in the name of imaginary goals. The struggle against hatred is thus not limited by humankind's biological nature but encompasses all the specifically inhuman, the perversions, and lies that comprise the anomaly of highly developed culture and cannot be destroyed until its existence becomes common knowledge. Free and perspicacious people someday will destroy hatred and create a world where no one will need to hate or oppose hatred. The human striving for freedom is incompatible with hate. Without going into complex definitions of freedom, one can agree that as it develops, freedom will steadfastly expel lies and hatred not only from the human heart but also from human relationships and the social order. Opposition to lies and hatred is thus already the first manifestation of human freedom. . . .

Having finished my investigation of hatred with this proud phrase, I turned over onto my back and looked around: I was lying in a meadow, on green grass at the end of the camp. The forbidden zone started five steps away and a tall palisade with barbed wire spread around. Several prisoners swarmed in the forbidden zone; they were cutting the grass and digging up earth. Under the windows of the hospital kitchen formed a line of medics with buckets for soup and kasha.

I again carefully looked over the manuscript, a stack of long strips of blue paper written in the most miniscule hand, and I erased all dangerous hints. I read it with the eyes of the security operative: it was an "antifascist" document written by a stranger, but it was not blatantly counterrevolutionary. Understandably, there was not a word about Soviet reality in this manuscript. I had to keep in mind that it could be taken away at any moment in a search. . . .

But I had pity on my manuscript. There was no chance of hiding a work of that size for a long time in the camp. Suddenly, I had a fantastic idea. I got up and went to the KVCh, where two girls were sitting at two tables. Both were free workers, recently taken from the settlement, typical civil servants in the deep Soviet provinces.

"What do you want?"

"This is what I want," I said slowly. "I have a manuscript of about a hundred pages. . . . I am an academic and wrote something in my specialty. In the barrack, you know, it's dangerous. They'll tear it up to use for rolling cigarettes. I want to give it to the KVCh for safekeeping. When I leave here, you'll return it to me."

The girl was taken aback. She and her friend looked at me in dull astonishment, suspiciously, as at someone abnormal. I spoke, however, very calmly and reasonably.

In the end, she went to the phone and asked the guardhouse to connect her to the security supervisor.

"Comrade supervisor, someone came here, brought a manuscript, and asks that we take it for safekeeping. He says that he is a scientific worker."

She repeated this several times over the telephone, then she turned to me:

"Your name?"

I gave it.

The girl conveyed my name, listened to the answer, and hung up the receiver.

"The supervisor said," she turned to me, hardly keeping back laughter, "let him throw his manuscript into the outhouse."

33

An Invalid's Lot

THEY MOWED THE field on which I was lying. They sent the zeks who slept next to me on *etaps* to Udmurtia, to Izhevsk camps. I also had to get moving. The heavenly condition of a nonworking invalid was ending.

There were two reasons for the change. The first was economic: one cannot survive on 400 grams of bread. An invalid eats 200 grams of bread in the morning and 200 in the evening. They give it to him in two portions, otherwise he would immediately swallow his chunk of bread and remain without anything for the next twenty-four hours. The food given in addition to the bread is not worth much: a meal ticket of the first or second category ration can be exchanged in camp for 150 or 200 grams of bread. Inevitably, all of an invalid's thoughts focus on how to earn more food. He cannot, in fact, earn much. He cannot possibly be allotted the Stakhanovite or shock worker's ration; for what kind of invalid would he be if he surpasses the norm? At physical work, the maximum he could receive would be equivalent to fulfilling the norm, which is another 200 grams of bread. In 1941, the difference was only 150 grams. Aside from bread, the difference in food between the first and second category was insignificant. Ten grams of vegetable oil was served in the kasha, and in Kruglitsa, only hospital patients received 20 grams of sugar daily, and not always.

Not only the quest for bread forced me to return to work. There was another serious reason. As a great number of invalids accumulated in the camp, they sent them to special camps so that they would not be in the way. Invalids from the medical settlement were sent to Ostrovnoe or Medvedevka. The human dregs, spent and worn out, were gathered there. They had a special regime and special work, whose evil reputation circulated in Kruglitsa. A person who landed there, as in a swamp, could no longer get out. It contained a concentration of unneeded, superfluous elements that no longer interested the

administration. The threat always hung over us invalids: "They'll send you to
Ostrovnoe; there you will croak." Being an invalid among healthy people in a
normal work camp is a great advantage. It is easy to find a place in the office or
with the service personnel, and they feed you better. When everyone is an invalid like you, however, it is impossible to climb out of the common mass, and
everyone shares the same lot. I thus clung with all my might to my wonderful
medical settlement. Approximately once a month, there was a purge: they
assembled the nonworking invalids and sent them out of the camp. In order
not to be included in the fatal list, one had to fulfill some useful function, be
a "working invalid," and, in general, have the reputation of a person who does
not sit around idly. Again, I thus "got down to business."

While it was not yet freezing, I would go the guardhouse. From there, the
invalid brigade was sent somewhere to do odd jobs—collect garbage, clear
fields of stones, and so forth. It was a motley crew: old people who were still
brash and had not given in, work veterans whose knees had given way and
whose cheeks were sunken, consumptives who were not yet ready for the hospital, cripples, gimps, oddballs from the four corners of the earth—Yugoslavs,
Koreans, Armenians, and Finns; a person who had known Professor Langevin
in Paris stood next to a shepherd from a *kolkhoz*. Each one cut a stick for himself and leaned on it heavily when walking. I also walked with a stick, stood in
line, and waited while they checked us. And they checked us by name to make
sure that someone healthy had not accidentally slipped in.

The invalid procession got underway. The rows of four quickly fell into disorder and stretched out in a chaotic crowd on the dusty or dirty road. A guard
walked on the side, also an invalid rejected for the war front, or a woman soldier in a jacket and cap with a red star, who held her rifle like a rod to chase
away geese. "Pick up the pace! "Close ranks! "Stop talking!" And when the
line was in complete disorder: "Stand!" Here the front ones would stop and
wait until the stragglers caught up. The guard would recount the people and
place the stragglers in front. The weakest ones always went in front and those
following behind would step on their feet.

Having covered half a kilometer, the brigade would sit down to rest
without asking. They would sit on stones along the road, laying aside the
walking sticks, while some dropped directly onto the ground and lay on their
sides or on their backs. "Rest, weak team!" said the guard, and he patiently
smoked a cigarette on the side. According to the rules, we were not supposed
to get closer than three to four meters from the guard, but that prohibition
was often violated. The brigade leader, as a representative of authority, often
sat alongside. The guards' attitude toward the prisoners was neither hostile

nor overbearing. It was too evident that we, the prisoners, were made of the same cloth, were neither enemies nor criminals but just that gray, working cattle whom the regime had decreed to live in camps.

The brigade leader did not work. According to the rules, only in large brigades of twenty-five to thirty people are brigade leaders freed from work, but in smaller ones, they are obliged to work with everyone else. In fact, however, the brigade leader never works: he only organizes people, instructs, demonstrates the work methods, and hustles; in the evening, he composes the work reports, receives bread for the brigade, and goes on brigade matters to the office and the general supply unit. Understandably, in the invalid brigade, he does not have much work.

We wove mats of thin wooden strips in the yard of the *selkhoz*. These mats were used to cover the glass frames of the greenhouses.

In the fall, they sent us to the field where the potatoes had already been gathered to collect the little potatoes that had not been noticed in the harvest. All day we poked around in the furrows and found a mass of little potatoes. They did not allow us to eat them, and there was no fire to cook them. Only the guard baked potatoes all day in the embers of his bonfire. Some zeks could not hold back and went there to beg. They pleaded in false, sweet voices, like little children, and sometimes the guard grumpily would throw them a little potato so that they would leave him in peace. We all ate raw potatoes, on the sly, barely cleaning them with a sleeve. I was able to eat twenty raw potatoes. If they had allowed us to cook them, half would have been enough. No one, however, had the right to permit us to do this. Every potato belonged to the state.

With the arrival of the frosts, I became the orderly at the Special Supply Unit (ChOS). My job was to clean two small rooms. The first room served as the office for food products and for clothing. The second was the office of the head of ChOS, Gordeeva. A table, a large wooden armchair, a portrait of Stalin, a cabinet with papers constituted the furniture of the little office; on the table was a large glass carafe, an unusual, attention-getting item in camp. Every morning, I filled the carafe with fresh water. I had to go to the other end of the camp, to the boiler room, for the water. Aron Shternfeld, a dark-haired Ukrainian Jew in charge of the boiler room, was my friend. He would give me, out of turn, a bucket of boiling water for the ChOS.

In the first room, behind a wooden barrier, sat the accountants. The chief accountant, a bald Armenian, would tell jokes and jest with the women. In the corner, at the clothing desk, sat a sixty-year-old man. He seemed to be grafted to the stool; he was an excellent office worker, an ideal accountant. The third person—in charge of calculating the bread distribution—one-armed (the other had withered), with a shaven, firm face and broad shoulders, was always ironically polite and inscrutable. All three were well-fed, cheerful, and liked to crack jokes. One could live with them for years and not know who they really were in the depth of their souls. These were the Soviet bureaucrats in camp, *pridurki*.

During the day, I would stand by the stove and run their errands. You cannot say that I ran: my feet barely dragged along. The accountants would go to the products warehouse and bring potatoes. They baked them in the stove, and tact required that I not notice this. God knows what efforts it cost me not to show them how much I was drawn to the smell of cooked potatoes or not to filch even one little potato. They divided them among themselves and shamelessly ate everything in front of me. Not one of them ever offered me anything, and I think that they even derived pleasure from the presence of a person by the stove who was clenching his teeth and looking away.

In the evening, I filled the oil lamps in case of an electrical failure (which used to happen every other day) and closed the windows with the heavy wooden shutters. From eight to ten o'clock in the evening, the ChOS was filled with a crowd of workers. A dense crowd stood behind the partition, and a long line formed by Gordeeva's door. Here they filled out orders to the clothing warehouse for gloves, shoes, blankets, and clothing.

In addition to my work as an orderly, I wrote all kinds of orders and accounts, composed mail and sent it with people who were dispatched from us to Ertsevo and neighboring camps. For this work, I was allotted the first category ration and 500 grams of bread, the norm for an orderly. The difference between this and an invalid's ration was just 100 grams of bread. As orderlies cannot live on this ration, unofficially, they are fed extra in the kitchen. I, too, was fed extra; it was a humiliating and repugnant procedure. At eight o'clock, after the distribution of breakfast, I went to the closed window of the kitchen and knocked. I did not have any friends in the kitchen, and no one hurried to open the window for me. Frequently, after standing for half an hour, I left with nothing. "There isn't anything!" This tin of *balanda*, the pitiful camp soup, was my entire payment for my work in the ChOS (aside from 100 extra grams of bread), and they always gave it to me as if giving charity, with annoyance and anger.

The people in the ChOS, too, were all completely alien. Gordeeva, the head of ChOS, a free worker, was there for about two hours daily. She once allotted me a new shirt but later was intimidated by my "letter to Ehrenburg," and, ultimately, she sent me to the punishment cell for the theft of fish.... Her assistant, with the title of "inspector of ChOS," was a young zek, Pavel

Ivanovich. The two seemed to be European types, but an abyss separated me from them. They belonged to the camp intelligentsia. No one forced Gordeeva to take part in searches in the barracks, but both she and Pavel Ivanovich loved to do so. Prisoners often kept camp property—a second pair of padded socks, a stolen blanket, or other "extras." Sudden random raids on barracks would take place in order to confiscate excess items. Gordeeva would come with her assistants, but she always conducted the search herself. This gray-haired woman with a schoolmarm's look would pick up the prisoners' bags, shake them out herself, rummage in the rags, climb to the upper bunks, and turn over the straw mattresses. Seeing the skill and enthusiasm with which she searched, I understood that she had the soul of a tsarist policeman. I must have been unable to conceal my disgust with the search procedure because soon they began to tease me in the ChOS and threaten to send me to conduct a search. "Margolin," said Pavel Ivanovich sternly, "you cannot work in the ChOS and evade participating in searches!" "But, really, I am blind, Pavel Ivanovich; how could I see anything!" "You will collect and record the confiscated items and hold the lamp for us." I joked as best I could but decided that I would leave the ChOS soon rather than make the rounds of the barracks with them. In any case, however, my work there ended in three months.

At that time, urgent measures were introduced to sustain the invalids. Both the working and the nonworking ones were dying. The advantage of being in the medical settlement was manifest: in no way could it permit the massive mortality of the prisoners. The trick used by the medical center was to rename the invalids as "chronic cases" or "chronics."

"Chronic cases" are sick people who were hospitalized until discharged without improvement, that is, people who do not want to get better or to die. There is no sense in keeping them in the hospital any longer, and it is impossible to place them with the healthy ones. Their place is in the middle. Their barrack is under the special supervision of a nurse and doctor. Chronics receive the second category of rations and 500 grams of bread, which is comparable to the food of the office and camp service workers. They did not raise the norms for invalids (only Moscow could do that), but they thought up a new term for them, a word that made it possible to remove them from the circle of those doomed to die or at least to slow, temporarily, the rate of death from depletion. Only temporarily because, of course, the rations for chronics also were insufficient for weakened people. We had so little physical reserves left that any hitch such as the theft of a bread ration or loss of a meal ticket could finish us off.

The cold season arrived, and the camp roads iced over. I started to fall in the snow, most often in the dark evenings, on my way back from the kitchen window to the barrack with my supper in my tin. These tins, made of rusty iron, rarely had a handle, and one had to carry them with two hands, carefully, while the feet fumbled for the road in the snow. My feet were made of straw, not my own feet. They tripped and slid apart like a one-year-old's, only there was no mother to hold me up at the last minute. Setting out on the 100- to 200-meter route, I was already prepared for the inevitable fall somewhere along the way. I learned to fall without spilling the contents of the tin. This was a special art. When there was a disaster and my tin spilled, however, I remained without food until the next morning. This was sufficient to weaken me noticeably. A clear link was established between the daily intake of food and the ability to move my arms and legs. The meager balance of input and output was evident: the daily piece of bread and the calculated number of calories in the morning and evening were expended on the body's movements. If this input was missing, I froze and stopped like an unwound clock. My body became brittle and fragile. Every sharp shock or abrasion left cuts and bruises, and the flesh did not heal for weeks; it bled and abscessed.

All the invalids of Kruglitsa were classified as chronics and divided into two categories. Sixteen tuberculosis patients were placed together in one room. Their disease was developing slowly, and it was too early to put them into the pulmonary ward. They had their own dishes and were under a doctor's special observation. The remaining twenty-five chronics were placed in another barrack. With us was another brigade and a "weak force," that is, a group of weakened workers who were given easier work conditions for two weeks.

Our barrack, the sixteenth, was spacious, dark, with double-decker bunks arranged in train car formation. The best places were near the stove. The brigade that was lodged with us went to wood sawing, and, therefore, that winter, we were well supplied with firewood. Toward evening, the doors would open and in single file, a procession of wrapped up, freezing people covered with snow would enter. Each one carried wood, and immediately a pile of logs and boards was heaped up by the stove. They sawed quickly, and soon the stove was so hot that the iron glowed red. The stove was covered with tins and mugs; the orderly brought two buckets of hot water, and arguments started about water and a place at the stove—the usual picture, the same thing the fourth year. There was one novelty that winter: potato skins. The Kazakhs, who came from torrid Central Asia, crowded around the stove more than anyone else, and they brought with them potato skins, the "peels," which they had managed to collect near the kitchen or beg from the cooks.

They dried these "peels" on a metal sheet until they turned into thin, crunchy brown chips, and they ate them that way. A yellow-complexioned, slanty-eyed Kazakh would stand by the stove and guard the peels, but the other zeks would take some from him "to taste them," and soon everyone began to chase after the potato skins and everyone liked them.

Every week a doctor would appear in the barrack; he would stand by the table and check the chronics. In the middle of the week, a nurse dropped in and sat on the bunk to talk with her acquaintances. All this, however, was merely a formality. No one could help us because we needed not medicines but bread and meat, fats and sugar, home and freedom. Most of all, we needed liberation.

We would now work infrequently and very little, as the difference between the food of a "chronic" and a "worker" was only 100 grams of bread, which later declined to only fifty grams. On a day that we worked, we received 550 instead of 500 grams of bread. Nevertheless, even these fifty grams were worth our keeping busy for a few hours.

In the morning, the camp commandant, the head of the bakery, or someone else who needed workers would drop in at the chronics' barrack.

"Guys, who is willing to clear snow or chop wood?" The commandant would promise to use his pull to get us soup; the head of the bakery would not promise anything, but immediately bodies that had been lying motionless under jackets on the bunks would start to move. Someone would get up with an effort, someone would look at his neighbor:

"Should we go? Maybe they'll give us some bread."

Those who no longer could walk performed various jobs on the spot, including in the barrack itself. Three people plucked needles from pine branches: Belovchenko, Mykola, and I.

The pine needle cook lived in our barrack. He was always sleepy: whenever we looked at him, he was sleeping or yawning. He worked at night: in the kitchen, he cooked the "pine infusion" or kvas,[1] as the prisoners called it. The pine infusion was the Soviet preparation against scurvy.

The brew was made from fresh green needles of young pine trees in three stages. In the first stage, Konev (a namesake but not a relative of the marshal [commander on the Eastern front]) would go to the forest, cut down

---

1. Kvas was a popular drink in Russia usually made from fermented rye bread or barley.

pines, and carry them to the camp yard. He would drop them in the empty lot between the kitchen and the bakery. Second, our group carried the pines to the barrack and plucked the needles from the branches. In the morning, we would sit by the table in front of a wooden box and in an hour or two would fill it to the top. No one checked how much we plucked, and no one took this work too seriously. In the final stage, the pine needle cook would take the box from us and cook a bright green, sharply bitter brew, which was poured into bottles and buckets and distributed among the barracks and hospital wards.

A bottle with the pine kvas stood in a prominent place in the clinic, and there always were people willing to drink a little mug of it although no one was forced to, and the drink was so sharply bitter that only the palate of a camp inmate, who had grown unaccustomed to sharp taste sensations, could find it attractive. More of this kvas was spilled out than was drunk, but half a dozen chronics were always busy making it, and each received an extra fifty grams of bread, not to mention the pine needle cook, who worked in the kitchen and had his own reasons for that.

Belovchenko, my neighbor on the bunk, was a young person about thirty, with a meek, pale, exhausted face, and a melancholy, downcast look. He was a sensitive, gentle person, broken by fate, dying without protest or commotion. Somewhere he had a young wife and child, but he no longer recalled them. Belovchenko was a fisherman; he had grown up in the home of his fisherman grandfather by the Black Sea near the Romanian border. "What is a mullet, Belovchenko, and how do they catch it?" Lying on his back next to me in the evening after supper, with his head on his sack, he would begin to tell me in detail, calmly, better than any book, about the marvelous fish and catches, about night trips with a casting net, about the fisherman's life and the sea's secrets, in a low, weak voice, trailing off like his life in camp.

The invalids would gather around the stove and begin endless conversations on the basic camp topic: food. The "national minorities" would tell about kurdyuk[2] and rice pilaf; the Baskhkirs about lamb; the Siberians about pelmeni,[3] and the Germans from the Transcaucasus about the time when wine from the Caucasus cost 3 kopecks a bucket. Hungry people could talk for hours about bread, flour, and various methods of baking bread. Their eyes shone and their imagination was fired up. Judging by the stories, everyone came to camp from a country of incredible abundance. A Ukrainian

---

2. Lamb tail fat.

3. Meat dumplings.

described the borscht that his old lady served him every morning in a way that turned our heads.

Only then, I realized how superficially and in what a mediocre way I had eaten in my former life. Before the camp, I had lived surrounded by miracles, not knowing how to utilize them, not knowing what hunger is nor what is a real appetite. Then I did not get hungry from breakfast to dinner or from dinner to supper. I ate five times a day, but did I really understand what food was? Could I appreciate, for example, peas? A Pole, the owner of a farm near Vilna,[4] began to explain to me about the different kinds of peas and what one could prepare from them. He spoke non-stop for an hour. I was dazzled. I did not know that in the hands of a culinary artist, peas, like a word in the hands of a poet, turns into a chef d'oeuvre. It was an epic about peas with Homeric force. Only many years of hunger—and homesickness—could bring a person to such ecstasy, fire his imagination and his speech. We all were abnormally aroused. It would have been healthier to speak and think less about food. But life in general, and camp life in particular, is a very unhealthy phenomenon.

Sometimes we listened to folktales. There was a Belarusian storyteller among us, and for the first time in my life, I listened to folk tales, which I knew only from books, in a masterful telling and with all the freshness of folklore when it is intended not for children but for adults. I heard soldiers' stories, where the hero dupes his superiors and marries the general's daughter, and Soviet folklore, very unpleasant, where it is not Baba Yaga who is enticing children in order to eat them but a band of criminals in Moscow that lures victims and sells human flesh. Some stories were about "Count Yusupov, who killed Rasputin." The Cheka arrests him but in some miraculous manner, he escapes from prison.

I began to record—not these stories, for which I did not have paper—but words and expressions of camp language. It was a language unlike Russian literary language. Earlier, I was unfamiliar with such words as *balanda* (camp thin soup), *tufta* (sham work for appearance's sake), *blat* (to signify secret pull), *ptyushka* (the camp bread ration), or *baldokha* (sun). In the ChOS, a female prisoner asked the person allotting the bread: "Vanya, list me for a bigger *ptyushka*," and at work, the zeks yelled to the work boss: "Citizen boss, the *baldokha* is shining!" I recorded dozens of such words. Some derived from the language of prisons and thieves, others arose in camp. The camp enriched the Russian language with the word *shizo* (Russian abbreviation for penalty isolator). The phrase *po blatu* evidently comes from the Hebrew language.

4. Now Vilnius, capital of Lithuania.

B'laat in the language of the Bible and the poet Bialik means "quietly." This word traveled a complex, long way from the shores of the River Jordan to the extreme north of Russia, to Soviet camps.

One winter evening, as I approached the stove, where, as always, there was a crowd of people, I suddenly heard strange sounds. A thin, pointy-nosed goner was dozing off on the bench, huddled in the warmth, and with eyes closed, was mumbling something to himself. I listened:

"Menin aiide tea, pelenadeo akhileos. . . ."

This man with thin blue lips, a cadaverous, lead-colored face, of an indeterminate age, in a jacket covered with patches, who appeared to be a *kolkhoznik*, like the majority of invalids, sat hunched up and was whispering the opening of the *Iliad*!

"Who are you? How do you know Homer?" The invalid opened his eyes and stared at me with no less astonishment. We introduced ourselves, then began talking, and then became fast friends.

Mykola was an entirely new person for me, from a different world. He was a Ukrainian from Dnepropetrovsk,[5] where I, too, had spent some years in my youth, when the city was still called Ekaterinoslav. By profession he was a Ukrainian language teacher, by temperament a gentle dreamer and a bibliophile. The two rooms of his bachelor apartment on Pervozvanovskaya Street contained two thousand books. In Soviet conditions, only a maniac or scholar who has collected books all his life could have such a private library. Mykola was forty years old, and the sole passion of his life was literature. He landed in camp because of a "nationalist deviation." During one of the ideological mass purges in Ukraine, when people were arrested for excessive Ukrainian patriotism, they called him to task for some remark of his in print where he had praised some Ukrainian communists who later were liquidated at Moscow's order. That sufficed to separate him from his beloved books and let him rot in the subterranean kingdom. He had been imprisoned for six years and was holding up fairly well. Aside from extreme physical depletion, mentally, he was still full of strength. He remembered Homer.

He devoted exceptional attention to me. He was somewhat stronger than I, and therefore he helped me pluck the pine needles, helped me with everyday details that determined a person's mood and well-being. I felt that I had an ally in the barrack and became attached to him with all the tenderness and gratitude of which my weakened, feral heart was capable.

What people there were in this god-forsaken Kruglitsa backwoods! How much refinement there was in this person, how much musicality in

---

5. Now Dnipro, Ukraine.

his ear, which reacted not only to Homer's hexameters but to every subtlety of modern poetry. Mykola understood everything, and he was the first to teach me to respect Ukrainian culture, which had nurtured such people. He transmitted his adoration of Ukrainian literature to me. From him I first heard the names of Maxim Rylski,[6] Pavlo Tytchina,[7] and others; the names of Franko[8] or Marko Vovchok[9] acquired real meaning for me. I had heard these names, but I did not know anything about them. I had only to ask Mykola, "Tell me, who is Marko Vovchok," and suddenly, it turned out that this was a woman and such a marvelous person and writer that Mykola simply beams in talking about her.

In order to give Mykola something in return, I began to teach him English. We did not have paper. Every day he brought me a wooden board, and I would write on it ten to fifteen words in English. Then I wrote an entire short text for him. Finally, I obtained a textbook from Maxik. Mykola knew how to study. In three months, he no longer needed my lessons. He manifested steely persistence and perseverance, true Ukrainian stubbornness. At midnight, when the barrack was sleeping, he would wake up, descend from the upper bunk to the table, on which a dim kerosene lamp was burning, and with his stony, pointy-nosed face would sit for hours on end over a textbook. By springtime, he was already reading English books by himself.

The Jewish and Ukrainian people have old, hostile accounts to settle. It is difficult to imagine what in the wide world could impel a Jew to take an interest in Ukrainian culture or the opposite. In a Soviet camp, however, a Jew and Ukrainian were brothers, and I understood that it was possible to sympathize with this people, the most musical and most unlucky among Slavic peoples. The Ukrainian folk song tradition is one of the richest in the world, and there are as many Ukrainians as Frenchmen, but they did not give birth to Chopin, and this people was never politically free. The time will come when Ukrainians and Jews will meet in the international arena, not in a concentration camp nor in a pogrom or conditions of inhuman police oppression but as free peoples. Mykola could have been an agent of Jewish-Ukrainian rapprochement or cultural ties. I lost track of him, however, in the subterranean kingdom, and I do not know whether he is still alive. . . .

------

6. Maxim Rylsky (1895–1964), Ukrainian poet and translator; arrested in 1931. Broken by the imprisonment, he came to support communism.

7. Pavlo Tychina (1891–1967), Ukrainian poet.

8. Ivan Franko (1856–1916), Ukrainian writer and poet.

9. Pseudonym of Maria Alexandrovna Vilenskaya (1833–1907), writer, poet, and translator.

In January 1944, Shulga, the brigade leader of the chronics, who was kindly disposed toward Mykola, offered him work in the vegetable warehouse. Mykola refused to work there without me. I thus became part of a group of four invalids: Shulga, Mykola, and Belovchenko—three Ukrainians and I. We got up at six in the morning, left for work at seven, and worked until one o'clock in the afternoon. For six hours, we sat in a dark, spacious cellar, where the light entered through a vent. The cellar was divided into bins, in each of which were sorted potatoes—dozens of tons of them. Our job was to look through the potatoes and throw out the rotten ones.

It was cool in the basement. The temperature in the vegetable warehouse must not drop below zero (so that the potatoes do not freeze) or rise above four degrees (so that they do not sprout). The manager of the warehouse regulated the temperature with the aid of a little stove, and he watched that we did not steal potatoes. He sat in a little warm room by the warehouse. Upon entering, we would sniff the air and look for the location of the potatoes that he had cooked for himself. In every raid by the administration, they would first check the stoves to make sure no criminal tin was standing somewhere. The administrators knew that the warehouse supervisor could not refrain from taking some potatoes but, nevertheless, they strictly monitored him so that he did not exceed the limits. The administration monitored the warehouse supervisor and he monitored us—and everyone, without exception, stole; even the guard, when dropping into the basement for a minute, would fill his pockets.

Our boss was a hook-nosed Ossetian from the Caucasus, a moderate person, very sensitive, who never cursed or hit anyone. Usually, warehouse managers are ferociously tough, but our Ossetian was not an ordinary person. . . . By chance we found out that he understood English and even had a wife in London; he did not, however, say anything more about himself. Our Ossetian understood that no one will sit for six hours in a cold and dark cellar for 50 grams of bread and that we had to be given something. He was afraid, however, to feed us; he was afraid that we would spill the beans if we received something from his hands. At midday, an hour before the end of work, he would bring each of us a cooked potato. Sometimes, it was a turnip. That was all, but we were not offended. We fed ourselves.

We had three means of doing this. First, we brought potatoes out on our bodies. They searched us when we left the cellar. At the guardhouse, we were threatened with another search, and if a potato was found, not only the thief but also the warehouse manager would land in the punishment cell for five days. Understandably, our boss carefully frisked us when we left and begged us not to cause him any problems. Nevertheless, we took them out. We sewed pockets under our armpits, between the legs, and in the most varied places, in the hope that one place would go unnoticed in the search. We hid small potatoes under our caps, in padded socks, in the *cheteze*. In the lining of our jackets, we carried out potatoes cut into flat slices. Sometimes this succeeded. In general, however, it is difficult for one prisoner to hide something from another. We therefore did something different.

Workers would leave the locked cellar to relieve themselves. The warehouse manager would unlock the outside door and let us out for a minute. Then there was no search, and we would gather potatoes in our pockets—the largest tubers there—and around the corner of the cellar, we would throw them into a snowdrift and make a mark at that spot—we would place a branch or little stone. Then with a clean conscience, we let them frisk us upon leaving work. "Margolin does not have anything!" the Ossetian would say, barely touching me. For a minute, he was busy locking the lock on the heavy outer door, and during that time, we extracted our treasure from the drift. Every second was precious; there was no time to hide the potatoes, and we carried it to the guardhouse in our pockets, relying on luck that they would not search us. Sometimes we did not manage to take out the potatoes from the snow. Sometimes they had already been stolen by someone who had noticed when we hid them. On the road, one hundred paces from us, the TsTRM brigade would line up: dozens of zeks stood in pairs and yelled at us to hurry up.

If the escort guard came close to the warehouse, it was impossible to take potatoes under his eyes. If we succeeded, however, we would bring two to three kilos of potatoes to the barrack. This was a victory. Then we had to cook and eat them without attracting general attention. Here Mykola relied on me. I had a friend in the boiler room, Aron. Under my jacket I would carry the tin to the boiler room and Aron himself would put it on the coals. Then on the upper bunk, Mykola and I would eat from one tin, and our neighbor pretended not to notice, and he envied us.

Such success, however, was rare. The magnet that induced four barely alive invalids to work in the warehouse was something very different. On the first day, we discovered that at the very end of the cellar, among the partitions with the potatoes was a bin with carrots. We had not eaten carrots for several years.

You do not have to cook carrots. It was the most healthy and greatest delicacy. From the morning, we meekly sat over the rotten and frozen potatoes, but all our thoughts were focused on the other end of the cellar. Having watched over us for several minutes and seen that the work was underway, the supervisor would leave for his room. As soon as the door closed after him, one of the invalids would get up and run as fast as he could to the dark corner where the carrots were. It was not possible to clean them; we scraped them with a small knife or simply wiped them on the edge of our jackets. In another ten minutes, the warehouse manager would return and stand, looking over our shoulders. The one whose mouth was not full would start a conversation with him. The others chewed as quietly as possible and swallowed in a hurry.

The warehouse supervisor sensed something. He looked suspiciously at us. Our cheek bones and our jaws stopped moving. We were still. He listened. Is someone munching something, is something crunching between someone's teeth? "What are you chewing?" he asked suddenly, approaching Belovchenko. "Well, let's see, open your mouth!" Poor Belovchenko hurriedly gagged, shook his head, and opened his mouth. "It's nothing," he vindicated himself, "I just found a little shred among the potatoes." The Ossetian merely shook his head reproachfully. Between us prisoners, this was a family affair, not dangerous. It would have been a different matter if a representative of the regime had found a carrot in Belovchenko's mouth. Then he would have been sent to the punishment cell, and if they had written a charge and opened a case, because of a carrot, they could have pinned another three years on him for embezzlement of "socialist property."

This "carrot heaven" or "carrot oasis" in January 1944 was the outstanding event in the story of my Kruglitsa imprisonment. We lived in carrot ecstasy. Everything else receded into the background. Every day from eight to eleven o'clock, we ate carrots. Every five minutes, one of us would run to the enchanted source. At eleven, we could not swallow any more. In my former life, I did not love or understand carrots. Now I valued them. In two weeks, I ate around 30 kilos of carrots. Carrot flowed in my veins; the world was decorated in its cheerful color. Mykola and I perked up; a carrot glow colored our cheeks. We got into the taste. If they had left us there for another two weeks, we would have eaten the entire bin.

Everything, however, comes to an end. The exile from carrot heaven was hard for us, but we consoled ourselves with the thought that we had not wasted our time. "We filled up a bit," said Mykola. Around that time, Mykola was already the brigade leader of the chronics instead of Shulga, who had been released at the beginning of 1944. In the spring, I parted with Mykola, who was sent to Ostrovnoe. I inherited his position, and until July 1944, I administered the chronics in Kruglitsa.

34

The Brigade Leader of the Invalids

I DO NOT need to describe Comrade Koberstein. He was a live, spitting image of Patachon.[1] The first time that I saw his gangling, sad figure, with blue, child-like eyes, his hands sticking out of the too-short sleeves, I involuntarily glanced around: "But where is Pat?" And I immediately felt cheerful, as at the movies.

Comrade Gustav Koberstein was a sixty-year-old German colonist from near Zhytomyr. A grandfather. Someone in the *kolkhoz* did not like him, and they sent him to a camp. All the Germans from his area were deported to Central Asia. He received a letter from his wife from there, which I read to him, and I also wrote a reply. All zeks' letters were the same: "Send a package." Gustav, however, was embarrassed to ask his wife for a package. Something was not right in "free" society either. The censorship crossed out half of his wife's letter, but in the other half, she said, "Aunt Mathilda died of hunger."

Two million Soviet Germans were crushed by the Soviet government even before they showed Nazi sympathies. They were deported to the Kazakh steppes; the youth were taken into the "workers' army" and sent to the Urals, where the conditions were approximately the same as in the camps. Children from mixed marriages where the mother was Jewish and the father German were registered as Germans. The father could die, but at age seventeen, the son, as a German, would be sent to the workers' army even if he did not know a word of German and considered himself Russian.

There are "democrats" who contend that hostility to the Soviet order justifies the forced resettlement of entire groups such as the Volga Germans,

---

1. Part of a Danish comic duo, Pat and Patachon (Ole and Axel), which appeared in about fifty film comedies between 1921 and 1950. Like Laurel and Hardy, one was tall, the other short. Margolin mixed up the two: Pat was the tall one.

the Crimean Tatars, or the Caucasus Karachai from their historical locations
to the depths of Asia. Possibly, from the viewpoint of the brotherhood of
peoples, Aunt Mathilda deserved her fate. Koberstein, however, was simply
an old peasant whom it was not worth sending to camp. They arrested him
just in case, as a potential enemy. In camp, where the radio daily repeated the
slogan "Kill the German," Koberstein, as an invalid and chronic, found suitable work in the drying room.

Behind all the barracks and hospital wards, at the end of the world, in the
farthest corner of the camp quadrangle stood a miserable shanty. Its logs had
darkened and cracked, the glass in the windows was broken, and they were
stuffed with straw, rags, and boards. The door hung on one hinge and did
not close properly. The entryway, with an earthen floor, led to two rooms: on
the left to the boiler room and on the right to the drying room. Aron and
Koberstein, who worked, respectively, in the two rooms, did not complain
about the cold. Water gurgled in the enormous vats in Aron's room; a pipe
went outside, and under the window stood a line of orderlies with buckets.
Thrice daily, Aron gave them boiling water: he would open the faucet and
look out of the window to keep track of the recipients. Inside the boiler room
was a large stove, bunks, a table, a lot of firewood under the table, under the
bunks, and on the stove. In addition, there was always a group of guests with
whom the hospitable host, Aron Shternfeld, hairy and dark as a gypsy, would
converse.

It was good to warm up in the boiler room in the winter, but I soon
discovered that it was even warmer in Koberstein's drying room. It was a
narrow room, along the entire length of which ran two iron pipes about 30
centimeters in diameter. The host was Patachon, with the frightened-looking
blue eyes. I conversed with him in German, wrote a letter for him, and he
allowed me to come to him to warm up.

At two o'clock in the afternoon, I would come from the chronics' cold
barrack (there they began to heat only in the evening) and stretch out under
the pipes. Curled up in fetal position on my jacket, I sank into the blessed
warmth. I lay there until dusk. There was my Africa, my equator. Somewhere
the winds were blustering, the snow circled in the open field, people froze
and tried to recover by bonfires, but I lay in a stream of hot air until the red-
hot pipes and late hour drove me from my shelter. Ultimately, Koberstein
proposed that we work together.

A drying room is an around-the-clock operation, which is difficult for one
person to run. It is a room in which the ceiling and walls are full of wooden
hooks. There were around two hundred in ours. In the evening, when the

brigades lay down to sleep, the procession of orderlies from the barracks to the drying room began. Each one carried an incredible heap of damp items. The brigades worked all day in dirt, out in the snow and rain. All their clothing was soaked and full of mud. They brought in the heavy mud-soaked padded pants, damp jackets, soaked padded socks, worn out shoes, felt boots, and *cheteze*. With the aid of a long pole, the worker hung all these items on the hooks. It is not easy to hang one hundred damp, heavy jackets under the ceiling. Each item must be hung skillfully, flattened out, and turned inside out; you have to put shoes on the stove or hang them very low over the pipes so that by morning they are completely dry. At the same time, one must not mix anything up, one must keep track of the things of each brigade and hang them separately. This hanging process takes place in the light of a dim kerosene lamp without a glass cover.

The stove is stoked from the entryway. At ten o'clock, the temperature begins to rise. The shadows tremble and flutter in the narrow dusky room, bedecked with fantastic rags, which one can pass under only bending down. The air is unbearably heavy—it is the air of a laundry in a cellar where everything gives off vapors and stinks. Hot, acrid waves traverse the dryer room. From ten o'clock, the dryers work naked. And that's not enough. At midnight, when the pipes are red hot, it is impossible to remain on the bunks. The sole possible place is on the earthen floor by the door, where the icy air is drawn in from an opening. Koberstein sleeps. I stoke at night. Every half hour, I jump out naked to the entryway and fill the stove with wood. All night, I continue to dart between the entryway and the red-hot drying room. By ten o'clock, people who drop into the drying room cannot remain there more than five minutes, but the real heat begins only after midnight. From this heat, as if from an oven, the nude dryer jumps into the yard, into the snow of the minus thirty degree cold of the Arkhangelsk night and back. These transitions do not harm him; he is used to it.

An hour before reveille, in the darkness, steps rustle outside, and the first orderly knocks on the door. The dryers get up and light the lamp. The stove has burned out. The suffocating night heat has gone. The first orderly does not hurry; it is pleasant to sit in the warmth, to talk about yesterday's news. He sits like that for about five minutes, then gets up and turns his back, spreading his legs apart. They throw on his shoulders a dry, hot jacket, then a second and third; over his arm they hang a bunch of padded socks, and a bundle of shoes on the other arm. He is so burdened that he cannot open the door on his own. They open the door for him and say, "Don't stumble on the threshold." Like a prehistoric monster, the orderly shuffles off, doubled up under the weight. . . .

In half an hour, the entire drying room is emptied out. The day turns gray. . . . The dryers lie down until eight o'clock, that is, until breakfast.

They do not summon us for the roll call. Twice a day, in the morning and at five o'clock in the afternoon, the guard or assistant work supervisor yells from afar: "Hey, how many of you are there?" Either Aron from the boiler room or one of us quickly checks how many people are at the neighbor's and yells from the door: "four" or "five," and that is the end of it. We are forbidden to go outside until the roll call is over and we hear the all-clear signal from afar.

At nine o'clock in the morning, they begin to bring the underwear and bed linen. The camp has a general laundry and one for the hospital. They also do the washing for the free workers. Everyone has the same thing: coarse calico with the stamp of the camp or the medical sector, torn shirts, tattered underpants, yellow sheets, gray tunics, blue undershirts. The women wear the same camp underwear as the men. Enormous bundles of linen are bound with a pair of rolled long underpants. If you open the door to the dryer room in daytime, you cannot see the windows or the walls because of the impenetrable curtain of damp linen. Soap in the camp is the greatest rarity, and therefore, linen washed without soap or with black-green paste that resembles tar is almost as dirty after laundering as before. One has to keep an eye on the linen lest some uninvited guest filches something.

There is a lot of work in the fall and spring, whereas in the summer, the drying room rests. If it did not rain during the day, there is nothing to dry. Linen does not come every day. Then the dryer room is like a dacha. Two invalids live an isolated life there. The administration rarely drops in. There is no radio or electricity or the bustle of the barrack. Real provincial backwoods. At midday, Koberstein and Margolin sit on the earthen embankment and warm themselves in the sun. Inside, the drying room is clean and empty.

Warm days arrived. Gustav no longer needed my help. I continued to live in the drying room, but my chief occupation now was different. I became the brigade leader of the chronics.

The two visible signs of a brigade leader's responsibility are the plywood board with the list of the brigade members and the bread box.

Ordinarily, a brigade leader and his workers are lodged together as one family, but not my chronics. There were from twenty to thirty of them. My people were dispersed throughout the camp—in the ATP (administrative-technical barrack), in the women's barrack, and in the workers' barracks. A brigade leader's day started early. I got up a quarter of an hour before the waking signal, went out to the yard, washed from a mug, and with the breadbox on my chest, set out for the other end of the camp. A line already formed under the bread cutter's window. The window was locked. Only when the reveille sounded from the guardhouse would the plywood window rise, and the robust, broad mug of Senya the bread cutter would appear: "Come for bread!"

The bread cutter is the aristocrat and rich man of the camp. He lives in the ATP barrack and eats as much bread as he wants. In the evening, the food supervisor gives him the exact calculation of rations by brigades. In Kruglitsa during the night, the bread cutter and his assistant cut about seven hundred rations of various weights. I gave him the least trouble. My chronics all receive 500 grams. Those who do physical work—of whom there are eight—receive 550. As the dryers' work is not considered physical, Koberstein and I do not receive anything for it. Why, then, do we work? First, so that we are not sent on *etap* to some deadly place as nonworkers. Second, for the possibility, on the basis of our unpaid work, of cadging a "scurvy" ration from the medical sector. People like us receive priority for that. Once a month, they prescribe a "scurvy" ration for me or Koberstein or both of us for two weeks. In the Kruglitsa medical settlement, it is exceptionally good: 200 grams of turnip flavored with vegetable oil.

In the morning at the bread cutter's, I receive identical rations for the entire brigade, 200 grams each, and meal tickets. After the roll call at five o'clock, I receive "small" rations of 300 grams and for my eight "workers"—350 grams each—"large" rations. Having received and signed for the bread, I carry my box to the drying room. In some camps, it is dangerous to walk with bread. Guards from the members of his brigade accompany the brigade leader. In Kruglitsa, however, everything is very civilized and decent. I walk alone, and along the way, my chronics come out of all the barracks when they see me. When I come to the drying room, a long line of chronics trails after me.

The bread distribution begins, with its special technique. First, the bread box has to be placed so that the zeks do not see it, do not stick their hands in, or poke with their fingers: "I don't want this ration; that one is better." Otherwise, you cannot avoid arguments. Prisoners argue like children over rations.

The bread cutter cuts the two-kilo loaves of bread into ten rations of 200 grams each. Two of these are end pieces. They are considered the tastiest and most desirable, and every zek demands the end piece for himself. They have to be distributed every day so that no one is slighted. Another difference is between a whole chunk and one made up of odd pieces. Some rations have cut corners and others have "added pieces." A small addition of bread is attached to the ration with a wooden stick. Sometimes, in order to make the weight equal to 200 grams, two to three additions are needed. A whole log is needed for wooden sticks to attach the additions to seven hundred rations cut by the bread cutter. Having received his portion, the zek suspiciously turns its around in his hands: was an addition taken off? Sometimes there is a little hole in the bread; that means there was an addition, which either fell off or was stolen. Rarely does the distribution pass without ardent protest: "Is this really 200 grams?"; "Is this really 300 grams?" Sometimes an insulted zek will force the brigade leader to go with him to the bread cutter to check the weight. The brigade leader therefore does well to examine attentively the received rations and, if there is the least doubt, demand a reweighing on the spot. Sometimes, he thus succeeds in time in discovering a missing 10 or 20 grams.

What is the good of wasting one's time as a brigade leader in such a pitiful brigade as that of the chronics? A working brigade is a different matter: there the brigade leader does not work, and he allots himself the norms of the Stakhanovite ration. Why does the brigade leader of the chronics bother? I did not understand until I myself took on the job. The secret was revealed rather quickly. The bread cutter—a healthy but uneducated fellow—regularly erred in distributing the rations. Our Senya constantly made mistakes in distribution. I, however, knew the exact calculation very well. If the bread cutter did not give enough, I raised a cry. If he erred in my favor, that is, gave extra, then without further ado, I took the box and left quickly. Fortunately, the bread cutter Senya erred primarily in my favor. One unforgettable May day, instead of twenty-one rations, he gave me twenty-eight of 200 grams each. After distributing all the rations, seven times 200 grams—a kilo and 400 grams—remained in the box. I was so prudent that I did not eat it all at once but in two sittings. I was so full that day that I ceded my midday snack to Gustav. He was unaccustomed to such generosity on my part, saw that I had stuffed myself with something, but he could not understand what or from where.

It was obvious that I was not the only one to whom Senya gave excess bread. There were fifteen brigades in Kruglitsa. How did he settle his accounts in the evening? That gave me a notion of the scale of theft in bread cutting. There was always excess bread there. And not only there. The bakery in particular stole on a grand scale. There they placed buckets with water under the dough so that it swelled from moisture—they stole the difference between the weight of the dough and the baked bread. No monitoring or analysis of the bread helped. Quality control of the baked product was carried out by hungry zeks. There was no one to supervise the supervisors.

That summer I ate a lot of excess bread. Something always happened. Either the bread cutter made a mistake, or the food supervisor forgot to take off the list a chronic who had been hospitalized or sent on an *etap*. I was thus fed on account of the disorder and imperfection of the camp mechanism. All of us in camp were caught in a net and incessantly were seeking some loophole in it. We lived like people shut in a basket who survive on the air that the sides of the basket let in. I grasped the dialectic of Soviet legality, which the petty, mouse-like illegality of private existence counteracts not only on the camp scale but also on an all-Soviet scale. In order for people to survive, the state's merciless exploitation of the individual is constantly balanced by the similarly merciless and widespread embezzlement of state resources everywhere where the least opportunity offers itself, in accordance with the Leninist formula: "Steal what has been stolen [from you]!" In a system where the state has a monopoly of the economy, and no competition acts as a regulator, corruption is inevitable.

It was obvious that a camp prisoner unscrupulously would eat every extra piece of bread that the state gave him by mistake. The bread distributor has to watch during distribution, but if a mistake occurs, it is too late to make demands. It is understood that the bread already has been eaten. The guilty party is the one who made the mistake during distribution, and he remains silent. It is ridiculous to demand that Senya the bread cutter, who himself eats as much bread as he wants, feel bad about the loss of "socialist property." The prosecutor, the NKVD, and organs of control exist to guard state interests. In a system that dooms millions to absolute submission and undernourishment, it is impossible to put an end to universal abuses. There is only one way to do so: stop measuring bread in grams and counting the population of the camps in the millions.

Having received their bread, the chronics did not disperse. They would sit near the door of the drying room and patiently wait until they were called to breakfast. The chronics' turn was after the workers' brigades. In the summer of 1944, a mess hall was already functioning in Kruglitsa; food was served to brigades, not individuals. When I led my "forces" to the mess hall, it would still be full of people. We would stand in a cluster by the door and wait to be called. The room was the same one where movies were screened in the evening. We would settle down near the wall at six or seven tables, four to a table. The brigade leader would seat them, count his people, and send for the tardy ones.

The mess hall was connected to the kitchen by a door and two windows in the wall for food distribution. When everyone had assembled, the brigade leader took a position by the kitchen window, and the distribution began. "Waitresses," that is, women working in the kitchen, took wooden spoons and ladled soup (half a liter) into clay bowls and then 200 grams of watery kasha.

In a quarter of an hour, everything was finished, the people left, but a few remained in place. Why?

The chronics were not the last group at breakfast. After them came the *pridurki*, the office or service workers who began work at nine o'clock. Some of them, such as the manager of the food warehouse or head of the bakery, were sated, and scorned the camp gruel. Something would remain in their bowls after they left. Women from the sewing workshop, laundry, and office often ate only the kasha and left the soup untouched. The kitchen workers sat down for breakfast last. They ate only for appearance's sake. They would take full bowls of gruel, taste a few spoonsful and then give it to one of those who sat by the wall and looked at them persistently and wistfully. Usually, each of those waiting had someone who would give his or her soup precisely to that person. They constantly drove away these waiting "beggars" from the mess hall with jabs and curses, but it was impossible to get rid of them.

They would be driven away, but in five minutes they would return, sneak past the orderly, and again sit in the corner. Glancing around the mess hall, a goner immediately would figure out near whom it was worth sitting, where there was a chance to get something. It was particularly advantageous to sit near Goshka, the supervisor of the punishment cell. One of the women "waitresses" was in love with Goshka. He would sit down with casual grace, his Cossack cowlick drooping over his swarthy face; with submissive devotion, the woman would serve him a full bowl and would sit down to watch him eat. He, however, looked neither at her nor at the bowl; he would take a spoonful or two and look around to see to whom to give it. Everyone then adopted an unusually dignified appearance and tried to look away, because Goshka did not like beggars and would never give to the one who looked at him pleadingly.

When my brigade finished its breakfast and dispersed, my turn came. I did not eat at the table and would receive a "brigade leader's" double portion of soup in my tin. There is no law that gives brigade leaders two ladles of soup instead of one, but that custom existed in Kruglitsa with the knowledge and consent of the administration. Twice a day, in the morning and evening, I received a supplement.

After breakfast, I demonstratively sat with Koberstein by the door of the drying room: a heap of pine branches lay in front of us and a large box at our feet. This was necessary because as the brigade leader, I regularly allotted a worker's ration to Gustav and me for plucking pine needles, that is, an extra 50 grams, which we did not earn for our work in the drying room. This was a fiction. The pine needle cook would daily sign for receiving pine needles from three to four people, but, in fact, one to two were working, and sometimes no one wished to do that.

At five o'clock, I would receive a form for the "work report" from the work supervisor, and I would fill it out, noting which chronics were entitled to an extra 50 grams. Some received this via the ChOS, others via the commandant, or some other way. It was a complex procedure. In order to "register" the pine needle pluckers, I had to receive a receipt from the pine needle cook, and on it, the endorsement of Gordeeva or the senior accountant of ChOS. If Gordeeva did not come to the ChOS in the evening or the bald Armenian accountant was capricious and did not sign the papers, then the pine needle cook's receipt was invalid, and we did not receive the extra bread for that day. On the following day, I went to Gordeeva to request a note for the 50 grams that had not been received. Although, in fact, we were not entitled because no one had plucked needles, if one calculates the hours that I waited in ChOS, argued with the accountant, explained things to Gordeeva, and looked for the pine needle cook in the kitchen, indeed, I expended an enormous amount of time, energy, and nerves on these 50 grams of bread. On paper, it all looked in order: one zek, 2 kilos of pine needles, and 50 grams of bread. In reality, there were neither pine needles nor labor, nor normal work relations; there were unfortunate people who foundered in the camp mire and wasted their lives in chasing after an extra crumb of camp bread, which the state had snatched from other similarly unhappy people.

Although officially I was a chronic invalid, who had been written off the accounts, my days were very busy. I would rise at dawn and handle dozens of bread rations, bundles of linen, troughs with pine needles; I sawed firewood with Gustav, twice a day I was counted for roll call; in the evenings, I dealt with documents, distributed meal tickets, and would run to the office for an endorsement or to the commandant for kerosene for the drying room.

The brigade was particularly excited when once a month they would give the chronics 100 grams of home-grown tobacco root and 400 grams of turnip "jam," which was not at all sweet but was a sugar substitute for us. I would receive it for everyone, borrow a scale from the hospital kitchen and divide it publicly in the drying room. The monthly portion of "jam" was eaten on the same day. Many would swap the tobacco for sugar with the patients in the wards, who did not receive tobacco but did receive 20 grams of sugar daily. They would exchange 100 grams of tobacco roots for a portion of sugar.

In the spring of 1944, the camp regime became stricter: they introduced "overseers" or supervisors who were supposed to reinforce the discipline in the camp and, in particular, see to it that every zek was in his place in the barrack after the bedtime signal. Now, when late in the evening I would sneak over to Maxik in the surgical ward, I had to be careful. If the supervisor caught me on the way, he would send me back to the drying room. I would wait five minutes and again set out, hiding in the shadows. At midnight, I would return to the drying room. A flame would sputter in the entry way; inside was an unbearable heat, a horde of roaches were crawling on the table, the bunks, and walls. Water was boiling in a tin on the red-hot pipe. The tin blackened, and half of the water in it boiled off. Gustav was lying naked on the ground, having placed a board underneath his straw mattress. I also undressed completely and lay down on the bunk by the window. My head was spinning from the radio news that I had just heard, from the names of liberated cities; hot air circulated in the room, the roaches rustled, and the moon looked in through the broken, dusty window. I had left home five years ago. What is happening there now? Do they still remember me? Shall I ever return home? And what shall I find if I do?

In the summer of 1944, I was able to obtain soup in the kitchen and bread from Senya the bread cutter, but I needed vegetables. The fall harvest was still far off. There were, however, vegetables in camp. The food warehouse stood directly opposite the guardhouse. The warehouse held products not only for the zeks but also for the free workers of the medical settlement, who received their monthly rations there. The guardian of these treasures was a short old Jew, Kremer, red-faced, with bloodshot eyes and the familiar appearance of a village shopkeeper. His eyes always looked as if he just had a good cry. Kremer was in his element in the food warehouse. He would receive, record, weigh, and distribute merchandise, but he did not wrap it, because Soviet stores had neither wrapping paper nor containers. Kramer slept in the ATP on a separate bunk and was not friendly with anyone in camp because of his job. Friendship entails obligations, and doubly so for the manager of the food warehouse in camp. You can't feed everyone. Kremer was inaccessible, but I soon found a path to him.

Once a week, they would bring damp sacks from the warehouse to the drying room. We dried them with special care, and I myself brought them back to the warehouse. Usually, the dryers receive something for this service: a few potatoes, a beet, a carrot. These sacks gave me a pretext to enter the warehouse. Normally, entry there was strictly forbidden. I tried to choose a time for bringing the sacks when Kremer was alone. How disappointed I was when Kremer did not give me anything the first or second time. The third time, he told me bluntly that he did not welcome my visits. "Let someone else bring the sacks!" "Why?" I asked, and I received a very characteristic explanation.

"You know," said Kremer, "that I would love to help you. After all, I used to give something to your predecessor, whose name was Edward. He was a German, but you are a Jew, and I am a Jew. For this reason, I cannot give you anything. They are watching us from all sides. They don't suspect anyone else. But if you enter the warehouse, now the guard in the guardhouse, the ChOS inspector, or everyone who sees us thinks: 'Margolin went to Kremer, aha! Two Jews.' And they will watch you until they see you take out of your pocket that miserable potato or carrot. Then I am finished. They will remove me from my job. There are many who covet my place."

This was the truth. The doors of the warehouse were under special observation. The goners kept a vigil nearby, the *urki* hung around, looking to see whether something was brought in or something drops accidentally to the ground, or grain spills from a hole in the sack. By the door was a chopping block on which Kremer cut meat for the free workers. Microscopic pieces of raw meat would stick to the chopping block; zeks would instantly pick them up and swallow them on the spot. Burning eyes looked at each person who entered and left. There was a risk that they would search me upon leaving the warehouse.

"That means," I said, "if I were a German, you could give me a couple of potatoes. It's too bad that I am a Jew."

I was overcome by anger. I was fighting for my life. A person in a state of alimentary dystrophy is deaf to the voice of reason. What do I care if they dismiss you? Either you lose your place or I die in this hole from starvation?

I did not say this to him. I did not even reveal my dissatisfaction. I turned and left.

My pockets, however, were full of potatoes. While the old man was preaching to me that a Jew should not put another Jew on the spot in a camp full of antisemites, I stuck my hand into the nearest bag, and to the sounds of his speech, while he stood half turned, I filled my pocket. I had no doubt about my right.

Kremer nevertheless was a compassionate old Jew. When I stopped going to his warehouse, he began to give me his meal ticket from time to time. Remember, any help given me was accompanied by risk. I was not "like everyone else," an anonymous goner drowning in the crowd. I had the misfortune to stand out like a sore thumb: they observed me; I was nearsighted, clumsy, a Westerner, a strange being. In my third year at Kruglitsa, everyone knew me. Even in the drying room, I was unable to hide from prying eyes, and everyone took an interest in where I obtained food and why I had not yet died.

In the meantime, I continued to live with Koberstein. With the arrival of the warm season, my lanky roommate's attitude toward me changed markedly. I felt that I embarrassed him in some way. He resembled Patachon, but I in no way resembled the small, cheerful little Pat. And I clearly lacked a sense of humor to balance the melancholy, silent disapproval that he displayed toward my presence.

What was going on? In the summer months, the fire in our stove attracted special clients. It had barely turned to dusk, when dark figures furtively began to creep into the entryway of our drying room, open the stove door, and stick pots inside. The pots contained grasses, mushrooms, or stolen potatoes. Some turned to the "patron" to ask for permission to heat the tin, for which he was entitled to a kickback. Others tried to do it without asking and slip away with a heated tin, giving nothing. Someone was always rustling like a mouse in the dark entryway, squatting by the fire. The profits from the stove belonged to Koberstein. He permitted and forbade, drove away smugglers and placed tins on the fire. I refused income of this sort. In the evening, while I was busy in the office dealing with the chronics' affairs, Koberstein presided over a gathering with tins by the drying room stove. Every tin yielded him a small mug.

Soon it turned out that melancholy Patachon had yet another source of income. There were two low bunks inside the drying room—boards placed on wooden stumps. On my bunk, a red pillow of simple cloth brought from Pinsk lay above the mattress stuffed with wood chips and a gray camp cotton blanket. Koberstein did not have a pillow; he would put a log wrapped in his jacket under his head. In the evening, when I had already undressed and was lying by the window, in the twilight of the white night, in the oppressive heat of the drying room, Koberstein had visitors. One was Mitya, a zek with whom I had worked reaping the previous summer in the brigade of the late Semivolos. Now he was a foreman—he had made himself a career in camp. With him was a woman. The three of them sat on Koberstein's bunk and conversed quietly. Mitya and Gustav were smoking. Having finished smoking, Koberstein rose and went to the exit. At the door, he stopped: "He's sleeping!" he said, looking at me.

"No, no!" replied the woman. "How can that be! Wake him."

She laughed uneasily. Koberstein called me and signaled that I should leave. In the entryway, he asked me to stay with Aron in the boiler room for half an hour.

The dilapidated drying room at the edge of the camp was the camp trysting site. It was one of the very few places where two people could be alone without attracting attention. Now I understood why Koberstein was uneasy from the start of the warm season and was continually trying to convince me to sleep in another place. I was in his way. He was afraid that I would demand my share.

Poor camp Patachon. He, too, probably, had not been prepared in life for such a career and would have been very surprised if he had been told in those years when he was a respected father of a family at liberty that his life path would end like this in a corrective labor camp. I did not say anything to him. An hour later, when I returned to the dryer room, he was already lying quietly on his bunk, and we did not discuss this topic. A week later, however, guests arrived again. This time I did not wait but immediately got dressed and left "home."

How nice it was in the drying room! In the winter it is warm, you can cook and dry as much bread as you want. You have your own corner—without the noise and din of the crowded barrack, without the daily fights and arguments, without eyes that are watching you from all sides, without thieves, even without bedbugs. Only roaches. . . . And suddenly, this unexpected complication. I was at a loss what to do and where to go.

The next day at supper in the mess hall, the grateful Mitya cheerfully waved to me: "Do you want soup? I'll leave it for you."

I imagined how this would look in another two months if I remained: two invalids in a wretched hole to which guests arrive in the evenings—with and without tins. . . .

This was the bottom rung. From here my path would lead only to the cemetery, Square 72. I had to do something, change something in my life, but I was no longer master of my fate, unable even to choose the place and circumstances of my death. Only a miracle could tear me away from the spectral procession of millions of shackled and doomed people.

In July 1944, my life changed drastically.

35

The Road to the North

ON MAY 30, 1944, a document arrived in Kruglitsa concerning four Poles, that is "Westerners," who had been deported from Poland. They immediately were to undergo a medical test to check their suitability for military service in Polish army units. This paper aroused indescribable excitement among the dozen Kruglitsa Poles. It was not clear why precisely those four were chosen. I was one of them.

That summer, a new Polish army was formed on Soviet territory under the leadership of Colonel Berling.[1] This army was destined to participate in the Red Army's march to Berlin under the supreme Soviet command and to take part in the expulsion of the Germans from Poland. Its organizers asked the Soviet government to release from camps the Polish citizens who were able to serve in the ranks of the new army.

I had more than a year left of my term. I had been excluded from the first "amnesty" for Poles under the incredible pretext that I was "a person of non-Polish nationality" (simply—a Polish Jew). Now, however, they proposed that the medical sector in Kruglitsa immediately check my suitability for service in the ranks of the Polish army. I was not surprised. This was a "new course." I was happy. They brought me and three other Poles to the food warehouse, where there was a large scale on which Kremer weighed produce. There they determined my weight: on May 30, 1944, I weighed exactly 45 kilos, whereas before camp, I had weighed 80. Then the head doctor of Kruglitsa, Valentina Vasilevna (a free worker) checked me. Here I suffered a cruel disappointment.

---

1. Zygmunt Berling (1896–1980), a Polish army officer who deserted from Anders' Polish army and, while in a POW camp, agreed to collaborate with the Soviet regime. He was promoted to the rank of general and took command of the Soviet-controlled Polish army in July 1944.

Valentina Vasilevna refused to certify that I was suitable for military service. I knew that she was well disposed toward me and did not wish to harm me. How could she close the door to freedom in my face? I implored her to write that I was suitable at least for noncombatant service, but she categorically refused.

"I cannot write absurd things," she said. "People in your physical condition are not sent to the army. You are a basket case. You need to sit in a rest home for six months with extra nutritious food, and even then, it is not clear whether you will get back on your feet."

I then wrote a petition to the head of the Ertsevo Camps. "They rejected me," I wrote, "but that is incorrect. I know languages. I graduated from university, and the army can use me for work that does not require physical strength. A front-line ration will quickly put me back on my feet, whereas in camp, I have no chance of recovery. I beg you to give me an opportunity to fulfill my duty as a Polish citizen and antifascist."

All four Poles were categorized as unfit for military service, and all wrote petitions similar to mine but did not receive an answer. Instead, an unexpected change occurred. In June, I lost my status as an invalid—that very designation that I had grown accustomed to as my natural condition to the point that I had forgotten the basic camp law: "Nothing is eternal." The administration, which had made me an invalid, could at any moment make me capable of work. All that was needed was a stroke of the pen. In the summer of 1944, the NKVD camps suffered from an acute labor shortage. There were too many invalids! It was decided that, henceforth, only cripples or those who were dying would enjoy the advantages of an invalid's status. A commission arrived in Kruglitsa to re-examine the invalids. In half a day they looked over everyone, literally "looked over." Two minutes each. We already knew that the commission had arrived to "abolish invalids." I did not even have to undress. They did not ask me any questions and wrote: "Suited for work. Third category, individual labor."

The notation "individual labor" was something new. It meant that every time I was sent to work, they had to check and decide whether I was suitable for that particular job. I knew, however, that in practice no one would pay attention to my "individual" condition.

After the verdict, nothing, in fact, changed. Everyone in Kruglitsa knew that no matter what you write, invalids are of no value. They therefore let me live as before in the drying room and remain in charge of the invalids' brigade. Now, however, the ground was opening under my feet. As a "worker of the third category," I could be taken from my accustomed place at any time and sent with a work reinforcement to any camp that needed workers. In the new place, where no one would know me, they could drive me to deadly exhaustion and catastrophe.

What could I do? I turned to the security officer, the representative of the Third Sector, with a request to help me receive an assignment to the Polish army at the front. This was the same security office who forbade giving me Lenin's works, who took away my son's picture, who threatened me openly in the summer of 1942: "They feed you," he said to me then, "they give you work, and you still are dissatisfied! People like you should be put on trial! Now we are at war, we don't have time for you, but just wait, when the war is over, we'll take care of you!" I now turned for help to this person who had once threatened me with a second term.

"Your case is being reviewed," he replied. "Your case will soon be decided."

The morning of July 13, 1944, an order concerning seven Poles arrived at Kruglitsa, including the four whom they had planned to send to the Polish army. We decided that this meant liberation. The work supervisor said so, and the entire camp believed it instantly. Everyone hurried to congratulate us. I spent the entire next day in feverish excitement, in a dream, not believing it myself. I simply could not imagine freedom; my imagination was blinded as if by the sun. Strangers came to say farewell. Maxik brought me a gift for the road—an English book, the stories of Jack London. My neighbor, a professor of bacteriology in his former life, brought me a white shirt: I had nothing but rags; you could not go free looking like that. All my things were arranged in my knapsack; at the bottom lay my manuscripts and a bag with a kilo of rusks for the journey. After lunch, I handed in my camp property to the ChOS. They took away my blanket but let me keep my jacket. I handed over the uncomplicated affairs of the chronics' brigade to a successor. In the evening, I went to the bathhouse, the last time at the camp bathhouse, where I had washed for four years. I could not resist going to the Second Sector, the Registration-Distribution Bureau, to ask the boss: "Where are they sending us? Is it true that we shall be released? Perhaps it is just an *etap*? You know, after all; why don't you tell us?"

The woman at the table in the office only pressed her lips: "Tomorrow you will know." She knew but it was not her business to inform zeks what awaited them. I left with a dark presentiment that all this was a terrible mistake, a misunderstanding.

I spent a sleepless last night in Kruglitsa, awake, but not thinking about what lay ahead. That was unimaginable. Four camp years rose in front of me like an impenetrable wall, like a mountain range, blocking the horizon. How far away did one have to go in order not to see them anymore? How could I tear out of my heart the memory of those who had perished and those who remained?

That night, I recalled an episode at Square 48 that had completely escaped my memory. Suddenly, I clearly saw myself in the office in the camp of the second division of the Onega BBK. I had night duty; it was past midnight. The kerosene lamp smoked on the table; I lowered the flame and shivered from cold. The autumnal night wind howled and tore at the shutter. The forest stirred steadily and loudly. Its booming, like sea surf, assailed the camp on all sides, an island in the forest ocean. The melancholy howling of the guard dogs resounded from the forest. I was alone.

Suddenly the door opened and an old man appeared on the threshold. I cannot remember his face. He was a Polish peasant, in tatters, almost bare-foot, semi-naked, bent and dirty, as if he had emerged from a puddle. He mumbled something disconnected and extended his hands. . . .

"Panie, panie, panie. . . ."[2]

"What happened? And why are you wandering around the camp at night? It's cold. Go to your place in the barrack, there you'll warm up. . . ."

"Panie, panie, panie. . . ."

The camp night guard passed by and chased him off the porch into the dark autumn night. I locked the door and forgot about him. An hour passed, and suddenly, I thought I heard knocking at the door. Barely audible. I went over and listened: no one. I opened the door. No one. The icy air took my breath away.

In the morning, they found the old man in a damp hollow behind all the barracks. He was sitting, leaning against the edge of the well, his head hanging on his chest, dead. He died alone although a thousand people surrounded him. This was the first case of death at Square 48. Four years later, I recalled him. Again, a sleepless night. Of everything that I had seen over these four years, I remembered precisely this face with the blurred features that I no longer could recreate in my memory. The face of the unknown zek. . . . And that barely audible knock on the door. I turned over endlessly on the boards and thought that this knock on the door in the deep of the night—I had heard it somewhere earlier. A knock on the door. Knock. . . . Where had it been? And who told me about it? Or was this merely the beating of my own

2. "Sir" in Polish.

JOURNEY TO THE LAND OF THE ZEK

heart, my pulse, and noise in my ears, silenced in daytime and heard only on a sleepless night, when people die in silence?...

In the morning on July 15, they brought the seven Poles to the guardhouse. They searched us at the exit as usual. We waited a long time until the escort guard came. Farewell, Kruglitsa! The sun was high in the sky. They escorted us along the street of the settlement to the crossing, where we sat on a stack of boards, waiting for a train. Now I knew for sure that this was not freedom. Released people were sent to Ertsevo without an escort. We, however, were under escort, which means that we are prisoners, as before. An armed guard sent specially from the guardhouse came up to me. "Untie!" The security officer had ordered the guard to shake out my sack and take away all the books. Only my sack. He knew that he did not need to look for books in the others'. The guard took away Maxik's gift to me, Jack London's tale. He did not pay attention to letters and notebooks. The security officer had forgotten to tell him about papers.

The train arrived—an antediluvian locomotive and two train cars. The first was a third-class car for free workers. The second was a freight car, for prisoners. It was already overcrowded. We scrambled in, took our sacks off our shoulders, and settled down in the midst of the crowd. The guards closed the car doors, and we set off.

In Ertsevo, they handed us over at the guardhouse, according to the proper count, like a consignment of merchandise. We entered a large camp, much larger than Kruglitsa, with spacious barracks and a broad wooden pathway. Immediately we went from the guardhouse to the bathhouse. We hung around the changing room for half a day. In the evening, they led us to a barrack for those on *etap*.

On the following day, we learned our destination—the first train to the north, to Vorkuta. The seven Poles were overcome with horror. We knew very well about Vorkuta—that area in the north is the same as Karaganda in the south—work in the mines. It is a frozen waste, far past Pechora, beyond the Arctic Circle. There, at the end of the world, near the northern Arctic Ocean, they established a city similar to Medvezhegorsk, the capital of slave labor by the Onega. Vorkuta is the capital of the Arctic region. The earth is frozen down to several meters, and nothing grows there. The food is brought in. During the long polar night, people do not see the sun for months. There are no free settlements there. Tens of thousands of zeks work underground in the NKVD coal mines. It is the hardest work in camps, and people who work there receive vodka and a fortified polar ration. A miner receives 900 grams of bread in comparison to 550 in our parts. If you only have the strength for it. . . . "Go," they told us, "you will be miners."

I understood that I would not return alive from Vorkuta. The next day, in the evening, they called us to the bread cutter and gave us a kilo and 300 grams of bread; this was our ration for a two-day *etap* until Vologda. They advised us to hand over the bread to the KVCh for safekeeping overnight. The advice was prudent, as in the common barrack it would have been taken away from us at night.

In the morning, we left Ertsevo. Right before we passed through the gates, at the last minute, they gave us back the bread that had been sitting in the KVCh overnight. My ration was complete, but some raised an outcry: their rations had been truncated. "They stole from us!" The woman in charge of the KVCh sent us to the bread cutter for a reweighing. Four hundred grams were missing from the rations. The woman was mortified but there was nothing to be done. It was too late to look for the thief. They hurried us out the gates and to the train.

I never saw such a train before. Until that time, I had traveled around Russia in cattle cars with bunks inside. Now I saw a real prisoner train of "Stolypin" cars—a prison on wheels.[3] It is constructed like a Pullman car, with a corridor and compartments. The windows, however, are small and square, high up in the corridor and covered with a grating. The doors also are grated. The compartments are locked; each contains three tiers of benches. Inside it is dark: light enters from the corridor through the locked, grated door.

This time we were a large group. They led an entire column to the train. The seven Poles tried to stay together. We were surrounded by people in caps with piercing, darting eyes, with malevolent, sharp faces. I already knew what kind of people they were. I heard them go to Kowalcyzk, a young fellow from our group, and begin to question him: "Who are you and who are your friends?" Kowalcyzk answered, "Poles." These people already knew that Poles were in this train, and they were looking for them. Poles might have Polish stuff. Now we were surrounded; we were separated and did not succeed in entering one compartment together.

Before embarking on the train, Kowalcyzk and the other Poles ate up all the bread allotted them for two days. I was stubborn. One of my eccentricities was to leave bread for the evening. I decided not to touch my bread until it became dark.

The train had barely gotten under way when my neighbors began to tug at the coarse, cotton red pillow that had accompanied me on all my wanderings

3. Pyotr Arkadyevich Stolypin (1862–1911) was a prime minister and minister of internal affairs in the Russian Empire from 1906 to 1911. The Stolypin carriage was designed in the context of his agricultural reforms and the deportation of peasants to Siberia.

since the Pinsk prison. Until now, the thieves had disdained it. "Give it to me for under my head!" But I did not let go of it. The guard stood by the door grating. They left me alone. At midday, we arrived at Vologda.

The convict train stopped 200 meters before the train station. Upon exiting, we saw in the distance the hands of the railroad station clock, the platforms, the crowd, as in a dream. The guards surrounded us and drove us across the tracks, bypassing the station. We reached a long street with small wooden houses and a cobblestone road. This was the regional city Vologda, where Alexander Herzen[4] had lived in exile one hundred years ago. Now there was a Herzen Street in Vologda, along which a long, dusty column of Soviet zeks was marching. My neighbor was barefoot. We walked a long time, and I became exhausted and started to fall behind the line; they pushed me. I kept expecting to see the tall palisade and watch towers of a camp. Infrequent pedestrians at the edge of the city turned away without looking at us. Finally, we turned off the street, the road went up a hill, and in front of us, we saw a massive white tsarist-era building. It was the Vologda transit prison.

The people traveling with us were, evidently, here not for the first time. They welcomed the prison like an old acquaintance. The commandant Volodya (a prisoner) met them at the entrance and received them like old friends. "Hello Vanya! Hello Petya!" Instantly, they exchanged winks, whispered, and led the seven of us to a cramped cellar-cell with a small window on top. Several of the "commandant's "friends" in caps with the look of apaches entered immediately after us. They included Vanya and Petya and the ones who had tried to take my pillow away from me on the train.

As soon as the door closed and we settled on the floor in the semi-dark, damp cell, the looting began. Efficiently and simply, as if it were the most natural thing in the world, they took from us our possessions, sacks, and bags. Kneeling, Vanya untied my knapsack and began to pull my things out of it. I lunged at him. His friend held me by the shoulder.

"Sit quietly! Otherwise it will be worse!"

I looked with helpless fury as they divided my things among them. Not only the bread ration for two days but also the kilo of rusks that I had collected for the road were eaten in a flash.

---

4. Alexander Herzen (1812–1870), an illegitimate son of a Russian nobleman, was a prominent socialist thinker in Russian intelligentsia circles in the 1840s. He left Russia in 1847, eventually settling in London, where he tried to influence the situation in Russia with publications such as the periodical *Kolokol* (The Bell).

"This here will be my cushion," said one, fondly patting the coarse cotton red pillow, which he had taken a liking to in the train car. "A nice cushion, brothers."

All seven Poles were robbed clean. They left us only rags. They took away the clean white shirt that the Kruglitsa professor had given me "for freedom." In its place, they threw me a torn, dirty camp shirt.

"You just squeak and we'll kill you."

I lay on the floor, stupefied, frightened, and ashamed. "You got money?" one of the *urki* approached me. "Give me the money or you'll be in trouble if we find it." He frisked me, turned the pockets inside out, did not find anything, and waved his hand in frustration.

It grew dark. The *urki* began to pound frantically on the door. Immediately someone approached the peephole from the other side. "What's the matter?"

"Tell them in the kitchen," shouted Vanya through the door, "that we're hungry! Let them bring something or we'll take off a head."

Silence ensued. Ten minutes later, the cannonade on the door started again. Again, someone came to the door. "What do you want?"

"To stuff ourselves this minute! Did you forget?"

"But there's nothing left. Only soup."

"Bring soup."

We were not entitled to any food in the Vologda prison that day, but to my surprise, they brought them soup in a large bowl, which the five of them ate. The sixth person did not belong to their group. He was their "prisoner," a person with an intelligent face, who did not take part in the theft or division of the booty. He was a young Leningrad doctor, Vakhrameev. He was completely terrorized by his traveling companions.

"You see," they told him, "we treated you well. We hardly touched your things. We took a trifle. Why? Because our joint destination is Vorkuta. There, if you act intelligently, no one will touch you. You're a doctor, we will need you and you'll need us. Do you know the law of the camps? You need to live in peace with us; you can't hide from us anywhere. . . ."

Vakhrameev, still a very young man, looked at them in fear. He was a novice, just out of prison. They "educated" him.

"Look, suppose you complain to the bosses. So, they'll take you away from us to the neighboring cell. But the same kind of people are sitting there. I'll knock on the wall and say, 'Crush the rat,' and they'll crush you in a second. You won't make it alive to Vorkuta. Remember this."

For the rest of the day, sated and pleased with their success, they boasted of their thievish exploits with unusual bravado and drilled Vakhrameev. One of the robbed Poles, a young fellow, already went over to them, "the masters of the situation," and began to worm his way into their company. Until the evening, they told obscene stories, and he sycophantically laughed, moved closer, and pitched into their conversation; he was already halfway to becoming one of them.

At night Vanya woke me. Everyone around was sleeping. He was waiting for this minute, he dragged my bag out from under my head, and again rummaged through it. This time he managed to find 109 rubles, the entire sum that my friends had collected for the way, thinking that I was "going free."

"Cunning you are, cunning," Vanya mumbled and looked around at his sleeping comrades, "but you can't hide anything from me. And now, watch it, be quiet."

He thus hid this money from his comrades in order not to share it with them. With this money, one could buy about five glasses of homegrown tobacco.

For two days, I lay without bread. On the second day, they brought us lunch—soup and kasha. They distributed the food through a serving hatch in the door; the *urki* did not let the Poles near the hatch; they took our food. They gave us the soup, thin as water, and one portion of the kasha for two of us. They thus took half of our kasha. Then a supplement was brought to them. We could see that these were truly dangerous people: even the prison personnel feared them. In fact, it was not a matter of fear. Volodya the commandant was their man, one of them. He brought them people from whom to steal, and they split the proceeds with him: the usual camp "cooperation."

Our "food product certificate" noted that we had received food for two days. We were, therefore, entitled to bread in the Vologda prison only from the third day. Weakened by our fast, we could barely wait for the third day. Only at one o'clock in the afternoon did they open the serving hatch and hand each of us our ration. I took the bread carefully, as the greatest treasure, but as soon the hatch closed, Vanya came to us:

"Half of the ration!"

I did not immediately understand what he wanted, I was so far from the thought that people who had taken my bread for two days could do the same on the third day. Bread is the very basis of life. I watched in stupefaction as the Poles obediently handed over their rations, the *urki* cut them in half with a knife, and left half. I looked at these insolent brigands' faces, and a fierce wave of anger and hatred rose in me and blood flushed my face.

"I won't give it!" I said quietly and distinctly to Vanya. I was ready for everything. I had ceased to fear them. They could take this ration from me only with my life. I thrust it into the deep pocket of my jacket and prepared to defend it, as a wounded bear defends her cub.

I saw near me the threatening, disgusting face of the hooligan, his teeth bared. He grabbed me by the throat. I could not release those fingers, and I grabbed him by the gullet and hair. We both tumbled to the floor. He was young, and I was a half-alive invalid—skin and bones. My glasses, attached by a string, flew to the side. He crushed me under him, and I tried in vain to loosen his iron grip on my neck, ten iron leeches. I began to choke. My mouth opened, and it emitted a wheeze and disconnected words together with spittle. My knees rose but my chest could not draw in air. He choked me calmly and slowly, while by the wall, the six Poles sat in a row and impassively watched, maintaining strict silence.

I experienced a childish astonishment at the awareness that I could be choked in a cell full of people, without a hand, without a voice raised in my defense.

The cell was full of my wheezing; in my brain floated a distant memory that I once had studied philosophy in the West, and this wheeze, if it could be translated into human language meant: "Me! Me, a doctor of philosophy! Me, a well of wisdom, created in the Divine image and likeness!"

I underwent what precedes death by strangulation, my consciousness dimmed. My thoughts disintegrated, but my body, taut as a bow, still held life, like an unreleased arrow. After a very long minute, I heard some voice through the fog:

"They'll add a year for that, fellows, and that's not worth it. . . ."

I realized that I was free. I, alone of all of them, did not hand over bread. I jumped up and ran to the door. I began to kick it with my feet and strike with my fists, yelling savagely, "They're killing me!" Behind me the *urki* were yelling: "He's gone crazy!"

From the other side of the door, a live human eye appeared in the peephole, and I heard or understood: "We see everything!" But no one opened the door or entered the cell.

Then one of the fellows jumped up and with all his strength flung my own metal tin at me. I did not feel pain. I grabbed the tin and flung it back at his head. I missed, and the tin whacked his neighbor's head, struck the wall, and clattered down in the middle of the cell. The injured one jumped up, looked at me, and again sat down.

My victory. Now I felt as if I had thrown off my chains. I showered them with savage curses. At the same time, I turned to my companions the Poles:

"Bastards. Cowards! There are more of you, and you let those scoundrels humiliate you!" Two days of suppressed fury, humiliation and fear poured out of me with the smoke and roar of an avalanche.

"Be quiet! Don't get on our nerves!"

Half an hour later, I saw two of them approach a Pole and start to pull off his shoes. He was a sick, consumptive shoemaker who had come from Kruglitsa, and those leather shoes were all he owned. He burst out crying. Tears flowed down his hairless, womanish face.

I was still full of a fighting spirit. I went up, and I did not say, I ordered: "Return his boots!"

"What?" said the gang. "You want to give commands, you measly Yid? We'll get you all the same. You won't make it alive to Vorkuta."

They took the shoes and went to their corner. "Don't cry *psia krew*" [Polish—son of a bitch, but literally, blood of a dog], I said angrily to the shoemaker. "You'll get your boots back."

Toward evening, the on-duty warden, wearing an official cap, entered. We stood in a line. When he had counted us and turned to leave, I stepped forward:

"Allow me to make a declaration."

"What's the matter?"

"I request to be transferred immediately out of this cell."

"Why?"

"Here my life is in danger." The warden raised his eyebrows and whistled.

"Whaddya say!" he exclaimed, "and who else wants to leave this cell?" The six Poles wavered and then together stepped out of the line. Vakhrameev, the Leningrad doctor, fluttered like a bird, hesitated for a moment and suddenly, gathering courage, stepped forward.

"Me too . . . take me."

The warden looked at the remaining five and understood everything.

"What is your complaint?" Dead silence.

"Citizen warden," I said, "don't you see that they are all terrorized by this band? In their presence, they won't say anything. Take them to another cell; there, no doubt, their tongues will loosen."

"Take your things, leave."

They led us to an empty cell in the same corridor on the other side. The warden summoned the commandant. Now everyone perked up as if they had just awoken. Complaints rained down. The commandant compiled a list of items stolen from us over the past two days. They could not have gone out of the cell where we were sitting together.

"You don't need to look for one hundred nine rubles," said the commandant. "Yesterday I received one hundred thirty rubles from this bunch to purchase tobacco. I wondered where they had stolen the money."

An hour later, the door opened and they tossed a heap of things onto the floor. The Poles gathered their possessions instantly. The shoemaker received his shoes back and I got my red pillow. We were so happy that we ignored the odd circumstance that somehow some things were not found. That was the honorarium for the commandant Volodya.

"What about my money?" I asked naively.

"I already told you that I have the money. You'll get it later."

That "later" never came. Alone in the cell, we rejoiced and laughed like children. We felt as if a burden had been lifted from us. One of the Poles came to me, shook my hand, and thanked me for the successful intervention. I settled down next to Doctor Vakhrameev, who also had cheered up noticeably. We spent two days together in friendly conversation, after which our paths diverged forever. He was a very pleasant person, and I hope he is still alive and well in the Soviet Union in one of the camps of the north, no longer a novice but an experienced, hardened zek.

I was apprehensive about one thing—how not to wind up in too close contact with "Vanya and Petya" in the future.

We left Vologda two days later. They led us—a group of fifty or sixty people— into the yard of the transit prison. The five bandits from our cell were in the first row. I stood farther away from them, in the back. The usual procedure before dispatch on an *etap* began. The administrative personnel sat at a table placed in the courtyard. We approached one at a time and undressed completely.

Here, in the yard of the Vologda transit prison, on July 22, 1944, occurred what should have been expected long ago. The guard, with a pockmarked, indifferent face, shook out my bag and found a bundle with papers including my mother's letters. In one, she wrote about my father's final days; that was the last letter that I received in the BBK camp from an old woman, a half-year before her martyr's death at the hands of German murderers. Without even looking, this sleepy, dull-looking man took this letter, which for me was like a sacred relic, and a bundle of papers—the manuscripts of my three works: "The Theory of the Lie," "The Doctrine of Hate," and "About Freedom." I was not supposed to possess any papers. No one cared about their contents. In my presence, they threw everything into the dirt, into the garbage heap. Standing naked nearby, I witnessed the disappearance of three years of my thought and work—not Soviet labor based on quotas but that which arises unsolicited, unexpectedly, in solitude, and is as unique as the life that engendered it.

My book was lost! And it will never be written by me or anyone else in the form in which it was created in those years, when I did not have access to libraries or the most elementary amenities, when every line was attained through struggle and was a challenge to fate. The book was lost that had been written in camp with fear and apprehension, with all the precautions, which for years had been hidden from searches and spies. A tragic and strange paradox was gone—a book about the lie written among lies, a book about hatred written among hatred, a book about freedom written in imprisonment. For years, I carried it with me like my child, and it grew with the years of suffering, even as my flesh declined, as if my life passed into it. The twenty-eight chapters of "The Doctrine of Freedom" were, no doubt, the sole literary document where a rational analysis indistinguishably merged with madness, and life with death, which stood relentlessly behind me. I shall never repeat the years spent in gloomy captivity, and I shall never be able to restore that train of thought nor separate it from the conditions in which it arose. Other times, other songs! The book was lost! Clearly, one must not write books in camps. But is this the only book in the world that was lost? Is this really the place and time to recall one, sole book—over the graves of millions, over the fresh ashes, over the ocean of human blood and evil deeds behind us, around us, and yet to come?

One book was lost and here is another in its place, but one book cannot replace another just as a new love does not replace a former one cut off by death. A person dies once in a lifetime, but this decisive experience is not useful to him and is not very convincing to others. After a war, they erect a "monument to the unknown soldier"; this, too, is little help to the unknown living. One should also erect a monument to the unknown destroyed book—the one that was destroyed at the hands of the annihilators of the spirit, the one that was crushed in embryo, and the one that was not allowed to reach readers.

Standing naked in the yard of the Vologda prison, I vowed implacable hatred toward people who kill books. Woe to the country where they kill books! In the country where the pages of so many books are stained with blood, writers die as Pilnyak and Kulbak died, but writers also die—not accidentally—in the way Mayakovsky and Esenin did.[5]

---

5. The poet Moshe Kulbak and writer Boris Pilnyak were shot during the purges in 1937 and 1938 respectively. The poets Sergey Esenin and Vladimir Mayakovsky committed suicide in 1925 and 1930.

When I left the yard of the Vologda prison, I saw the commandant Volodya at the administration's table and recalled my 109 rubles.

"Where is the money that you took into custody?"

He laughed in my face. I turned to the people at the table:

"This man took my money. Order him to return it!"

But they, too, laughed, and someone remarked to me:

"From whom are you asking this? He is a prisoner, after all. You shouldn't have let it get out of your hands."

36

Kotlas

THE PRISONER TRAIN traveled for two days from Vologda to the northeast. In the morning, the guard distributed the food for the day: 500 grams of bread and a piece of salted fish. The food stunned us: after eating, we felt heavy and fell asleep.

My place was on the floor under the bench. I would crawl there, stretch out, and spend long hours in the darkness in a stupor, dozing or in a deep, dreamless sleep. We slept for half of the day, and the other half, we suffered from hunger and thirst. We were not entitled to food until the next morning, but we received water at the stations. The guard would fill a bucket, make the rounds of our cages, and, opening the door slightly, would fill our tins and mugs. We drank a lot, greedily, and then began the nagging: "Dear guard, let us take a leak. . . ."

On July 25, 1944, they brought us to Kotlas, a city on the bank of the Northern Dvina with a population of 15,000 people. It is the center of Kotlaslag (Kotlas camps) and also a transit point for masses of prisoners who are dispatched from there to the camps of Pechora and the Arctic Circle region. The train stopped a few kilometers beyond the city. They led us past unending wooden warehouses, granaries, barns, shanties, and barracks to our destination. Upon reaching the guardhouse, it was the same picture in infinite variations, always the same, in any corner the entire length of this gigantic country: a wood stave fence with barbed wire, massive wooden gates, and a guardhouse through which one enters the camp.

"Lie down," ordered the guard, and with this one word, he mowed us down like grass in the field. We fell to the ground and lay there for a long time, waiting for the person from the URB (Registration-Distribution Bureau) who was supposed to receive us.

The first thing that I saw on passing through the gate of the Kotlas transit center was a familiar pair of shoulders. There could be no mistake. Only one person in the world had that shoulder posture and manner of tipping his head back. I hastened my pace, caught up, and looked him in the face. Now I knew that I was saved. This meeting was salvation.

In front of me stood Doctor Spicnagel, who three years earlier had kept me in Kruglitsa by putting me in the pulmonary ward for three days and with whom we went on strike together and sat in the punishment cell in Osinovka in September 1941.

"Spicnagel!" He turned around and . . . extended both hands to me.

They hurried the group from the *etap* into the "club," a small wooden house on the edge of the camp, and then led us to the bathhouse. Before that, however, Spicnagel ran into the club, looked at me, and sighed; when he heard that I was being taken to Vorkuta, he laughed. "Your journey ends here; you won't go any further."

Spicnagel himself could not remain in Kotlas, and he was sent away from there a week later. During that week, he extracted me from the mass of prisoners and brought me to the attention of the doctors at the Kotlas transit point who examined the arriving trainloads. Kotlas was another turning point in my camp life; here I "went underground"—disappeared from the surface of the camp in order to emerge into the sunlight, to freedom in another ten months, to arise from the dead.

If the camp system as a whole is a "subterranean kingdom," the gloomy cellar of Soviet Russia, then it, in turn, has its own catacombs and dungeons. This "descent into the underground" was my salvation, for as long as I remained on the surface of camp life, in the "daylight" of spying and political supervision, under the vigilant eye of the security agents, I had no chance of living to see freedom. The following occurred in Kotlas: a serious illness detained me halfway to those places to which they had sent me never to return. They took me off the train to the polar region. Vanya, Petya, and the rest of that group traveled on to Vorkuta, while I remained in the transit point, this godforsaken hole, where very few knew about my existence except for some kind people who cared for me with infinite patience and rescued me from the verge of death. It was as if I had disappeared from the NKVD's view and ceased to exist for the camp administration.

August arrived with cold nights, but it was still warm in the daytime. New groups arrived daily, and every day a commission sat in the medical sector and examined the arrivals. They immediately sent some on further and left some "to recuperate." I was among those who were left behind. Every few days, the latter were summoned to a commission to verify whether they had recovered sufficiently to continue on the way to the north or to surrounding camps.

The area of the transit point was divided into zones. The "communal" buildings were to the left of the guardhouse: the club, the bathhouse and laundry, the boiler room, the medical sector, kitchen, bread distribution point, and the office. The punishment cell was also there. To the right of the guardhouse, the low hospital barracks stretched out on two sides of a wooden pathway. Here these buildings were called blocks [in Russian *korpus*]. The hospital sector was closed on both sides by gates, which were locked during roll calls. The patients were not able to leave their zone, and the healthy zeks were not allowed into the hospital sector. "Watchmen" stood at the gates and regulated the traffic: they let some in and detained others. Beyond the hospital zone stood a women's barrack, some barracks for those on *etap*, and at the very end, something new to me: "BUR."

The BUR (a disciplinary barrack; literally of reinforced regime) stood behind a separate fence in a separate yard and was locked tight twenty-four hours a day. Either the commandant or the guard at the door held the key. The people living there were condemned to forced labor (*katorzhane* in Russian): this was a new camp category that developed as a result of the war. In the footsteps of the Red Army, which cleared the territory of the Soviet Union from external enemies, the army of the NKVD moved in to purge it of domestic enemies. The real enemies, that is, the active collaborators, were hung and shot. There remained, however, a mass of people who had sullied themselves by collaboration with the Germans—those who were employed under the Germans, got along well with them, kowtowed to them, or expressed satisfaction at the Bolsheviks' departure. All such people—and there were many of them—were now seized, and the old tsarist term *katorga* (forced labor) was revived for them. Whereas at that time, the maximum term for ordinary political prisoners under Article 58 was ten years, these people faced two possible terms—fifteen or twenty years. In other words, they tore them away from life. A wave of a million forced laborers flooded the camps, shattering the illusions of those who had hoped that in post-war Russia, the camp system would be liquidated or at least modified.

The forced laborers signified a renaissance of the camp system, a fresh influx of a work force—not for just a year or two but for a long time. They arrived just in time. Here at the transit point, the terrible physical degradation of the camp population at the end of the war was particularly evident. The trainloads that arrived every few days consisted of semi-cripples, former, present, and future invalids. Alimentary dystrophy mowed down the prisoners. In Kotlas, I saw women who had not been in the "rich" Kruglitsa *selkhoz*: their looks shocked me. Nothing womanly remained: they were bony shadows with hands and feet like sticks, in smelly tatters and dirty rags. One easily could photograph them and write the caption: "Victims of German atrocities released in Bergen-Belsen by Allied troops." This was an ominous sign: women always founder last, after the men. And, indeed, soon I was told about terrible places around Kotlas—about a camp where out of 2,400 people, 1,600 were in bed, unable to rise, and people died at the rate of thirty a day. The Soviet regime sent doctors and medicine there, but it did not touch the root of the camp system, which always was linked to the systematic mortality of depleted people. People on the spot were unable to help much. The real murderers of the prisoners were located in Moscow and in every place on earth outside of the USSR where knowledge of this terrible crime was consciously silenced. Looking around, I thought that an American with a camera who would manage to snap sixteen pictures at the Kotlas transit point and bring them to Europe would convince worldwide public opinion better than all accounts and descriptions.

Theoretically, a person was supposed to spend a week or two in the transit barracks and then travel on. In reality, however, people remained at the transit point for months and years. All their efforts to escape from this deadly place did not help. They were not sent on because of the state of their health, but, at the same time, they were not sufficiently ill to be hospitalized. They lived in barracks which were large, half-collapsed sheds, damp and moldy. I was placed in one of these barracks, number 15. It was a dark hole where half of the boards had rotted or had been broken off. The barrack was torn down and rebuilt in the fall of that year, but by that time, I no longer was there. Despite my vast experience and endurance, I could not sleep in Barrack 15 because of the bedbugs. The Kotlas bedbugs could cause a motorized division with tanks and armored cars to flee. In the cold August white nights, half of the barrack escaped to the yard. It was already damp and impossible to lie on the ground for a long time. At night, I would wander around the yard with my knapsack and jacket; I did not have a blanket.

On the other side of the camp fence flowed the Northern Dvina River. It was very close—a few meters, but in all my eleven months in Kotlas, I never managed to see it. For several nights, I slept on old boxes, or on a large barrel, then I stole into another barrack (which is rather dangerous, as they could mistake you for a thief and drive you away with blows), but there were more bedbugs there than in Barrack 15. Finally, I found a place without bedbugs—the club, at the other end of the camp. In order to reach it, I had to slip through two gates and enter very quietly so that no one saw me. In the club itself, a spacious, recently constructed cabin, carpenters had begun to set up bunks. Some select brigade was supposed to be lodged there, but while all the bunks had not yet been set up, I escaped there from the bedbugs. A door opened from the club to a side room where the "educator" of the KVCh and his orderly lived. The orderly of the KVCh was my new friend Nil Vasilevich Eletsky. I owed the opportunity to sleep in the club to his influence. I can acknowledge this openly without fearing to harm Nil Vasilevich, who has been beyond the grasp of the NKVD for a long time.

Besides the bedbugs, during the first week, I was seriously annoyed by my "friends" from Vologda prison—Vanya, Petya, and company. One of them was my brigade leader. I did not see them all day as they worked outside of the zone. At night we slept in different places. But unpleasant incidents occurred during the distribution of bread. On the first day, the brigade leader handed me a suspiciously small hunk, but I kept silent. On the second day, I was not given any bread. When my turn came, the brigade leader simply pushed me away: "Where are you butting in? You already got yours."

Now, "witnesses" were found from the same gang, who asserted that I had already received bread. I did not argue and went to the commandant. The commandant had several prisoner assistants, and one of them, fortunately, was a Jew called "Moseich." He was a rare instance of an intellectual who in the camp was also a "strong man," solid, energetic, with cold gray eyes, and the bearing of a boss. He knew how to keep his "public" in hand. Hearing about the matter, Moseich summoned my brigade leader to the office and did not let him utter a word.

"I know you! I don't need your stories. Put on the table what you stole. If you don't, tomorrow we'll take yours."

The next day, at the commandant's order, the bread cutter withheld the brigade leader's ration and it was given to me. Before that, I sat for a full day without bread. Now the gang was out to get me. A new unpleasantness occurred during the next visit to the bathhouse. The dressing room of the bathhouse is the locale for all thefts. The moment they bring the steaming hot, damp bundles of clothing from the disinfecting room, the free-for-all and crush begins. On this occasion, zeks exchange things and steal everything of worth. I was searching for my belongings in the crush when they pounced on me and knocked my glasses off my nose. They immediately disappeared. Without showing how important this was to me, I dressed and went to the barrack.

I was afraid of only one thing: that out of malice, they would break my glasses. In that case, I would be "out of order" for several months, as there was no normal way of obtaining optic lenses in camp. The demand in camp for glasses with low optical numbers is very great, and one could obtain a lot of bread for them. My glasses, however, were nine dioptrics! Who needs such glasses? I was the most near-sighted person in Kotlaslag. I calculated that they would bring them back to me eventually because I was the sole person who needed them. I had to wait patiently.

For several days, I lived in a foggy, unrecognizable, and blurred world. They wrote me down as "needing rest," and I spent the entire day lying on the grass, unable to distinguish faces or follow what was happening more than three meters away from me. Every day I received news about my glasses. Like a bird that flew out of its cage, they fluttered around me throughout the camp. One day they offered them to the head cook. Another day they were outside the camp zone. Dozens of people tried them on. I waited imperturbably. Finally, in the evening, a fellow came to me and said that he had "won my glasses at a card game." I reacted indifferently to this news. "Don't you want your glasses back?" The bargaining began. The fellow started out high: three bread rations and 50 rubles. I offered him 200 grams. We settled on a bread ration. I thus had to pay back the bread ration that Moseich had got back for me; fortunately, they sent the whole band—Petya and Vanya included, on an *etap* the next day, otherwise, God knows what would have happened to me. The Poles left with them. Only I remained in the transit point.

Then they made me a watchman in the inner zone—a suitable task for an invalid. Sometimes I guarded by the fence of the disciplinary barrack, sometimes by the entrance to the women's barrack so that no male zeks sneaked in. The focus of my guarding, however, was in the very center of the camp, at the passage from the hospital zone to the general one.

In the morning, barely splashing my face with water from a mug and wiping it on my sleeve for lack of a towel, I would take my knapsack with my things (the main item was my red coarse cotton pillow) and bring it for safe-keeping to Ivan Ivanovich, the superintendent of Block 5. It was impossible to leave it in a transit barrack because it would be stolen immediately. Then I took my place at my guard post by the gates, which consisted of wooden frames with barbed-wire netting. People streamed toward the kitchen: the transit brigades, the women's brigade, and the two disciplinary brigades from the BUR, each in a line under the direction of the brigade leader. Each one had to be let through in turn to avoid excessive crowding by the windows of the kitchen and bread cutter. A crowd of disciplinary zeks approached, pressing their chests against the barbed wire:

"Open up!"

"I can't; it's forbidden!"

"Open this minute!" roared the fellows on the other side of the barbed wire, and a squabble broke out. In the midst of the argument, the free workers or medics would arrive from the barracks with buckets for water. The commandant would yell constantly: "Let this one through! Let that one through!" I would crack open the door, and immediately another ten men would push through. I was too weak to stop the breakthrough. Long after a brigade had entered, the stragglers were still piling through the gates: "I'm from brigade 15! Look, my brigade is already getting food! Let me in, or I'll whack you in the head!"

Suddenly, looking around, I saw that the distribution of breakfast was ending. I would leave my place and run to the serving window. The gates remained open. Sometimes a nimble kid, a prisoner around twelve years old who worked at the office, would take my place. He was supposed to replace me during breakfast. He was a much better watchman than I was. His tongue was as sharp as a razor blade, which is the first requirement for a guard. I cursed half-heartedly and let all and sundry go from zone to zone. After standing for half an hour, my feet became numb, and I would sit down on the ground. What kind of guard sits on the ground? Ivan Ivanovich, the superintendent of Block 5, allowed me to take a footstool to the gates. I sat on the stool for an hour, and suddenly they stole it from me! Mahmud, the superintendent of Block 9, a Tatar, passed by, saw the stool, and said, "Hey, that's our stool! Who let you take it!" and he simply removed it from under me. I ran to Ivan Ivanovich: "Mahmud took away the stool!" Ivan Ivanovich ran over to Mahmud. The two superintendents quarreled, and I no longer received a stool.

I was glad to leave everyone alone, but they would not yet leave me in peace. Suddenly they ordered me to go past the guardhouse with a brigade . . . to carry boards. This clearly was nonsense. I went—I was a prisoner, after all— and carried about three boards. The people around me had scattered; the brigade leader and guard, cursing, tried to round them up. It was no longer possible to force them to work properly, but I did not even try to pretend. The *etap* and nights in the bedbug barrack, in the yard, and wherever I landed had deprived me of my last strength. I lay on the grass, spread out my hands, looked at the blue sky, and listened to the uneven beating of my heart. The guard approached: "Are you going to work?" "No, I've had enough." "Well, let's go back to the camp." They led me and three others like me to the medical sector. The woman in charge of the medical sector, a free worker, looked as if she was dying to run away from Kotlas to the end of the earth. She cast a glance at me and said hurriedly, "Leave him alone; who sent him to work?" and turning to me, she said, "Calm down, you won't go to work anymore. . . ."

But I could not remain that way: every day my condition deteriorated. I no longer could remain in the barrack. My life was slipping away. I had a recurrence of an old illness that I had completely forgotten about while still at liberty. Sharp attacks of pain tortured me at night. In the morning, I would rise with a severe headache, and barely waiting for eleven o'clock, went to the medical sector. "Put me in the hospital!" I importuned incessantly, but this was not Kruglitsa; here they waved me off. They prescribed medicine and sent me back to the barrack. A war began for the right to be hospitalized. Only through the intervention of several doctors from various barracks was I sent to a bacteriological unit outside of the zone. An analysis of the gastric juice showed a high blood content, but they still did not hospitalize me. During the day, I burned with fever and lounged around the camp, while at night, I lay sleepless on bare boards without a blanket. Now, truly, nothing remained but to die.

Before that, however, I went again to the head of the medical sector and warned her that failure to hospitalize in time is punishable by law, and I would send a declaration to the security officer that I had been left to lie in an ordinary barrack while I had internal hemorrhaging. Mention of the security officer had an immediate effect: I was sent to the hospital.

37

Block 9

"THREE MONTHS," SAID the doctor, having examined me thoroughly. "Three months" meant that I had approximately ninety days of life in me, that is, given my current state of physical depletion when I was hospitalized in Block 9 and given the food norm allotted me, I ought to kick the bucket in approximately three months.

One could rely on the doctor's evaluation. He had vast experience and rarely was mistaken. Sometimes a patient did not want to die at the designated time. Let's say, he was supposed to die in February but he was obstinate. In February, he became better, not worse. He did not know that three months ago, the doctor had written him off to the other world by the end of February. We sometimes knew this and looked at him curiously: here is a man defying medicine. The doctor would circle around the stubborn patient with a worried look, examine him out of turn, and write something in his notebook. We, his neighbors in the block, some similarly sentenced, watched, holding our breath, the duel between the human will and death. When we had already become accustomed to the idea that some miraculous exception had occurred (how we wanted to believe it!), a month later, in March or the beginning of April, the stubborn one would die nevertheless. Suddenly, his condition would decline sharply, and, without obvious reason, he would die in twenty-four hours. Like a chess player, who, realizing that he is in a losing position, makes a last desperate effort with some unexpected combination, tortures his opponent for a while—and, finally, gives up and surrenders.

What occurred in block 9 resembled a session of simultaneous chess games. One hundred and twenty people played the game of their life against the great Champion. Death circled around. Without looking at the faces of the players, Death, the grand master, made his move every day—a little move leading to the endgame. We defended ourselves as best we could, but we did not have great hopes. We were overcome by timidity.

The doctor was our judge. Like an arbitrator, he saw to it that everything went according to the rules. For every move of the Opponent, there was our countermove. Don't surrender ahead of time. He did everything possible to support us. The only thing he was unable to do was to give those dying of depletion a sufficient quantity of food.

"Look," the doctor told me, "here are two identical cases—you and your neighbor. You both have three months left to live. In this situation, however, it is still possible to save both of you if you are fed properly. But where can we get food? In our hospital situation, one could create special conditions for one person by collecting the leftovers, the scraps, occasional extras. I could cut out something from my own ration, not eat enough myself. Somehow, for one, we could scrape by. I can't do it for two. What should I do? I must choose one of you. Your neighbor has no family; no one will mourn him. You have a family abroad; someone is waiting for you. God knows which one of you deserves more to stay alive. I choose you."

And thus it was: they began to bring me leftovers in addition to the camp ration. The doctor contributed his lunch, his assistant gave part of his bread. They decided not to surrender me to death. They assigned work to me for which one was entitled to a supplement. This was called "support." They did everything so that I would win the chess game. The doctor deceived fate: he put extra figures on my chessboard. Three months passed: I was alive but my neighbor died. They came to remove the corpse, and when they carried away the stretcher, I understood that my life and his death were one.

Block 9 at the Kotlas transit point in the winter of 1944-45 was a simple wooden barrack. The doors to the entryway were covered with matting, all the crevices were carefully covered with straw and felt cloth to keep the wind from blowing in. The hospital aides bustled around in the entryway; some of the patients themselves did part of the work because there were not enough personnel allotted to handle everything. The patients served themselves, or healthy people were registered as sick in order to have the right to use them as medical aides. On the side, behind the partition was the storeroom and distribution point where they prepared and handed out portions for the sick.

After passing this anteroom of block 9, one entered the catacombs. The darkness (the light barely passed through the broken windows stuffed with whatever was handy), crowding, and noise created an impression of a dungeon or overcrowded beehive. The barrack resembled an extended cave. An unsuspecting person who entered the barrack would recoil in horror. It was a hospital for zeks but without beds. On two sides stretched double decker wooden bunks in Pullman style. Each bunk had room for two people above and two below. There were seven bunks on each side. Normally, one could hold 4x7x2=56 people. The size of the room was calculated for this number, but there were over 120 people in the barrack. Two people occupied each place designated for one. In the passageway between the bunks, at both ends, they had built two low brick stoves with metal pipes; one was insufficient to heat such a large barrack. Between the stoves stood another eight cots arranged in twos. These were simple boards placed on trestles. Three patients lay on each of the two cots. A narrow passage remained between the cots and the bunks. Here, in the center of the barrack was a real ship of death—the most seriously ill patients, on the verge of death, who could not be placed with the others because they soiled themselves, and others would object to their proximity. Behind the ship of death, in the depths of the barrack, on the opposite side hung an iron wash basin above a bucket—one for everyone—and a door led to another, locked anteroom, where there was an unheated toilet. For those who were unable to go there on their own, a slop pail stood by the door near the wash basin.

By the entrance to this ward, on both sides, two "cages" measuring about two by three meters were partitioned off. Behind the partition on the left in a tiny, dark room lived the medical assistant, the doctor, and the record keeper. Behind the partition on the right was a table and medicine chest. This was a "treatment room" with a window, where patients were examined. In general, the treatment, eating, and all of the patient's life took place on bunk boards.

I received the best place in block 9, the first on the left, next to the door, in the corner. To the right was the wooden wall of the dark cage where the medical personnel lived. We lay near the window, which, on the one hand, was a big advantage because we were able to utilize the daylight, but, on the other hand, was a minus because the cold came in through it. On the boards were straw mattresses and thin pillows stuffed with straw. There were not enough blankets: four patients lay under two blankets. In those conditions, people had to be placed on the narrow bunks in such a way that they could get on with each other, sharing one blanket for two.

A select society lay on the first bunks: first from the wall was Nil Vasilevich Eletsky; I was second; third was Nikolai Alekseich Burak, a forester from the village Parichi in Belorussia. The fourth person would change, but if possible, they left us as three, out of respect for the "intelligentsia." My place was the best as I lay in the middle, and both neighbors warmed me with their bodies.

It was worse for Nil Vasilevich; he lay near the wall, which crawled with bedbugs, and he sustained their main attack at night. We therefore gave him a whole blanket, and whenever we were only three, I lay with Nikolai Alekseich under the other blanket. The person on the edge had it the worst because at night, he inevitably was pushed to the very edge, and he had to cling to his neighbor desperately in order not to fall on the floor.

Sleeping four people in a narrow space calculated for two requires a high degree of social sensitivity, tact, and self-discipline. It educates a person and suppresses harmful individualism. Before my camp experience, the thought of lying in a strange bed or allowing a stranger into my own bed would have made me shudder. In block 9, however, we were not fastidious, perhaps because the bunks on which we had to lie were not *ours*, and we all were forced to occupy the indicated places. We "met" on the bunk boards and, naturally, as civilized people, tried to adapt to each other. Some nervous people turn from side to side every few minutes and have their favorite positions. Someone sleeps curled up, another on his back. Here that is impossible. For four to fit in, each person has to lie on his side and extend his feet. If one of the four turns to the other side, then all four are forced to turn to the same side. This leads to the body disciplining itself; it automatically reacts to the neighbor's movements and to a significant degree relaxes. No doubt, communism has an excellent educative and "corrective" tool in forcing adult individuals to sleep closely together.

There is a Talmudic saying, according to which a person recognizes another person by three things: "*bekoso, bekiso, bekaaso*." This means: "by his [liqueur] glass, his pocket, and his anger." I did not know this saying at the time, but, had I known it, I could not have applied it to camp conditions, where people do not drink and therefore do not reveal themselves when drunk; they do not have money and therefore one cannot meddle with their pockets. Only the third criterion, anger, remained valid in camp. Lying between Nil Vasilevich and Nikolai Alekseich, I came to the conclusion that there are three ways of getting to know with whom you are dealing in camp. The first is joint work. Until you work with a zek, you do not know him. The second (here I, unaware, reiterated the Talmud) is to get involved in a serious argument. Until we quarrel with our neighbor, our friendship has not yet passed a genuine test. The third condition that the Soviet camp taught me is sleeping together. Until you have slept next to a person, you do not know him. The body does not reveal itself so fully other than in sleep, when flesh touches flesh, when the tiniest, concealed movements affect us, when a person's unconscious nature and character are revealed.

On the basis of the last criterion, I can say that N. A. Burak, with whom I slept under one blanket, was an excellent person. Without knowing his social views or professional abilities, I am ready to vouch that both were in full harmony with his milieu and time. We were ideally adjusted to each other; our hands and feet never got entangled, we did not bother each other, and he always knew how to find a position in which it was easy for me to lie next to him. This was not so simple in a crowded barrack where people argued crudely and savagely because of the inability of two people to share one blanket.

He was a Belarusian over fifty, from the area of Mozyr, calm, sensitive, and meek. One could sleep next to such a person. He had not yet become fully accustomed to his new status as a forced laborer. He was given fifteen years of forced labor because, as a senior forester, he had continued to practice his profession during the German occupation. He had two daughters, both Komsomol members, a small house, and sufficient means for a peaceful life of the semi-intelligentsia, semi-peasant type. Life had already begun to wane when the Germans arrived in the village of Parichi. He should have abandoned his house and family and fled into the forest, but Nikolai Alekseevich remained and tried to live as he had before. The Gestapo arrested his daughter but released her. A German forester slapped him on the face when he met him in order to emphasize the racial difference. . . . The real trouble, however, occurred when Parichi was liberated. They arrested him, and the NKVD charged him with responsibility for the felling of timber on his plot. The old man, even before reaching the camp, collapsed on the way. He was stunned, did not understand the meaning of a fifteen-year sentence, and he thought it was a terrible nightmare from which he would wake up the next day in his comfortable home in Parichi. For days on end, he would tell me about the life of the deep Belarusian backwoods. In fact, he did not live so badly before the war.

A no less terrible criminal lay to the right of me. Nil Vasilevich Eletsky had been a colonel in the tsar's armed forces; after the Civil War, he had emigrated to beautiful France. Between 1920 and 1943, he led the life of a White émigré, was a chauffeur in Paris and on the Riviera, married, outlived his wife, and ultimately was a chef in an émigré Russian restaurant in Nice or in Cannes. He was nearing sixty. France became his second homeland, when suddenly. . . .

After twenty-three years, Nil Vasilevich suddenly became homesick. How could he die without seeing Russia? Hitler occupied the Ukraine and was approaching Leningrad. Nil Vasilevich went East and arrived in Rostov. The Germans withdrew, and Colonel Eletsky remained. He appeared at the Soviet headquarters, introduced himself, and offered his services to the Red

Army. Nil Vasilevich had his profound reflections on how to fight against the Germans; moreover, he was writing a study of "military psychology," his life's work. Nil Vasilevich was a short, vigorous old fellow, with a resonant bass voice, graying sideburns, very lively dark eyes, who liked to drink or converse in good company. The young Soviet officers surrounded him curiously, took an interest, and showed respect to the old warrior. First, they put him in the hospital. He had become somewhat weak from his experiences, from the excitement, and from the long road from Nice to the foothills of the Caucasus. They visited him every day in the hospital, bringing gifts and wine and asking questions. They discharged him after ten days and put him in a car that headed straight to Moscow. Nil Vasilevich thought that they were taking him to the main headquarters, to the marshals. On the way, they were extremely polite and attentive. In Moscow they dispatched him—straight to the Lubyanka [prison].

"We did not invite you," the interrogators told him. "You may be a very charming person and inspired by the best intentions, but who knows? What if you are a German agent? You came to Rostov via Berlin. In any case, we are going to isolate you. Sign this protocol." Nil Vasilevich signed and received ten years imprisonment in camp. In Kotlas he spent the first year out of ten. The first and the last. He did not live to the second.

Nil Vasilevich wrote a petition to the Supreme Soviet asking for special conditions in order to write his work about military psychology; he tried to be an orderly in the KVCh, and found himself in block 9. Here he became so thin that his face and body began to resemble Gandhi's. Yet he remained talkative as before, and in his stories, sunny France came to life. He also explained to me how to prepare capon in wine with truffles. Once I asked him (it was in the evening; we had already eaten our supper of barley kasha and 100 grams of bread, and we were lying down, getting ready to sleep): "Nil Vasilevich, you have seen so many countries and beautiful places; you wandered all over Europe and lived in France for twenty years. What is the most beautiful place in the world that you saw? Where would you want to live?"

Nil Vasilevich screwed up his eyes, thought a bit, and answered: "The most beautiful place in the world, my dear, without doubt is the city of Ostashkov by Lake Seliger in Novgorod *oblast*. That is my native place, you should know. I was born there. The more I saw of various things, the more I longed for home. There is no place like home. . . ."

The old man began to describe the beauty of Russian forests, Russian lakes and rivers, and fishing, and I understood that he was never so happy in his life as in the years of his Ostashkov childhood. That was his soul's dream.

From the camp he wrote to Ostashkov and—a miracle!—it turned out that his sole brother was alive and living in the same house on the same street where the Eletsky family had been living since time immemorial. His brother answered him in sparse, cautious words. Nil Vasilevich asked him to send him a package without delay, if possible—tobacco. He did not receive a reply, but Nil Vasilevich kept waiting for an answer, and until his last day he was convinced that in Ostashkov they were preparing a large package for him that would contain everything necessary for an old, tired person.

My day in the block started with the sensation, in the midst of sleep, that it had become roomy. That means that my neighbor has already gotten up to work. It is still completely dark in the barrack. The heap of sleeping people does not stir. Nil Vasilevich has thrown a blanket over his thin shoulders, eyeglasses on his learned nose (a military psychologist!), in slippers that had been hidden since the evening; he is already walking along the bunks, pulling at feet, waking people up, and sticking a thermometer into each one. Having taken the temperature, he goes to the window and writes it down on a plywood tablet. For this work he is entitled to extra soup at lunchtime. Taking the temperature of 120 patients twice a day (the second time is at five o'clock in the afternoon) means four hours of work. The sick people do not like the disturbance and curse loudly. Nil Vasilevich is quick to wrath and gives no quarter. There are two or three thermometers for the entire ward. Annoyed, Nil Vasilevich shakes the thermometer too strongly and breaks it. He surrenders half a kilo of his bread for the broken thermometer, as a result of which he loses more calories than he earns. When Nil Vasilevich finishes his rounds, it is already light and they are preparing breakfast. Ten to twenty people crowd around the wash basin. There are no towels. Not many people wash. A medical aide goes to the seriously ill with a bowl.

Now it is my turn. The medical assistant David Markovich has already come out from behind the partition. He is a stocky person, no longer young, with bulging light eyes and light eyebrows, and swollen cheeks. David Markovich is the real father of block 9. Doctors come and go, but he is invariably present. He puts all his energy, his heart and soul, into his daily work. At his signal, I set up the table and bring flasks with medicine and little glasses. He pours and my job is to distribute the medicine. I grab two or three vials and run to the recipients. The sick people do not believe in the medicinal preparations, and they are right. David Markovich's entire arsenal is five or six potions. These are used to treat all possible illnesses, but often even they are lacking. "You can lie down," David Markovich then says to me, "today the medicines did not arrive." The patients divide all medicines into bitter and sweet ones. No one wants the bitter one; they push away the hand giving it, or the angry ones take it and immediately spill out the contents on the floor. There is a big demand for the "sweet," and whoever does not receive it becomes irritated. "David Markovich," they shout from their places, "again they skipped me." Having received the small glasses, the patients swap them, and if someone does not drink his own medicine, he gives it to his neighbor. There are many aggravations in this work. I have to go five times to one semi-conscious patient: to insert the thermometer, give medicine, remove the thermometer, again give medicine—a different one, and finally, put a pill on his tongue. The patient does not stir; he does not have the strength to sit up and only mumbles quietly. He opens his mouth, and I pour in the contents of the small glass. The same glass goes from mouth to mouth throughout the entire ward.

Mahmoud and the medical assistant bring buckets with breakfast from outside. The ward becomes alert. The kitchen allots food for the entire block in bulk. The distributor has to prepare portions for 120 people. First comes the bread. Two people carry in trays with hunks of bread. The majority receive a "pellagra ration," that is, 400 grams of bread divided into three servings: 200 in the morning, and 100 each for lunch and supper. The "general hospital ration" includes more bread—550 grams—but less kasha and other items. The breakfast for pellagra patients consists of a piece of salted fish and 10-18 grams of fat. The amount of fat depends on whether it is butter, margarine or "mixed fats." Then they ladle out "tea," that is, hot water. Sometimes the water is boiled with something dark, which derives from the dregs of the jam factory. At the end, the server brings a clay bowl of green "horse" peas, flavored with vegetable oil. The patients on a "scurvy" ration—there are fifteen of them in the block—each receive a tablespoonful of peas. Those who perform some function in the block receive a scurvy ration. Nil Vasilevich and I receive a spoonful of peas.

During meal time, the patients sit in a kind of lotus position but haphazardly, not in a row, in order to fit better on the bunks. I sit next to the window, Nil Vasilevich at the foot of the bed with his back to the wall; Burak is in the middle, and the fourth one sits with his feet dangling to the opposite side. As a veteran zek, I have a piece of plywood that I place on my knees instead of a table. The others place their bread and other food on the window sill, but they must be very careful. People come from the yard to the windows of our barrack. The windows are low, and these people see not just that the patients are eating but also what they are eating: through the window pane, they see food that they, the "healthy" ones, do not receive. They are attracted to the sight of butter and fish. They look through the window, persistently, greedily, and wistfully. They are not entitled to anything in the morning except for bread and the miserable camp gruel. They crowd around with thin, savage faces, in tatters, with burning eyes. Watch out! The window pane is smashed into smithereens. A hand stretches in and grabs bread, butter, and fish from the window sill—and the goner runs away, stuffing his mouth on the run. He is not afraid of the punishment cell or the blows of our Mahmud: what he has grabbed is gone. In the block there is a commotion. David Markovich yells at the guilty one: "why did you put it on the window?" The guilty one is thus punished twice: he not only loses his breakfast but also, he and his companions will freeze on the bunks all day until Mahmud somehow gets hold of a piece of glass or plywood to place in the broken window.

All day, the noise, cries, and quarrels in the barrack do not cease. The 120-people mass, crowded into close quarters, incessantly shifts around. Mattresses are constantly rearranged. Above us lie Lithuanians. Skeletal Yunaitis, a teacher from Kovno, constantly shifts and turns. Dust, dirt, and straw from the mattress fly down on us from the cracks between the boards of the upper bunks. The neighbors yell at each other: one has stolen from the other. Farther away there is a search: they call David Markovich and point to a patient who is hoarding butter. Indeed, two uneaten portions are lying there. The patient is an incorrigible smoker who has set aside butter in order to exchange it for tobacco. People who swap bread and other food for tobacco are doomed to die. Every calorie that they deprive themselves of brings the end closer. David Markovich takes away the butter and yells: "You are killing yourself, you scoundrel!" The incorrigible swappers are led to the table in the middle of the barrack and forced to eat their food publicly under the eye of the medical assistant. At each distribution, they are seated on the side and watched closely to make sure they are not hiding any crumbs. If they catch a sick person buying someone else's food, then they take it away, and David Markovich, at his discretion, gives it to one of the weakest patients.

Two punishments are applied to those who violate discipline, to persistent thieves, hooligans, and trouble-makers. Either they give them their food two hours after the others or they undress them completely. In the latter case, they call in Mahmud, the fierce Tatar with a gloomy face. He pulls off the underpants and shirt, takes away the blanket, and the one who has broken discipline remains lying naked among his companions. Understandably, he is not silent. Savage cursing, hysterical crying, pitiful attempts at resistance. Even the threat of discharge from the barrack does not stop the aggrieved party, who runs to the doctor behind the partition, shouting: "Discharge me! This minute, discharge me! I don't want to remain here!" There are cases where they indeed discharge hooligans who cannot be dealt with in any way. This is a severe measure. In two or three days, they again land in the hospital, in this or another block. This time they are quiet and calm: several days in the general barrack among healthy people broke them and subdued their unruliness.

Tension arises as the time for lunch or supper approaches. The sick people are actually always in a state of waiting for food. They spend all their life in this expectation. For lunch they are given cabbage or turnip soup and 250 grams of watery kasha for the "general" ration. The pellagra patients receive 300 grams of kasha with some supplement in the form of a "gravy" or a sprinkling of grits or fish. In the evening we receive a little kasha and milk: 200 grams on the general diet and 300 on the pellagra ration. The milk is replaced by a piece of fat or cheese. In the evening, they distribute 200 grams of "sweet tea" (if there is sugar at the transit camp). This "sweet tea" is not the least sweet and has nothing in common with tea; nevertheless, it is different from the simple boiled water, and the sick people wait for it impatiently.

When lunch has already been served, they bring a small bowl of soup for each of the "workers," that is, those who distribute medicines or take temperature, the tailor who mends underwear for the sick all day, and so forth.

The portions are ridiculously small. "Like for a kitten!" says the patient, taking the kasha at the bottom of the bowl, where they have tossed him a tiny groats cutlet or a potato pancake. It would take fifty such for a mouthful. Having eaten, the people are angry, as if they had been deceived. That is how they feed the ill and depleted. It is impossible to restore one's strength on this food: it only delays the inevitable process of alimentary dystrophy. Somewhere abroad, in sated America, or even in Europe, which considers itself "starved," there are people who rationalize all this on account of the war. These people would be stunned into silence in block 9. Indeed, what can you say to zeks who are convinced that at liberty they would find something to eat? The state that is incapable of feeding its captives should at least not cut them off from any help from abroad. For millions of Soviet prisoners, the war did not begin in 1941 or end in 1945. In this state's domestic relations, war—in accordance with the doctrine of Leninism-Stalinism—never ends.

Aside from food, there are not many exciting events in the barrack. Once a week there is a "hygienic procedure." After breakfast, they bring in a tin bathtub, which they place in the middle of the block. Two medical assistants tirelessly drag buckets with hot water from the boiler room. Two patients assist with a scrubber and a rag. There is no soap. A board is placed across the bathtub. The patients line up. Each one approaches and sits—not in the tub but on the board. Only his feet are in the tub. They hand him one or two tins with water; he pours the water over himself from head to feet, they scrub his back, and that's it. Those who are unable to get up without help are supported to the bathtub. Finally, there are those in the "ship of death" in the middle of the barrack. These are not bothered: the medical assistant goes to them with a bowl of water and washes them there.

After the first twenty to thirty people, the water in the bathtub becomes yellow-gray and smelly. The patients lower their feet into it fearfully and try to leave as fast as possible. Each person is washed for two minutes, but, as there are 120 patients, the operation drags on for half a day. Neither the sick people nor the personnel are interested in cleanliness, which is unattainable technically in the conditions of block 9. One has to carry out one's duty. In the evening, a report will be sent to the medical sector: "a hygienic procedure was carried out for 120 people," and that is all the administration needs.

Before going to the bathtub, the sick person sits on a stool, where the camp barber cuts his hair and shaves him. One person cannot handle all this; volunteers from the patients help (all for a small bowl of soup). This is a difficult and unpleasant operation. Each one lathers himself from a common soap dish. There is one soap dish for the face, another for the pubic area and armpits.

After leaving the bath, the people hurry to the heated stove and dry up, standing around the pipe. In the meantime, laundry is brought in, and the nurse hands out a fresh round of linen. The camp underwear is gray, unwashed, without buttons, worn out, and patched, with the stamp, block 9. The sick person has taken off the buttons from the old pair—they are his property, and he sews them on the new pair for a week. Attendants shake out the mattresses and blankets and bring them to the yard to air out. They are all identical; and after airing, it is impossible to receive one's former bedding: everything is mixed up; they put things back randomly. All this work is accomplished with the aid of the patients. For half a day, the barrack has the appearance of complete devastation and disorder, like the deck of a ship during a storm. By lunch time, everything starts to look normal. The patients lie resting, exhausted as if after a severe jolt.

After lunch come the rounds of cupping glasses, enemas, and the like. In particularly complex cases they summon doctors from neighboring blocks for help. Among the doctors there are many great specialists—from Riga, from Lithuania, or Poles with European diplomas. They have been brought from the territories occupied by the Red Army and are serving ten-year sentences. "Boom!" a sick person fell from the bunk in a fit of epilepsy. We have a few such, and one must watch them so that they do not hit their heads or wound themselves when they fall. When a person writhes in convulsions, his neighbors from the bunks crowd and press on him, holding his arms and legs firmly. After several minutes, it passes. The sick person lies taut as a string, with eyes closed and bitten lips.

It gets dark early in the barrack; a dim lamp is lit by the entrance. The barrack quiets down immediately after supper. A nurse and night medical assistant are on duty all night.

The human heap sleeps, but its sleep is restless, anxious, full of murmurs, sighs, and angry cries. "Nurse!" "Orderly!" "Give me water!" There is so little water that they bring it in a little glass to the most severely ill. It is not cold in the cramped quarters, but the bedbugs force people to jump up from their places and do not let them fall asleep. You must not crush bedbugs or they become fiercer. People constantly rise, sit up, and go to the slop bucket at the dark end of the barrack. Around the nurse there are always two- or three-night owls who suffer from insomnia and cannot wait for morning. Only the guard's appearance at the door, in his army overcoat and cap with the five-pointed star, forces them to disperse to the bunks.

The most basic of all experiences and events in the block is death. People lie around for months. Their illness is simply hunger depletion. There is nothing with which to cure them. All that block 9 can give them is physical repose, tranquil bed rest under the doctor's supervision. And they lie that way until death. Everything in them is unsteady, deceptive, and fragile. Yunaitis, the restless neighbor above, does not bother us for long. He, who not long ago was garrulous and busy, willing to work, gradually drops all work, become more and more mild and quiet and dies as imperceptibly as twilight behind the window. Only this line in the book of an accidental witness of his life and death remains of him. Even that does not remain of others. You cannot remember everyone.

At one time, the fourth person lying with us was a young Ukrainian fellow about twenty-two years old, jowly, sluggish, and docile. He, apparently, is healthy, and they discharge him and send him to work. After several days, he returns to the block, to a different place. Now he is even more docile and quiet. While distributing the medicines, I greet him as an old neighbor:

"Enough of faking it, Havryushka, get up, you have to work."

"Yes, I have to," says Havryushka," "I must."

The next day, the same thing: "How do you feel, Havrylo?"

"All right, okay." On the third day, he does not answer at all. He died at night and is lying on his back, the third from the edge, very calm, as in life, with a look as if this is not his first time. His neighbors have moved to the side, but not much. The stretcher is already brought in and placed in the passageway.

"The second one this week," said David Markovich with chagrin.

In block 9 people are not supposed to die too frequently. This is a barrack for uncomplicated cases. When a patient requires serious treatment, they send him to a more suitable place.

38

Block 5

AFTER THREE MONTHS, my time came to leave Block 9. My illness took an unpleasant turn. The surgeon who was consulted suggested transferring me to Block 3 for an operation. I did not consent. After an operation, one needs fortified nutrition, but the surgeon did not promise me that. He was prepared to cut me but not to feed me. A compromise decision was taken, to move me to Block 5.

Only a few steps separated Block 5 from Block 9, but they were two different worlds. Block 5 was an oasis in the Kotlas transit point, a place where all sick people dreamed of landing, but only the select made it—those with complications, who needed the greatest medical skill. The head of this block was a doctor,[1] a Westerner, whose face resembled that of Anatole France as an old man. He was in charge of a relatively small barrack of about fifty people. Here there were no bunk boards. Along the walls stood hospital beds, gleaming white. A white sheet hung like a curtain by the patients' feet. The block looked like a genuine hospital ward. It was a shrine. The medical personnel were all dressed in white. The patients, subdued by the grandeur and solemnity of the setting, behaved more politely and quietly than in all the other blocks. As much as they could, they tried "to conform." Even cases of theft were rare. Here one could leave bread overnight in the night table between the beds without fearing rats walking on two legs or on four.

The doctor's silver hair and bearing made the appropriate impression on the patients. The doctor was the embodiment of science and moral authority, not only among the patients. Once a week there was a meeting of the doctors from all the blocks of the transit camp in the treatment room of Block 5. Only

1. Benyamin Berger (1880–1948), leader of Lithuanian Zionists, arrested in 1941, died in the Gulag.

the head doctor was a free worker (that is, he had already served out his term), while the others were still serving sentences. At the meeting of this "medical society," they would read research reports and discuss problems of camp medicine. Our doctor was the recognized authority in the medical world of the Kotlas transit point.

The meeting of medical personnel took place in the afternoon, during roll call. The on-duty guard would enter the ward accompanied by the tally clerk, who would tell him the number of patients and personnel. The guard would walk through the ward in front of the beds, pointing with his finger. Having counted, he delicately would open the door to the treatment room, where about twenty doctors were sitting. Without interrupting the learned session, he would count the people in the white coats from the threshold. Science and State Security thus coexisted in harmony.

Everything in Block 5 was extraordinary. Behind the distribution room were two monastic cells—one could not call them anything else. They were added onto the barrack at the personal expense of the doctor who served his term in Block 5 before our doctor. Now the medical assistant lived in the first cell and the doctor in the second. Looking around this second one, as in Maxik's little room where Kotro's watercolors hung on the wall, I felt the presence of an individual personality, that is, of that quality which is altogether expelled, destroyed, devitalized in camp. Here lived a human being. A shelf with books hung above the bed, which was covered with a totally improbable yellow quilted blanket from another world. In addition to medical books, there was a pocket Bible in the original Hebrew and several math books. In his free time, the doctor studied advanced mathematics.

The first thing that they did for me in Block 5 was to restore my status as an invalid. The head doctor, the free worker, did this. He came into the ward one morning, sat at a table in the middle, and about twenty people filed past him. For all of them, he wrote "A-D" [alimentary dystrophy] and a secret mark, which we later found out meant "invalid."

The move to a new block, where they gave me a separate bed, accomplished a miracle. I immediately felt better. Then they appointed me night attendant. At this work, I could get extra food. I could not do this job in Block 9 because it held 120 people. Here there were only forty to fifty. I was able to handle that. I could not be a daytime attendant: that required working in regular clothing, going out to the yard, carrying water and firewood and going to the kitchen for food. Because my legs were too weak, I could work only in the block itself.

The night hospital attendant was not supposed to live in the ward. They put me in the entryway. Behind a partition, bunks for three had been set up. The superintendent Ivan Ivanovich, a small, strict old man and the daytime attendant Kolya, an engineer by training, were lodged with me. I worked from eleven o'clock at night until eight in the morning. I slept during the day, getting up only for breakfast, lunch, and supper. I was fed liberally, as is due a night attendant. Finally, I stopped feeling a bestial hunger. I consumed enormous amounts of soup and kasha, sitting on my bunk behind the partition. At night, the on-duty nurse gave me her portion. The doctor gave me his soya porridge, which he could not stand. In my first year at camp, I, too, could not eat soya porridge. Now I ate everything. My gluttony astonished Sonya, who distributed the food.

Sonya the distributor, on whose generosity I depended, was a small, dark woman who resembled a Jewess, although, in fact, she was a Muslim, a Karachai. The Karachai are a small ethnic group in the Northern Caucasus. In 1942, they suffered a disaster: they presented Hitler with a white horse when the German army occupied their district. When the Soviet authority returned, they put the Karachai in freight cars and punished the entire tribe by deporting them to Central Asia. Sonya, a local primary school teacher, was sent to a camp. When she arrived at Block 5 in the summer of 1944, she was a pitiful runt, a skinny chicken at her last gasp, but the doctor cured her and made her a distributor. Now Sonya held the ladle in her hands like a scepter. She had rounded out, ate moderately, carried herself with dignity, and with unlimited reverence looked at the doctor with her almond-shaped dark eyes.

Eleven o'clock at night. The attendants wake me as they leave. I lock the outer door after them. Everyone is already sleeping, and only the night nurse sits in the middle of the ward at the table, but soon, she, too, disappears into the treatment room. I am alone with the patients. I begin by carrying in firewood from the shed—all kinds of sticks, boards, and logs, which Ivan Ivanovich, the superintendent, had placed under his bunk. I put a tank with water on the stove and place the firewood around the stove to dry. I shave off chips with my knife and start a fire. One has to stoke the oven carefully so that the meager reserve will last until the morning.

I bring a large bucket with a wooden seat from the cold latrine. By the cots of the seriously ill patients, I place clay bowls. These are the same kind of bowls as those from which we eat. All night, I pour them out into the bucket and put them back, and I do not permit those who are able to go to the bucket to use the bowls. The slop bucket is full in an hour or two, and I carry it out to the cold, dark latrine. An old, torn jacket and cap hang on a nail by the entrance to the toilet; tattered shoes stand nearby. You have to get dressed for the toilet as if going outside: it is freezing and the floor is dirty. In the ward, people go barefoot, wearing just their underwear.

Fifty people lie on the cots along the walls and in the middle. The middle of the ward is occupied by cots, where, just as in Block 9, three people lie on two cots pushed together. The ward also contains an iron stove and a table with two stools.

It is quiet in the ward. The strong electric lamp burns with a bright light above the table in the center, but in the corners it is shadowy. Rats begin to dart around under the beds. . . . One of them jumped onto the night table between the cots, and I go to check whether bread or a towel in which bread had been wrapped remained there. It is already past midnight. A patient stirred and called me—a Ukrainian who does not have long to live. I drag over the bucket with the seat and put it at the foot of his bed. The sick man is lying on his back; he threw off his gray soldier's blanket, bent his bony knees. He is helpless like a child. All his ribs protrude. I bend over to him: "Grab my neck!" With my right hand, I encircle his shoulders, with the left under his knees, I lift him like a child from the bed. I, an invalid staggering from weakness, am a hero in comparison to him. I feel in my hands this impotent sack of bones, and I am afraid that these bones may break in my arms, the desiccated thigh may break off, or that he may die on the slop pail upon which I seat him. He sits on it for a long time, his entire body sagging, until I come and wrap him in a blanket. He mutters something, quietly whines to himself. . . . "It's hard, it's hard. . . .," disconnected words of complaint and reproach. Before I manage to put him back in place, a second one like him calls me, and then a third.

A dying person is lying by the door to the latrine. They put him in the worst place because it no longer matters to him. For two days already, everyone has been expecting him to die. He no longer speaks or groans; he only stares with blank eyes. A bad smell emanates from him. The neighbors call me. I cautiously take off his blanket and pull out the soiled sheet from under him. There are no more bed sheets for him. I put an oil cloth under him, directly on the mattress. He lies naked. The neighbors curse him in low voices. . . . "It is not my fault, brothers," the dying man whispers, "bear with me a little longer. . . ." Toward morning his death agony starts.

At that time, the lamp goes out, and the ward is enveloped in darkness. This happens frequently, and from the evening, a kerosene lamp is prepared for such an event. Today there is no kerosene in it. This, too, happens often. The sick people are restless—a light is needed. I go to the shed for thin resinous wood splinters the width of a finger and about seventy centimeters long. Such a splinter torch is a *luchina*: the very same about which Pushkin [in *Eugene Onegin*] wrote: "In the hut, singing, a maiden / spins—and the friend of winter nights / a *luchina* crackles in front of her. . . ."

Here it is—the torch, friend of winter nights—in Block 5 of the Kotlas transit camp in 1945. Communism is not only "electrification plus the Soviets," as Lenin said. Twenty-eight years after the October Revolution, it is also a torch plus camp. An old friend is better than two new ones. A splinter torch is more reliable than electricity and kerosene. Eighteen-year-old Vitya expertly lights it with an ember from the stove and places it aslant on a wooden pole in the middle of the ward.

The torch glows with a yellow, smoky light; we don't let it burn down and every ten minutes replace it with a fresh one and throw the residue of the old one into a small tub with sand on the floor. Several dozens of these splinter torches are ready for use. In an hour, however, the electricity is restored, and we return from the eighteenth century to the twentieth.

Someone knocks energetically at the door. It is the nightly round. Before opening the door, I warn the night nurse, who was lying down in the treatment room. She quickly enters the ward and sits down at the table. The armed guard goes around the ward, looks in at the doctor, checks whether everyone is sleeping according to instructions and what is lying on the patients' night tables. He then goes to the thermometer in the middle of the ward. If it is below 16 degrees centigrade, the superintendent has to answer to the administration, and I to the superintendent. I show the guard that there is no more firewood—nothing with which to stoke.

The guard leaves and in half an hour knocks at the door: "Go outside! Two boards are lying behind Barrack 16. Take them and stoke!" It is easy for him to say "Go outside!" I have not left the block for about four months. For me this is a big expedition! I put on someone else's padded pants, jacket, and felt boots and creep over the threshold.

A dark winter night outside. I wade through knee-high snow. Not a soul is out. Only smoke billows from the pipes of the low hospital barracks, and an electric lamp flashes on a column on the other side of the barbed wire camp fence. Far, far away the locomotives whistle on their tracks. That is the Kotlas station through which the trains pass. And we are lying here, hundreds, thousands of people—for what? I feel like a mole that has emerged from his underground burrow. I look with amazement at the alien and strange world of a winter night. The stars are shining on high. Where am I? Hurry, take the boards, hurry back to the ward, to the warm lair, where I have my place and the title of night hospital attendant. Here in this severe frost, in the nocturnal silence, under the dome of the northern sky, I am only an apparition, a shadow, a phantom in a stranger's jacket.

Having returned and revived the fire in the stove, I sit by its iron side and talk with the nurse and with Vitya, a boy with a round face and closely cropped hair—a very polite and diligent helper in the block. He has a three-year term for a not negligible crime: with a group of friends, he stole a sheep. They ate the sheep immediately—they hadn't seen meat for ages. The temptation was great and hunger spurred them on. He only tagged along with older fellows; they received longer sentences whereas Vitya received only three years because of his youth.

At two o'clock at night, there is another knock on the door. This time two or three messengers enter from the guardhouse, carrying boxes covered with cloth—packages for the zeks. They distribute packages to the patients in the block at night rather than in the day, in order to avoid prying eyes. No sick person will get angry if they awaken him at night with the words: "Take your package." Only two or three of the fifty in the block receive packages. The awakened ones sit up in excitement. A package is a radical change in their lives. Starting tomorrow, for several days in a row, they will not be hungry. The messengers rip open the cloth, pull off the top of the box, and, in the presence of the addressee, take out the contents item by item. One package is of the usual kind from a *kolkhoz* of Central Russia: rye rusks, dried potatoes, onion. The onion is frozen but even so, it won't go to waste in camp. At the very bottom is a piece of lard, 200 grams, wrapped in a rag. If the package is from Central Asia, it will contain a small bag of dried fruit (raisins, dried apricots) and *kurdyuk*, that is, a fat lamb's tail, a particular favorite of the national minorities. Popov receives the best package. His wife sends it to him from Sochi, the Riviera of the Caucasus. It contains not only butter, honey, and sugar, but also that magical fruit that causes Vitya's eyes to shine with delight: several mandarins. Mandarins in camp! Mandarins in the north, where for years people do not see an ordinary apple and live to old age without knowing the taste of a pear. Vitya receives the mandarin peel from Popov. He puts the peel in boiling water and affirms that the "tea" acquires a special flavor from this. The nocturnal conspiracy does not help Popov. By the morning, the entire block will know precisely what was in the package. He has to treat his closest neighbors and give the entire package for safekeeping in the distribution room so as not to tempt those near him.

Popov is the aristocrat of Block 5. He is a young man of around thirty years, with brown hair and a delicate, pleasant face. He is a chauffeur by profession.

Before his arrest, he was the driver of one of the people's commissars (he did not want to say which one), and he lived in Moscow. Despite his proletarian profession, Popov is well educated, has excellent manners, and reads books in French. He has several issues of the Moscow journal *Literature Internationale* and a Soviet edition of the anti-German stories of Maupassant. Thanks to Popov, during the winter, I have the opportunity to read "Boule de Suif" ten times in a row. He is the most educated chauffeur that I have met in my life; it turns out that he is the son of an actress and from an intelligentsia family. Popov is aloof, restrained to the point of haughtiness, and supercilious toward the other patients. Even his bed is separate—it is the first from the door, at some distance from the other cots. His isolation is explained by his illness: he has tuberculosis. One year in camp was enough to contract the disease, and he has ten years in front of him. His song is sung. Were it not for the packages with mandarins, he would have died already, but in camp there is no hope for recovery. In the morning his temperature is normal but after lunch it is 39 centigrade, and thus it is from day to day.

When everyone disperses, Popov calls me and gives me several sheets of paper in which food was wrapped: the pages are from the French *L'illustration* from before World War I and from an old English journal. All this is a treasure. Later on, we shall read every letter and every line, including advertisements, as an echo of the world from which we are cut off. An extraordinary excitement seizes me at the thought that this is not Soviet, it was not submitted to the censor and was written by people not under the rule of the NKVD, who did not even know of the NKVD's existence.

At six o'clock, the gong sounds outside. The night is over. Reveille! But it does not concern us sick people. I wake up Kolya, the daytime hospital assistant, and bring water in a bucket for washing. The first patients begin to stir. My night watch is coming to an end. Sonya and the two helpers appear around seven o'clock in the morning. I go to sleep in the cold entryway, at the "north pole." I sleep in my clothing and freeze even in sleep. How I envy the sick ones who lie in the warm ward and do not worry about anything! It is impossible to have everything: to be sated and to lie in the warmth.

I worked as a night time attendant for only one month. During that time, I ate a lot, and my weight went up from 45 kilos to 51. That was my maximum weight in camp. At the end, I could not endure it and I was moved to the ward with the other patients. My successor was Vitya.

It was 1945, and the war was coming to an end. Soviet troops entered East Prussia, and we agitatedly followed their advance. Every issue of *Izvestiya* or *Pravda* that fell into the hands of the medical personnel for "half an hour" was avidly read and discussed in a small circle of people. At the end of the winter, the first trainload passed through Kotlas—women from East Prussia. The massive deportation of Germans began in accordance with the tried NKVD system. One morning, a group of German women went through the bathhouse of the Kotlas transit point; they were wearing light dresses and shoes, unprepared for the severe winter of the extreme Russian north. "Kalt, kalt ist in Russland!" they repeated and they huddled together. The train had been traveling for four days from Moscow. During this time, eighty people from the group froze and died. It was not permitted to bury them on the way. A car with the corpses was at the end of the train. "Half will die on the way—half at arrival," appraised the Kotlas people, who had already seen everything. No one felt sorry for them. Countless of one's own were dying all around.

I lay for month after month on a cot across from the stove. Again, they declared an amnesty for Polish prisoners. It was an amnesty in coordination with the new Polish democratic government. There were around ten Poles at our transit point. Only one of them was released; the others remained imprisoned. They protested and wrote complaints. This time I neither complained nor protested. I was convinced of the uselessness and, moreover, of the harm of too frequent protests. During the years in camp, I had protested sharply and ardently against my detention several times, and there was no sense in repeating what I had said. Now, I did not want to attract any more attention to myself. I felt that this time, the less the representatives of the regime dealt with me and the less they knew or remembered about me, the better it would be.

Month after month, lying on the cot, forgotten by the entire world, even by my enemies, I watched as people were dying.

Here there was no war, but nevertheless great carnage surrounded me. Echoes of the terrible slaughter reached me, as the noise of a storm reaches the hold of a ship. Block 5, covered with snow, reminded me of a ship sailing on the sea to an unknown destination. The waves boomed on the sides of the ship, and the heap of human bodies in the hold tossed and turned. Scrutinizing this, I realized what a monstrous murder machine had been brought into motion on the expanses of Russia—a machine that grinds up human "garbage" and daily tosses out the refuse to the Kotlas hospital barracks.

Next to me, Vasya was bewildered. He was dying; he was a twenty-year-old youth, and his sentence also was twenty years. For what crimes did they give Vasya twenty years of forced labor? Whom did he kill or betray? In the corner of our ward lay a seventy-two-year-old *kolkhoznik* who in a drunken fit had murdered his wife. He received two years, but Vasya got twenty because he had swept the floor for the Germans in the police station. Perhaps this was "state wisdom," but I could not but hate and scorn a state that defended itself in that way. Two years or twenty—it made no difference, and they both—old and young—died that winter in Block 5. Vasya died from fulminating laryngeal tuberculosis. Until his last moments, he did not understand the danger of his condition, and he did not even know the nature of his illness. The doctor ordered him to eat from a separate dish. This offended Vasya: "Look at when they realized it," he said, "when I am already getting better!" When he was dying, he was still sure that he was recovering, and he did not understand why the other patients in the block turned away from him, did not allow him to sit on their beds, and did not lend him their belongings. He thought that they scorned him and did not want to have anything to do with him. Vasya, with his laryngeal tuberculosis and twenty years of forced labor, was helpless and uneducated, a boy who understood nothing in life, who fell along with millions of others under the wheels of life. "The only human being in the block is you, Margolin!" he said to me, plaintively, insulted by the general boycott. I did not boycott him. I took no precautionary measures; I drank from his mug and sat on his bed. I was not afraid of infection, and death did not frighten me. On the contrary. Death, at worst, was salvation from slavery, an exit from the dead end which I had entered.

Vasya was overcome by bewilderment in his last days when the catastrophe arrived: "It's bad!" he said to me, finally, in a whisper, and I saw unbounded astonishment in his eyes. When Vasya began to wheeze and choke, it was already known in the ward who would be given his bed. He still lay in his death agony when the usual robbing of the dying began. They snatched all his pitiful belongings from the night table. The hospital attendant took his bread, which had not been touched the last two days. Nothing remained, and when they had already carried him out, I ate his last kasha at the bottom of the clay dish, which had grown cold from yesterday, and took for myself the nicked metal mug that we had shared.

Alimentary dystrophy most often led to edema. First, the feet swelled monstrously. Then the stomach ballooned like that of a pregnant woman. The entire body was filled with water, the eyes puffed up, and when the water reached the heart, the person would die. In the ward, there were a half-dozen patients from whom they periodically would pump water from the stomach. The sick person would sit on a stool in the middle of the ward; they would prick his belly and insert a tube from which water flowed out. It would flow for a long time into the basin placed there, and then the nurse would calculate how many liters of water had come out. Fifteen liters were pumped out of some patients. That offered some relief, and the sick person could lie in bed for two weeks in expectation of the next pumping operation. Death in this condition was inevitable.

The death that produced the strongest impression on people in the block was that of a Lithuanian who had been lying in the ward with us for four months. In general, there were many Lithuanians at the transit camp. Two waves of mass expulsions from Lithuania met here—in 1941 before the war and in 1944 after the expulsion of the Germans and the recapture of the country. Lithuanians were dying in all the blocks of the Kotlas transit camp. The one in our ward was a railroad worker from near Kaunas, middle-aged, very solid, apparently a peaceful, ordinary citizen. He was still rather strong, and during the hygienic procedure he volunteered to wash the patients. He was very taciturn, with the phlegmatic dignity of a person who knows his worth. At night, he occasionally would wake up, sit on his bed and, as if ossified, look straight in front of him for an hour. Then he would go to the stove to smoke (in the daytime, our doctor strictly forbade smoking in the ward) and silently returned to his place. His death came as a surprise to us. He swelled quickly and died rapidly in a few days. He died painfully and without any dignity: he shouted with a high childish voice, which no one had expected to hear from him, and he filled the whole ward with his agony. Others become silent before death, but with him, the opposite happened: he had been silent all winter, withdrawn, but in his last hours, he raised a commotion. For an entire day he raved loudly, cried out, and sang. He sang before his death, dying with songs. To this day, his cry rings in my ears:

"Lietuva mano! Lietuva mano!"

The Lithuanians in the block told me that it means "My Lithuania, my Lithuania!" We all were so impressed by the dying man's longing for his native country—not one of us had remembered that he, too, had a native country which, perhaps, he was not destined to see.

On the first cot by the entrance to the ward, opposite Popov's bed lay Father Serafim. He was over seventy and looked like a biblical patriarch, with a broad white beard and shoulder-length gray hair, which from one side was braided so as not to bother him. Father Serafim was an archimandrite and prior of one of the Moscow churches. There must be people in Moscow who know more about him. Apparently, he was unable to get along with the regime and was sent to camp already after the change of course—a rapprochement with the church. At his interrogation, they asked him why he had prayed for the tsar before the revolution but he does not pray for the members of the Politburo. Father Serafim answered that he was willing to pray for the members of the Politburo when they would attend church.

Twice a day, morning and evening, the archimandrite got up and prayed, turning toward the wall, bowing at the waist; watching him, our half-wit Alesha also began to pray, but he soon got tired of praying. Father Serafim prayed for everyone, and when Easter arrived, he received a package with a sweet Easter cake. He shared it with everyone in the ward, and everyone received a tiny piece of the "holy cake." The patients came up to thank him, and I, too, thanked Father Serafim. On this occasion, I conversed with him about the Holy Land. Father Serafim had visited Palestine in 1902, and before that, he had been to Athens, Greece. He remembered Palestine through a pious haze—holy places, monasteries, churches, donkeys on mountain paths, fish that they had served him on the shore of the Sea of Galilee. I remembered it differently: asphalt and gasoline, cement and the dark green of plantations, tractors, and power stations.

Father Serafim had a golden cross, which the doctor had given him. One of the prisoners had given it to the doctor before he died. That prisoner, too, had not brought the cross to the camp but had taken it off the neck of his dying neighbor. The gold cross was thus the property of the entire block. The worthiest person wore it, but the doctor guarded it. He himself was a Jew and an uninvolved party, but he had been chosen by fate to transmit it from hand to hand. This cross was a golden link of an invisible chain. Father Serafim was not the last wearer; he received it for a while, a very short while. I do not know who is wearing it now. The archimandrite died in the fall of 1945.

Fifteen people died in Block 5 during the winter. This means that one can assume an annual mortality of thirty people for Block 5 and three hundred for the entire Kotlas transit camp, at a very moderate estimate. Let us lower this figure by half to 150 people. Let us say that people die in the Soviet Union only in five thousand camps. This yields three-quarters of a million victims for one year, given the most moderate, cautious, and low estimate. The true figure may be much higher. It is not a matter of statistics. These figures give a notion of what we have in mind when we call Soviet camps one of the greatest death factories in world history. One or two million—that is not what matters. All those who died and are dying there to this day are captives, involuntary, defenseless victims of the regime, people who did not deserve their fate and, in the vast majority, did not commit any crime in the European sense of the word.

I can imagine that many readers of this book will try to justify the Soviet Union because of wartime circumstances. Many millions of Soviet citizens died at the front and in the rear. The blockade of Leningrad alone caused millions of deaths from starvation. At the end of the war, entire provinces in China were struck by starvation. That is true. It is difficult to understand, however, how one can equate the death of people during an elemental disaster such as war or a crop failure with the death of millions of people deprived of freedom, driven into camps and condemned by the state consciously and cold-bloodedly to dying off. In the Soviet camps, the killing of politically undesirable elements takes place every year, and the end is not in sight. Each person who died that winter of 1944–1945 in Block 5 of the Kotlas transit camp could have lived if the Soviet Union had removed its strangulating grip and if it had permitted help from abroad and the supervision and aid of international humanitarian organizations.

I can also imagine that people will allude to historical necessity in justifying the mass murder: under the given conditions, it was the only way to build communism. This is an argument of degenerates. One must ask those people: how do you determine the limit of sacrifices for this goal? What I saw in five years of my stay in the Soviet subterranean kingdom was an apparatus of murder and oppression acting blindly. For the goals of communism, undoubtedly, what they did to me and hundreds of thousands of foreigners was unnecessary. I dare to think that it rather harmed their cause.

By sheer chance, I avoided death in the winter of 1944 in a Soviet camp. In the spring of 1945, I had been so debilitated by months of lying in bed that I had forgotten how to walk. In order to accustom the residents of Block 5 to using their feet, they introduced an obligatory fifteen-minute walk in the fresh air. The snow was still lying on the ground in March, when processions of survivors from the other world began to appear among the barracks, in groups of four or five, accompanied by a nurse. We did not want to go out voluntarily; we had to be coerced and forced out of bed. They brought us special clothes from the clothing warehouse for walking outside; it was cold as ice. I would try to go out with the second group as by then the things were warm: they went directly from body to body. Unaccustomed to the air, we became dizzy outside and our feet became stiff. Fifteen minutes lasted interminably, but they did not allow us back into the block before they were over. I fearfully thought about the inevitable day when they would discharge me, and I would walk out of the doors of Block 5 without the right of return.

39

Release

ON THE MORNING of June 1, 1945, a young zek from the Second Section brought a letter to the head of Block 5 stating the following: "Report immediately about the state of health of prisoner Yuly Margolin."

My five-year term of imprisonment ended on June 20. On that day, I was supposed to go free. Everyone around was sure that they would detain me in camp just like the other Polish citizens who had served their term. If they had wanted to free me, they could have done so in the winter, in accordance with the amnesty. Together with me in Kotlas were about ten Polish citizens who had already served their terms; all of them had been informed officially that they were "detained until special instructions." One of them had already been waiting for these "special instructions" for three years. What grounds did I have to go free before them?

The difference between us was that they had finished their terms before May 9, 1945, before the end of the war, and the orders in that case had been to detain until the end of the war. My term, however, ended six weeks after the end of the war.

I was supposed to be excited and worried, but I was indifferent. I lived in a dreamy state, on my guard, but externally and internally completely calm. Dry bones and the souls of the dead thus could await the Archangel's trumpet calling to resurrection. Is a miracle possible? I could not imagine freedom, and I did not want to toy with the idea of freedom after the repeated cruel disappointments of the last years. I explained to myself that the Second Sector's inquiry was motivated by my long, drawn-out stay in the hospital. A person lies in bed for ten months without getting up; the case needs to be checked. Perhaps they wanted to send me on an *etap*. The practice was to send zeks who were not released on time to another place. Before including me in the lists for an *etap*, they would want to know whether I could withstand the trip.

I thus interpreted this issue. The head of the block replied honestly that I was recovering after a serious illness and my condition was satisfactory. After that, several days passed in waiting—will they demand that I join an *etap*? When that did not happen, a week before June 20, I was discharged from the hospital. Indeed, I had already recovered sufficiently, and it was not possible to keep me any longer in the block. In the case of release, I needed a few transitional days in order not to be released directly from a hospital bed.

The great events of that summer—the storming of Berlin and the end of the world war—overshadowed the camp routine. Everyone in camp was excited, and it seemed to many that the time had come for some unprecedented mass amnesty. This "genuine" amnesty would astonish the world with the magnanimity of the Soviet regime. We all were expecting an amnesty on November 7, the anniversary of the revolution. I could not imagine that they would release me the next day. It was easier for me to expect it half a year later.

June 20 arrived, and no one came to call me to the Second Sector for release. Until eleven o'clock, I lay on the bunk in a dusty, dirty barrack. Finally, I could not help going to the Second Sector without a summons. It was in a tiny hut of two little rooms.

"What do you want?"

"I came to find out why they are not summoning me for release."

"What's your name?"

The prisoner clerk started to fumble through the papers, looked at me, and said:

"Come tomorrow."

I did not ask anything more and left confused. Why tomorrow? My sentence ends today! Why didn't he tell me: "Stay put until they call you!" or with a wry smile: "They will tell you, don't worry, when necessary!" Instead, he said, "Tomorrow." What did that mean?

Tomorrow, tomorrow. . . .

Suddenly, my heart fluttered. I must get ready for tomorrow. . . . Just in case.

I had two possessions that were not standard camp items: leather shoes and a heavy peasant coat that reached to my knees. The medical assistants in Block 5 had obtained these two things for me before my discharge from the hospital. After they had saved my life, they considered themselves responsible also for my wardrobe beyond the walls of Block 5. I did not possess anything else. My camp work pants were full of holes and patches. One could not leave in such pants. In the Karelian camps there were instructions to give released prisoners clothing—not new but clean and decent looking. Here, evidently, there were no such instructions. David Markovich from Block 9 came to my rescue: he gave me his own padded pants. They were slightly brownish, but they were whole and suitable for the journey.

In another place, I received good underwear. This was all given on the condition that if I was not released, I would return it. Finally, they collected 50 rubles for the trip. In the evening, I pulled out my old knapsack, mended the holes, and affixed new straps. This completed my preparations for the road.

All day people came to me with requests to write down the addresses of their relatives and loved ones in the Soviet Union and abroad. All these people were sure that I would be released the next day. In the course of five years, I had asked other people many times what people now were asking me; my turn came to give promises to others. Those people did not fulfill their promises. I asked myself that evening whether I would be better or would that incomprehensible force of forgetting, alienation, and indifference prevail over me, too, as soon as I left the camp.

The last person from whom I parted was Nil Vasilevich Eletsky. He was still in Block 9. Block 9 had been transformed into a tuberculosis barrack, but that did not prevent Nil Vasilevich from remaining there: he already had tuberculosis, which he had caught in Block 9. During the day, they brought the cots outside, and the patients warmed up in the sun. Nil Vasilevich, wrapped in a blanket and looking like Gandhi, also went out for some sunshine. Something was bothering the old man; something had not been said. Suddenly, he embraced me and whispered: "My dear, I don't know whether I will see you. . . . There's one thing I must tell you. I am guilty toward you. I cannot part without saying it. Do you remember when we were lying next to each other at the beginning of the winter? I committed a sin against you then. . . . I took your bread from under your pillow. I took a little, a piece, a crumb, but I took it. I felt bad, but I took it. I couldn't control myself. Forgive me, and here . . . here. . . ."

Nil Vasilevich handed me a small fish cutlet in a mug; he had saved it from lunch in order to give it to me upon parting, and, thus, at least partially to atone for his sin. . . . I was confused, embarrassed, and moved to tears. Why suddenly this ridiculous sentimentality, and in this place? I embraced Nil Vasilevich in farewell and promised to send him tobacco from freedom. I did not manage to fulfill this promise: Nil Vasilevich died two months later.

On the morning of June 21, I went to the Second Sector. They told me to wait for the director. I still could hardly believe it. I waited a long time, about two hours, went out to the porch, and sat on a step. I could not go farther, as if I were bound.

The director could simply give me a paper to sign: "Detained until a special order" and send me back to the barrack. What then?

Of course, of course, that's what will happen. I'll return to the barrack and lie in my place. I have a good bunk and a quiet neighbor. The neighbor will ask, "Well, what happened there?" I'll answer, "They are leaving me for the time being," and I shall pretend that I did not expect anything else. I'll turn to the wall and pretend to be asleep. My neighbor will yawn, sigh, and also lie down. The commandant will enter with a shout, "Oh, you damn invalids! Get up, take the brooms, at least sweep the floor. . . ."

The director went into the second room, and I followed him.

"Citizen director, my term ended yesterday." He glanced at the paper on the table.

"No. Your term wasn't until yesterday but today. Where do you want to go?"

I was silent. My breath was taken away.

He raised his eyes to me, and I tried to look indifferent. What's special about this? A prisoner served his term, and, understandably, now nothing remains but to release him. A simple matter.

"I am a Polish citizen," I said slowly, almost with regret. "Where should I go? To Poland."

The director laughed. "They don't let people go to Poland. You have to choose a place in the Soviet Union."

"If I can't go to Poland, then as close as possible to the Polish border."

Here he looked serious and explained to me that the territory of the former German occupation is closed to me. I also could not go south, but I could go to Asia, for example, Kazakhstan.

At that moment in front of my eyes, I pictured a white triangle of a letter. In the winter, the doctor had received a letter. Where had it come from" Aha! From Altai region (Russ.—*krai*).[1]

"Can I go to Altai region?"

"You may."

---

1. A *krai* (territory or region) was a form of geographical-administrative division in the Russian Empire and later in the RSFSR in the Soviet Union. The term "region" is not used here in the official administrative sense of the word.

Altai region has a good reputation in the Soviet Union. There people eat well, bread is cheap, there is a lot of milk and meat. And there—exactly there—the doctor has a friend, a compatriot somewhere!

"Excuse me, citizen director, I need to leave for a moment."

I went out, leaving him in astonishment. It was a few steps from the Second Sector to Block 5. Through the open doors of the ward, I saw the rounded back and the white coat of the doctor. It was eleven o'clock in the morning, the time for sick rounds. I dashed into the little room behind the distribution room. "Faster, faster!"

"Call the doctor," I said to the distributor Sonya. "This minute."

The doctor stopped his rounds and hurried to me.

"What's the matter?" "They are releasing me! Doctor, who do you know in Altai region?"

He gave me the name of the city Slavgorod, the street and address. I did not need to write it down; the address was immediately imprinted in my memory. I parted with him and ran back to the Second Sector. No more than three minutes had elapsed, and the director had not had the time to change his pose by the table where I had left him.

"I am going to Slavgorod, Altai region," I said firmly.

Immediately a barrier arose between me and camp inmates. They did not let me leave the office, and everything that followed occurred at a speeded-up tempo. They literally chased me out of the camp. They did not allow me to take leave of the others or to converse with them. A person from the Second Sector went with me to the barrack; in his presence, I took my knapsack. Then they escorted me to the food warehouse. They gave me a ration for the twelve-day journey to Siberia: 400 grams of bread and 100 grams of salted fish per day. The warehouse superintendent tossed me two loaves of bread and a large fish. With that I was supposed to travel to my destination.

They took me to the accountant's office, where they issued a document certifying my release. They gave me money for a ticket to Slavgorod—131 rubles. In addition, I received 19 rubles, a ruble per day for nineteen days. I could not buy much for that money (one egg in Kotlas cost 15 rubles), but if I was detained on the way, and I ate all my bread, then, starting from the thirteenth day, I could pay from this money for "travel" bread at the state price.

"Escort him to the guardhouse!" said the director of the Second Sector to the work supervisor. This was to prevent me from stopping on the way at any barrack. Here, I protested. They gave me bread from tomorrow, but what would I eat today?

"You're right!" said the director. "Take him to the kitchen. Let him eat out of turn and then immediately to the guardhouse."

The work supervisor sat down next to me while I ate, for the last time, the camp gruel, and he ate a tiny portion of kasha. We left together. I did not look to the right or the left. In front of the door of the guardhouse, the work assigner turned sharply to the side. I pushed open the door and went to the on-duty guard. He looked at my certificate of release, wrote down something, and showed me the exit.

"Get going," he said, without any expression, evidently no longer interested in me.

I adjusted the strap of my knapsack where the twelve-day bread supply was lying, and I went on my way.

This was not yet freedom. It was "the other side of the guardhouse." How many times in five years had I gone out of the guardhouse with a brigade or on an assignment, and there was nothing extraordinary about that. But now, I left without any task. I left altogether; it was unbelievable. . . . It was several dozen meters to the railroad tracks.

I walked slowly along the railroad ties. It was 5 kilometers to town. I was supposed to appear with my certificate of release at the police station and receive a permit for Slavgorod. With that permit, I could go to the train station and buy a ticket to Slavgorod. It was 2,700 kilometers from Kotlas to Altai region.

It was a bright, sunny June day. Five years before, on a day just like this one, the prison gates had closed behind me. Now, gray and shattered, I walked along the tracks of the Kotlas railroad. The sack pressed on my shoulders. I was free, but the burden weighed not only on my back. Heaviness filled my heart, and I was still far from feeling relief.

Everything in me was tense, gloomy, and stark. With every kilometer that I went away from the camp, I felt as if its shadow stretched out and trailed after me. This entire area—fences, warehouses, little houses, fields on both sides of the way—was still the vicinity of the camp. People came from the opposite direction toward me along the railroad ties. A lean worker in a cap was leading a girl by the hand. Some peasant women in kerchiefs passed by, conversing quietly; they glanced back at me in curiosity. It was clear where I was coming from, but their look was not hostile. I later was convinced that although they do not mention the camps and never ask about them, Russian people feel something similar to compassion for former prisoners. An atmosphere of very cautious and silent sympathy forms around a person who has come from the camps. This is understandable: almost every free person has some relative or friend in camp.

Many months passed before my normal sense of self returned, and I truly felt out of danger. I returned to my homeland by a difficult, long, and circuitous route. On that summer day on the outskirts of Kotlas, it was still very distant from me. On that day, I was still solidly in the grip of Soviet discipline—and fear.

I walked about 2 kilometers away from the camp and sat by the side of the track. Here I encountered a minor problem: my right leg became numb. I had impulsively covered 2 kilometers but, after all, I was only an invalid who had been discharged from the hospital a week before after ten months of hospitalization. Something had happened to my leg. When I got up to continue on my way, I was able only to limp, dragging one foot.

At that moment, I did not think any more about freedom or my past or my future. I thought only about how I could reach the police station in Kotlas without being late.

Fortunately, an empty freight train approached quietly and stopped. I hobbled up to the locomotive and asked the engine driver: "Comrade engineer, may I ride to the station?" It was the first time in five years that I had used the word that was forbidden to prisoners: "comrade." The driver looked at my foot.

"Get in."

I scrambled onto the tender and wiped the sweat from my brow. The train moved on.

40

Conclusion

EVERY DAY AT dawn—in the summer at five o'clock, in the winter at six in the morning—the signal to get up to work sounds forth in thousands of Soviet camps spread over the vast expanse from the Arctic Ocean to the Chinese border, from the Baltic Sea to the Pacific Ocean. A shudder passes through the mass of human bodies. At that moment, people who are close and dear to me, whom I shall probably never see again, wake up. Millions of people arise who are cut off from the world, as if they were living on another planet.

It is a long time since I was with them. I live in another world, where people are free to think, to act, and to struggle for a better future as their conscience dictates. Their happiness and unhappiness differ from the happiness and unhappiness of Soviet zeks as light from darkness. I live in a wonderful city on the shore of the Mediterranean Sea. I can sleep late, I am not counted at a roll call morning and evening, and I have enough food on my table. But every morning at five o'clock, I open my eyes and experience an acute moment of fear. This is a habit from five years in camp. Each morning the signal from that world rings in my ears.

"Get up!"

Reader, I do not know with what feeling you close this book, what you were seeking in it, and whether you regret having wasted your time. This book about the camps was not written for your entertainment or to satisfy your curiosity. This book is not a memoir. It is too goal-oriented for that, and it relates not to the past, which people who have grown wise with experience recall in their declining years, but to the present. This book will not accomplish its purpose if it does not convey to you a lively sense of the reality of the camps, which exist today just as they existed yesterday and five years ago. Nothing has changed. These camps are a basic fact of our reality, and it is impossible to understand the epoch in which we live without knowing how and why these camps arose and how they are growing and expanding in the world.

Make no mistake and do not confuse Soviet camps with Nazi ones. Do not justify Soviet camps by asserting that Auschwitz, Maidanek, and Treblinka were much worse. Remember—Hitler's death factories are gone, they have passed like an evil dream, and in their place stand museums and monuments over the graves of the dead—but Square 48, Kruglitsa, and Kotlas are functioning as before, and people are perishing there today just as they perished five or ten years ago. Strain your ears and you will hear what I hear every morning at dawn from afar:

"Get up!"

This account of my five-year incarceration in the Soviet subterranean kingdom is a story of human grief and the limit of human degradation.

There is hell on earth, created by those who lay claim to the title of Builders of the New World. This book was not written, however, for the sake of polemic or "anti-Soviet propaganda." There are people among us who are prepared to deny indisputable facts if they do not fit in with their notion of the Soviet Union. For those people, a book about the camps is only "anti-Soviet propaganda," and they turn away in dissatisfaction. "This cannot be true," they say. Unfortunately, it is true. The gray mundane daily routine of the camps is presented in this book without exaggeration, without the piling on of horrors and cruelty.

This book is anti-Soviet propaganda in the same measure as Harriet Beecher Stowe's *Uncle Tom's Cabin* a hundred years ago was "propaganda" against Southern slave owners in the United States. The condition of millions of Soviet zeks is much worse, and the degree of their moral oppression and physical exploitation is much greater than was that of the blacks, which evoked such a fiery protest, even armed intervention.

Each of us is obligated to know the truth, and if one is a political supporter or fellow traveler of communism, then one is doubly obligated to know what is happening behind the facade of the Soviet regime. If one has the slightest doubt, then one is obligated to demand the opportunity to verify every assertion about Soviet camps that is made in this and other books written by camp survivors. This book is not intended for those who consider any statement against the Soviet system as "insolence" or who would like to suppress any cry of pain from the mouths of the victims. It is for readers who want to know what is happening behind the smokescreen of false official propaganda in order to come to the aid of those who need such help.

One can say that this book was written *against*: against oppression, against terrible evil, against great injustice. This definition, however, is insufficient. Primarily, it is written *in defense*. In defense of millions of buried alive, suffering, and suppressed people. In defense of those who today are still alive but tomorrow may already be dead. In defense of those who today are still free, but tomorrow may share the fate of those buried alive.

On the basis of my five-year experience, I affirm that the Soviet government, utilizing specific territorial and political conditions in its country, has created a subterranean hell, a kingdom of slaves behind barbed wire, inaccessible to monitoring by world public opinion.

The Soviet government has used its unlimited hegemony over a sixth of the earth's surface to recreate slavery in a new form and to keep enslaved millions of its own citizens and a mass of foreigners, not because they committed any genuine crime but as a "preventive measure" at the discretion and arbitrary will of the secret police. This charge may seem unbelievable to whoever grew up under Western democratic conditions and personally never saw or experienced the lot of a slave.

Something else seems improbable to me: that millions of people in the West can reconcile democratic convictions and a protest against social injustice in any form with support for this flagrant and abhorrent outrage that one can no longer ignore in our days.

I call the attention of people who are capable not only of seeing but also of foreseeing and thinking to the ominous fact that slavery—incompatible with the essence of the capitalist order and the moral consciousness of mature humankind—becomes technically possible and an economically meaningful phenomenon in the framework of twentieth century totalitarian ideology.

The technological revolution led to a situation where governments that would have been unable to retain power with bayonets can rely superbly on tanks and automatic weapons. Slave labor again pays for itself both politically and economically. Hitler demonstrated one variant of rule based on suppression and enslavement of "inferior races" and weak peoples: a stupid and irrational variant. If you want to see how the Soviet variant looks—no less cynical but more intelligent and perfected—try and obtain a face-to-face meeting with millions of Soviet slaves. Throw open the doors of the camps to people of independent science and free thought! Let them enter not as captives under escort with ten-year sentences of forced labor but as envoys of nations, free researchers and observers—for a great uncorrupt investigation.

The Soviet government created living conditions for two hundred million people that sharply deny the elementary needs of the minds and bodies of ninety percent of the population, thus arousing ineradicable and perpetually growing dissatisfaction. Among the Soviet masses, this dissatisfaction takes the form of blind—not protest! —but merely discontent and a sense of hardship, but one that endures, and despite all the purges and preventive imprisonments, it grows anew just as inevitably as a person's nails and hair grow after being cut. For people who manifest any form of dissatisfaction or critical attitude—even if it is only suspected that at some time, they will manifest it—the Soviet regime has created an unprecedented reservation of slavery, unequaled in world history. On the basis of an arbitrary selection by local organs of power and at the orders of central organs, this reservation is filled with elements that are "unsuitable" or "superfluous" in the eyes of the regime, where the value of human life is estimated as not higher but in practice often as lower than that of the beasts of burden. That is the state of things in the greatest power of our time. The camps, with their multimillion population, are the Soviet Union's corrective; under conditions of totalitarian violence against human nature, they are ineradicable.

If in reply, the "devil's advocates" will allude to racial or national discrimination beyond the border of the Soviet Union, one should answer that these do not derive from the essence of Western democracy, and eliminating them—sooner or later—will be a triumph of active, struggling democracy. The forced labor camp, in contrast, derives from the essence of the Soviet regime and is inseparable from it. They are two sides of the same coin. Western literature speaks openly and bravely about all the social defects of democracy and throws light on all dark corners, whereas censored literature of the slave-holding system is silent and tries not to look where it is dark. It has no answer to charges other than abusive language and denying the facts.

It is necessary to protest against the camp system as the most monstrous contemporary phenomenon containing the seeds of universal catastrophe. A moral and political catastrophe begins at the moment that methodical and mass torture, displacement of people, and murder practiced under the cover of Marxist and democratic rhetoric is passed over in silence or justified by progressive people, people of the Revolution and of good will.

No matter what our understanding of the essence of democracy, it is clearly possible only in an atmosphere of absolute transparency, openness, and visibility. The democratic world must be observable from one end to the other. Where there are concealed places or forbidden zones, where something is carefully hidden from view behind prison walls and camp fences, we can be sure that evil deeds are occurring. Camps in their present form can exist only at the price of the strictest and most hermetic isolation and inaccessibility to the outside world, similarly to the way that the Nazi regime hid its shameful secrets not only from the outside world but also from the mass of its own population.

What happened to the author of this book between 1939 and 1946 is in itself sufficiently appalling. A person who committed no crime and was completely extraneous to the Soviet state could be seized on foreign territory, and without a trial, in conditions of strictest anonymity, cut off from the world for several years. They sentenced me to slavery, transported me to the end of the world, and submitted me to physical and mental torture for several years, when there was every possibility to return me to my homeland, where my home, family, and work were waiting for me. Chance saved me from death. Nothing can repair the harm done to me and my family. That, however, is not the main thing. Millions of people remain in the condition that I was in. We are talking about them.

What I experienced in the Soviet Union was a terrible nightmare. My obligation and my first act upon my return to Europe was to give an account of my experience and to convey the cry for help of people cut off from the world. But only here, among free people of the West, did I understand the depth of misfortune of those who remain imprisoned. Emerging from behind the barbed wire of the camps, I ran up against a stone wall of indifference and treachery.

I became aware that in certain circles, precisely those whose help is most needed, it is unacceptable to speak aloud about certain phenomena taking place in the Soviet Union because it is shocking and, moreover, compromising. Not once, but ten times did I hear that only enemies of progress and allies of reaction can accuse the Soviet Union.

This book was written under the silent and patent disapproval of my milieu, and were it not for my personal experience and the force of conviction borne of five years of camp, I might have succumbed to the collective admonition as do other participants in the "conspiracy of silence."

In my opinion, the attitude toward the problem of Soviet camps is the touchstone in evaluating a person's decency, just as is one's attitude toward antisemitism.

Indeed, just mention the victims of camps to people who on every other occasion are full of honeyed goodness and democratic sensitivity toward the smallest imperfection in the world, and they suddenly develop wolf-like fangs and absolute deafness and a hardening of the heart—as in Stevenson's tale of Doctor Jekyll and Mister Hyde.

These people, are convinced, as I am, that the Soviet regime cannot do without camps, but they draw opposite conclusions. Progress, in their view, fits in excellently with a system of modernized slavery.

The people who justify Soviet camps, who say, "Let them sit in camps," or "Perhaps this is not true," or simply, "What do we care?" may consider themselves anti-fascists and wear a mask of rectitude. It is clear to me that these people are preparing a second edition of Hitler in the world. These people are living testimony to the impotence of pseudo-democracy.

No better are those who in private conversation are willing to acknowledge that not everything is in order behind the border of the greatest police state in the world but view open protest or the least attempt to influence the organs of Soviet power as detrimental and dangerous, even when some of their closest ideological friends are perishing in prison. I understand these people's motives. The more I understand them, however, the less I sympathize with them. Their line of conduct is dictated by fear. They are weak people.

Every crime that occurs in the world ought to be identified publicly by name. Otherwise it is impossible to fight against it. No trampling of human rights should remain anonymous. The slogan of weak people—"Don't say it out loud! Don't name it!"—is a dishonest slogan. To a certain degree, it makes them accomplices to crime.

"Woe to the weak!" My five-year stay in the Soviet subterranean kingdom taught me this wisdom. The lot of the weak is slavery or death. One must understand the harsh, terrible meaning of these words in order to avoid submitting to blind force that threatens us all around. "Woe to the weak!" I saw and shared the fate of the weak in the Soviet country. Thousands of kilometers from the centers of terror, far beyond the borders of the Stalinist regime, I still saw the base, cowardly fear of weak people. I learned to hate violence in its embryonic form. The seed of all violence is in the meekness of the weak.

The sole reply to the harsh truth "Woe to the weak!" is that right must be clad in force. Against the forces of illegality stands the force of right. The consciousness of right engenders the bravery to defend trampled human rights—and the necessary force.

As long as the democratic world is reconciled to the existence of reservations of slavery in the Soviet Union, there is no hope of averting the threat of slavery in our own midst.

Tel Aviv 12/15/1946–10/25/1947

The Road to the West

I

Slavgorod

I ARRIVED IN Slavgorod on July 1, 1945, a memorable date.[1] Behind me were five years of forced labor camp and ten days on the road from the far north. Tucked inside my shirt was my certificate of release from Kargopolag. I was hungry, ragged, and wild looking. I did not have any money. I had eaten my last piece of bread at the railroad station early in the morning. I had one address in Slavgorod: On 52 Lunacharsky Street lived one Soloveichik.

Slowly, I trudged down the streets, looking in all directions. I was disappointed. Associating Slavgorod with Gogol's Mirgorod, where once upon a time Ivan Ivanovich had quarreled with Ivan Nikiforovich,[2] I had imagined it like the Ukrainian village with shady gardens and greenery. . . . But this was Central Asia: heat, desert, a burning hot, stifling wind, mud huts with flat roofs. . . .

A wretched little wooden house stood at 52 Lunacharsky Street—a detached hovel with a door on one hinge. . . . I cringed: who could live in such a hole? Now, probably, a strange, unpleasant person will open the door and, without hearing me out, will slam it in my face. . . . Thus will begin my Soviet "freedom," which could be worse than camp. But I had no choice. I mustered my courage, pushed the door open and went into the entryway.

---

1. The section on Slavgorod is a composite of material taken from Julius Margolin's article "Chudo v Slavgorod" [Miracle in Slavgorod], published in the newspaper *Novoe Russkoe Slovo*, July 5, 1953, and an unpublished story "Vostochnoe vospitanie" [An eastern upbringing] located in the Central Zionist Archive in Jerusalem.

2. "The Tale of How Ivan Ivanovich Quarreled with Ivan Nikiforovich" is one of the stories in Gogol's short story collection *Mirgorod*, set in a Ukrainian village.

The landlady pointed to a kitchen piled with dishes, buckets, and odds and ends. The Soloveichiks lived past the kitchen in a single little room. I knocked; a soft, old-mannish voice asked: "Who's there?"

"I am straight from camp! And I have greetings for you from Doctor Benyamin Berger."[3]

I named the magic name. Immediately Leonty Albertovich and Lina Grigorevna got up from their beds. Still not believing my success, I removed my heavy knapsack from my shoulders. They invited me to the table. Under a window between the beds was a small table piled with books.

"You haven't had breakfast? What should I prepare for you?"

Lina Grigorevna is already bustling by the table, and I cannot believe my eyes: for WHOM? For me, a camp zek, they are covering the table with a white tablecloth, placing genuine cups, plates, butter, fried eggs, tea, and sugar? I was overwhelmed: this was, indeed, a return to family! It was as if I were at home here! This Soloveichik, whom I did not know, became my support and anchor of salvation in a new, alien place. Leonty Albertovich first gave me money and took me to the telegraph office. I sent a telegram to my wife in Tel Aviv. THAT was the first greeting after long years of silence from a person missing without a trace.

"Will the telegram get there?"

"It will!" said Leonty Albertovich, "and now let's think how to arrange a lodging for you." We went out to the street, sat down on stools under the sole tree, and Leonty Albertovich held court.

I could see that the person to whom fate had led me was a significant individual in the Slavgorod exile colony. Leonty Albertovich Soloveichik had been living in Siberian exile in Slavgorod since 1941, but he was not alone. In the summer of 1941, the Soviet regime deported tens of thousands of "undesirables" from Lithuania. A large colony of Lithuanian exiles gathered in Slavgorod. Together with the exiles from Poland, they comprised a "family" of several hundred people—an island in the midst of the Soviet population, which itself was far from homogeneous.

Slavgorod was teeming with people from Leningrad who had been evacuated during the war. Kazakhs and deported Volga Germans[4] also lived

---

3. Benyamin Berger, b. 1880, died in camp in 1948. In Chapter 38 about Block 5 (written when Berger was still alive), he is referred to simply as "Doctor."

4. Ethnic Germans had been living in the areas around the cities of Samara and Saratov in the Volga region of southeastern Russia since the eighteenth century. The Soviet Union established the Volga German Autonomous Republic in 1924. In a "preventive measure" to avert collaboration with the invading Germans, the Soviet regime deported them en masse by a decree on August 28, 1941, and the Republic was abolished in September of that year.

in the region. At the *kolkhoz* market in the center of town, however, where the motley crowd swarmed, one could easily spot the "Westerners"—not only by their looks but also by the goods they were selling—items from packages that they received in an uninterrupted stream from New York and Tel Aviv.

The passers-by all greeted Leonty Albertovich and came up to exchange a few words. In his fifth year of exile, he knew everyone, and everyone knew him. A thin, dark-eyed girl approached:

"This is Klara, the planner at the factory where you will go tomorrow to apply for work."

A thickset, round-faced man approached: "Meet Kirshenberg, a well-known Warsaw lawyer. He and his wife were imprisoned for three years for refusing to accept a Soviet passport. You will sleep at their place today."

Two hours had not passed, and I already had a large circle of acquaintances in Slavgorod.

Thus began my friendship with the Soloveichiks. Both were highly cultured people, who were well acquainted with Europe, and Europe knew of them. In his *Autobiography*, which was published in 1950, the English poet Stephen Spender devoted several pages to the Soloveichiks' Berlin home at the end of the 1920s. Their Slavgorod home, however, differed sharply from the Berlin one: it was a hovel to which, over the years, they gave a civilized appearance. While I was living there, they affixed wooden shutters to the windows and put together something like a table lamp. As an exile, Leonty Albertovich did not have a normal Soviet passport, and he was obliged to appear at the police station every two weeks. He was prohibited from leaving the city. He was over seventy years old, did not work, and survived on income from the packages that arrived regularly from abroad.[5]

The technical division where I worked occupied a one-room wooden cottage in the back of the factory yard in Slavgorod. On that morning, there were two girls in the division: the eighteen-year-old Komsomol member Marusya,

---

5. In a section of "Miracle in Slavgorod" that is not included here, Margolin recounted the story of how the Soloveichiks miraculously succeeded in leaving Slavgorod and moving to Paris. In brief, when Margolin was in Paris in 1946, he personally delivered a letter to their daughter, which gave an uncensored picture of their situation. The daughter was married to a relative of the writer André Gide and thus was able to bring pressure on the Soviet side, which finally provided them with a visa to Paris in 1948. Margolin visited them in Paris two years later. Noting that Soloveichik continued to write and send packages to those remaining in Slavgorod, Margolin wrote that in a certain sense, he never left Siberia, "like all of us, his friends in Soviet captivity, who left part of their hearts in camps and exile, forever, possessed by the specter of the past, which remains in the present."

thin, timid and quiet, and twenty-six-year-old Shura—an energetic, round-faced, bold individual, as talkative as Marusya was taciturn. Shura was a party member and held a responsible post as a draftsman at the factory.

Shura's day at the factory began very successfully. Sitting at a large table in the middle of the technical division, I witnessed her successes and defeats. I was an "alien" at the factory, a stray "Westerner," who worked as a translator of technical literature from English. Shura sat at the table to my right. A large portrait of Voroshilov hung overhead.[6]

On my table that morning lay a description of a "Cincinnati" milling machine, an American brochure on coated paper with sketches, which I translated in good faith and literally, but not only without the aid of a technical dictionary but also without the slightest technical knowledge. In translating the word "---"[7] with the word "cogwheel," I had no knowledge about the object it designated, but no one demanded this knowledge from me. Shura's efforts were much worse than mine. The workshop heads were able to make some sense of my translations, comparing the "Lend-Lease" American machines with my makeshift terminology. Shura suffered at her draftsman's work—her two semesters at a Sverdlovsk technical institute, from which she had fled, unable to withstand hunger in the dormitory, were insufficient to cope with what was demanded of her. Her self-esteem suffered terribly, and she would have left the factory long ago if permitted. As there was no one to replace her, the senior engineer merely waved his hand in resignation: "Stay, stay!" and Shura continued to draft designs that amused the senior metal workers and brought her to bitter despair. She went around in a torn coat, was wasting her youthful years, but once a month she was on night duty at the Party municipal committee and on that night, she represented Party, Revolution, Power.

Shura flew into the technical division, pathetically brandishing a pair of leather shoes. She had succeeded in receiving one of seven pairs of women's shoes that had arrived at the factory. This was a great victory: hundreds of women worked at the factory. Marusya watched agitatedly as Shura tossed away her worn old boots and tried on the shoes. She put her foot on the stool and, her arms akimbo, threw back her head with playful pride: "Take a look at me!"

---

6. Kliment Voroshilov (1881–1969) was a Soviet military hero and close associate of Stalin. A Politburo member, after Stalin's death in 1953, he became chairman of the Presidium of the Supreme Soviet. He joined other members of the Presidium in the "anti-party" group that tried unsuccessfully to depose Nikita Khrushchev in June 1957.

7. The word is missing in the manuscript.

At that moment, a tall, dark-complexioned peasant, in a dirty worker's shirt entered and stood by the lintel. Shura unhurriedly removed her foot from the stool, straightened her dress over her solid calves, and wiped the smile off her face. They began to talk, and I suddenly heard the word "Papa." It was Shura's father, an unskilled worker at the same factory. Shura and Marusya both grew up in the village, both retained some features of village girls. As a party member and draftsman at the factory, Shura, however, had already climbed higher on the social ladder, and she addressed her father as if from an invisible higher step. It was not so much that her father embarrassed her, but he could no longer be her equal. He addressed her respectfully, gently, and cautiously.

"They get tractors, and they still complain!" said Shura, shrugging her shoulders.

"Because they're not very useful." The old man looked at her askance. "Consider how much time you lose while you wait for them . . . and how much they will make us pay. . . . You see, it turns out that I manage better with horses."

The old man began an extended explanation why *kolkhozes* do not need tractors, clearly an old regime explanation; in the middle, his daughter stopped listening to him and just looked at him condescendingly and patiently, waiting for him to finish his nonsense, and the father, just as condescendingly, as if to a child, explained things to her, which, because of her learning, she was unable to understand.

It was unpleasant for Shura that her father spoke about this topic in my presence, a foreigner after all. No sooner had he left, cautiously leaving the felt-lined door slightly ajar, then a new visitor opened it with full force, and the girls jumped up:

"Petya, Petenka!"

From the autumn, the first soldiers on leave or demobilized began to appear in our town. The market was swamped with trophy German watches, stockings, and suits from hundreds of packages arriving from Germany. The soldiers coming back from Eastern Prussia or from the environs of Vienna could not always refrain from expressing their feelings, and at first reacted sharply. One of them, stepping over the threshold of his hut, sighed, "How do you live here! We must leave, the sooner the better!"

That was easier said than done. Taking a seat at the table, Petya [? missing word in text] began to talk. He was a curly-headed, lively fellow in a military uniform, fresh as a berry, with swift movements. His long forelocks bobbed in all directions. I was busy with my work, but suddenly I began to half listen, involuntarily. I recognized a "pebble." In my terminology from childhood, "pebbles" were things that fly in through the open window of memory and remain there for a long time, perhaps forever.

In general, we do not have great control over our memory. Events and things leave nicks, without asking for our consent. The important thing is forgotten; the unimportant clings forever. In those days, my life was like a weed-infested field full of tossed stones. It would take cartloads to haul away these stones. But the pebbles remain, like that first Polesian pebble, which for some reason I picked out, standing by a train window in my distant youth, long, long ago, at either the Brest or Drohiczyn station, at a clearing in a birch grove. It was early dawn, a cloud hung over the damp grass, buttercups colored the slopes of the tracks yellow. The train was traveling past, and I was seized by remorse and despair at the impossibility of embracing this life, incessantly losing itself, at the impending doom of each blade of grass in this lonely spot, and I fixed my gaze for one long second, while the train sailed by, on a pebble lying two meters from the track, and remembered it forever. With the hope, which then I was unable to express in words, that my life, too, like this chance pebble, would be snatched away from the indifference of things and come into someone's view, that can see everything. . . .

Petya started to relate his tale:

"The fellow was a real combatant. And he was calm, neat, not a drinker. We became very friendly over three months. We were together from the very start of the offensive. But, as we approached Orsha, he became very agitated. It was his native area. Near Orsha was a *kolkhoz* from which he had been taken in the first year of the war. He had not been home for three years. At home he had a wife and mother.

"He told us a lot about his wife. Everyone talks about something, but he used to talk about his wife all the time. We made fun of him: 'You'll succeed, soldier, in returning to your feather bed, just be patient; it's not long now; from Berlin you'll go straight home, with all your medals, a hero.'"

"He himself was short, drab, red-headed, and pock-marked. His wife, however, was a beauty; we all knew this. He bored us with his stories. When the front just passed by Orsha, he asked for a leave. They gave him a week off for domestic matters, to go to his native village. You have to give it to such a hero. Our Vasya washed up, shaved, put on a new overcoat, and left."

"And here an evil thing happened. His wife, it turned out, had taken up with a German lieutenant. There were many such cases. It happens that when our men enter a village, the kids run to meet them; 'Let's go,' they yell, 'We'll show you all the German wives. . . .' But here it turned out very badly."

At this point, Petya's story began to expand outside the framework of his words, and I pictured clearly, just as clearly as that Polesian pebble—a damp spring evening, a dark muddy street with the last patches of snow—a hut, the soldier in a long overcoat, cautiously making his way on the dry spots. A bottle stuck out from his pocket, and in his wooden soldier's chest were presents for his young wife and old mother, prepared in advance for this occasion.

"But his wife did not come out to meet him. She looked out from behind the door and hid in a corner of the kitchen. Only his mother received her son, wrung her hands, threw herself on his chest, and between her tears, told him everything in the first minutes: 'No, dear son, you do not have a wife any more. And the German did not buy her with money or gifts, but she went to him of her own free will, like a wife, she looked after him, like a bitch she lay at his feet until the last day. The German bewitched her completely. What a disgrace! What shame! For over a year they did not part, and what to do with her now?...' "

"Vasily calmed down, sobered up in a minute. Three years at the front had taught him not to lose control. And there were worse things. Love, it's that way: love. We know."

"He stood up, went to his wife: 'How come the German didn't take you with him?' "

"And here is that pair: the small redhead with a bristly moustache, piercing, malign eyes, unchanged, and a hated voice, like all that life, from which there is no exit. . . . And opposite him, by the wall, his wife in savage, frenzied despair, in a state where nothing matters anymore, and the sooner it's over, the better."

" 'I had no life with you, Vasily! Not one good day! I didn't know life, I didn't know people; I didn't know myself! Now, at least, I know what people are like. . . . Your return is my ruin.' "

"Vasily stood for a while, looking. He shook his head."

" 'Did you really like the Fritz so much?' "

" 'Well, everything is clear.' "

"Vasily returned to the room. Unhurriedly, he took off his jacket and looked around. Evidently, no simple fascist lived here. There were books in the corner. 'Well, let's eat.' "

"His mother prepared to serve him, but before eating, Vasily filled a liqueur glass for himself and his mother, got up solemnly: 'For victory, for the Motherland, for Stalin!' They drank."

"Having eaten without haste and having exchanged a few words with his mother, he concluded, 'We'll talk tomorrow.' Vasily rose, nodded to his wife: 'Let's go' and went out to the yard through the kitchen, fastening on his belt with his pistol holster as he went. In less than a minute, a muffled shot rang out in the yard. Vasya entered, wiped his feet on the doormat, sat on his bed, and took off his shoes."

"His mother looked at him with a stony, expressionless gaze. Vasya himself drank the entire bottle and lay down to sleep. In the morning, having rested and recovered his spirits, he took his wooden chest and went back to his unit."

"That's the army, that's how it is with us." Petya smiled with a triumphant look. I'll never forget the solemnly frightened faces of Marusya and Shura. Marusya opened her mouth like a child and pulled in her neck, as if the bullet had passed by her ear, while Shura quietly and firmly nodded her head. After Petya left, I asked the girls what they thought about the heroic tank driver's deed. Did Vasya act correctly in this case?

The meek Marusya did not answer, but Shura proudly lifted her head: "Of course! She got what was coming to her! We punish treason mercilessly!"

"But for what treason did Vasya shoot his wife? For personal treason?"

"With us, there is no personal treason! If she simply had fallen out of love with him and gone to another, her husband would not have touched her. But she fell in love with a GERMAN!"

Probably my face expressed some lack of comprehension because Shura, after a pause, added: "Soviet education erases the boundary between the personal and social! In the West, you can fall in love with anyone you please, but here, don't get out of line! And remember who is your enemy!"

This was said so resolutely that I understood: in Shura's life, no one will succeed in destroying the ideal harmony between the personal and social.

Before leaving Slavgorod, I parted from Shura, my coworker during that Siberian year. The train that was to take the Polish repatriates from the city and surrounding areas was already standing at the station. We had received our payments and travel documents. On the eve of our departure, I arrived at the factory to say good-bye to the people whom, I knew, I would never see again. Shura sat in the technical division at her usual place. I shook her hand, expressed regret that I had to return to the West, the rotten West, above which the Stalinist sun had not yet risen. There would be no more of those heartfelt conversations, in which she, a Party member, had shown such enthusiasm and understanding of world politics, while I—so much modest loyalty and respect for the great Soviet power. No more of the idylls in the technical division, when Shura would bring yet another portrait of the Adored Leader, and I would find nails; she would choose a place, and I would climb on a stool and hang up the portrait, not too low and not too high, and then we both affectionately would admire the new decoration.

Shura accompanied me to the door. One more instant, and I crossed the threshold and turned around for the last time.

Shura stood, pale, biting her lips, her eyes blazing. A change occurred in her in a second. I did not have time to collect myself when she drew herself up, threw back her head and flung words at me, impulsively, angrily, as if something that had been boiling up inside suddenly, against her will, burst out from the depth of her being: "How fortunate you are, that you are leaving this cursed country!"

I was dumbfounded, and for a long second, we stood, looking intently at each other, so close and so distant, from two sides of the half-open door. Then, without saying a word, I cautiously closed the door and went away forever from her, from the portraits of the leaders, and from the comedy that we would have played to the end of our days if fate had doomed me to spend my life in the technical division.

2

The Freedom Train

MY ROAD TO the West began on that frosty morning at the end of March 1946, when an overcrowded train full of Polish "repatriates" set off from the Slavgorod Altai station, from the depths of Soviet Siberia. The freight cars were stuffed with agitated people; on the double-decker bunks a crowded human mass lay among bags, bundles, and wooden chests. In the middle of each car, like an iron monster on four paws, stood a squat stove, radiating heat. I was wearing the heavy homespun peasant coat that reached to my knees and padded quilted pants—a souvenir of camp. Women, youths, and children were all crushed together in a heap; there were not many old people among us: the harsh Siberian earth had swallowed up the old people during the years of exile and disasters. Our train traveled twenty-five days and nights toward the West across the endless Russian plains. Along the way, we stole boards and logs at the stations for fueling the stove. At the stops, market women brought eggs, milk, pancakes or pies, even pieces of roast meat: ineradicable, unsuppressed, unofficial "private initiative."

The train passed through cities—Omsk, Chelyabinsk, Kuibyshev.[1] It crossed rivers: first the Irtysh, then the Volga by the Syransk bridge, slowly, solemnly. At the beginning of April, the Volga was still covered with snow and ice; only in the very middle did the ice darken, and on the right bank, a long train of sleds stretched out along the river. In Kuibyshev, for the first time in many years, I saw a European-style railroad station: evening time, lights, in the heated corridor—a barbershop with a mirror and the fragrance of eau de cologne, a first-class buffet with palm trees and music. They did not let us in, and I remember only the people in rags who crowded by the entrance and

---

1. The city of Kuibyshev reverted to its original name of Samara in the post-Soviet period. During the war, many Moscow institutions and the elite were evacuated there.

peeked into the hall behind the back of the doorkeeper and the second-class buffet, for which we were sufficiently decently dressed; there we sat down to drink "Moskovskaya" vodka with the train's commandant.

The train then passed through the cities of Kharkiv and Konotop,[2] Gomel and Baranovichi.[3] At the main stations, we would stop for a long time, send delegations to the traffic director, and there, on the side tracks, ducking under the train cars, among the immense herd of massed cars, we came across others just like us: echelons from all sides, from the Urals, from Tashkent, Krasnoyarsk, "Westerners" streaming to the Polish border, and among them, like the last foam of a fleeing wave, were Jews. This was "repatriation" according to the treaty of 1945. In those months, 350,000 Poles returned from Russia, and almost half of them were Jews. Our cars were decorated with pine branches and inscriptions about the friendship of peoples; in the course of a week's travel, we lost the slogans, placards, and green decorations. We Jews were not deceived by the word "home." We knew that we would find only graves and ruins in Poland, and even before we arrived, our hearts were far away—over seven seas,[4] where everything was different—people, the sky, and memory.

The train crossed rivers: the Don and the Dnepr; days passed, and we felt the first breath of spring. Escaping from the stuffy, crowded car, I would stand for hours on the narrow open platform, avidly breathing the pungent air, watching as the fields flowed by, where the avalanche of the German invasion had rolled. We began to encounter German prisoners. . . . They were working along the tracks at the stations and approached to beg for bread. A woman from our car heaped curses on them. "We are not guilty. . . ." And remembering that my tortured mother lay in a mass grave by Pinsk, with a feeling of fastidious horror, I gave them bread. . . . In Russia I had learned to take camp bread from the hands of jailers and to convey it further with a thought about the miserable human rabble who found themselves steeped in blood and misfortune between their own and another's death. And I did not think about guilt or retribution in those weeks when the wheels thundered toward the West any more than a thirsty man thinks, when he thrusts his head back and is splashed by water from a jug.

---

2. Ukrainian cities.

3. Cities in Belarus. Now Baranovichy; in Polish – Baranowicze.

4. A reference to Palestine.

In those dark years, at the very bottom of the Soviet pit, I had often tried to imagine the "freedom train" that someday would transport me across the border of that horrible country. Then, it seemed to me that at the moment when the last kilometers before the border would fly past the windows in the corridor (I imagined a Pullman . . . half empty, like before the war), my face would harden, my throat would constrict, and in the very depths of my eyes, tears would form without spilling out. . . . But now, standing in my peasant coat on the platform of the freight train, I was not thinking about anything, and I did not recall anything. . . . It was like before an exam, when the studying is completed and nothing remains but to be yourself. Nothing to add and nothing to subtract. . . . I was borne rhythmically and smoothly, keeping time with the thundering wheels, toward the future, just as a river flows toward the sea—without disturbances or waves.

At Gomel, one of the former Jewish centers of Belorussia,[5] I went into the city. People were milling about in the dark April mud; the gray sky hung over the gloomy plains, and finally, I found what I had been looking for. In a side alley, I saw a shanty, just like in a Chagall painting: the roof was slanted; the windows were crooked, the door rested on one hinge, and in front of it was an old Jewess in a kerchief and a man's boots. From what kind of Turkestan evacuation had she returned to her old hearth? I went up to her and said, "I am going to Palestine." She became animated.

"Yes, I know. . . . I have a sister in Tel Aviv. . . ."

"Do you want me to give her a greeting?"

She gave me a confused and suddenly cautious look. She was silent and then said indifferently: "No, it's not worth it. We are Soviet people. I don't even know her address." I understood that she did not trust me, and I regretted that I had told her about Palestine. I said good-bye, and I went on my way. I was looking for a post office. In every city where we stopped, I would write or send a telegram saying that I was on my way. At the corner, I turned; the old women stood frozen in her place just as I had left her, and she stared at me intently. I waved to her. She did not respond or stir. We stood, looking steadily and silently at each other from afar.

I thus retain in my memory that figure against the background of ruins and a gray sky, like Lot's wife, turned into a pillar of salt, like a question mark, like a symbol of everyone who is silent and waiting over the Soviet border. Silent and waiting until this day.

---

5. Now independent state of Belarus.

And another recollection—about the final hours before the train left Slavgorod. It had turned to dusk, and everyone was impatiently waiting for the signal to start moving. In our car, the heavy door was partially open. . . . In front of our eyes, something harsh unfolded. In the corner of the car was a family of three women with two children. In the middle was a very young woman with an infant and near her the grandmother, with a somber, severe face. On the other side was a young woman of about twenty-six, with a six-year-old girl. They had been deported from Poland five years ago—the old woman with her daughter and Vladya, her son's wife. Understandably, during the five years, both young women found friends—the younger legally, according to registration at the marriage bureau, but the already-married Vladya—under her mother-in-law's disapproving eye and without any registration. The little girl grew up obstinate and wild, and when she was six, her grandmother explained that her father was not the person she thought but someone else. When the time came to return home, Tanya's husband, a towheaded lieutenant, did not detain her and immediately gave a divorce—a free pass from the Siberian drifts to the wide world. Vladya, too, parted from her man. It seemed as if everything was settled between them—and now in the last hours before departure, after boarding the train, everything broke down.

Beside himself, frenzied, with wild, unseeing eyes, Vladya's Nikolay arrived, entered the car, and lay down on Vladya's place.

"Go away, go away!"

She wrung her hands, jumped up, went out into the cold, returned, all agitated. . . . But he did not leave, and tension began to mount in the car, as if a bomb ready to explode at any second had been placed on the bunk.

"Don't worry, I won't remain. . . ."

By then, we knew for sure that he would not let Vladya leave. In those last hours, when there already was nothing to talk about, he, wordlessly, solely by his presence, with each hour, broke the woman's resistance, just as one breaks a slender tree, bending it until it cracks at the very root. . . .

The Polish commandant in charge of this train arrived, warily, cautiously. "I beg you honorably, comrade lieutenant, you do not have the right to be here."

By the door, his loyal friends appeared, military youth; they led the commandant aside: "Don't worry, dear, you can count on us." Nikolay got up and nodded to Vladya; she went out after him. We saw fear and dismay on her face. She was afraid of her husband in distant Poland. The train had not started to move, but her mother-in-law was already threatening her, hissing: "Just you wait, wait, your husband will know everything. . . ."

It was frightening to stay behind—the only one from everyone!—it was a greater betrayal than betraying her husband—it was her soul's eternal damnation. I, however, was not watching her, nor Nikolay, nor her mother-in-law, who, having turned away, seemed all busy with the infant. For me, the main personage in this drama was the small, thin, six-year-old girl.

She sat the whole time on her bundle, in a bonnet, warmly wrapped up, with a tiny, tense, completely understanding face. What kind of a disaster would it be for her to remain: she had grown up in Siberia, did not know any other language nor any other life than that in Slavgorod—the little room with a kitchen and entryway, where the exiled Poles lived and young cadets gathered in the evenings to drink vodka, unbuttoning their uniforms? I do not recall, however, that I ever saw such an expression on a child's face: horror and frenzied grief. . . . She was quaking from despair and hatred. . . . When her mother approached to fix her coat, she repulsed her and shouted, not to her, but to those of us around: "She's going to take me; she's going to take me!"

Nikolay paid no attention to her. The girl suddenly pounced on him: "Get out of here! Go away! I don't want you, I don't want, I don't want!"

Vladya then took her in her arms, kissing her and weeping, and both were flooded with tears. This tiny being already knew that resistance was useless. All her life was decided in that moment. . . . Her mother would take her with her, as her own property, and she would never see her father. She disappeared from the car, obediently let herself be led, as if paralyzed by a nightmare. Then they began to take Vladya's things out of the train. Nikolay and his friends had prepared a sled. The mother-in-law began to scream and call the commandant for help: Vladya's bundles included joint possessions. At the last minute, Vladya, wildly distraught, ran up to say good-bye and calm her mother-in-law. The whole car turned away from her as if she were a leper. . . . At that moment, I was not thinking about her or about the passions that deprive a person of free will and reason, and then, like a burned-out bonfire, leave only a heap of ashes. I thought about that little girl whose fate had been decided, who did not make it to her father, and sank into the gloomy, inhuman Slavgorod night, like a stone, without a trace or hope, without anyone being able to interfere.

She could have gone away from there, from that pit of unrelieved need and savagery—and she remained! And who dared to take her out of the car— her own mother! I had the impression that this unlucky woman flung herself head first into this whirlpool, and not alone but with a child, who felt that something irremediable was being done to her. And I could not regain my equilibrium, as if a murder had been committed in front of my eyes. . . . Yes, and it was a murder—thus to uproot and decide another's fate, eternally to condemn a young life to staying in the wretched atmosphere of the Stalinist Siberian backwoods, a life in falsehood, alienated from the free world, in the rancid, cold fumes that penetrated all the daily life of these people, from childhood until death. . . . And everything in me cringed from outrage and pity.

During the seven long years that I lived in Soviet captivity, I thought solely of liberation, a return to that distant world where people do not fear each other, boldly say out loud what they think, choose their own path, where and how to live, and eat unrationed bread. . . . You have to touch death to know what life is, you have to disappear from the West to know what the West is. At that very time, many voluntarily returned to Russia or dreamed of being permitted to become citizens of that country. Fate, ignorance, personal calculations—what difference does it make? The train traveled to the West, and weighing down relentlessly on my shoulders was the memory of those innocent people who had perished, trampled into the ground, shamed, exiled and simply deceived, like children led forcibly by the hand, concealed from the human eye and from human judgment, floundering, betrayed, and buried alive.

3

Non Omnis Moriar

LYING ON A cot in the camp hospital in 1945 in a state verging on insanity, I painfully collected my thoughts. One of the signs of alimentary dystrophy is the loss of memory. I felt that I was sinking into forgetfulness while awake, and the past was leaving me in clusters. In that state of exhaustion, every day I felt divested of some memories, knowledge, and names. . . . What are the names of my sister's children? Who is the author of *City of the Sun*?[1] I was losing my spiritual possessions, and every day I discovered that something else was missing. . . . Then I began to review my life, by years and months, in chronological order and randomly; I learned it by heart in order not to forget. Nevertheless, gaps appeared.

Repeating the lines from the ode by Horace that, when free, I had always remembered distinctly—"Exegi monument aere perennius" [I have created a monument more lasting than bronze],[2] I began persistently and tensely to retrieve it from memory, word by word, verse by verse. I would repeat the first six lines endlessly, lying on my back with eyes closed. But on the seventh, I failed: "Non omnis moriar. Multaque pars mei. ... Vitabit. ... Libitin. ... [I shall not wholly die and a greater part of me will evade Libitina (the goddess of death)].

Here the thread was broken and I could not remember any more. Then, with the exasperation and fury of a drowning man who is being carried away by the current, I promised myself that I would not die—non moriar!—before opening Horace and repairing the torn thread. That was my pledge. Two

---

1. *La città del Sole*, Utopian novel by Tommaso Campanella (1538–1639).

2. The translation of Horace, Ode 30, vol. 3 comes from the site http://www.kniskern.com/robin/classics/horace/03.30.html.

years later, already in Tel Aviv, I sought out a copy of his *Odes*, and my hands trembled while I read: "...usque ego postero Crescam laude recens..." [continually I, newly arisen, may be strengthened with ensuing praise].

What is happiness? In the summer of 1943, when we were working in the field in the strict regime camp Osinovka 1, a tall, gloomy Finn approached me during a work break. He was an exceptionally serious and taciturn person. He was not close to anyone, and I knew nothing about him. Suddenly he addressed me—for the first and last time—and he turned out to be a sectarian and a mystic.

"I read the Bible differently from everyone else!" he told me. "I know how to deduce the fate of every person from the Bible. And I know your fate: you will be happy. And remember: your happiness is in a distant country where your home is. When the time comes, go directly there, don't hesitate or linger anywhere. Do not be tempted by anything, do not detour, hurry home; you will be happy there."

At that moment, the meaning of "happy" was completely clear to both of us: it was the opposite of our present situation. What they had done to us was so terrible that a return to normalcy—to one's home and family, to the absence of fear for one's life, to satiety, and the opportunity to choose one's work, meant assured happiness to us.

Over the long years of Soviet imprisonment, I had forgotten the taste of an apple. There were no apples in the north of Russia or in the Altai region to which I was exiled after my release from camp. Occasional travelers from Alma Ata (Kazakhstan), thousands of kilometers away, brought several apples and sold them by the piece at the market. There were enthusiasts who would buy them in order to learn "what an apple is like." I was not attracted to that kind of apple stolen from fate. Gradually, however, the apple—juicy red or an aromatic light-green rennet apple of the pre-war years—turned into a symbol of freedom for me. A free country is precisely one where apples are sold on the streets, as many as you like.

As soon as the train reached the Brest station, at the Polish border, I immediately headed toward the market—for apples. The city of Brest, associated with a variety of memories for me, lay in ruins. A Soviet movie house was located in its intact, monumental synagogue. I was not, however, searching for the past: I was looking for apples. . . . That was the sign that we were approaching freedom.

Finally, late at night, we—several passengers with insomnia—opened the heavy lock of the freight car. The train stood in the profound silence of the night on a bridge over the Vistula River; to the right, we could not see but inferred the walls of sleeping Warsaw. The river flowed in the moonlight and the cold—another marker of freedom. Not a soul was around the sleeping train, which stood motionless on its solitary heights, over the deserted and gloomy "diluvian" valley.... The nocturnal cold forced us to close the door. During the night, the train circled, circumventing the city, and in the morning, we saw that Warsaw was behind us; fields and meadows shone in the April sun. The curtain of night rose over the Polish spring, and little stations with half-forgotten cheerful names, like music, came to meet us. . . . Where were they taking us? I decided to leave the train at the first opportunity. At midday we arrived at the Skernewice station, which before the war, I had traveled past dozens of times. Opposite our Siberian train stood a peaceful, calm, sparkling clean passenger train Skernewice-Łódź. It looked unbelievable, as if there had been no war, no German invasion, nor Soviet hard labor camp. "Ten minute stop." Without much hesitation, I grabbed my wooden chest and sat down in the third-class car of that train.

The car was overcrowded, and people surrounded me. "A repatriate from Siberia." The Sovietization of Poland was just beginning in the spring of 1946. The people who showered me with questions did not look like Soviet people; they spoke differently, were dressed differently, smiled, moved.... As if awakening after a very long sleep, I felt deeply aroused, which was not expressed outwardly, but suddenly I stopped hearing what people were saying to me. Rogov—Koljuszki—Andzejow. For two hours, the train was approaching the city where I had spent ten years of my life and from which I had fled in 1939. The circle was closing, the past was returning to me. . . . And now I saw the familiar Łódź suburbs of Widzew, Park of the Third of May, and the white building of the train station.

As if nothing had happened, and there had not been seven years of exile, I checked my suitcase in the baggage room and went out, unhurriedly, to the square. My first impression was that nothing had changed. There had hardly been any destruction in Łódź. Here on Brzezna Street, 6, in September 1939, I had left an apartment, library, manuscripts, pictures on the walls. . . . I automatically went from the train station along the customary route "home." Gradually, a sensation of amazing lightness and blitheness seized me. . . . I did not walk, I flew. Having reached the main street, I opened my arms wide, as if I wanted to embrace homes, passers-by, the sun on the sidewalk.

"Hey!"

I turned around and saw a newspaper vendor imitating my gestures, making fun of me. "Did you lose your marbles?" I nodded to him. My body was suffused with spring and joy. "Non omnis moriar,—multaque pars mei—vitabit Libitinam." First, don't delay (remembering the Finnish mystic) and second, find the continuation, what follows after "Libitinam." I walked along Piotrkowska[3] Street, still not knowing where I would spend the night and how I would spend my first "European" day.

Suddenly, something struck me. At the site of the Gothic synagogue in the center of town—one of the most monumental buildings in Łódź—there was nothing. This was so fantastic that I recoiled. Green grass was growing on the wasteland, and two horse-drawn cab drivers were dozing peacefully in the April sun. The synagogue had disappeared.

It was not so much that I was surprised; I had been expecting this, but I experienced something similar to what a Parisian would have felt had he not seen Notre Dame in its place. There were not even ruins. Not the slightest trace remained. Now I went further, with the anxious awareness that I was moving in a semi-spectral world; for me, the synagogue was standing as before in the empty space. I could not stop seeing it.

People die; that is understandable. Others come in their place. Piotrkowska was teeming with people as before the war. But when suddenly buildings disappear that had been calculated to last for centuries, leaving a smooth, even place, temples in whose shade generations were supposed to come and go, then this is unnatural and uncanny, like the Gogolian face from which the nose disappeared.[4]

That evening I found a place for myself on St. Jakub Street, on the fourth floor of a house for repatriates. A crowd of thousands was housed on all floors and in the halls of the former factory. These people were Jews—not "repatriates," but simply refugees from Stalinist Russia, people at a rest stop. In the large dining hall, crowds of people would sit on wooden benches by the plain tables until midnight—a variegated group—turmoil, a ruckus, a veritable Noah's ark after the flood. I looked for familiar faces. . . . It seemed to me—I shuddered—I noticed an old friend from Łódź in the crowd. I saw his ruddy face, fleshy lips, and characteristic forehead. I recognized his gestures and stride . . . and rushed to him.

I knew very well, however, that this man had been killed four years ago. The Germans had murdered him, but at that moment, I ceased to believe that. I often get mixed up about the facial features of people whom I have not seen for a long time. I had not seen Lubliner for six years. I used my usual trick

---

3. A main street in Łódź.

4. Allusion to Gogol's short story "The Nose."

in those cases: I walked in front of him so that he would see me first and recognize me.

He, however, as ill luck would have it, did not look at me.

Then I resolutely shouted from the other end of the table so that everyone would turn around:

"Lubliner!" With the passionate thought, like a prayer: let a miracle happen!

I waited for him to lift his head . . . look in astonishment, and suddenly, in a second, his eyes would sparkle, grow wide, his face would light up with the joy of meeting, and he would rush to me.

But the miracle did not happen. Lubliner's double gave me an indifferent, absent-minded glance and returned to his conversation with a neighbor. And my friend, who had almost returned to life, again disappeared into nonbeing, this time forever.

Two days later, I settled into an excellent room in the Hotel Savoy in the center of town, with hot water and an elevator, a carpet in the corridor, a restaurant on the first floor, and an elegant lobby. The Zionist organization, to which I turned (now all traces of it disappeared long ago), provided me with money, sent me to a tailor, who dressed me from head to foot—and while waiting for the first opportunity to continue on my way (I remembered the Finn's warning), I lived like a person convalescing from a serious illness in a sanitarium.

The bag with the rye rusks and the tattered camp pants were still lying in my wooden chest. My time, however, now belonged to me, and with each day, the habits and needs of a normal person returned. In a month, I received a visa to Palestine. After another three months, I obtained a passport for travel abroad. During those four months of my stay in Łódź, the ordinary passing of the hours, the life processes, and the chronicle of daily events were full of such intensity and interest, it was as if I were starting my life for the second time.

This second beginning, however, was not so simple. Life is not a record player where you can put the same record on twice. There was neither repetition nor continuation in what was happening to me. There is a law according to which with the years, we change our relationship to people and things. We flow with time and change with it, but a black chasm had opened in my life across which I was unable to stride—neither then, in my first days after my return from the subterranean kingdom, nor now, when I am writing these lines. . . .

Two hundred and fifty thousand Jews had disappeared from Łódź without a trace, but to me, they continued to populate the city. The streets and houses were full of yesterday's warmth; I had friends in every courtyard; familiar children were playing in the sandboxes in the parks; each intersection was full of memories and mementos. I felt acutely that I was surrounded by the unfinished, yet enduring, practical bustle of life that had been truncated seven years ago. After seven years of otherworldly sleep, I had returned to the starting point—and two different time frames, two worlds intersected inside me.

In broad daylight, in the bright gleam of the sun, like a lunatic, I moved among shadows. It was inconceivable that in this city, where I had known hundreds of people and could not walk a hundred meters without encountering a reciprocal glance, gesture, or word in greeting, now no one recognized me. The truncated life of the people of Łódź cried out inside me. I circled around many houses, climbed staircases, and entered courtyards. The houses were standing but no one was home. Those who were no longer there were more real than the random passers-by around. I knew what had happened to the Jewish people in this city and throughout the country, but knowledge did not help. If I had been put to sleep for a hundred years and then awakened, I would have felt the same way in the new world.

I did not return to a cemetery or feel as if I were in a cemetery. People go there in order to remember the way of all flesh, which has reached its natural limit. But my people did not die; they disappeared in broad daylight, just as I myself had disappeared from life in one instant when they threw me into the cellar for those doomed by the Soviet regime.

I walked on the sidewalks of Łódź, and the kingdom of shadows swayed around me. There were more people close and dear to me in this shadow kingdom than among the living. And I realized that to the end of my days, I would not leave this circle of shadows; I would remain faithful to them; I would be more with them than with new friends. So many had perished that I could not encompass all of them in my memory. Who will remember the murdered children in this one city of Łódź? I was unable to remember them and unable to forget; I felt that they surround me in sleep and in waking, in the deep shadow of consciousness.

In those first days, I wandered the streets of Łódź endlessly and aimlessly, hoping only to meet someone. If not here, then where? If I had returned, why should others not return? I vigilantly looked all around and kept waiting for someone to call out to me. . . . No sooner did I go up to my excellent room in the Hotel Savoy, then I was drawn irresistibly to the street. In the street, I still could meet someone, and every meeting would be a salvation and victory over death, but locking myself in the room, I betrayed them all irrevocably and hopelessly. Could I do that? I knew that my departure date would be a day of great parting, and then I would remain alone in the gigantic kingdom of shadows, like a diver whom they had lowered to the bottom and had forgotten to raise.

A week passed before I found the courage to go to my old apartment. Going up to the ground floor, I was impressed by the gleam of the front stairway, and the steps seemed steeper than I recalled them from the summer of 1939. I did not expect to find anything behind the door: I had been told that the Germans carted everything away, leaving bare walls. But I had to enter; the law of return required it. I had to enter in order to close the circle, to wipe out or to smooth over the memory of flight when, not looking back, I had abandoned my nest. Part of me remained behind those doors, to which I owed a last visit.

On the door was a sign "Bilasiewicz, municipal employee." An unfamiliar woman opened the door. The entryway was unchanged: the same furniture, only it had faded over the seven years. I was surprised. . . . What if further on everything was as before, and it was not true about "bare walls." I would enter the study now, and I would see the books, the Underwood typewriter in the corner, and above the sofa a woman's portrait, in silvery-green tones, which was dearer to me than Leonardo's *Mona Lisa*. I hastened to assure the tenant that I had no claims to the apartment; I only wanted "to cast a glance" before traveling abroad forever. Warily and cautiously, they led me into the rooms, and the tenant explained that the Germans had been living there; he moved in recently and he received the furniture according to a list from the administration in charge of abandoned Nazi property. . . .

Indeed, everything was alien. The Germans had left their books, and suddenly, among Goebbels' brochures and *Judenpest* of Hermann Esser,[5] I noticed familiar book bindings.

"You see," I said to the tenant, "the Germans left several of my books: I recognize them by the bindings. Here, this one, and this one, and this one. . . ."

Which of my books did the Nazis leave? An illustrated guidebook to Palestine, a collection of East European Jewish humorous anecdotes by Olsvanger,[6] two volumes of Sombart's *Der Proletarische Sozialismus*,[7] and a

---

5. Hermann Esser (1900–1981) was a functionary in the Third Reich. The full title of his book is *Die jüdische Weltpest* (Munich, 1939).

6. Immanuel Olsvanger (b. 1888 in Poland, d. 1961 in Israel), folklorist and Hebrew translator. The work, first published in 1920 was entitled *Rosinkess mit Mandlen: Aus der Volksliteratur der Ostjuden. Schwänke, Erzählungen, Sprichwörter und Rätsel.*

7. Werner Sombart (1863–1941), sociologist and economist.

thick volume in a red binding *Wahrheit und Wirklichkeit* by Heinrich Maier,[8] my university instructor, which was scribbled all over with my student notes. I showed them to the tenant as proof that I truly had lived in that apartment. In the dining room, the heavy metallic lamp was still hanging, and in the bedroom, where my wife's mother had lived during the final summer, her closet and the old-fashioned ponderous bed of yellow wood with gilded garlands were still standing.

"If you want to take your things," said the polite tenant, "there is a procedure for this: you have to apply to the district court, it will issue a permit, but otherwise, I am responsible for the things, according to a list. . . ."

I had no idea what I would do with this junk, but, following the advice of the polite Bilasiewicz, I submitted a request to the court. I thought it was a simple formality. My surprise was great when, appearing according to a summons on the designated day, I found, instead of the polite Bilasiewicz, two lawyers, who, as representatives of "the opposing side," requested an extension until the next session. At that time, they would present the receipts of the firm where Mr. Bilasiewicz had purchased the items that I had listed and also proof that I never had lived in that apartment and therefore none of my things could be there.

The extension was granted, but I did not appear at the second session. Seeing that I would have to fight for the bed, the lamp, the closet, etc., I pusillanimously gave up on the idea. The polite Bilasiewicz had calculated correctly: after a few weeks, I left Łódź forever, leaving him my mother-in-law's bed with the gilded garlands.

That was not difficult for me. It was more difficult for others to leave their belongings—attained by the labor of generations—in the rapacious hands of those who inherited it while they themselves were still alive. More than one Siberian Jewish repatriate who appeared unexpectedly on the threshold of his home or village estate, where his existence had already been forgotten, evoked an indignant cry and the sincere curse: "They liquidated everyone, but this one survived. . . . May you disappear, cursed dregs. . . ."

Before leaving, I spent many hours at a marble table by the large window of a café in the center of town; there I wrote my letters and observed the street. I dropped in at the municipal library and asked for all the newspapers for the first half of 1939, the last half year before the destruction of my Atlantis. Did you ever try to read old newspapers with screaming headlines and the

---

8. *Wahrheit und Wirklichkeit* by Heinrich Maier (1867–1933) was published in 1926.

ludicrous bustle of people unaware of what tomorrow will bring them? Newspapers that in the perspective of several years look like curved mirrors of an assemblage of the tragic absurd, arousing bewilderment. Had this been my world? Looking through the large glass windows of the café, I saw the street of 1939 so clearly that I could do nothing but take up my pen.

At the intersection of Piotrkowska and Cegielniana, where the bagel vendors swarmed, where the cries "*Haint!*, *Moment!*,[9] *Frische beygels!* and the rumble of tram wheels does not cease for a second, at midday, it was like a frying pan with boiling oil: streams of pedestrians swirled around, the sidewalks could not accommodate all of them, and people stepped off onto the road. Under the horses' muzzles and in between the cars walked old Jews in tatters, dragging on their backs bundles of fabric, unbelievable piles of cardboard boxes with dry goods. They walked, bent at a right angle, catching their breath, staggering, beards thrust forward, with bulging eyes and gaping mouths. At the gateways of the houses, which were clammy and damp even on that clear May day, with the yards thronging with people, stood porters awaiting a penny's worth of work—scraggly Jews from Baluty and Starówka,[10] with rope harnesses on their shoulders, in worn shoes and "kapotes" [long coats worn by orthodox Jews], affixed to the spot like galley slaves. They stood at the entrances to innumerable shops with yarn, with print design or white cloth, near the warehouses, offices, and windows piled with knitted wear or jute. The hungry crowd swarmed by the windows of the kosher stores of Dishkin and Diamant, while the chivalrous Kosciuszko, perched on his high pedestal on Freedom Square, turned away from it indifferently.

The entire first kilometer up to the corner of the Passage and Andzej was a Jewish commercial center. Jewish betting offices and banks alternated with cafés, the refuge of salesmen and agents. Deals were concluded there under the café signs "Ideal," "Astoria," and "Italy." Currency exchanges alternated with editorial offices of newspapers in three Łódź languages [Polish, Russian, German, but also Yiddish], gigantic wagons rumbled into the narrow yards, heaped with goods in colorful wrappings with the labels: "Adria" of Steinert, "Sotka" of Widewska—"Receive 500 pieces!" Here street photographers circulated, debonairly focused on foppish passers-by, and around the corner, in the alley, where the traffic dwindled, street musicians were singing in Russian and Polish: "My Natasha," "I jeszcze coś . . . O jeszcze coś!"

---

9. Titles of popular Yiddish newspapers.

10. Poor neighborhoods in Łódź.

In the center of Piotrkowska, among the Jewish silks and fashion workshops, one opposite the other were located the editorial offices of the pogromist Polish newspaper *Orendownik* and of *Freie Presse*, a Nazi-oriented German paper; on the side, directly on the sidewalk was a kiosk where a gaunt fellow with a gangster's mug hung Streicher's *Der Stürmer* with the screaming headline "Jude verrecke"[11] and a disgusting cartoon. Right nearby on the second floor was located the Club of the Jewish Intelligentsia. Jewish intellectuals and nonintellectuals made their way past *Der Stürmer* and *Der Schwarze Corps*[12] with real or feigned indifference, and only occasionally some unemployed melamed[13] in a tattered jacket, tieless, would freeze with a naïve and nearsighted gaze in front of the antisemitic caricature, ready, it would seem, to ask the ironic, cold vendor, "Aren't you ashamed? How could you?" But all around there were too many display windows with crystal, Framboli chocolate, Van-de-Vega roses, caviar, and wines, and an advertisement for the Rialto cinema—the scent of cakes and black coffee drove away the vision of blood—and nothing remained in the heart aside from a light shadow of anxiety: there is plenty of everything, and everything is at the service of the person with money. You just have to know how to earn enough. On Piotrkowska Street, especially at midday, when the traffic reaches its peak, it is difficult for a Jew to think of anything other than what the next day and hour dictates.

Make a living! Somehow, we'll manage. God will not leave us. Three and a half million Polish Jews, that means something!—Make a living! Behind us are Democracy, Culture, Europe, and America, the working class, and what else?

Make a living!

On the corner of Piotrkowska and Cegielniana, I sat behind the large glass window of the café and beyond the shoulders of the passers-by, I saw the doomed ones.

Let's look with a stranger's eyes—such as those of a peasant or an English tourist. Narrow chests, gaunt, sinewless, deformed bodies, rounded backs, impotent and crushed, weary, wrinkled faces, a jumble of straggly ears, crooked noses, twisted lips, awkward or too fussy and restless movements. Crooked shoulders, everyone squints, looks back, or runs forward without looking

---

11. "Death to the Jews!"

12. Official weekly paper of the Nazi SS.

13. Teacher in a Jewish "heder."

ahead, and in every case, a screw is loose. Limping, bobbing figures, broken, worn down, wobbling people, tired before they were born, sickly and tragic eyes, black kapotes, the coat of idleness, flat black hats, the sign of the ghetto, women without charm, men without pride or calm strength. The human stream rushes about and gesticulates, laughs too loudly, reacts too sharply, and in some way is always defective, unrestrained, unbalanced, beyond the limits of harmony and fullness of life: an unfortunate product of three factors: the large city, Jewish poverty, and the Slavonic-German intersection, where all influences are transformed into deviations, mental instability, and a lack of equilibrium, constant looking over one's shoulder, imitativeness, or wild sectarianism.

Enough! I dropped my pen. These people died—did I have the right to judge them? Can one judge the process of dying? But they began to die even before Hitler's arrival. They were ready to fall under the knife or the gas, and all that we could do—we who hated this misfortune and tried to shout something into their deaf ears—was to flee from there—fleeing even without the certainty that the same shock as in Łódź would not repeat itself. Doomed people! The person has not yet been born who could tell the truth about their end, hurl the angry story at their descendants and brothers without choking on his words, covering his eyes with his hand, or turning away.

The person who will dare, who will have sufficient spiritual strength, like Dante, to descend to the underworld and tell how the death of his people unfolded, the loss of the will to life and passion for freedom—let him take as his epigraph the ancient line of Lucretius, the classic image of the *facies hippocratica*, the face of the dying: with the advent of the final hour, the nostrils contracted, and the nose, pointed at the end, became thin; the eyes and temples sank; the lips grew cold and stiffened; the mouth gaped; and the skin on the forehead tightened.

In the summer of 1946, while awaiting my departure from Łódź, I began writing a story about what had happened in this city in the last months before the Holocaust. The very first pages, however, destroyed my mental equilibrium, and I felt that it was not yet the time for this truth.

4

The End of Maria

IN THE SUMMER of 1946, Warsaw was a chaos of ruins while Łódź was on the verge of a Stalinist re-education. Nevertheless, Łódź represented a very acute and sudden contrast with Soviet Russia.

During my seven-year exile, I had become accustomed to the sight of women lacking charm or a shadow of coquetry, who went around in boots and male jackets and in winter wore kerchiefs and hats with earflaps. The female workers and prisoners had clipped hair and the morose, gray faces of sexless and prematurely faded Soviet civilian workers. On the streets of Łódź, however, in the summer of 1946, it was always Sunday. People would dance in all the cafés, and the very gait of young women on a clear day on the overcrowded sidewalks seemed to me like a ballet, a miracle of elasticity and suppleness. They all seemed like dazzling beauties. I was overwhelmed by the way they dressed and moved and by the sound of their voices. I was struck by the unfolding spectacle of sunny, bright fullness of life. I was entranced by the carnival-like, triumphal summer of 1946.

Sometimes I would encounter women with powerful hips and uplifted chests, proudly tossing their heads. Like animated statues, they moved in marble beauty, and they looked to me like reproductive machines, live automatons—you drop a coin in the slot and exactly nine months later the apparatus delivers a baby, with mechanical precision multiplied by the generative force of nature. When they smiled in my direction, however, I turned my head to see at whom the smile was directed—I did not think it was for me.

By the porch of a church, I watched the small square, where women entered with empty carts and glowing faces. Children, waving their little hands like swimmers, paddled the air. Young mothers, near whom desire dies away, were leaning over their children. A radiant woman passes by, smoothly carrying her large body, swinging her shoulders, and the flowery silk of her dress shimmers in red and blue, hugging her body down to her strong, golden calves. A girl in a red sweater flies over the square like a bird, lightly touching the ground with her shapely legs, as if borne by an invisible force. The force of youth. I was enamored of her without desire or jealousy. A girl wearing red shoes tests with her feet an invisible wave that approaches her. The wave recedes and surges, and the natural grace of the surf, mirrored in her movements, is repeated. The waves of the sea surround the Łódź square, and it turns into an island inhabited by ghosts. . . . I bit my lips and closed my eyes in order to regain self-control.

I needed to free myself of a memory that adhered like a stain and gave me no peace. It was a camp memory from the time when I had skidded to the lowest point of physical decline. There was no mirror in camp, I did not know how I looked, and I did not care. I saw myself reflected in my pitiful neighbors, hideous goners. I did not shave for weeks, slept in my clothes, and I was disgustingly filthy, like everyone else or even more. For some reason, I happened to drop into the office of a director, a free worker, a pedantically neatly dressed woman. She was sitting at a desk, and I, forgetting myself, walked right up to the desk. She looked at me with undisguised horror and hastily warned me in the middle of the conversation: "Don't come close!"

I was taken aback by the panicked fastidiousness in her expression. I suddenly became aware of the incredible filth of my jacket, unwashed for years, the odor of the rags clinging to my body, all of my unbelievably repulsive appearance. I was stung to the quick. This was not the cry of a boss: no, it was a woman's involuntary reaction to my coming two steps closer to her desk than she could bear. Having returned to the barrack, I felt like a leper, like Job with a shovel on a stinking pile of manure. I looked at my hands as if they were not mine. Is it possible that these very hands once touched others . . . and did not repel them . . . on the contrary . . . ?

With a frozen gaze, I fell into a reverie. I recalled an episode from a time when no one told me "Don't come close."

The Savoy Hotel. The very same hotel, not far from the square. Then it had a different name, but it was the same six-story building on a small side street, detached, with a bakery on the corner and a flower vendor at the entrance.

At the time, I lived rather far away, on the outskirts of the city, in a large, bleak apartment that had once belonged to the sausage maker Karpuze. He had gone bankrupt and died, and his widow rented out rooms. The apartment was full of tenants. My student room was the smallest and led directly to a large, carpeted vestibule with mirrors and red wood panels.

The lanky, gaunt landlady, with a despondent face and deep voice as if emerging from a barrel, requested that I pay her directly for the cleaning of the room instead of giving the money to the house cleaner. Her niece did the cleaning; she supervised it and could not allow her to have separate sources of income as this would undermine her authority as landlady and aunt. The widow Karpuze had a particularly glum and sour look when talking about her niece.

Maria was a distant, poor relative, taken directly from the village. I was nineteen; she was seventeen. My experience with women was inversely proportional to my knowledge of Kant (from whom I was inseparable). The Kantian philosophy of space and time stimulated my imagination early on, resulting in a relative decline in empirical and practical knowledge. This was my first year away from my parental home. Maria had a fresh, round face, open and affable. Her face inclined one to trust. It radiated innocence and willingness to obey her elders. Her aunt was too strict with her. Although, pressing her lips, Mrs. Karpuze told me that Maria was mischievous and even very much so, I preferred conversing with Maria than with her aunt. We quickly became friendly.

In conversations with Maria, I limited myself to short replies and remarks, letting her express herself. She complained to me about her aunt, who worked her to death. She would tell me very movingly about life in the village, about her mother and father, a schoolteacher; she was the sixth but not the last child. Our friendship grew stronger in these conversations—we were natural young allies among the grumpy and sullen residents of the apartment. It was completely understood that she would not only serve me breakfast but also sew on missing buttons. She was attractive and merry, always neat and well-mannered and did not arouse any passionate feelings in me. I teasingly called her Cinderella. A prince in a golden carriage ought to come to save her from her Aunt Karpuze. Everything was fine while she would sew buttons on my shirts from the laundry, but once, when she had to sew a button directly under my neck, and she sat down so close to me that her round, rosy cheek, upturned nose, and ash-blond curls almost touched my face, and I felt her fresh, light breath on my cheek, I could not help but cautiously embrace and kiss her.

We sat on the little couch in my room. Behind the door, we could hear the landlady's deep, bass voice. Without dropping the needle and thread from her hand, Maria whispered very seriously: "You mustn't!" She continued to sew, but her eyes were laughing. I also started laughing and firmly kissed her ruddy cheeks. Her lips slid along mine; she quickly finished sewing, tore off the thread, and ran away. I was very pleased with myself. I got up from the couch smiling. That was enough for today.

But at that minute, the door opened, and Maria again appeared on the threshold. This was unexpected but even more unexpected was the expression on her face—shining, jubilant, full of an inner laughter which she could hardly hold back. All my life I had never seen such an expression of expectation and joyful astonishment on a face. She stepped toward me, opened her mouth in agitation, and hesitated. She had not prepared what to say.

"I . . . wanted to ask. . . ."

I was silent and waited. She said, looking straight into my eyes: "Don't you need something else sewn on?"

Then I embraced her with all the strength of my philosophical youth, bogged down in transcendental analysis and the antinomies of pure reason. I forgot about the landlady and the door through which someone could enter momentarily. A minute later, I heard her agitated whisper: "Away from my legs!" and old lady Karpuze, as if she saw through the walls, began to call from the dining room: "Maria!" She partly tore away from me, clinging, not clinging, breaking away, but I knew beyond doubt that everything that I was doing was as desirable and pleasing to her as to me. In five minutes we ceased pretending or fearing each other, and for the first time, I addressed her with the familiar form of "you."

Nevertheless, I was not sure how I should behave toward her. I felt much older than she and more responsible for my deeds.

A few days later, I was returning home from a meeting where the discussions had dragged on until three o'clock in the morning. On the way, a light rain fell, soaking me, although I paid no attention to it. I walked on the damp asphalt, the collar of my summer coat pulled up, thinking about anything but Maria. I had completely forgotten about her.

When I reached the third floor, I put my key in the door, but it had been locked from inside with a chain. How annoying! Usually, the last one to return in the evening would lock the door with the chain, but until then, I had never been the last. The person who had returned before me that evening had not thought to check whether I was home. I had to ring the bell! I was embarrassed about waking people up at night, but I had no choice. I started to ring; I rang for a long time, but no one responded. The house, full of people, was sleeping. I began to knock, to break down the door. No answer. A quarter of an hour later, I was still standing on the landing, and I had begun to despair. These people were sleeping so soundly! Despite the hellish noise that I was making, my fellow tenants were sleeping like the dead. Old lady Karpuze was sleeping in her room with open doors that led into the dining room. And there was no way of reaching Maria: she slept in an opposite, distant part of the apartment. Her room was right next to the kitchen, at the end of a long corridor past the dining room.

Convinced that no one would open the door for me, I went down to the courtyard and climbed up the back steps. In the darkness, I counted the floors. At the third floor, I knocked on the kitchen door. At that moment, from behind the door, a frightened girl's voice could be heard: "Who's there?"

"Open fast!" I said impatiently.

"But I'm not dressed," whispered the voice behind the door. That was simply an awkward remark.

"Open the door already!"

Upon entering the kitchen, in the darkness, I saw her delicate, slim figure through the thrown-over housecoat. She was waiting for me. And again I embraced her, but my coat was in the way. My coat was saturated with urban dust and smelled of the rain. In my overcoat, I felt uncomfortable and strange embracing a girl who still radiated the warmth of the bed. I felt her firm breasts through the coat, and I discovered something that disconcerted me.

I had grown up in a city, and the only nightgown that I considered natural for a woman was made of elegant, light silk. I was not familiar with anything else. On movie screens, in store windows, and in the circles to which I belonged, that was the only kind. Pajamas came into use several years later. Hugging Maria, I felt that she was wearing a gown of rough, coarse material, home woven linen from her parental home in the Polish village. I was embarrassed. I heard her heart beating through the rough fabric, and she stood motionless. . . . Suddenly, I felt that not for anything in the world would I be able to touch this adolescent's chaste and absurdly long clothing. I left her and returned to my room through the corridor and dark dining room, past Auntie Karpuze's open bedroom door. But the thorn had already entered my flesh. I was unable to rest or sleep the entire night; I was agitated. The next day, I firmly resolved to drive this nocturnal meeting from my head. I succeeded during the first half of the day, when I was away from home, but (I dined at the landlady's) my feet carried me to a store on the main street, where I bought a silk nightgown. It was neither the most expensive nor the cheapest, pale rose, very attractive looking, such as I knew that Maria did not possess. Given my modest student budget, this was a significant expense. The saleslady approved of my selection and taste.

When I came home, I threw the package onto the table and called for Maria: "This is for you," but she did not touch the package. Seeing that she

was embarrassed and did not dare take the gift, I took the package, brought it
to her room at the end of the corridor and threw it on the bed.

I imagined the expression on her face when curiosity would finally impel
her to open the package. Would she return the gift to me? Or try it on?

Guests gathered in the evening in the landlady's dining room. They were
playing cards. I lay down in bed early and read, waiting for the guests to disperse so that I could cross the dining room on my way to the bathroom. I customarily bathed in the evenings. The line for the bathroom in the morning
was too long.

Guests were rare in this house, but precisely that evening there was a big reception with cakes, flowers, and noise: it was the landlady's birthday. I waited
patiently. After midnight, the farewells began, the good-byes in the hallway,
then the noise of chairs being moved and dishes washed. When everything
became quiet, I crawled out of bed and went to see whether the water for the
bath had cooled.

The bath, however, was excellent; I sat in the water, and at first, I still heard
steps in the corridor and the voices of the landlady and Maria. Then all the
sounds grew quiet. Silence ensued.

I dozed, lying in the hot water. Thousands of thoughts passed through
my mind. I lost my sense of time. The silence swelled around me. I was the
sole person not yet sleeping in the entire apartment. The bright electric
bulb shone above my head in a double glass casing. Suddenly, I woke up
and opened my eyes: drowsiness had overtaken me so imperceptibly that
for the first second, I did not know where I was. The mirror was clouded
over, but I was not looking for anyone there. Throwing a robe on my damp
shoulders, cautiously, trying not to make any noise, I entered the dark
corridor.

Before I managed to close the bathroom door behind me, immediately,
in one brisk movement, the door from Maria's lighted room opened. She was
standing on the threshold in a ray of light, smiling wordlessly. Immobile, like a
mannequin in a store window, she modeled her new, genuine silk nightgown,
the first in her life. Rapture shone on the girl's face, and she looked at me as if
into a mirror, rounding her bare arms.

I immediately lost my head. Still damp from the bath, I immediately dried
off. Between me and her there was nothing but fine, smooth silk, full of dim
reflections and tender shadows.

I approached and touched her. I turned off the light behind her shoulders
and closed the door of her small room. We lay down next to each other on her
narrow, hard bed, and then I felt that she became heavy from fear.

She began to say strange things in a subdued voice, as if something had constricted her throat. I was afraid of being the first in Maria's life. I began to calm her cautiously, like a child to whom one brings new food. "You'll see how good this is . . . just try, then you yourself will ask for it. . . ."

"Maria, you really never slept with a man?"

In the same agitated whisper, she told me what had happened in the village when she was sixteen . . . how awful it had been . . . how she had wanted to kill that man . . . wanted to break his window with a stone . . . and never again since that time, never. . . . I immediately stopped listening to her.

It was all the same to me. Even if she was lying, it didn't matter. You can lie in love with words, thoughts, feelings, but the body never lies. At least that is what I thought.

But if the body does not lie, that does not mean that its truth is always fully accessible. Sometimes it is like deep water, into which the swimmer dives on a hot day, and upon returning to the shore, feels just as if he had not entered the water. I was constrained and restricted by the close presence of the widow Karpuze. On the following morning after that accidental and hasty encounter, I felt deeply dissatisfied. What could be more humiliating than the necessity of glancing at every door in an apartment full of strangers? Or more absurd than a nocturnal journey across the dining room past the open doors of the madame?

In the morning, as always, Maria knocked and brought in a tray with breakfast. Her face showed nothing but imperturbable, cherubic clarity. Perhaps I had dreamed yesterday's happening? I looked at her inquisitively. "How do you feel, Maria?" She raised her trusting, artless eyes at me and said: "Fine . . . only I have a little pain here, and she placed her palm on her thigh with an unexpected movement, full of calm intimacy.

The next Sunday was a day off for Mrs. Karpuze's niece, when she was permitted to be away from the house after dinner. I left the house early in the morning and took a room in a hotel. I chose a hotel in the center of the city that was large and full of people, where no one noticed who entered or left. I chose the Savoy, the very same hotel where, twenty-five years later, I rediscovered Europe. Until midday, I remained in my room; I prepared fruit, cake, and even wine. Then I returned home and told Maria that after dinner, I would expect her as my guest in the Savoy Hotel, room 413. The effect, however, was unexpected: Maria was frightened. She had never been in an elevator, never been in a hotel, and my explanations frightened her even more. She refused. We almost quarreled. I turned away, gloomier than a cloud. Seeing my cruel disappointment (tears welled in my eyes), Maria relented. We decided that I would wait for her at the entrance to the hotel and would take her to room 413.

Maria appeared from around the corner at 3:05. She walked slowly and hesitantly, barely moving her feet, and peering into the distance. She was dressed to the teeth: a hat, veil, and white gloves up to the elbows. The gloves, evidently, came from Madam Karpuze's closet. In her hand she held a handbag and modest package, which, I guessed, contained the pale rose silk nightgown. Altogether, it was very touching, but I asked her to remove the gloves so as not to attract attention.

We entered the lobby and went up in the elevator, pretending that we did not know each other. The dark, empty corridor was carpeted. I felt as if this was not only the first time in my life, but also the first time in the history of the Savoy Hotel, in the history of mankind, in the history of the world.

To this day, I do not know whether Maria was a depraved, scheming girl, and this was no more important than a dull sediment at the bottom of a glass of clear water: I drank the water and did not touch the sediment. She was as overwhelmed and enthralled as I, even more so because during the six hours that we spent together in the large, nickel-plated bed, as if in a boat that had been torn away from its mooring by a storm and carried to the open sea, she did not touch the food; she did not drink anything, and she hardly spoke. I recall the marvelously supple movements when she let me unfasten her hooks and shoulder straps—and the brief naps during which her body on the edge of the bed gave off a warm, animal-like warmth that was so unusual and strange to me. It seemed as if she was sleeping, but the minute I stretched out my hand and lightly touched her shoulders, she immediately turned toward me so obediently and precisely, as if we were one ideal mechanism, whose parts a great craftsman had fit together.

Dusk came; it was evening and the pale electric bulb lit up beneath the ceiling. We discovered that it was 9:15 p.m. It was time to return. The bed looked terrible. The pillows and sheets formed swirls, as if some prehistoric dinosaur had chewed and swallowed them and spit them out. Maria took her time, carefully getting dressed in front of the mirror, combing her hair. Then, ready to leave, she came to me and leaned over the bed where I was lying, like God after the sixth day of creation.

She kissed me and said very simply:

"Thank you."

I did not respond, but a minute later, when this word reached my consciousness, I experienced something like an electric shock. Until then, I knew only theoretically that in love and via love an extension of one's life opens up to another life. This "thank you" filled me with immeasurable pride, as if I had passed the first real test of my life.

In the labor camp, many years later, when another woman said to me "Don't come close," just as instinctively and directly as Maria had said her "Thank you," it was a sign that I again had fallen out of the circle of normal people. That "don't come close" wiped out Maria's "thank you" and made me an outcast. All my years in Russia, I carried it inside me like a stigma until, in the summer of 1946, fate brought me to the very same Hotel Savoy, and I saw this as a stage of my return to the West, to freedom; like Mayakovsky, that summer I waited for the return of Maria.[1] All the floors and corridors of that building had been trodden by her feet. I awaited her impatiently, as I had many years ago, despite the obviousness, despite the dead burden of years, and the impossibility of repeating anything from the past. . . .

The windows to the garden were open. The light hum of the fan's movement reached my ears. On a low podium a violinist in a tailcoat was standing. The white front of his shirt blended with the silhouette of the amber-gold violin. To be precise, it was the color of strong tea. At the first crystal-clear sound, I placed my hand on the hand of my companion and gave her a small key.

The violinist was playing a sonata by Handel. The accompaniment followed on the side like a shadow, but soon a dialogue developed between the violinist and the instrument. He was like a rider, leaning toward the horse's neck. And, how marvelous! The duo turned into a trio when the melody split and the soul of the violin was lifted above the passionate monologue of the sonata.

Turned at an angle, the violin began to grow and spread . . . its coves and bays, expanding, seemed to fill the entire hall, and the bow of the violin moved like a sail into the open sea, shimmering in the sun with a gleaming edge.

In the intermission, my companion got up and left soundlessly. I remained alone, my head lowered. At ten o'clock, I went to the hotel dining room on the first floor. We were all dining together for the last time at the round table in a niche, before my departure.

Malwina, my friend's sister, a large blonde with a sleepy, calm look, had survived the war precisely because of the tranquil, undisturbed expression on her face. She did not need to pretend; she had been that way from birth. In the Polish family where she spent the period of the German occupation as a housemaid and where they would not have hesitated to turn her in to

---

1. A reference to lines in Mayakovsky's poem "A Cloud in Trousers," where the poet is feverishly awaiting the arrival of his lover Maria. She arrives to tell him that she is getting married.

the police if her secret had been discovered, they used to say, "Look, no one would take our Zosia for a Jew! Jewish women are all so nervous and agitated, but our Zosia, although her face is similar, look how she behaves!"

Malwina's friend Krystyna was eighteen years old. She was a charming, porcelain-skinned beauty with large, shining eyes. The gleam of those eyes saved Krystyna when a German gendarme stopped her on a street in Warsaw, asking "What are you carrying in your handbag?" She was carrying illegal proclamations of the patriotic alliance.[2] Krystyna raised her eyes and with a most coquettish smile showed him her bag with the proclamations at the bottom. The gendarme gallantly let her go without checking.

Nevertheless, Krystyna had her tragedies—not one but three: in the past, an unhappy love at age sixteen for an older man, who did not take her seriously; a terrible, painfully concealed fact that her mother was an ethnic German who had fled to Germany after the war; and her father, ultimately, took up with another woman. Krystyna left her father's house and even tried to poison herself. She took a large but insufficient dose of a barbiturate, and lived. Her heart, however, was damaged; we all felt sorry for Krystyna and admired her angelic beauty. The young student Jacek particularly admired Krystyna and wanted to introduce her to his mother, which Krystyna avoided. Jacek had a pleasant voice and performed on the Łódź radio station. When he sang, Krystyna would sit near the receiver and listen with a divine expression on her face. This did not prevent her, however, from breaking the heart of the faithful Jacek and even telling Malwina laughingly that Jacek yelled, grasping his head and rolling his eyes: "You are inhuman! It's the Jews, with whom you associate, who made you so cruel!"

On that farewell evening, we drank more than usual. I was sad that I would never again return to this country, but I would have been even sadder if I had to remain there.

"Each of us must choose his or her own happiness and unhappiness, good and evil; don't let anything be foisted on you; fight. Krystyna believes in God. It is not enough to believe, you must love. But I cannot love that which is above our good and evil, our understanding and anxieties. I love Krystyna because she has the face of an angel and the body of a dancer. Each of your movements is a dance, but you don't know this. If you learned to control the movements of your body, you would become famous. I can read every movement of your heart on your face. If you controlled the movements of your

2. Union of Patriotic Poles (Zwiazek Patriotow Polskich, ZPP) organization formed in March 1943 to unite Polish refugees in the USSR under the communist banner.

face, what a marvelous actress you could become! How frightening it is that we do not have control over our bodies!"

Krystyna smiled modestly and sat motionless, like someone who has put on ice skates for the first time and knows that she cannot avoid falling on the ice.

"When I leave here, I shall write a drama about the life of a person who wanted to be a leader. When he did not succeed, he became a teacher. When his students rejected him, he wanted to be merely a comrade, a good friend. And in the end, he remained alone."

"How sad! And what became of him?"

"He defended himself the best he could. His attitude to life was one of defense. He was like a swimmer in a boundless sea. His fate was to drown in a hostile element. While he still had strength, he floated on his back, gazing at the sky. Above him—the sun, beneath him the cold deep. But for one short minute, closing his eyes, he feels so good and calm under the sun."

"Had I been in your place," said Malwina, "I would have written something not connected to anyone, only for myself, for my other self. I once dreamed that I was lying on the bottom of a deep stream, at the bottom of a river, separated by a thick wall of water from the world and people. The dead weight of the water pressed me to the sandy bottom. I saw the play of shadows and light around me and in me for the last time before dying out forever. I knew that I would die along with everything in, around, and above me. And all this was unnecessary, but it existed! Existed! Existed! As in a haunting dream that so resembles reality that you do not notice when you wake up. . . ."

In parting, I cautiously kissed Krystyna's smooth, rosy cheek. She looked at me reproachfully, and we both laughed. In the publishing house where she worked as a typist, the young authors, the rising stars of Polish literature, called her their mascot and kissed her for good luck when they entered the office. Krystyna resented it, but her protests did not help. I myself was not even a Polish author and had no chance of being published in her press.

Carrying a tray with a nocturnal glass of tea, I went up to the third floor. It was eleven o'clock at night. I looked around the door of my room, but there was no one to open the door for me. I put the tray down on the floor and cautiously turned the handle of the unlocked door.

The lamp at the head of the bed was lit. My companion was sleeping, her curly, golden-haired head placed high on the pillow. Her pale, thin lips were luminous like coral. The face of a doll. Her hands were lying on the blanket.

She was sleeping soundly. Here in this room, she felt "better than at home." That is what she said to me when I brought her there for the first time after a chance acquaintance at a movie theater. Then she had entered the room with ceremonial politeness, calmly, unhurriedly looking around, and she said, "Do you live here? This is a very good room, better than mine," and she sat down in the armchair by the window.

I called and ordered tea. Then I asked her how long she could stay.

"At six o'clock in the morning, I must leave," and she was silent for a moment: "You won't have any problems because of me?"

"I have been living here for a long time. No problems. I have special rights."

"And you often invite women so late?"

"No, my dear, you are the first."

"Over the entire summer, the first?"

"Oh, no, for seven years." She laughed.

"What happened to you for seven years?"

We continued our conversation in bed, gradually getting used to each other. Gradually she overcame her uncertainty. Learning that I was a foreigner, she noted, "I, too, was abroad once, at relatives in Dresden."

"Really? You mean, you are German?"

She became frightened. "So what? I don't hide that I am German."

"That means we can talk in German. It is a long time since I spoke German."

In that first post-war summer, it was not good to be a German in Łódź. She told me her story. She was born and spent her entire life in Łódź. Her late husband had been a Pole, a mechanic. Her child died a year ago. Her name was Maria. Now she was working as a salesperson in a store. The other salespeople were not supposed to know that she was German. The storeowner knew; of course, he had to know.

"I have not touched a woman for seven years. I'm afraid I'm out of practice," I joked.

She said very seriously, "No, you're not."

Late at night, I turned on the light and took a book from the night table. I read for an hour, feeling her even, warm breathing behind me. Occasionally, I extended my hand and touched her. Peace, silence, calm. Then I fell asleep, firmly embracing her. Her right breast was in my left hand.

She woke up at six o'clock in the morning. We agreed to meet the next day.

On the second night, she suddenly burst out crying. There is no city more terrible than Łódź. In the whole world, there is no city more terrible. Could I take her with me abroad? It doesn't matter where. She is a good housekeeper. She would be faithful to me. She would work.

I barely calmed her. "You don't know anything about me. You are still young; everything will work out."

Indeed, she could not know anything about me. She also did not know that this, our third meeting, would be the last. In the morning, I would travel far away, to the West, and even farther. Everything was ready, the suitcases were packed, the farewells were done. In the final hours, she alone remained with me.

In sleep, her body was hard and firm, like a statue. Slowly she woke up, came to life, and warmed up. A spark ran through her body. Her knees and shoulders trembled. Flexibility, resilience returned to her limbs. In the darkness, she opened her eyes and sighed.

In the morning, when she was leaving, I detained her.

"Don't you need some money?"

"Money is always needed. But I prefer that you buy me something... later... when you want to."

"Buy it yourself. Open the desk drawer. The money is on top."

"How much?" she asked, finding a heap of bills.

Lying in bed, I looked at her for the last time. "Take half."

"But that's too much."

"Keep it with you. I might lose it at cards."

"No, no!" she said. "Then it's better I take it."

In leaving, she turned around: "Will you call me today?"

"Not today and not tomorrow," I said, drifting off to sleep. "I am going away... to Warsaw." "For a long time?"

But I was already sleeping. The door closed behind Maria. In my dream, I saw her carrying her head held high, slowly, with dignity, descending the steps of the wide staircase, walking across the carpeted lobby, past the sleepy guard. On the empty street, she is greeted by the gray dawn, which is so out of keeping with her evening appearance and dress.

The end of Maria. *Finis.* An end to old insults and accounts, to old passions and emotions. The start of new paths and excitement, new joys and disappointments.

5

September 1946

EARLY IN THE morning on August 29, 1946, friends accompanied me to the airport in Warsaw. I belonged to the group of refugees to whom Poland had temporarily granted the "privilege" of emigration. Many at that time envied me, knowing that I was traveling to the West; I was crossing the border separating two worlds. When people in the hotel where I had spent the entire summer—the room cleaners, waiter, and guard—learned about my departure abroad, they took turns sighing about my happiness ... you could think that they were foreigners in their own country, forcefully riveted to their place.

I recalled the farewells five months earlier at the Slavgorod factory in distant Siberia. Then, too, there had been the same parting looks and sighs: "The Poles are getting out." When we fortunate ones with Polish documents in our hands hypocritically regretted that we could no longer bask in the mighty sun of "Stalinist freedom," the workers only smiled with a silent glance that said they understood us and were sure that we understood them just as well. Only one party member, privy to secrets, consoled us then: "Don't worry! We shall follow in your footsteps; we shall meet again. . . ."

All those who were accompanying me were preparing to leave Poland soon themselves, and that morning, they rehearsed their upcoming departure. They remained in a crowd behind the barrier, and I felt their eyes on my back when the small cluster of passengers walked out onto the airfield toward the plane.

People showed us the way, waited for us, inviting us: "This way, please." The plane was basking in the rosy glow, but it was an illusory calm, a minute before take-off, and the steady hum of the motors intensified, making our hearts beat faster and causing us to lower our eyes in order not to reveal our inner anxiety.

We entered an American transport plane hastily adapted for travel to Paris. Benches lined the walls on both sides under the round little windows;

in the middle stood a heap of baggage. The lady sitting next to me was flying to her husband in Bolivia; one could hear English and French spoken. The plane had barely taken off when a ruddy, good-natured American pulled out a box with salted almonds and shared them with his neighbors. I sat uncomfortably, on the side, my eyes glued to the window.

The asphalt lines of the air strips gleamed in the bright sun. The land was divided into colored squares. A toy-like train appeared in view, crawling like a little worm, and I saw both the station from which it departed and the one to which it was headed.

An hour passed . . . and from one end of the horizon to the other stretched the gleaming, narrow ribbon of the Oder River with its sandy shoals. The Polish border. Only now was I truly free. We flew over Frankfurt on the Oder, and I recalled that the last time that I had passed through that city was eighteen years ago. The "Soviet adventure" was over.

"I'll even cross myself with my left leg if they let me out alive," said the work boss Zelemotkin, a pot-bellied fan of pancakes in the snowy camp.

"Farewell, Zelemotkin!"

WE WERE SUPPOSED to fly nonstop to Paris, but after two hours, we landed in the Landsberg airport, about 25 kilometers outside of Berlin. The massive buildings constructed in the Nazi era remained intact. I was still in the Russian occupation zone. Soviet army uniforms surrounded us. While the plane refueled (the operation took two hours), we walked across the broad airfield to a restaurant. We stopped near a guard with a high-cheek-boned Mongolian face.

"Where are you from?"

"Near Kazan."

Someone pointed to a worried-looking German cleaning woman who was dragging a broom and buckets past us. "Are the German women here good?"

The Tatar spit: "Damn them! They are all infected."

"That one, too?"

He squinted and smirked: "No, this one is all right. . . . She is clean. . . ."

That's what befell Germany from the war.

We entered the restaurant, where the German waiters bustled around the young Soviet lieutenants. The latter behaved with unbelievable dignity, "putting up a good front." I looked at them with the sympathy of a person who not only appreciated their external deportment of victors but also understood what no foreigners comprehended: all the suppression and mistrust of children of Soviet Chukhloma[1] and my former Slavgorod (in the starving steppe) in an alien and difficult environment.

My traveling companions were extremely indignant: the restaurant at the Landsberg airport accepted only German marks and Soviet rubles. Their dollars and pounds sterling were useless here. I was not yet hungry and did not have any money with me, but suddenly, I discovered in my pocket what none of the European passengers could possibly have: seven Soviet rubles. I had accidentally kept them from April, from the Siberian transport.

These crumpled little papers were of no use in Russia. One could barely buy a little roll at the Slavgorod market for seven rubles. But here the Soviet ruble had value! The victorious ruble! I ordered breakfast—an omelet, coffee, butter . . . and to the waiters' surprise, I proudly paid with seven Soviet rubles. But there was not enough for beer. . . . I asked the young German woman at the buffet to bring me water. Two clean, neat, cordial girls immediately brought me one glass. I looked at their rosy faces. From lack of practice, I had trouble speaking German. I could not pull myself together: I am in Germany! In front of me is post-Hitler Germany, like the earth after the flood, full of ruins, sinister ghosts, and sprouts of new life. Yesterday these girls were in the *Hitlerjugend* [Hitler youth organization]; what new *Jugend* group awaits them tomorrow?

The plane took off. The movie performance continued but the magic screen could not contain the aerial expanses. In front of my eyes, the geographical atlas turned into a flourishing world in which I was a spectator, participant, and contemporary.

We flew over Germany, bypassing large cities, and nowhere were traces of war visible. What richness, population density, and variegated landscapes! The green hills and forests alternated with picturesque towns and villages. Church towers, the tiled roofs of homes, gardens, and fields were intertwined with roads and rivers. The lakes reposed like mirrors in precious frames. Everything exuded an indestructible peace, calm, and contentment. This country was so evidently better off than Poland, so incomparable to the Russian wilderness and monotonous plains, and yet it was precisely from here, from this blessed fullness and strength, that misfortune had spread over the world.

I recalled my former German friends who had betrayed me, who had voted for Hitler, whose hand I could not shake were I to meet them—what happened to them? What was their place now in Germany over which I was

1. Reference to a small town in the Russian north, i.e., the backwoods.

flying? Where are you now, dear auntie Hedeke, who would not take money from the poor Jewish tenants, but later on...? Where is the kind Fraulein Rohr from Dresden, the rhythmics teacher, who spent years with us in Poland and then ... and the mixed families of former friends, whose children must now be young adults, if they remained alive ...? My thoughts moved on to the helpless, meek people who, undoubtedly, had been taken away to their deaths; my thoughts whirled around, froze, dissipated, died out.... And suddenly I saw the Rhine and far away to the side, the towers of the Cologne cathedral. Already? So soon!

Westward! Westward!

OUT OF THE abyss, from the kingdom of the dead night, traversing the shadows of the past to beautiful, luminous France, a country which itself had suffered but was not guilty of the drab evil or the gloomy barbarity of its neighbors. How long had I been waiting for this border, as if there really were a border in the world between the kingdoms of Good and Evil. No matter how many times I told myself that there is no such border on the map, that it passes, indistinctly, through a person's heart and not on the earth—for me this was the threshold of freedom. Now we were flying over the white little houses of French cities; the sun started to set when we began to descend over Paris, over the city about which I had spoken so much with my camp friend Oleg.

Oleg was the son of the former Soviet envoy to Paris, later a professor in Tashkent. As a schoolboy, he had spent two years in Paris, and he loved that city. By the bonfire in the open field under the northern autumnal sky, he told me how his father took him to dine with the distinguished Professor Langevin. The professor volunteered to initiate them into the secrets of French cuisine, bringing them to the gourmets' inner sanctum. There the dishes were prepared in front of the diners and served on dozens of small plates. The envoy praised this. Later, when he was alone with Oleg, he asked, "Well, how did you like it?" Oleg replied decisively, "I would trade all forty dishes for one bowl of buckwheat groats." His father laughed: "Oleg, you are right."

"Farewell, Oleg, farewell, buckwheat groats!"

Paris was spread out before us in indescribable beauty; the giant city unfolded over hills, and Le Bourget airport came in sight with dozens of airplanes on the airfield, with the ant-like bustle of machines and people around them. We made a smooth landing, the plane rolled and rounded a corner, and then a signal man ran toward us with a flag, indicating where to stop.

That's it! We have arrived. I descended and walked with the Bolivian lady across the field to the terminal; suddenly, from the side, behind the barrier, someone rushed about, waving his hat and crying out. . . .[2]

It was Sanya, my Alexander, Vusya's brother,[3] whom I had not seen for eight years (since 1938)! Now my nomadic existence came to an end: the first contact with family. Sanya, if it is possible, had grown younger during those eight years!

After the formalities, we got into the car—an excellent make! "My car," noted Sanechka modestly, and twenty minutes later we were in the city, which is comparable to Łódź as Łódź is to Slavgorod.

Half an hour later, Alexander brought me to Faubourg Poissonière and Nina hugged me. I was speechless.

Although Sanya's wife Nina had turned gray as I had, she was the same as she had been seven years ago (in May 1939, we parted in Tel Aviv), and we talked until late at night. They gave me two letters that Vusya had written to me back in July.

One could write for a year about our dear Sanya and not tell everything. Suffice it to say that during the German occupation, he did NOT register as a Jew, which saved his life; he participated in the Resistance, accomplished miracles, supplied London with information, indicated where to bombard German airfields, and personally ignited a gas depot. Voilà! He played with death, was arrested, but I shall not relate all his heroic deeds.

That evening I did not leave the house. These were the first relatives whom I met after eight years. Each of us had more to relate than it was possible to express. I was overwhelmed, dumbfounded, in a state when agitation does not let you finish a sentence. I had known nothing about my relatives during all those years, and they had known nothing about me.

I gradually came back to myself. I looked at them as from a great distance. How strange! Finally, here were the first people who loved me. Unbelievable! I looked at them from the perspective of the Altai mountains; I smiled my toothless camp grin. My wedding ring was missing. Yet, we were the same people as eight years ago. In those eight years of bondage, I did not experience as much warmth and love as I did that one evening. That, however, was

---

2. The next few paragraphs constituted a very short chapter, "Paris," which is not printed separately in this edition.

3. Sanya—nickname for Alexander; Vusya—Evusya or Eva, Margolin's wife.

only a prologue, only an advance on what awaited me; after all, I was not home yet.

Nina and Alexander's apartment was full of pre-war coziness, solid comfort, the tranquility of past generations: seven rooms, of which three were for an office and four for just the two of them, with a grand piano in the living room. And an upright piano in the study, which contained excellent paintings. A Rodin sculpture on the mantelpiece. Beautiful pictures hung in the living room, where they settled me for the night on a broad couch. The hallway was long and dark, the old parquet floor boards creaked under foot, and there were several side doors on the way to the kitchen. Thick curtains draped the windows. Alexander sat at the piano and played a work that he had composed, and then, for comparison, Bach—exactly as eight years ago. Then they showed me how to turn off the large chandelier and left me alone.

I woke up early the next morning in the living room. I dreamed of Barrack 9. After waking up, for a long time, I contemplated the chandelier, the ceiling, the lowered shades, the wall-to-wall carpet, armchairs with colored upholstery, the grand piano, and a large portrait of Alexander in a silver frame.

THE NEXT MORNING, Alexander went to purchase a ticket for me for a steamship to Palestine. He returned with a long face: there were no places until October or November. . . . This was 1946! Maritime transport was not yet functioning normally.

"Nonsense! I'll fly."

Planes to Lod airport flew via Cyprus. I went to the Egyptian Royal consulate. They received me courteously, but when they discovered that I was a Jew, they refused to give me a visa. The Egyptian government would not allow me to pass through their territory because I was an alien in Arab Palestine. Here for the first time, an echo of that hatred from which I had fled in Siberia and Poland reached me. They were not communists; on the contrary. They were not Nazis. They merely preferred that I remain in the place whence I had come.

My departure suddenly turned into a problem. How to get away from here? Paris was too grandiose for me, too beautiful, too eternal. I strolled along the boulevards and came out on Place de la Concorde. This was not my first visit to the French capital. Once, I had spent a month in the quiet suburb of Clamart, conscientiously following the schedule of a carefree foreign tourist. Much had changed since that time but for me, this city, as before, remained a somnolent bulwark of millennia—in contrast to all Utopias—an earthly, concrete achievement of human genius. I did not believe in any "fall of Paris," nor in any "Paris is burning."[4] Only now, I was in no state to promenade along the Champs Élysées.

I wanted to continue on my way. I wanted to return to that city not from Siberia but from Tel Aviv. I saw its streets with the eyes of one blinded by agitation, by love for everything that this city signified to me. But I could not dawdle. In my imagination, tomorrow was pushing out today. Alexander's living room with paintings by Kisling and Mane Katz was flooded with the azure and sheen of the Mediterranean.

Go! Go! Go! Sail, fly, rush evermore forward, freeing myself of all that dead burden, away from the circle of hate, there to my homeland, where, finally, I would acquire the gift of speech, where I would recall all the forgotten words. . . .

On the third day—it was Sunday—it suddenly turned out that there was an available place on the steamship leaving the next day, Monday, from Marseille to Haifa. They reserved the place for me by telephone, and that very evening I left for Marseille.

The platform of the Gare de Lyon railroad station swam past the windows, with the evening bustle of lights and those who saw the passengers off. I remained alone with a familiar, childhood feeling: again alone, lost in the night, in the enormous world, like a swimmer who fell overboard from a ship into the ocean. This time, however, the ocean was not stormy, icy, and hostile but warm, without waves, and tranquil . . . and the steamship, all lit up, did not sail away, but stood and waited . . . in the Marseille harbor.

I stood for a long time near the window in the empty corridor, looking out into the dark. The train clanged along, slowing down and speeding up; the semaphores indicated the way, and the dispatchers signaled its passing. At stations, it shook, changing tracks, and I heard snatches of conversations that the nocturnal passengers were exchanging, sleepy words, the language of France. I was in the West, the best proof of which was that I could stand by the window, without fear, so carefree and calm! Tomorrow at this time, I would sleep in a warm cabin to the hum of the engines, somewhere along the Italian coast.

A young man stopped near me and glanced inquisitively. He looked like a student. What was interesting about me? I was elderly, tired, and stubbornly silent, looking out into the night. He initiated the conversation.

---

4. References to the novel of Ilya Ehrenburg, *The Fall of Paris*, written in 1940 and awarded the Stalinist Prize and to the novel from 1928 by Bruno Jasieński, *Je brûle Paris*.

"So far away, from Siberia!" he said, when he learned whence I had come and where I was going. "And to Palestine! You have seen many countries. And so, what? Were people satisfied or happy anywhere? Soon I shall travel very far from here, over the sea to Indochina!"

"Why? To fight?"

"No, we have fought enough. We are seeking peace. Perhaps we shall find some country overseas where one can start everything anew. The world around us is crumbling. France is impoverished. France is in mourning. Where will the light come from? From the East? From the West?"

"Nonsense," I said. "You are young. You have a beautiful, rich country. Go to work and don't trust strangers. Don't seek light elsewhere. What kind of light is there in Siberia? There one finds cold and need, and they would be happy to have your worries."

The young man continued to solicit details about Siberia. He was less interested in Palestine. He had, apparently, become thoroughly disenchanted with France. I bid him good night and went to sleep in the compartment.

WE ARRIVED AT Marseille in pouring rain at ten o'clock in the morning. I hurried to the Rue de la République to the steamship office. The place on the steamship was still available. I drew out my Warsaw passport and a heap of French currency to pay for my ticket. But the clerk's face darkened when he saw my passport.

"You are a foreigner? In that case, by law, you must pay for a ticket in foreign currency. Do you have dollars or pounds sterling?"

"No, but if I need dollars, if you please, I shall go now and change money."

"Impossible," said the clerk. "You must pay only in the currency which you brought into France, which you declared at the border when you entered. How much did you bring in?"

"I did not bring in anything, sir. But I have relatives in Paris, and they gave me money."

"In that case, we cannot sell you a ticket."

I got worried.

"Listen. If it is like this, I shall never be able to leave France. Judge for yourself: I am a foreigner to whom you sell tickets for currency noted down in the passport, but if nothing is written down, what am I supposed to do?"

The clerk suggested that it would be better for me to return to Paris and appeal to the ministry.

"But in the meantime, my transit visa will expire! Here is the stamp: 'without the right of extension.'"

"Oh," said the clerk, "what a pity. Will you really have to return to Poland?"

I remarked mildly that I had an immigrant's passport. Without the right of return. If I returned, Poland would not accept me.

"Well, that means, stay," the clerk admitted. "Do you have someone in America whom you could ask to buy you a ticket? That's a way out: America."

I took a room in a hotel on the Rue Colbert, not far from the Cannebière, and after dinner, I went to the office of the Zionist Organization. There they explained to me that I could leave France only with the next transport of refugees, which, in coordination with the French government, the Zionist organization periodically dispatched from Marseille to Palestine. They promised to include me in the next transport but could not say when it would leave. Perhaps this week or perhaps next week.

I remained to wait for a steamship and waited three weeks. The prefecture extended my visa despite the stamp "without the right to an extension." In the Soviet Union, that would not have been so simple. There a stamp is a stamp. For not departing on time, that is for "violating the passport regime" in the Soviet Union, you could receive several years of forced labor in a corrective labor camp, as I had learned in my day. But the French are a carefree people.

I THUS WAS stuck in Marseille, but I did not regret it. It was pleasant to be in a "state of departure" in southern France, in a large port city, which you see for the first time in September when the sky is blue and the streets are flooded with sunlight. A feeling of mindless lightness, dreamy weightlessness possessed me. I knew that this was not for long, but it was the fulfillment of a long-cherished dream. In 1943, in a Soviet camp, I wrote, promised myself, and confirmed:

> *I do not need gold coins or ducats,*
> *Nor family silver.*
> *I do not expect to derive any benefit from the*
> *Society of bankers and magnates.*
> *But if I come home,*
> *I shall feel cramped in my urban apartment—*
> *My habitual and warm corner*
> *Will seem, after a day, like a prison,*
> *And I shall go out to wander freely in the world.*
> *Neither yesterday's affairs nor yesterday's friendship!*
> *Nor the drab web of sleepy days—*
> *I shall not accept job obligations*

Or the ritual associated with them.—
"Reception hours," checking at the doors.
Not for that did I live in captivity for years.
Where an enemy dictated every step,
So as not to desire fierce freedom,
As God desired on the first day of creation.
Marvelous books, hitherto unread,
Enchanting countries not yet seen,
Spring thunderstorms and blues skies in April
Are fervent temptations for me.
My train approached Paris in the morning,
And Sacré Coeur shone in the heights,
I shall again see this city, however,
More beautiful and brighter than in a dream.
More beautiful and brighter and desired
My youth will return to me,
Like a swallow in the aerial ocean
Flying to distant lands. . . .

With these lines in my subconscious, I spent my days on the streets and boulevards, in the cafés where they served coffee without sugar, and every day, I dined in a different restaurant. I learned to eat bouillabaisse and drink wine in water glasses. I drank grape juice at the kiosks that were called *station uvale.*[5] I went to the movies to see Marlene Dietrich and Fernandel.

In the fall of 1946, France was experiencing food shortages, but I did not notice this, as I had more than enough. At midnight, I ate sandwiches on the street and stood in line for roasted chestnuts. I traveled to the Isle d'If by the outer harbor, with the famous fortress in which Mirabeau had been imprisoned, and, if I remember correctly, Portos died, having killed 106 men before his heroic end. I took the elevator to the top of Notre Dame de la Garde and viewed the city of a million inhabitants in the rays of the southern sun and platinum gleam of the sea. I went to Corniche to swim in the sea. I received and wrote letters. I had plenty of patience. I was satisfied with life. Everything that was happening to me seemed like a divine miracle. I had just enough money to wait for the steamship, living modestly and not leaving Marseille, where the signal to board could come any day.

---

5. Kiosks in Marseille specializing in grape juice drinks, which were supposed to have a therapeutic effect.

Naturally, I used my three weeks in Marseille for reading in French. For seven full years I had been cut off from Western culture, from current literature; for seven years I had been nourished by what I could find in the Soviet camp and in the deep backwoods. Now, for the first time, I could get close to the source, and my thirst was indescribable. "Marvelous books hitherto unread. . . ." What had happened in the years of my absence in literature and philosophy? I humbly lifted my eyes to the throne of the wise and meekly extended my hand. In Paris I asked Alexander to give me something new, from the latest works of French thought.

"Existentialism!" said Alexander. I did not know what that was.

Alexander give me two books for the road by an unfamiliar author: a "novel" and a thick volume on "phenomenological ontology": *Being and Nothingness*. The author's name was Jean-Paul Sartre. I read both books in Marseille.

I began to read precipitously, flipping through the pages of the novella in the hope that it would hold my attention. Indeed, my interest was soon aroused.

THERE ARE BOOKS that attract and win over the reader and others that tease and stimulate through repulsion. *La nausée* was a philosophical novel of the second kind. The hero of Sartre's novel, a middle-aged scholar, living in provincial France and writing a historical work, made a discovery, or, one could say, contracted a hitherto unknown illness: he discovered his own existence.

Just as Parmenides, 2,500 years ago, discovered "being," so he discovered the bare truth of his presence in the world. But Mr. Roquetin's existence, like that of his entire milieu, first revealed to him in all its inevitable reality, was the polar opposite of Parmenides's "being": it filled him with horror and repugnance, like the head of Medusa, who destroyed anyone who dared to look at her. Disenchanted with the humanism of the fathers, the hero of the story drops the work that he had started and loses the ability to love or hate; in short, he turns into a living corpse.

All this would have been astonishing if Sartre had depicted his hero's adventures as only his personal experience with no applicability to others. The work, however, is not merely a novel with psychological adventures; it is a kind of introduction to the philosophy of existentialism. Existence, in general, evokes repulsion and fear. People who have not experienced these states simply do not exist properly. They are deceiving themselves.

It is difficult to imagine a book that was less suited to my mental state in Marseille. I was a camp inmate who had escaped from prison to freedom. I needed the bread of freedom, and here was a dish from the French cuisine, Roquefort. In one respect, the first book that I held in my hands after my return to the West did not disappoint me: nothing like it, of course, could be either written or published in those places from which I had arrived.

The entire book was freedom and a quest. But Sartre's freedom recalled death (he himself stated this on occasion), and as for the quest. . . . I tried to imagine what Mr. Roquetin's life was like before he discovered "existence" with all its nauseating reality. I followed the philosophical struggles of Sartre's hero with sympathetic curiosity. *La nausée* seemed to me to be the ridiculous experience of an old bachelor who unexpectedly comprehended what it means to exist in the world. And before that? What "slumber of his soul," what painted decorations hindered him from acquiring this basic knowledge that initiates the true seriousness of life?

IN MY YOUTH, I was full of wonder, hope, expectation, and enthusiasm. My fear of life was the happy fear of an inexperienced lover. I first experienced the nausea of life when I was five years old at the sight of the enormous bare soles of the first corpse that I saw. I then felt a flaming desire to dissociate myself from my own feet, and for the first time, I sensed that this was impossible. I grew from these feet, and I myself was these soles. I was "trapped" in life.

But disgust and fear could never prevail over a child's soul. In reading Sartre's book, I felt not infantile repugnance but indignation. When was this book being written? Before the world war, when Hitler was preparing to conquer Europe and annihilate millions of people in death camps. In those years, an infantile fear of life gripped many people. To some degree, this book was responsible for my mother's death in the ghetto. There was a subterranean link between the mental attitude and the "climate" of this book and the future successes of Hitlerism . . . or of Stalinism. There they did not read Sartre; nor did they deal with his problematics. France's defeat was predetermined in this book . . . and more than that. The philosophy whose starting point was *la nausée*, physical disgust at life, inevitably led to its logical result—moral and political indifference and politically, capitulation to its opposite, that is to brutal mass movements, full of primitive energy, charged with masculine force. Sartre's man who made the "discovery" could evidently continue to "exist" only by relying on something outside himself, on something powerful and victorious . . . to which it was worthwhile to cling: as a child who fears to cross a bridge suspended over an abyss grabs the hand of anyone who crosses without vertigo: "Take me along."

I could picture that "take me," but it was difficult to imagine a movement, revolution, or a counter-revolution that could have need of Sartre.

I opened *Being and Nothingness*. I had been prepared for this difficult and convoluted book by my familiarity with the philosophies of Husserl and Heidegger. The introduction immediately returned me to the atmosphere of the Heideggerian *Being and Time* [Sein und Zeit]. Even the style was similar:

> And because the essential definition of this being cannot be accomplished by ascribing to it a what that specifies its material content, because its essence lies rather in the fact that in each instance it has to be its being [Sein] as its own, the term Dasein, as a pure expression of being, has been chosen to designate this being [Seinden].[6]

Is this not simply and elegantly expressed? But Sartre did not lag behind: "The Being, by which Nothingness arrives in the world, is a being such that in its Being, the Nothingness of its Being is in question. *The being by which Nothingness comes to the world must be its own Nothingness.*"[7]

Wonderful. His own Nothingness! I felt that, finally, I was in the West, where there are proprietors of Nothingness.

Being and Nothingness was a philosophical continuation of *Nausea*. The former is philosophical belles lettres and the latter literary philosophy. It was not easy to make my way through Sartre's analysis; ultimately, each analysis turned into the most tenuous and completely arbitrary spider web, suspended on the border of experience, where the darkness becomes impenetrable, and fantasy and fact become indistinguishable. Sartre's analysis was an expression of freedom, as the author defined it: "the possibility for human reality to exude the Nothingness that isolates it." I began to view Sartre's analysis as an entertaining game of concepts, an eccentric tightrope dance and pure art. I rejected the hope of harmonizing Sartre's world with the one in which I lived, and only after this did reading the book turn into an undiluted delight,

---

6. Martin Heidegger, *Being and Time*, Trans. Joan Stambaugh (Albany: State University of New York Press, 2010), 11.

7. Jean-Paul Sartre, *Being and Nothingness: An Essay on Phenomenological Ontology*, trans. Hazel E. Barnes (London: Methuen, 1969), 23. In the original French: "L'Être parqui le Néant arrive dans le monde est un être en qui, dans son Être, il est question du Néant de son Être: l'être par qui le Néant vient au monde doit être son propre Néant" (Jean-Paul Sartre, *L'Être et le néant* [Paris: Gallimard, 1943], 59).

full of disinterested curiosity. I ceased seeking objective truth in it and found in it a precise self portrait of my contemporary, the son of our harsh epoch.

Precisely in that way and in no other, despairing Western thought had to react to the labyrinth of reality where it had hopelessly lost its way and remained alone in the darkness, alone with itself. Sartre's intellectual experiment began with the distinction between *en soi* [in oneself] and *pour soi* [for oneself]. This initial dualism was unacceptable to me, as I knew that for something to exist "for itself," at the same time it had to be and not only be thought of "in itself." Everything that exists, exists "in itself." *La réalité humaine*, the human reality, also exists "in itself." The terrible confusion of the epoch spoke from Sartre's pages which, in, contrast to Bergson, affirmed the suicidal *élan vers ne pas être* [striving toward nonbeing] and where *le temps se révéla comme chatoiement du Néant à la surface d'un être rigorousememnt atemporel* [the time reveals itself like the shimmer of Nothingness on the surface of a strictly a-temporal being], while the continuity of time is acknowledged as a pure phantom, and where, in the same breath, it is asserted that consciousness does not create anything and that abstraction is necessary for there to be things and a world.

This world was quite simply not the one in which I lived, and I resolutely refused to submit to Sartre's "nonbeing."

In Sartre's eyes, nonbeing—primary and nonreducible—was the precondition for every difference and distinction. I considered "alterity" as a positive sign of being, which any human negation relies upon and toward which it leads. In transiting and disappearing, being does not turn into nothingness (a process for which Heidegger and Sartre respectively thought up the words *nichten* or *néantiser* [nihilate itself]); it merely retreats into the past, to a potential condition. But the potential is not, as Sartre thinks, that which we lack but that which endlessly exceeds the power of our recollection and does not fit into our present and future. It is neither "lack" nor "deficiency" that constitutes the fundamental definition of human existence (which thus is a priori deformed in Sartre's notion) but rather the ability to participate, however imperfectly, in what surpasses the bounds of each separate individual life.

Sartre tried to replace the antithesis "Being and God," which had nourished human thought for millennia, with the antithesis "Being and Nothingness," and, consequently, in his vision not only the integrality of the world but also the integrity of our spiritual life turned into a phantom. Negation took the form of evasion from reality, and the image of "stream of consciousness," operative for two generations of psychologists, was replaced by the image of flight, the fall, the uncontrollable lapse into Nothingness. Face to face with the puzzle of the world, Sartre, with his insurmountable Nothingness, expressed in his own way the impotence and fear, the embittered despair of a deceived son of his century.

I do not know how this philosophy would have affected me in other circumstances, but the Soviet camp years and the experience of spiritual resistance to the distortion of human reality as practiced there made me immune to such philosophizing.

The uniqueness of this existentialism consisted of a racy and reckless pose, which ultimately spread from the everyday and political realm to the spiritual one. The human tragedy was presented as a piquant and light-minded sketch.

> *It is good*
> *When thrown into the jaws of the scaffold*
> *To shout*
> *"Drink Van Huyten chocolate!"*[8]

That same mentality led the political existentialist Mayakovsky to communism, and to his "nowhere other than in Mosselprom"[9] and the philosophical existentialist Sartre to the concept of Nothingness. Pronouncing the word "nothingness" already gives it a positive ontological meaning. There are no "empty" intentions just as there is no intentionality outside of being. I acutely felt the enormous vitality and boldness of Sartre's book, steeped in the energy of thought. The audacity with which the philosopher recycled Nonbeing in order to construct the complex skyscraper of his thought upon it was in complete contradiction to both the thesis of despair and the conception of freedom, understood, ultimately as "that terrible necessity to be free that is my lot."

I did not, however, see any "necessity" in either the author's life, which could have been cut off at any minute by his free choice, or in his thought, which so easily could have been given a different direction. From the moment when I began to peruse the pages devoted to the concrete structure of human consciousness, Sartre's self-portrait ceased to interest me. Neither my love, my passion, nor my vices accorded with this analysis. The interpretation of an alien consciousness as a threat, as something that disrupts the wholeness of my perception of the world, was alien to me, despite the years of persecution

---

8. A quotation from Vladimir Mayakovsky's poem "A Cloud in Trousers."

9. The Soviet food conglomerate in Moscow.

and suffering in a foreign country. I stopped reading it halfway through. Not because I was bored by the evident subjectivity of the pseudo-analyses but because his kind of subjectivity did nothing for me.

I wanted to live! I had just escaped from the abyss, and I was seeking allies, friends, companions in the struggle with real evil. But primarily, I was overwhelmed by a feeling of life in me and around me.

When a person's consciousness is not distorted by illness or vice and is full of things and events, people and others' lives, it enters another consciousness and does not only stand on its threshold—"Everything is in me and I am in everything"—and the world opens up in the intersection of consciousnesses. Philosophy that is unable to indicate how consciousnesses intersect—even through the example of a glance exchanged by two lovers with entwined hands on the boulevard of a populous city—is not worth much. What could this first "greeting" from the West teach me? And how could it help me? How could it help my friends whom I had left in Russia, in the camp hell, and whom it would have been so easy for me to *néantiser* [turn into nothingness] according to Sartre's prescription?

The refrain of the Marseillaise rang in my ears: *Aux armes, citoyens!* The people who composed and sang the Marseillaise, however, believed in the reality of the world, of good, evil, and freedom not according to Sartre. In the substratum of this philosophy, I felt hidden hostile forces, a secret betrayal, an attempt to evade that which obsessed me not as a "phantom of the past" but as an absolute statement, here and now, in me and near me, with me and against me. That which firmly welded me to the world was an incontestable debt and flexible freedom whose bounds I could not even think to deplete with my meager forces.

I felt strength and future possibilities within myself, and it was a source of joy. *Aux armes, citoyens!* Onward to the struggle against indubitable and real evil, without fear of the night's shadow! I was happy to live in Marseille for three weeks, like the son of the gods and a transient guest, foreign and close to everything, an outsider and at home in the intermission between two acts of the universal drama, in the pause between the strokes of the bow at a concert—a swimmer on the crest of an enormous wave that lifted me up from the abyss of death toward people, the sun, sky, happiness, and new trials of still untested suffering.

6

Heliopolis

IN MID-SEPTEMBER 1946, the small Greek steamship *Heliopolis* left the port of Marseille. The ship, with a displacement of about two thousand tons, was heading toward Haifa and carried about three hundred passengers. Among them were Palestinian[1] citizens returning home after vacation or work trips, but the majority were immigrants, refugees uprooted by the recent catastrophe in Europe. For them, this journey was the greatest turning point in their lives, the end of wanderings and the ascent to their homeland. The extreme expression of the mystique of Jewish nationalism, which reaches an almost religious tension, terms the move to the land of one's fathers *aliyah*. *Aliyah* means ascent. The *Heliopolis*, lost in the azure of the Mediterranean Sea, in the bright sun's rays, was one of the ships of the heavenly fleet of Ascent.

The voyage did not cost anything. Jewish organizations paid the fares of immigrants and the expenses of Zionist delegates in Europe. I was the sole paying passenger on that ship, as I did not belong to either of the two categories: I was neither a delegate nor a new immigrant. I was returning home after a seven-year absence, not knowing what my home would look like or in what condition I would find my family. I was happy, but I tried to control my excitement. I was externally calm, like everyone else, although my entire being was full of inner quivering and concealed joy. The preceding seven years had compressed me like a spring, and now I almost felt in my blood the jangle of the bent metallic spiral, similar to the vibration of a running motor.

The small steamship was overcrowded. At night, the people settled down to sleep in the dining room and bar; they spent the day on deck. I was given

---

1. When mentioning Palestinian citizens, Margolin is referring to residents of Mandatory Palestine, a geopolitical entity established between 1920 and 1923 after the defeat of the Ottoman Empire. The British terminated their mandate over Palestine in May 1948.

an excellent place: the cabin of the telegraph operator on the upper deck, near the captain's bridge. It consisted of two tiny rooms: in the first was the radio transmitter; in the second, the bunk of the telegraph operator. Twice a day, a bald, middle-aged Greek sat by the transmitter, tapped on the keys and received and sent radiograms. Lying on the bed, I saw a slice of the sea and sky through the window. The line of the horizon rose and fell calmly; beyond the half-open door, I could see the railing, chaise lounges, and freshly-washed decks. Lying down, I heard the splash of the waves, laughter and conversations, the measured humming of the steamship engine, keeping time with the beating of my heart.

Alone among hundreds of passengers, I drifted into memories, returning to the blessed days when my original journey to Palestine had begun early one morning in sooty, smoky Łódź. In an hour and a half, the "rocket"—a train car—transported the traveler to the capital, where the last formalities before departure were arranged successfully. A feeling of marvelous ease, the sweet, enchanting charm of separation, flight, transition to another world, with different dimensions. The morning of leave-taking from Warsaw, already foreign to me, with its parks, the red trams on Marszalkowska Street,[2] and business-like bustle. The express train leaves at four o'clock in the afternoon, and life becomes a movie in Technicolor played at an accelerated speed. The wonderworking power of the blue booklet with many stamps opens walls and borders, and even the police move back politely and salute. At midnight, we arrive in Lvov[3] and transfer to the silence of a sleeping car, where during the night, full of whispers and lullaby humming, the first travel miracle occurs. In the morning, green ravines, hills, and white train station buildings of Moldavia pass by the train windows.

Henceforth, everything is possible. In Bucharest, we have time to get a glimpse of the Rumanian capital while they attach our car to the evening train "Regele Carol" that is leaving for Constanta. We dine at Victoria Street and write our first postcards from the road. In the dusk, the train carries us to the Black Sea; we cross the River Danube and the starry night wafts a breeze to us from the nearby sea. At eleven o'clock at night, we arrive at Constanta. A small locomotive, slowly touching the tracks with its wheels and clattering on the railway switches, brings our car to the port, where in the inky darkness we see the illuminated body of the sea monster *Polonia* or *Transylvania*. The

2. A main street in Warsaw on the left side of the Vistula River.

3. Now Lviv, Ukraine.

steamship seems enormous at night and the sea truly black. It takes an hour for the passengers to settle down, and many, aroused by the encounter with this novel force of nature, do not lie down to sleep until the ship sails into the open, swelling sea.

The next morning, the mosques of Istanbul rise in the pearly haze. After a long day in Constantinople, during which we made an obligatory visit to Aya Sofya, Büyük Mecidiye Camii,[4] the Blue Mosque, and the Serail[5] with a view to the Golden Horn, drank coffee at the Hotel Takatlian, and saw the Monument of the Republic, we passed through the Bosphorus Strait, above which the crescent moon rose majestically, and the evening star of the Levant shone in the orange glow of the sunset. Our hearts softened and were moved in expectation of future miracles.

Across the Sea of Marmora and the Dardanelles, past the reddish islands of the archipelago, we approach Greece on the evening of the second day. At Omonia Square in Athens, we see the first palms and make the traditional pilgrimage. "In order to grind the marble dust, we climb like squirrels to the Acropolis."[6] There in the marble dust, we, too, find a little stone. As we move farther south, our mood picks up, the joy increases, and at sunset, the youth join hands and dance the hora to the tune of Palestinian songs. The steamship goes farther and farther south, toward the sun of a new life, until finally, on the morning of the sixth day, Mount Carmel—the mountain of the prophet Elijah—appears like a light cloud on the horizon. Looking at the contour of the land, we know that the silhouette of Mount Carmel appeared precisely this way two thousand years ago, when our ancestors left these shores on their way to exile and their eyes caught the outline of the coast for the last time.

Crossing the sea from the old world to a new Homeland is like recovering from an illness. That is how it should be: between the old, corrupt world of sorrow and misery, hatred and injustice, and the new beginning on the land that awaits us like a bride, there lay several otherworldly days of azure sea and sunshine, solitude between the distant sky and the desolate sea—time for everyone to shake off yesterday's dust, purify him or herself, and prepare for the future. This is not a simple change of place or movement in space and time! We broke away from one continent and arrived at another separated by four

---

4. Also called Ortaköy Mosque, an Ottoman mosque built in 1911.

5. Probably a reference to the Topkapi Palace.

6. Inexact reference to a poem by the poet Osip Mandelstam "An American Girl of Twenty": "To crush the sugary marble/ [She] Climbs on the Acropolis like a squirrel (https://allpoetry.com/-An-American-girl-of-twenty-).

seas, as in the fairy tale. The steamship, lost in the watery expanse and the columns of light, sailed and sailed; dolphins danced around it, and behind the hull flowed a broad trail, a foamy road to the edge of the horizon, with diamond splashes, as if a miraculous plowman made a furrow for new planting, and, like a wrinkle, it disturbed the sea's eternally smooth surface for a minute, only to disappear, and along with it our worries about the past and memories of the misfortunes and evil that we had endured.

My journey in September 1946 was entirely different from the earlier one. Again, there was the watery basin, but this time I was covered not with dust but with blood, from feet to head. How do you wash off blood? I read somewhere how the steel was tempered,[7] but how is blood washed off? And the passengers around me were not at all like those young, carefree, happy youths full of life's joy. They were not *halutzim* (pioneers). This was the rearguard, the vestiges of a destroyed army, the last spray and foam of a receding wave. They were returning from afar, from the fires of war and places of exile; many bore the branding of Nazi concentration camps. In this context, the Jewish Palestinians seemed like successful officials of a colonial region. Their gestures and intonations displayed an ironic self-confidence. Their look seemed to say: "Rely on us, don't worry! We know how to take care of you!"

The *Heliopolis* held course toward the East, but for me, it was still traveling westward. For me, only now the West was beginning in earnest. I calculated it not from Paris or Marseille. In my calculation, the road to the West led away from Siberia, from Lake Onega, from the five-pointed star over the camp kingdom. From there, from the tundra and taiga, from the famed forests and blocks of barracks, from university auditoriums and military settlements, a shadow spread over the entire world, and from there a direct line, fractured on the map, led to the West, to Freedom, to the Homeland. My West was where I could finally stretch out to my full height, where no one would force me to lie anymore. Europe, like a continent from which the flood's wave had just receded, lay in filth and ruins, full of monstrous vestiges and memories. The *Heliopolis* had left Europe, and the sea around it was deserted and clean, untouched by human baseness. It was good to dive into its unlimited expanses. It was good for a while to get away from the deafening, millennial clamor and to listen only to one's inner voice. The sea, however, was only a stage on the way to the West.

---

7. A pejorative allusion to the 1932 novel by Nikolay Ostrovsky *How the Steel Was Tempered*, considered a model of Soviet socialist realism and its hero, Pavel Korchagin, the model positive hero who ruthlessly overcomes all obstacles.

On one of the evenings, we passed by Stromboli. A thick fog hung over the sea, and distant clouds reflected the subterranean flame in the depths of the volcano's mouth, which we discerned, looking out in the dark night. My heart contracted as I recalled the pale dawn of the north seen through the barred window of the prison train car, day after day, night after night, traveling toward the east, toward the subterranean prison camp kingdom. Blinded eyes feared the light, the tightly packed car with its human cargo, like a coffin, sunk into the abyss without an exit or name. Now, however, a floating cradle carried us, like newborns; the sea exuded warmth and light, and gradually the icy cold left the heart, and the mind cleared.

How is blood washed away? The ominous nocturnal silhouette of the volcano disappeared behind us, drowned in the darkness of the night, and in bright daylight, we saw the strait between Messina and Regio Calabria. We traveled between Sicily and Calabria, past the populous cities situated in the midst of green mountains, with forests and groves descending to the sea.

That morning, when I sat down at the table in the small bar of the *Heliopolis* in order to write my first article after seven years of silence, a strange, unaccustomed feeling gripped me.

I feared my pen, which, finally, was free. For seven long years, my thoughts had been outlawed, my very silence was illegal. Now I held a pen in my hands as if it were a flag pole. My every word ought to flutter in the wind like a banner. I wanted to return to my homeland with a banner, but that morning I felt a weakness in my fingers, fear in performing the first action of a free person. If I could delay this writing. . . . But I could not wait any longer. I glanced around at my fellow travelers. The *Heliopolis* hummed like a beehive with a sleepy midday sound; children were running on the deck; adults were speaking in calm voices. Nothing disturbed their repose. This calm was transmitted to me: I felt pride and gratitude to fate for having put a pen in my hands. I began to write, without considering for whom I was writing. I wrote above the heads of the peaceful passengers in the bar and on the deck. Like a wireless operator sending a signal on short wave for everyone who will hear it. The *Heliopolis* sailed to the West, to the West of the heart, the West of thought. My words flowed to that very West. It was not a complaint or protest; it was a Declaration. A declaration of independence, my personal Declaration of the Rights of Man and of the Citizen.

I wrote:

Between the fall of 1939 and summer of 1946, I spent almost seven years in the Soviet Union, of which the first was on occupied Polish territory. There I witnessed the process of Sovietization of a conquered country. . . .

I spent the following five years in Soviet hard labor, in the so-called "corrective labor camps." There I understood the secret of the staying power and strength of the Soviet regime.

I spent the final year in a little town in the Altai region, participating in the dull working routine of Soviet people.

I think that I have the right to speak about and to judge that country. "No one knows what a state is like who has not spent time in prison," wrote Leo Tolstoy. I think that no one knows what the Soviet Union is like who has not spent time in a Soviet prison.

I thought to myself: Your every word must be checked and weighed. Is it true that the secret of the Soviet regime's staying power and strength lies in the prison camps? Indeed, such a sentence has the power of a blow to the face, but not to the face of those who created the camps. Words will not affect them. But how many good people will recoil, how many will be offended? What does it mean: the secret of the staying power and strength of the Soviet regime is in the camps? After all, millions of people work in that country not out of fear but in good conscience. Why don't you seek the secret of the staying power and strength of the Soviet regime in their enthusiasm and devotion, in the voluntary discipline of the masses? They withstood the German avalanche. What did you do to help the Russian people and all peoples of the world, including your own, to crush the beast?

Nothing. The imprisonment in Soviet camps of millions of honest, militarily fit people weakened the Allied struggle against Hitler, but, simultaneously, it helped the Soviet regime to survive at a critical moment. If we had all united in a common front of struggle, we would have overthrown both Stalin and Hitler. That is why they kept us in prison. There is no greater demonstration of the power and bestial cruelty than that very ability to imprison and torture millions of people at the very time of a historical hurricane. The existence of camps was and remains proof of Soviet strength. Only the camps endow this regime with staying power, just as a deep hold sustains the hulk of a ship.

Guests from another world, journalists, neutral observers, and tourists travel around the Soviet Union for a month, study its prose and poetry, praise some things and disapprove of others. No one is able to see everything and does not claim to do so. . . . Do they know, however, that the life of this country has a secret? And that the secret, guarded from enemies and friends, lies at the basis of the staying power and strength, at the basis of achievements and fame, at the basis of daily life and holidays, of the laughter and jokes of passers-by, of parades and demonstrations, symphonic music, the latest novel by Leonov or Ehrenburg, children's games in the playgrounds of "parks of culture and rest"?[8]

Was Tolstoy correct when he said that the person who has not done jail time does not know the state? How much could Count Lev Nikolaevich know, sitting in his retreat in Yasnaya Polyana, in the shelter of his enormous fame and popular love? Such people do not need a state, and prison does not frighten them. A person who was never abroad is unable to value a state, just as one who was never ill cannot value good health. Only in Soviet captivity, in a bleak, alien land can one understand what "one's own state" means. One's "own" state, where there is no hand on one's throat, no camp hell, no forced lying. We shall build our home with labor, and, if necessary, with blood, but there will be no slavery in it! No lying! No secrets!

I wrote: "The past seven years made me a convinced and passionate enemy of the Soviet regime. I hate it with all my heart and all my mind. Everything that I saw there filled me with horror and disgust for the rest of my life. I am happy that I am in a situation where without fear, I can openly say everything that I know and think about this regime."

I write these lines on the deck of a ship that carries me to the shores of my homeland. My return to life is a miracle, a genuine resurrection from the dead. What can a person think about who has returned from the grave, from the underworld? Time does not wait. There are things that must be said immediately, without delaying for a minute. I write like a person who has only one day of life left, and on that day, he must say what is most urgent and important! And as fast as possible because tomorrow may be too late!

I thought: How many people have ceased to believe in the word! For the end of things is silence, and they maintain silence to the last day of their lives. What is the most important of all? For me this is simple: to break through the wall of silence behind which people are suffering. End the silence, pour out everything that seethed in the heart. Wisdom is unnecessary if like a spider web it covers all the corners of an uninhabited home. Happiness, too, is unnecessary, if the price of happiness is oblivion.

How many people will turn away from me! But at this moment, I don't care. My duty is to speak. And I know there will be an echo. It is a matter of

---

8. The official name of public parks in the USSR.

honor for me to attain a response, and I know that I shall find friends among free people, and companions will come to help me. There, in the country that I left, people lowered their eyes and looked away. There, together with them, I lowered my eyes and looked away.

I wrote: "Millions of people are perishing in the camps of the Soviet Union."

"You keep on writing and writing," said my neighbor to me, smiling. He was a middle-aged, solid person with a tanned face. He introduced himself as Doctor Falk from Tel Aviv, an administrator in one of the large Tel Aviv newspapers.[9] He exuded benevolence, tranquility, and a good mood. I told him that I was returning from Siberia. This interested him. He began to question me, smiling at my every word.

"Listen," I said to him, "I am in an abnormal state. Have you heard of something called a 'moral affect'"?

"What's that?" asked Dr. Falk.

"Let's say: you meet a beggar on the street. He does not affect you at all. You can put a coin in his outstretched hand or pass by. In both cases, you are not responsible for him. He is none of your business. He is nothing to you. You didn't create this world or its structure in which someone invariably is condemned to flounder at the very bottom of the human scrap heap.

"But what if just yesterday, you yourself were extending your hand? And at the edge of the sidewalk you meet your double?"

Doctor Falk continued to smile. "What do you want to say?"

"A year ago, I was passing through Sverdlovsk, formerly Ekaterinburg in the Urals.[10] You know, the city where they murdered the tsar's family in 1918. I had just been released from a camp in Kotlas and was heading toward the Altai city of Slavgorod. A trip of 2,748 kilometers, with a change of trains at Sverdlovsk. It was summer, June. I had no money; I had eaten the salted fish provided by the camp authorities for the road; and all that remained was the bread ration calculated at 400 grams per day. I spent two full days in Sverdlovsk, sleeping in the railroad station under the ticket seller's window. This was my first 'free' city after five camp years. Sverdlovsk surprised me with the contrast between the enormous barrack-like buildings of new Soviet construction and the old, small wooden houses of the pre-revolutionary

---

9. According to the editor of the 2016 Russian edition, the passenger list of that voyage of the *Heliopolis* does not include a Dr. Falk. Perhaps Margolin did not want to reveal the name of one of the passengers.

10. After the end of the Soviet Union, the name of the city reverted to Ekaterinburg.

province. This architectural cacophony somehow corresponded to my state of mind. The entire city consisted of torn scraps lacking any unity. On the main street was a restaurant with palm trees in the windows, but I did not have money to go there—you needed hundreds of rubles. In the flea market, a fellow was selling dates for six rubles a piece. Dates in the Urals from God knows where. I myself felt like a date in transit.

"Suddenly, in the square, I saw schoolchildren eating ice cream in paper wrappers. This ice cream was the last straw. I picked up a wrapper thrown away by the children. By inertia, after the camp, I could not bear the sight of unfinished scraps, little pieces. . . . The station was crowded with passengers waiting to switch trains. They lay side by side on their bundles; at night everyone was awakened and driven out to the square so that the station might be cleaned. On the second day, I already had a few acquaintances. And here I began to beg for money.

"Why did I do that? Not from hunger—I still had a supply of bread in my bag—but from some kind of mental annoyance that everyone had money except me. From fear that until the Altai region itself there would not be another such opportunity. And also, something in the manner of curiosity or hope for a miracle that impels people to look into a stranger's eyes and wait for a response. Some do this arrogantly, as if they have it coming to them, others timidly. The reaction of a camp inmate who, having landed among 'free' people, hurries to take advantage of the situation. Among the Russian prisoners, at the first railroad station on the way home from camp, many were unable to resist the temptation, got drunk in compensation for all those years and debauched themselves, after which their documents were checked, and they were sent back to camp. I did not get drunk but just in case, I decided to collect a little money at the Sverdlovsk station. And again, I was very interested in how various people would react to my request. Who knows whether there would be another occasion in my life to beg? What do you think, if I asked for a loan from that dark one with a big nose who is sitting with a group in the corner, would he give?"

Falk looked in the indicated direction and smiled.

"Do you know who that is? One of our most prominent figures, a labor leader, a Marxist-Leninist by the name of Meir Yaari."[11]

---

11. Meir Yaari (1897–1987) was the leader of the socialist Hashomer Hatza'ir movement. A founder of the Mapam Party, he served in the first through seventh Israeli parliaments (Knesset) from 1949 to 1973.

The name Yaari did not mean anything to me. "That means, he won't give."

"At the Sverdlovsk station, they also gave very little. I approached selectively, not everyone. I especially chose Jews who were simpler, older, without Marxism-Leninism, with ordinary city faces—'my kind of people.' I would start up a conversation and inform them that before the war, I had been living in Palestine. This evoked surprise and inquiries among some of my interlocutors, and after a half hour or so, when I had succeeded in gaining their interest, they responded with warmth and cordiality. In the old days, people would wander through peasant Russia begging in the name of Christ; I acted differently but similarly, with a magic name concealed in people's hearts. Having talked as long as necessary, I would take the bull by the horns and state directly that I remained on the road without money: 'Can you loan me something? I shall return it by mail as soon as I arrive home.' And now I could judge what kind of an impression the preceding conversation had made: the facial expression changed immediately, and precisely the kindest and most good-natured people, with potbellies and sated looks, gave nothing but were willing, nevertheless, to continue the pleasant conversation, whereas others, with embarrassment and regret, gave me five rubles—a pittance, as to a professional beggar. I accepted them, and both sides were ashamed. There was nothing more to talk about, and I walked away.

"Suddenly, I was lucky. I spoke to a young woman with a serious, intelligent face and lively eyes. I immediately aroused her interest with my knowledge of 'overseas' and of Western literature. We discussed French writers, the Thibault brothers and the films of René Clair. In the end, I felt bad about spoiling the impression from the meeting. Nevertheless, I said the same thing to her that I had to the others: 'Can I borrow a few rubles from you?' She was embarrassed for a second, took out her purse, and offered me one hundred rubles. My breath was taken away. An enormous sum! And it means that she believed me, believed that I was not a 'moocher,' but a person who had encountered misfortune on the road. I was so grateful to her! And I wrote down her address in order immediately to pay her back from the first money upon arriving at my destination. She was traveling far, to somewhere in Ussuriisk region, by the Amur River, the terrible backwoods, to her husband. Thus, our paths parted, but I was immeasurably happy, and I remembered her for a long time. I lost the piece of paper with the address and did not return the money. What can you do? She, no doubt, forgot about this money, but I did not. To this day I keep returning those hundred rubles. Every time that I have an opportunity to give a 'former person' a little more than he expected, I am returning that Sverdlovsk debt. Do you think that I shall every repay it?

"Let us now return to what I term the 'moral affect.' It is that abnormal situation when you feel that you are obligated to someone, obligated to do something although it is unpleasant in order not to be a scoundrel in your own eyes. You, for example, are you obligated to give alms? Are you obligated to write about what is happening in another country near the North Pole, about which no one writes?"

Falk smiled politely. "And you don't need to answer. You, Mr. Falk, are completely at peace with your conscience. You never robbed anyone, never insulted, never stole, and never did anything punishable by law. That is completely sufficient. Over there is our neighbor who is involved in politics and public affairs, of course, a very respectable person. He suffers from no moral affects and therefore has no obligations. I would like to be in his place. Regrettably, I am in a situation where I am obligated to help a person who remains in camp. This person is counting on my help, not without foundation, as he saved my life in very dramatic circumstances. Now it is my turn to save his life. He is an imprisoned Zionist, and he is dying in a Soviet forced labor camp."

Doctor Falk smiled politely. "You can send a package to him in camp. If I am not mistaken, there is an organization in Tel Aviv that sends packages to Zionists in the Soviet Union."

"Very kind. They send us packages from America, but we send them to those who are poorer than we are. But I want to give that person's freedom back to him. He is now in the situation that I was in yesterday. I know that what he expects from me is not packages with fats and sugar but a resolute public statement, a struggle for his freedom and life. If you saw that a person fell over the side of a boat, what would you do?—sound an alarm, ring the bell, stop the ship, throw him a lifebelt, lower a lifeboat into the sea?"

"This comparison is not apt," said Dr. Falk. "Our ships do not sail on the sea of Soviet justice, and your friend is not a victim but a criminal: he is a Soviet prisoner."

"All Zionists are criminals against the Soviet order, and all are potential victims of the Soviet regime."

Silence and heat enveloped the *Heliopolis*, lost in the watery desert, in the incandescent gleam of the sun. In the infinite expanse of the sea, our little ship carried a cargo of human passions, anxieties, and contradictions to an unknown destination. Doctor Falk was the first person from Israel whom I chanced to encounter. He was the first with whom I could talk about the moral situation of a Westerner who emerged alive from the camp kingdom. That evening, I read him my first article written on the steamship: I was in a hurry to test its effect on the first Israeli resident whom I met.[12] When I had finished, Doctor Falk still smiled politely, but now I sensed a certain astonishment in his smile.

"I must warn you," he said after a brief silence, "that no one in our country is ready to accept such things. It will be very difficult to make people listen to you."

"Do you believe me?"

"That is not important. I believe that everything is possible in our world. But nothing will be changed because of my belief."

Doctor Falk pointed to a group of passengers who had taken a table in the corner of the bar. They were playing cards, laughing loudly, and joking.

"These people, like yourself, went through a lot in Siberia during the war. Some of them have a tattoo from the Nazi camps on their arms. But these people drew a line across the past. It is healthier for them. I think that you will end up the same way."

"But my article is the line across the past! I am drawing it sharply, crudely, with ink, as befits a man of the pen. In that way, I draw the line in my life between what was and what will be."

"You don't know how to forget; you don't know how to be reconciled. And I foresee that for a very long time you will have to ward off the specters of the past. They weigh on you; they go with you on the *Heliopolis* to the West. Look around: over there, in another corner sits a group of respected public figures, and, incidentally, they are the friends of those with whom you spent time in Soviet imprisonment. Do you think that any one of them will talk with you? You attacked communism and therefore your truth has no meaning for them. By this single article, you drew a sharp line between them and yourself."

"How strange! I see among them a person who together with me was arrested in the summer of 1940 and tried for Zionist activity. At his trial, he delivered a fiery speech in defense of his ideas. He argued that his party serves the cause of progress and socialism in Palestine. They did not interrupt him. They let him speak for three hours; he said everything that he could. Then they sentenced him to ten years in camp. The intervention of the Polish government and an amnesty restored his freedom to him. What is he doing now among the defenders of the camp system?"

---

12. Margolin used the term "Israeli" although this was before the establishment of the State of Israel.

"The same thing that he did in the Soviet court," said Doctor Falk: "He continues his service to 'social revolution.' He and those like him express a blind and pitiful, impotent and touching striving of our people for humaneness and goodness on earth. Precisely these people, however, will suffocate you with their inert mass. Don't think that only they will obstruct your way."

"I know," I replied, "opposing me will be the cowardly fear of the little man, the herd-like fear, collective cowardice, covering itself with phrases about 'responsibility,' the resignation of those condemned eternally to follow someone else's lead, fear of what might happen, which, if it happens, does so precisely because of this fear. And petty bourgeois self-satisfaction, the false idyll of others, erecting monuments to themselves in their lifetime, with gilded inscriptions on the pedestal, people who are preoccupied only with their own party careers."

"In order not to reduce everything to another's weakness," said Doctor Falk, "add: the pressure of life, which goes its own way, deaf to others' grief. It is not easy to shout over the street noise. The human voice is incapable of doing that in our machine age. Perhaps, in several years, what now seems important to you will lose its significance, and you will renounce your attempts to shout louder than life. Perhaps, you will forget about today, too, about the long September day that you spent at sea, en route from one Mediterranean port to another. . . . Your recollections will fade, your thoughts will change. You will come to see that there is evil in what seems good, and some measure of good in what you hate today. . . ."

I no longer was listening to him, however. A dark premonition of calamity took hold of me. "My friend will die in imprisonment," I thought. "He is too distant from them." The sea expanses lay all around, sparkling, glittering, steadily rustling; they streamed, gurgled, and the platinum gleam turned to dull silver, the silver gave way to dark azure, the azure changed to a greenish tinge, which turned into steel, and the eyes had nothing on which to focus, the eyes glided over the flood of light without firm contours or the least shade in the cloudless sky.